ROBERT
The Hard Road of Dreams
REMEMBERING NOT TO FORGET

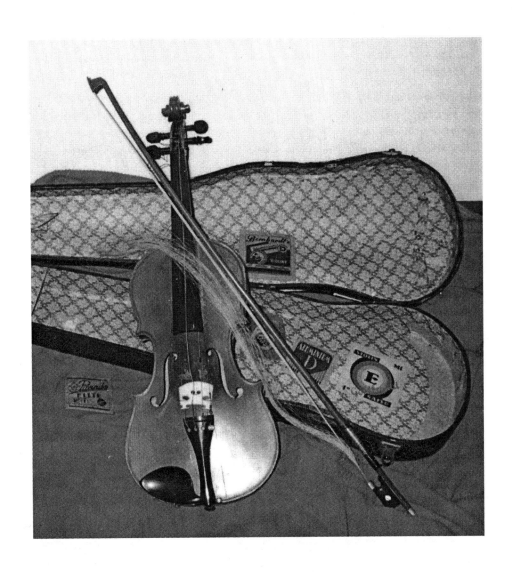

An Expanded Autobiography

The Hard Road of Dreams, An Expanded Biography, was written, researched and edited by Robert B. Kahn, copyright 2016, and published for limited, select distribution, and sale.

All rights reserved. No part of this book, including photographs, may be reproduced for commercial use in part or whole. No part of this autobiography may be stored in a computer retrieval system in any form or by any means, or otherwise recorded without permission in writing from the author, spouse, or heirs. For permissions or further information contact Braughler Books LLC at info@braughlerbooks.com.

Printed in the United States of America

Second Printing, April 2017

ISBN 978-1-945091-19-3

Library of Congress Control Number: 2016952691

Ordering Information: Special discounts are available on quantity purchases by bookstores, corporations, associations, and others. For details, contact the publisher at sales@braughlerbooks.com or at 937-58-BOOKS.

For questions or comments about this book, please write to: info@braughlerbooks.com.

Braughler Books
braughlerbooks.com

Remembrance

I want to wrest from the darkness a day, an hour,

a moment, belonging to my vanished home.

Dear God, it is so hard to draw out a fragment of bygone life

from fleshless memories!

And what if they should flicker out, my lean memories,

and die away together with me?

I want to rescue them.

Bella Chagall, *Burning Lights*

To Aledanra

Whenever possible your life should be a pattern of experiences to enjoy not to endure!

Bob Kahn

With best wishes

Table of Contents

Recognitions and Acknowledgments vii

Introduction ix

Chapter One: *The Western Europe of My Forefathers* 1

Chapter Two: *Laufersweiler* 7

Chapter Three: *My Father's Early Years* 17

Chapter Four: *My Hometown of Mannheim* 39

Chapter Five: *My Early Childhood* 51

Chapter Six: *Growing Up Under The Swastika* 99

Chapter Seven: *The Noose is Tightening* 125

Chapter Eight: *Luxembourg: Short Reprieve from Persecution* 167

Chapter Nine: *Precarious Journey* 209

Chapter Ten: *The New World of Hope* 241

Chapter Eleven: *Caught Up in the War Again* 269

Chapter Twelve: *Modern Warfare Among a Stone Age Civilization* . . . 303

Chapter Thirteen: *Invasion of the Philippines* 331

Chapter Fourteen: *Japan Surrenders – I'm Going Home* 355

Chapter Fifteen: *Life After Victory* 369

Chapter Sixteen: *Away from Home and Marriage* 401

Chapter Seventeen: *New Branches for the Family Tree* 435

Chapter Eighteen: *The Tranquil Years – Part I and Part II* 485

Chapter Nineteen: *How We Won The West* 543

Chapter Twenty: *1968 and Beyond* 561

Epilogue 603

Appendix: *Supporting Photos and Documents* 607

Additional Copyright Notes 771

Archival Sources and Literature 773

Recognitions and Acknowledgements

As soon as I had put together the outline for what I viewed as an Expanded Autobiography, I began to realize that none of the autobiographies that I had researched had gone into the depth of their ancestors' lives as my plans demanded. The book written by my friend Ernest W. Michel "Promises to Keep" picks out certain important years of his life and fortunately our miraculous meeting. My idea was to go much further, requiring greater genealogical as well as historical research. Once my undertaking became known, my children, Dr. Ronald Kahn, Susan Kahn Rapoport, and Karen Kahn Weiss, my sister Irene Kahn Poll, as well as some of my cousins urged me on, some by sending me useful information and photos about their lives and of others. My thanks to all of them for their thoughtfulness.

My dear wife Gertrude who not only urged me on was also the one suffering the most because of her love of my companionship and many social activities over the years. I remember her coming into my study many times past midnight urging me to come to bed. Her understanding and patience is a testimonial to my successful completion of what I started.

Others must be recognized for their dedication to my project. At the very beginning there was my dear friend, the late Reverend Elwood Rose, who on his word processor spent hours putting into type these sentences I had written out in longhand. And when disability of Woody as he was affectionately known brought his effort to a close, another neighbor and friend, Jane W. Fagan, to whom I'm indebted, generously offered her time and expertise until I was sufficiently comfortable with my new computer and programs. My nephew, Marc Diament, was a resource for creating maps and layout of my childhood home. My appreciation also goes to my long time friend James Cooper who, after my several years of using "Word Perfect" to key in my story on the computer, installed Microsoft "Word" which became a huge help to me.

Indispensable became my granddaughter, Emily Rapoport, who at last offered and applied her professional skills in editing and prepub-

Emily Rapoport

lishing knowhow to advise me on bringing my effort to fruition. Her filtering of the manuscript rendered it more meaningful and concise. If in the end the book is applauded for its arrangement and quality, she deserves much of the credit for which I'm immensely thankful. Finally, I must thank G'd all Mighty for giving me the strength and the years to accomplish what I started.

Introduction

To remember, respect, and learn from the past should be a prime concern of my generation and generations to come. Yet, our preoccupation with today's needs and desires for the future do not always allow us the time or the inclination to dwell on the past, especially on events beyond the immediate past. It is a syndrome caused by an almost unavoidable collision between the many priorities we are required to sift through in our daily lives.

Let me try to explain why I think our history is so important and why we should be concerned about events in our past and be able to review them. It is my belief that no matter what environment we are born into, it is the past which is the birthright of us all. Growing up as I did, the past became a constant source of my strength, a fountain of inspiration and perhaps wisdom. Eventually, it became a pillar from which I derived a sense of honor as well as comfort, and above all, the will to survive when I needed it. The knowledge of this living history passed on to me in anecdotes and stories by my parents and others, and also as I experienced it, provided me with a splendid opportunity to recapture and preserve it on paper. Many voids remain in spite of my research to make this history more complete. These accounts can now be conveyed to my children and their children's children since they have never been presented in written form before.

As I organize my thoughts, I recognize the dynamics of the world we live in. It is a world that creates and demands changes with ever-increasing tempo, requiring immediate responses and adaptations. Each day presents new situations and issues that have varying impacts and require selected adjustments on a global, national, and personal level. This environment can produce misunderstandings among family members, mistrust and recrimination in the business world, crime in the streets, and death on our highways. Our ever increasing pace of life is responsible for new diseases, poverty, bigotry, hatred, and all forms of discrimination, including veiled and open anti-Semitism. If that were not frightening enough, constant warfare, spontaneous revolts and natural disasters occur in many parts of the world. The threats of environmental pollution, nuclear miscalculations, and international terrorism are ever present. The extinction of cities, countries, continents, and even the world are remote but distinct possibilities. We need to be concerned with all of these problems and build social, political, scientific, and religious bridges to overcome these evils for the good of America, the preservation and prosperity of the state of Israel, Jews everywhere, and the well-being of the entire world. At the same time we must diligently nourish our Jewish identity and maintain an awareness of our German and other European ancestry. This heritage is particularly important because of the bitter experiences forced upon Jews by the German people, climaxing in the Holocaust. Every effort should be made to educate ourselves and our children in understanding and practicing Jewish traditions at home, in temple or synagogue. This is vastly important to maintain our noble identity as the Kahn family, and its descendants, becomes larger.

Vigilant, alert, and proud, the Kahns have always stood together in happiness, and more importantly, in despair. Husbands and wives, like tall trees in a forest, have maintained a deliberate and high spirit in times of trouble and have weathered the storms amid confusion and calamity. My father and mother always managed to portray a ray of optimism, even when events were bleak and their expectations were controlled and manipulated by others.

As I look back at good times and bad, there were never any easy solutions or answers. My parents, Joseph and Martha, made no ivory tower decisions. They spoke to my sister and me as their parents spoke to them, sometimes protectively vague, at other times blunt and direct or simple and compassionate, but always with a vision filled with love. By trial and error, I have imitated their styles, modifying some and adding to others, but always upholding the principles they instilled in me: fairness, goodness, honesty, pride, and a lust for life.

Now as I enter the final and most important phase of my life, I experience a burning urge to explore my past with you as well as the lives of others in the midst of what was once a more extended family. It all began on the "old continent," with a large family, some of whom, but not others, survived the Holocaust. Against high odds, the remnants of this family have blossomed again in the "new world continent," my beloved America.

To tell you this fascinating story, I must first take you into the past. I have searched my memory, talked to relatives and friends, reviewed old letters, documents, archives, chronicles and memorabilia, and obtained information from European countries. For certain time periods, my memories are somewhat blurred, either because I was too young or because an inner psychological mechanism automatically suppressed the unpleasant and sometimes terrible happenings. However, many painful memories have survived and will be revealed here. There are also many interesting, happy, funny and odd tales, which I hope will bring smiles, laughter, and perhaps raise a few eyebrows.

If I succeed in providing some insight into my life, the lives of our ancestors, and the world in which events took place, you will be able to draw strength to carry on and also remember old traditions for future generations to come. I ask you to add to my writings from time to time to ensure that the family's written thread will not be broken even if certain branches of the tree wither because of a lack of male descendants. I urge others of the extended Kahn family, regardless of name, to carry on.

What you will read comes closest to an expanded autobiography: the story of my life as viewed and written by me. This story also spills over into the lives of others and covers the world events of their times. Frequently, you will note a departure from the personal to the historical, the political, the philosophical, and perhaps the abstract. However, all of this material is interwoven to fulfill my desire to capture the feelings of when, where, how and sometimes, why. I hope to create a text of multidimensional quality that should awaken the reader's intense curiosity. Nothing I write, however, will provide satisfactory answers to many deeper questions I have alluded to thus far, namely the events of senseless, shameful, inhuman persecution and the attempted total annihilation of European Jews. You will not find answers to why brutal savagery was perpetrated by the German people and their allies under the banner of Nazism against me, my family, all other Jews, and other minorities on the continent. The "why" will be discussed, argued, speculated and written about by others for eternity. One important fact however, arose from the ashes of the concentration death camps: namely that a people can be nearly destroyed but never defeated. I am the proof of this statement. The will to survive must serve as a lesson and inspiration to those who at times may think that life has little or no meaning. It has for me, and it must for you and those who come after you.

I have made many mistakes in my life, but fortunately, many more of my decisions have been rational, prudent and sometimes farsighted. In retrospect, even those made on the spur of the moment have been mostly correct, or at least headed in the right direction. Although not necessarily spectacular or often noticed by others, my accomplishments have been many. I have received many formal recognitions, honors, and compliments. In my earlier years, I learned to live with disappointments, disillusionments, and frustrations, while harnessing my relentless optimism, enthusiasm, fantasies, and sometimes unrealistic goals.

Through more than sixty-nine years I have loved my wife Gertrude passionately and completely, as well as our three children. As time has gone by that love has grown to encompass the families my children have created, including our seven wonderful grandchildren. All my life, I have reached out to my dear parents whom I respected and adored, my sister, Irene, whom I admired, and a wealth of relatives including aunts, uncles, cousins, nieces, and nephews. I also include in this circle many old and new friends who have shown me kindness and understanding.

Some of these details will be forgotten after I am called away by my maker. Other memories will withstand the passage of time, but eventually those, too, will vanish as in a fog. Nevertheless, I hope that the pages of this expanded autobiography will endure. Perhaps someday you, my children, grandchildren, and great-grandchildren will read and reread these accounts and understand your rich heritage. The generations to come must always, as I have, cherish old memories, dream about rainbows of happiness and tranquility, and work relentlessly to bring those dreams to fruition for yourself, your loved ones, and for the benefit of all mankind. Then and only then will you understand the purpose and meaning of "The Hard Road of Dreams."

CHAPTER ONE

The Western Europe of my Forefathers

Much thought has been given on where and how to begin. On one hand I would like to present a short overview of the period in which my forefathers lived. While my genealogical research goes back to the early 1700s, going back that far has its drawbacks. Names, dates, places, and other information become sparse and are often not easily verifiable. Also, genealogical and historical references are not always in agreement. However, I was able to reconcile most of the inconsistencies.

By beginning with my great-grandparents, Joseph Kahn, and his wife, Karoline (née Wendel), I hope to enrich the reader's understanding of the 19th century without giving the appearance of a history lesson. This also gives me an opportunity to generalize or detail certain aspects of my research with commentary. In the next few chapters I will endeavor to cover these and earlier years, detailing facts, events, and circumstances because of their relevance to the objectives of my expanded autobiography.

The Holy Roman Empire vanished around 1806 when Emperor Francis I abdicated the throne. The decades following 1830 were generally viewed as a sort of golden age of Europe, the bourgeois era. Capital was amassed by relatively few entrepreneurs to fuel the establishment and operation of industry. The profits derived from its output would go primarily into the pockets of the owners, with very little going to the men, women, and children of the working class. In those days child labor was in vogue to the detriment of the children's well-being. The pioneering of factories in England were adopted in varying ways and degrees by the countries on the continent, and experiments with running factories were no longer limited to steel and textile production. Although all of the German states were producing only a fraction of the amount of iron produced by England, and less than half of that produced by France, in 1840 the German Cunard Shipping Lines entered four steamships in transatlantic service. Prior to this date Germany exported solely to European states, so the new shipping routes clearly indicate Germany's interest and ability to increase global trade.

The financial, political, and social gaps between capital and labor groups of that period created strains that led to the formation of unions and the beginning of socialistic ideas. The struggle between the classes was felt across all borders and was the eventual cause for the collapse of governments everywhere. It gave rise of another Napoleon, a nephew of the great Bonaparte, and a chain reaction of revolutions, wars, and Marxism. Germany, consisting of many individual states, failed to solve its problems by unification all the while stirring up much provocative nationalism. This nationalism contributed to the animosity between Germany and both Western and Eastern countries for many years to come. Migration to the United States by disappointed Germans was one of the results.

Between 1859 and 1871, a new German empire was created, and so was a unified kingdom of Italy. A dual monarchy of Austria and Hungary came into being, while many changes took place in Russia under a tsarist regime. The expansion of railroads, telegraphs, and steamships brought about profound changes in the economies and societies of European countries and also the world. Ideas were more easily transmitted, and material goods, even people, were more easily transported. On the other side of the Atlantic Ocean, a central authority had been established in the United States as well as the Dominion of Canada. The empire of Japan opened a crack and revealed itself to the modern world. All of this change was accompanied by many wars in Europe: the Crimean War in 1854, the Italian War in 1859, the Danish War in 1864, and the Austrian-Prussian War in 1866. The years 1861-1865 also saw the tragic civil war between the Northern and Southern states in a young America.

Until 1866 there were thirty-eight states in what was then considered Germany. In 1866, Bismarck, the minister-president in the Prussian Parliament was able to enlarge Prussia by conquests. In 1867, Mecklenburg, Saxony and other states joined with Prussia to form the North German Confederation. Bismarck was then able to persuade Bavaria, Württemberg and other German states to form the German Empire in 1871. Next, he conquered Alsace Lorraine from France and ejected Austria from the Empire. The boundaries thus formed remained by and large unchanged until the end of World War I in 1918.

In the years between 1871 and 1914, world peace, the formation of basic democratic governments, material and industrial advances were tremendous influences on the world. A high regard for the sciences, philosophy, and the quest for progress prevailed. However, all of these forces, economic, political, scientific, and liberal thinking, started to undermine and weaken European civilization by pitting materialistic ideals against non-materialistic ideals as the population suddenly increased. These rapid changes of the modern age heavily impacted religions as more and more people looked to science and philosophy for answers to life. Although this period caused many great divisions among Protestants, the Catholic Church proved to be more resistant to changes taking place around it.

Judaism and the Jews themselves had become a widely dispersed minority, noticed and tolerated primarily in the larger cities of Europe where they had to wear special clothes to mark them as Jews. They had survived the pressures of conversion to Christianity (or suffer the consequential penalties of death), and finally confinement to ghettos under papal decree over the course of several centuries. These were some of the penalties during and after the crusades of the Early and Middle Ages. Later, Martin Luther (circa 1500), and thereafter Johann Wolfgang Goethe (late 1700s to early 1800s), expounded on forced integration of Jews by baptism to Christianity or suffer expulsion. Because Jewish populations were small in number, by decree or law, they had to conduct their lives now basically separated from the rest of the population where they could easily be observed.

Strangely enough, they were now looked upon somewhat like a barometer of the well-being of the communities at large, and even the well-being of the entire continent. Jews everywhere were affected much like other religions, but with diverse repercussions. Emancipation and conformance as a form of social and political assimilation were basic evolutions over the course of the late 17th century into the 18th century. Jewish orthodoxy was probably most affected by these trends giving rise to a new movement of reform known as Reform Judaism. Based on new emancipation laws, Jews were technically allowed to exercise their rights as citizens and participate in every type of business and profession. The legal distinction that had singled out Jews as second-class citizens for centuries no longer existed. But, in everyday life, on the streets and in the business community, deep mistrust and discrimination against Jews were still very much alive. The general population still considered them a threat to society.

Between 1890 and 1910 against this background of change, Jews in Western Europe became concerned with two basic situations. One was the fear that their general acceptance would eventually lead them away from their Jewish rituals, their distinctive characteristics, and their Jewish way of life. Observing nationalistic movements designed to strengthen countries and their people, Western European Jews also began to embrace their own nationalistic thoughts. The outgrowth of these ideas led to the first Zionist Congress in Basel, Germany in 1897. As a result, the term and ideology of "Zionism" became deep-rooted. From then on, the dream to establish a national homeland in Palestine for Jews from all corners of the world became the fervent goal of Jews who embraced Zionism.

Now that Jews were becoming citizens of equality, the second area of concern was that gentiles were noticeably aware that Jews were now competitors in all types of businesses, occupations, and even politics. On another plane, capitalists and the rich feared the theories expounded by the Jewish radical thinker, Karl Marx, and the encroachment of his theories into the existing political and social system. This fear, coupled with the gaining momentum of nationalism, gave rise to muffled, but noticeable, renewed anti-Semitic behavior in various disguises.

While these were the trends around 1900 in Western Europe, in Eastern Europe, particularly Russia and parts of Poland, Jews were actually mistreated, abused, molested, and even killed. This time became known as the period of the pogroms. In 1896, French Captain Alfred Dreyfus, the first Jew to serve on the general staff of the French military establishment, was sentenced for treason amidst trumped up charges. This manifestation of unusual deep-seated, anti-Semitic hatred was characteristic not only in France, but also in the rest of Europe. Only years later was Captain Dreyfus exonerated. These events and others drove an increasingly large number of Jews into the Zionists' national movement that became their rallying cause and a unifying goal. Other Jews, however, firmly believed the goal of Zionism to be wrong since Judaism was meant to be only a religion, void of any nationalistic aspirations. A third faction believed that Christians and Jews should generally be equal in all aspects and support the political, economic, and nationalistic aspirations of the country in which they happened to live.

This should suffice as a general frame of reference of the difficult and confusing times in which my forefathers and later my parents were born. My ancestors lived and struggled to survive economically while raising their families in the Jewish tradition. They were my paternal great-great grandparents: Leopold Lowe (sometimes recorded as Lob or Löb), born in 1789, his first wife, Judith Wachtern; and after her death his second wife, Jettchen (née Gartner), living in the village of Rhaunen, in an area known as the Hunsrück, Germany. Later in 1808 by decree of Napoleon, Jews were required to change their surnames. My great grandfather and his family did so by changing it to Kahn. One of their sons, my great grandfather, Joseph Kahn was born in 1815, and his wife Karoline (née Wendel), was born in 1816, both from Rhaunen Germany. Next came my grandparents, Isaak Kahn, born in 1848 in Rhaunen, and his wife, Johanna (née Levy), born in 1853 in nearby Hottenbach. And finally, there was my father, Joseph Kahn, born 1889 in Laufersweiler, and mother, Martha (née Joseph), born 1892 in Schieren, Luxembourg. To avoid confusion, it should be mentioned that hundreds of years ago, it was customary to give Jewish boys the first name of their grandfathers. Hence my great-grandfather and father share the same name, Joseph.

EXHIBIT 1.1 My maternal great grandparents, Bernard and Elise Joseph. His parents, my great-great grandparents were Moses Joseph born 1798 and his wife Marnel (née Mendel) who resided in Aach (near Trier) Germany.

Because I remember much of my grandfather Isaak, how and where he lived, worked and died, my story will start with him and his family. Not wanting to slight my mother's side of the family, her paternal grandparents were Bernard Joseph (born January 12, 1828) and Elise née Kan (born 1835).

Their son (my mother's father, and therefore my maternal grandfather) Raphael Joseph was born 1860 in Aach, Germany. He would eventually marry Amalia (née Levy), who was born 1865 in Laufersweiler, Germany. As strange as it may be, the wives of both my grandfathers, Amalia, the wife of Raphael, and Johanna, the wife of Isaak, were sisters. Exactly how these relationships with their husbands came about I could not determine and therefore can only be left to speculation. It should be pointed out that the two small towns of Aach and Laufersweiler are approximately 60 kilometers (or 37 miles) apart. Had I known I would be writing this 70 plus years later, I could have asked Raphael or Amalia.

CHAPTER TWO

Laufersweiler

The village of Laufersweiler, even today, is primarily a small farming community surrounded by many forests located in an area of western Germany known as the Hunsrück. Formerly occupied by France, then part of the North German Confederation (1866-1871), Hunsrück finally became part of the German Empire. It is a hilly but fertile area cradled between four rivers. The Mosel lies to the north, and a smaller river, the Nahe, lies to the south. Both are tributaries of the Rhine River, the largest of the four, which borders the Hunsrück to the east. The Saar River, which empties into the Mosel, forms the area's western demarcation. Today, the Hunsrück region is bisected by the Hunsrück Hohenstrasse, a scenic highway similar to the Blue Ridge Parkway of western Virginia. The region is part of the Rhineland known as Palatinate. The Hunsrück is a very scenic area roughly 1600 sq. miles, its west edge bordering on the small Duchy of Luxembourg where my mother was born.

The region then was sparsely settled with farms, where raising livestock was the primary occupation. However, there were some industries of note such as vineyards making semi-dry Mosel wines and semi-sweet Rhine wines famous. These wines were highly regarded in Germany then, and are highly valued all over the world today. There were also slate and stone quarries. Slate was used in early European years as a durable roofing and siding material for houses and for making slate boards for school use and children's homework. Even I used a slate board and chalk for my homework. There were also glass and crystal factories teeming with talented glass blowers and polishers. A few of these businesses have survived to the present and are still renowned and valued for their craftsmanship.

The immediate area around Laufersweiler was also known for its abundance of agates, a semi-precious stone with striped or clouded coloring. These mineral stones were polished by men lying prone in front of a large, crude sandstone wheel that was turned by another man (or boy) who also applied water to the wheel to keep the ever-present grinding dust down. My dad told me that because of this dust, many of these men died of lung disease at a young age. The beautifully colored stones were in great demand in the youthful days of my father and in prior years for jewelry and other art objects.

Aside from river transportation, there were eventually a few main rail lines that connected to the bigger cities of the region, which then connected with even larger cities inside the Hunsrück such as Trier, and then to cities outside such as Saarbrucken, Koblenz, Mainz, Luxembourg, and cities in Belgium and France. Primitive roads, connecting the small hamlets around Laufersweiler were passable with ox or horse-drawn wagons, by foot, and later by bicycle. These kinds of roads were common, and one could see old and young traveling from one town to the market in another town. There they would sell their homemade or homegrown wares and buy or barter things for their own needs. The area was somewhat remote, and news from other areas and the continent traveled slowly.

Laufersweiler lies in the foothills of the Idar Forest at an elevation of 1,400 feet. According to old records researched by Gabi von Brug, the town is mentioned for the first time in documents dealing with real estate property division dating from the year 1283. Since that time the town has been known as Lauferswilre and Loffinswilre, derivations from the words Laufari and Liuvo without further explanation of where those words came from. By 2002, the population had grown to only about 860 residents, and the size of the incorporated area was 6.79 square kilometers, or approximately 2.6 square miles. However, no Jews lived there at that time, and none live there now. Most of them left because of Nazi persecution, emigrating or moving to safer havens. Records, however, show that twenty-five Laufersweiler Jews were deported and exterminated, among them relatives and persons I knew.

While the documented history of Jews in Laufersweiler in earlier centuries is almost non-existent, and in later years was still sparse, it is believed from research and oral accounts undertaken by Hans-Werner Johann that the first Jews settled there in the 17th century. At that time Jews were identified as *schutz juden* or *geleit juden*, which translates to "protected jews" or "safe conduct jews." Then, whenever Jews wanted to settle in a town, they had to obtain a *schutzbrief*, a letter of protection from the local authorities, which cost 6 Florin 45 Kreuzer during the 18th century in Laufersweiler, which in my understanding was not a small sum. This protection fee had to be paid yearly. The number of Jewish inhabitants in 1748 had increased to five, presumable five families. Also in 1748, a decree was published whereby Jews had to obtain permission from the *schultheis*, the village clerk, when they wanted to move livestock to pasture and also provide proof that the stock was healthy and carried no disease.

Jews were treated not only as second-class citizens, but more like outcasts, criminals, and pariahs, and every opportunity was taken to make their lives more difficult and miserable. What made matters worse, they had no rights, and their sources of income were limited by law to paltry trading in livestock, new and used haberdashery articles, and other shabby occupations.

In 1756, Herr von Schmidtburg, the reigning lord of the region, issued other decrees that no visiting Jew could stay longer than one night in a town under his domain. Only an inn could be used for their stay. Anyone who stayed overnight at a Jew's house was severely punished. As if such chicanery of blatant anti-Semitism was not enough, an earlier decree issued in 1753 provided that a Christian who bought a house from a Jew had an entire year to reconsider the purchase

EXHIBIT 2.1 Germany with today's borders showing Rhineland Pfalz, also known as the Palatinate, within which the Hunsrück, and its capital city of Mainz, lies. It is one of 16 states of the Federal Republic of Germany.

contract and cancel the sale within that period without recourse. Jews were not trusted even when important business matters were put in writing. They were additionally required to give a special oath. This was the situation in the area of the Hunsrück where my ancestors lived. In other parts of Prussia, other states and European countries, Jews fared no better. In many larger cities Jews were restricted to ghettos and had to wear special items of clothing to identify them.

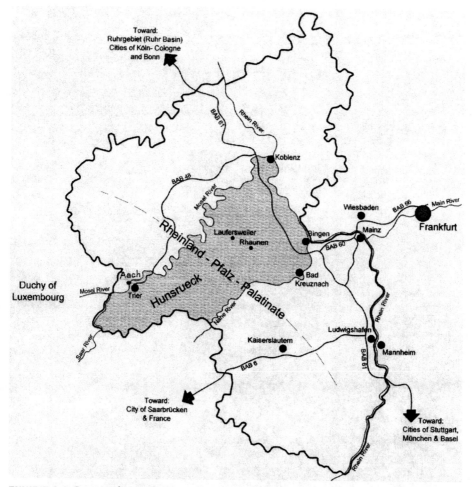

EXHIBIT 2.2 Germany's Hunsrück and Environ. Part of the Rhineland-Pfalz-Palatinate Region. For an additional map that shows a detailed view of the Hunsrück, see exhibit 2.3 in the appendix.

In a letter dated April 1760, the *Kurtrier*, a local area official, made a request to Freihern von Schmidtburg to deny the settlement of additional Jews in Laufersweiler. After several years of negotiations, he issued a decree in April 1788, "that the present Jews in Laufersweiler should die out (*aussterben*) until the number of Jewish households would number no more than four families."

No one knows how the Jews of Laufersweiler and the surrounding area might have fared had it not been for the French Revolution in 1789. In 1791 the French National Assembly decided to bestow equal rights for Jews of France with full citizenship. It became law on September 20, 1792. As a result of the French territorial conquests in 1794, of the areas west of the Rhine River, which included the Hunsrück, Jews under this French occupation and administration were also granted full citizenship in 1798. This citizenship extended to the areas between the Maas, Saar, Rhine, and Mosel rivers. Later, Emperor Napoleon issued several other decrees that shamefully reneged on some earlier provisions that had been good for the Jews. One of these decrees, issued on June 28, 1808, required all Jews to select a permanent Christian first and family name within three months. There is much speculation as to Napoleon's motivation for this latter decree. Prior to this change in law, it was regular practice to skip over Jewish sounding names when conscripting for his army; therefore, the argument can perhaps be made that a change in name would end this unofficial policy. Conscription into the army was a very plausible reason since Jews had been excluded to serve in the French Army before that time. This decree also specified that the last or family name could not be the same as biblical first names or the names of cities, geographical identifications, or Hebrew words. Records indicate that Jews of Laufersweiler registered their new names on October 19, 1808, at the registrar's office (*mairie*) in Sohren, a larger town approximately five kilometers north by northwest. At this time, the Jewish community of Laufersweiler had increased to approximately thirty-six people.

On November 11, 1808, my ancestors by the name Löw or Low (the document shows the spelling both ways), appeared before the assistant to the Mayor of Rhaunen, and adopted the family name Kahn. The name "Kahn," which met the requirements of Napoleon's decree, was a less recognizable Jewish name at that time than it is today; however, it allowed my ancestors to clearly remain identifiable as Jews to other Jews. The document, written in French, bore the seal of the Empire of France. Isaak Kahn signed his new name only in Hebrew. Jews retained their Hebrew names for use during religious worship services but were required to learn to read and write French and German. Hinnele Low and Rebecca Löw were apparently unable to sign their names. Until the Napoleonic wars and French occupation, Jews primarily used Hebrew characters to write German. French occupation of the German areas, including the Hunsrück, ended January 1814 after French, Prussian and Austrian armies were defeated in their war against Russia. Napoleon's armies were decimated giving the remaining Prussian armies the opportunity to free the French occupied territories. In 1826, the royal Prussian government advised the district president in the town of Simmern, Hunsrück that Jews who wished to become Christians should not be given any difficulties as long as a set fee was paid to the local parish. The records, however, do not show that any Jews of Laufersweiler converted to Christianity. Jews who wanted officially to become members of a local community had to pay a fee to the town's treasury. In Laufersweiler, 1843, the amount was three Taler (or Thaler) a silver coin.

An enormous catastrophe occurred on July 27, 1839, when a fire that started around 1:00 p.m. destroyed 130 homes in the village of Laufersweiler, including ten Jewish homes. The fire occurred in the town's center and also gutted the Protestant and Catholic churches, which were both built in 1738, as well as the *shul* (Yiddish, based on the German word for school), the Jewish house of prayer

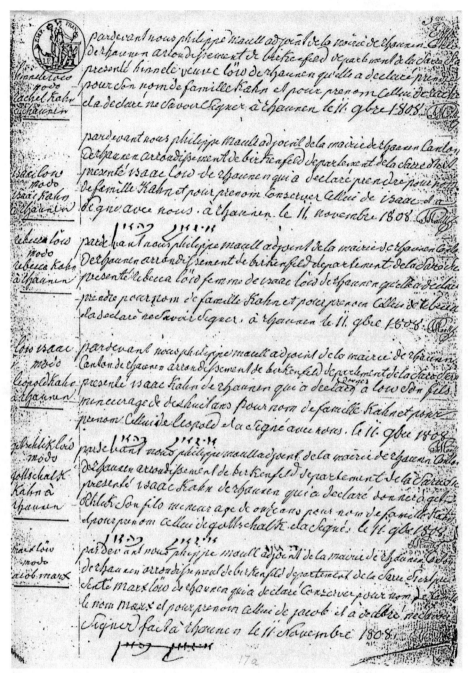

EXHBIT 2.4 Copy of the change of name document with the French Empire seal. See exhibit 2.5 in the appendix for the English translation.

and learning. The shul was very small consisting of one large room also used as an elementary school (we called it *cheder*, the Hebrew term) for Jewish children. There were ten small benches for cheder and religious services and two special chairs, one for the cantor (in Hebrew known as *chazon*, also referred to by Germans as *vosänger*), and the other presumably for the officiating head of the Laufersweiler Jewish community. A strong southwest wind had fed the fire that spread so fast that the townfolk, who were largely occupied with harvesting, could not contain it. Nearby townspeople and fourteen pieces of horse-drawn fire equipment came to help fight the blaze.

The Jewish banker, Baron Rothschild of Frankfurt, came to the rescue of the town by granting a loan of 30,000 Talers to rebuild the town. Rothschild made one important contractual stipulation however. It stated that the town elders had to agree to accept ten to fifteen additional Jewish families into their midst. It was a shrewd way to persuade the townspeople to allow additional Jewish families to settle and earn a living in Laufersweiler, thus overcoming earlier restrictions on the numbers of Jewish residents. At the time of the fire, there were about fifty-five Jews living there among a total population of 560.

According to the history research by Gabi von Brug, seventeen Jewish families, perhaps almost all, were responsible for building a new synagogue with their own money and a 100 Taler loan. Construction costs were approximately 1,492 Talers. The synagogue was completed in 1844 according to a design by the architect Baumeister Hahn from the town of Kulz. The worshipers who came from nearby towns, or those not born in Laufersweiler, were required to purchase or rent seats. These funds provided adequately for the interest and principle of the loan as well as for the maintenance, lighting, and heating of the synagogue. A request to the town council of Laufersweiler for a supplement from town funds was rejected since there was "no legal obligation." However, in 1841, when the town agreed to make available 500 Talers worth of building lumber from the community forest, the head forest ranger (*kreisforster*) for the region rejected the request on the grounds that "it was not possible to furnish that much lumber from the community forest."

After the synagogue was built, two seats were forever allotted to those seventeen congregational families and their descendants who made the synagogue financially possible. The historical record about Jewish life at Laufersweiler indicates that by 1843 the German language was not used during religious services. Presumably the service was conducted entirely in Hebrew or perhaps Yiddish. However, sermons and speeches were made in German, which was also used for the benefit of the invited non-Jewish neighbors to weddings, funerals, and circumcisions. The synagogue could accommodate 150-160 people, including standing room. There was a small apartment for a teacher and a *mikveh*, a ritual bath for women. On the right side of the sanctuary the seats were marked with odd numbers, the left side with even numbers. Spaces for standing room were also marked. Seats were assigned by age of the congregant, the oldest sat toward the front of the sanctuary. Women and visitors of other denominations sat in the mezzanine. In 1875 my great grandfather, *kaufman* (businessman) Josef Kahn, approached the congregation to purchase seat #35. At that time, the eldest congregants could purchase seats toward the front, so I don't know where his seat was previously, this is merely the only surviving record of a seat purchase.

In a letter from Hans-Werner Johann, a local Laufersweiler area historian, to me dated November 15, 1991, he stated that "a Josef Kahn surfaces in the records of this area (Laufersweiler) in the beginning of the 19th century. He came from Rhaunen, a town about eight miles away, with his family and settled in Laufersweiler sometime between 1849 and 1854." It is pure speculation on my part that my great grandfather, and his brother Manuel who never married, relocated from Rhaunen because life in Laufersweiler at that time seemed somewhat more favorable for Jews from an economic and social viewpoint. A larger number of Jews living there made it easier to live a Jewish life and raise a family. According to today's standards, the Laufersweiler of old would probably not be the ideal place to live and raise a family, but in those years the concept of mobility was extremely limited especially for Jews who did not have much choice of where to live.

By 1885 the Jewish population had increased to 114 thanks to the stipulation by banker Rothschild, while the town's total population, including 225 Catholics and 366 Protestants, had increased only to 705. The incoming Jewish families were settled near the rebuilt town hall, an area which today is still called *Judeneck* or "Jew Corner." While the overall population increased 26%, the Jewish population had more than doubled. By 1895 when my father, Joseph, was six years old, the largest number of Jews (156) lived in Laufersweiler. Because the synagogue, completed in 1844, had become run down, was structurally unsound, and hard to maintain, it had become a hazard for its occupants. The congregation therefore decided to sell the building for salvage in January 1909. A new one, which I still remember from later vacations and visits, was designed and built to plans by Nickolaus Eltz, from the nearby town of Hirschfeld, and dedicated in 1911. Until its completion, worship services and the teaching of religion and Hebrew took place in the Catholic school. This accommodation indicates a somewhat harmonious existence between Jews and other townspeople. The opening dedication ceremonies of the two-story synagogue took place on Thursday, June 1 and Friday, June 2, 1911. To finance this construction, a loan of 4,000 Mark was required.

From the records of Hans-Werner Johann, I have been able to reconstruct the history of the town's cheder during the 19th century. These details were only brought into my writings because they are historic, peculiar in their details, and attest to the strong beliefs by the Jewish families in their God. This information will survive in archives somewhere, but the readers of this expanded autobiography will not have to go out of their way to find and research them. The history of Jews in Laufersweiler needed to be told and preserved. Making them a part of this autobiography was a natural way to do it. To read additional history about the development of the Jewish cheder of Laufersweiler, see the appendix.

The struggle of Laufersweiler Jews to make a living, raise a family, and provide meaningful religious and elementary educations for their children created problems that they had never before encountered and were only partially solved. In spite of emancipation laws, these Jews felt insecure. Anti-Semitic undertones were always present, and the public atmosphere was generally, but not always, openly hostile. All of these circumstances led to a confusing spiritual and mental transfiguration that was partially to blame for the confusing attitudes in relation to teachers, and Jewish learning. The Kahn children, my father, his brothers and sisters, never complained about the cheder or their teachers. Why would they? They had never experienced anything else, and therefore were naively satisfied.

Because very small towns had no synagogues, Prussia enacted a law in 1847, which among other stipulations, established synagogue districts, depending upon which town Jews traveled to for worship. The statistics that resulted over the ensuing years gives further insight to the evolvement of the Jewish population in the area surrounding Laufersweiler. At the time, only two synagogues were shown for the geographical district: Kirchberg with nineteen Jewish families consisting of eighty-nine people, and Laufersweiler with one hundred one Jews of twenty families. Jewish families of Kappel, Dillendorf, and Lindenschied, with a total of six families, visited the Kirchberg synagogue. In 1855 records showed two Jewish persons from nearby Niederkleinich joining the religious services at Laufersweiler. Again, in 1864, the Royal Prussian government established the following synagogue districts:

Simmern: with all towns within the mayoral jurisdiction including Ohlweiler and Kastellaun

Gemünden: with all towns within its mayoral jurisdiction

Rheinbollen: with all towns within its mayoral jurisdiction

Laufersweiler: only the Jewish inhabitants of Laufersweiler

Over a period of seventy-eight years, from 1817 to 1895, the Jewish population had exploded almost three-fold, yet between 1895 and 1925, the Jewish population declined about fifty percent. See exhibit 2.7 in the appendix for a graph that shows the religious affiliation of the townspeople between 1817 and 1925.

No one knows exactly how records were kept. Most Jews came to Laufersweiler for reasons already mentioned, and left for reasons not well documented. Much reading and research convinces me that those reasons must have included the freedoms that became available to Jews once the laws of emancipation took effect. They certainly included a new freedom of movement to other and larger cities and countries, the ability to enter institutions of higher learning, and a desire to learn and enter new professions formerly not open to them such as commerce, medicine, and law. The exodus of Jews from Laufersweiler was further motivated by greater opportunities for social affiliation in much larger Jewish communities. Jews were able to shed ingrained and crude anti-Semitism prevalent in small towns like Laufersweiler. For the most part, inhabitants there had very little or no education and were not open to new ideas brought about by the movement of the enlightenment.

With more freedom of movement, new economic and social opportunities, some of Laufersweiler's Jewish population emigrated to America and other overseas countries. World War I, 1914-1918, gave young Jewish men an opportunity to heed the call of the German Kaiser to join the ranks of the German Army and fight for the nation that had given them citizenship and equality under the law. Most of the Jewish men living in, or were born at Laufersweiler, who were the right age and physically fit, joined the army. This included my father and his brother Simon. Many of those who came back from the war, having seen or heard of other parts of the world, soon left or never returned to their families in Laufersweiler to start a new life elsewhere and take control of their destiny. As a result by 1925, only seventy-six Jews remained in the town. A small World War I memorial in the village indicates that at least five Jewish soldiers from Laufersweiler died serving their country. By 1930, only about twenty-five Jewish families lived in Laufersweiler, operating two businesses, a tavern and a combination grocery-butcher shop. Dad's other two brothers, Ernst and Herman had immigrated to America several years before World War I.

CHAPTER THREE

My Father's Early Years

November 1889 was already a cold month. On the 7th of November, a proud Isaak Kahn was on his way, either on foot or by horse-drawn wagon, from Laufersweiler to Kirchberg, the district seat about ten kilometers away. Certain local government offices responsible for many of the legal affairs of towns in that area were located there. Most towns were too small to have a mayor and other administrative offices. Isaak entered the Kirchberg-land district registrar's office and announced to the clerk (*schulze*) that a child of masculine sex had been born to him and his wife, Johanna (née Levy) on Tuesday, November 5th, at 2:00 a.m. by the name of Joseph. According to an interpretation of an entry on the birth certificate, the schulze knew my grandfather Isaak well. Isaak had made that trip five times before, three times to record the birth of baby girls, Jenny, Ida, and Bella, and twice to record the birth of boys, Herman and Ernst. Three more trips followed after the birth of my father. Opa (grandfather in German folk dialect) Isaak made that trip to Kirchberg for the births of Simon, Gertrude (later known only as Gerda), and Martha. Isaak and his wife Johanna (known to most people as Hannchen) had nine children and raised them in a very modest house that seemed to burst at the seams.

According to her children (my aunts and uncles) and others who knew her, Hannchen was a wonderful woman, mother, and wife. I never knew her since she died in 1909, long before I was born, but my dad always talked about what a wonderful mother she was. During her childhood, Hannchen's family lived in Hottenbach, about ten kilometers from Laufersweiler. In 1859 her father, Herz Levy, was hired by the *kille* (congregation) of Laufersweiler to teach religion and Hebrew. Herz Levy and his wife, Babette (née Frank) were the parents of four daughters, Johanna ("Hannchen"), Amalia ("Malchen"), Henrietta ("Yennchen"), and Magdalena ("Lenchen"), who later became the wife of Isaak Löser in Laufersweiler. As a linguistic note, the diminutive *-chen* was often used alongside German words and names, especially the latter as an endearing way to say "little." As mentioned earlier, Johanna, married Isaak Kahn, my paternal grandfather. Amalia married my grandfather on my maternal side, Raphael Joseph in Luxembourg. Thus, Herz Levy became my great grandfather on both paternal and maternal sides.

Levy was paid a yearly teacher salary of 165 Taler in Laufersweiler. Two Christian teachers continued to teach reading, writing, and arithmetic to the Jewish children. Although Herz Levy had passed a required test at the teachers' seminar in Neuwied to teach religion, the parents of the pupils became

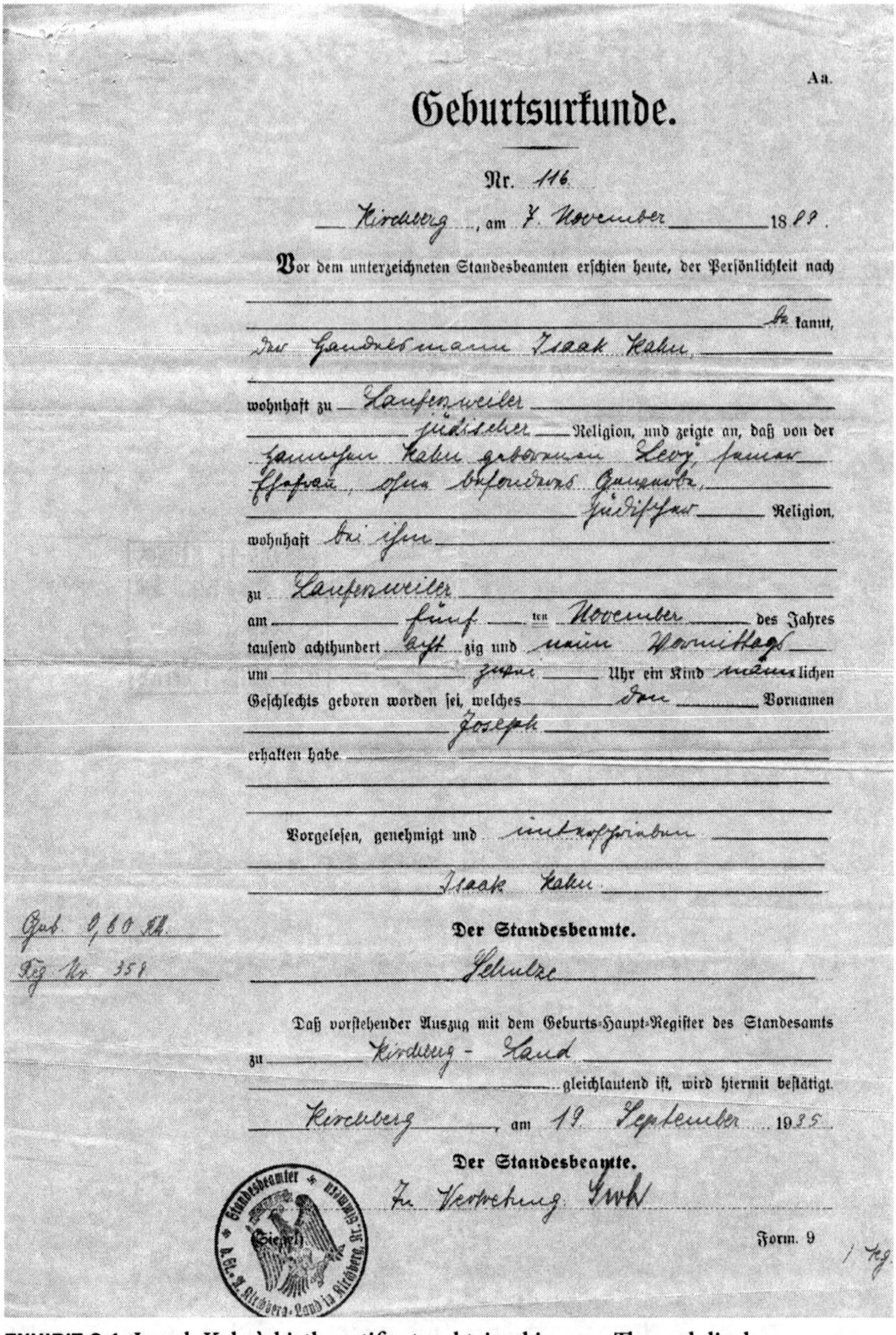

EXHIBIT 3.1 Joseph Kahn's birth certificate, obtained in 1935. The seal displays two swastikas in the circumferencing text that reads "God with us."

dissatisfied with his teaching ability by year 1863. Many parents therefore sent their children to the public parochial schools in town, making it necessary to operate classes in shifts. Levy was released from his teaching job in 1867. In 1868 a new religion teacher, Mendel Mossbacher, from the town of Gleicherwiesen, was hired. Two years later, as part of the curriculum, all Jewish girls began to learn the art of knitting from Mossbacher's wife.

In those days there was almost no knowledge of contraception, and large families were the order of the day rather than the exception. I often heard my mother quote her father, who lived in Luxembourg at the time and whom she always called "Pop": *Kinder kriegen ist nicht schwer, aber keine haben, so viel mehr!* This translates to "Having children is not difficult, but to have none is much harder." When Isaak was thirty and Hannchen twenty-five, their first child, Jenny, was born on September 2, 1879. Every two years thereafter, except for the ninth and last child, a birth in my family was registered in Kirchberg. Herman was born on June 25, 1881, Ernst on July 9, 1883, Ida on August 1, 1885, Bella on August 25, 1887, my dad Joseph, November 5, 1889, Simon on September 2, 1891, and Gertrude on November 11, 1893. The last child, Martha, was born three years later on June 23, 1896. By that time Opa was forty-seven years old with a newborn in a basket, and his oldest, Jenny, was seventeen. Today one would say, "Oh my God!" My dad, in later years, would often exclaim, *Bist du Meschugga!* a combination of German and Yiddish that means, "Are you crazy?"

For the two years after Joseph was born, there were other little toddlers around creating much work for Oma Hannchen. Jenny, age ten, Herman, the oldest boy, eight, and Ernst, six, were all going to public school and twice a week to cheder. In addition, the boys went with their dad to synagogue every Shabbat evening and morning as well as on Jewish holidays. Ida was four, Bella only two, so they were not old enough to go to school. There was no such thing as kindergarten in the village or anyplace else.

In 1888, the year before my dad was born, William I, King of Prussia, the Kaiser, died. His empire included a federation of monarchies that consisted of twenty-five German states. He was succeeded by his son, Frederick III, who was incurably ill and died about three months later. His brother, William II (also known as Wilhelm II) took over as Kaiser at the young age of twenty-nine. He reigned from 1889 through 1918. No one knew at the time that Kaiser Wilhelm's reign would be the beginning of a new and decisive course for the German Empire leading to more

EXHIBIT 3.2 Johanna "Hannchen" Kahn (née Levy) and husband Isaak Kahn.

aggressive and ambitious colonial and nationalistic policies. These actions eventually led to the First World War and perhaps created the atmosphere for the events leading up to World War II.

In 1889, the year my father was born, Benjamin Harrison became the twenty-third president in America, and in the land rush thousands of homesteaders, known as Sooners, staked out claims in the Oklahoma territory. Floods killed more than 2,000 people in Jamestown, Pennsylvania, while Montana, North and South Dakota, and Washington became states. Also during that year, the first Army-Navy football game was played at West Point, New York, with Navy winning 24-0. The U.S. Marines took over Guantanamo Bay, Cuba, during the Spanish American War, and William Gray was awarded a patent for a coin-operated telephone. In Europe, Crown Prince Rudolph of Austria allegedly committed suicide at Mayerling, and in Paris, France, the Eiffel Tower opened. As coincidence would have it, in this same year of my father's birth, Adolph Hitler was also born in Braunau, Austria, on April 20th. He would grow to become a man who would set out to conquer Europe, then the whole world, and who would become responsible for the death of six million Jews and millions of others during World War II.

Joseph, like all of his brothers and sisters, was born at home, helped into the world by a midwife. There was no doctor living in the village, and hospitals were remote. This sixth child of Hannchen and Isaak created an even busier and more crowded house. Conditions became even more pronounced when Simon, Gerda, and Martha were born. On July 10, 1975, during a trip to Europe and Laufersweiler, my wife Gert and I, along with our daughters, Susan and Karen, visited the house, but were only able to see the much remodeled house from the outside. It was located on Kirchstrasse (Church Street) the main street of the village that ran perpendicular to the major county through-road that led from the northwest town of Sohren to the southeast town of Rhaunen. Supposedly, the wealthy farmers lived on the uppermost of the three major streets of town. In the vicinity of the large community water well, center of town, lived the smaller farmers and the so-called middle class. The poor lived in lower part of Laufersweiler. The Kahns lived near the center of town, and so were considered middle class.

Many events made news in the 1890s. The first person was put to death in the electric chair in a New York state prison, and the Duchy of Luxembourg became sovereign by separating from the Netherlands. Chief Sitting Bull was shot by U.S. troops and died in South Dakota. The first electric lights were installed in the White House, and in 1891, Thomas Edison invented a motion picture camera. In 1892, an immigrant reception station in America formally opened at Ellis Island and in 1893, Hawaii became a territory of the United States. In 1894, French Jewish Army Captain Alfred Dreyfus was convicted on trumped up charges and banned to Devil's Island in French Guiana. That same year Turks murdered 6,000

Armenian Christians in Kurdestan. Also in 1894, the first Stanley Cup in hockey was won by Montreal, who beat Ottawa 3-1, and the last Czar of Russia, Nicholas II, was crowned. In 1895, William Roentgen discovered the x-ray, and George B. Selden of Rochester, New York, received the first patent for an automobile. In 1896, the first modern Olympics took place in Athens, Greece. U.S. Marines landed in Nicaragua, Henry Ford drove a car at night in Detroit, and Utah became the forty-fifth state. In 1897, *The New York Sun* ran an editorial that answered a question from an eight year old girl, "Yes, Virginia, there is a Santa Claus." In 1898, the Spanish-American War started and ended with a treaty between the U.S and Spain, and the element radium was discovered in France. Emil Zola's famous defense of Captain Dreyfus, *J'accuse*, was published and Dreyfus vindicated. The first automobile insurance was issued in the U.S. for $11. Theodor Herzl, the father of Zionism, met with Kaiser Wilhelm II in Jerusalem, and in 1899, the first World Zionist Congress convened in Basel, Switzerland, under the leadership of Theodor Herzl. These world news events give some perspective of this period of time in which the Kahns lived.

It was during these eventful years in Laufersweiler that my father, Joseph, grew up. At first little Joseph slept in his parents' bedroom upstairs in a wooden crib called a *schaukelwiege*, the bottom cut in the shape of an arc, enabling it to be rocked from side to side. Herman and Ernst slept in the second bedroom, while Jenny, Ida, and Bella in the third. The rooms were small, each one holding a large bed, a wardrobe, and a washstand with a mirror. After Simon, Gerda, and Martha were born, the two bedrooms became too crowded, and other sleeping arrangements were needed. Opa Isaak and Oma Hannchen couldn't just go out and buy a larger home or even add on to their existing one. Also, farmers and merchants usually built their homes according to their own needs and abilities, and did some of the carpentry work. Isaak arrived at an ingenious idea which, as described shortly, solved the problem. See exhibit 3.3, 3.4, and 3.5 in the appendix for photos of buildings that my father would have seen at this time.

Since Isaak raised, traded, bought, and sold livestock, primarily cattle, there was originally a large stable attached to the house with a hayloft above. There was also a large barn containing all sorts of equipment for a horse-drawn carriage, collars and bridles for the horses, a hay wagon, a horse drawn sleigh, as well as all kinds of farm implements. There were logs, wooden planks, leather belts, buckets, barrels, tin cans of all sizes, ropes, broken chairs, hand woven baskets and things I can only describe as curious stuff. As a youngster I just loved to spend time there and hang out. The entrance to the house opened onto the side of a large courtyard facing the street. In the courtyard's center, conspicuous by its size and smell, was a large dung pit surrounded by a low stone wall. Near the house and barn was a cistern that supplied water for the family. It looked like what we today think of as a wishing well where one throws coins and makes a wish. A bucket hung from a rope that was wound over a winch. By turning the crank at the end of the winch,

EXHIBIT 3.6 Children in front of Cheder at Laufersweiler circa 1895-1898. First row sitting on ground, sixth from left: Joseph Kahn. Second row, second from left: Ida Kahn; last from right: Gerda Kahn. Third row fifth from left: Jenny Kahn. Third row second from right: Bella Kahn. Fourth row eighth from the left: Simon Kahn. The other three Kahn children, Herman, Ernst, and Martha, could not be identified in the photo. Perhaps they are not in the photo.

the bucket could be lowered into the water; turning the winch in the opposite direction brought the filled bucket back to the top of the well. The bucket of water was then carried into the garden behind the barn and courtyard where potatoes, lettuce, onions, carrots, cucumbers and other vegetables and berries including goose berries were grown for home consumption. There were also a few apple, pear and cherry trees. Most of the water, however, was taken to the barn to feed the livestock. Opa Isaak and Oma Hannchen were fortunate to have a well on their property. Many of the townspeople did not. They had to go to the water well in the town square that delivered water into two basins, one for drinking and watering livestock, the other for washing clothes. The well was referred to as the *bohre*, perhaps because bohre in German generally means a large hole. Families who had no well on their property had to carry water from the town well to their homes or put the containers on a pushcart. The well was a likely place for women to gossip and share news of their families and the town. This was long before I came to Laufersweiler; communal well-usage had gradually decreased as most families began to rely on indoor plumbing.

On occasions when the weather was warm enough, Oma Hannchen and Opa Isaak would bring out a large sheet metal tub, fill it with water and let their children bathe. On a hot day they could play in the water and cool off. Can you imagine the scene in the courtyard with as many as nine children playing while chickens, ducks, and geese ran around making their peculiar noises, interrupted occasionally by the loud mooing sounds from the barn? Of course, Oma Hannchen kept a watchful eye on her children while she was doing laundry, cooking, canning, baking, or mending clothes. There was a lot or work, so much that the children did chores around the house as soon as they were able to walk. The girls sewed and did housework. The boys helped with housework too, but they tended mostly to heavier work like tilling the garden, feeding and milking livestock, taking livestock to pasture, cleaning the barn, and sawing, chopping, and stacking firewood.

Life was hard in those years. Bread was baked at home or in the community *backhaus* bakery. Likewise, there was a community mill where wheat grain was ground into flour. Each family's name was entered into a lottery that determined what days they would take their turn to grind grain or bake bread. Opa and Oma had to decide how much flour they needed for the entire year for all their baking and cooking needs. Grinding flour was done primarily once a year, but the baking in the community bakery took place monthly. Breads were round, dark ryes about twelve inches in diameter except for the challah, also known as *berches*, eaten on Shabbat. It was a braided loaf of white bread, sixteen inches long, glazed with egg white. Oma Hannchen would always bake two loaves each week for the large family. Visiting my grandfather as a boy, I was always filled with great excitement when I went to the *backes*. Even though I did not do the hard work of kneading the dough or firing the ovens with wood, I enjoyed being there, watching and inhaling the wonderful aroma of baking bread, and sampling cakes and cookies.

Can you imagine the activity, the hustle and bustle, the commotion in the Kahn's house every day? In the morning, the older children washed themselves either in the laundry tub adjacent to the kitchen, in the water trough outside the barn, or in several glazed pottery wash basins that were in the three bedrooms upstairs. Matching water pitchers were filled the night before and stood waiting in each washbasin. On the outside wall of the house next to a stone trough was a water pump with a handle. The handle had to be primed four or five times or more to bring the water from the well up to the pump faucet. The same type of system was in place in the laundry room, also used for bathing and washing, and in the kitchen by the sink. During those years running water was only for people in big cities, not in Laufersweiler. The only running water came from rain. The water would run off the slate shingled roof and into large barrels standing at the far ends of the house and barn.

What about toilets? There was a two-hole outhouse near the barn with pieces of newspaper, catalogues, and other paper serving a unique purpose. This arrangement was not very convenient, but that was the way things were when my father Joseph was growing up, and as I remember from later visits. During the night, everybody, especially in winter, used chamber pots that were conveniently located under the beds and had to be emptied out in the morning.

In those years, kitchens were big, as it was in this house. The kitchen was a very busy place, located directly adjacent to a large combination living and dining room. It held a coal and wood-fired cast-iron range that was between six and seven feet long and about thirty inches deep. The only other heat source was an iron potbelly stove in the *gute Stub*, local dialect for the living room. With no heat in the bedrooms upstairs, feather bedding and feather-filled quilts made sure that no one froze during the winter. Heat traveled up the stairs and readily went through un-insulated ceilings from below. Standing inside the stable, I could tell that the house was built from logs laid lengthwise, filled in between with mud and straw. Inside the house the uneven walls were covered with paint while some logs were visible in the ceilings.

Each of the children and grownups wore hand-knitted bed shoes in winter. Opa Isaak and the boys wore flannel nightshirts that almost reached the floor and nightcaps with tassels. Oma Hannchen and the girls wore similar nightshirts and very simple bonnets for warmth. The bonnets also served to keep hair in place. When darkness fell, the family lit candles and kerosene lamps and lanterns that they carried about the house and barn as needs arose, always careful of the ever present danger of fire. When going out in the evening or early morning, a lamp was carried. In the early darkness of winter the Kahns' would read, learn how to crochet or weave by hand or with a loom, do homework, while Opa would read Rabbi Rashi's teachings.

Because there were no streetlights, only moonlight and lights from lamps and candles inside houses and taverns shone the way after dusk. There was really no place to go in the evening unless one visited neighbors, went to shul, courted, or made trips to the butcher, Simon Baum, the grocery, or the seamstress, tailor, the tavern, or Löser's general store. My great-uncle Isaak Löser and great-aunt Lenchen (sister of Hannchen and Malchen) owned the store. There were no fixed hours for any of these businesses, and people would come in not only to buy, but also to talk and find out what was new in the area, country, and the world. News traveled slowly and came by word of mouth, mail, and out of town newspapers. Laufersweiler did not have its own newspaper. A town crier came each day to the center of town at noon, rang a large bell, and then read national, world, and local news. Local news included deaths, births, marriages, accidents, illnesses, and fires, etc. in nearby villages. In the 1920s and 30s, the town crier stopped just a few houses below Löser's general store. From what I remember, he came on bicycle.

The large kitchen opened into an even bigger room that served as a combination living/dining/family room. It was here that this large family of eleven, hired help, and visitors ate and gathered for all of their activities. This room saw celebrations including Passover meals, *holekrashs*--a religious celebration where a baby girl received her Hebrew name, *b'rith milah*, circumcision of baby boys held on the eighth day of life, birthdays, and bar mitzvahs. On many of these occasions the *mischpocha* (relatives), the kille, (Jewish community), Christian neighbors, village fathers and sometimes clergy, as well as friends from Laufersweiler and surrounding towns participated and celebrated. In addition to several unmatched chairs, high chairs and several footstools furnished the room, I remember a large, ornately carved rocking chair that Opa Isaak used most of the time. In the center of the room was a huge, plain, rectangular oak table with twelve uncomfortable solid wood chairs. Hidden underneath this table was a trap door. When opened,

EXHIBIT 3.7 Laufersweiler, late 1920s. A typical house for the area, belonging to Sally and Erna Mayer (née Baer) and their son Heinz. Heinz, later called Henry, married my cousin, Lorie (née Lerner) Mayer.

EXHIBIT 3.8 Same house in Laufersweiler 40 years later, with some modernization.

a ladder led down into a large cellar where flour sacks, baked breads, potatoes and homemade wines were stored. Benches ran the entire length along the outside walls of the living room, each below a large window. They were approximately two feet wide and twenty inches high, made of solid wood, with hinged lids spaced every five feet or so. Pretty homemade pillows sat on top. When the pillows were removed and the lid lifted, inside was stored a down pillow, a small homemade mattress, a blanket, and feather bedding. It became apparent that these so called bench boxes were Isaak's solution to sleeping accommodations for the older children for whom there was no room upstairs. As ingenious as these makeshift beds were, their dimensions somewhat constrained the movements of the children sleeping in them. However, they assured that all nine Kahn children grew up with straight spines, backs and gaits. I have no idea who slept in the bench beds, but I assume that Herman and Ernst were the first. Later, my dad also slept there from what he told me in later years. Whether any of the girls ever slept in the bench beds, I never found out. As I remember, whenever I visited my grandfather and years later after he had died, these bench beds were very comfortable, and I enjoyed sleeping or just playing in them. The additional hinged benches along the walls were used for storage of toys, books, extra kosher dishes, and more. For me, they were chests filled with curious treasures.

My father was, according to his three brothers, a nice, quiet, dependable, and industrious fellow. He had apparently inherited those traits from his mother and father. Not to give the wrong impression, I must add that I discerned in later years that all of the nine children grew up to be exceptional individuals. None of them ever had any type of criminal record, and the courts would have gone out of business had they been dependent on the Kahn clan.

Kahn's Joseph, as he was known in Laufersweiler, was a good student and was particularly adept in arithmetic. He enjoyed adding, subtracting, multiplying, or dividing series of numbers without writing them down. This was a big asset for my sister Irene and me when we went to school because dad was able to explain and drill arithmetic with us. For him it was a big advantage later in his life when he was on his own and established himself in business. One should also remember that in the early years of dad's life the abacus was still being used. Dad, like the rest of the kids, had chores to complete before and after school. Taking care of the vegetable garden was a job for everyone from providing natural fertilizer to the soil, to planting, cultivating, and harvesting. Dad told me about watering the garden which had to be done by carrying water buckets and large sprinkling cans. Harvesting different crops of wheat, hay, potatoes and other plants was hard work, but everyone, including neighbor families, pitched in. There seemed to have been a very cooperative spirit among the town's folk for making the hard, rural life more acceptable.

The community spirit also existed when women and girls got together at different houses in the evening with their looms, spinning wheels, and knitting needles to make fabric for shirts, dresses, linen, mend articles of clothing for their families or worked on items for their dowries. The men also pitched in together to fell trees in the community forest and cut them into firewood for winter. Some of the cooperative activity was sheer necessity like fighting fires and other unforeseen calamities, or helping with the annual *kirmes*, town fair and harvesting. Neighbors helped each other when it became necessary to repair or build a new home or barn, a marked contrast from what happened many years later when the Nazis came with their hate propaganda destroying existing cooperation and good will.

All activities stopped at the beginning of sunset on Friday, Shabbat evening, and resumed only after the evening of the next day. Hannchen and Isaak observed the Jewish traditions and were true to them including the holidays when the family went to shul. Each of the children learned to read, and to some extent, write Hebrew since prayer books at that time did not have a German transliteration. Because Opa did his livestock business in the surrounding villages, he was seldom home to help raise and teach the nine children or taking care of the household. That was left to Oma and was quite a responsibility and loads of work from early morning to late evening. They both worried about the future of each of their children as they grew older. The hired help attended primarily to the livestock. Hannchen and Isaak knew too well that there was no future for their children in this small village of perhaps no more than 750 people.

The only industry of sorts was the matzo, unleavened bread, bakery in the village that employed about seventeen people for the three month period prior to Pesach, the Passover festival. Located in the Kirchgasse, the same street on which the Kahns lived, it was last operated, prior to the Holocaust, by August Joseph. I remember when we lived in Mannheim that Mom and Dad, his brother Uncle Simon and Aunt Hilde also living in Mannheim, would order the Passover matzos in big, round, ten pound packages from Laufersweiler. A smaller package contained the "mizbe matzo," short for *mizbeach* - place of sacrifice, which were only to be eaten at the Seder table. In other parts of the world they were known as shemurah matzo. The quality of the matzos was so well known that they were shipped all over Germany and adjacent countries. It was probably the only product for which the town was well known.

Then came the saddest day for Opa and the children when, on October 17, 1909, his beloved wife and their mother, Hannchen, passed away after a number of illnesses. She was not quite fifty-six years old, too young for a wonderful wife and mother to leave her husband and precious children. Her death was due, in part, to bearing nine children in a matter of nineteen years coupled with the hard work of raising them and conducting a household in a farming community where life was primitive and without doctors or hospital. I would love to have known her, but it was not to be. Hannchen was buried in the only Jewish cemetery in the village that consisted of one long row of graves. Only in 1911 was it finally possible to buy additional adjacent ground to enlarge the cemetery. At the time of their mother's death, Jenny was thirty years old, the youngest, Martha, was thirteen, and Dad was nineteen. What a pity to lose your mother at such a young age, unable to have her see her family grow and prosper and for her children to return the love that she had heaped on them. Following her mother's death, Gerda, the second youngest of the Kahn siblings, took care of the chores at home until she became married in 1920 at age 27, to Manfred Ackerman.

EXHIBIT 3.9 My Opa Isaak Kahn and his daughter Gerda, who took care of him and the house after his wife Hannchen died. Notice the stone and timber house construction.

Public school in Laufersweiler was at best a patchwork of rudimentary learning, particularly for Jewish children who went additionally to cheder where Judaic subjects were taught. As the Kahn children graduated from eight years of public school, there was really nothing else to achieve but to help at home, as most of them did, or leave Laufersweiler for some larger city where there were some relatives or friends. Needless to say, Isaak and Hannchen did not have the means to send any of the boys or girls to a Gymnasium, a secondary school generally located in a larger city. Grants, scholarships, or state subsidies were not available in those days so basically only the well to do could move on to a school of higher learning and eventually a university. As a result, after my dad graduated from school in 1903, Isaak and Hannchen decided that it was best for Joseph to learn a trade. A friend of Isaak's was a shoemaker in the town of Saarlouis located fifteen km. northwest of Saarbrücken, a much larger city about fifty miles southwest of Laufersweiler. He took Joseph on as an apprentice to learn the trade and to learn all there was to know about leather. Dad was not quite fifteen years old and told me often how homesick he had been, and how strange it was for him at first to live with the family of the shoemaker, one of the *Gebrüder Bickart* (Brothers Bickart, the name of the business).

The work was hard, but he learned willingly and was interested in every phase of leather working. Later in life, after Irene and I were born, I can still see

EXHIBIT 3.10 Simon and Joseph Kahn on a postcard from Saarlouis Germany where Joseph learned the shoemaker trade. The card was mailed September 1907 to relatives wishing them a happy Rosh Hashanah.

him taking care of our shoes. He not only polished them, but also bought the right kind of leather to put new soles on when they were needed. In fact, Dad had a box where he kept all the tools necessary to make shoe repairs. Of course there were shoemakers in Mannheim, but Dad was frugal, plus he enjoyed the filing, gluing and nailing.

Since Dad's mom, Hannchen, and my mother's mom, Malchen, were sisters, it was only natural that the two families would get together either in Laufersweiler or in Luxembourg. It was on one of those occasions that the two cousins, Joseph Kahn and Martha Joseph met as children. Since she had been a school girl, Martha kept a *Poesie*, a leather-bound book in which friends, family, and visitors wrote short dedications. I found a poetic entry by Joseph that told a lot about their courtship. At one of those early family visits Dad recalled that Martha had a special nickname for him. Later in 1918 he wrote, "as fate would have it I found you again in 1910 in this praiseworthy land." Both the nickname and the reference to meeting again ten years before to this letter was written, indicates they most likely met as children. He was now twenty-one and Martha eighteen, just the right age to fall in love.

That's exactly what my parents did, they fell in love. He wrote that the evenings were long until they met again in Hollerich, Luxembourg, at the home of her parents, Raphael and Malchen. Then there was the continued exchange of letters between them from Luxembourg to Saarbrucken and from Saarbrucken to Hollerich. Since most of his letters had to be written in the evening after work, he was tired and told Martha that he once fell asleep while writing her. The letters continued for some time until they decided to meet in Paris, France for a few days, where Martha was a governess or a companion to a lady. They had a wonderful time, although, according to Joseph, as written in her Poesie book, they had a few quarrels. He went on to write that none of them were lasting and, "did not create a wall between us!" Eventually, Joseph was able to find a job in Luxembourg City with Berthold Lieben Lederhandlung, a leather business. He worked there primarily as a sales person doing extensive traveling, calling on

EXHIBIT 3.11 The Poesie Album – still in my possession.

EXHIBIT 3.12 Joseph, 1910

shoemakers and manufacturers of leather goods throughout the area. It was a better paying job, while working and living with a nicer family, and the added advantage of being near his love, Martha Joseph.

In the meantime, time did not stand still at Laufersweiler. Jenny, the oldest daughter, had left home years before her mother, Hannchen, passed away, and moved to Frankfurt at the Main River. The latter designation is important because there was at least several other Frankfurts in Germany. There she became a dressmaker and was quite good at her job. A few years later her younger sister, Bella came to Frankfurt and they both worked on making dresses to order, which was customary in those days. In 1912 or 1913, Bella became a little homesick for her two older brothers. She was somewhat adventurous and decided to visit Herman and Ernst who had earlier, before World War I, traded the village of Laufersweiler for the big American city, Chicago. At the time America was touted as the land of opportunity, and Bella wanted to see for herself.

For almost a century America's immigration policy was extremely liberal and encouraged all who wanted to enter with few restrictions. As a result of increased arrivals of immigrants each year, questions arose as to whether a head tax instituted in 1903 and the disbarment of objectionable individuals from entering the country was working. At one time the greatest influx of immigrants came from Ireland, but now the preponderance were coming from Italy, followed by Poland, Russia, Belgium, and other countries. These numbers included many Jews fleeing persecution. American workers also raised increasing concerns that immigrants would threaten their livelihoods by working longer hours for less pay. However, American industry leaders, business owners, farmers, and mine operators were only too eager to hire the newcomers because of their work ethic and satisfaction with lower pay and tolerance of inferior working conditions compared to what American workers expected.

Immigrants continued coming to the land of opportunity, a land where, at least up to that period, wars and soldiering were far from the horizon and racial and religious persecution were not officially condoned. As a matter of fact, most of the immigrants had never seen a Negro in Europe.

How my Uncles Herman and Ernst came to America is an interesting story in the history of the Kahn family. You may remember that their mother, Hannchen Kahn's maiden name was Levy. One of her brothers, Simon Levy, had immigrated to America years earlier, between 1870 and 1880 where he first became what was then known as a peddler. Today we would call that same person a salesman. Enterprising as he was, he later established a business distributing supplies needed by the wine and liquor bottling industry. A considerable part of his business was geared to farmers and small vintners who grew grapes and bottled their own wines, or through fermentation of certain fruits, and distillation of their own vinegar. The business came to be known as the Chicago Specialty Box Company. From what I remember, the warehouse and offices were located at 20 East Kinzie Street, Chicago, next to the Chicago River. I do not know whether this was the original location of the business. Probably not.

After Simon Levy was well established in Chicago, around 1900 he returned for a visit to Laufersweiler, to see his family and friends. He used the occasion to brag about America, his accomplishments, and the good life. He also used the occasion to suggest and urge his sister, Hannchen, and her husband, Isaak Kahn, to send their oldest son, Herman, to America, since there was no future in the farming community of that village. I have been told that Herman didn't want to go, so instead, his brother Ernst became the first of the Kahns to venture to America. There he started to work for his Uncle Simon's business as a stock and errand messenger boy. Several years later brother Herman made the decision to emigrate from Germany, and he, too, got his start at Specialty Box Company in Chicago.

As mentioned earlier, Bella missed her brothers and yearned to see them and America. The letters from Ernst and Herman confirmed that it was the land of opportunity, and Bella wanted to see for herself. And so in 1912 or 1913, she went for what was to be only a visit. She decided to extend her stay and took a job doing dress alterations at the department store, Carson Pirie Scott & Co., French Room dress shop, in downtown Chicago.

While the nine Kahn children had grown up and most of them had left home, the world around them in Europe was marked by unprecedented growth and progress. Other countries of the world envied the industrial and material wealth that had been infused by important inventions and scientific discoveries. However, on the political, economic, and social fronts there were undercurrents that would create a boiling pot of troublesome issues, eventually leading to an unprecedented world war.

All nine Kahn children grew up in those years while many important events, some of enormous consequences, developed. After the turn of the 19th century, political, social, and economic, upheaval all over Europe became responsible for large emigration movements to North and South American countries.

Far away in India millions of people were starving, while in South Africa the fighting between the Boers and British soldiers seemed endless. In 1900, at the World Exposition at Paris, the wonders of electricity were on display to the world while 99% of the world's inhabitants were still living with kerosene lamps, gas lights, candles, fire, or complete darkness. Attempting to open up China to the outside world produced anti-foreign attitudes that led to the Boxer Rebellion in China between 1899 and 1901.

In pursuit of its imperialistic designs, Germany decided to build no less than thirty-eight battleships over the next twenty years. The German ship, *Deutschland*, broke the eastward ocean crossing time in five days and eleven hours, while in Morristown, New Jersey, an Automobile Club member was arrested for exceeding a thirty mph speed limit. American President William McKinley was assassinated, and the newly invented Kodak Brownie Camera sold for $1.00. At the same time, German Kaiser Wilhelm did not have peaceful endeavors on his mind. He called for the "Germanization of all Slavic people"!

In 1902, the United States made the decision to build the Panama Canal, while in Russia, the Czar encouraged pogroms resulting in the murder of thousands of Jews despite the pleading by President Teddy Roosevelt. The Ford Company sold the first automobile in 1903, and in the same year Theodor Herzl told the sixth Zionist Congress in Basel, Switzerland, that Palestine was the best area for a future Jewish state. In Kitty Hawk, North Carolina, the Wright brothers of Dayton, Ohio flew the first heavier-than-air craft giving birth to the engine powered airplane.

In 1904, Japan and Russia engaged in a full-fledged war that ended with a Japanese victory. While the Italian tenor, Enrico Caruso, made his first recording, and the New York Subway System opened. San Francisco experienced the most catastrophic earthquake in 1906 that killed thousands, and in France the Jewish Army Captain, Alfred Dreyfus, after being accused of being a traitor, was vindicated and bestowed with honors. German troops crushed tribal uprisings in its colony, Southwest Africa, and told the world that it had developed the first self-propelled submarine. Expressing its imagined superiority, Germany demanded additional colonial territory in 1907. Attacks and murders of Jews continued in Russia, while Germany, Italy, and Austria signed a triple alliance.

The Boy Scout movement was born in England, and the Pope issued a decree warning against secular influences. In the same year, the Women's International

Socialist Congress denounced German militarism and its colonial policies. Germany ignored the denouncement, and its army bought Zeppelin dirigibles for aerial reconnaissance. Also, Cuban rebels attacked Americans in Havana, while the International Peace Conference at The Hague, Netherlands, agreed on the rules of war.

The year 1908, saw the Russian Czar praise leaders of pogroms against the Jews by calling them heroes, and in London discussions were held on arms reduction, while France introduced the invention of an electric gun. In the meantime, Germany passed legislation to increase ship building, in spite of England's protesting the numerical growth of German war ships. England's King Edward, concerned with the ever-growing military might of Germany, tried to persuade Germany's ally, Austria, to oppose aggressive German designs. His attempts failed. Belgium annexed the Congo, Turkish troops massed near the Bulgarian border, while Austria and Hungary annexed Bosnia, and Serbia threatened war against Austria. Europe had become a tinder box.

In 1909, Serbia's Crown Prince warned England of German militarism. America noted Germany's bullying and the increasing unrest in Europe and funded the construction of new battleships each with fourteen-inch guns. Great Britain announced building six new battleships, and Russian troops invaded Persia. France requested an army made up exclusively of men from its colonies, and in 1910 French troops occupied Morocco. In the same year Jews were expelled from the Russian city of Kiev, and the Japanese Army invaded Korea. In 1911, Germany increased its so-called peace time army by one-half million men, and Great Britain decided to build five more battleships. If all this saber rattling were not enough, Italy went to war with Turkey for control over Tripoli.

Also on June 1, 1911, Laufersweiler inaugurated a new synagogue since the old one was run down and no longer fit for religious services. It was built at Kirchstrasse 6, only a few houses from the Kahn's house. The Laufersweiler synagogue was renovated on the outside after World War II. The inside currently serves as a museum of the Jews of Laufersweiler before the Holocaust, an area for study, and a library (where the original sanctuary stood).

Germany was in its glory when its ally, Italy, bombed Beirut in 1912. Germany used dirigibles for military use and occupied the island of Rhodes. Bulgaria and Serbia declared war on Turkey. On the other side of the ocean American Marines landed in Cuba. Finally in 1913, Germany accepted British requests to limit the size of its navy, but then went ahead and voted an additional $510 million for its army and increased its number by an additional 135,000 soldiers. Seeing the handwriting on the wall, France ordered the draft of all twenty-year-old males.

All of Europe was involved in a never-ending arms race, and talk of war increased to a fever pitch as 1914 approached. Russia also increased its military budget. But the straw that broke the camel's back came on June 28, 1914, when

Archduke Ferdinand and wife, heir to the throne of Austria and Hungary, were assassinated. This tragedy upset the political equilibrium that had existed in Europe and led to an unexpected chain of events. Austria and Hungary declared war on Serbia. Russia immediately mobilized and so did Belgium. On August 1, Germany declared war on Russia, and also invaded France, Luxembourg, Belgium, thereby declaring war on them as well. England next declared war on Germany, and World War I had begun!

Historian purists argued that based on the assassination that triggered the events leading to war, Germany could not be held responsible for starting the war. Nevertheless, Germany, by virtue of its expansionistic, militaristic, arrogant policies, as well as military alliances, had divided all of Europe into two camps for the sole purpose of pitting one against the other.

To what extent my father and his other siblings were conscious of the events that finally led to war, I can only guess. Later, however, based on brief discussions, remarks and overheard comments as I grew up, Dad was proud to be a German and believed in Germany's superiority in many ways, at least until the Third Reich under Hitler led to other conclusions.

So strong was Dad's allegiance to his fatherland and his obligation as a Jew that, although he had a job in neutral Grand Duché of Luxembourg at the time of the all-out German mobilization, he left on August 1, 1914, for Trier, Germany, and then Koblenz where he enlisted in the German Army. He did so after a long and sad good-bye with his sweetheart, Martha Joseph, in Hollerich Luxembourg. Both hoped for a quick end to the war. Near Koblenz, Germany, he was trained with a *Fuhrparkkolonne*. This is an outdated military term for which there is no adequate translation. To explain, Dad was assigned to a regiment whose mission was to supply troops with guns, ammunition, food, medical supplies, clothing etc., to sustain them on the battlefront using horse-drawn wagons and caissons which required considerable care. The horses, especially, had to be fed, kept strong and healthy. They were trained to pull heavily loaded wagons in pairs, and in foursomes to pull heavy artillery guns and other extremely heavy loads. Motorized vehicles played an insignificant role in this war until about 1917, when the British Army introduced tanks for the first time. When my dad enlisted in the German Army he was twenty-four years old, five-feet, five-inches tall, and weighed 150 pounds. Although he was small of stature, he was very muscular, having helped with chores at home, later working as a shoemaker, handling heavy reams of leather and supplies. His unit supported the battles in France along the river Marne, and he later often mentioned locations like Soissons, Reims, Chalons, Chateau-Thierry, and Verdun where battles raged nearby. Dad did not dwell on how terrible the war was, although he laughingly mentioned an incident when one of the horses he was tending stepped on his foot, and really hurt him.

By the time he had recovered, the horse stepped on his other foot. Dad's brother Simon also served in the Kaiser's German Army.

In summer of 1915, Dad was ordered back to Germany for additional training with the infantry and was assigned to a heavy machine gun company on the Western front. According to his military identification he was, "Musketeer (rifleman) J. Kahn, Ersatz (reserve) Battalion, Reserve Regiment No.25 4th Company, Coblenz." He was infinitely more vocal about the fighting there. He told us about the trenches both sides had dug and the constant artillery barrages day and night from both sides. There were rats that would not let him sleep, mud everywhere, and water standing in shell holes. He told about the skirmishes into the no-man's land between the enemy positions, and the dead and those wounded by machine gun fire. Seeing the dead and injured was the worst, especially those who had succumbed to machine gun fire which was at knee height. Therefore, many of the wounded had to have their legs amputated at the knee or worse. There was also reconnaissance by manned balloons, dirigibles, and even an occasional airplane. He also told of sharing a cake that Martha had sent with other comrades. When he returned to his post, a shell had hit and killed some of his soldier buddies there. He claimed that Martha's cake had saved his life. She smiled when Dad told me and my sister Irene that story.

EXHIBIT 3.13 Martha Joseph, circa 1917. See exhibit 3.15 in the appendix for a photo of Martha and her siblings.

EXHIBIT 3.14 Joseph in German uniform. Photo taken circa 1916/17 when courting Martha. Translation of back of the postcard in the appendix; see exhibits 3.23, 3.24, and 3.25.

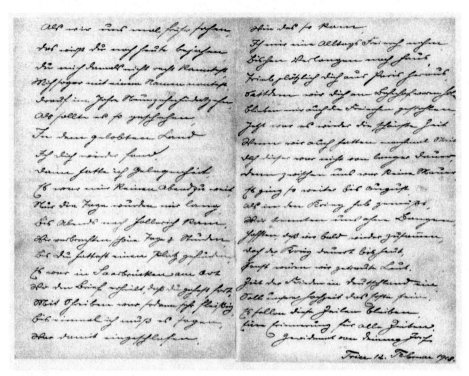

EXHIBIT 3.16 Dad's dedication to his sweetheart, Martha. The English translation is in the appendix, exhibit 3.18.

EXHIBIT 3.17 Dad's signature and date of his dedication. It is interesting to note that my father spelled his name sometimes with a "ph" as recorded in his birth certificate, and other times, such as here, with an "f". For more samples from the Poesie, see exhibits 3.19 and 3.20 in the appendix.

When Dad had time he wrote letters to his loved ones including his sweetheart, Martha, whom, apparently, he had promised to marry when the war was over. This became obvious from a dedication written to her several years later at Trier, February 12, 1918 in her Poesie book, which is now in my possession.

When the war broke out, Germany immediately overran the small neutral country of Luxembourg and proceeded to sequester lodgings for some of its soldiers, horses, and wagons for convoys. My Oma and Opa, Raphael and Malchen Joseph, in Hollerich, Luxembourg, had three good looking daughters at home, Martha (my mother), Helene, and Irma. It was only a matter of time before some of the German soldiers befriended them. Beginning the summer of 1916, one of them, Otto Winkler, often came to the house, and all of them had a good time. From a piece written by Winkler in Martha's Poesie book, it appears that he knew

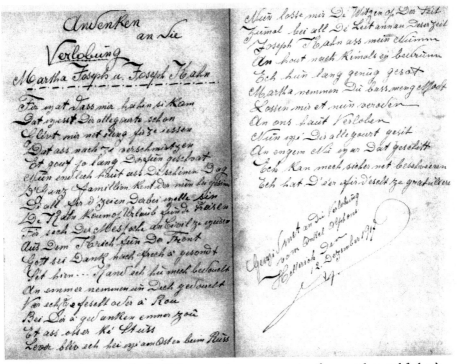

EXHIBIT 3.21 The poem Uncle Alphons wrote as a memento of my mother and father's engagement. See exhibit 3.22 in the appendix to read the full English translation.

about the relationship between Martha and Joseph, and even when they were all having a good time, she would cry thinking about her sweetheart soldier Joseph.

Due to the unsanitary conditions under which the soldiers lived and ate, Dad came down with a bad case of dysentery. He was treated in field hospitals for intestinal inflammation and great abdominal pain. Several times he was sent on furlough for rest, and took the time to visit Martha in Luxembourg. On one of these visits, December 12, 1917, they became engaged. Uncle Alphons, brother of Raphael Joseph, wrote a short poem of congratulations as a memento for the happy couple. It was written in the Letzebourg dialect, but I managed to read and undestand most of it.

By 1918 the war against Russia was going well for Germany, but the battles on the Western front were at a stalemate. As American Doughboys entered the war, hope for victory was snatched from the Germans. Then in October, during a French offensive, Joseph, along with many thousands of other German soldiers, was taken prisoner in the vicinity of the French town, Aisne. Ironically, Joseph's capture was only weeks before the German surrender on November 11, 1918. When Dad's family and his sweetheart, Martha, heard about his capture, they were very relieved, aware of the tragic alternatives. At the end of the war, however, victorious France did not free the German prisoners. Joseph was held captive for another eighteen months, and was not released until the spring of

1920. He was assigned a desk job, since he understood some French. He was not treated badly and had decent food as well as cigarettes. Yet time went ever so slow.

After more than six years of long distance romance, praying and waiting, my Father and mother kept their promise to each other. On July 27, 1920, 27 year-old Martha Joseph, born to Amalia Levy Joseph and Raphael Joseph at Schieren, Grand Duché of Luxembourg, married 30 year-old Joseph Kahn, born to Johanna Levy Kahn and Isaak Kahn at Laufersweiler, Germany. Although most of my dad's family was unable to attend the wedding, all of the Luxembourg mischpocha, family and friends of the Josephs provided for the happy event and customary celebrations. It was not long after that the happy couple moved to Mannheim where they started their life together. I'm not sure why they chose Mannheim, other than it was an industrious and cultured city that had a fairly large Jewish community, especially in comparison Laufersweiler.

Overshadowed by the events of war, an event had occurred, primarily significant to Jews around the world, and especially to those who had suffered from the ravages of blatant anti-Semitism for hundreds of years. It was the surprise announcement by the British government on November 2, 1917, in a declaration drawn up by Foreign Minister Lord Balfour. In essence it stated His Majesty's Government views with favor the establishment in Palestine of a national home for the Jewish People. While no one at the time had any idea of the far reaching consequences of this bold promise, it was the spark the Zionist movement needed to formulate imaginative plans for the future, to make aliyah, settling in Palestine to cultivate the land and drain the swamps, of what is now the state of Israel.

CHAPTER FOUR

My Hometown of Mannheim

Is it possible to describe a city and tell about its buildings, streets, stores, theaters, restaurants, sports stadiums, railroad stations, parks and more, after a childhood so long ago? A childhood I was later robbed of by being terrorized, traumatized, cast out, and finally exiled? Shouldn't this darkest period of my life cloud my view about the city I was born in? One would think so. Yet, my early childhood was normal, pleasant--even happy. Therefore, I have fond recollections of the city and its environs, and in all fairness, I must maintain a complete separation between this beautiful place of my youth, the places within it, and the people who later became demons after Adolf Hitler came to power.

As I remember, Mannheim, including the suburbs, east of the river Rhine, had a population of approximately 300,000 inhabitants. The city was and still remains one of the largest cities in that geographical area, and one of the more important industrial centers of Germany. Steel products, special metal and non-metallic materials, processed agricultural products, manufactured automotive, aeronautical, and electronic components, and chemical products were just a few of the commodities for which the city was known. Winemaking, textile production, tobacco growing, and cigar making were other sources that sustained Mannheim economically.

The city is huddled between the Rhine and the confluence of the smaller river, Neckar, and the city of Ludwigshafen. Situated on the other side of the Rhine River, Mannheim had the second largest inland harbor in Germany, and as I remember, it was always endowed with a spirit of progress and vitality. I assume this bustling urban center, compared to Laufersweiler at the very least, is what led my father and mother to settle there. I remember the cleanliness of the streets and parks. There were signs that admonished everyone not to litter or wander off pedestrian walks into lawns or flower areas. There were uniformed guards and policemen who enforced the rules and fined those who disobeyed.

The heart of the city was arranged in a large grid of squares, a layout unique in Germany, and as far as I know, anywhere else in the world at that time. Uniform sized blocks of buildings separated by streets were identified by letters followed by numbers rather than names. Originally there were at least 140 or more of these city blocks encircled by a wide boulevard. Seen from the air, the main part of the city would appear to be in the shape of a horseshoe. The heavily traveled boulevard was called The Ring, with more specific names for certain parts of it. Our last permanent address was L14,14 at the Kaiserring. The entire ring traced, more or less, the long gone fortification walls. At the open end of the horseshoe was

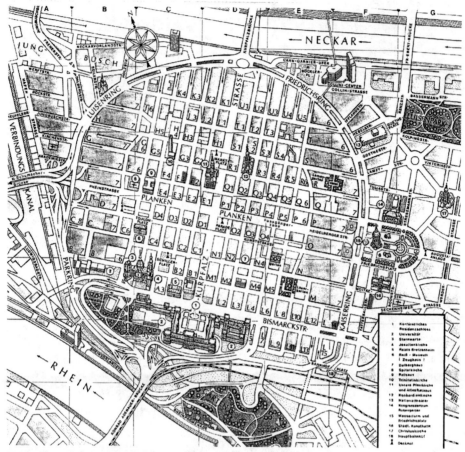

EXHIBIT 4.1 Schematic of Mannheim with places identified in German.

the enormous palace built in the 18th century. Elector Prince Philipp began construction of this palace in 1720 with the intention of it being the second largest Baroque palace in Europe, after Versailles. His palace took 40 years to complete. Although it was heavily damaged by bombs during World War II, it remains one of the largest baroque palaces in Europe. Prince Philipp and thereafter Prince-Elector Karl Theodor and their large entourage lived in this splendid palace that had 500 rooms, and 1,387 very large windows. It extended over an area equivalent to seven city blocks. Its inner courtyard measured 858 sq. yards. A huge monument of the Emperor Kaiser Wilhelm I, on horseback in full military regalia, stood in its center. When I was about ten years old I played with a small balsam wood airplane propelled by a strong rubber band. I was standing at the foot of the monument when I let the airplane go. It landed on the twelve foot high marble base of the statue. I waited until the groundskeeper briefly left the area, and then climbed up to rescue my toy, much to my mother's chagrin.

The city gained notoriety in 1606 when Prince Friedrich IV built a fortress there and named it Friedrichsburg. Over the course of its 400 year history,

EXHIBIT 4.2 Mannheim Castle. Germany's largest Baroque Castle, the second-largest of Europe, built during the reign of the Electors Charles Philipp and Charles Theodor in the course of 40 years (1720-1760). Main view of castle with monument of Emperor Kaiser Wilhem in center.

Castle courtyard with huge monument of Emperor Kaiser Wilhelm in full military regalia. See exhibits 4.3 - 4.8 in the appendix for photos of additional locations around the Mannheim of my childhood.

Mannheim was destroyed three times, and rebuilt each time because of its strategic and economic importance. The first destruction occurred during the Thirty Year War of 1622, the second during the Palatine War of Succession 1689, and the third and most severe destruction occurred during the Allied bombing during World War II. However, after this third time, the city was partially rebuilt without some of the pre-war ornate architectural details. Modern buildings have replaced those destroyed by Allied air attacks.

Some of the sites and places of Mannheim have made ever-lasting impressions on me and are forever entwined in my childhood memories.

The Haupt Bahnhof was a train station of great importance as a key rail junction between northern and southern destinations for passengers and freight. Of all the train stations and terminals I have ever seen, this one was among the largest and busiest with many small stores and restaurants in the side terminal. This is particularly noteworthy because movement by rail was vital to the economy of Germany in terms of goods, raw materials, coal, and passengers. In the 1930s and 40s, this movement also included troops and war materials.

The Wasserturn, was a gigantic, ornate water tower that pumped filtered water into homes. It formed the Friedrichs Platz (Frederick Square), a beautiful park with cascading water displays flowing into a series of small pools and hence into larger pools, each with many large and small fountains. It had more than twenty-five magnificent statues and sculptures bordering walkways and arcades, many of which were surrounded by manicured shrubbery and beautiful flowers. I may be able to connect my childhood with some of these places, while for others brief descriptions will satisfy a general interest while they jog my memory.

The Zeughaus, literally translated as the "Arsenal," was built around 1778 by order of Crown Prince Karl Theodor to provide storage of weapons. It later became a museum of area antiques of sorts with two World War I cannons standing back-to-back in front of the building as a monument. Between the two cannons stood a larger-than-life sculpture of former Field Marshall, Count von Moltke. From my history lessons I remember that he was responsible for winning the battle against the Russians at Tannenberg and the Masurian Lakes during World War I, and for taking an enormous number of Russian prisoners. This Zeughaus Museum was located at city block C5. Inside the museum there were many archaeological exhibits, some items dating back to the Roman period. Included in its archives were many research documents, early astronomy, and early maps of the area where Mannheim is now located. In the lower level there were exhibits of stone pillars that stood on Roman built roads indicating respective locations, directions, and distances. I remember other artifacts dating back to 400 C.E., such as pitchers, pots, pans, keys, porcelain, weapons, bronze statues, and items used in idol worship. Many of these were finds discovered through archeological digs around the nearby town of Ladenburg. I spent many hours there satisfying my youthful curiosity.

The Luisenpark was a park located outside the Ring which was the demarcation of the inner city. It contained a large planetarium where my sister Irene and I would go to see children's movies on Sunday afternoons. In front was a lake that was referred to as Kutzerweier. A short distance from the planetarium was a large glass-enclosed botanical garden. I also remember the Parade Platz at O1, a public square with beautiful flowers and a magnificent large multi-figure bronze pyramid. The large square was finished with cobblestones, which was typical as it was used in earlier times as a parade ground for troops.

At a bend in the Rhine, south of the city and perhaps a thirty minute bicycle ride away, there was a beach that I knew as the Strandbad. To get there one had to travel through the Waldpark, a forested park with walking and bicycle paths that extended for many kilometers along the east shore of the Rhine on the side of Mannheim.

The Planken, a street also known as Heidelbergerstrasse, was one of the few that had a name. It bisected the city inside the Ring starting at the Wasserturm and ending at the Parade Platz area. Lining the street were specialty shops, a number of department stores, a movie theater named Alhambra, restaurants, and cafes. Today it still exists, although much more modern, as one of the main elegant shopping areas of the city.

Another street, the Breite Strasse ("wide street") ran perpendicular to the Planken and the two intersected in the center of the city. This area, not as elegant, contained a shopping arcade and department stores that were interspersed with office buildings, banks, and insurance companies. The Breite Strasse extended from the palace to the Neckar Brücke (bridge over the Neckar) to the suburbs. It was purposely laid out to be exactly one kilometer from the palace to the Neckar River. Between the bridge and the palace, one could find the historical Untere Pfarrkirche (lower parish church). It was connected by a tower, from which could be heard musical chimes at certain hours, to the Altes Rathaus (old town hall). The entire structure was in Baroque architecture, built between 1700 and 1723. In front of the multi-purpose structure was a vast open area that contained an imposing and ornate fountain with unusual sculptures. The figures represented the two rivers, the Rhine and the Neckar, as well as the god, Mercury, and the sun. In this open area in front of the town hall and church, *Marktplatz*, an open market was held three times a week, if I remember correctly. On those days one could find every type of food possible including meats, fresh fish, produce, dairy products, chickens, flowers, spices and more. It was an exciting sight to see hundreds of colorful umbrellas above each of the food stands with a variety of smells enveloping everyone and reaching beyond the confines of the market. I am not surprised that I remember all of this because walking and cycling all over the city in my youth left deep, lasting impressions.

The Rosengarten ("rose garden") was an impressive concert and theater hall complex in which the best musicians, singers, and performers known throughout Europe performed. At the time it was the largest facility of its type in Germany, with a capacity of 5,000 people. The Friedrichspark was a private park for relaxation and enjoyment that required a daily admittance fee or an

EXHIBIT 4.9
Haupt Synagoge: Main Synagogue located at F2,13 with entrance portal and its two side entrances.

annual membership. Although it was a twenty minute walk from our house, we were members. There were playgrounds, a restaurant overlooking a terrace, a lake, and on weekends music from a band filled the air. Across from the park's entrance was the Sternwarte (observatory), an unusual octagonal tower about seven stories high. It was built in Baroque style and at one time served the prince's court astronomer as a sky and star observatory. The Jesuiten Kirche, the Jesuit Church, was located in the immediate vicinity. Built between 1733 and 1760, the church connected via a theological seminary to the Palace. The church, according to current reference literature, was considered one of the most important Baroque churches in southern Germany. There was also the Tattersall for which there is no meaningful translation. It was a key junction and transfer point for streetcars and their passengers. It has particularly disturbing memories for me that I will describe elsewhere.

As my mind and thoughts go back many, many years, I can think of a variety of other places in Mannheim. Perhaps I will bring them up later. A few very

EXHIBIT 4.10 Inside view of the Haupt Synagoge highlighting the overwhelming Byzantine interior design elements. Ceilings were of wood construction with oriental patterns. Note the elevated sermon pulpit on the right front.

important exceptions are my recollections of institutions relevant to my Jewish upbringing, which I would like to share now.

Foremost of these memories is my beloved synagogue, known as the Haupt Synagoge (main synagogue), to which my parents, my sister, and I belonged for as long as I can remember. According to local history there was a place of worship in a private home for about thirteen families as early as 1660. Later, different versions of a synagogue rose in the city block F2, including a community house, a clinic, a house for the poor, and school facilities. After many years of modification the buildings were torn down to make room for the synagogue that I eventually became familiar with and that was finally dedicated June 29, 1855, at a cost of 85,000 Gulden. It's a coincidence that years later my sister Irene's birthday fell on that same date.

The synagogue accommodated about 700 worshippers, and from my perspective, was enormous. The inside was awe inspiring and absolutely stunning. It faced east: a Jerusalem orientation. The ceiling was extremely high, reminding me of a cathedral. It had a unique Byzantine architectural style with gold colors and beautiful ornamentation. The imposing huge entrance doors at F2,13 led to the sanctuary that was about 100 feet wide and 200 feet long. The very high ceiling was configured by two ornate domes. There were primarily two stories. On the ground floor center were pews for adult men with a wide aisle running down the middle. Long, theater-tiered pews for boys of all ages, which were perpendicular to the pews for adult men, lined both sides of the sanctuary under ten beautiful black marble arches to remind us of the Ten Commandments. I usually sat on the right side.

Upstairs in the mezzanine on theater-tiered benches sat the women and young girls. Along the mezzanine railing were seven foot high bronze candelabras, each gold-plated with seven arms on which lights were mounted in a circular fashion. Downstairs, almost identical hanging chandeliers were placed at different intervals, and two more candelabras flanked the *aron hakodesh*, where the Torah scrolls were kept.

EXHIBIT 4.11 Inside view of the Haupt Synagoge showing the ornate architechture.

The walls of the synagogue were covered with gold arabesque frescos, and the floor consisted of alternating color mosaic stone. The windows were alternately clear and frosted. To the rear of the edifice, on the upper level, stood a huge organ with nearby seating for a large choir complement. There were also side entrances that were used when worshippers were late or wanted to leave early. To the right of the *bima* an oak spiral staircase led about ten feet off the ground to a pulpit from which the rabbi preached the sermons. A massive and beautifully decorated roof or cupola towered above that pulpit. Obviously with a Jewish population of about 6,400 in Mannheim, the Haupt Synagogue was too small to accommodate all of its members who wanted to worship, especially on the high holidays. Therefore the synagogue council rented additional halls elsewhere for adult and youth services, which were conducted in the conservative style familiar to our congregation. I have such fond memories of this synagogue that I could spend

EXHIBIT 4.12 Notice the mezzanine reserved for women.

more space describing what it was like. Today, I appreciate those memories more than I did in my youth. Already in 1933, after Hitler came to power, SA men, also known as "brownshirts," entered the synagogue for the first time and damaged it. I was just ten years old when I heard about this incident from my parents at the dinner table, and then from others, including my own friends. It had never happened before, and nobody knew what to make of it or what to do about it. From then on, the Geheime Staatspolizei, the German secret police (better known to history by their abbreviation GESTAPO), was always present during synagogue services so that free speech, open sermons, or pertinent and timely remarks by Rabbi Max Grünewald were no longer possible except at neighborhood get-togethers in someone's home. During these prayer meetings in private homes, Dr. Grünewald was able to read from the scripture, detail current event topics, and lead discussions. He also used that format to give comfort, advice, and courage in the face of Nazi harassment and uncertainty. Mom and Dad attended such prayer study groups for a number of years to discuss different issues. Later at home, with my sister Irene and I present, my parents talked about some things yet never included us in the conversation. From those discussions, I learned about their concerns, the options of emigration, and their reactions to Nazi hostility. It was a time to learn about fear, and a time to be vigilant outside the home. Behind the safety of our home, I pondered our future and often cried myself to sleep.

In addition to the Haupt Synagogue, there was also a second synagogue, the Klaussynagogue, located one city block away from the Haupt Synagogue, at F1,11. This synagogue was built in 1706. In 1888 a major modification of several connected buildings at the "Klaus" was completed, including a Hebrew school and living quarters for a caretaker and the cantor. Again, in 1929, a major interior modification was made to the building which was dedicated in the spring of 1930. The synagogue, as I remember it, differed from the Haupt Synagogue in several ways. First, from the outside of the building, there was no visible sign that this was a synagogue, even though the façade had an Islamic motif. Compared with my synagogue, the interior was not ornate or exquisitely furnished. The mezzanine level was designed for about 200 women in a tiered theater fashion, while the main floor sanctuary was divided into three groupings of pews for 250 male congregants. Perhaps the relatively austere interior had to do with the fact that this was an Orthodox congregation, while ours was considered Conservative. Although there was no organ, there was room for a thirty-six voice choir. In addition, there was a special section for children.

I vividly remember a third synagogue which was referred to as Ostjuedische Gebetstübel. It was a prayer hall for Eastern European Jews who had emigrated or had come as refugees, beginning around 1880, primarily from Russia and Poland. They continued coming to Mannheim during and after World War I. Among them were also Austrian and Hungarian Jews. Most of them spoke Yiddish as well as their own mother language. In addition to bringing their own religious customs, they were generally poor. While some of them joined the Haupt and Klaus Synagogues, the majority preferred to conduct their own services and form their own association at F3,13a, in an upstairs hall of a commercial building just a block from our synagogue. None of them ever came to ours. I remember that several times a year, the rabbis from the other two main synagogues were invited to give sermons at Gebetstübel.

As young children before we became teenagers, and before bar mitzvah, my friends and I would leave our synagogue during Simchat Torah services after we had received candy, chocolate, and fruit from adult worshippers. Included in our group were Max'l Kaufmann and Kurt Müllner, whom we called *Floh* which means flea, the kind you didn't want on your skin. Also with us were Erich Dreifuss, his younger brother Herbert, and Fritz Landman (murdered in a concentration camp) whom we called Frieda, a girl's name because he appeared to us, rightly or wrongly somewhat feminine in his demeanor. Also included sometimes were my two cousins, Ernst Kahn and his younger brother, Walter. I do not want to miss the opportunity to relate a little saying or verse we had for Fritz aka Frieda that we used to get his attention and his dander up: *Frieda das Negerweib mit einem verstellbaren Unterleib!* Freely translated "Frieda the black woman with an adjustable lower abdomen." It had no particular meaning and made no sense, but in German it seemed to rhyme with his nickname. My inconsiderate friends and I had no notion of what we were saying. It was strictly nonsense. Certainly, it had nothing to do with black women since we had never seen one except in the movies. It wasn't until the circus Sarrasani (a well-known German circus of that time) that I ever saw a black person and he was billed as the strongman of the circus. Yes, while everyone considered us different because we were Jews, underneath, my friends and I were just boys doing what normal boys do, except we did it among ourselves, somewhat cautiously, quietly, and without malice.

After we left our synagogue we would go to the Klaus Synagogue and then to the Gebetstübel where, again, we and other children would get more sweets. Simchat Torah was a minor Jewish holiday when we rejoiced with the Torah, paraded with it, and danced around in the synagogue with all the Torahs available at each synagogue. In Mannheim the celebration involved the entire Jewish community, young and old. There was laughter, joy, and singing processions inside the synagogue where children were given little flags, candy, and fruit. Adults, as well as children, danced in the aisles. It was exhilarating, exhausting, and loads of fun for the young boys while girls of our age were more reserved. Later we would look over our loot of candy to see who got the most and traded the sweets we didn't like for sweets from our pals that we liked better.

During the worship service, the last of all Torah portions, Deuteronomy 33-34, was read. At the Klaus Synagogue it was customary for as many men as possible to be called up to the Torah. The fifth Aliyah, or call to the Torah, was traditionally given to all of the children as a group, while a large tallit, prayer shawl, or several were spread over our heads as we together recited the blessing over the Torah. As the last section of the Torah was read, it brought to a close the Torah reading cycle for the year. Then a different Torah was brought forth, from which the first reading of the Torah, Genesis 1:1-2:3 Beresheit, the beginning of creation, was read. I didn't know it then, but this was to be my reading at my bar mitzvah years later. A great honor! The Simchat Torah at my synagogue was always more disciplined and perhaps more reserved. That is why we young children enjoyed the upbeat, more informal, uninhibited Simchat Torah festivities at the Orthodox synagogue. The other, the Gebetstübel of the Eastern Orthodox Jews, was even more unrestrained, while wine and whisky flowed freely during that holiday celebration. Whether it was that reason, or because we didn't understand their language, and their chanting, we did not fit or feel comfortable with the congregants and were unable to participate in the service. Sometimes when a few of us visited there, just being nosy perhaps, we were asked to leave. While this should have bothered us, it did not at the time. To the contrary, we laughed and snickered going down the stairway and down onto the street. We weren't old enough or mature enough to understand why we were considered a nuisance and shown the door. Today I am ashamed of my behavior, attitude, and lack of tolerance then and wish I had acted differently.

CHAPTER FIVE

My Early Childhood

After a long courtship which started prior to and extended through World War I, Martha (née Joseph) married my dad, Joseph Kahn, on July 27, 1920, where she and her family lived (Hollerich, Luxembourg of the Grand Duché de Luxembourg), after he was released from the French as a German prisoner of war in March 1920.

He had been a prisoner of war since October 1918. After my dad was discharged by the French, it took only a few months to be discharged as a German soldier and leave his birthplace, Laufersweiler, for good and settle down in Mannheim. Dad must have determined that settling in a large industrial city with his bride would provide greater opportunities than elsewhere. Besides, there was an established Jewish community as well as a variety of great cultural opportunities and good educational facilities. It appeared that my dad had coordinated this move with his younger brother, Simon, who had also served in the German Army. Simon also settled in Mannheim where the brothers became partners in a dry goods business in June 1920. The registered name for the business was "J&S Kahn" (J for Joseph, S for Simon), a wholesale enterprise that sold men's and children's socks, ladies stockings, gloves for both sexes young and old, as well as handkerchiefs, underwear, and scarves.

EXHIBIT 5.1 Martha Joseph and Joseph Kahn, married Hollerich Luxembourg, Grand Duché of Luxembourg on July 27, 1920.

By the time my sister, Irene Johanna Elizabeth, was born on June 29, 1921, the two brothers

EXHIBIT 5.2 On the left is the main entrance to the Haupt Synagoge. Next to it on the right is the youth assembly building known as Schiff House. And to the very right is the first location of the Kahn business shared with Berg.

were hard at work getting the business off the ground so that its revenue could support not just one Kahn family, but two. It was assumed that eventually Uncle Simon, who was still single, would also become a family man. Their offices and merchandise were located at E7, beginning in 1921, almost across the street from where Irene would later attend secondary school, after first sharing space with Berg's paper goods store next to the synagogue in F2.

A huge explosion occurred on September 21, 1921, at a chemical plant at Oppau, approximately eight km away. The shocks were so great that my 3 month old sister fell out of her cradle. There was much damage everywhere, and 500 people were killed in the immediate area of the explosion.

The day I was born, September 30, 1923, must have been a gorgeous day. If this were a novel, I would elaborate at length in vivid colors what the day was like. However, it is impossible for me to describe the day of my birth because, despite notions to the contrary, I did not keep notes at such an early age. Nevertheless, the world I entered had already experienced a terrible war with much suffering on both sides. Germany was still in a state of disillusionment but trying to break free in order to move toward one of hope. The terms of the Versailles Treaty were still in the mind of every German, and it hurt their sense of honor and pride. On a lighter side, "Yes, We Have No Bananas" was then a hit song in America.

My parents had chosen my name to be Robert Bernhard Kahn. Both names were popular at the time. My research indicates that the name Robert had its origin from the Teutonic, members of early Germanic people who believed in racial superiority. Had my parents anticipated the events of years later and known the derivation and meaning of that name, they may not have chosen it for me. The Name Dictionary by Alfred J. Kolatch indicates an additional meaning of Robert as "bright or famous council." My middle name, Bernhard, supposedly came from the old high German and means "bold as a bear." My parents' choice of these two specific names indicated their enthusiasm at my birth and their hopes that I would grow up to be a person of honor and strength. All through my later life I have tried to be both.

EXHIBIT 5.3 Amalia (née Levy), a sister of my Dad's mother, known to everyone as Malchen, and her husband Raphael Joseph, 1930

EXHIBIT 5.4 Malchen in earlier years.

I was born a proud "Kohen" because my forefathers and ancestors were also "Kohanims." This means in the Jewish tradition that my father and I, as well as all of my descendants, are also descendants of the high priests of the first temple at Jerusalem. According to biblical accounts, after the Jewish exodus from Egypt, Moses's brother, Aaron, was selected as the first high priest, a Kohen. The designation was also given to his sons, thus providing the basis for a firmly entrenched Jewish tradition in which a male Kohen bestowed the status upon his sons. Several nice privileges go with this honor for my entire life. I, as a Kohen, am given special recognition and honors during religious worship services. There were also a number of restrictions which my dad made sure I would observe. As a Kohen I could not enter a funeral home, synagogue, cemetery or private home in which there was a corpse unless it was of the immediate family. Consequently, I did not attend a funeral until many years later in the U.S. Exceptions became the primitive burials of my comrades and enemy soldiers while I was overseas during World War II.

Following my birth came my *b'rith milah*, Hebrew for the Day of the Covenant, which symbolizes a covenant between Abraham and me, when the circumcision took place. Since it was performed as required on the eighth day of my life, it gave Opa, my grandfather Raphael Joseph, and Oma, my grandmother Amalia (Malchen) from Luxembourg a chance to travel by train to Mannheim for the once-in-a-lifetime event. Opa Isaak, my dad's father from Laufersweiler came alone because Oma Hannchen had died in 1909. His travels to Mannheim were more complicated and time consuming since there were no trains from Laufersweiler. He had to travel first to another town that had train service.

On this occasion, Opa Isaak gave my mom and dad a gift of 100 Mark, a lot of money in those days. Opa Raphael and Oma Malchen from Luxembourg presented my parents with a beautiful emerald green crystal goblet, 11-½ inches tall. The goblet is still in our possession and has its place of honor in our dining room breakfront. Of course Uncle Simon and other family members, sisters and brothers of both my mother and father from other cities and towns were present. The b'rith milah was performed at the rented apartment where we lived at the time, which was in one of the "J" city blocks of Mannheim.

During the circumcision, as was customary, I was given the Hebrew name "Bär Ben Joseph" (Bear, son of Joseph.) It may have been a coincidence, although I doubt it, that "Bär" also had the same meaning as my middle name, Bernhard. Also, I learned later the German word "Bär" and the English "Bear" have the same meaning.

Frau Klett had rented a small one-bedroom family apartment to my

EXHIBIT 5.5 The most beautiful green crystal goblet given to my parents by Opa Raphael and Oma Malchen in honor of my birth.

EXHIBIT 5.6 Robert, 3½ months, with Mother. It was customary in those years to take photos of naked babies on rugs.

EXHIBIT 5.7 Robert, age 5 months, and Mother. It was customary in those years to dress little children in short gowns.

parents sometime in the summer of 1920. It was, according to my sister Irene's recollections, on the second floor of the house where Frau Klett also lived at J7,28. It must have been a wonderful relationship between my parents and the landlord, Frau Klett. She took a liking to my mother, father, Irene and me, and we also cared a great deal for her. We spent many hours together. Irene remembered that Frau Klett had a lot of plants, and that beggars came to sing in the large courtyard which prompted other tenants and Mom to wrap up some coins to toss to them. The area where we lived then was known as Jungbush, more commonly known as Filzbach, an area where common harbor and factory working people lived. It was not the most desirable area for a family with two small children, but it was acceptable and affordable for a start of my parents. Even after we moved to another apartment in the city quite a distance away, my mother, with Irene and me in tow, would visit Frau Klett often.

These were very difficult times for my parents and the German people. The defeat of Germany by the allies several years earlier put tremendous strains on the economic and political situation of the Weimer Republic. Germany had lost a considerable amount of territory and its colonies, including their scarce natural resources. In addition, Germany was obligated by treaty to pay huge reparations approximating $56 billion over many years, a sum that it could not possibly pay. The coal and timber which were used as reparations to the victorious allies began falling behind schedule and was one of the reasons that in January 1923, French and Belgian troops occupied the Rhineland, including Ludwigshafen, the city immediately across the Rhine from Mannheim. Almost simultaneously, American troops were withdrawn from occupied areas of Germany. Mannheim, however, was spared from occupation armies. The Germans responded with general strikes, slowdowns, and other passive resistance.

Rising prices resulting from inflation, high taxes, unemployment, and welfare expenses created catastrophic economic conditions. The German Mark was devaluating not only on a daily but hourly basis. The country was bankrupt. Paper money was printed in enormous quantities and ever larger denominations, including million and billion Mark bills. This, and the humiliation of a war lost, produced the first Nazi Party meetings and demonstrations, with Adolf Hitler at the helm at Munich and elsewhere. The monster had been let out of its cage.

EXHIBIT 5.8
Front and Back of 1000 Mark bill. This is a sample of the kind of inflation money Irene and I played with.

EXHIBIT 5.9 Uncle Simon, Dad's brother, and Aunt Hilde, his wife, in 1925. See more family photos from this time in the appendix, beginning with exhibit 5.10.

In this chaotic economic and political climate, dad and Uncle Simon had an almost impossible task not only keeping the business going, but also earning an income. What helped them was that the merchandise they sold as wholesale distributors were not luxury items, but bare knuckle items that every man, woman and child could not do without. As a toddler, I remember Dad brought home boxes full of paper money that was practically worthless. Irene and I played with the bills. A pound of sugar at the store cost 250 billion Marks.

It was June 25, 1925 when Uncle Simon married Hilde Betty Ullmann of Wiesbaden, who became our aunt. Of course, Mom and Dad attended the wedding at Wiesbaden, but Irene and I stayed home under the watchful eye of our nanny. Our two families became very close and often got together socially, especially after my cousin, Ernst, was born July 19, 1926, and Walter in March 1929. During the week mom and Aunt Hilde would go for walks in the nearby parks with children in tow.

We moved to a large and very comfortable apartment about 1925, the location L11,25 was very close to the Haupt Bahnhof, the main railroad station. Not counting *paterra*, the ground floor, we lived on the fourth floor, high enough so we could overlook the railroad yard in the near distance. The advantage of living on the fourth floor was that it was not noisy from street traffic. The disadvantage what that there were many steps to climb. The attic above us, a mansard, was made into a number of small comfortable rooms where the live-in maids and housekeepers would sleep and store their belongings. Kate, our nursemaid, who used to come every morning and go home every evening when we still lived in the Klett house, now lived with us around the clock except on weekend days when she had a day off. She was gentle, kind, and both Irene and I loved her. A second live-in maid took care of the housework and cooking.

Irene was growing up fast and was a pretty girl at an early age, as confirmed by some early photographs.

Irene and I got along very well considering she was four and a half and I was only one and a half. There was the usual rivalry especially since we shared a bedroom, but with separate beds, of course. Irene had some nice dolls, and I had

EXHIBIT 5.14 My sister Irene, about 3 years old.

mostly wooden blocks, other similar toys, and empty cigar boxes dad brought home. Mom or Kate took us for walks to the Palace grounds, the Friedrichs Park, Waldpark, or the gardens and fountains at the Wasserturm. Irene usually walked holding onto the carriage in which I rode. Mom and Dad believed in fresh air, walking and hiking, something that was in the nature of all Germans. Of course, Mom always found occasions to correct people by stating that she having been born in Luxembourg was a Luxembourgeoise. She was no dirty *Bosch*, or dirty German as the French called them. I remember that once we took a walk past the Palace toward the Rhine Bridge. The French had occupied the industrial areas left of the Rhine, including Ludwigshafen, and occupied the bridge so that no one could cross the Rhine via this bridge without a special pass. One of the French soldiers approached my mother and complimented her in French about the beautiful children. Surprised that mom could understand and speak French, he asked my name. Hearing that it was Robert, he replied that his name was also Robert but with a slightly different pronunciation. Since I was young and thought I was the only Robert, I was very much surprised and disappointed. It was an unforgettable moment although not an important one in later years of my life.

EXHIBIT 5.16 Joseph and Martha.

Soon it was time for Irene to join a kindergarten. She started going to a well-established one operated by Fräulein Gertrude Traub, Moltkestrasse 6, around the corner from the Luisenschule, public school, where Irene and I would go later when we each turned six. The Traubs belonged to the orthodox Klaus Synagogue, and in addition to playing games, listening to stories, painting, etc., Irene, and later I, learned much about Judaism and Jewish customs. Her father, Josef Traub, always wore a yarmulka, a cap worn by observing Jews, and helped with telling Bible stories and festivals. When festival Sukkot came, we children were happy and excited because we were allowed to assist in building a sukkah, a temporary outdoor hut. It represented the journey of the Israelites through the desert when they lived in temporary shelters. It was a season of joy when we dwelled, ate, prayed, and entertained in the hut fully decorated with flowers, fruit, nuts, an entire range of agricultural products and leaves. This thanksgiving festival always took place in the fall during harvest time, and gave one respite from the high holidays of Rosh Hashanah and Yom Kippur. The children at kindergarten created most of the decorations for the sukkah and helped hang them up. It was loads of fun. We celebrated Sukkot for nine days. We prayed and held processions with a *lulav*, a palm branch, a myrtle branch, and a willow branch tied together, and the *ethrog*, a citron fruit that smelled lovely. This fruit came from what was then Palestine and was twice the size of a lemon. Mom and Dad had a special and ornate ethrog box which I gave as a present to our daughter Susan.

I remember Fraulein Gertrude's father, Josef, leading the boys to the bathroom at certain times each morning while Gertrude took the girls. Kate, our

EXHIBIT 5.18 Kindergarten, November 1928. I am third from the right with Gertrude Traub standing behind us. She, her sister, and her father became victims of the Holocaust.

nanny, whom we respectfully referred to as Fraulein Kate, first walked Irene in the morning to kindergarten and back again in the afternoon every day except Saturday and Sunday. I joined them two years later. Years later, the family Traub, mother Betty, father Josef, and two spinster sisters, Gertrude and Hedwig, were deported by the Nazis October 22 or 23, 1940, with the remaining 2000+ Jews of Mannheim to a concentration camp, Gurs, in southern France which was not then occupied by the Germans. From there, those who had survived were eventually shipped beginning July 1942 to their certain death at Auschwitz. I mourn and think of them often since there were many friends and acquaintances among them.

As I was growing up, I contracted many childhood sicknesses, some of which I vividly remember. At age five I had the measles. Dr. Balkasar Berthold, whose office was located at P7,1 was our pediatrician. Dr. Katzenstein was our family doctor. Each would make house calls, but I also remember that Mother took Irene and me to each of their offices for examinations and therapy via a sun lamp which required wearing dark goggles. Depending on the circumstances, our nanny or Dad would come along. During some research, I located my vaccination certificate dated June 8, 1925. Between four and six years of age I was plagued with very painful middle ear infections (otitis). That is when Dr. Richard Gumpertz came to the rescue. He was an ear, nose, and throat specialist who pierced my ear drums to provide me with some relief. (Some years later Dr. Gumpertz immigrated to Haifa, Palestine, where he became very well known in his profession.) I remember my mother heating up what appeared to be an oily solution and then squirting it into my ear with an eye-dropper where it produced a soothing, bubbling sensation. During those painful episodes when I also ran a temperature, I would put my ear on a hot water bottle or on the warm ceramic tiles of the large coal oven, a *kachel ofen*, glazed tile stove, in the living room. This was the primary heat source in our large five room, plus kitchen and two bath apartment except for the coal cooking stove in the kitchen. Both were kept burning all day during the winter season, and at night they were banked. At age nine, I contracted scarlet fever, but had no noticeable after effects. Curtains had to be closed to keep the room dark, a requirement for scarlet fever at the time. My temperature was very high and since antibiotics had not yet been discovered, this was a serious, life threatening illness.

We had one small but important luxury, a small gas heater that hung from the wall in the bathroom that had to be lit with matches. All other rooms, bedrooms, dining room, and guest room had no heat sources and were cold unless doors from the kitchen or living room were strategically opened. Yet, when Irene and I played on the linoleum floor in our joint bedroom, it was never too cold. Irene played with dolls, especially one called *Mystangette* named after a well-known French female entertainer. She also enjoyed reading and needlecraft. As she grew older, she read books from a series titled *Nesthäkchen*. I will not even try to translate the title for fear of misleading, but they were typical young girls' books for different age groups. My favorite toy was a castle with towers, moats, bridges and fortifications. There were cast iron, tin, and lead soldiers, either on foot or horseback, with different kinds of weapons of the Middle Ages. I played with them for hours. I also had a *märklin baukasten*, a construction erector set with many metal pieces that had to be screwed together according to instructions. I had other toys, but these were my favorites.

This was a time for collector's cards that were attached to certain grocery and tobacco products. Irene collected film stars and female sports figures and got me started on collecting other sports personalities, and then we would trade the cards with other children. There were cards of Albert Einstein, Amelia Earhart, Charles Lindbergh, Primo Carnera, Sonja Henie, Greta Garbo, Al Capone, Gandhi, Marlene Dietrich and others. There were also cards of all types of airplanes and race cars. Those were just a few I remember, but there were hundreds more. It was the rage, and every boy and girl collected and traded them.

As I think back to our apartment, the different rooms come clearly into my mind, along with the entire layout and placement of furniture. To share this view, I drew a sketch (professionally rendered by my nephew, Marc Diament, Irene's son, who is an architect) that is probably 95% accurate except for relative dimensions. However, the rooms were very large indeed. Nostalgia overcomes me, as if looking through a rear vision mirror of a life. I can see myself ringing the bell at the front door of the apartment building. Through a speaker I hear someone ask, "Who is it?" to which I reply "it is I." The buzzer sounds and I push open the heavy steel door.

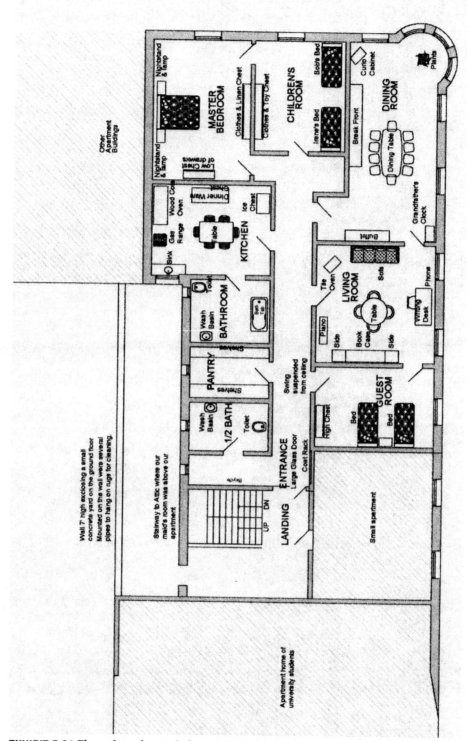

EXHIBIT 5.21 Floor plan of our 4th floor apartment.

There were perhaps six steps up to a landing and the entrance to the first floor apartment where Frau Keller lived. She owned the building, and we brought the monthly rent to her. Behind the landing to one side there were another six steps going down to an open area where tenants stored their bicycles. At the same level there were two additional doors, one of which led to a basement subdivided into individual storage for each tenant. Our compartment was used primarily for storing coal briquettes and fire wood for the kitchen stove and the massive, glazed tile oven in the living room used in winter. Every day the maid had to go to the basement to retrieve coal. The basement was dreary, dirty, scary even spooky. I never enjoyed going there, especially when it was dark since there were no electric lights.

The second door opened into a drab courtyard with a six foot high wall on one side, the building providing the other three sides. There were long pipes mounted on the high wall that were used for hanging and cleaning large and small room sized rugs. Wall-to-wall carpeting was not known yet for many years. Cleaning them consisted of beating the dirt out with a *klopfer*, a bamboo carpet beater. Vacuum cleaners were not known at that time, and all area rugs had to be cleaned this way several times a year. It was a hard job. First, the rugs were rolled up and carried downstairs by two people. They would methodically beat the rugs to rid them of dirt and dust and then carried them back up four flights of stairs. By the time I was six or seven, I enjoyed helping with this chore. Essentially, we had parquet floors, which had to be scrubbed with steel wool and oil. Few of which were carpet covered. The kitchen, pantry, and a full and a half bathroom had tile floors. The children's bedrooms and hallway were covered with linoleum.

Come with me now as I climb the stairs to our apartment. From paterra, the first floor, we had to pass three additional apartment floors before coming to a door, the upper half made of milk glass so that no one could see inside and from the inside we could look out but only see shadows. As you entered the apartment, my bicycle stood on the floor to the left. I didn't trust leaving the bike downstairs where all other tenants kept theirs. Again, to the left, down the hallway past the half bath, the pantry had many shelves with staple food items plus hundreds of canning jars filled with fruit, hard boiled eggs, and a variety of vegetables such as red cabbage, beans, white asparagus, and red beets. Mom also prepared and canned marmalade and jam. There were canned pickles and little white onions in glass jars, and in several stone crocks meat was pickled and salted for later use. I remember with nostalgia an oblong china terrine about ten inches long, four inches wide, and five inches deep, used for marinating herring. What was fascinating for me about this dish was the lid; its handle was fashioned into a true color glazed likeness of a herring. Also on the shelves of the pantry were apples, pears, and other fresh fruit in season along with onions and a limited amount of fresh vegetables including potatoes as well as wine and cider.

The pantry was an important room especially since our ice chest in the kitchen was relatively small and primitive by today's standards. In summer we needed about fifty pounds of ice per day, while in winter we needed less. Each morning we heard a certain ring of a bell, the distinctive sound of the ice man on the street below with his horse drawn wagon. Mom, Dad, or the maid would open the window and shout down, indicating with their fingers how many pounds of ice he should carry up.

There was a ventilator in the kitchen over the sink. It was an opening perhaps nine inches by nine inches with overlapping horizontal metal slats, similar to a Venetian blind that could be opened by a long chain to let air in or out. It was also the perfect niche for swallows to nest and raise their young. Occasionally, the young swallows would fall or fly into the kitchen when someone would unsuspectingly open the ventilator. You can't imagine the commotion this created among those of us in the kitchen. Mom, Irene, and Kate, the nursemaid, and the domestic help would shriek and carry on while Dad and I tried to catch the bird in a large paper bag. The women were afraid that the swallows would fly into their hair and get stuck. We had flocks of swallows in the area where we lived, particularly in spring, summer, and fall. Often Irene and I would stand at the open window in our room and almost touch them as they flew by screeching. When they flew at our elevation or lower, there would be a chance of the weather worsening. If the swallows flew higher than our fourth story then the weather was likely to become nicer. Dad, who as you know was raised in the country, told us that and had a very good explanation for it. At lower barometric pressure, indicating possible rain, the insects after which the birds were chasing would fly low. If the barometric pressure was high, it indicated good weather, and the insects would fly higher.

Our hallway, about forty or forty-five feet long and at least seven feet wide, was like another room, a perfect place for Irene and me to play. It was a natural extension of our own room where we kept all of our toys. Quite often when Irene's or my friends visited, or when we had a birthday party, we would play on the swing mounted on the hall's ceiling or play ball which was always great fun. Other times I would set up an entire collection of soldiers, forts, and a menagerie of building blocks and other things so that I wouldn't interfere with Irene's activities in our joint room. Of course we played marbles with other children in the street, hide and seek or other fun games or soccer. Irene and I were very considerate of each other, but even so, we had our quarrels, and often I would pull her pigtails in fun or to provoke and get her attention. Generally Irene was very proud of her little brother and I loved my sister very much.

One day when we were having the best time playing ball in the hallway with friends, we accidentally broke a pretty large vase that stood on top of a Chinese motif lacquered chest. We all felt bad and cried, but that didn't bring back the

EXHIBIT 5.22 This is the vase Irene and I bought to make up for the one we broke.

vase. By this time I must have been at least seven years old and Irene about nine and a half. We both felt so remorseful about breaking the vase that we decided to buy a new one for our parents. On a Saturday morning on the way home from synagogue services, we went to a very fine china and glassware store in the high class shopping area, the Planken. We saw a beautiful vase although it bore no resemblance to the one that had bit the dust. We indicated to the saleslady that we wanted to make this purchase. We had brought with us about 10 Mark, a lot of money for us, but insufficient for the vase purchase. The clerk called her superior who questioned us as to why we wanted to buy the vase. Apparently, she was impressed by our story and after checking and finding that our parents had been customers, she let us buy the vase provided that we would come back every week and make payments with our weekly allowance. Mother laughed and cried with happiness being proud of her children and surprised with our restitution effort. We did not tell her or Dad that we still owed the store a considerable amount of money. Irene and I went back to the store for many weeks to make our payments until one day they told us that we were all paid up. Astounded, we thought they had made a mistake, but we were emphatically told the vase was paid for in full. Only later did it occur to us that possibly Dad and Mom had made the remaining payments. We were curious but never asked. Today, that vase has a place of honor in our dining room breakfront, and before you come to the epilogue, you will discover how it was salvaged.

Every room in our apartment holds many memories for me, both pleasant and some not so pleasant. As I write them down, all become anecdotes of the time and the people that played a part in them. The living room held a particular fascination because, after the kitchen, it was the most lived in. We ate breakfast in the kitchen unless we had overnight guests, and our main meals at noon and evening were served at the massive round table in the living room that could seat eight persons comfortably. Dad came home for dinner at noon since the business was closed from noon until two p.m., a European tradition. My parents had a strict policy that we had to eat from whatever food was put on the table. For me and Irene that was sometimes difficult to do, and therefore, she and I often wound up leaving the table crying and still hungry. Many times we would end up later in the kitchen where our nursemaid would sneak us something more palatable. Going to bed still hungry was always an unhappy event, and even Mother would relent most of the time and offer me something to eat later. Irene fared somewhat better, but then she was two years older and adapted more easily to the rules. In the end, this rule of eating whatever was put on the table conditioned me, and as time went on, I tried all sorts of food and finally learned to eat just about anything, even things I didn't really like. My dear parents had an interesting expression concerning eating: "*Ess dass du was wirst*," or "Eat so you amount to something." These were words of encouragement as well as admonishment. I may not have been eating great amounts then; however, I have been eating ever since. Yet, only you, the reader, will be able to tell whether I, in one sense or another, did "amount to something." If in the affirmative, it must be because I listened to the words of Mom and Dad and ate!

The living room holds other memories. During my bouts with middle ear infections, I would lie on the sofa and stare at the huge, captivating oil painting which hung above it, of a mountain and lake scenery by the artist, Capellman. Lying there in pain, I would often be covered with a blanket, and in my hand I would hold a small porcelain figurine, about one and a half inches in size, of a ladybug sitting on a green leaf. It was a pacifier of sorts, a tranquilizer that had a calming effect on me. My wife, Gertrude, and I have this small but wonderful "bug" in a place of honor in our curio cabinet. It is small but precious! Today, the large oil painting hangs in my study. Four more paintings by this artist were hung in different rooms in our Mannheim apartment and were often admired.

The huge bookcase, which held about 200 books, a massive writing desk, and an enormous round table were matching pieces, with exquisite owl carvings that served as handles and decorations. The wood was a beautiful, black walnut. Irene used the desk for homework and letter writing, while I used it to draw pictures. Sometimes we worked there together. Later I also used the desk for homework and my stamp collecting hobby. Of course, Mom and Dad used it for writing correspondences and many other purposes. The living room, in many respects, served also as a study. Irene and I were always admonished not to scrape our shoes on the pedestal of the table. If there was a conflicting need, the large table in the kitchen was also available. Mom and Dad acquired most of our furniture, dining room, living room, and bedrooms, during the terrible inflation and depression years right after the war. Instead of banking the income from the business, Dad and his partner, Uncle Simon, immediately bought merchandise, art objects such as paintings by Capellman, or household furniture. In that manner they protected the value of money that otherwise would have become worthless overnight.

One of my fondest pastimes was to look out the living room window and watch the marshalling yard of the train station. The constant coming and going of passenger trains and the coupling and uncoupling of freight cars in the switchyard were infinitely intriguing. To watch freight and passenger cars shift and switch from one track to another, locomotives puffing black and white smoke was not only fascinating but spellbinding. We lived so close that I could see the yard signals and the trainmen clearly. From another window toward the rear of the apartment, I could look to the next courtyard of a university fraternity house and occasionally see men engaged in fencing duels and hear the attending noises and verbal signals of fencing etiquette.

The most secluded of all rooms, as if behind a veil of secrecy, was the formal dining room. This seclusion was intentional because irreplaceable handed-down linens (some from Mom's trousseau), silverware, elegant and expensive bone china, stemware of every kind and for every occasion, silver, crystal, or china cake platters, lead crystal bowls, and more were displayed or neatly stored and locked away. Additionally, a beautiful antique curio cabinet housed some of the most sensational and valuable figurines, collector plates, ornate spoons and other tableware, decanters, and a wealth of keepsakes a museum would have been proud to have in its collection. On a wide ledge of a huge, elegant breakfront, stood a large, tall, heavy bronze sculpture (two feet long by seventeen inches tall) of a nude boy on a galloping stallion. It was created by Heinrich Splieth circa 1865 and was fairly valuable. Through almost miraculous events, which will be described later, the sculpture and other household things are again in our possession. In the center of the room stood a long, oak table with two extension boards that would comfortably seat eighteen people. Above the table hung a large crystal chandelier with many light bulbs that often burned out.

In the far corner of the dining room was a large semi-round bay with windows all around. It contained a large, specially crafted, tiered rack on which many types of cacti stood, some with spine-like leaves, others with showy, colorful blooms. Most of them, however, had prickly needles that were unforgiving. Mom loved them and was the only person in the household permitted to tend them, and she was always mindful and concerned when someone came near them. On another wall stood a tall grandfather clock with a slowly swinging pendulum and several heavy weights. Every so often the weights had to be hoisted up so that the clock would run again for a week or so. It had chimes that imitated the deep sound of Big Ben at the House of Parliament in London. It brought forth a deep sound, but since the doors of the room were always closed and usually locked unless in use, we were used to its muffled sound.

It was amazing how this room came to life when Mom and Dad entertained for a *kaffeeklatsch*, an afternoon dessert party or an elegant dinner in the evening. Mom and Dad had many good friends and loved to entertain. Some of the friends whom I remember were the Steckelmachers and Martin Zlotznitski. I do not remember all of their first names. The latter had a son, Egon, several years older than Irene, who later immigrated to France when anti-Semitism became unbearable. They lived around the corner from us at L11,2. Then there were Theo and Erna Kiefer and daughter, Edith, a schoolmate and good friend of Irene's, who last lived in Israel.

Selma and Benny Loebenberg and their daughter, Dinah, also a good friend of Irene's, lived at Charlottenstrasse #2 next to Albert and Regina Prinz at Charlottenstrasse #1, all about a fifteen minute walk from us. The Prinzs were unable to emigrate and were deported in October 1940 and eventually murdered by the Nazis.

One of the first families Dad, and later, Mom became good friends with in Mannheim was Isidore "Isi" Berg and his wife, Mathilde. They lived at M3,6 and operated a small paper products and bookstore at F2 near the synagogue where Dad's business was first co-located with that of the Bergs'. A few months later the Bergs moved their business to the Breitestrasse, and Dad re-located to E7, almost across from the Elisabetten Schule, the school that Irene would later attend. Disillusioned by the anti-Semitism that later caused him to lose his business and other harassments, Isidore Berg took his own life on March 20, 1938. Their son, Kurt, born March 1, 1910, became a Doctor of Literature, although he had first studied law at his parents' insistence at the University of Heidelberg. After teaching for a short time in Switzerland, he married Doctor of Philosophy, Marie Hirsch, in 1935. Later, Dr. Berg became one of my teachers, and I grew very fond of him. His mother was deported on October 23, 1940, to Camp Gurs, France. After being rescued, she lived for some years in Chicago where she later died from life's disappointments.

Around the same time that Dr. Berg was my teacher, he also became editor of the *Juedische Gemeinedeblatt*, the Jewish community newspaper in Mannheim. In addition, he taught classes for the young and old on how to prepare for the eventuality, consequences, and expectations of having to leave Germany. Both the newspaper and his teaching were stopped by the Nazis in 1938, and in the following year he and Marie were deported to a labor camp near Berlin. Kurt Berg, as most of us but in different ways, was tormented and persecuted to no end by the Nazis.

EXHIBIT 5.24 Mathilde and her husband Isidore Berg, with son Kurt, age 3, 1913 in Mannheim. Good friends of my parents.

While his spirits and hopes were shattered, he, his wife and infant son, Michael, managed to survive and immigrate to the United Sates in May, 1940.

He settled his family in Milwaukee, Wisconsin, where he found work in a factory. After a move to Chicago, he worked in a shoe factory. Only years later was he able to obtain a teaching position at the University of Michigan. He died November 13, 1960, in St. Paul, Minnesota, a broken, disappointed, distraught, unhappy, beaten, and homesick individual. For reasons not clear to me, he and the family had turned away from Judaism and converted to Catholicism. During his life in Germany and the United States, he wrote many poems and lyric reflections which were published in 1962 entitled, *Führe Mich Zur Abendinsel*, (*Lead Me to the Island of the Evening*) a book ranging from unending love and happiness to the contemplation of suicide and death. The book published in Mannheim is written primarily in German. His wife and I continued to correspond, even after she celebrated her ninety-third birthday on March 20, 2002. She has died since.

I have digressed somewhat from the tour of our Mannheim apartment. I did so because I wanted to give some insight as to what happened to very good friends of my parents and their son, to whom I had taken a liking for his optimistic, yet somewhat naïve, philosophical approach to our dilemma.

And so I return to describing our dining room which became a particularly festive place on Pesach, when we celebrated Passover, one of the most cherished of Jewish holidays. It is the festival of freedom Israelites dramatic deliverance from slavery in Egypt some 3,200 years ago. On the evenings of the first and second night, the Seder was held. It was a combination banquet and family religious service. Usually invited were Aunt Hilde, Uncle Simon and their children Ernst and Walter after they were old enough, as well as Dora and Gustav Zimmern and daughter, Stephanie. Their son Heinz had halis own ideas and would not attend. Dora was a sister of Aunt Hilde. Lotte, her brother, Herbert, their mother Therese Isaak, and father, Emil, second cousins, were also often invited, as were several of our parent's friends mentioned earlier. As was customary, special dishes, flatware and utensils were set aside for the occasion. *Matzo*, unleavened bread, bitter herbs, a shank bone, a roasted egg, *charoseth*, a mixture of chopped apples mixed with wine, chopped nuts and cinnamon, were served as a symbol of the slavery the children of Israel had undergone. There was a special sweet, kosher wine for Passover on the table.

The head of the household, my father, began by reading from the Haggadah, the story of the exodus of the Israelites from Egypt. Our Haggadah was beautiful. It was an oversize book about eleven inches high, perhaps nine inches wide, in color with pictures, and the story in Hebrew and German. It was a product of Vienna produced by Joseph Schlesinger. One passage early on in the reading always fascinated me: "Next year may we be in Jerusalem!" It was more than an idle saying; it was a wish and our fervent hope. The Haggadah was brand new to me in

1929 when, for the first time, I had to read the "Four Questions" in Hebrew. Until then Irene had read the questions. After I was done, my dear father read the questions in German and then read the answers. Next, Dad told of the nine plagues that visited the Egyptians so that Pharaoh would witness the power of Moses's G'd. These plagues were only directed toward the Egyptians, and symbolically Mom and Dad would hang a white sheet or towel on the door identifying the household as being Israelites, and so each of the nine plagues would not affect us. It was another of so many religious worship activities that gave us children much to ponder and ultimately left a life-long impression to continue the tradition.

Everyone at the table participated in the reading, chanting, singing hymns, and performing symbolic acts. The service was long, often lasting until after midnight. There was plenty of opportunity for Irene, cousins Ernest, Walter, and me to laugh, giggle, and have fun, but we were always reminded by our elders to behave. Of course, halfway through the solemn recitations came the meal that always started with a bowl of matzo ball soup. The charoseth, the sweet mixture of apples, nuts, cinnamon, and wine, eaten between two small pieces of matzo, was always a savory treat. After the meal, the reading, singing and chanting continued until attention was drawn to a large goblet that was mysteriously filled with wine for the Prophet Elijah. One of the children was told to open the door, welcoming him to the table as the Messiah. Hiding the *afikomen*, half of the middle piece of the matzo by the house elder, my dad, at the beginning of the home celebration was also fun for the children. At the end of the meal, we were asked to find this missing piece. My dad gave a small present or a coin to whomever found the afikomen. Of course, the others also received a present or coin, so they were happy too. The second evening of the Passover Festival was conducted very similarly at Uncle Simon and Aunt Hilde's apartment. The two families rotated hosting the first or second Seder, continuing this practice until Uncle Simon and family immigrated to America on June 21, 1938. I never heard what prompted them to leave earlier than we did, especially since the two brothers were business partners and the two families were very close. It dawns on me now that Mom and Dad had other plans, because of different circumstances, which will be explained elsewhere.

There were other occasions when the dining room was used, like family and friends birthday parties. Mother enjoyed preparing for parties and often we helped with decorations and setting the table. Mom and Dad were known for their hospitality, good food, and good times at their parties.

Mom and Dad's bedroom was very large with heavy furniture for storing bed linens and clothing. Two queen sized beds were pushed together flanked by nightstands with lamps, whereby two bronze angels held the lampshades. I remember the room well because many times Irene and I crawled into our parents' bed when we couldn't sleep, didn't feel well, or were scared of something. I would always crawl into what we called the *gräbelchen*, the little trench between the two beds. We couldn't just barge in, however, and we always had to get our parents' permission to keep it from becoming a habit. During a heavy thunderstorm we often sought refuge and comfort in the grabelchen of our parents' bed. Irma, our maid, was also very scared of thunderstorms, and she would come down from her attic room at night and join us in the bedroom on the floor. My dear mother was particularly frightened of thunder and lightning. If storms occurred during the daytime, she and the rest of us hid under the beds. Irene and I were therefore conditioned to also be afraid of thunderstorms.

One of the most memorable places in the apartment was the kitchen that always had an unwritten welcome sign for anyone. It was always warm and it seemed that someone was always stirring, baking, or cooking. Once I opened the door, aromas of all sorts greeted me. I was always nosy as to what was being prepared by Mom, Irma, or Irene. My mother affectionately called me *dippe kooker*, or pot watcher. Often I would offer to help Mom, and she let me put on an apron and stir whatever was in the pot or skillet. When Mom was mixing ingredients for a cake, I was right there to lick the pan or spoon with my fingers. There was the wood and coke oven in which the fire was banked unless more than the four burners on the gas range were needed. In wintertime, that wood and coke oven was wonderful to be around especially in the morning when the rest of the house was still cold. The main bathroom tub, accessible from the kitchen, was very convenient for similar reasons since we had to go there to wash up before we got fully dressed. The other half bath at the far end of the hall was used when needed and by guests.

In our own bedroom the drapes had a design of large dark brown and black circles that, in my imagination, often turned into wild animals and monsters, giving me nightmares. However, I was never able to explain this scary phenomenon to anyone at the time, and therefore, no one ever knew what bothered me or why I cried. Irene and I got along fine together in one room, after I was a few years old. Before, I slept in my parents' bedroom while Fraulein Kate, our nanny, slept in Irene's bedroom.

Irene and I went to kindergarten together for about a year. When she started going to public school at age six, I stayed behind in kindergarten. Time passed quickly, and in 1929, I graduated from kindergarten to elementary school. That first school day was something special, as it was customary that each child received a surprise gift from parents. This gift was called a *Zuckertüte*, a cardboard cylinder, similar to a New Year's Eve hat, about three feet tall with an eight or nine inch opening on top. This upside-down cylindrical hat was covered with very colorful paper, ribbons, and bows. Inside was a variety of commercial and home-baked candy. Some was chocolate, but also included was a very delicious, sweet marzipan, a confection of ground almonds, sugar, and egg white made into a past of varying colors and wrapped into large or bite-sized pieces. The Zuckertüte also contained various kinds of nuts and small fruits. It was an unusual one of a kind present to remind me of my first school day and be proud of it. And I was! Dad and Mom made it a special day by taking pictures with me and walking me to Luisenschule school with the Zuckertüte. It was a glorious day for me! I liked sweets and as fond of Mannemer Dreck, a chocolate covered pastry for which Mannheim was then, and even today, famous for (see exhibits 5.26-5.30 in the appendix for more on this sweet treat).

EXHIBIT 5.25 My first school day with Zuckertüte.

As in all children, I possessed certain traits that my parents noticed at an early age and tried to correct. I seemed to do more activities with my left hand than with my right. Being left-handed was considered undesirable and perhaps even detrimental to me as I would grew older. Of course, I had no idea what all the fuss was about, and no one explained it to me. Lefties were simply thought to be at a disadvantage physically, mentally, and socially, and would even be shunned by society. It was considered a sign of bad luck, possibly causing the person to be prone to all sorts of calamities, even suicide. Mom and Dad were constantly after me to do everything with my right hand especially when I was drawing pictures or writing in kindergarten and elementary school. It made learning much more difficult for me, interjecting some elements of confusion and anxiety within me. These notions about lefties were scary, made up by prominent psychologists and other meddling professionals and perpetuated by society at that time. Today we know that there is no shred of scientific evidence that being a southpaw is detrimental in any way to an individual. We no longer condemn people for being lefties, and teachers no longer try to change students' writing habits in school. As a matter of fact, we celebrate lefties every August with a special "Southpaw Day."

I learned to write with my right hand with great difficulties but thank my parents in spite of that. While writing left-handed is no longer a taboo, it is still looked upon as a novelty. However, my left hand and arm developed greater strength than my right, and that is why today I am still a southpaw playing tennis.

Around that time I also went through a period of fingernail biting. It is questionable whether this habit resulted from all the constant attention, prodding by parents, their friends, relatives, teachers, and even my sister regarding my left-handed problem. I am the first one to admit that this compulsive nail biting was a nasty habit and totally unacceptable, but it still took me a number of years of shame and self-discipline to overcome. Sometimes Mom, Dad and others would bribe me by promising special gifts of money and other incentives if I would stop and pass fingernail inspection. Conquering this undesirable destructive habit at an early age although difficult, had a real positive effect by raising my self-image, confidence, and determination.

Until now, I have not mentioned that I had a minor but noticeable and annoying speech problem. I lisped, which meant that the sound "th" sounded like "z." I was aware of it, but my parents and Uncle Max and Aunt Helene, mom's sister, worried about it and searched for a speech therapist who could help. Aunt Helene had heard of a doctor in Cologne (Köln in German) who specialized in ailments of this type, and she took me to him. Dr. Moses was his name. This was an odd coincidence because Moses from the Bible had an aversion to speaking, and now this doctor with the same name was engaged in correcting and restoring speech difficulties. The whole idea of corrective speech therapy was a little frightening, and I was somewhat reluctant to go. After examination he prepared a retainer for my mouth that prevented my tongue from being placed in a way that caused the lisp. I had to wear it for weeks of practice, and finally, I was able to speak correctly without the mouthpiece. My aunt, uncle and parents were thrilled to no end, and I have been forever thankful to Aunt Helene and Uncle Max for their caring and concern. There was no way to repay them for their kindness except to show my continued affection. After I was able to discard the retainer, I received no more strange looks from anyone. The event changed my life. As a child it was almost impossible to realize that harsh sounding words from my parents regarding this disability really reflected their love and caring.

In spite of these glitches, these were tranquil years for me. I had a very satisfying feeling of belonging to a happy family. Nothing else could have ever given me the same sense of belonging, being loved and appreciated as I was by my dear parents, sister, and others around us. There was a great sense of comfort and happiness. The close-knit family, grandparents, uncles, aunts, and cousins living elsewhere wrote to us often and us to them. Writing letters was the means of staying in touch even though many people like us had a telephone. It depended on where one lived. Every beginning of Shabbat, Friday evening, we telephoned

Opa Raphael and Oma Malchen in Hollerich Luxembourg, to see how they were doing and to trade news back and forth. It was a weekly tradition. This was how my mother kept in touch with her parents. In those days, operators knew the callers and recipients by name. When we called them, operators came on the line, first at our end and next at theirs, since it was a long distance call. Both Oma and Opa on my father's side, in Laufersweiler had already passed on in 1909 and 1927 respectively. Had they been alive, we surely would have phoned them also and often. Regardless of the long distance telephone calls to mischpocha relatives, most of the news came by mail. Irene, too, wrote or added to letters. When I was able, I also added greetings after Mom or Dad drew some lines on the stationery.

It was during the late 20s and early 30s that I saw for the first time that huge cigar-like dirigible, *Graf Zeppelin*, flying very low above our apartment building, usually in the early evening. We could hear the whirring of its engines and see this enormous shape approximately 775 feet long, maneuver in the sky. It was an awesome sight. All Germany and the world was proud of this engineering and navigation feat when the LZ127 Zeppelin managed to complete a trip around the world in 1929.

In the meantime the wholesale business of J&S Kahn was doing well. Both Uncle Simon and my Dad sought out and called on local as well as out-of-town customers. Since the business owned only one automobile, a four door Opel, the brothers alternated days in soliciting business from merchants. When Dad called on customers in surrounding towns and villages, Mom prepared sandwiches and a thermos of coffee for him. However, on some days customers would ask Dad to join them for lunch, in which case he brought the sandwiches back home. These sandwiches were then referred to as *hasenbrot*, which literally translated meant "bread from a rabbit," since it had dried out during the day and tasted slightly different. It was that difference and the peculiar name that I enjoyed, and I looked forward to hasenbrot whenever Dad returned from these day trips.

There was always much to talk about at the dinner table, and we children listened intently. Much of the conversation consisted of what had transpired at home while Dad was away, what Mom and the maids had

EXHIBIT 5.31 The Dirigible Graf Zeppelin above our apartment.

EXHIBIT 5.32 Irene loved her little brother and I loved her, 1930.

done to keep the home livable and attractive, and what we children had done at school and play. Even though Dad was tired at the end of the day, he always took time to help us with homework, reading, writing, and arithmetic. Dad was always quick to compliment Mother on a good meal and us for doing well in school. After dinner Dad would relax and smoke a cigar while we all listened to Irene as she practiced her lessons on the piano. Sometimes Dad and I played checkers or chess, games he had patiently taught me.

Now and then, usually after a meal, Dad would pace the floor because of stomach cramps. He attributed these pains as being the residual of the poor hygienic conditions soldiers lived in during World War I and from contaminated food and water which gave him typhus and typhoid fever. This cramping prevailed during the remainder of his life although he was often medically treated.

I also enjoyed listening to Dad's stories. The ones that I liked the best were stories passed on to him by his mom and dad and dealt with happenings in the Hunsrück area where he was born. In the late 1700s a band of robbers and thieves led by Johannes Bueckler, known to everyone as *Schinderhannes*, was feared as well as admired by the populace of the entire area. His band of men stole horses and other livestock, often re-selling them to their original owners. At other times his band robbed mail and bank carriages on the road or businesses in small towns. He threatened the townspeople not to reveal his whereabouts.

Apprehended several times, he managed to escape but was eventually caught and executed by hanging in Mainz, Germany in 1803.

I have not mentioned anything about the peculiar dialect spoken in Mannheim that every child learned from parents, friends, people in general and on the street. It was simply called *Mannemerich*, and on the street everyone used it. It appeared to be a Palatine dialect but was very difficult to understand and harder to speak. The early influences of people migrating from Holland, France, Belgium, Switzerland, Bavaria and other places apparently had left their marks on the local dialect. The family Kahn spoke it well, but preferred to use high German when not conversing with locals. Without malice, Mannheimers were referred to as *Bloommaul*, or "Blue Mouth," which was looked upon as a title of recognition. There were books, poems, and stories written completely in Mannemerich, along with dictionaries that explained the strange words. Blumenpeter, real name Peter Schafer, epitomized the Mannemerich dialect. He was born in 1875, was somewhat mentally and physically challenged, and never went to school. This gnome-like fellow sold flowers on the street, in pubs and told stories in Mannemerich that were perceived as humorous. He died June 15, 1940. I still remember a few of his stories. Today, my German is not very fluent, and my spoken Mannemerich has suffered substantially, although I can still understand it. A book as published with many of his stories and a monument of his likeness was erected after World War II.

EXHIBIT 5.33 Blumenpeter- Manneheim.

EXHIBIT 5.34 Blumenpeter sculpture Mannheim created after World War II.

On Shabbat J&S Kahn's business was closed, and in the afternoon if it was not Uncle Simon's and Aunt Hilde's turn to have the automobile, we would go for a drive. Roads were not crowded and the drives were pleasant. Depending on the time of year, we would take a ride to Bad Durkheim, an old, interesting city with castle ruins and fortification wall and spa with mineral springs. Each year there was a sausage festival with parades, music, and good food which we enjoyed. We didn't have a strictly kosher house, but ate no *trayf*, pork, oysters, nor shrimp. On other weekends we took leisurely drives along the scenic Weinstrasse, the center of the Palatinate wine growing area. Neustadt, the sleepy little town where my future wife, Gertrude Wolff, was born and lived, was located along this route. Speyer was another nearby town that we enjoyed visiting. One of the oldest cities in Germany, it contained the largest European Romanesque Cathedral containing tombs of former emperors and kings, and the remnants of the oldest synagogue and mikveh in Europe.

Nearby, Schwetzingen was a beautiful ancient town with one of the loveliest flower parks and water fountains in Germany. There was a palace with an adjoining indoor and outdoor theater where musical performances took place, all in Rococo period costumes. Normally we parked the car and walked for a while, then sitting to admire the performance and the scenery. Since this was the heart of the white asparagus country, we would stop at a roadside stand and buy some ready to eat and have a picnic. All of these weekend trips were within 20-25 miles of Mannheim and provided relaxation and fun from the prior week's chores and stresses.

My favorite place for excursions was Heidelberg. To me, it was like a jewel in our backyard. A large majestic castle built of red colored stone was erected on a mountain overlooking the city with its university of world prominence, and the river Neckar with a beautiful bridge spanning its banks. From this 12th century castle, with additions added hundreds of years later, one could enjoy the most romantic views imaginable. There were iron gates, draw bridges, moats, towers, stables, carriage houses, split towers, banquet halls, gardens and sculptures. The city, with its narrow and colorful streets, led up to the largest and grandest of all castles in Germany. A wine cellar harbored the world's largest handcrafted wine barrel with a capacity of 55,000 gallons. Stairs on both sides of the barrel led to its top with a floor where people once danced, and still do today on special occasions. Below, in the same wine cellar, was an unobtrusive metal box on the wall with a handle on the bottom. Nosey people, like myself, pulled on the handle and were shocked when a small door on the metal box opened with a loud noise and a long foxtail sprang out into their faces. Farther up from the castle grounds was a lovely restaurant, known as the Molkenkur, with a large terrace where people could sit, order drinks and food, while taking in the splendid panoramic view of the castle below and its surroundings. On a clear day we could see Mannheim in the distance. The road up to the restaurant by car was winding and steep. There

EXHIBIT 5.36 Heidelberg Castle with town below and the river Neckar.

was a cog railway that could be boarded from Heidelberg below to the castle or the restaurant for a small fee. We spent many an afternoon at this terrace while my parents enjoyed coffee and a smoke, and Irene and I had ice cream or some other snack. These outings were always enjoyable, relaxing, educational, and good family fun.

On other weekends when Uncle Simon's family had the car, we planned outings closer to Mannheim so that we could combine a walk with a ride on a streetcar or suburban train. One exciting time was in February/March of 1929, when the Neckar and Rhine were frozen solid. The Neckar was a much smaller, slower flowing river and had frozen over before, but the fast-flowing Rhine had not frozen over for centuries. Shipping was halted, and people enjoyed ice skating, skiing, sledding, or just walking on the ice, which we did. We lived less than a mile from the Rhine, and after dressing properly with long underwear and heavy outer garments including hats, gloves, and earmuffs, we set out on the once-in-a-lifetime expedition.

Diagonally across the street from us was a long underpass tunnel for pedestrians. It led us under the rail yard to the Waldkpark, a forest park, past Monte Gogelo, a name given to the only natural hill in town where sledding was supreme. After walking for about ten minutes, we arrived at the bank of the frozen Rhine, a magnificent sight. Thousands of people from both sides of the Rhine, Ludwigshafen and Mannheim, were walking, sliding and skating on the ice. The Rhine had fought to keep from freezing, however, as evidenced by big plates of ice that had been thrust on top of other plates until the river finally gave up.

EXHIBIT 5.38 Restaurant Molkenkur. See the appendix for additional photos of Heidelberg.

We were brave to fight of the cold, and when we arrived back home, a cup of hot chocolate felt really good. Every winter, like all children, we built snowmen and engaged in spirited snowball fights. Sometimes Irene and I and a gang of other kids went to Monte Gogelo for sledding. Dad often came along. It was so much fun coming down the hill, but it took a long time and a lot of effort to climb back up, pulling the sled behind me. Irene was a big help. I don't recall Mother ever coming along on these sledding excursions; she was not the athletic type.

There were a number of times over the years when Mother took ill with kidney problems. Afterwards the doctor recommended that she recover at Bad Herrenalb, a health picturesque resort in the foothills of the Black Forest, known

EXHIBIT 5.41
Sledding on
Monte Gogelo.

as Schwarzwald. Irene and I took vacations in Cologne (Köln) with my mother's sister, Aunt Helene, and her husband, Uncle Max Cohen. They had a profitable business that cleaned, mended, sorted, and sold burlap sacks of all sizes and for different types of commodities. The *Sackgrosshandlung* business was located at Landmannstrasse 5, in Ehrenfeld, a near suburb of Cologne. The business was dirty and very dusty, yet their two-story home right next to it was elegant and clean as a whistle. A stairway led to the living quarters on the second floor, and bedrooms were on the third. Aunt Helene had a live-in maid who did some of the cooking and most of the cleaning. Uncle Max was very fond of Irene, and because he and Aunt Helene had no children of their own, they took her to concerts, the theater, and opera. Since I was a boy and younger, their love for me was expressed in a different manner and was never jealous of my sister and her close relationship with Uncle Max and Aunt Helene.

In March of 1930 the family got ready to take a big trip to Luxembourg to celebrate Opa Raphael's 70th birthday. There were suitcases to pack and passports to get ready. The trip was about seven hours by train, and because there was no dining car, Mom made sandwiches for everyone, filled thermos bottles with coffee, and packed some apples. Everybody carried a suitcase, and there was also a hat box for the ladies as well as a "rucksack" or backpack for me containing the food. The seats on the train were hard and made of wood; luggage was stored above. I had my *mundharmonika*, harmonica, with me and played a few tunes until the more scenic route along the Rhine appeared beginning at Bingen. There were many interesting castles nestled in the hillside.

There was the *Mäuseturm*, Mouse Tower, built on a very small island in the middle of the Rhine. According to legend, a pied piper played and the mice who had invaded the town of Bingen followed him and drowned in the water. Then came the old scenic towns of Bacherach, St. Goar, Boppard and the Stolzenfels Castle near Koblenz, then the towns of Assmannshausen, Lorch, and then the big castle on an island of the Rhine at Kaub. I can still see the castle as if it were here today. Then came St. Goarshausen with the bend in the Rhine and the high, rocky mountain, the Lorelei, written about in literature, and in mythology. There, the fabled Rhine sirens bewitched sailors with their singing, causing their ships to run aground or sink. Immortalized by the poet, Heinrich Heine, and others in literature, the "Lorelei" was also captured in operas and song. The words of one song, "Ich weiss nicht was soll es bedeuten dass ich so traurig bin…" ("I don't know what it means that I am so sad…") had a beautiful melody and was always sung by passersby on ships and is still sung today. We did the same on the train while I played the tune on the harmonica. Then came the towns of Oberlahnstein and Rüdesheim, famous for their grapes and wine making. It was all so picturesque, so unforgettable, so fairytale like. Then after Koblenz-Coblence, where the Mosel River empties into the Rhine, the train traveled west and we had our picnic on the train. Irene and I broke the shells of our hard-boiled eggs on each other's heads.

EXHIBIT 5.42 Uncle Max and Aunt Helene were deported and murdered by the Nazis at Izbica Poland or some other killing center nearby.

EXHIBIT 5.43 Aunt Helene, mother's sister, and her husband Max Cohen.

EXHIBIT 5.44 Uncle Sally Cohen, brother of Max Cohen, murdered during the Holocaust. Irene is pictured standing next to him.

It didn't hurt and was fun. And now, I have exposed this nonsense to my seven grandchildren!

We had taken this trip several times, and the route and routine were always the same. Mom, and especially Dad, pointed out the *Deutsches Eck* at Koblenz, the German Corner, where, high on a mountain, we could see the former fortress Ehrenbreitstein, the big stone of honor, a huge monument with a statue of a heroic warrior on horseback. Regardless of wins or losses, it seemed that Germans revered war and loved their heroes. Their monuments everywhere attested to that fascination.

Leaving the Rhine, we traveled west until we came to a stop and a town called Igel. This was where uniformed German border patrols entered the train, checked everyone's passport, and searched luggage for contraband. It

EXHIBIT 5.45 My sister Irene with her dear friend Irmgard Isaak (on left) from nearby Cologne. Irmgard and her parents perished during the Holocaust.

was scary because the German soldiers were not friendly when they asked where and why we were going to Luxembourg. It was always quite a relief when they stamped our passports, left, and the train started to move again. Five minutes later the train stopped again. The German locomotive was uncoupled, and a different locomotive and crew from the Grand Duché de Luxembourg pulled us into the Luxembourg border town of Wasserbillig. Seemingly friendly Gendarmes from Luxembourg came on board, politely asking us for our passports, first in French, then in German. My Mother, born in Luxembourg, replied in French, and thereafter conversed with the officials in their native dialect. What a relief to be finally on the other side of the border. Twenty minutes later we pulled into the *gare*, French for rail terminal, at the capital city of Luxembourg of the Grand Duché de Luxembourg. Uncle Berney, my mother's only brother, greeted us. After we carried the luggage outside the terminal, we piled into his large American made Oldsmobile and proudly drove us to Hollerich where Opa Raphael and Oma Malchen lived.

Hollerich was a section of town rather than a suburb. In my imagination, their house at cobblestone Rue de Hollerich #83 always reminded me of a gingerbread house. In reality, it was nothing like that, although compared with city apartment buildings of Mannheim, it did look small, odd, and dainty. It

EXHIBIT 5.46 This is the only photo I could find of my grandparents house in Luxembourg, Hollerich Strasse #83, before the war.

EXHIBIT 5.47 The house was sold to a lumber company after the war and later demolished.

was two stories high, with an attic. Behind the house stood a large animal barn, a manure pit, in front of which was a large courtyard closed in by a five-foot high stone wall and a wooden gate through which livestock and vehicles entered and exited. At the end of the courtyard was a large fenced in vegetable garden.

Although they led a hard and modest life, Raphael and Amalia were kind, gentle, and loving grandparents. From her childhood Amalia was called Malchen, and the nickname stuck. To friends, neighbors, and family she was known only as Malchen. Of course, grandchildren didn't have to worry about nicknames; she was simply Oma to us.

Another reason why their home reminded me of a gingerbread house was its old, dreary stucco appearance from the outside, the low ceilings inside, squeaky wood plank floors, and the small, low-mounted windows covered with hand-made curtains. In the kitchen old and odd looking cooking implements such as pots, pans, wooden spoons, and cake forms hung on the wall. There was also a huge wood and coal fired stove. In the dark hallway that led to the annex where milk, cream, butter, cheese, and eggs were processed, was a trap door in the floor with a ladder leading to the cellar where bread and homemade wine were stored. The three rooms on the first floor, including the living room, a dining room which was rarely used except on

Shabbat when guests were there, and the kitchen, were not large. Neither were the four bedrooms upstairs, accessible via a narrow squeaky, wooden spiral staircase. Light fixtures were few, old, and used low wattage bulbs, making rooms somewhat dark and dreary, and reading tedious. All of these things added to my gingerbread house perception, while enjoying the warm and loving outreach of Oma and Opa. A live-in maid, Anna, while sort of chubby and smelly, could be charming, but mostly was not.

Soon after we arrived and our luggage was stowed away, the house began swarming with relatives, aunts, uncles, and cousins, all there to greet us and celebrate Opa's 70th birthday. The relatives included my Mother's two sisters, Aunt Helene and her husband Max Cohen from Cologne (Köln); Aunt Irma, her husband Charles Ehrlich, and their young son, Claude, from Lille, France. Also present was my Mother's only brother, Bernard Joseph, who had picked us up from the railroad station. They called him sometimes called Benny or Berny, his wife, Marthe, and their son, Georges, all of whom lived not far from Oma and Opa's house. Georges was a year younger than I, and we got along fine. He showed me the barn with the cows, the chicken coop, and the garden.

EXHIBIT 5.48 My cousin Georges Joseph and me, March 1930. Fifteen years later he was executed by a German firing squad in the city of Cuneo, Italy with other partisans.

When I slept at Oma and Opa's in the morning after I awoke, Oma Malchen, who had snow white hair, came to my bed with a big cup of milk, fresh from the cow and still warm. She recited numbers in French and asked me to repeat so I would learn them. Then she gave me a "Su," a Luxembourg coin that had a hole in the middle. She also sang French nursery rhymes to me like *Frere Jaques, Au Claire de La Lune*, and *Sur Le pont Avignon*. Oma had started that custom on prior visits when I was younger. Although I was now just 6-1/2 years old, I always enjoyed her loving gentleness and animated singing. She had soft facial features that my mother had inherited. Opa, while good-natured, was somewhat more authoritative and had toughened over the years. With the assistance of the hired hand, Anna, who lived in the attic of the house, his work started at 5:00 a.m. every day. He was a remarkable man at age 70. He wore a cap on his bald head and often used it to kill flies, of which there were many, that landed close to him.

Windows had no screens in those days. This feat required a very quick reaction, and in most instances, he was successful, and definitely fun for me and Irene to watch. Some years later when he had become older with more sluggish reaction time, he would not be as successful. Noticing this he would shrug it off by saying, "They are flying faster than they used to!" I think of this remark when I miss a ball playing tennis. Since he lived in a primarily residential area, neighbors came in the morning and late afternoon with a pail or jug to buy fresh milk, butter, cream, eggs, or cottage cheese. The front door was always open except at night when it was locked with a very large key. When people came to the house, a bell attached above the entrance door rang loudly. Especially in the late afternoons, neighbors left their containers in the kitchen, walked into the living room and spun tales with Oma and Opa. It was a daily ritual that included me and the cat sitting under the table, listening to the gossip, and inhaling the aroma from the tobacco of Opa's odd looking, long curved stem pipe, despite his owning more conventional looking pipes.

A few years after that when Mother and I vacationed at Luxembourg, I remember playing some pranks and getting in trouble. One time cousin Georges and I saw Opa smoking his pipe. It was bent similarly to a walking cane, and adorned with several tassels. Opa was sitting inside the house by the window, with the end of the pipe dangling out the window. Georges and I went to the barn and cut some hair off a cow's tail. We then proceeded to sneak outside to the window and deposited the hair into the bowl with pipe tobacco which Opa was smoking. The rest you can imagine! Opa coughed, choked, shouted, and swore as we ran away and hid. He never knew what really happened.

That brings to mind another time when Oma asked me to feed the chickens. There was chicken feed inside the barn, but I had other ideas. I went into the garden, and without further thought, pulled out many heads of lettuce and fed them to the chickens. When Oma and Opa found out what I had done, they were angry and read me the riot act. During another vacation which coincided with the apple harvest, an older boy, Gaston Leib, who lived across the street, and I walked to a large estate with an apple orchard. We climbed over a high, iron fence, and filled our knickerbocker pants, the ones that tied just above the ankle, with apples. Suddenly, as we heard dogs bark, we became scared and ran toward the fence. Just as I got to the top of the iron spikes, my knickerbockers tore. Not only did the pants tear beginning at an embarrassing part of my anatomy, but I also lost most of the apples in one leg and some from the other. I had a lot of explaining to do when I got back to the house. It was embarrassing and not funny then, but is sure is funny now.

I remember Opa having the simplest but most accurate weather barometer nailed to the barn door. It was a donkey painted on a piece of wood with a tail made from a strand of yarn. The instructions under the donkey read: "When tail wet – rain; when tail frozen – sleet and ice; when tail covered with snow – snow; when tail dry – nice weather." The instrument never failed in its accuracy! I was always amused when I saw this donkey.

Returning to Opa's 70th birthday celebration in March of 1930, a professional photographer came to Hollerich in the afternoon for a family portrait. It was taken in the courtyard in front of the barn, and required a lot of patience especially for the four children, Georges Joseph, Claude Ehrlich, Irene, and me. Georges, Irene and I wore sailor suits which were in vogue at the time. That evening a festive dinner was arranged at Uncle Berney and Aunt Marthe's home at Rue de Strassbourg 16-18. Their dining room was large, and on this special evening, it seated twenty-five people, including immediate family, children, grandchildren, brothers and sisters, several cousins and a few good friends of Opa's. There were prayers, toasts, speeches and poems dedicated to Raphael. His nickname sounded like "Raph." He was called Pap (short for Papa) by his children, and Opa by the grandchildren. It was a memorable event, one that instilled me the seeds of family values at an early age and reminded me always of the Fifth Commandment: "Thou shalt honor your Father and Mother."

Three months later on June 30, 1930, the French pulled their last troops from Germany's Rhineland, five years earlier than set by the Versailles Treaty. In turn,

EXHIBIT 5.50 Photograph taken the week of March 31, 1930 on the occasion of Raphael Joseph's 70th birthday, in the courtyard in front of the animal barn at Hollericherstrasse or Rue de Hollerich, Luxembourg. A detailed listing of everyone in this photo can be found in the appendix, exhibit 5.50.

EXHIBIT 5.53 Gertrude "Gerda" (née Kahn) Ackerman, my father's sister, and her husband Manfred, circa 1920 in Bad Schwalbach, later Frankfurt, Germany. Both would become victims of the Holocaust.

Germany agreed not to rearm itself nor put any military forces on the right bank of the Rhine into a thirty mile demilitarized buffer zone. Now we could walk across the bridge from Mannheim to Ludwigshafen without a written pass. Then came a big surprise to the world and Jews everywhere. The elections held in September of that year resulted in Hitler's Nazi party winning a total of 107 seats in government, raising an alarm in all of Europe. The German people were attracted and seduced by his speeches, vitriolic hatred of the Jews, his unwillingness to continue paying war reparations, and his promises for a greater "1000 Year" Germany. His megalomaniac rantings were without comparison, particularly his promise to revenge for Germany's loss of World War I by creating an Aryan nation above all other nations in the world.

In addition to visits to Luxembourg to spend time with family, during school vacations Irene visited Aunt Helene and Uncle Max in Cologne (Köln) and Mom and Dad drove me to Bad Schwalbach, not too far north from Wiesbaden, to spend time with Dad's sister, Aunt Gerda, and her husband Uncle Manfred Ackerman.

Bad Schwalbach, where Uncle Manfred was born, lies in a mountainous region known as the Taunus. It was known as a health spa with unique health-inducing mineral water for drinking and bathing. There were many mineral springs in the area, and people living in town would drink that mineral water for their health. Because I was not used to drinking this water, I came down with diarrhea and learned not to drink too much of it, even though it tasted pretty good. Each day my job, which I enjoyed, was to fill up a pottery jug at the public pump house and carry it to my aunt and uncle's apartment. The Ackermans lived on the second floor overlooking a large courtyard. Uncle Manfred was a salesman for milk centrifuges, devices that separated cream from milk. He had a motorcycle, and with many catalogues he would call on farmers in the area to sell these machines. However, he would never let me ride with him. I have a hunch that my parents were behind that. I always had a good time staying with them. Often we would go on hikes in and around the resort park and forests. Sometimes I would play with kids from the neighborhood as long as Aunt Gerda knew where I was. Once a week she or Uncle Manfred took me to a private bath house where I would be given a warm mineral bath for about thirty minutes, which was said to be good for my health.

On the ground floor where Gerda and Manfred lived, was a butcher. Once a week they would slaughter a pig in the courtyard and I could watch from the window above. The whole procedure sickened me, and I could not stand the merciless squealing of the pig until it died.

My aunt and uncle were religious people and recited Hebrew prayers before and after each meal. I quickly became used to saying grace in Hebrew from memory, even though I was not taught to at home except on Shabbat and Jewish holidays. Uncle Manfred also taught me to play a board game known as *mühlchen* that had some vague similarity with the game of checkers. According to Hoyle, the American authority on cards, board games, and games of chance, this game is called "the Mill." Each of two players played with nine pieces that could be simple buttons. Afterward, Dad and I played the game that he had also learned to play in the Army during World War I. Uncle Manfred also taught me to play a better game of chess so that I could be a stronger opponent when I played against my father or anyone else. After two or three weeks' vacation, my parents came with our Opel car to pick me up again.

In other years, I would spend part of my vacation at Ehrenfeld, with Aunt Helene and Uncle Max, unless Irene was there. She and I would alternate vacation there. They would show me different parts of the big city and take me to big department stores like Tietz where I experienced my first walk on escalators and a huge toy department. Uncle Max, who loved music, took me to concerts, theater, or the opera, but I was probably a bit too young to fully appreciate them. One evening he took me to see the play, *Der Schneider Wibbel*. It was a hilarious comedy about a tailor who wanted to find out who would attend his own funeral. I have never forgotten the plot. Another time Uncle Max, who always used a walking cane, took me to the zoo. As we stood in front of the monkey cage, another viewer used his own walking stick to tease the monkeys. Thinking that was funny, I asked Uncle Max for his cane and proceeded to do likewise. To my surprise, the monkeys held onto the cane and pulled it away from me into the cage. I was so astonished that I didn't know what to say. Neither did my uncle. Mistakenly, I had given the curved end of the walking cane to the monkeys, which provided

EXHIBIT 5.54 Uncle Manfred and Aunt Gerda (née Kahn, my Dad's sister), Irene, my mother and father. I am kneeling. Photo taken at Bad Schwalbach circa 1934.

EXHIBIT 5.55 Manfred and Gerda were murdered during the Holocaust.

EXHIBIT 5.56 Robert and Irene, 1933.

them the strength advantage. Uncle Max was good natured and finally laughed, and I with him. The story was all over town in no time, and I learned a lesson not to "monkey around."

Another fun part of taking vacations at Ehrenfeld/Cologne was that Uncle Max had several married sisters: Aunt Berta was married to Karl Katz, lived in Cologne; Aunt Johanna and Uncle Moritz Capell lived in the small farming community of Rommerskirchen, thirty minutes away by automobile. Irene and I would alternate spending vacation time at Rommerskirchen as well. There Aunt Johanna and Uncle Moritz lived in a large farmhouse. Part of the farm estate was a large barn with five or six milk cows, a hayloft, a separate stable with at least one horse, a chicken coop, and many ducks and geese. I was particularly fond of several small gnome statues in the yard. The gnomes had long beards, smoked pipes, wore red caps, and colorful jackets and pants. One was sitting on a rock, and the other was pushing a wheelbarrow. Aunt Johanna and Uncle Moritz also had a large vegetable garden behind which was a pasture where the cows grazed most of the day. In the pasture were many fruit trees that were the source of delicious cherries, pears, plums, and apples.

Once Aunt Johanna asked me to pick up *fallobst*, ripe fruit that had fallen to the ground. I went to the pasture with a large basket, shook the trees branches until much of the fruit not yet ripe fell to the ground. Of course, that was not what Aunt Johanna had in mind, but in my eagerness and intent to please I was able to fill up several large wicker baskets with fruit. At first there were some strange looks of disbelief on Aunt Johanna and Uncle Moritz's faces. Later at the dinner

EXHIBIT 5.57 Aunt Johanna Capell and Irene, 1930.

EXHIBIT 5.58 Erich Cappell and me (and the horse), 1930.

EXHIBIT 5.59 Änne Capell and her husband.

EXHIBIT 5.60 Erich, Ilse, Uncle Moritz and Änne

table the discussion of the day's events turned into laughter, especially after it was explained to me what I had done. Their three grown children, Ilse, the youngest, Erich, and Änne, the eldest, tried to reassure me, but I had learned an important lesson, not to take instructions literally, nor to do a job without knowing exactly what was to be done.

Uncle Moritz and Aunt Johanna certainly had their hands full managing the farm and all the chores that had to be done from sunup to sunset. They had several hired hands from the village, and their own three children helped as much as possible. When I arrived at Aunt and Uncle's, I could not wait to be turned loose in order to explore the estate. I would fill a pot with chicken feed and disperse it in the enclosure where chicken, ducks, and geese were held. Later I would pull several sugar beets from the neighboring field and feed them to the horse. If I didn't do things myself, I would watch whatever was going on at the time. In the morning, after the cows were milked, I was allowed to lead them from the barn to the pasture. I remember being in the barn when the cows were milked early in the morning. The barn was warm from the bodies of the cows, and a certain amount of steam would rise from the warm milk in the buckets and cans and was noticeable against the windows. In the late afternoon I helped round up the cattle and herd them back to the barn. Once a day Aunt Johanna gave me a basket to pick up the eggs in the hen house. Sometimes I picked up a number of baby chicks and played with them up in the hayloft above the barn where they couldn't get away. As a city boy, it was all enjoyable to me.

When it was harvest time for wheat, I would sit on the horse drawn wagon. In the field, men and women cut the wheat with long-handled scythes. I and others raked and bundled the wheat into stacks for drying. It was hard work for them as

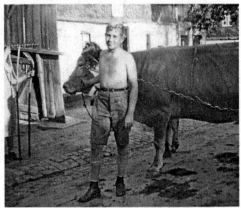

EXHIBITS 5.61 & 5.62 Vacation on Uncle Moritz and Aunt Johanna Cappell's farm, Rommerskirchen, Germany. Aunt Johanna was Max Cohen's sister. Irene feeds chickens and I tend to the cows.

adults, but the demands on me were minor, and I looked on it as a form of fun. I played hide-and-seek in and around the stacks with other kids whom the farmhands brought along. Days later when the wheat was dry, the stacks were loaded onto wagons and brought to the Capell's farm where the wheat was threshed, the grain separated, and the leftover straw baled.

Next to Uncle Moritz's farm stood a single house where a priest and housekeeper lived. The priest's nephew, Herbert, spent vacation time with him, and since he was perhaps only a year older than I, we were good companions for each other. One day when the two of us were in the pasture, he pulled two cigars out of his pocket that he had taken from his uncle. He also had matches. He lit his cigar and encouraged me to do the same with the other. I did, and both of us puffed away where no one could see us.

By now it was the late summer of 1933, and I was not quite ten years old. When I returned to Mannheim from my vacation on the farm, I became very ill. At first, neither my parents nor the doctors had any idea what my ailment was until one doctor mentioned that my symptoms were similar to nicotine poisoning. At that point, in tears and with remorse, I confessed my cigar smoking to my parents. I learned a bitter lesson, one that had given my parents much anxiety and worry. At the movies, news reels showed the bitter fighting, the agony of homeless civilians, the destruction of cities in China inflicted by the Japanese Air Force and Army. But it was so far away, no one seemed to care or worry too much. What intrigued me more were the daily newspaper articles with details on the kidnapping of the infant son of the famous American aviator Charles Lindbergh. The headlines were highly sensational, and the massive search ended when the baby was found dead. Less attention was given to the German elections that resulted in increased

EXHIBIT 5.63 Herbert, the Priest's nephew, who lived next door to the Capells. He persuaded me to join him to smoke a cigar; cigars that he had taken from his uncle.

strength of the National Socialists, the Nazi party, from 107 seats in the German government to 229, leading to fierce street battles between the Communist party and the Nazis in different cities of Germany. The continued strengthening and political pressure by the Nazi party finally led President Paul von Hindenburg's yielding to Adolf Hitler, allowing him to become Chancellor of Germany on January 30, 1933. While his political opponents feared the flamboyant and power-hungry Hitler, there was jubilation in Berlin and other big cities, including Mannheim. Large crowds greeted columns of Hitler's storm troopers as they marched in torchlight parades, singing and carrying large banners as we watched from our windows. It was something the German people had never seen before, but seemed to enjoy and relished participating in.

What diverted my attention at the time was the arrival in Mannheim of the largest amphibious passenger airliner in the world, the Do-X, built in Germany by the Dornier Werke. The flying boat anchored on the bank of the Rhine had ten pusher-type engines and could carry one hundred passengers transatlantic. It was as determined much later the beginning of Germany's quest for world aviation superiority. Several of my friends and I went by bicycle to the Waldpark to see the 150 foot long giant.

Other highlights occurred during 1933: On February 28 the German Reichstag parliament building in Berlin was destroyed by fire, and the Bolsheviks were blamed. The first concentration camp near the town of Dachau opened on March 20, and on March 23, Hitler was granted dictatorial powers by the German parliament. On April 1 the Nazis' enforced a country-wide boycott of Jewish owned stores by placing placards and uniformed storm troopers in front of stores, denying entrance to customers. I was really scared and did not venture out of the house. May 10 was the beginning of the crackdown on intellectuals, scientists, and cultural leaders by burning their books in public squares with great hoopla, books that were determined to be "un-German." A hundred years earlier the

German writer and poet, Heinrich Heine, wrote: "Where they burn books, in the end they will also burn people." His books were also set on fire by the Nazis. Jews were evicted from civil service, and on July 31 German newspapers reported that 27,000 persons were being held as political prisoners. However, thousands more who were incarcerated remained unreported. Finally on July 26, the Nazi government announced a program to sterilize Germans who were mentally ill, had physical handicaps, including blindness and deafness. It was the beginning of Hitler's quest to perfect the Aryan race.

The world heard, saw, and listened to the German maniac but did nothing. The countries of the world had their own problems. President Roosevelt of America was trying to determine how to collect the huge debts owed by foreign countries in spite of a world depression. In Miami, he was the target of an assassination attempt prior to being sworn in. At the swearing-in ceremony, March 4, he tried to calm the economic crisis of the country with the maxim, "The only thing we have to fear is fear itself." Bank failures, closed factories, bankrupt farms, enormous unemployment, and poverty were rampant. In England high unemployment resulted in riots and attacks on the King's palace. In Russia dictator Stalin conducted limitless purges in his government. Revolt in Spain, which included rioting, bombings and fighting, led to martial law. There was unrest and bloody strife in Cuba. Angry mobs fed up with their government rioted in France. There appeared to be no end to the world's problems and unrest.

While all of this turmoil was going on in the world, at the age of ten I was not very concerned since I didn't understand what was happening or its consequences. I did, however, read about the completion of the world's tallest building, the Empire State Building in New York. I also read about Picard's balloon flight into the stratosphere, gangster violence in America's big cities over prohibition, Gandhi's acts of civil disobedience in India, Tarzan movies, and the Chicago World's Fair. It was also the time that I started reading my first Karl May book about American Indians and was thrilled every moment of every page. There was school, homework, and I heard the first discussions at home about the possibility of Irene leaving and going to school in Lille, France. There, she would live with Mother's sister, Aunt Irma, her husband, Uncle Charles, and their two children, Claude and infant Eliane.

Irene was encountering all sorts of subtle anti-Semitism in the Elizabetten Schule, an all-girl gymnasium. My parents and Irene were alarmed. For me, anti-Semitism at elementary school had become noticeable, but at this point manifested itself as more of a nuisance. Some harassment by teachers and students did not seem a serious threat to me or my education, although I began to dislike school. These occurrences which we would call bullying today, resulted in frustrations that probably led to my nail biting along with experiencing nausea at breakfast time. To keep me from vomiting, my parents told me to breathe

EXHIBIT 5.67 A wedding photograph of my mother's sister, Aunt Irma, and her husband Uncle Charles Ehrlich.

deep with a wide open mouth while they gave me water to drink to which an inhibitor, *Alcool Du Monde* had been added. It was an over-the-counter medication produced in France that had a strong peppermint flavor. Literally translated it meant "People's Alcohol." Surprisingly, it helped me most of the time. Little did I know what harassment and anguish I was in for in the not-too-distant future.

Meanwhile in Luxembourg, Oma Malchen who had been ill for some time and had a nurse at her side night and day, died at her home on September 22, 1933, the day of the Jewish New Year, Rosh Hashanah, at the young age of sixty-nine. She had been taken care of by Niederbronner Sisters, a Catholic Order dedicated to help the elderly and sick. The order was founded over one hundred years ago in Niederbronn, a small community in Alsace-Lorraine, which at that time was part of Germany, not France as it is today. On September 24 she was buried at the Jewish Cemetery Luxembourg in the presence of her children and those who loved her. The eulogy by Rabbi Serebrenik of Luxembourg is still a treasured document in my possession, which can be read in the appendix,

EXHIBIT 5.68 Eliane and Claude Ehrlich, the two little French cousins who welcomed Irene into their home in Lille, France.

as well as her obituaries and photos from her final years, (see appendix, exhibits 5.64-5.66).

Now my dear grandmother, Oma, who had sung French nursery rhymes to me as I awoke in the morning, was no more. Opa Raphael Joseph was now all alone in what, as a young child, I had perceived as the Gingerbread House. It was my first experience of a family tragedy. While Dad and Mom traveled to Luxembourg for the funeral, Irene and I stayed home. We both went to our respective schools, and I couldn't fall asleep, wondering what it would be like to be dead.

When spring came to Europe and Mannheim, feverish preparations were underway to get everything ready for Irene to leave us for Lille, France. Dad and Mom were hoping that while staying there with her aunt and family, Irene would be able to obtain a good education, which as a Jewess in Mannheim was becoming more difficult. She was resigned to leaving her hometown under the circumstances, although I had mixed feelings, and knew that I would miss her terribly. A few days before her departure in April 1934, Mom had arranged a farewell party in the afternoon for all of Irene's Jewish friends: the ones I remember being there were Dina Loebenberg, Edith Kiefler, and Lilo Wartensleben. Christian students could not be invited because of the race laws that precluded associating with them. Of course, as the only boy at the party, I was in my glory. At some point in the party, Irene read a farewell speech and made everyone a little sad. Somehow, her speech has survived through all the ensuing years and serves as a reminder of that day.

Irene's departure and Mom accompanying her on the trip brought forced smiles to Dad's face as we all embraced over and over, first at home and then at the railroad station. Although she was my older sister, she was still a child, not quite 13 years old. I was close to tears. In Lille, at Aunt Irma and Uncle Charles', Irene had her own beautifully appointed room on the third floor with a small balcony overlooking a nearby botanical garden. The children, Claude, five, and Eliane, two, taught her to understand and speak French quickly. After mom returned from Lille to Mannheim, Passover came and went. Reading the ancient biblical stories about the exodus from Egypt and be free of slavery gave us hope. Pharaoh had become Hitler and Egypt had become Germany. And now we were all looking for a modern Moses to perform miracles to help us.

In the meantime, Irene had enrolled in school, taking the streetcar every day but Thursday, which was a day free from school. Uncle Charles and Aunt Irma kept a strictly kosher home, and their friends were often invited for Shabbat meals. Irene told me how embarrassed she was when she was mixed up the *milchig* and *fleischig* mustard, dairy mustard and meat mustard. Not being raised in a strictly kosher home, she had no idea that there was such a thing in kosher dietary laws. Their maid, Martha, and Irene went to the market on Thursdays. She learned to love Claude and Eliane and played with them in the garden sandbox, sang to and with them, and told them fairy stories. Above all, she became an excellent student. The entire Ehrlich family spent summer vacations at the Atlantic sea resort, Blankenberg, Belgium. Irene had started a new life.

With all of the things Irene had to do as a teenager, she made sure to write to us every Thursday. Likewise, my parents wrote to her, allowing me to add a few lines. Now and then we sent her small packages with home baked cookies, chocolate, and other surprises. My parents, of course, contributed to Irene's upkeep, but there was never any talk about that subject, the amount of money, or whether it was a hardship on my parents.

Summer 1934 we were visited by Aunt Martha, Dad's sister who was married to Julius Lerner, and their daughter, Hannelore, who was seven, three years younger than me. They lived in Eberswalde near Berlin. Hannelore, now called Lorie, told me that once she was bored and asked my mother, "what can I do?" Mom was washing and gave her some socks to wash. Lorie had not forgotten this all these years. In that year, I had the last vacation of my youth and the last vacation for many years to come. My parents had made arrangements for me to spend two weeks at a children's health camp operated by a Jewish family since I was under emotional stress and nervous tension from constant intimidation at school. The camp was located about 140 km west by northwest of Mannheim at Bad Münster am Stein. The area was well known for its spa and its quiet scenic location by the river Nahe, only a few kilometers from another, perhaps better known spa, Bad Kreuznach.

It was a very nice vacation with perhaps twenty other children of similar age. From this large private home we went on daily walks and hikes, sometimes whistling or singing and then had to rest for hours. I was not homesick as some other children were, and enjoyed the fresh air and the peaceful and quiet, rural setting. The name of the spa, Bad Münster am Stein, referred to a steep rock cliff located near the town. At its bottom the unassuming river Nahe flowed slowly. The ruins of a Middle Age castle and fortifications were located at the top of this cliff. Although we could see some of the castle from below, we never hiked up.

There were times when we had fun playing soccer, handball, and other games. All of us ate together in a large dining room, and I remember eating *Himmel und Erde*, sky and earth, for the first time. It consisted of applesauce (sky) and mashed potatoes (earth). A main dish came with it, but I thought the term H&E was unique, and I have never forgotten it. I didn't know that in the not too distant future, sky and earth would be just fine even without a main dish. It would be all we could buy with the ration stamp allotted to Jews.

Not quite eleven years old I was a typical boy and in all probability behaved as such. Mother now and then would refer to me as "*Raschiveschen aus der Äppelkammer.*" It was an expression in the dialect of Luxembourg people and I had no idea of its meaning at the time. Nor did I care. Today, after considerable research, this saying among Jews in Luxembourg embraces the name of the famous Rabbi and scholar Rashi (1040-1115). Literally it means "a little Rashi from the apple storage room." Or as it was explained to me, "a little wiseguy." Perhaps I behaved that way on occasion, but don't remember whether this was a realistic perception or just a way to express endearment. On the other hand, my mother's sister, Aunt Helene, often referred to me as "Nicodemus Sanftmut." Nicodemus is prominently mentioned in the New Testament as a Jew having belonged to an extremely pious sect, who was perceived as a confident, kind hearted person. Could both of these utterances convey some sort of image of me? And did these distinguishing traits carry forward as I grew up?

Fall had come to Mannheim when all of a sudden much concern and anxiety befell the Kahn home. An official letter addressed to my dad had come from the police department requesting that he make an appointment to appear at police headquarters. My parents feared the worst with the internal political situation and the Jew baiting being what it was. He went while Mom and I were nervously waiting. He returned and with an awkward smile on his face showed us a velvet case containing a medal, the Cross of Honor awarded to him as a soldier in World War I. A certificate which accompanied the medal read in part that it was awarded, most astonishingly, by the Führer (namely Hitler) and "Reichskanzler" Chancellor of Germany Hindenburg dated November 3, 1934. It was indeed a completely unexpected, and to say the least, a perplexing event. Both, medal and certificate, are now on exhibit at the National Air Force Museum, Dayton, in a special area devoted to the Holocaust. I have my doubts that visitors viewing this display realize its ironic significance.

EXHIBIT 5.70 My father's Cross of Honor and certificate awarded for his service during World War I. See the appendix for larger image of exhibit 5.70.

CHAPTER SIX

Growing Up Under The Swastika

In early fall of 1935 I was not quite twelve years old when on September 12th the Nazi hierarchy invoked the terrible Nuremberg Laws (see the appendix for the full details of these laws), I was too young to comprehend the meaning of the laws or their far-reaching, dreadful consequences on the Jewish people of Germany and on our family in particular. Yet it did not take very long for me to begin sensing and feeling the ghastly impact. These laws quickly destroyed and brought the cultural life of Jews to an abrupt halt, forbidding social contact with the now so-called "Aryan" population and stifling the participation of Jews in the economic sphere of Germany. Mom and Dad didn't explain to me the repercussions of these laws, but I knew from overhearing grownups talk that the winds of Jew hatred had picked up.

Somehow I was glad that Irene had left in April the year before to live with Aunt Irma, my mother's sister, and her husband, Charles, in Lille, France, with their two children, Claude, aged seven, and Eliane, aged three. There she was able to go to school without being harassed by her schoolmates or teachers as being a "dirty Jew."

EXHIBIT 6.1 Mom's sister, Irma Ehrlich, with Claude and Eliane, 1934

EXHIBIT 6.2 Charles Ehrlich, Aunt Irma's husband.

I was two years younger than Irene and so I didn't realize how concerned she was about our parents and me. She wrote us at least once a week, as we did to her. Occasionally we telephoned each other, and it was a treat to hear each other's voice. Absence does make the heart grow fonder, but it would have been nicer being together as a family.

For me, going to the elementary school, Luisenschule, was not enjoyable anymore. The school was perhaps half a mile from our home and an easy walk four times a day since we came home at noon for lunch. In those days all children walked to and from school. Bicycles were used mostly by teachers. Each day I walked past a large villa on the corner of L13 and Bismarkstrasse. A high, heavy metal fence fronted its courtyard in which two huge St. Bernard dogs kept watch. Even if I walked on the other side of the street, the dogs were provoked to bark at me loudly making a peculiar deep sound. They would stand on their hind legs, their front paws pressing against the heavy, ornamental, iron gate bars. They were enormous and looked very threatening. Somehow I imagined they did this because I was a Jew. They were very scary, but I always managed to make it past the villa and continue my walk to school. Along the way I also passed a dairy store, almost at the corner of Bismarkstrasse and the Kaiserring. The name of the store was *Vonderheit*, after the name of its Dutch owner. It was the first store in the neighborhood to display a large sign in the window that read, "*Juden werden hier nicht bedient*" "Jews will not be served here!" Because of the store's proximity to our home, it was there that we bought our milk, cottage cheese, butter and eggs until the sign appeared. It was very uncomfortable for me to walk past that store. Pretty soon signs like this one and others reading "*Eintritt für Juden verboten*," which translated to, "It is unlawful for Jews to enter," showed up all over the city. Not only did these signs appear on stores, but also public buildings, restaurants, movie theaters, all types of entertainment venues, parks and more. We had become prisoners in our own city.

As I continued on to school I came to a major intersection of the Kaiserring and Bismarkstrasse. Here, in the center of the boulevard on a large marble slab stood a ten-foot tall, impressive, black bronze statue of General Otto von Bismark in full military uniform. Otto von Bismark (1815-1898), was a "Junker," a large land owner from the old German Brandenburg State east of the river Elbe. He was a diplomat, and later general of the Prussian Army and was considered a hero for unifying the thirty-eight German states into a German Federation (1867). In 1871, after winning a number of wars, he formed what became known as the German Empire, the boundaries of which did not change until 1918, the end of World War I. The statue of this hero of the German people stood in all its glory, pith helmet on his head, saber on his side, wrapped in his General's coat. At his feet was a winged angel with drawn sword and shield, supposedly depicting might and right.

EXHIBIT 6.3 The statue of Otto von Bismark in Mannheim.

I was always very impressed as I walked by each day, having learned about him and other German heroes in class or on short field trips. From this point I walked across the Tattersall, a very busy traffic area where a transfer station depot for streetcars and public restrooms stood. One could also buy fare tickets, newspapers, candies, cigarettes, and cigars. From there it was only a few hundred meters to my school. I had to walk past the *Mädchen* girl's entrance to the *Knaben* boy's entrance, as the school was divided by gender.

My classroom was either on the second or third floor. My teacher would often come to class in the Nazi SA (Sturm Abteilung) uniform. It consisted of a brown brimmed hat, brown shirt and tie, brown flared trousers similar to riding breeches, a swastika armband, and dark brown boots that came to just below the knee, and other paramilitary Nazi trappings. His name was Pfeiffer; he was a little on the heavy side and very mean to the two Jewish students in his class. We had to sit in the last row of desks in the large classroom. When he came into the room in the morning, the entire class had to get up, raise and stretch our right arms, hands extended forward, and yell, *Heil Hitler.* To say and give the Hitler salute for me was an insult and a despicable task, but I had no choice. The consequence would have been a beating with a wooden rod on my buttocks. I also often got beatings on my bottom for other minor infractions for which Christian pupils only received mild verbal reprimands. Of course, the others laughed when I was singled out, and I shuddered most of the time knowing that I was always at the mercy of Herr Pfeiffer. I remember one episode that revealed Herr Pfeiffer's quickly aroused temper and left a lasting impression on me. One late winter morning, with closed windows facing the street, Herr Pfeiffer was explaining something on the blackboard with a wooden ruler. All of a sudden, there was a noise outside which annoyed Herr Pfeiffer. While making noises outside of school was against the law, a coal peddler with a horse-drawn wagon was ringing a bell, shouting "coal for sale!" It disturbed and irritated Herr Pfeiffer so much that he became angry, turned toward the window, shook his fists, swore, and hit the glass windowpane so hard with the ruler that the glass broke into a thousand pieces. The class thought it was hilarious, which it was, and burst into loud laughter. As punishment all of us had to stay fifteen minutes longer after the morning session was over at noon. I ran home so that I wouldn't be late for lunch, the customary main meal of the day, which was always lovingly prepared by Mom and our maid. Dad had already come home as he normally did each day unless he had to go out of town to see customers. As we sat down to eat, Mom asked me about my morning at school. I couldn't resist telling them what had happened. I even proceeded to demonstrate by acting it out. But I got so carried away imitating Herr Pfeiffer that I too broke a window using a broomstick as my prop. I was embarrassed and my parents gasped as we were all caught by surprise. Then Mom and Dad laughed at my unfortunate re-enactment and settled down for lunch.

In some schools, as it was in ours, especially at lower grade levels, there existed another system of disciplining students. That system was known as *tatzen*. The literal translation is "paws," like the paws of cats, lions, bears, dogs, etc. If a student received tatzen, he had to put out one of his hands palm up, and then the teacher

EXHIBIT 6.4 The building on the left, Luisenschule--my school.

hit him across his open hand with a stick or a long wooden ruler. Depending on the severity of the disciplinary action, tatzen was administered once or a number of times on one or both hands. It resulted in painful welts and served as a grim deterrent while preventing the pupil from doing many things he would normally do with his hand for the rest of the day or the next. I can't remember which of the two punishments, the tatzen or hits on my bottom, was worse. I received both almost daily and feared both of them. Under the circumstances I learned very little, and this showed up on my report cards. I was not intellectually stimulated, my emotional state was less than desirable, I was scared and I was very confused. I had lost all perception of why I was going to school, and moreover, what the ultimate purpose of learning was. I seem to remember that I thought the only purpose of school was to make my parents happy and deliver good report cards to them. But the grades were always wanting, and Mom and Dad never realized what the causes were. Perhaps they knew but kept it to themselves.

There were other matters in the Luisenschule that caused me nightmares and made me wish that I didn't have to go to school. During the study of religion and German history, the other Jewish boy and I had to leave the classroom and stand in the hall as if we were outcasts until the bell rang at the end of the session. Sometimes I would go to the nearby art museum and spend time there. The school's boys' toilet facilities, according to standards even then, were somewhat primitive. The urinal consisted of a long vertical wall that was painted with something that smelled like creosote. We urinated against that wall and the urine ran off through a wide groove in the floor toward a drainpipe. I always tried to get there either first or last. If I did not, other boys, knowing I was Jewish, shoved me against the wall without recourse and considerable embarrassment to me. Complaining to my teacher or the principal was of no avail and further led to recrimination by teachers and the students whom I had reported.

There was a recess in mid-morning when everyone received a small bottle of milk that we took outside into a walled-in courtyard, provided it was not raining. My classmates and others, who had been taught that I was a dirty Jew and worse, would gang up on me and others, taunt and push us, and made us spill the milk or drop and break the glass bottle. Teachers who supervised the yard during recess did not interfere with anti-Semitic gang activity until they heard glass breaking or saw fighting. Then they ran to us, inquired what had happened, as if they didn't know, and then made me pick up all the broken glass while everyone stood around laughing and taunting me. These were unhappy and hurtful experiences for me that, unfortunately, colored and distorted my mind toward school for many years. It was disillusionment in a big part of my early childhood that stands out in the long chapter of persecution because it was inflicted on me daily. These were such traumatic experiences I was unable to comprehend or convey it to my parents even remotely, and I cried often and hated school. In turn, my parents were confronted with other, much bigger problems. The results and consequences of the Nuremberg Laws and others impacted my father's business (and his brother Simon's) livelihood and our way of life. My parents never talked with me about their problems, their concerns, or their heartaches. They wanted their son and daughter to be happy, and they could not do that by telling us that their own life was at the brink of a catastrophe.

The open hostility in my school, the open and vicious racism was finally coming to its fullest fury. I was on my usual trek to the Luisenschule one morning, past the St. Bernard dogs, past the store that would not serve Jews, and past the Bismark monument, and approaching the Tattersall, when I was attacked by a group of perhaps eight Hitler Youths. All were dressed in their well-defined Nazi Youth uniforms. Stripped of my book satchel, I was kicked and hit with clubs on my legs, body, and face, time and time again until I was bleeding from my forehead, nose, ear, and mouth. I was hurting everywhere. It was only after I came to America many years later and was being examined for service in the United States Army that I learned that the beating had probably left me with a deviated septum of my nose.

They, the pride of Hitler and National Socialism hollered, "Why don't you fight, Jew pig? Coward!" and worse. There were people walking past who saw the altercation, but didn't intervene because it was only a dirty Jew who was being beaten up. I made every effort to protect myself and finally was able to run away while being pursued by this gang. I reached the streetcar switching station, the Tattersall, and ran down the steps of the small building leading to a women's public toilet facility where the Nazi hoodlums didn't dare follow. There, a wonderful and compassionate woman restroom caretaker attempted to treat my wounds, washed me and tried to calm my fears. On previous occasions when I was harassed, scared, and threatened on my way to school, I took refuge with her in the lounge of the ladies' restroom. However, I never told her I was Jewish. Somehow, with all of the shouting from my pursuers, she must certainly have suspected it. I am forever grateful to her for being such a kind humanitarian. It proves that it takes more than humility. It takes courage and action. Humility without taking action makes one a bystander, and in this instance an accessory to the crime. However, during that period of time, beating an innocent Jewish boy was encouraged. It was even considered macho!

This courageous woman asked someone to telephone our apartment, and it was not long before my dad came and carried me, crying, and scared, to our car. He drove me to two hospitals, neither of which would medically treat a Jew. He then drove me to Heidelberg, about 15 kilometers from Mannheim, where he was able to admit me to the Moro Kinderklinik (children's clinic) and where Dr. E. Moro, Professor, was the director. When I visited Mannheim and it surroundings in 1993 with my wife Gertrude, Moro's Clinic was still there; I found it in the phone book. It was now known as Luisenheilanstalt, located at Mozartstrasse 46,

EXHIBIT 6.5 The Tattersall. To the left, the railing where steps would lead down to ladies restroom and temporary safety.

Heidelberg. Once I was admitted to the hospital, doctors and nurses attended to my bruises, cuts, lacerations, swellings, and the pain and anxiety that I was suffering from the ordeal. I was hurting, devastated, and scared. Had the hoodlums wanted to maim me or worse? Kill me? Those thoughts ran through my mind as I lay there crying from pain and fright. For fear that the doctors and nurses would not treat me, my Dad told me not to tell anyone that I was Jewish and that the bullies who had beaten me up were Nazi Youth, but to say only that they were hoodlums. He said this in spite of the fact that one of the Hitler Youth ringleaders was a boy in my class, somewhat older than I. His last name was Boslet, and he had shown his animosity often before in school. Yes, it was sad that neither my parents nor I could tell the hospital staff the truth, and my father did not file a police report since molesting a Jew was not considered a criminal offense. In the hospital for that moment I was safe, but I was alone, and at night I had terrible nightmares. Ants, which I had noticed during the day crawling on the floor and on the white walls, turned into vicious monsters at night. Even weeks after my body had healed physically, the trauma left a permanent mark on my soul and life, and had turned me into a nervous wreck.

During my stay, I remember being taken on crutches to a huge lecture hall with inclined theater seating where men and women, interns and doctors from the University of Heidelberg sat. There my case, which included photographs and treatment, was discussed. Yet no one knew that the Nazi Hitlerjugend, Hitler Youth, had inflicted all of this pain on me. I was referred to by case number, so that no one knew my name. Sounds familiar, doesn't it? Only a few years later

Jews were stripped of names and given numbers, some tattooed on arms, as they arrived at their final destinations, the concentration camps. Finally, I was discharged from the hospital and went home where Mom lovingly took care of me as she had always done for as long as I could remember.

While there were numerous other incidents of abuse and discrimination that I could describe, there is one other that stands out in my mind because it illustrates how callous the German people were and how merciless and cynical they could be to Jews, even children. Once a week we had swim classes. The irony was that with all the hatred against Jews, a very prominent Jew, Bernhard Herschel, a past member of the city council, had many years earlier donated 500,000 gold Marks for the design and construction of a very large indoor swimming facility located in city block T4, Mannheim. The facility at the time was the most modern in Germany, and had been completed and dedicated in November 1920. There were actually two pools, one for women, and the other for men. Floors and walls were tiled, as were showers, toilets and lockers. The ceilings were very high, and boys swam in the nude. I don't know about the girls but often wondered.

There was a low and high diving board. Most of my schoolmates were only beginners or could not swim at all. All of us had to jump off the one-meter board and swim or paddle toward the side where the exit ladder was located. The swim instructors had very long poles that they used to help each student in the event they needed assistance. Since I was a Jew, my turn came last. Instead of jumping from the one-meter board, my lot was to climb to the three-meter board (about ten feet) to the delight and laughter of my classmates. Of course I was frightened of the height and stood there shaking as the instructor blew his whistle, and with his long pole, pushed me off the board. Fortunately my dear mother had enrolled me in swim lessons before this at Frauenbad Arnold, a women's swimming pool, but I did not learn to jump off a diving board. And yet when I came to the surface in panic, the instructor intentionally let me gasp for air and thrash around while the whole hall reverberated in loud laughter. Finally, but reluctantly, the instructor gave me the pole. I climbed up the ladder, scared, cold, shivering, and embarrassed. I was being conditioned that Jews could be made fun of and treated unfairly. It was no fun for me! My dear father went to the school and complained. It was an exercise in futility.

In the meantime my dad, and I am sure my mom also, made arrangements to enroll me in a local private school. Privat Realschule Schwarz was located in city block quadrat M3, in a mansion of a former aristocrat and only one city block from the palace of Karl Theodor. Herr Georg Sessler was the school's principal. The school was also only a few blocks from my dad's and Uncle Simon's business (see exhibit 6.6 in the appendix for a sample advertisement). The school itself was old, not very large, and clearly not designed as a school. To my best recollection the school had approximately 450 students. There was a small courtyard surrounded by the building with classrooms. My room was on the second floor.

Because of the proximity of the school to my father's wholesale business and my previous experiences with harassment, he accompanied me to school after we ate breakfast in our big kitchen. Mom often made a soft-boiled egg for Dad and me. But often, I could eat nothing but a slice of toast or an apple on the way to school. At noon I waited for Dad in front of the school and then we walked home together, talking about various topics until we arrived at our apartment on the fourth floor at L11, 25. My school days at Privat Realschule Schwarz were relatively tranquil except for the occasional taunting and exclusion from certain Nazi dogma related courses, events, and rallies. While the classroom teacher knew I was Jewish, my classmates did not. However, they may have wondered why I was not present for certain periods or events. Instinctively, I knew how to conceal that I was Jewish without raising suspicion. It was almost a game that I conditioned myself to play without any formal training. What also helped was that, according to physical race profiling, which by the way was taught in school, I looked more like an Aryan than a Jew. My hair was wavy blonde, and had no facial features, crooked nose, floppy ears, or other features that were so-called Jewish traits, except for my flat feet. You could say that I faked my identity outwardly while I had no illusion that I was Jewish. It was a conditional response I assumed for years to come, and which may have, ultimately, helped me to survive.

The problems of living in a country that had stripped me and all other Jews of their citizenship, and more importantly, all civil rights, became more acute every day. Our family life became more restrictive as to things we used to do as a family. My parents were precluded from doing what they used to do in public, and I was no longer able to do some of the things I liked to do. Simple things like playing with children in the neighborhood, taking walks as a family to different parks on the weekends, driving in our Opel car to nearby towns, attending festivals, or just sightseeing became somewhat dangerous. Restaurants, taverns, cafes, side-of-the-road kiosks that we used to frequent, were off limits for us. Formerly, when it was customary and fun for Mom and Dad to go together with their friends for a picnic, movie, theater or musical performance, it now became impossible. It even became a risky liability to be seen in small groups and be recognized. To go out as they once did was now unlawful, and signs forbidding Jews from entry were everywhere. Our lives became more concentrated on doing things within the four walls of our apartment, the homes of our friends, or at the Haupt Main Synagogue and the youth center next to it. At least in that manner we were safe, from intimidation and worse or so we thought. Long gone were my pleasant childhood days. Remembering and reflecting on these events herein is like recalling a bad dream after many years.

It was almost ironic that after I had transferred to the private school, the Director of the Jewish Community had obtained permission from the Public School Board to conduct religious study classes for all Jewish boys and girls of Mannheim at the Luisenschule, the very school I had left. Rabbi Max Grünewald, the rabbi of my synagogue, served also as the elected president of the Mannheim Jewish Community Council. He was able to make these arrangements against all odds in spite of the public school board dominated by anti-Semites. Classes were conducted in the afternoon once a week for two hours. Reluctantly and with some fear, I went to study Jewish history, Torah, and Hebrew. We had a number of wonderful teachers among whom were Berthold Baruch Stahl and Leo Hanauer. Contrary to our regular public school teachers, our religious teachers had little authority or clout, and therefore, had a hard time enforcing discipline. We, the boys, took full advantage of the situation and did things we normally wouldn't have done in a regular class. Sometimes we spread ground pepper on the teacher's desk blotter so that he sneezed. Other times we threw stink bombs, small thin glass vials the size of small marbles. I have no idea where they were bought, by whom, and what putrid smelling, chemical mixture was inside of them. However, the odor always had the desired effect and made our teacher very angry.

Around 1936 religious classes had to be moved to study rooms of the Klaus Orthodox Synagogue where older boys and girls also received their Judaic teachings. In 1937, we also took special classes there to learn conversational English as a foreign language which was meant to help us if and when we were able to emigrate to England, Australia, America, or other English speaking countries. In that English class, I remember a teacher, whose name I cannot recall, writing on the blackboard at the beginning of the first session, "The sleeping fox catches no poultry." From that day on, his name became the "Sleeping Fox." The emphasis shifted to learning about the things and subjects that would enhance our ability to survive economically in another country if we ever got the chance to escape Nazi Germany. Girls fourteen years and older learned about general housekeeping, sewing, needlework, stenography, typing, and other allied subjects. Similarly, older boys learned mechanics, metal and woodworking, which I will explain in more detail later. At that time I was not yet fourteen, and so had to wait. Dr. Kurt Berg, the son of my parents' friends, was in charge of this initiative known as *aufbauklassen*, for which, unfortunately, there is no good translation. It is sufficient to refer to it as "preparatory to emigration" courses. I will write more elsewhere about Dr. Kurt Berg, who was very dear to me.

By now it was the fall of 1935 and my bar mitzvah was to take place in October 1936. What would have normally been an exciting and happy event, looked to me to be an event that would be exciting and meaningful, but not necessarily happy under the constant Nazi threats. I tried to put these sad thoughts into the back of my mind while my mom and dad calmly spread the word about the forthcoming event to the mischpocha, relatives and friends. Rabbi Robert Raphael Geiss, who had been the youth advisor for boys and girls of the Haupt Synagogue since the prior year, was to be my teacher and tutor, helping me learn to chant my Torah portion, the blessings, and also understand the meaning of my portion.

When I went to his home for the first lesson, I was so surprised to learn that my *parsha*, the specific part of the Torah that I was required to read based on the corresponding date in the Jewish calendar year, would be the very first in the Torah, the holy scripture. It was *Beresheit* in the Book of Genesis, or as it is often called, Book of Creation. Beresheit is Hebrew, meaning "In the Beginning," and is the first of the fifty-four week Torah readings on Shabbat morning prayer service. Naturally I assumed that this was a great coincidence and honor for me because the portion I would read is a majestic narration of the miraculous origin and creation of the universe and the creation of the world by *Elohim*, G'd. With this in mind, I studied at home and looked forward each week to receiving my tutoring in the Hebrew reading and chanting. I jealously guarded my day in the spotlight, hoping that no other boy in Mannheim would have this honor, now less than a year away. Sometimes, it took my thoughts away from the everyday uncertainties and tribulations of life under the Swastika.

In the meantime the Nuremberg Laws passed by the Reichstag, September 15, 1935 had caught up with us. The law stated that to qualify as a German Reich citizen, one must be of German blood and prove his or her willingness, by specific conduct, to serve and dedicate him/herself to the German Reich. The law stated Jews no longer had voting rights, could no longer participate in political matters, and could not occupy any local, state, or national office. All Jewish officials had to retire as of December 31, 1935. Accordingly, and through implementation and interpretation, Jews were no longer citizens of Germany and would no longer receive the protection by all institutions such as courts, police, fire, first aid, etc. It was a shock to realize that this could have happened in a country that once prided itself on having one of the oldest and highest cultures, next to none other in the world, having the greatest and most distinguished history, and the foremost poets, painters, composers, writers, architects, scientists, engineers, statesmen, military and medical geniuses, philosophers and on and on. Now, Germany and its Nazi regime also showed the world that its true nationalistic and racist instincts encompassed the most despicable aims the world had ever known. World domination and the eradication of Jews and all other undesirable were necessary to create an Aryan Nation that would last one thousand years according to Adolf Hitler's rhetoric. All of a sudden we were undesirable and despised exiles in our own homeland.

Even so, my father had volunteered and served almost six years in the World War I German Army, a year and a half of that time spent as a French prisoner of war. Though he had been a good German citizen, all that was for naught and was now completely ignored. Then there were laws put into effect that dealt with the protection of German blood and German honor. These laws forbade intermarriages and intercourse between persons of Aryan blood and Jews. The laws further decreed the unlawfulness of employment of Aryans by Jewish households and was later extended to making it unlawful for Jewish owned businesses to employ non-Jews or so-called Aryans.

Beginning in my early childhood, my mother had live-in housekeepers or nursemaids, and was now in a sudden quandary as was my father who employed non-Jewish people in his small but thriving business. I remember well when Mom had to tell our live-in housekeeper, Irma, who had been in our employ for perhaps six years that she could no longer work or live with us because we were Jews. It was a very moving and emotional scene, one you could imagine better had it been possible to capture the interaction on video. We did not consider Irma as a housekeeper but rather an integral part of our family. She was fairly tall, but not a pretty girl. However her heart of gold made up for her lack of physical beauty. She begged us to go to the authorities with her and ask for a special exception at her behest. She cried bitter tears with her head on my mother's shoulder while she also held my hand. She had no place to go since our home had become her home.

Irma had helped raise Irene and me, took care of us when we were ill, and she had shared birthdays, anniversaries, and other special occasions with us, including Jewish holidays. She knew how to cook what we liked because Mom had taught her over the years. All of that had now changed because of the Nuremberg Laws, the prelude of further radical restrictions placed on Jews. I can still picture my father, mother, and myself kissing her goodbye. She stood in the hall leading to the door and stairway thanking my father for giving her an additional month's wages in cash. She was wearing a winter coat and hat that my mother had bought her for a recent birthday. I carried one of her suitcases down the four flights of stairs to a waiting taxi that took her away. We heard from her several times until it became too dangerous for her to send mail to us, her Jewish family. Mail was being opened by the Gestapo, the secret police, and people were being punished if they were corresponding with Jews. Whatever happened to Irma?

Dad and Uncle Simon had to let go some of the help at J&S Kahn and hired Jewish help who had lost their jobs elsewhere. The laws forbade us to fly the Reich's (Nazi) National flag with the Swastika, not that we would have done so. On the other hand, the law said that we could display Jewish colors. At the time none of us had any idea what Jewish colors were, and no one dared to try the system. It sounded like a cruel joke. The law went on to restrict Jewish religious and cultural community organizations and required their registration and approval for their continuation under curtailed and supervised conditions.

My father belonged to the Reichsbund Judischer Front Soldaten (RJFS), a National Jewish War Veterans Organization, and its bowling league that was able to continue with certain restrictions. After a while, non-Jewish bowling alley

EXHIBIT 6.7 With hiking cane and backpack on an excursion with the RJFS. See exhibit 6.8 in the appendix for another photo of me, the honorary member of RJFS.

owners denied entrance to Jews, and likewise, RJFS lodge meetings could no longer be held in the usual public places. Details of a proposed meeting's agenda had to be supplied to the local authorities for approval and had to be held at facilities operated by Jewish owners. During the meetings, however, the members did discuss non-listed agenda items of interest to the veterans, their families, and the Jewish community in general. I realized what was being clandestinely discussed at these meetings because Dad would converse with Mom and explain timely specifics of the new oppressive laws, how to cope with them, and how to evade them. I could tell how depressed they were, but was unable to help them.

There was conversation between my parents about immigrating to countries like Cuba, Palestine, America, and temporary flight to other European countries. Similar discussions occurred between my parents after each meeting of the bowling club members. Members got together at someone's home since there were no Jewish-owned bowling facilities. I was never an active participant when Mom and Dad talked about these matters. When I would ask a question, "butt in" so to speak, either my Mom or Dad would say something like "Robertchen," a loving nickname for Robert, "this is nothing to concern yourself with." That usually ended my involvement in the conversation, but I was still very much concerned and worried realizing the ever-mounting pressure on my family, the Jewish community, and the uncertainties hanging over our heads. Yet in the back of my mind, in denial of the realities, it all had a sound of fantasy, intrigue, mystery, and disbelief.

The best part of Dad belonging to the RJFS bowling league was their occasional outings in spring and fall. I prided myself on being the only son going along with his father and ten to fifteen other adult club members. With my backpack full of picnic food and my special hiking cane we set out to nearby forests and scenic mountains in brotherly camaraderie, always concerned about the possibility of outside (Nazi) interference. That is why the initial meeting points for the wonderful outings were always somewhere outside the city of Mannheim, away from the populated areas so we would not be too noticeable. My hiking cane was special because it was covered almost from top to bottom with small souvenir metal plaques. Each had been bought at a well-known place where we as a family had been, either on vacation, or where I had been at summer camp or excursions with the RJFS.

For these excursions I loved to buy *landjäger*, flat sausages about six or seven inches long. They were not kosher but tasted good, somewhat softer than beef jerky. At the time Karl Herzberg, whom I knew casually, was the president of the local RJFS which had perhaps as many as five hundred Jewish World War I veteran members from the greater Mannheim area. 12,000 Jewish German soldiers, including many officers, lost their lives in World War I fighting for what they thought was their *vaterland*, their homeland. 130 Jewish soldiers from Mannheim were among those who lost their lives. I was very proud of my Dad who had been a courageous soldier in World War I and for the subsequent eighteen months as a prisoner of war to the French.

Until I was twelve, Mother, Irene, and I would go swimming at Frauenbad Arnold, a female only large, specially-built, barge anchored above the Rheinbrüke Rhine Bridge. Boys under twelve were able to swim, sun, and enjoy the surroundings with their mother or sister while the Rhine flowed through the huge barge-like installation. When I reached the age of twelve, I had to go to Rheinbad Herweck, a similar but much larger barge anchored only a short distance from Arnold. It was a great place for swimming and spending a few hours. It was always enjoyable, and many Jewish friends and acquaintances, old and young, found temporary refuge from the oppression by the Nazis. Everywhere in Mannheim were signs prohibiting Jews from entering stores, museums, movie theaters, restaurants, public buildings, parks, benches on public streets, forests, beaches and railroad stations. There were even signs stating "Jews Not Allowed" on entrance roads to near-by villages. Yet, the swim installation, Herweck, once owned and operated by Mr. Herweck, had refused to issue the edict forbidding Jews to visit their swim facility.

On June 27, 1935, I rode my bicycle to Herweck for a swim. I was not expecting anything out of the ordinary, but in the mid-afternoon I heard voices that became louder very quickly. Then I saw people running, screaming, mothers holding their children's hands, boys picking up bath towels, and others running with their personal belongings. It became clear to me what it was when I heard men shouting in unison, "*Juden raus! Das ist nicht ein Judenaquarium!*" "Out with Jews! This is not an aquarium for Jews!" It was a staged raid by the SA, normally brown-uniformed Nazis. However, most of them were in civilian clothes, giving the impression that this was a random group of German citizens who undertook a spontaneous pogrom action. As the Nazi hoodlums came into the Herweck, they abused, swore and insulted everyone, especially the Jewish bathers who frantically tried to gather their belongings and leave. Using megaphones, the Nazis ordered the Jews to leave immediately or they would be taken into custody, which meant jail, or even worse, a concentration camp. This was a work day, and so the Jews consisted primarily of women and children.

I grabbed my towel, left my clothes and shoes in the dressing room where I had checked them earlier, and helped a woman with two small children by carrying her little boy, who was about four or five years old. Not only were the Jewish women harassed, some were assaulted, pushed into the water, kicked, and worst of all, thrown into the Rhine. I noticed one incident where a Nazi took hot coffee and hot water from the restaurant and hurled it against several women and children. Mothers and children were screaming and crying. The fear and humiliation were indescribable. It was utter chaos. Once we were outside and standing in small groups by the bank of the river, people began shivering. In the rush and panic, most of them still wore bathing suits and even swimming caps. No one was allowed to go back and retrieve their clothes and other belongings. Of that the brutal SA men made certain. They were enjoying the misery and panic they had created and stood there laughing, taunting us. That day was the last day that a Jew could go swimming anywhere in Mannheim. Even at the only indoor pool in the city, the Herschelbad, Jews were forbidden to enter by order of the local police. Normal Jewish optimism had turned into confusion.

As I rode home on my bike through the Waldpark a park alongside the Rhine, everyone looked at me dressed only in my swimming trunks and wrapped in a towel, barefoot. I was shaken by the events and felt helpless. The soles of my feet hurt from pedaling barefoot over a fairly long distance. As I finally stood in front of my mother telling her in a stammering voice what had happened, she put a

EXHIBIT 6.9 Jewish bathers expelled from swim facility Herweck, June 27, 1935 by the Nazis.

heavy blanket around me, and with tears in her eyes, tried to console me. It had been another heroic day for the Nazi master race and agonizing terror filled day for me. Later, after my dad arrived home from the office, tired from the unending harassment he was dealing with on a daily basis, we talked about the afternoon events while eating supper. He tried to explain to me about anti-Semitism, that it was an ideology that blamed Jews for all the problems of the German people. I heard, but did not understand, and wondered when anti-Semitism would end. I was physically and mentally exhausted, confused, and went to bed early not being able to sleep until past midnight, feeling sad, excited, and angry on the inside. The next day after I managed enough courage, I went back to Herweck. All of the clothing had been piled on the riverbank and it took me some time to find my clothes and shoes. Years later on March 29, 1945, after the Allies won the war and the American Army occupied Mannheim, numerous depositions were taken from interrogated Nazis that established, without a doubt, that this action in the summer of 1935 had been organized, planned, and executed by the direction of the local Nazi SA party. However, I could not confirm whether the people responsible for this event were found and taken to court for their cowardly act.

Even though we were under a constant cloud of intimidation, persecution, and isolation, our life went on as best as the family could manage. Much of the isolation from cultural and social life had to be overcome by interjecting other activities that Mom and Dad often encouraged. Most of these activities were confined to our home, yet I managed to derive some satisfaction and a limited form of enjoyment from them. Postage stamp collecting, introduced to me by my dear cousin, Kurt Strauss, a few years my senior, became an exciting and fascinating hobby for me.

Reading became another enjoyable avenue of escape from reality. I couldn't get enough of *Robinson Crusoe*, an adventure novel by Daniel Defoe, *Leather Stocking Tales*, by James Fenimore Cooper, and especially books by Karl May. May mixed realism, fiction and fantasy in such a superb manner that once I started, I couldn't put his books down. He wrote about 70 adventure books of which I read about 50. I believe I was addicted to them and in the evening I continued reading after lights out at 9 p.m. Since electricity was expensive, I read under the blankets by flashlight not to be noticed by my parents. Each book was more than 500 pages, dealing mostly with the American Wild West and American Indians, for whom I learned a great respect and reverence. The books were written in the late 1800's and dealt with the "Red Man's" love, peace, hate and fight for his territory and quest for continued existence. The "White Man's" forceful encroachment into Indian Territory by introducing money, fire water, material for trade, disease, hate, lies, and guns seemed to have vague similarities with the plight of us Jews vis-à-vis the Nazis. I know now that this similarity of suffering was one of the reasons for my fascination with May's writings, although I was not conscious of that at the time. Also it was the alluring tales about the life of the American

Indian and the description of the rugged but beautiful Wild West that left an everlasting impression. Those descriptions haunted me for years to come and drew me in thought to the land of the wild mustangs like a magnet and perhaps a state of nirvana. Only much later in the U.S., when I came across a copy of a Karl May book, did I notice endorsements on the back cover by Albert Schweitzer, Albert Einstein, and Herman Hesse, the latter a German/Swiss novelist, poet, and essayist, who received the Nobel Peace Prize in 1946. Certainly these were impressive references and endorsements.

My other hobby was playing one of several harmonicas, often in my bedroom when I was lonely. On a more serious level I was learning to play the violin. Irene had been playing the piano for several years. She was pretty good at it, and my parents enjoyed listening to her play. Even though we had a piano in the living room, she took lessons at her teacher's home, and later practiced at home. For me it was a little different. I started playing the violin in early 1934, shortly before my sister left for France. This allowed for some musical continuity after Irene left and the piano went still. My violin teacher came to the house once a week and taught for one hour. Of course he had to be Jewish. A man of small stature, in his fifties or early sixties, with white flowing hair, he was somewhat pathetic looking, but an excellent violinist. He was the typical *nebbish*, an unfortunate person to be pitied. Knowing that giving lessons was his only income, my mother always served him a meal after we ended our session. It was her way of doing a mitzvah, a good deed, *tikkon olam*, Hebrew for making it a better world.

I can still see Herr Levy coming slowly up the stairs to our fourth floor apartment carrying his violin case. He would stop at the landing of each floor for a brief moment to rest. He was one of those outstanding musicians who had lost his fame and musical identity and could no longer perform with the symphony because he was born a Jew. Under his coat he always wore the same suit, a specially cut swallowtail that musicians wore to performances. Not only did my mother feel sorry for him, but I did also, sensing the plight and frustrations imposed on him by the Nazis. He was not alone.

Besides the hobbies and activities I have described, I was eagerly continuing my studies with Rabbi Geiss in anticipation of my bar mitzvah. Among other things I had to learn about the tallit, the prayer shawl worn at religious services. More complicated was learning about the *tefillin*, the phylacteries. They were worn in a fairly unique and elaborate symbolic manner on the forehead and on one of the arms. Then there were prayers that had to be said while donning the tefillin in the morning. In the meantime, my dear mother worked on two velvet pouches, one to store my tallit, the other to hold my tefillin. The material was a medium blue color with beautiful ornate gold embroidery. She sat for many hours happily and lovingly doing this tedious work for G'd and her coming-of-age son. I would learn how to continue the religious rituals as my father, my grandfather, and all my ancestors had done, under circumstances that were, like now, bleak. As recorded in history, for Jews, worshipping Elohim, the sacred name of G'd was never easy.

Mother did a lot of needlework in addition to mending socks and doing all sorts of repair and alterations on clothing. She worked diligently putting together a fine trousseau for Irene so that she would have beautiful, personalized garments and linens when she became a bride. Of course that would be years away. For my mother these activities filled part of the day and took her mind off the dark clouds overhead and on the horizon. No one knew then that Irene would never see the trousseau.

It was summer vacation 1936, when Mom, Dad and I packed couple of suitcases and drove our Opel automobile to Laufersweiler for a visit. I don't remember whether Dad and Mom stayed for the entire vacation. Somehow, I doubt it. However I remember staying for several enjoyable weeks. We also visited the Jewish cemetery where Opa Isaak and Oma Hannchen Kahn were buried to pay our respect (see exhibit 6.10 in the appendix).

For the time being, anti-Semitism in this small village had not reached the proportion as in the large cities. Therefore, restrictions and economic or verbal abuse of Jews in the community was not immediately noticeable, at least not to me. This was the time of Heinz Hanau's bar mitzvah. He was a third cousin of mine, and there were a few other visiting relatives and friends in the village for the occasion. Lieselotte Boehm, who was my age and a cousin of his from Lampertmühle, was one in attendance. There was also Heinz's sister, Trude, a year or so older than I, and a somewhat younger Beate Berney, the daughter of Lina (née Löser) and Heinrich Berney. Their son, Alfred, was a few years older than I, and therefore didn't want much to do with us. The five of us, and a few others from Laufersweiler, palled around together and had a rip-snorting good time without getting into too much trouble. We did manage to get into some mischief; we just didn't tell anyone.

I stayed with cousins, Hilde and Albert Hanau, the parents of Heinz, who lived in the same large house with Hilde's parents, Isaak and Lenchen Löser, whom I called Uncle and Aunt. Her given name was Magdalena, and was a sister of my Omas Hannchen and Malchen. Although our family relationships were several times removed, everyone in Laufersweiler was very close and regarded themselves as family, including those who were not related at all. It was the Jewish spirit of small town mishpocha, members of a clan. In effect, most Jews considered themselves mishpocha, with underlying feelings of a common bond and friendship. That feeling was truer then than now. There were others attending Heinz's bar mitzvah, but not my sister Irene, who intended to come to my bar mitzvah later that year from France.

The bar mitzvah was held in the small synagogue of Laufersweiler, paradoxically located in the Kirchengasse 6, Church Alley 6, and was filled to capacity. The synagogue's outside dimensions were only about thirty-eight feel long and thirty-feet wide. The interior, used for a sanctuary, was much smaller since there was a stairway to the mezzanine where the women worshipped, and there was a small social room downstairs on the opposite side of the stairway. The synagogue was by no means ostentatious, but had its small farm town charm. It was of a very simple, traditional architectural design, except for the mosaic windows upstairs and downstairs. There were also several gothic pillars and an arched ceiling. On the outside, small medieval type ornate towers graced each corner of the steep high-pitched roof, and a small iron fence surrounded a small front courtyard. The roof was covered with black sheets of slate, which, in all probability, was locally mined, and a Star of David graced its peak. On each side of the synagogue entrance, which looked eastward, was a stone relief of a large crouching lion, undoubtedly representing the Lion of Judah. Aside from several churches in Laufersweiler, the synagogue represented the most unique building in town and the immediate area.

EXHIBIT 6.11 The Laufersweiler synagogue dedicated in 1911 was ransacked November 9 and 10, 1938 by Nazi thugs and the inside was completely demolished. After World War II, the synagogue was designated as a cultural monument and reconstruction began. The synagogue was restored primarily on the outside and today serves as a museum honoring the Jewish community that once existed in Laufersweiler. The inauguration of the restored synagogue took place January 31, 1988 with a meaningful ceremony. However, the inside is completely changed from what it was.

EXHIBIT 6.12 Löser's House. Isaak Löser standing in the doorway and Hilde Hanau with fur coat at left window. Lenchen next window. Albert Hanau, sitting in front of store.

    The festivities of the bar mitzvah took place at the Löser's house. Hilde and her mother, Lenchen, and some other Jewish townspeople, had prepared the most wonderful dinner and luncheon for all the Jewish and non-Jewish guests attending the service at synagogue. Since the Lösers and the Hanaus managed a combination grocery/bakery/variety store attached to their house, every type of food, including wonderful baked goods, were served. Since no special meal could be served without wine, there was plenty of it. Heinz and I had a good time going from room to room, pouring all of the leftover wine from glasses into empty bottles after the guests left. With a couple of the bottles refilled with wine, Heinz and I proceeded upstairs to his room to hide. There we began to drink all of the wine in the bottles until we were so *shikker*, drunk and sick, that we didn't know what had befallen us. The bed was moving around, as were the ceiling and walls, and finally we were tumbling around like drunken sailors. After much giggling and laughing, holding our heads and stomachs, we finally fell asleep. It was an afternoon I will never forget and neither has Heinz. From then on I had more respect for wine, although I did not shy away from it on Shabbat, and other religious, ceremonial occasions. Today, I still enjoy a good glass of white wine now and then. Now you realize why I have gone through such length to tell you about my summer vacation in Laufersweiler. I will never forget it!

    I have fond memories of Laufersweiler, particularly of the Löser's house. Attached to the left of the house was a large barn where chickens and goats were kept, along with all sorts of farming and gardening implements. Above it was a hayloft accessible via a vertically mounted ladder. In the hands of young girls and boys this combination of strange things lent itself to many activities, pranks and escapades that we wildly enjoyed. It was a real playpen! In the valley below the town was a very nice swimming pool that we frequented and enjoyed although it was a goodly walk to get there and a tiresome walk back up from the valley.

As the day of my bar mitzvah neared, it was customary for relatives and acquaintances of ours to ask what kind of gifts I wanted for that special occasion. As a young boy I had many realistic and some unrealistic wishes and ideas for gifts. To everyone's surprise I had developed a very unique gift idea. My thoughts had to do with the political situation at the time, the persecutions of us Jews, and my aspirations and ideals at the moment. There were a number of Jewish youth organizations that had sprung up in response to the depressing isolation of children, young and old. All of us who belonged to one or another group under adult supervision had dreams of a better, happier, more just world in the future. We were being taught to become idealists and futuristic thinkers. It was a form of mental resistance in our feeble struggle to cope with Nazi oppression. However we and our parents knew that an overt attempt, like a revolt, by the Jewish population along even with the support of underground resistance movements and Christian sympathizers, would fail miserably in any attempt to overthrow the Nazi regime.

Those youth groups formed earlier by Rabbi Max Grünewald held the children and teenagers of Mannheim together. Approximately 450 youths belonged to different groups with names such as *Kameraden, Werkleute, Kadima, Haschomer Hazair* (the young Guardian), *Habonim, Esra,* and *Hechaluz*. All of them had various Zionist aims and ideals. They either wanted to participate in an *aliyah*, emigrating to what was then Palestine and working in a *kibbutz*, a collective agricultural settlement, or simply participating in the creation of a Jewish homeland. I belonged to *Betar* which believed that in order to create and maintain a homeland in Palestine, it would be necessary to add some paramilitary training to vocational, agricultural, and industrial endeavors to protect the fields, harvests, and family settlements from outsiders, ostensibly Arabs. In later years it was proven that such personal defense was crucial to survival.

We met in the *Schiff Haus*, a building next to the Haupt Synagogue with ten different rooms where the various named youth groups met on different days. Our leaders tried to steer our mental aptitudes into practical, idealistic, creative directions through learning about *eretz*, the land of Palestine and the problems and hardships that settlers would face as pioneers. We sang uplifting Hebrew songs including *Hatikvah*, "The Hope" which many years later, with some minor changes in wording, became Israel's National Anthem. We also learned to dance the *hora*, the now popular Israeli folk dance. We always collected money, money, and more money, which included much of my allowance so that land could be bought from the Arab owners to establish more collective farms and the essential establishment of a Jewish national homeland. These activities and my love for a land that I had never seen germinated an idea for what I thought would be a fitting bar mitzvah gift.

The ceilings in our apartment were about ten feet high, and so I proceeded to obtain four-foot wide white wrapping paper in ten-foot lengths from our business. Next I spent many hours drawing on this paper an outline of a map of the then British Mandate, Palestine. It was a difficult task since I had to transpose outline dimensions from a small map to one ten feet long. Next I drew lines horizontal and vertical so that they formed rectangles ½ inch by 1½ inches. Then I cut blue paper strips the identical size. The idea was to sell each space for 50 Pfennige, then to be affixed to the map which had been mounted to the dining room wall with straight pins. I would then donate the proceeds to Betar for buying more land in Palestine. It was a unique project and a great mitzvah, with which I wanted to fulfill my covenant with G'd on this once-in-a-lifetime day, my bar mitzvah. I solicited no gifts and hoped that I would cover the entire map of Palestine in blue. At my young age I had become an ardent Zionist.

The week before my bar mitzvah, Rabbi Raphael Geiss asked me to practice at the synagogue. It was the last chance for rehearsal, and I was a little scared. Then the big day arrived, October 10, 1936. It was Simchat Torah, the day of rejoicing in the written book, the Torah, when the last chapters of Deuteronomy would be read. Immediately thereafter I would read from a different Torah, the first chapter

> **Aus der Gemeinde Mannheim**
>
> **Barmizwah**
>
> **Hauptsynagoge:**
> 19. September: Werner Levi, R 7, 24.
> 19. September: Walter Ullmann, C 1, 1.
> 19. September: Hans Zwang, D 7, 1.
> 3. Oktober: Walter Oberländer, Chamissostr. 7.
> 10. Oktober: Robert Kahn, L 11, 25.
>
> **Claussynagoge:**
> 3. Oktober: Jakob Goldmann, R 3, 9.
>
> **Trauungen:**
> Hugo Zimmern aus Mannheim mit Hermine Sonnheim aus Worms.

EXHIBIT 6.13 A segment of what appeared in the newspaper of the Jewish community of Mannheim, September 1936, listing my Bar Mitzvah and others.

of Genesis. Thus I would become the *Chatan Beresheit*, the "bridegroom of the beginning of creation."

Many of our relatives had come to Mannheim for the big event, among them my maternal Opa Raphael Joseph from Luxembourg. Mom's sister, Aunt Helene, and her husband Max Cohen also came; Aunt Irma Ehrlich, Mom's youngest sister came all the way from Lille, France, with my dear sister, Irene. Irene had been staying with Aunt Irma and her husband, Uncle Charles, for about two years already. Aunt Gerda, one of Dad's sisters, and her husband, Manfred Ackerman, came from Bad Schwalbach. Ilse Isaak and her brothers, Helmut and Norbert, first cousins on my father's side, and their mother Ida, sister of my dad, came from Aschaffenburg. Uncle Berny, my Mom's only brother, with his wife, Marthe, and their son and first cousin of mine, Georges Joseph, came from Luxembourg. Unfortunately my other Opa and Oma from Laufersweiler had passed away years earlier. Of course, Uncle Simon, my Dad's brother, his wife, Hilde, and their two sons, Ernst and Walter, didn't have to come far since they also lived in Mannheim. We had only one spare room at the apartment, and I don't remember what hotel the out-of-town guests stayed except Opa Raphael Joseph stayed with us.

For Shabbat evening Mother had set the dining room table beautifully, and during the prior weeks had baked and cooked for the customary Shabbat meal along with some additional special dishes. The usual prayers, blessings for candle lightings, wine, and the *berches*, which we refer to in America as *challah*, a braided loaf of white bread glazed with egg white, preceded the meal. Since we no longer had a maid, Irene helped Mom with serving and clearing the table. A soup course was followed by the traditional soup meat, potatoes, white asparagus, and salad, and a third course of *kartoffelshalet*, which is like a huge potato pancake about ten inches in diameter, three or four inches high with a delicious crust. Dad and other guests gave toasts in honor of the great *simcha*, the happy event. After the meal I recited the blessing for the meal, generally referred to as *bentshen*, along with several prayers for health and welfare of the entire family and all others present. The prayer expressed hope for the rebuilding of Zion and ended with a prayer for peace and reprieve from Nazi oppression. Then came coffee, tea, and dessert with pies, cakes, and tortes with different kinds of fruit. It was, indeed, an unforgettable evening albeit the dark clouds of oppression.

On Shabbat morning we all got up very early so that we could take turns with the only bathroom. I wore a new suit, shirt and tie, and had to comb my hair several times until my dear mother thought it was right. Mom and Irene dressed in their finest, and Opa and my dear father looked sharp with their heavily starched shirts and separate collars. My father wore gray spats over his shoes, and both he and Opa took along collapsible top hats. Mother and Irene wore pretty fall hats and gloves, proper etiquette in those days when going to the Synagogue. I donned my tefellin, said the morning prayer, and sat down for breakfast with the family.

Afterwards we all walked to the synagogue. I carried the beautiful blue and gold trimmed pouch for my tallit that my mother had presented to me earlier and inside of it was a blue striped tallit presented to me from my father. In addition, Opa had given me a beautiful wristwatch with my initials engraved on the back. I wore it proudly. I should hastily add that watches at the time were costly, and the majority of people, especially young boys, didn't have them. I was very excited and already felt somewhat grown up, since I was wearing a felt hat for the first time in my life. Soon I would reach the status and assume the duties of a man, at least in accordance with Jewish tradition. I felt proud!

We arrived before anyone else except for the *shammes*, the sexton and caretaker of the Synagogue, and the Rabbis, Geiss and Grünewald. Only the choir and the organist were practicing. We went into the Rabbi's study where Dad and Opa received their last instructions, and I received encouraging words so that I would not stand at the bima platform with stage fright. For the first time I was able to be with the grownups, the men, in the center pews, a privilege reserved for boys after their bar mitzvahs. All lady guests, including Mom and Irene, sat upstairs. By the time the service started, the edifice was populated with congregants, and my girl and boy friends.

The holiday service was festive, as it should have been on Simchat Torah. Happiness abounded as Dad, Opa, the Rabbis, Cantor and I each carried a Torah through the sanctuary while chanting the usual *niggun* melody (A niggun is a traditional tune or melody, sometimes with repeating words or phrases, such as bim-bim-bam). I was proud to carry the heavy Torah scroll adorned with the finest silver breastplates and crowns. Other male congregants took turns carrying the scrolls until we had made several rounds through the synagogue. Children followed the parade while congregants handed out candy and chocolate. The women in the balcony also threw small bags with cookies and other sweets to the children below.

By the time I was called to the Torah, my Father, Opa and my Mother were seated in the chairs on the bima, a raised platform where the Torah was read. Since my ancestors claimed to be descendants from the high priests of the Temple in Jerusalem, I had been designated a Kohen, as were all of my other male family members. According to ancient tradition, I was therefore the first called to read from the Torah. After the Torah service, I briefly addressed Rabbis, thanking them for teaching me the ideals of Judaism. Next, I thanked my dear father and mother for all they had done for me, including standing by me in health and sickness. I acknowledged the presence of my sister, Opa, and all the other mischpocha, family members and friends. Then Rabbi Geiss spoke to me and admonished me not to build my life around Karl May books and American Indian lore, but to dedicate myself to the lofty precepts of our ancient people and traditions. Next, Rabbi Grünewald blessed my parents and Opa, and gave me a

Chumesh, a Pentateuch, a book containing the first five books of the Bible, the Holy Scriptures. The Chumesh, printed in 1936, contained a personal dedication for me by Dr. Max Grünewald as the President of the Synagogue Council of the Jewish Community of Mannheim. I still have the Chumesh today, a most valuable possession, even though it is not in the best conditions anymore. But then, it has been through a lot of turmoil and seen a lot of happiness and sadness.

Because of all the well-wishers, it took some time to get back home. A huge surprise greeted me when we arrived there. A big box was standing in front of the door of the apartment. In it was the most beautiful bicycle I had ever seen, and with it a card from my Aunt Helene and Uncle Max from Cologne (Köln). Until now, I had only a bike that was used when we bought it. Now the new bike was the Mercedes, or Cadillac of bicycles. Except for the frame, the bike was clad in chromium – spokes, handlebars, it had a generator for a front and rear light, balloon tires, and a loud bell. I was elated and promised myself that I would not leave the bike downstairs in a rack with others, but instead, carry this bike up and down from our apartment whenever I wanted to use it. As heavy as the bike was, I kept my promise and made sure that it was cleaned after I rode it in the rain or snow.

Later that afternoon, relatives, friends, and acquaintances came to congratulate me and wish me mazel tov, good luck. Many brought gifts, including fountain pens, which were just coming into vogue and were very expensive. Others brought money that I converted immediately into the small blue paper strips for the big map of Palestine. On each piece I wrote the person's name who had made the donation. I was complimented not only for how well I had done at synagogue, but for my clever and unselfish idea of raising funds to buy land in Palestine. Even people who had brought gifts reached into their pockets and bought tickets to cover the map. Since I had started at the top of the ten-foot high map, a ladder came in very handy. By the end of the day, my *mitzvah*, my good deed, had been completed. Palestine was all in blue, and I was going to be able to donate 250 Marks for the land in Israel– *Eretz Israel*. It was a day in my life that was very important to my parents, my sister, and especially me. It was a part of my life that I would always remember and cherish. Now I could be counted as an adult in the *minyan* of the ten males required before public prayers could begin. I would count as part of the required quorum.

The next day after most of the relatives had left, there was a phone call for me. My Uncle Max had asked an insurance man to contact me regarding insurance on my new bike. I listened intently to what he had to say. A day or so later I found out that the insurance salesman's call was just a lark foisted on me by Uncle Max, who was not only a generous man but also a prankster. Slowly the reality of the time came back as my bar mitzvah faded into the past.

My teacher, Rabbi Geiss, left Mannheim the following year (1937) for Kassel, Germany. After World War II, I found out that he had survived Buchenwald concentration camp, immigrated to Israel and later returned to Germany where he functioned as the Rabbi of the entire province of Baden, dying at the resort Baden Baden in 1972.

CHAPTER SEVEN

The Noose is Tightening

With my bar mitzvah fading into the past and my life taking on some semblance of normalcy, the oppressive conditions came to the foreground again and again. As a matter of fact the threat was with us all the time. It was time to leave the Institute Schwarz and enroll in the Jewish School that had provisionally opened around Easter of 1936 because the law required the separation of Jewish students from Aryan students. The school, known simply by its location as the "K-2 Schule," was built around 1873 at K2,6 in the central part of Mannheim. It was a fire trap to say the least, and was referred to as the Judenschule, the school for Jews. Principal Berthold Stahl, known in Israel where he eventually settled as Baruch Stahl, was fifty years old and had his hands full designing a teaching and learning environment for nine grades of about 400 students.

This number grew smaller by the months and weeks because students were leaving Germany for safety in other countries, alone or with their families. The Jewish teachers, who had been removed by the Nazis from public and private

EXHIBIT 7.1 Berthold Baruch Stahl (born 1876) became principal of the Jewish school Mannheim, which was open to grades three to eight. He and his wife Johanna née Cahn (born 1886) were deported October 22, 1940 first to Gurs France and hence to Auschwitz in 1942 where they were killed.

EXHIBIT 7.2 Dr. Kurt Norbert Berg. He was an important teacher at our Jewish School and an important person in my life. It was his job to prepare us for an unknown future by instilling in us courage, self-reliance, and optimism. His life was full of disappointments and he died never having been able to benefit from what he taught us.

schools, were thrown into the breach along with students who came from many nearby city and suburban schools, including the city of Ludwigshafen. The teaching and administration staff numbered about twenty. Nothing was more important, under the circumstances, than a good education with emphasis on all things Jewish. Education was thought to be one of the most important aspects for assuring the survival of children and our families.

Although this was a public school, normally financially supported by the state, the Jewish Community of Mannheim was tasked to pay all of its operational costs. In addition to standard subjects, we received instruction on how to deal with eventual emigration. Hebrew studies were also emphasized, including singing, bible study, and the familiarization with the land of Palestine and the English language. Dr. Kurt Berg, whom I mentioned in an earlier chapter, was, by and large, responsible for instilling in us the confidence to deal with all sorts of difficult, changing lifestyle situations, and developing sufficient backbone to survive anticipated hardships here and in other countries. However, the Nazi regime made certain that we would not be exposed to the thinking of many well-known poets, writers, and philosophers and the vast amount of world literature because their ideas and thinking were not in consonance with Nazi ideology.

The school curriculum was under constant review and censorship, and under the best circumstances, learning was difficult because of few teachers and large classes in a dilapidated three story building. We had a large number of outdated books, and teaching aides were not available. Behind the antiquated school building was a walled-in courtyard with a few large, beautiful chestnut trees. We parked our bicycles in that yard since only a few of the students walked. We also spent recess there playing games and chasing each other around. Although we came from different directions to school, we always had to be on our guard that we weren't waylaid by gangs of Nazi hoodlums. However, attacks happened numerous times, not only to me but others also. After a while we worked out a system whereby several of us living in the same neighborhood, including girls, rode our bicycles together for protection. On several confrontations some of our bikes were damaged, but we were able to run away. In other instances a few of us suffered minor cuts and bruises along with wounded pride. Girls were less frequently attacked. I guess there was some reluctance by the HJ, Hitler Youth, to hurt or intimidate Jews of the weaker sex. I was always scared on the way to school in the morning and on the way home in the afternoon, and my parents were always happy to have me home again.

My homeroom teacher was the Principal Baruch Stahl. Other teachers were Professor Emil Friedrich Zivi, whom we nicknamed Zeus because of his autocratic approach, Dr. Kurt Berg, Professor Darmstadter, Mr. Kalberman, Samuel Liebermensch, and Arthur Kohn. It was only several years after World War II that the news trickled out that twelve out of the twenty teaching and clerical staff did not escape the tragic end designed for them by the Nazis. Gertrude Traub, my former kindergarten teacher, was also teaching at the school and was among those who were deported to their death. Her sister and parents suffered the same fate. Three others from the school's staff, including Manfred Kälbermann, had taken their own lives before deportation.

It was in the K-2 school that I made good friends with a number of boys and a few girls. Several boys were from the Jewish Orphanage located in a large building at R7,24, right off the Friedrichsring. Since those children had no family, Mother always encouraged me to bring several to our apartment for a home-cooked meal and some kind conversation. One of the boy's names was Adolph Lippschitz; another boy was named Paul Levi. I was able to determine that they and thirteen other orphans were deported with most other Jews of Mannheim to Camp Gurs, France. Their final fate is unknown.

Every day in school we heard about someone else leaving Mannheim, with or without their parents, to another city or country in Europe. Others were receiving affidavits for America, Brazil, Australia, or elsewhere. Still others were signing up for "Hashara," preparation and training for Palestine, and eventual aliyah, immigration to Palestine. My cousin, Kurt Strauss from Frankfurt, about five years older than I, was an ardent Zionist who planned to join a kibbutz, a collective farm in Palestine. He wanted to be a *chaluz*, a pioneer in Palestine. He never saw his dream become reality. He was arrested and taken to several prisons, concentration camps and was finally murdered at Camp Sachsenhausen. Through my research efforts I was able to obtain a copy of his death certificate in 2002, acknowledged by the brutal camp commander. Turn to the appendix to see exhibit 7.3, the original death certificate document and translation.

In Berlin, the Nazi Ministry advised the League of Nations that the treatment of Jews under German jurisdiction was none of their business. The world had no response to our plight and stood idly by while the armies of Italian dictator, Mussolini, had invaded Ethiopia on the African continent months earlier. While Edward VIII was crowned King of England in London, Josef Goebbels, the German Minister of Propaganda told Britain of a plan of mass deportation of Jews to the British territory of Palestine. The plan provided for the British to reimburse Germany for the re-settlement costs and financial losses Germany would incur as a result. The alternative, Goebbels asserted, would be greater, continued persecution. England did not respond and ignored the German proposal. The 1936 Winter Olympics had long concluded, and the Norwegians walked away with most of the important event medals. Yet, Hitler, with a gleam in his eyes, introduced to the German people and the world the "Volkswagen," the people's car, which took the world by surprise. Its much improved and completely modernized version was phased out July 30, 2003, at its final production site in Mexico.

Next, in a daring move, Hitler sent his troops into the Rhineland, including Mannheim, in gross violation of the Versailles and Locarno Treaties which had declared that area a demilitarized zone. The major powers and parties to the treaties, primarily France and Great Britain, admonished Germany only with words and no action followed. Thus, Hitler became even bolder, forbidding Jews the vote in the forthcoming election where he received 99% of the German vote. Britain's response was the announcement of a fifteen year arms production program that included the building of thirty-eight warships. What made political matters worse was that General Francisco Franco, a Fascist and ally of Hitler, had installed himself ruler of Spain and was fighting the Loyalist forces of Spain with the massive assistance of weapons and incognito German forces. It was the beginning of the Spanish Civil War, and with that, another escape route for European Jews was closing. Everywhere, the situation for Jews was becoming more precarious and desperate, and Hitler's noose around us was tightening.

While all of these events weighed heavily on our home life, particularly on Dad and Mom, my day to day schedule continued although in a much more constrained mode. Our minds were less concerned with learning than with the day-to-day survival. Erich Dreifuss, Max'l Kaufmann, Ernst Michel, and others like Adolph Lippschitz, Alfred Selig, Hans Zwang, Heinz Kuhn, Günter Kaufmann, Friedl Landmann and I palled around and played *Kellerlöchel Fussball*, basement window soccer. Let me explain: In all the Mannheim neighborhoods, apartment houses had small glass basement windows covered with wire mesh about two feet wide by one foot high, and, perhaps, three to four inches above the sidewalk called *Kellerlöchel*. We used such a *Kellerlöchel* as the goal for our impromptu soccer games. It was fun, challenging, and we could move around quickly and easily to different buildings and neighborhoods. Sometimes we got together and played in a grassy area near the river Neckar, known to us as the *Neckar Wiese*. At other times a few of us met in some out-of-the-way hiding place, like a cellar, and smoked a cigarette, unbeknownst to our parents. Had they known, we would have received some sort of punishment. My younger cousin Ernst Kahn was often among us. We also compared notes about girls we had crushes on, or less plausible, girls who had crushes on us. Of course, all were Jewish girls, their names I still remember but wouldn't want to mention here with several exceptions. There were the pretty Doiny sisters, Alice and Meta. Not only were they good looking, but also very athletic. They were always seen together whether in the Synagogue, during Hebrew classes, *Bar Kochba* athletic club, volleyball, soccer games, or just out for a walk. Ernst Michel, perhaps because he was better looking than I, was Alice's boyfriend, but I could never get to first base.

My flame was a cute girl, Marion Grodsinzki. She lived next to Friedrichspark, and she and I often walked there until it was against the law for Jews to enter that private park and all other public parks. I remember her being at one of my birthday parties. Her father, Friedrich, was a Polish citizen who had settled in

Mannheim after World War I, but by law was never able to become a citizen of Germany. He and thousands of others in the same situation were deported on October 29, 1938, and were never heard from again. It was the first selective mass deportation of Jews from all over Germany. Neither Marion, her sister, Ruth, nor her mother, Hedwig, survived the Holocaust.

I am getting chronologically ahead of myself because it was still 1937. Often in the evening when it was dark, Max'l Kaufman, who lived in an apartment across the street from me, and I would communicate with each other by using Morse code signals using a flashlight. We had learned Morse code by attending *Betar* meetings, a Zionist youth organization. Communicating like this was fun and entertaining.

On the darker side of things we, including many of our other friends, tore off automobile emblems fastened to winter radiator covers. We only did this in winter since the radiator covers were to protect the water in the cars' radiators from freezing. The ornamental metal emblems were colorful, between two to three inches in size, and were sought after by collectors, ourselves included. Several of us were lookouts while someone paraded down a line of cars in the railroad terminal parking lot, for example, where we tore the well-known automobile insignia emblems from the cover material. Later we traded different car emblems among us, including Opel, Hanomag, Adler, Mercedes, Horch, DKW, and others. I collected about twenty-eight of such winter radiator cover ornaments that were expensive for owners to replace at a garage. Thinking about it now, the prank was utterly dangerous and stupid. As Jews, had we been caught, we would have been paraded through the city and put in jail or concentration camps, our fate certainly not certain.

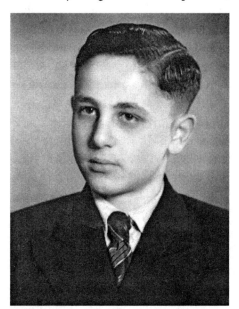

EXHIBIT 7.4 My friend, Max'l Kaufman, around 1938.

As young rascals, we engaged in various other pranks. We put matchsticks into doorbells so that they would keep on ringing until the match was removed. Worse, we would sneak up on glazier Lechner's motorcycle sidecar. Inside he stored glass and tools, and we took some of the putty. Then Max'l Kaufmann, Alfred Selig, myself and others smeared putty into car door locks so that the cars could not easily be opened with the key. It was a prank we really enjoyed and caused much havoc for the automobile drivers.

EXHIBIT 7.5 A few of my friends, all of whom cheated the Nazi henchmen. From left: Unknown, Alfred Selig, Hans Zwang, Max'l Kaufman, me (age 13).

Sometimes I rode my bike aimlessly through areas of the city or nearby suburbs where I hoped no one knew me. Whatever I did, my Jewishness was with me like a dark shadow. Thus I never felt alone, but I was always on my guard. I wondered what it would be like to have non-Jewish friends and be able to do whatever they were able to do. What a strange thought! I had been singled out to suffer the punishment for being a Jew. As a teenager it wasn't clear to me, and I could not understand what I had done as an individual or as part of a religious group to be constantly tormented by all of the people around me. This hatred was visible everywhere and was not only condoned by the government, but inspired and nurtured by it so that the people believed and acted upon the propaganda.

In spite of the great burden my parents and I endured, along with my sister in France, we always hoped that life for us would eventually become better somehow. Our optimism never wavered, and we prayed that the German people would suddenly relent from their ruthless persecution and experience a transformation to reason. My father occasionally talked to me about his hardships when he was young and told me about his goals and how he achieved them. He admonished me not to lose courage. I believed him and promised myself to maintain my strength and willpower. I would try hard to shape my destiny in spite of the evil forces attempting to destroy my aspirations to live a meaningful life in the future. I continued to concentrate on constructive activities that in today's world would seem trivial. At the time these activities kept me healthy and helped me keep my sanity. Unfortunately, there were those who could not or were not willing to be treated as sub human, and chose to end their lives by unnatural, radical measures. Many men and women chose this road, as well as young people, including some in my age group, also chose this destiny. I can still see them as they were, and my eyes blur as I think of their vitality. Sadness overcomes me to think of their needless ending. Among these young people was Robert Süss who was a congenital, bilateral leg amputee and moved about leashed to a board on wheels similar to a skateboard. Four of us carried him up and down stairs at school each day. It was a pathetic sight to see him moving about using his gloved knuckles. We treated him as our friend with utter respect and tenderness. He shot himself because he stood in the way of his family obtaining an immigration visa from other countries No country wanted a cripple unable to sustain himself.

Most Friday evenings, to usher in Shabbat, I went to synagogue and then again the next morning for the youth services even though it was dangerous for a Jewish boy to walk alone. I competed with other boys for an aliyah, a mitzvah, a special honor designated for participation in the religious Torah service. Services were conducted either by Rabbi Max Grünewald, Cantors Hugo Adler or Erwin Hirsch. After Rabbi Grünewald had departed Mannheim, Rabbi Geiss or Rabbi Karl Richter officiated. Brothers Walter and Hans Salomon often conducted the youth services as lay cantors. See the appendix for their images, listed as exhibits 7.6, 7.7, 7.8, and 7.9.

On Saturday afternoons, boys and girls who basically had no place to go, met next door at the Schiff Haus where Zionist youth groups met, groups such as Habonim, Makkabi, and Betar, of which I was a member. There, our leaders told us about Palestine and the hardships the Jewish settlers had to endure. They drained swamps, cultivated the land, and lived in communal settlements, all in an effort to create a land where all Jews could someday live in peace. We also learned patriotic Hebrew songs and danced the horah that were all part of the chaluzim, the settlers' way of life.

My favorite activities continued. I still took violin lessons, collected stamps, played the harmonica, and read books about the American Indians and wild animals in Africa. That's how I fell in love with the Indians and the wild life, primarily elephants in Africa. In the meantime the rationing of food and clothing was becoming more prevalent, and Jews were further humiliated because we were allocated 50% fewer food rations than all other Germans. Fortunately, Herr and Frau Anna Kress, who operated a tiny grocery store next to the police headquarters at L6,5, ignored our meager ration stamps and gave us additional quantities of eggs, meat, milk, cleaning products, etc., that we were not allowed to have. Mr. Kress had lost his leg below the knee in World War I, and had a wooden prosthesis. As customers entered the store, he made all sorts of tap dancing sounds as he walked around waiting on them. He was dejected because of his lot and the fact that Germany did not compensate him sufficiently for his loss. He told my parents about this, and he never joined the Nazi party although everyone else had to join provided they could march which he could not. His favorable and humane treatment of our family singled him out as one of the very few Jew friendly Germans of Mannheim. A year later, this kindness on his part resulted in quasi heroic deeds for us, which my parents and I have not forgotten.

We continued to hear from my sister Irene, Aunt Irma, and Uncle Charles in Lille, France, through letters, which had been opened by the Nazis as was most of the mail from foreign countries to Jews, and occasional phone calls. Therefore, everyone had to be very careful of what was written or said because of

EXHIBIT 7.10 Selma Weil, dad's business secretary, sitting on our apartment balcony. She wrote a dedication on the back of the photo, August 4, 1938. This balcony was to become a very important place within the tragedy that unfolded several months later. She and her sister Sofie did not survive the Camp in the East.

the censorship imposed on Jews corresponding with others in foreign countries. It was a long-standing tradition at our home that Mom and Dad called Opa and Oma in Luxembourg every Friday evening. Aunt Helene and Uncle Max called us on Saturday evenings from Cologne (Köln). The other aunts and uncles called less often, but we kept in touch by mail or phone. Dad also corresponded with his two other brothers, Herman and Ernst, who had left Germany before World War I for Chicago, Illinois. Basically, the Kahns were a close knit family, and now even more so, as living in Germany had become a nightmare for everyone.

The wholesale business, J&S Kahn, located at B1,6, only a few blocks from the former regent's palace, had become far less profitable in supporting both families due to the ever-tightening boycott of Jewish owned businesses. Selma Weil, who was the secretary, bookkeeper and the only Jewish employee left, had to be let go. Selma and her sister, Sofie, never married. Sadly they were deported from Mannheim on October 20, 1940, to Camp Gurs in France and again in 1942 to other camps in Eastern Europe, where they were both murdered by the Nazis.

Both Dad and Uncle Simon took turns visiting those few remaining customers who defied the Nazi boycott edicts. They both packaged, mailed, or delivered the merchandise themselves, and could only procure goods from Jewish manufacturers, not yet taken over by Aryans. One of those manufacturers was the Marum Knitting Mill at Sobernheim, owned by Alfred and Amelie Marum. They were the uncle and aunt of Gertrude Wolff, who would later became my wife.

All over the city and throughout Germany were newsstands and *Litfasssäulen*, large, tall, round columns, approximately 2 feet in diameter and approximately 7 feet high, for posting advertisements and news, displaying one of the most vile and aggressive propaganda media known as *Der Stürmer*. It was the foremost racial hate magazine, containing offensive and vulgar anti-Semitic caricatures, with lies and fabricated stories about Jews, gays, lesbians and gypsies. Julius Streicher rose to fame with the publication of this Jew baiting, brass knuckle, and often pornographic trash. He had the full support of the Propaganda Minister, Josef Goebbels. Seeing it and seeing the German public reading it made me, and any other free thinking, intelligent person, sick to our stomachs. Several years later when my father had to sell, or better said, give away his business under threat to his life, a very cynical, hate-filled article about this transaction appeared in this magazine. (I will describe this further on pages to follow.) In retrospect, it was a magazine designed to incite the German people to hate us that eventually almost led to the annihilation of Jews through ruthless killings.

With the glory, excitement, and disappointments of the Summer Olympics at Berlin long faded into the past, German laws decreed that 25% of all Jewish financial assets were to be confiscated. The machinery to accomplish this was elaborate, and it was impossible for even the poorest Jews to be spared from this national robbery. All of a sudden, money and all other earthly goods no longer mattered to us. What did have meaning was maintaining our sanity and our lives.

Not a day passed that my Dad, Mom, and I were not in tears saying good-bye to good friends and neighbors who were fortunate enough to have the legal papers to leave Germany and enter some other country. What would be their fate? What would be ours? Every day was a new twist in our struggle to continue with anti-Semitic laws and decrees. From historical records it has been established that by 1937 approximately 1,460 Jews had fled Mannheim.

Among those who were fortunate enough to leave in January 1937, was my cousin, Norbert Isaak, age 18, the son of Ida (née Kahn) and Julius Isaak. My Uncle Max in Cologne (Köln) gave him sufficient money for a *passeur*, a smuggler, to take him across the German border to Belgium. His one year older brother, my cousin Helmut, had already left to join others to cultivate and settle the land of Palestine. Their older sister Ilse, age 21, was fortunate to flee Germany with her mother Ida to America. Ilse had married Otto Hertz shortly before. They were reunited several years later after his journey first took him to Cuba, where he waited to obtain his visa to immigrate to America. Each of the cousins

EXHIBIT 7.11 & 7.12 My cousins Norbert (age 16), Ilse (age 19), and Helmut (17), and their mother, Ida, my father's sister.

came to Mannheim at different times to say goodbye since my parents were their favorite aunt and uncle. It was time for young Jews to leave and save themselves. Unfortunately, many were unable to do so.

There were many others, like my cousins Ernst and Walter Kahn, who would be fortunate enough to leave with their family, Uncle Simon and Aunt Hilde to America in 1938. I remember in years past watching from their balcony the religious procession in conjunction with the Catholic holiday of *Fronleichnam*, the Feast of Corpus Christi. Thousands of people, including their priests, participated in the procession wearing their ritual dress while First Communicants wore white dresses and robes. They carried banners, monstrances, large crucifixes, statues of the Virgin Mary, and other holy sculptures. They were accompanied by musicians, children, and occasionally, very loud firecrackers. The smell of incense was in the air. We were very curious, but also observant and respectful, as were many others watching from their balconies. The event usually took place in mid-June each year.

One day Cousin Ernst, three years my junior, and I biked in the Waldpark, a park nearby that stretched for miles along the east side of the river Rhine. We didn't obey the signs that restricted some roads to bicycles and rode on a path for pedestrians only. A forest ranger caught us and issued citations to us. Accordingly, we had to meet him the next day at *Kaffee Stern*, a restaurant with a small animal sanctuary several miles into the park, and pay a relatively small fine that came from our allowances. It was raining heavily when the two of us delivered the money, and we were glad when it was over and never told our parents about the incident. First I was told that during the ensuing war, the Allies destroyed *Kaffee Stern* during a bombing raid. Later I found out that after the war, the restaurant fell on hard times and was finally razed.

In stark contrast to the aforementioned, everyone watched with awe and astonishment as the huge, beautiful dirigible Zeppelin, "Hindenburg," flew gracefully over the city. It was the first commercial, lighter-than-air craft to make scheduled Atlantic crossings to America. It was a marvel of technology that, unfortunately, was fueled by hydrogen gas which was prone to ignite. In May 1937, news came over the radio that the Hindenburg had gone up in flames as it tried to land at Lakehurst,

EXHIBIT 7.13 The Waldpark.

New Jersey. It was a tragedy not easy to forget. Had they used helium, which is not flammable, instead of hydrogen, it would not have exploded. An American embargo prevented its use by Germany.

Also in May 1937, specifically mid-morning of May 10, Rudolf Hess, deputy and confidante to Adolf Hitler and second in charge to head the Nazi Party, visited Mannheim and stayed at the hotel, Mannheimer Hof. In earlier and happier years Irene, dressed in Rococo costume, and I in a chimney sweep costume, enjoyed elaborate and fun-filled *fasching*, carnival parties there for children. But now, the grounds in front of this grand hotel, located at the beginning of the Augustaanlage Boulevard had become the staging area for a huge rally. I was a young thirteen, naïve and curious. Without my parents' knowledge, as they would never have given permission, I decided to become a spectator. For hours the crowd shouted slogans which were so rhythmic that one of them I have not forgotten: "*Rudolf Hess sei so nett, zeig dich doch am Fensterbrett.*" "Rudolf Hess be so nice, and show yourself at the windowsill." Had someone in the crowd recognized the Jewish boy among them, they would have killed me on the spot.

With drum and bugle corps, fanfares, songs, and the waving of swastika banners, the crowd had hypnotized itself into a frenzy, when finally the balcony window opened. The mayor of Mannheim, Carl Renninger, in Nazi uniform, introduced Hess to the masses. Renninger was a feared, ruthless, and unrepentant Nazi who was in office from 1933 until the surrender of the city to the American Army when he went into hiding.

Hess, of course, was in uniform. He was of slender build, not tall, and thrust his right arm and hand straight forward to give the Hitler salute. He stood there smiling while the crowd around me went berserk. During the speech that followed, I managed to extricate myself from the crowd. It was a day for me to remember, not because it was enjoyable, but because I realized the spell and power Hitler's propaganda had been able to cast over the German people that had led to their blind obedience, world disaster, and a sad chapter for European Jews.

Hitler showed off his new technologies to the world for advancement, weapons, including fighter and bomber aircraft and war ships, and conducted massive military maneuvers filmed for the entire world to see, envy, and fear. Military attachés from foreign countries had been invited. The AXIS pact between Japan, Germany, and Italy was in effect, and German bombers and fighter aircraft were deployed, in open defiance of the world, to support Spain's Franco Nationalists (Fascist) forces against Republican defenders. Heavy casualties were inflicted on civilians by German dive bombers since Spain became a testing ground for the German Wehrmacht's armies war machinery, in particular JU-87 Stuka dive-bombers. These aircraft made a horrible siren-like sound as they dove almost vertically toward their targets.

The German people were very proud of all their accomplishments. Fritz Todt, a civil engineer who had risen to the position of Secretary of Transportation, had designed and was constructing the *Reichsautobahn*, the first four-lane, divided, limited access automobile expressway to eventually crisscross Germany. Shortly after Hitler came to power, Todt and Hitler recognized that the construction of such an undertaking would be the salvation for the economic depression Germany was suffering by putting all of the unemployed men to work. These men were drafted into a paramilitary *arbeitsdienst*, a uniformed work force. We could hear the sound of the dynamite charges and the hordes of men singing while they marched to work with shovels on their shoulders. By this time, late 1937, more than 3,000 miles of concrete roads and bridges had been completed. It was a masterful piece of engineering. Formerly, it took Dad forty minutes to drive from Mannheim to Heidelberg, and now it took only twenty minutes. The roads became a huge advantage when the war started a few years later by enabling entire armies to move from one battlefront in the West to others in the East in a matter of hours or days. Again, the world took notice of Hitler's achievements but not the plight of the handicapped, gays, lesbians, political opponents, gypsies, blacks, and Jews who were oppressed under his grip.

As I continued to attend the Jewish school, I learned more about the world around us and how isolated, shunned, and despised we were from the brainwashed population Mannheim, who daily, became more hostile to us. Now and then I read or heard about someone having been arrested and removed for having spoken out about his or her disagreement with excessive laws and unethical and immoral Nazi conduct. The Reverend Martin Niemoeller, a Protestant church leader, became one of those. Even in his high standing in the church, he became only another voice stilled while being openly ridiculed by the Nazi media. The concentration camps, Sachsenhausen and Dachau, were filled with undesirables and political prisoners. Another so-called correction camp had to be opened and became known as Camp Buchenwald. Like the others, it was administrated by the feared and ruthless SS guards. Anyone who did not openly support the Nazi regime or methods was subject to forceful correction efforts in concentration camps.

Whenever we had an opportunity, my small circle of friends would get together at Günter Kaufmann's #47 apartment at the Jewish Altersheim, home for the aged. It was located on Collinistrasse, today Bassermannstrasse, a nice, quiet, almost suburban area between the river Neckar and the Luisenpark. I knew Günter's father, Ludwig, his mother, Amalie, and his younger sister, Ellen, well. Ludwig was the caretaker engineer for the Altersheim. Because the apartment's location was below ground level (*gartengeschoss*) at garden level, we felt safe in meeting without being noticed by anyone coming or going or being surprised by the Gestapo, the Nazi Secret Police. When this institution was built in 1931, it could accommodate fifty Jewish seniors in small apartments. However, in 1936, it was modified to absorb the Jewish Hospital and its functions that until then was located elsewhere in Mannheim. Therefore, it became necessary to eliminate and make smaller some of the apartments for the elderly.

When we gathered at Günter's apartment, we talked about our mutual concerns, fears, and problems. We discussed all the anti-Semitic turmoil around us and also the situation in Palestine where constant violence resulting in the death of Jewish settlers and Arabs was the norm. The British administration of Palestine, who were supposedly pursuing a policy of neutrality, were truly aligned with the Arabs and seemed unable to maintain order. There were rumors about a partitioning of Palestine into an Arab state and a Jewish state, restricting immigration and other news. Our most important quest for knowledge was by way of the radio, a course that was also very dangerous. Had we been caught listening to a foreign broadcast, you would not be reading this. It was considered a high act of treason by the Nazis, and the punishment was death. Unless one had purchased a radio prior to Hitler coming to power, the only radio available for purchase was the Volksempfänger VE 301, the people's radio. It was made of Bakelite with a small swastika under the dial. It was not possible to receive any foreign broadcasts because of its design. It was perfect for keeping German listeners isolated from the outside world and the truth. In spite of the risk, we sat very close to the radio speaker while Günter fiddled around with the dial trying to tune in on a foreign country transmitter until we could hear a commentator from Radio Luxembourg, London, or Bratislava. If we were lucky we were able to tune into short wave from America. When the static on the radio subsided, it was so quiet we could practically hear each other's hearts beat. We listened to the voices of

EXHIBIT 7.14 The Altersheim Jewish home for the aged where we listened to foreign broadcast radio stations at great risk. It was a death sentence crime had we been caught. See exhibit 7.15 in the appendix for a photo of my friends at this time, including Günter.

truth and freedom, hoping to hear some good, encouraging news, perhaps words that could finally give us renewed hope. But, time and time again, it seemed that the world didn't realize our desperate situation, didn't have the resolve or clout to intervene or help us, or simply didn't care about our plight. Perhaps it was a combination of all of these.

Günter's entire family, including Günter's grandmother, Hedwig, who also lived with them, were deported on October 20, 1940 to Camp Gurs in Southern France. Only Günter and Ellen survived. Both of their parents and grandmother perished after being transported from Gurs to other camps in Eastern Europe. From my research, I have determined that both Günter and Ellen Kaufmann came to the United States after the war, but, regretfully, after repeated attempts year after year, I have still been unable to locate them.

Business opportunities and income for Uncle Simon and my dad had worsened, and the lease for the business was not renewed because we were Jewish. Knowing that Uncle Simon and his family had all the documents to leave for America within six months, Dad decided to find a sufficiently large apartment with the intention of combining our living quarters and the business. He found an ideal place with a large, lovely balcony at L14,14 that met those conditions. It was not far from where we had been living located at the Kaiserring Boulevard, where once stood the Bismark monument. The move was logistically difficult, but the layout permitted my dad to move the office and remaining textile stocks to the front of the apartment while we lived toward the rear of the building in smaller surroundings than before. Several large pieces of furniture from our home had to be sold including Irene's piano. Uncle Simon and my dad carried on as well as they could, and instead of selling only wholesale as they did before, they now sold retail to individuals, primarily Jewish customers. Sometimes I took packages to the post office, strapping them to my bike. Several times when the clerk at the counter noticed the sender's name, J&S Kahn, I was told, "The German Post Office does not accept or dispatch packages for dirty Jews." They made me feel like an outcast, dejected, without anyone around me showing any concern or sympathy. As a matter of fact, they were amused. On the way home, the package always seemed twice as heavy. I then had to take the package to another post office.

During summer vacation 1937, Irene came from Lille to visit us for the last time at Mannheim. It was enjoyable to see her maturing and becoming a lady. She no longer had her pigtails. However, it was discernible that she was ill at ease being in a home that was no longer her home, and in a city that now made her unwelcome. Most of her friends were no longer in Mannheim, and so we did a lot of sitting on the balcony talking and reading, while Mother and Irene often knitted. She missed the piano, which we sold since we moved to a smaller apartment. We went for walks, being careful to avoid places where many people

EXHIBIT 7.16 During Irene's visit we all spent much time sitting on our balcony. It was summer 1937 and we could not do much else.

gathered and also places where Jews were forbidden to walk or sit. Now and then I played my violin for her which she enjoyed. Mom and Irene went several times to department stores early in the morning before it was crowded to avoid being recognized by someone who would cause a scene. We all had been conditioned to feel as if we were criminals, and we acted accordingly. Yet we put on a false front to hide from Irene the trauma and fright which had befallen us.

One afternoon I asked Irene if she wanted to go swimming. She was excited and happy to be doing something with her brother. There was a hitch, of course. In Mannheim and vicinity, there was no place where Jews were allowed to swim by order of the police. Numerous times, however, during the past two years I had bicycled alone to Ludwigshafen, the large city located directly on the other side of the Rhine opposite Mannheim. Not telling my parents, I ventured to a place along the river's bank and went swimming there. No one there knew me, and I was careful not to swim where others did and did not have conversations with anyone. Still I took the chances since there were signs posted along the river by the police making it unlawful for Jews to sunbathe, swim, play, or even walk there. That is where I took Irene to go swimming. Everything was fine until something happened that neither of us had ever dreamed about or anticipated in any way.

The River Rhine is a very fast moving stream that travels a long distance and finally empties into the North Sea at Rotterdam, Holland. Ships and the shipping business on the Rhine were and still are big business. I estimate the number of ships of all types and sizes that traveled up and down the river, passing Mannheim and Ludwigshafen in those days numbered several hundred daily. When ships traveled up stream, good swimmers swam toward the ship, letting the current literally throw them on the deck of the heavily laden freighter. Irene and I had no intention of doing that, although, in the past, I had done so. I would sit on the deck for a short distance, jump off, and let the current carry me back toward the spot where I could easily swim to shore and rest from the exhausting, somewhat dangerous feat.

Irene and I swam away from shore into stronger currents of the river when a freighter approached moving upstream. Irene and I were about 100 feet apart from each other, and Irene was trying to close that distance. However, the freighter came between us, and when I saw Irene last, her two hands were raised and the current produced around the ship pulled her under the bow. I did not see her until she surfaced again, a considerable distance downstream behind the freighter, desperately gasping for air. Finally, I reached her and with all my strength and much luck, brought her to shore where both of us recovered from the ordeal. Luckily no one had noticed what had happened else the consequences would have been unpredictable. Silently I thanked our good Lord for the miracle of Irene's survival, and I never swam there again. And, you guessed it. We promised ourselves not to reveal any part of this scary event to Dad and Mom, and we never did. But the thought of the ordeal still makes me sick to my stomach.

Irene told us years later that on her trip back to France, she and her luggage were taken off the train at Aachen, the border. She was alone and scared while Nazi border guards questioned and harassed her. While she was being interrogated, the train left. However, she was permitted to continue on the next train. Yet the wait in the presence of unfriendly Nazi guards made her feel like a prisoner. It was an encounter too close for comfort. She promised herself never to visit us in Germany.

That summer was the last time that I rented a kayak. On some Sunday afternoons I would paddle up the Neckar River toward Heidelberg, enjoying the temporary freedom and the peculiar soothing sounds of the water flowing past the smooth hull of the boat. Now and then there were trees, high grass, flowers and houses that came into view. I wished that it would always be that tranquil, but then I realized that Jews were forbidden to rent kayaks at the boathouse. The posted sign said so by order of the police. In the past I had ignored the sign, paid, and was on my way. What an irony that I had violated the law of the lawless!

Before I went back to school, my parents went on a buying spree for all sorts of clothing items. I received a winter coat, hat, a new suit and two pairs of pants, shoes and so on. They told me that I had outgrown some of my clothing, but I suspected that we were getting closer to the time when we would leave Mannheim forever.

Soon fall came, and with it the Jewish holidays with prayers at synagogues in a subdued and almost cloaked atmosphere. There were fewer worshippers, as many stayed away, afraid of praying openly. The Gestapo had to review and approve of all readings and sermons by the rabbis. Danger was in the air, and people were arrested on the street, and simply disappeared, never to be heard from again. Jews had been stripped of all human rights, all personal freedoms, and practically all means of support. We were prohibited from participating in any cultural or

EXHIBIT 7.17 & 7.18 My new suit with two kinds of pants. The second pair of pants are knickerbockers.

economic endeavors. We thought that we could be safe if we stayed at home. Slowly, we found out that even the home was no longer a zone of genuine safety.

When I went back to school after a long summer vacation, it was very noticeable that some of my classmates were missing. Presumably they had left Mannheim for other destinations, not necessarily overseas but to towns where they were not known and thus were less noticeable. Some teachers were also missing, and the news as to what had happened to them was part of the rumor mill. It was hard for any of us to concentrate on our studies, as we were too preoccupied with events of the day and concerns about our future.

Although it was somewhat difficult to travel, we managed to attend my Cousin Georges's bar mitzvah on August 28, 1937 in Luxembourg. Today, I ask myself why we didn't stay there and leave everything behind. But, at that time, no one could really imagine what was to come. It was the last time I saw my sister Irene, who had come from France for the occasion, and did not know when I would see her again. Turn to the appendix to see exhibit 7.19, a family photo taken at this happy event.

Hitler's axis partner, Japan, was engaged in military actions against mainland China with many Chinese soldiers and many more civilians killed. It was the beginning of an all out war without a declaration of war. Again, the free world did only protest. In Germany the Nazi regime began to take children with disabilities away from their parents or if they were not educated according to Nazi doctrine.

We became more aware of military uniforms around us and saw more and more military infantry units as well as artillery and light armored columns near main roads and the train station. There were also more military aircraft in the sky. The military might was beginning to show more each day. In the meantime the propaganda rhetoric from Herman Göring, Adolf Hitler, Rudolf Hess and others against the Communists, western allies, Russia, and Jews became more vigorous, hateful, and shocking.

Some food items became very scarce, and coffee, which could no longer be imported, was replaced by coffee made from the roots of the chicory plant. Besides eggs and meat, certain kinds of bread also became scarce. We ate *komissbrot*, a dark, large grain bread about eight to nine inches long and about four inches square. For its size, it was very heavy. It derived its name during World War I when each German soldier received one loaf per day. Komiss means barrack; in other words, it was barrack bread. In general all formerly imported products were now either no longer available or the Germans had found substitutes. Some trucks were converted to run on wood fuel and we could see more of them every day with large containers mounted on top. The Germans were very innovative when it came to items in short supply.

In December 1937, I went to Cologne (Köln) to visit Uncle Max and Aunt Helene. Uncle Max had sold his business to an Aryan because as a Jew he could no longer stay in business. They had moved from Ehrenfeld, a suburb of Cologne, to an apartment in the city. They had purchased tickets for me and a girl, who was there vacationing from Berlin, to see *Fledermaus*, by Johann Strauss at the opera house on New Year's Eve. Her name was Hannelore Schuftan; she was very pretty, and we had a good time. I often wonder what happened to her and her family.

On March 14, 1938, Hitler declared the imminent unification of Austria with Germany. He marched across the border with all his military might, and within hours the annexation was complete without a shot having been fired. Austria, the country that gave birth to Adolf, embraced him as its own. All of those who tried to spoil his success were either incarcerated or simply done away with. Shortly thereafter, America, Great Britain, and France did nothing more than accept Hitler's conquest, while the civil war in Spain was considered to be over with Generalissimo Franco at the helm with hundreds of so called German military and civilian (Gestapo) advisors remaining in Spain.

For the Jews the situation was getting much worse. All kinds of laws had been implemented. If a person wanted to rent an apartment from a Jewish owner, he or she had to reveal to the potential leasee that he was a Jew. Names that many Jews acquired by state decree in 1808 could be withdrawn by the regime. Jews could only use the public libraries for genealogical purposes. Each and every Jewish person was required to declare in detail what he or she owned if the total value exceeded 5000 Mark. It was unlawful for Jews to vacation at any resort.

Streets that had been named after Jewish people had to be changed immediately to Aryan names. Beginning on September 30, 1938, my birthday, Jewish doctors and lawyers could only treat Jewish clients. The compulsory use of the middle name Sara for all Jewish females and Israel for males was another blow to our dignity. Compounding our distress was the revocation of all Jewish passports. New ones were issued incorporating the new middle name and a large "J" imprint. The implementation of these laws was more than an embarrassment and chicanery for Jews. They amounted to the denial of all human rights and the cold hearted persecution of innocent people.

Since Hitler's rise to power, more than 135 anti-Jewish laws had been enforced, and the conference of most of the world nations at Evian, France, July 1938, failed to solve the Jewish refugee problem. Chaim Weizman phrased it well when he said, "The world is divided into two camps. One camp consists of countries expelling Jews, the other camp of countries will not admit them." The world was taking notice of our plight, but was unwilling to help. All participating countries at that conference are to blame for letting the Holocaust happen.

Because we hoped to leave Germany and live temporarily with Opa in Luxembourg, Mom and Dad arranged for a moving company to construct a "lift," a large wooden crate, to store certain household items, select furniture, paintings, sculptures, and other art objects prior to shipping to Luxembourg. As you will see later, this was a wise decision and explains how I still have family heirlooms.

It was April 20, 1938 when I mounted my bicycle and rode to the suburb of Neckarau to begin my apprenticeship in metal working and fabrication at the *Anlerwerkstätte*, a vocational school for Jewish teenagers. Another phase of the school was devoted to instruction in carpentry. The curriculum was originally designed to be a two and a half year program but was later changed to allow graduation in only two years in recognition of the urgency of emigration. This career school opened in April 1936, after Sigmund Keller, a generous member of the Jewish community, donated a complex of factory buildings and an office building located at 47 Friedrichsstrasse. I learned later that Mr. Keller made available all of the tools, machines, other equipment, and furniture to provide the most modern, efficient, learning atmosphere.

For most of the morning we had theoretical instruction by engineer Georg Brauer, a man with a mustache similar to Hitler's. Different teachers taught English, spoken Hebrew, known as Ivrit, and current Jewish history that included the latest political and economic situations in Palestine. The actual hands-on metal working experience was under the supervision of Mr. Jacob Safran who brought his many years of experience with Heinrich Lanz, a well-known producer of small and large motorized agricultural equipment and diesel engines. At the time the company was engaged in producing heavy diesel engines for German Army tanks. Today Lanz has been bought out by John Deere & Co., a U.S. based corporation that makes motorized agricultural equipment for sale worldwide. Working in the blacksmith shop was intriguing, and I enjoyed the assigned time and projects that took me there.

Each morning, rain or shine, I rode my bike approximately five kilometers to the school and changed into overalls prior to class at 8:00 a.m. At noon I ate lunch that Mother had prepared before that morning. At 4:30 p.m., after washing up, I peddled home. The streets were mostly cobblestone, but I was used to the bumpy ride and was able to repair an occasional flat without too much trouble. Rubber tires were impossible to buy, and even synthetic tires could only be purchased with a special needs permit.

Since new classes began each year, there was an overlap in students' standing within the curriculum. For example, there were about thirty-five students who would graduate and receive their Craft's Master's Diploma in September (of 1938), another class in April 1939, and so on. My class of thirty, which was evenly split between metal craft and carpenters, would not graduate until September 1940. Who could know then what was to happen in the future?

Most of the boys I did not know beforehand because many came from other cities and far away places in Germany. After all, this vocational school was not only unique, but it was also the only school of its kind in Germany. Contrary to the regular Jewish school, I took my studies and shop work here very seriously. I understood that, just perhaps, the craft and skill I would learn here would be key to my economic survival if I ever got away from the Hitler's clutches and into some other country.

In normal times and under normal circumstances there would have been a big reception with dignitaries from all walks of life invited to fete and honor Rabbi Max Grünewald when he left Mannheim. But this was not the case. Rabbi Grünewald, who had presided over my bar mitzvah, very quietly left for Berlin after many productive years in Mannheim. This man, who had shaped, guided, and loved each of his constituents, was in turn loved and revered by each of them. As I wrote in my book, *Reflections by Jewish Survivors from Mannheim, 1990*, "Dr. Grünewald has touched thousands of lives, not only in Mannheim but the world over." It was true then and is still true today although he is no longer with us. He provided the spiritual strength for us to cope with life in spite of Nazi terror. He had left with his wife and son to serve as the executive of the *Reichsvertretung der Juden in Deutschland*, Central Jewish Council for Germany located in Berlin. I didn't know this right away and was saddened by his leaving.

At this point I must tell you something that happened during a sermon that the Rabbi gave at synagogue during the Channukah festival back in 1934. From the raised preaching pulpit, he rhetorically asked the question, "Do you know why Jews don't put the Channukah Menorah lights on the window sill anymore?" There was a young boy who blurted out, "So that Hitler doesn't see that we are

EXHIBIT 7.20 Dr. Max Grünewald, our rabbi, my friend, revered by the Jewish community of Mannheim since 1925.

Jews!" That eleven year old boy was, you guessed it, me.

Going to the Jewish vocational school was tiresome with little time to do much else but rest up for the next day. Nevertheless, there was always a little spare time, especially on weekends, to read, sort postage stamps and put them on album pages. I did not neglect my violin either and practiced regularly although my lessons had been changed to Saturday mornings. Mom, in particular, enjoyed my rehearsing a number of her favorites, among them, "Claire de Lune," "Largo," by Händel, "Nocturn," "Träumerei," by Robert Schuman, "Minuette," "Leise Fliehen Meine Lieder," by Franz Schubert, and other wonderful and exciting pieces.

Since Dad's business was barely surviving, and the business was an extension of the apartment, he spent much more time with Mom while attempting to complete all the paperwork to give us the opportunity to immigrate to Luxembourg. My parents were hoping to wait there until our magic quota number would be called for our turn to leave for America. Dad filled out forms and wrote letters to Pap, Mom's father, in Luxembourg since we hoped that we could stay with him. But first he had to obtain permission from the government of Luxembourg. My parents received permission in January 1938 (see exhibits 7.21 and 7.22 in the appendix for original documents and translations), but it did not include me. My parents were disappointed that I had not received permission to stay with them in Luxembourg. Renewed, but frantic attempts were made by my Opa Raphael in Luxembourg to obtain that permission.

It was a seemingly never-ending process. Dad sent other letters to his brothers, Ernst and Herman in America, to the American Consulate at Stuttgart, Germany, hoping to obtain an appointment to speak to someone, or better, to be summoned to appear for a physical examination. The latter was considered one of the first important hurdles toward obtaining a visa. If you were not physically fit, your chances to immigrate to America were nil.

Progress at the vocational school seemed very slow to me because I was eager to learn as much as I could as quickly as possible. However, one of the goals of our instructors was to instill an appreciation and respect for our tools, equipment, and different metals available for use. For weeks I had to practice with various types and sizes of files on a small cube of iron to make it perfectly straight on all surfaces and sides and perpendicular with respect to each other. I learned how to use precision gauges, calipers, micrometers, and other instruments. It was absolutely essential to acquire the discipline needed to accomplish these apparently simple tasks with accuracy, precision, and quality.

In the meantime Mom and Dad had engaged a private tutor, Blanche Schreiter, to teach French to the three of us since French was preferred over German in Luxembourg. (Although Mother was still fluent in French.) In addition, I was eagerly continuing to learn English at school.

Weekends and occasional national and religious holidays made our isolation from the rest of society more noticeable and uncomfortable. Dad and I played an occasional game of chess, checkers, or *Mühlchen*. Sometimes the three of us played a board game, *Mensch Ärgere Dich Nicht*, translated, "Man Don't Get Angry." Mom wrote letters, read, or knit. Often we listened to German news broadcasts on the radio. Only when I was at home alone would I try to listen to foreign news broadcasts on the short wave. I was very careful to draw all of the curtains and keep the volume barely audible. I knew the consequences only too well if I were caught. All the Nazis had to do was barge in, feel the tubes on the shortwave receiver. If they were hot, that was proof positive. No one was immune from unannounced searches and consequent arrest. Shopping for Mom became much more time consuming due to food scarcity and having to go to different stores several times on the same day or different days. Sometimes Mom had to wait in line for an hour or more. Nothing was simple anymore. We learned to eat stews most of the week, and Mom became pretty good at them. I had no idea that there were so many kinds of stews. Every two or three days Mom changed the flavor by adding slices of salami or other slivers of meat to the stew that consisted primarily of vegetables and cooked meat bones. It was also the first time I experienced eating dandelion soup or salad. Since coffee had to be imported, it was no longer available, likewise chocolate and cocoa to put into a hot cup of milk or water. We drank a lot of *kamillentee*, chamomile tea, a green tea that came from dried leaves of a plant with the same name. At least it was a warm drink. The rationing of food such as butter, eggs, meat products, and other food items was so acute that we resorted to what was known then as *schiebebrot*. A translation of the term would not mean much, so I will have to describe it. Imagine a large slice of rye bread on which one would place a small slice of salami. One would then take a big bite of bread while pushing the salami back, so that in fact, one would only get a taste of the salami. With the second, third, and fourth bite, one would again push the salami back on the bread, so that each time, one would bite off a large piece of bread but only a sliver of salami. In that fashion, a small slice of salami, cheese, meat, etc., was consumed with a large slice of bread, but still gave one a little taste of the scarce food. We got used to it, and it worked. By the way, *schiebe* means "push," and *brot* means "bread." Get it?

Food became so scarce that quite often there was not enough to go around for the three of us. Sometimes when I was still hungry, Mom or Dad gave me food from their plates telling me that they had more than they could eat. Only years later did I realize that they were not truthful and gave me their food when they themselves were still hungry. For my parents, loving their two children was their highest priority, and they expressed that love in many ways that Irene and I have never forgotten. Only on Friday evenings, erev Shabbat, did we have a more substantial and traditional meal. We lit the candles, had a sip of local wine, and said the appropriate blessings before and after the meal. It was at that time that we missed Irene the most; it just wasn't Shabbat without her.

On several occasions, curiosity, sheer spite of the rules, and the longing to see a particular movie made me risk sneaking into a very small and somewhat out-of-the-way theater. It was located at square U1 on the Breitestrasse, now renamed Kurpfalzstrasse. The theater had a maximum capacity of perhaps seventy-five people or less, and was known as the *Floh Kino*, a flea movie theater. It was a theater that most ordinary people did not frequent because it was rundown, dirty, and located in a not too desirable neighborhood. I wore a pair of overalls, raincoat, glasses, and a hat. I removed the glasses and hat once inside and tried to blend in as best I could, and hoped no one would recognize me. After all there was a big sign at the ticket booth stating that it was "unlawful for Jews to enter." Once inside it was dark and smoky. The national and international news were laced with racist and nationalistic propaganda, accompanied by applause and whistles from the audience. I, too, had to applaud in order not to draw attention to myself, but I felt very awkward doing so.

I remember seeing my first *Godzilla* movie there. It had been produced in Japan and the dialogue was spoken in English with German subtitles. The plot was a fantasy about a giant reptile monster terrorizing Tokyo. The film gave me a thrill that to this day I have not forgotten. It was also my first science fiction movie that mixed live photography with special cinematic special effects. But the best part of the entire episode was that I did not get caught. It was the last time that I saw a movie in Mannheim.

1938 was also the last pleasant summer vacation for Irene when she and Uncle Max met in London to see the sights there and also in Ireland. She pleaded and begged him to leave Germany with Aunt Helene, but her appeal was of no avail.

It was a sad day when the time came to say good-bye to my dear cousins, Ernst and Walter, and Aunt Hilde and Uncle Simon. They had received their visas for America, and their passage from Hamburg was scheduled for June 21, 1938, departure on the American liner, *President Harding*. There were handshakes, hugs, kisses, as well as tears. How lucky they were. Would we ever see them again?

EXHIBIT 7.23 My dad's brother, my Uncle Simon and his wife, Aunt Hilde.

EXHIBIT 7.24 AND 7.25 My cousins, Walter and Ernst, Hamburg Harbor, departed June 21, 1938.

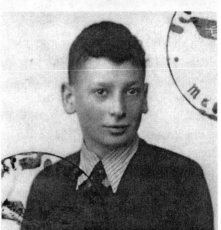

There was no answer. Finally, we received word that they had arrived at New York on July 2 and were well. They were able to start a new life, and we were relieved and envious.

If anyone thought that the Nazis had relented in their humiliation and ruthlessness, they would have been greatly disappointed. Mayor Carl Renninger of Mannheim directed the closing of the old Jewish cemetery located at F,7. This cemetery had been in existence since 1661 and had been in use until 1842. For almost one hundred years no one had been buried there. It was, however, a historical icon attesting to Jewish life in the city for hundreds of years. Now the Nazis demanded that the Jewish Community vacate it in order to create a parking lot. This closing request was not only against the laws of all world cultures and Jewish laws but was also a humiliating insult that hurt every Jew in the community deeply. After many meetings and attempts by the rabbis and Jewish Community

EXHIBIT 7.26 The old cemetery of Mannheim, which had 1113 grave markers. 3586 Jews were buried here before the city fathers decided they needed the area to create a parking lot. See exhibits 7.27 and 7.28 in the appendix for two more photos.

representatives, the city of Mannheim reluctantly agreed for the transfer of all 3,586 remains to the cemetery in use at the time. Mayor Renninger insisted that all the remains were to be buried in one communal plot. It was sometime in July 1938, that Rabbi Lauer of the orthodox Klaus Synagogue and Rabbi Richter, who had assumed Rabbi Grünewald's position, undertook the frustrating and sad task of transfer. Along with the *Chevra Kadisha*, the ritual burial society, and volunteers undertook the unearthing of the remains, the transportation, and the interment into a mass grave demanded by the mayor. He also prohibited the removal of the grave markers except a few. The remaining markers were crushed and their residual was to be used in the parking lot. It was against Jewish ritual laws, but under the dire circumstances, there was no other way. In the past I had gone past the cemetery surrounded by a wall, but never entered. The same was true for the new cemetery for reasons that will be explained elsewhere herein. As far as I was able to determine, the parking lot was never built.

As sad and ghastly as this was, I did not find out about the tragic event until weeks later when articles appeared in the local newspaper and leaflets described the situation as a big triumph for the city and dismissed the entire episode as a removal of an eye sore. Whether it was my preoccupation with my vocational training, or whether my parents wanted to spare me the news, I cannot say. This is for sure; Mom and Dad loved me very much, tried to shelter me from reality, and did not want to add to my frustrations although I was aware of the dire situation we were in more than they perhaps realized.

While the world looked at our plight as an inconvenient side show, Hitler's territorial ambitions toward the East, particularly the Sudetenland and Czechoslovakia, were on the front burner. I heard on Radio Bratislava that Czechoslovakia was mobilizing its army, while ethnic Germans living in those territories were agitating to be annexed by Germany. After threats by Germany and counter threats primarily by France and Great Britain that this could lead to war, a hasty meeting was convened in Berlin on September 30, 1938, my fifteenth birthday. This meeting was attended by the foreign ministers of France and Great Britain, but without consulting Czechoslovakia, a shameful agreement, dictated by the Führer, was signed. The provisions of the agreement permitted Germany to annex the territories of Bohemia and Moravia, the area designated as "Sudentenland," to avoid war. While Neville Chamberlain, prime minister of Great Britain, claimed to have achieved, "Peace in our Time," it was nothing more than a giveaway, another slippery step to war, not peace.

Emboldened by Germany's diplomatic successes, Hungary and Poland took the opportunity, with Germany's consent, to annex other parts of Czechoslovakia adjacent to their borders. Thus, when the German Army marched into the so-called Sudetenland on October 5, 1938, without any resistance, Czechoslovakia had virtually already been dismembered. This was only the continuation of things to come. Again, Hitler had successfully blackmailed the world!

In late October when I arrived at school, rumors were circulating that during the night all Jewish men who were Polish citizens and had Polish passports were being deported from Mannheim. Later that evening I went to see my friend Marion Grodzinski. Calling on the phone was always too dangerous because telephone conversations between Jews were often secretly monitored. Sobbing, she and her mother, Hedwig, confirmed that her father, Friedrich, was among those being deported. Seventy-five men over the age of eighteen were arrested in Mannheim and thousands more all over Germany. As a matter of fact, in most other cities women and children were also arrested. They were transported to the Polish border where they were left to their fate without food or water. Poland would not allow them to cross the border. The resulting chaos was indescribable and led to hardship, sickness, starvation, and death including untold suicides. Friedrich did not survive. Neither did Marion, her sister, and mother who were deported later. I wondered about Albert Kretschmer, a friend who was in the class below me, because he, too, had a father born in Poland. Albert's story did not come to light until 1994 when I watched a video taken by a Russian film crew at the new Jewish cemetery at Mannheim where he was visiting. It wasn't until his name was mentioned, that I realized it was Albert after sixty years later. He had survived.

The ruthless action that occurred on October 27, 1938 to 15,000 Polish Jews was the prelude of other Nazi cruelties to come. All of us, students, teachers, parents, and children were stunned by this action. We were finally convinced that what we had believed to be rumors was now, in actuality, fact. We sensed that other actions against Jews were just a matter of time although we had no idea then what they would be. We tried to determine how we could escape the fate others had already experienced. There were no answers.

It has been just a little over seventy-eight years ago since the incident occurred that I am about to relate. If it had been an inconsequential event, I would not have tried to remember, but this was not insignificant. In fact, it was monstrous. It has been so deeply entrenched in my mind over these many years that only a doctor's scalpel would be able to remove it from my brain.

Wednesday, November 9, 1938, began like any other morning as I rode my bike to the vocational school at Neckarau. Several streets away from my destination I smelled smoke and then heard the crackle of fire. I saw flames shooting upward. As I came closer, I realized that the fire was at the *anlernwerkstätte*. It was impossible for me to get close because of the many people standing around. They were outwardly jubilant, shouting insults against Jews and basically enjoying the calamity engulfing the three large factory buildings and several smaller structures. As I tried to compose myself, I thought it strange that there were no fire trucks, no water hoses, and no ambulances. In fact, there were only a few policemen. Then I heard the Nazi coined word, *aktion*, a word I was very familiar with by then. It meant an event staged against Jews, a pogrom.

I recognized a few of my fellow students standing nearby and exchanged a few words with one of them. He confirmed that, in all probability, this was not a natural random fire. The fire was well planned and executed; its purpose was to burn down all the buildings, simultaneously, although a safe distance separated each of them. He also told me that a truck had been there earlier to arrest and haul away forty students, most of whom I knew, who had arrived before I did. For once I was glad not to have been there earlier. This day, November 9, 1938, was the beginning of the most violent pogrom and public display of anti-Semitism in Germany and world history. There was no way for me to know what was yet to come.

A few days earlier a teenage Jewish immigrant in Paris, upon hearing of his parents' mistreatment during their forced deportation from Germany to Poland, shot the Third Secretary, Ernst vom Rath, at the German Embassy in Paris. Seventeen year old Herschel Grynszpan, the assassin, was caught but never heard from again. Jews expected some sort of reprisal but not the furor that was directed by Hitler and his ministers several days later on November 9.

Back at the scene of the fire I was distraught, frightened, and in a cold sweat panic. Confused, I began my return trip from the fiery ruins of the vocational school. I stood up as I peddled my bike in order to get home as fast as I could. When I turned into the Ring, the boulevard where we lived, I immediately saw a mob of people in front of several apartment houses, including ours. What I saw was unbelievable. Men in street clothing appeared on our balcony carrying armloads of our clothing and throwing them into a heap of other possessions in the yard below. The pile was burning and smoldering. What I didn't know at that moment was that shortly after I had left for school, Nazi storm troopers, disguised in civilian clothes, had broken down the front door of our apartment. They had put my dad under arrest and proceeded to ransack the apartment, demolishing furniture, taking kitchen utensils, glassware, bedding and then throwing it all off the balcony into the courtyard and setting it on fire.

Trying to push my bike through the agitated, cheering crowd, a uniformed SS guard stopped me and asked where I was going. When I told him that I lived there, he escorted me into the apartment house entrance. There, I heard for the first time in my life, screams of my father. The Nazi hoodlums had him lying face down on the floor and were brutally beating him with clubs. He had covered his head with both hands to ward off the blows, while three out of control Nazi beasts shouted profanities and accused him of all sorts of crimes. Dad's head was bleeding, and there was blood on his knuckles and shirt.

My entire body trembled and my voice quivered as I shouted at them to stop beating and kicking him. When that failed, I begged them to stop. They just laughed. Then I heard my mother calling me from the bedroom where she had been locked in. Her voice was tearful and whimpering. I couldn't find the key to the door, and I reassured her as best I could that Dad and I were all right. The brutes continued to break up chairs and other furniture. They carried drawers filled with our belongings down the hall, to the balcony, and then flung them onto the bonfire to the delight of the bystanders. I was in a total state of shock. Had the world spun off its axis? Was it no longer in equilibrium? Or had the world turned into savages?

Attempting to escape the madness, I went into my room that no longer held a bed. The two chests of drawers were gone, with some of the contents on the floor. My books were gone, including my beloved, treasured stamp collection. Pictures that had hung on the wall were smashed and glass was strewn all over the floor. The closet where I had spent hours hanging and arranging my clothes was empty, except for some hangers. I looked behind one panel of drapes where I had always stored my music stand and violin. To my surprise they were still there. Lovingly I picked up my violin case and looked inside.

Unexpectedly, one of the SS men came into the room and in a boisterous voice bellowed, "Is that your violin?" I said, "Yes," and he took it from its case and said, "Follow me." Reluctantly, but without choice, I followed him to the balcony where he then ordered, "Play!" My senses left me. All I could see was the

EXHIBIT 7.29 Mom and Dad sitting on our balcony a year before our entire household goods were tossed into the yard and burned, and from which I had to play my violin to the amusement of cheering people, November 9, 1938.

pile of smoldering rubble, the remains of our belongings that had been ruthlessly and savagely plundered and destroyed. The people below watched happily and applauded approvingly as I stood in complete helplessness. The SS man stood right next to me and prodded me again to play. I played, but I don't remember what or how long I played. Tears ran down my cheeks and blurred my vision. I didn't have to see; I could hear the people shouting insults, cheering, and jeering. It seemed as if I were playing happy melodies on my violin at my own funeral. It was a gruesome feeling I have never forgotten. It was Dante's Inferno.

I stopped playing when I realized that the SS man who had ordered me to the balcony was no longer standing beside me. When I retreated from the balcony into the apartment, Dad was sitting slumped over on the floor against the wall. I located the spare key and opened the bedroom where my mother had been locked up. One Storm Trooper was standing in front of our demolished apartment door. All of the others had gone. Suddenly I was aware of the quiet broken only by my Mom's sobbing and Dad's moaning. Most of the towels, linens, and first aid material was gone, but Mom and I did our best to attend to Dad's cuts and bruises, washing and wiping some. The irony was that I could not muster anger. I was too numbed and completely disoriented to think rationally.

The ferocity, brutality, physical and mental humiliation we had just suffered had not completely set in when two policemen appeared and ordered Dad and me to put on our coats and follow them. We no longer had coats, but we followed them without knowing where they would take us. Mom pleaded with them to tell her, but all they would say was "to the police station." Dad's legs hurt from the beatings, and he was limping. I put my arm around his waist to steady him and also tried to console him. People gave us dirty looks as if we were criminals. Some even spat at us and called us names. We passed other houses with destruction similar to ours, and we saw other Jewish men being escorted by police, presumably to a police station.

It seemed odd to me that we passed within the vicinity of the nearest police station. We were marched, no, *paraded*, through downtown on exhibit for all to see the dirty Jews and what had become of us. It was a degradation of the worst kind, but we could do nothing about it. It was cold outside, but in our physical and mental states we did not feel it, nor did it matter to us. We turned onto the street where our synagogue was located and received the shock of our lives. On the steps and in the street in front of our house of worship, pews, candelabras, carpets, prayer books, the ornate portal doors, the Torah scrolls, and other objects were all hacked and torn to pieces. Some of the stained windows had been forcibly removed

EXHIBIT 7.31 Our synagogue after it had been demolished during Kristallnacht, November 9, 1938 by the Nazis.

and smashed on the ground, the many colored glass pieces strewn all over the street. There was another pile of furnishings still smoldering. The synagogue itself seemed to have been torched because we noticed smoke coming from the inside. I could see a large opening in the wall where the *aron hakodesh*, the shrine for the sacred Torahs, had been. I found out later that the sanctuary, that wall in particular, had been blown up by dynamite.

The police had taken us past the synagogue to humiliate us and to show us that the Nazis could mistreat and destroy our culture, and us, at will. It was part of their ritual to prove their Aryan supremacy. From there they took us to a police station where we were separated. I was taken to a large room crowded with boys of various ages, most of whom I knew. At a table in front of the group, each of us had to answer a few questions and then was ordered to exit the room via one or the other of two doors. My turn came, and when I was asked my age, I uttered, "thirteen," even though I was fifteen. I had lied! The SS who had called my name kicked me in my behind and said, "Go home to your mother. You are too young!" With that he pointed to the door I was to exit and was free to go home.

I ran until I was out of breath. Then I slowed down and tried to figure out what the SS man had meant when he said, "Go home to your mother. You are

EXHIBIT 7.30 After the inside was looted and destroyed, specific structures were dynamited. The synagogue could not be dynamited in totality because of the damage it would cause to the other buildings in the immediate vicinity.

EXHIBIT 7.32 Another view of the inside of our synagogue after its destruction by the Nazis, November 9, 1938.

too young!" What was I too young for, and what was happening to my dad? No answers came to me. I arrived at the apartment and re-lived the chaos left by the perpetrators. Mother was sitting on a chair in the business section of the apartment that was, surprisingly, completely untouched. None of the cartons that held merchandise or any of the fixtures and furnishings of the business had been ransacked. What was the reason for that? Of course it was by design, just as the "spontaneous" break in and total destruction of our apartment had been.

Mother was visibly shaken and distraught, and my trying to console her had no apparent effect. On top of all her distress, I pleaded with her to let me go briefly to the train station because it had always been the best source of local, national, and international news. Luckily, nothing had happened to my bike since I had left it outside the apartment. Even though we were only a few blocks from the station, riding was quicker than walking. Upon my arrival I noticed more activity than usual. There were a number of Jewish acquaintances huddled in a small group. They were very agitated and whispered to me that all of the men arrested that day, including my Dad, had been brought to the station earlier in trucks. From there they were marched at double time through the railroad station and were herded into freight cars that were immediately locked and heavily guarded. Later, the train with several hundred men and boys was seen leaving the station heading south, destination unknown.

The news was devastating! In talking with others, there was high speculation that all of them would wind up at a concentration camp. There was also some bittersweet news. Of all of the boys who had been taken to the police station as I had been, many who were my age, and all who were older, were taken away on the train with the others. Because I had lied about my age, the SS officer had spared me from the transport ordeal and sent me home. Suddenly I realized what he meant when he said, "you are too young!" Why I lied about my age, I cannot say. At this stage, my thinking was not too rational. Perhaps, just perhaps, an angel had guided my answer.

When I returned home and told my Mother what I had learned, she sobbed uncontrollably and I could not console her. The janitor of the building, Mr. Brinkman, and his wife came to help clean up the apartment, and they helped put the few remaining things, including some from the front yard that could be salvaged, into different rooms. They did all that, very carefully, knowing full well that they were not allowed to lift a finger to help a Jew. The Nazis had special ways to deal with so called "Jew lovers and collaborators." The mob in the street had disbanded and it was frightfully quiet. Then Mom noticed that the safe on rollers, which normally stood in the business office, had disappeared. In the safe Dad had kept business ledgers, receipts, inventory records, documents, savings account bank books, insurance policies, and passports. Dad had also kept cash as well as all of our valuable jewelry therein. The Nazis must have taken it away.

However, for the time being, as important as the safe's contents were, possessions did not matter anymore. What did matter to Mom and me was the safe return of Dad and our safety.

We closed the wooden shutters on all of our windows, most of which were shattered. I helped Herr Brinkman repair the entrance door temporarily, although the door could not be locked since the brutes had broken the door down. We salvaged one large, partially burned mattress and placed it on the bedroom floor providing us a place to sleep. The last thing I did before going to sleep was to make a trip to the attic with my violated violin in its case. I had wrapped it in a bright red bedspread also salvaged from the yard. I found a good spot in a corner of the attic where I lovingly hid it, hopefully, from further savagery. Then I did one other thing. I made a silent oath to myself:

To remember, not to forget, not a minute, not a second, of what happened, and the faces and the fists that made it happen. This day shall not have happened for naught and those responsible would be held accountable so help me God.

Neither Mom nor I slept much during the night, and every unknown sound inside and out, created new anxieties. I tried as hard as I could to think of a solution to our immediate problem, but there was none. We both arose by 6:00 a.m., and as I opened one of the shutters on the side of the apartment, I got a big surprise. There on the outside window sill between the shutter and the window ledge was a bottle of milk, some eggs, butter and a loaf of bread. We immediately speculated as to who had brought this "manna" from heaven. A week or so later we determined that our hunch was right. Our grocer, Herr Kress, at great risk to himself, had brought the food items during the night. Yes, at the time there were still a few Germans who tried as best they could to help Jews who were now in a desperate situation. Alas, there were too few!

I biked again to the train station for the latest news, which was not encouraging. During the night the Nazis had set fire to the large building of the Jewish Altersheim, a Jewish home for the aged at Neustadt, a city about sixteen miles west of Mannheim (see exhibit 7.33 in the appendix to see a photo of the rebuilt facility). As fate would have it, this is where Gertrude Wolff, my future wife, was born and raised. Several people had been burned alive. The surviving old and sick people were evacuated from the burning building, loaded onto open trucks and, regardless of their physical conditions and the cold weather, driven to the Jewish Home for the Aged at Mannheim. There was a great need for volunteers to assist. Hearing that and in spite of my mother's pleading, I went to the Home for the Aged to help. The other bad news was that freight trains and trains made up of cattle cars escorted by heavily armed guards were carrying Jews from other cities in a southerly direction through the train station. There seemed to be no end to the tragedies unfolding.

The conditions that I witnessed at the Home for the Aged almost defy description and were desperate. The combination of the Home for the Aged and Hospital, which had a normal capacity of about eighty people, was now confronted with giving refuge and care to an additional 350 people, perhaps 300 from Neustadt. The picture was that of a hospital after a major disaster. These old and sick people still in nightshirts and without shoes, were covered with blankets and stretched out in the halls, the laundry room and operating room floors. Two person rooms were now occupied by five or more. There were people who had been beaten badly and hurt as evidenced by bandages. The moaning, groaning, crying, screaming, and pleading of these patients was almost unbearable for me. Rabbi Karl Richter, who was Rabbi Grünewald's successor, had been placed in an isolation room with a sign that read "Communicable Disease" in order to keep him from being taken away. He was twenty-eight years old, and from what I remember, had a pretty wife, Ruth, and an infant daughter. I was glad to see my friend Günter Kaufmann. He and I did what we could to carry food, drink, and blankets and consoled these poor souls who did not comprehend what had happened. Food staples had become scarce since no one had planned on feeding three times as many people and the usual suppliers were scared to make additional deliveries. It was only during the night's darkness that a few deliveries of bread and milk arrived. We assisted patients into wheelchairs and took them to different locations to be examined and treated. We even carried some on stretchers. Basically, we did everything we were told to do by the head nurse Pauline Maier, nurses, doctors, and those in charge. Men and several teenagers who had been badly beaten up arrived from different towns and cities because this was the only Jewish hospital within a forty mile radius. By order of the Nazis in charge, there was no destruction of this facility although there were unpleasant intrusions and confrontations.

The violence accompanied by indescribable savagery had not ended. To me it seemed as if the devil in hell had taken the upper hand on earth. The Nazis had gone berserk, and with them, all of Germany. I thought and hoped that if a reckoning was ever to come, all of the Germans who followed the Nazi regime's orders and wishes must then share in the blame and punishment for the hideous crimes perpetrated against the Jews.

Mom was afraid to leave the house although we desperately needed money. She did, however, write a check to Mr. Kress, our kind grocer, for him to cash it at the bank. I took the check to him and explained the situation. He understood and even gave me money from the cash register before taking the check to the bank. I was exhausted, distraught, and devastated.

Later that evening I went to the train station with slips of paper and pencils. As the trains came into the station with Jewish prisoners and stopped for change of guards, I passed pieces of paper and pencils through the small freight car openings, asking them to write down their names and addresses. After depleting all of the paper, I went home and from the office wrote postcards with several names and addresses of men from the same city, and mailed it to only one address. Basically I wrote, "I saw Mr. (Name) coming through Mannheim by train going south. Please inform families of the others listed below." I took postcards from Dad's business stationery supplies. It was a labor of love combined with sheer desperation. I mentioned what I was doing to some of my younger buddies who thought it was a great idea and did likewise. It was dangerous work and we watched out for each other and for ourselves to be sure we weren't caught.

News about what was happening in other parts of Germany and Austria came to us painfully slow. Our radio had been hacked to pieces, and the newspaper gave no specific details. It was rumored that all of the men arrested in and around Mannheim, along with others coming through Mannheim on trains going south, were incarcerated at concentration camp Dachau. Men arrested in other parts of Germany were shipped to concentration camps elsewhere. This was confirmed when some families in the city received form letters from Dachau stating that Mr. (Name) had died either during transport or for some other reason. In all, 35,000 Jewish males from all over Germany had been taken to concentration camps where they were humiliated, punished, beaten, and tortured not for crimes they had committed, but because they were Jews. If that weren't enough, in addition to the physical violations on those two days, 100 persons of Jewish faith had been brutally and publicly murdered. As I found out many years later, another 280 escaped that fate by taking their own lives. 8,000 Jewish owned stores and businesses were demolished, and sadly, 1,200 synagogues were shamefully desecrated, burned, and looted. That was the total tally in Germany. The shame on the German people for their barbaric and cowardly deeds will stay with them forever.

The police did not interfere with the perpetrators, the SA and SS in civilian clothes. Fire departments stood by to be sure that fires did not spread to real estate owned by so-called Aryans. If this were not enough, more evil arrived shortly after the so called *kristallnacht*, the Night of Broken Glass. As part of the further implementation of the "Four Year Plan," that was set into motion in October 1936 by Field Marshall Herman Goring, Jews were ordered to cease all economic endeavors. Operation of any and all Jewish businesses was to cease no later than December 1938, in other words, within the next forty days. All contracts regarding Jewish businesses, their owners, or employees were invalidated immediately.

On top of all this agony, and as an individual insult, a fine of one billion Marks, equivalent at that time to about $400,000,000 was levied on all Jewish communities in Germany, Austria, and the Sudetenland to pay for the destruction of all property caused by the Nazi hoodlums on kristallnacht. It was the ultimate insult for us, the victims, having to reimburse the Nazis for the destruction and suffering they had brought upon us. An additional 25% tax was levied on all Jewish property taken out of the country when people left Germany permanently. Both of these measures meant that some emigrants could hardly take any of their remaining belongings along. Some people had become so impoverished that they had no money for transportation to leave. They had been bled of all their savings and had no money left to pay this exit tax. I was baffled as to how this would affect our immediate family but was more concerned at this time about saving our family's sanity and our lives.

In the meantime, there was no word or news about Dad's condition at Dachau. I kept returning to the train station at night, and occasionally, I saw a returnee arriving from Dachau. I found out that they had been threatened and sworn to secrecy and would not talk to me for fear of reprisals. Each one looked as if he had risen from his own grave. One night in late January 1939, I was prowling around the station when the most wonderful miracle happened. As one of the trains slowed and stopped, I saw a compartment door open. A figure of a person stepped out, and as it came closer, I realized it was Dad. His head was shaven, his face unshaven, he was shivering because he had no coat, and he wore someone else's clothing under which he had stuffed newspapers to keep himself warm. I was ecstatic, but neither of us could do more than fall into each other's arms. I cried, but Dad was emotionless and only said, "Good to be home!"

I took a less frequented route through the terminal to avoid making a scene or being recognized by others who knew us. Along the way I shed my overcoat and cap and gave them to him to wear. He did not answer any of my questions; he had nothing to say to me. He seemed comfortable with the warm coat, and the cap hid his baldness. It was cold, but in the excitement I did not feel it. It was, perhaps, ten or ten thirty p.m., yet the boulevard was empty. I can't remember what Mom was doing as we entered the apartment. She let out a scream when she saw Dad, and then they were in each other's arms. Tears ran down her face, and looking at him, she said over and over, "*Ach nein, ach nein, ach nein!*" "Oh no, oh no, oh no!" She couldn't believe her husband had returned. Taking my coat and hat from him her tears flowed more because she barely recognized him with his mustache gone and head shaved. He looked more like a ghost than a human being.

This pathetic looking man, my father, had indeed come home. In spite of all that had changed him, Mom and I were happy, but most of all thankful. I got a chair for him, but he would not sit down until I brought him the only pillow we still had. I found out later from Mom, who had managed to undress him and give him a warm bath, that he had welts on his buttocks and sores on his arms from being beaten, kicked, and who knew what else.

During that night I could not sleep because of my anger toward my enemies, the Nazis. Their brutal excesses at Dachau concentration camp, where my father had been held, on thousands of innocent, helpless men and boys was disgusting, shameful, and degrading. All of a sudden I realized that I hated the perpetrators, the German people who had allowed this to happen and even participated in this savagery. Should I become another Hershel Grynszpan? No! That would be counterproductive and result in the loss of my life as well as many others. I thought of revenge, not now, but when the time was ripe. Would any of us live to see that day? I prayed for that day! In the meantime, many caskets had come from Dachau with the remains of those that had died. It was against the law for anyone to open the caskets and burials had to be undertaken in the presence of so called law enforcers. Urns with the ashes of loved ones were also received from the Concentration Camp Buchenwald. Several funerals took place day in, day out, for weeks and months.

In the morning as Dad still slept, the doorbell rang and a Frau Grimm demanded to come in, pointing to a big swastika button, a symbol of the Nazi party, on her long leather coat. She asked to see the business office and storerooms. Strutting around, she uttered suddenly, "All of this belongs to me! Give me the keys! No one is allowed in here without my explicit permission! Give me the keys!" She locked the doors to our business and left.

Later, when Dad arose, Mom and I told him what had occurred. We thought he would be surprised, but he wasn't. In a slow and halting voice he explained to us that while at camp he had been approached by an SS guard by the name of Karl Grimm. This man offered to free Dad from his desperate circumstances provided that Dad would sign over to him the ownership of the business, J&S Kahn, without any further financial consideration. This was not a legitimate offer, but a threat. Dad realized that he was not in a bargaining position, and recognized the offer for what it was, a buy-out of his life, a swap of his business to save his life. It was, in fact, the expropriation of Jewish owned business assets under conditions of threats of torture and possibly death. While SS guard Grimm became owner of our business and its assets through extortion, his wife, Frau Grimm, claimed ownership only one day after Dad had arrived back home. It was the perfect scheme by the Nazis to remove all Jews from the German economy through the most degrading public rituals and unconscionable humiliation. Dad's life at the concentration camp was worth nothing, and refusing SS guard Grimm's offer would have marked him a dead man. What could possibly happen next?

All of the fantasies that the Nazis had dreamed about, namely how to intimidate Jews and destroy their wills, had actually come about through specific decrees and laws and horrible pogroms. There was no longer any prospect of living in Germany, and hopes for some miracle intervention from the outside world were no longer realistic. Any form of resistance at this point was deemed futile. My question was no longer what country we would immigrate to, but how soon.

Dad recovered slowly, and Frau Grimm, for obviously selfish motives, had civilized discussions with him about the operation of the business. She managed to locate the office safe that had disappeared to the Gestapo headquarters and managed to have it delivered back so she could examine the books. You can imagine how difficult it was for Dad to talk to Frau Grimm and give her advice on many matters. This was the business that he and his brother, Simon, had established over many years, and now it had been virtually stolen from him. But all of this gave him precious time to plan for leaving the country. Unwittingly, Frau Grimm became instrumental in obtaining certain necessary papers and approvals from authorities that Dad would have had considerable problems with. It was somewhat of a hate relationship that, nevertheless, enabled a temporary, civilized discourse because of her need to know as much about the business, merchandise and customers as possible. It was through her Nazi party connections that Dad located our car that had been seized by the Nazi mob on November 10 and driven off to a garage. Although Frau Grimm assisted Dad in pleading with authorities, he was unable to get the car. They told him that if he made any further requests for the automobile they would send him to the KZ (an abbreviation of *Konzentrationslager*, or concentration camp) for good! Years later after the war I found out that Frau Grimm's maiden name was Guthman. I wonder if she had Jewish ancestors named Gutman? What did it matter!

This was a particularly distressing time in all of our lives. It was a period of utter darkness from which we had no means of escape. We were like animals in a cage, constantly poked with sticks, mocked and threatened without immediate hope of escape. It seemed as if we were alone on planet Earth, isolated from others. The phone lines had been ripped out by the Nazis, and since Jews rarely ventured out of their homes, there were no visitors. We knew that there were others in similar predicaments and worse, shut off from the outside world. Where was God? I had been taught that God All Mighty was with me and my loved ones in time of peril. Where was God now? Had he failed us? Had we failed him?

After determining how much of the November pogrom destruction fine we had to pay, Dad went to the Gestapo finance office to pay the ransom. There, completely surprised, he was given the letter from the Justice Minister of Luxembourg granting me temporary stay in the Duchy of Luxembourg, signed November 19, 1938. (See exhibit 7.34 in the appendix)

Through our sympathetic apartment building janitor, Dad also made arrangements to purchase some of the necessary furniture, like beds, linens, etc., to compensate for our burned and destroyed essentials. When I asked if there was enough money left to buy clothes, Dad smiled briefly and shook his head up and down. Over the next months, we re-acquired those things necessary for our immediate sustenance, and also items to use in other parts of the world if we were lucky. We needed dishes, tableware, towels, linens and hundreds of other things normally taken for granted that the Nazis had destroyed. All of this was very difficult for us.

Dad was smoking more heavily than before he was incarcerated. He was very restless, nervous, and wanted more cigarettes and cigars although both were rationed and hard to get. He continued his silence about Camp Dachau, but mentioned the names of some of the men he saw. His big secret was how he and others were mistreated by the Nazis. He took these images to his grave and did not want to open old wounds. I received a letter dated April 21, 1986, from Herbert Isaak of Mannheim, who lived in Myrtle Beach, South Carolina. He wrote, "In November 1938, I was taken to the concentration camp Dachau, and I was together with your Father. After my release I went illegally to Belgium to await my entry papers, the visa to the U.S.A. I made it to Belgium with the financial help of your Uncle Max Cohen in Cologne." Not a word about their treatment at Dachau! A bit of a side note: Herbie, as he was known to us, has a sister, Lotte, with whom I have been in touch for many years. Aunt Ida Kahn Isaak, my Father's sister, was the wife of Herbie's father's brother. Lotte and Herbie called my parents Uncle Joseph and Aunt Martha.

Mom, Dad, and I were able to obtain our passports with our new name added, "Sarah" for Mom, "Israel" for Dad and me. At the time I thought of these added names as an insult and badge of shame. Today I look at that entry in the passport as a badge of honor.

One of the very last things I did before we left was to obtain a letter from the Office of Economic Assistance of the Jewish Community to certify that I had been enrolled in the Vocational School for Metal Fabrication.

EXHIBIT 7.35 My new passport with the letter "J" for Jew and my new middle name "Israel."

Those last few months created an unusual struggle within me. The frustration of a useless fight against the barbarism around me was ever present although there seemed to be an unnatural calm without the realization of an end to our plight. The immediate world around me had collapsed, and I was a prisoner of devastating circumstances. Jewish life of any kind had come to an end. Our schools, synagogues, and every bit of economic and cultural life had been destroyed.

The whereabouts of my friends and their well-being was constantly on my mind and in my silent prayers. It is hard to describe the love I had in my heart for the friends who deserved that love and who had suddenly vanished. The cruelty of the Nazi bastards and

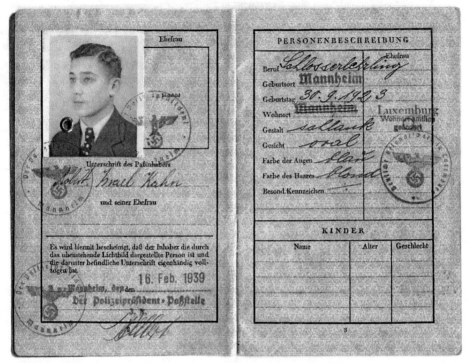

EXHIBIT 7.36 Inside my passport, my new middle name of "Israel." Also shown is the country to which I will soon move: Luxembourg. They've already decided I no longer live in Mannheim, and it is therefore crossed out.

their equally barbaric collaborators were however incapable of breaking my will to live except momentarily.

It was their sadistic slogans and the relentless silence by those I thought civilized that tore at my heart and soul. Dad, Mom and I could no longer depend on anyone with certainty. The idea of mutual trust and equality that had existed prior to Hitler's rise to power between Jew and non-Jew had disappeared. Often I had the feeling of being transplanted, as in a dream, into a strange yet undiscovered wilderness, constantly defending myself against wild animals and primitive people. And then, when reality set in again, my will to live under existing conditions was constantly challenged.

Desperation and utter despair lured my thoughts again and again to ending it all. Love for my family, my romantic yet naïve notion about life, the burning desire to tell the world what was happening to Jews, and the urgency to rid the world of these monstrous, out-of-control criminals made me put those thoughts aside. Today I know that I made the right decision!

Strengthened by his diplomatic and military victories, Hitler no longer had to fear intervention by other world powers into matters concerning his merciless mistreatment and terrorizing of Jews and other political opponents within his reach. Large public protests and demonstrations in France, England, and

America against Germany's excesses toward Jews fell on deaf ears. In fact, these activities increased our vulnerability and intensified the ruthless persecution. Ugly rumors abounded about how Jews were being treated elsewhere. Thousands of refugees from the Spanish Civil War had crossed into France, and Jews in Czechoslovakia were trying to flee in anticipation of an imminent German invasion. Meanwhile, Germany's pride of the fleet, the world's fastest battleship, the *Bismark*, was launched, an open threat to the world's navies.

The boldest move yet was Hitler's triumphant invasion of Czechoslovakia that reached its capital, Prague, within hours of crossing the border on March 15, 1939. This event stunned the world. Europe was a boiling cauldron, and we were in its midst not knowing how to save ourselves.

The conditions were ripe for people to panic and grasp at straws no matter how fragile. In earlier years, 55,000 Jews from all over Europe with the right immigration papers had been lucky to book passage on ships going to America. Others had taken chances on ships to Cuba hoping, eventually, to obtain the proper papers there. In June 1939, we heard about the ordeal that befell over 900 Jews who had used their remaining life savings to book passage on the S.S. *St. Louis* from Hamburg, Germany, to Havana, Cuba. When they arrived at the port of Havana, the Cuban government reneged on its promise and did not admit them. Pleas to the Cuban as well as the American governments to open their ports to the desperate refugees were of no avail. The ship had no choice but to turn back after this tragic, month-long odyssey. Belgium finally let the disillusioned, weary travelers stay in its country where their fate, again, was uncertain. There was no safe haven for us anywhere, and foreign embassies were giving the cold shoulder to asylum seekers. So far, only 43,000 Jews had managed to leave for Palestine, among them my cousin, Helmut Isaak. 32,000 others were displaced refugees somewhere in Europe, living fearfully under incredible conditions. We would soon be among them.

Not having been able to obtain all the necessary exit papers from the Gestapo and elsewhere, Mom and Dad decided that I should leave for Luxembourg alone, hoping that they would be able to follow me in the near future. Discussion of this and related subjects were heart-wrenching with tears, and sleepless nights for us all. In the meantime, we had been unable to communicate the true facts of our personal lives to Irene in France because of censorship. She had to rely on general French news coverage, which said nothing specifically about her family, and the horrendous drama we had been through.

CHAPTER EIGHT

Luxembourg: Short Reprieve from Persecution

It was May 1, 1939, and after many goodbyes, hugs, kisses, reminders of "do's and don'ts," tears, and wipes, I was on the train standing by the open window with my two suitcases. Mom and Dad held my hand; Mom cried and Dad tried to comfort her while giving me words of caution and encouragement. The locomotive whistle sounded and the steam poured out from under the wheels as the train lumbered into motion. All of a sudden my hands separated from theirs as they stood still and I moved away. Their voices mixed with the noise of the train, and I could no longer hear them; I only saw their hands wave and their lips move. As the train moved faster, Mom and Dad became smaller, and their waving white handkerchiefs finally disappeared.

I was alone on my way to Luxembourg, the first time making the trip without my family. I was a frightened fifteen and a half year old kid, and I knew that I would not see Mannheim and my friends for a long time, possibly ever again. After the trauma my family and I had been through because of the Nazi persecution, I didn't know if I would ever see my parents and sister again, although she was still in Lille, France. The trip to Luxembourg was not enjoyable, and the beautiful scenery, the river Rhine, castles, and towns were no longer important. The monotonous noises of the train as the wheels rolled over each section of track finally lulled me to sleep. I was glad when we stopped at the border town of Wasserbillig, and the German border police returned my visa for temporary stay in Luxembourg and the passport stamped with the big "J" and my new middle name, "Israel." They had searched my suitcases and asked many questions while I answered, perspired from fright, but at last it was over. The locomotive was changed and the train moved slowly to Igel, the border town of Luxembourg where I could finally breathe a bit easier. Upon showing the gendarmes my passport and my visa, and receiving a friendly salute, I settled down knowing that I had finally escaped the fangs of the Nazi hordes.

Luxembourg was a gem in the multitude of Western European countries. A nation about the size of Rhode Island, 999 square miles, even today it is overlooked by many who pride themselves as geographically and travel astute. Tucked between France to the south, Belgium to the west, and Germany to the east, it packed an unusual number of exciting things of interest into a small area. Back in those days, it was about seven hours by train east of Paris, and about four and one-half hours west of Coblenz on the Rhine in Germany. The capital of Grand

EXHIBIT 8.1 The Palace of the Duke and Duchess of Luxembourg. Additional photos of Luxembourg are shown in the appendix as exhibits 8.2 - 8.5.

Duché was also named Luxembourg City. It had picturesque medieval ramparts clinging to a steep ravine although the nearby newer city became very modern. The old section built upon the site of a tenth-century fortress and castle stood on top of a sheer rock ledge that dropped several hundred feet into narrow valleys. There, two tiny streams, the Petrusse and the Alzette, snaked their way through as if they were silver threads.

I will temporarily digress from my journey in May 1939 to recount some of the areas in Luxembourg I had enjoyed in my previous visits. There was a walk along the ledge, the Chemin de la Corniche, which was like nothing else in Europe. The spectator could look straight down into tiny medieval stone houses at the bank of the Alzette reminding one of pictures in a book of fairy tales. Making an about face, narrow, twisted streets of the old city led from the ruins of the original castle, the Grand Ducal Palace, built in 963. The Palace, where the Duchess and Duke lived had been constructed in the 15th Century in Spanish Renaissance style, with high pointed towers and an ornate balcony.

Behind the Palace, where the Duke and Duchess resided, was the Place Guillaume, a large square where a flower and vegetable market was held several times each week. Beyond the square, interrupted by the beautiful Cathedral of Notre Dame, were modern boulevards lined with cafés, *patisseries* (bakeries) and high quality stores. The center of the city was the Place d'Armes, surrounded by cafés, restaurants, and bars. In spring and summer tables were outside for people to enjoy the tranquility and the music that came from a bandstand centered in the Place. People generally spoke their dialect, Letzeburgish, although they were conversant in French and German. The cuisine at restaurants was basically French and German plus local dishes including *pommes frites*, french fries, which I learned to love.

Within a few weeks in Luxembourg I had explored this wonderful city with its large parks and the deep valley known as the Grund. The latter required a steep climb but a fairly easy descent. I also visited the ancient underground fortifications and tunnels known as Casemates, carved deep into the rock with fourteen miles of crisscross labyrinths under the city. Very interesting was the Pont du Chateau, the Castle Bridge built in the form of a Roman aqueduct dating from 1735. From there was a magnificent view of the suburb of Clausen at the foot of rocky cliffs carrying the remainders of ancient forts and also below the suburb of Pfaffenthal. The Grand Duchess Charlotte Bridge straddled both suburbs. In comfortable walking distance on a hillside was an old Austrian fortress dating back to 1733 known as Trois Glands, "Three Acorns," which I visited sometimes because of its charm.

The entire country's population was only 360,000, one of Europe's more sparsely settled countries. Thanks to its iron and steel industries, its agricultural resources, the great power output of Radio Luxembourg, it boasted one of the continent's highest living standards, and still does today. People living in the Grand Duché had always enjoyed the good life, and while it was mainly Roman Catholic, approximately 900 Jews of Luxembourg nationality lived there at the time. About 1,000 additional Jews lived there since 1927, not having obtained Luxembourg citizenship yet. Another 1,600-2,000 refugees, like myself and later my parents, had found exile there between 1933 and 1939. The additional influx of Jews seeking asylum became a considerable burden on the Jewish community because most were forbidden to engage in any economic endeavors and had to rely on welfare support. This made immigrants and refugees rather unpopular.

A beautiful and elaborate Moorish style synagogue stood almost in the heart of the business district on the corner Rue Aldringen and Rue Notre Dame. It was built around the year 1895. Since there was no separation between Church and State in Luxembourg, Judaism was treated as a state religion, and the state supported the upkeep of the synagogue as well as the salaries and housing costs of the cantor and rabbi. Because of these legal arrangements, the rabbi and the chairman of the synagogue board were always invited to official state events. In turn, the synagogue held services honoring national holidays that were also attended by government officials. Often the Grand Duchess or her son, Prince Jean, who was two years older than me (to the day), would be in attendance. I was informed that in the house across the street from the synagogue, Franz Liszt gave his last piano recital in 1886.

EXHIBIT 8.6 Synagogue in Luxembourg.

However, I did not come to this beautiful, neutral, freedom-loving country as a tourist. I had come to escape from the torment delivered upon my family and me by the brainwashed people of Germany. I lived with my grandfather, Opa Raphael Joseph, and prepared myself for further flight to whichever country would offer me a haven of freedom. How and when this movement was to happen was a total mystery to me and to others who had fled the Nazis to find temporary refuge here. I had been expelled with no place to go for safety since foreign governments were refusing entry to Jews who had become impoverished and destitute. Most countries were unwilling to shoulder such burdens. One could not plan future escapes, but lived only in the moment. In short, I lived one day at a time with words and prayers of hope silently on my lips and in my mind.

When I arrived at the gare, the railroad station in Luxembourg, I did not have to look very long before I saw Uncle Berny, my Mother's only brother, and his son, Georges, on the passenger platform. We waved to each other, and then after my suitcases were on the ground, I was hugged and kissed with a hearty, *Bonjour, Robert*. In French pronunciation, the "t" in my name was silent, and it sounded nice.

It took me only a split second to realize that I was in Luxembourg where Letzeburgish was spoken first, then French, and German last. That order was dictated because the Letzeburgers, living in close proximity to Germany, did not appreciate the recent years of Nazi propaganda nor the oppressive and aggressive

EXHIBIT 8.7 Uncle Berny and his pride and joy, the American made De Soto automobile. Next to him is his wife, my Aunt Marthe.

regime. As a matter of fact, I quickly realized that I had better learn the local dialect unless I wanted to incur dirty looks and verbal abuse for being mistaken for a *knaschtige Preuss*, a dirty German.

Uncle Berny, Cousin Georges, and I proceeded through the cavernous railroad terminal to the street where an American De Soto automobile was parked. I could tell how proud Uncle Berny was of that car. I found out later that he was one of the very few in Luxembourg who was able to boast owning an American car. It was one of his hobbies.

We drove down Hollericherstrasse until we came to Opa's house, #83. He was sitting in front of the door waiting for us. He was now seventy-nine years old, had tearing eye problems, and walked with a cane. He had aged visibly. After the traditional kiss on both cheeks, he hollered for Anna, the live-in maid, who then took my suitcases and backpack upstairs to my room. After saying *au revoir* to Uncle Berny and Cousin Georges, I went up the squeaky spiral staircase to my assigned room and threw myself on the bed, tired and confused. Without my parents and friends, I wondered when or if I would see them again. I fell asleep and awoke a few hours later when Anna came to my door to let me know that it was time for supper.

The three of us ate in the kitchen where, now and then, Anna was interrupted by neighbors who came with their containers to buy milk, and/or cottage cheese. They would stay a few minutes for an exchange of neighborhood gossip with Opa and Anna in the *stub*, the living room. I learned later that Anna was actually more than a housekeeper and maid. She was my Opa Raphael's absolute confidante. Months later this relationship would turn out to be an impediment.

When I was younger, I loved being at Opa's house, especially when Oma Malchen was still alive. Now, as much as I still loved being at Opa's house, there were certain things I had to get used to now that I was older. For one thing the only bathroom was the size of a large broom closet, and it was downstairs toward the rear of the house. It had been added not too many years before, making the outhouse near the dung pile pit obsolete. The toilet paper, however, still consisted of squares torn from old newspapers which were hung on a nearby hook. In the evening when darkness began to fill the living room and kitchen with their low windows and ceilings, Opa objected to anyone turning on lights until absolutely necessary because electricity was expensive, or so he asserted. Nevertheless, light bulbs were all of low 40 wattage, giving off barely enough light to see where one was going, and definitely insufficient for serious reading. What surprised me more than anything else was that Opa and Anna went to bed, she on the third floor in the attic, at 9:00 p.m. every evening. At that time it was *math luchten out*, lights out! And that was that!

Of course, I also realized that Anna and Opa rose at 4:00 a.m. every morning to clean out the barn, feed the cows with the hay stored above, and prepare slop, a heated mixture of malt feed and water. Then the cows had to be milked by hand as milking machines had not yet been invented. Next the cream had to be separated from the milk by running it through a centrifuge separator. All that work was accomplished while I was still asleep. By the time I awoke, Opa was resting in his *fauteuil*, armchair.

Another surprise and inconvenience was the absence of running water upstairs. Each afternoon I had to fill up one or two water pitchers in the kitchen with which I would wash myself the following morning. Under the bed stood a chamber pot for use during the night. Everything had to be emptied out downstairs in the morning. All of these things were a far cry from what I had been used to at home. But I was here now at age fifteen and a half, no longer a vacationing grandchild, but a young man in exile. I didn't dare question or complain about things, but I cried myself to sleep several times during the first few weeks.

One of my objectives while I was in Luxembourg was to continue my preparation to learn the metal-working and fabrication trade, and to complete my apprenticeship in that field. Some work permit approvals had to be obtained from the Luxembourg authorities for that to happen. It was my fervent hope that obtaining these permits would not be too difficult because of two important facts. One, this was a postage stamp sized country with an equally small bureaucracy. Second, two of my uncles, Berny Joseph and Eduard Salomon, who was married to Opa Raphael's sister, knew a few people in the right places of the Grand Duché.

Uncle Berny was in business selling specialized equipment, spices, and other supplies for butchers, restaurants, slaughterhouses, and farmers. His store and large warehouse were below his apartment. High demand items were natural sausage casings, primarily from hogs and cattle, which were stored in barrels with preservative brine. Often, as I found out later, the excess inventory was put in storage at Opa's barn. Bernard Joseph, as he was known in the business world, sold his products in Holland, Belgium, France, and Germany, but had discontinued sales in Germany for obvious reasons. He was a very charismatic, dapper looking, and suave dresser. He always wore a tie, hat or cap even in summer, and sported a rose or other flower from his small garden in his jacket lapel. I hardly ever saw him without one; it was like his personal trademark. His wife, Aunt Marthe (née Michel), was a very proper, proud woman who was always elegantly dressed and enjoyed wearing furs. She was born January 8, 1893, in Freisdorf, district of Lothringen-Lorraine, which at that time was a part of Germany. Prior to 1871, the Alsace-Lorraine area was a part of France; however, between 1871 and 1919, the area became under the control of Germany. Shortly after the First World War, it was returned to being a part of France. Aunt Marthe had two brothers who had served in the German Army during World War I and was a widow when she married Uncle Berny in 1923. Georges was born a year later. She enjoyed a large circle of primarily Jewish friends. They often frequented the famous Café Namur at Grand Rue, in downtown Luxembourg. It was where the elite met in the afternoons to sip coffee and eat some of the most delicate and delicious baked goods, *glace* (ice cream) chocolate, and the famous French *nougat*. That was a tasty confectionary consisting of nuts and pieces of fruit in a sugary paste. It was chewy and sweet and sold in bars of various sizes.

Uncle Eduard Salomon was married to "Tata" Aunt Julie, who was the sister of Opa Raphael. Eduard was the other uncle who had connections and friends in the inner circle of the Palace. He was a barber with his shop at Rue Lavandier 4, a minute from the Palace and Government offices. He shaved and cut the hair of some of the ministers who either came to his shop or summoned him to their offices. On occasion, I received a free haircut from him. From his barbershop "Moni" Uncle Eduard also sold postage stamps for collectors and had a big display in the storefront. With the connections from both uncles, it was no big surprise that I quickly obtained a permit to start my apprenticeship somewhere in Luxembourg.

A few days after I received my work permit, Opa took me to a long-time friend who owned and operated a large structural steel and fabrication plant. It contained all sizes of hydraulic vertical and horizontal presses, shears, and lathes. The plant included a large galvanizing facility, a welding and blacksmith shop. The business's name was "Feidert, Eisenbau, Presswerk, Verzinkerei," and was located at Rue Anvers, Antwerpenstrasse 69. It struck me as somewhat odd that this plant was located in a highly populated residential and small business area

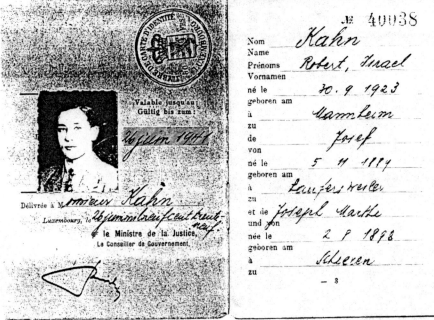

EXHIBIT 8.8 Luxembourg Foreign Identification Card, which was valid until June 26, 1941.

within fifteen minutes walking distance of Opa's house. The only outward sign of the plant was a huge metal gate that permitted large trucks to enter. The offices of Monsier Pierre Feidert were on the second floor behind his family residence where, I found out later, he lived with his wife Mariechen, a nickname for Mary.

This meeting was unusual to say the least. Monsieur Pierre Feidert was an enormous person, at least six feet tall, weighing about 300 pounds. He wore a fedora-like felt hat with a large brim, black trousers, and a long gray smock. He wore at least a size 15 shoe, although they could have been larger. His greeting was like the roar of a lion, and his handshake was like a vise. Although a faint smile was visible through the cigar smoke, I had no doubt as he and Opa conversed in Letzeburgish that he, and no one else, was in charge. I was unable to understand, specifically, what the two men were saying, which gave me the uneasy feeling as if I were being sold to Feidert. When the two men shook hands again, I knew that a deal had been reached.

The three of us went down a steel stairway into the noisy plant. Feidert primarily took us around to show me what was being fabricated and worked on. He pointed out large bank safes and vaults in various stages of construction along with small parts that were being stamped or pressed out. There were steel doors and frames ready for business and residential use. Some of the frames were very ornate and caught my eye with more than a casual interest. There were steel windows and frames along with vertical shutters for residential use, some of which were being painted. Nearby, horizontal metal shutters, the type that could be rolled up, were being assembled for installation on storefront windows. All products were custom made, and mass production was limited. He pointed to another area where large-scale roofing frames were readied for safety glass installation. He was noticeably proud of a new product, very heavy steel doors designed for air raid shelters. Of course we didn't get to see everything, but the variety of products and the diversity of machines and equipment as well as the cleanliness of the plant impressed me. I estimated the work force to be about thirty to thirty-five men.

On the way back to Opa's house at Hollerich, Opa explained to me that the understanding between Monsieur Feidert and him was for me to start my apprenticeship the very next morning, May 15 at 7:30 a.m. I was delighted! Since this job was to be a learning environment for me, my pay would be only sufficient enough to take care of washing my work clothes and buying new steel reinforced shoes every three months. I was disappointed about the money because I had hoped to save a few francs for miscellaneous expenses and an occasional ice cream, chocolate, soft drink, and, perhaps, even a movie. In spite of the low pay, I was upbeat to embark on this important opportunity to learn the trade I had been deprived of completing in Germany.

That same evening I called my parents and gave them the good news. They were happy for me and gave me words of encouragement. I questioned when they would be able to join me and other loved ones here, but their reply was very vague. Since the Nazis monitored all phone calls of Jews to foreign countries, it was difficult for them to speak freely. Even with the physical distance between us, yet so close, for thousands of other reasons we seemed a world apart. Though I

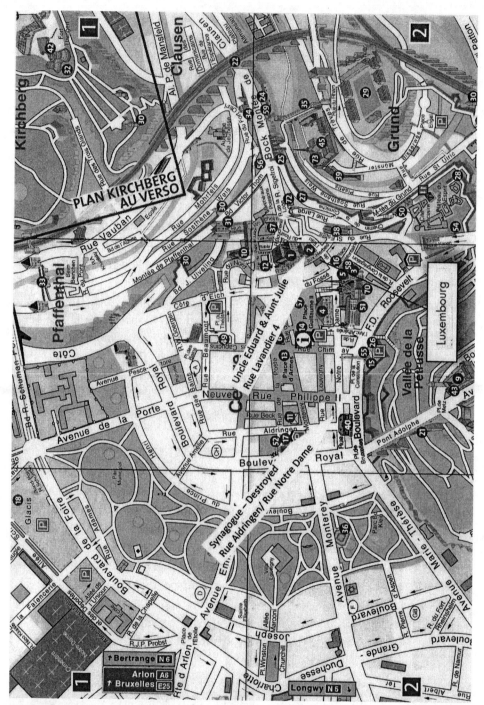

EXHIBIT 8.9 Partial map of the city of Luxembourg with personally important locations noted.

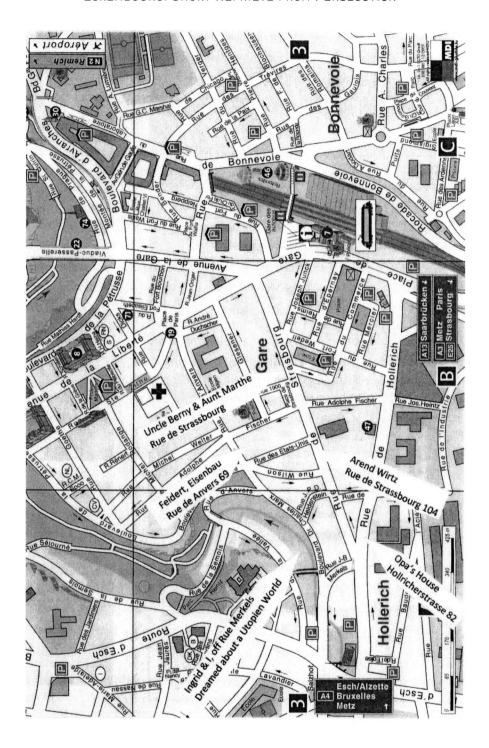

was no longer under the clutches of the Nazis, for a while after our phone conversation I missed being there with them and felt lonesome and homesick.

Cousin Georges came later to visit and spend time with me. He arrived on his *vélo*, his bicycle. Everyone rode a version of a racing cycle with handlebars curved downward, and so did Georges. From where he lived it was only a ten-minute ride, mostly downhill. We had hit it off well on earlier visits, and nothing had changed now. Georges was a year younger than I, and small for his age. Since he was an only child, his parents were very protective and strict. I felt somewhat sorry for him because one of his neck muscles was impaired so that he always held his head to one side. He endured neck-stretching exercises where he had to wear a halter, and although painful, they seemed to help. He had an artistic flair and enjoyed drawing, painting, and occasionally composing poetry.

The first morning of my apprenticeship I awoke early and donned my overalls. Anna had prepared a plain sandwich and a thermos bottle of milk for my lunchbox. Opa and Anna wished me good luck when I said *au revoir*. When I arrived at the shop, one of the workers showed me how to use my time card and then took me to my workbench station. So far so good! Then it happened: One of the manually operated overhead cranes stopped working because of a chain that had jumped off a pulley. The fellow who had directed me to my work station came over and gave me some brief instructions on how to place the chain back on the pulley that was suspended from an I-beam approximately thirty-five feet high under the shop's glass ceiling. My first day, and I had not been on the job more than fifteen minutes. It did not take long for my little brain to realize that I was going to be directed to perform this difficult and dangerous high-wire act. I had no choice to say no.

A vertical ladder mounted to the wall led to the eight-inch wide I-beam that I was going to have to traverse for about forty feet to reach the pulley. I straddled that beam in a sitting position, holding on with both hands. Scared as never before in my life, I moved forward ever so slowly, a few inches at a time. When I mustered enough courage to look down, I noticed that the workers below had stopped whatever they were doing and silently watched me. Among them I saw this big fedora hat and knew who it was. The easy part was when I reached the pulley to put the chain back into the groove. The hard part was sliding back over the I-beam until I reached the wall with the ladder. There, I had to catch my breath and wait until my legs stopped trembling. Then as I climbed down the ladder, I heard muffled applause and a few whistles that were then interrupted by a thundering voice, "Back to work!" by the man in the fedora hat. I had just successfully completed my unscheduled initiation to my new surroundings.

It turned out that there was one other apprentice who appeared to be older than I. The fellow who had initially taken me under his wings was my foreman, and I would report to him daily for my assignments. It took him a little

EXHIBIT 8.10 In my overalls working as an apprentice at Feidert.

while to realize how much or how little I had learned at the Anlernwerkstatte at Mannheim/Neckarau and make my work assignment accordingly. In Mannheim there had been classroom, but mostly shop teaching: here it was all hands-on doing and learning. The hands-on experience was an advantage in that I would be capable of becoming a "Master" in my profession much sooner and hopefully, be able to earn a good living wherever I would eventually end up. The drawback was that without theoretical learning I would not have the basic knowledge to study engineering. For the present, however, I saw no alternatives.

While most of the workers were Letzeburgers, others were Belgians who spoke Flemish among themselves; another group spoke French. My foreman, whose name was Schüssler, was German and spoke German with me while I tried to pick up on the Letzeburger language and some French. What helped me was that everyone around me spoke whatever language they felt like, and I picked up the swearing and curse words first.

The work hours were long and the work regimen hard. Monsieur Feidert was on the shop floor much of the time giving instructions or orders. The rest of the time he sat upstairs by a large set of window in his office where he could pretty much observe the entire work crew. He always made sure that everyone was working hard and not loafing, so much so that he timed how long his workers took to go to the "crapper." It was not uncommon for him to come down the stairs, go into the crapper where there was little privacy, and yell at the individual, *Du knaschtigen hond*! "You dirty dog! Get back to work!" He turned out to be a real slave driver without consideration for human needs or dignity. We had a fifteen-minute break in the morning, the same in the afternoon, and seventy-five minutes for lunch. He strictly enforced all rules and deducted a full hour's pay for any infraction including arriving a few minutes late for work. Knowing these stringent rules, I ran to Opa's house when lunchtime came and then ran back to the shop to make sure I was on time to punch my time card. Feidert, whom some referred to as "Jemp," a condensation of his first name, Jean Pierre, was the undisputed master, and everyone feared him. There was no kind word, no regard for personal problems, and no compliment for good work. It was my first experience with a true sweatshop. Safety was of little concern to him.

As time went on, I was either instructed on, observed, or operated every machine operation and all other processes including working in the blacksmith shop and the zinc plating (galvanizing) shop. The zinc plating presented the hardest and most dreaded work area because of the inherent hazards caused by chemical reactions of the process. First the sheet metal items had to be cleaned by pickling the items in acid baths. Next, the products had to be submerged in the super-heated zinc solution that often resulted in small explosions when the parts were immersed. The noxious fumes required us to drink milk periodically to avoid becoming ill. Additionally, everyone had to wear face masks, gloves, and long protective leather aprons. Fortunately, I managed to survive this and other ordeals.

No one can imagine how tired my body and mind were at the end of the day. I never had any problems sleeping. Twice a week I went to Aunt Marthe and Uncle Berny's home to take a bath since doing so at Opa's required my carrying buckets of water upstairs and emptying it into a large, round, galvanized tub. There were no shower facilities. Afterward, I would have to carry the dirty water downstairs again. It was a task I did only when I had no other choice. Honestly, I hated it!

On Friday evenings Opa and I made the thirty minute walk to synagogue for Shabbat services. The synagogue was somewhat similar to that of Mannheim. Although it was smaller, not as pretentious inside, and the architecture was that of a mosque. While the order of service was pretty much the same, I kept comparing Rabbi Serebrenik with Rabbi Grünewald of Mannheim. One interesting difference here was the shammes, or caretaker of the synagogue. Mr. Klein sported a white goatee and a moustache under his lip. More importantly, he wore a very impressive black tuxedo-like uniform with a large, heavy silver chain around his neck embellished with a big medallion. He wore an unusual pointed hat that protruded about five inches from the front and back of his head, a design that must have come from the

EXHIBIT 8.11 Monseur Klein, the shammes of the synagogue.

EXHIBIT 8.12 Inside view of the synagogue's interior (Luxembourg).

EXHIBIT 8.13 View toward the rear of synagogue with ladies emporium and organ. Notice the beautiful woodwork and ceiling design.

Napoleonic era. I found out later that the hat was also similar to one worn by King George VI of England. During Shabbat and holiday services, he carried out his responsibilities with dignity and authority and among many other things he decided who would be called to the Torah and in which order.

When we returned home on Fridays, we enjoyed a typical Shabbat meal with the usual prayers, conversation, and relaxation. The following morning we again walked to synagogue, Opa in a dark suit, white shirt, tie and hat. I dressed similarly except that I didn't have a dark suit. When Opa walked with his Shabbat cane, I could tell that he was proud to have his grandson accompany him. Often he would hum or whistle, an indication that he was happy. At shul his permanent seat was about six pews left of the bima, and I was in the seat next to him. Other boys my age sat with the adult men, while ladies and their daughters or girls in general sat upstairs in the mezzanine. Of course, this was a major distraction for me as I tried to make eye contact with one or several of the loveliest like Lilo Hecht and Denise Levy. Denise lived in a big house next to Opa. As a matter of fact, the Levy's and Opa shared part of the driveway separated by a four-foot high wall. The Levy's had a large livestock business, and their pasture always had about fifteen to twenty cattle and four to six horses grazing. I thought Denise was cute, but not her sister, Edith, who was perhaps two years older. Yet, I got along with both Denise and Edith. Lilo was tall, a real charmer, and a good dancer, but I thought she was somewhat aloof and stuck-up.

EXHIBIT 8.14 (left) Denise Levy, my friend who lived next door; (above) Edith Levy, her older sister.

When Georges came to shul, he either sat on the other side of Opa or with his dad in the center section of the synagogue. Neither Opa nor Uncle Berny allowed the two of us to sit together because we did more talking than praying. Georges had many friends and was instrumental in having me meet them, and through them I met others. After religious services everyone, young and old, met outside to greet each other and schmooze, conduct friendly conversation. The young people, like Georges and me, usually planned something for the afternoon. Sometimes we met others and walked to one of many scenic spots and then wound up buying some refreshments or baked goods at a bakery. Since I had very little money left from my work at Feidert, I often had to defer by making some excuse, and hardly ever had any money to treat my friends, especially girl friends. I never asked Opa or any of my aunts and uncles for anything like an allowance, and they never offered any even though they knew I made just enough to buy only the most essential personal items. Often I was very embarrassed, and on one occasion I went home to my room and shed a few tears because I felt so humiliated.

After morning synagogue services Opa walked to the the train station. Across the street were a number of hotels, one of which was the Hotel Metropole Kaffee. This was the gathering place for four or five friends with whom he played cards. It was a weekly ritual that Opa dearly enjoyed and never missed. Afterwards, he walked home, and as the sun set he made havdalah, a particular ritual ending Shabbat.

Usually, by that time I had also returned home to partake in this symbolic custom. While Opa chanted certain prayers, a specially braided candle with two wicks was lit. I held the candle symbolizing the divine in man. Next he passed an ornate spice box "bisame box," filled with cloves and other spices, and we inhaled the fragrances to enliven our spirits. We drank a sip or two from a silver cup filled with wine and then poured the remaining wine onto a dish and extinguished the candle on it. At that point we wished each other a *gut woch*, Yiddish for a good week to come. It was a short but festive ceremony that I enjoyed with Opa each Saturday evening, although it made me a little more homesick. At home in Mannheim we did not routinely conduct havdalah.

In the meantime, some of Mom and Dad's belongings, as well as mine arrived in a "lift", a large wooden shipping crate. Prior to Kristallnacht, my parents had packed many of our household items in preparation for our departure. They could not have known at the time that what they packed would eventually survive. With the help of the truck drivers, the furniture and other belongings were taken into the almost-empty dining room downstairs and the two rooms upstairs that were to become my parents' bedroom and sitting room. Meanwhile, my parents moved out of their apartment and had rented a furnished bedroom at Mannheim next to Vetters Beamtenkaufhaus, located at N7. As much as we were looking forward to their arrival, they were unable to tell us about their impending travel plans. At their end there was so much red tape, required authorizations, declarations, payments to Nazi authorities, and bribes under the table. All of these things were necessary for Jews to leave Germany. It seemed like a never-ending maze, and it made me very uneasy not knowing if they would ever be able to emigrate so that we could be together once again.

And so it was a complete surprise to all of our loved ones in Luxembourg, and especially to me, when I came home tired and dirty after work at Feidert to find my dear parents waiting for me at the door. It was an unforgettable June 27, 1939, and an exciting reunion with no dry eyes at #83 Hollericherstrasse. The three of us were together again, no longer in the clutches of Adolf Hitler and his evil regime. We had saved our bare skin but not much else. The life my parents had built for themselves, for my dear sister Irene and me, with hard work and toil over many years, close to all had been left behind, destroyed by the senseless hate of the Nazis. That evening we telephoned Lille, France, to tell Aunt Irma, my mother's sister, her husband, Uncle Charles, and Irene that we had been reunited at Luxembourg, and we thought it would not be long before Irene would also be with us again. Irene was elated. She was happy staying with Aunt and Uncle in Lille, attending school, and sharing the love with her young cousins, Eliane and Claude. However, she missed her parents and me and was concerned about our well-being.

Mom and Dad didn't tell me very much about the ordeals that happened to themselves and others back in Mannheim except when I asked them about certain things and specific people. However, they did talk about an article published in the hate propaganda newspaper, *Der Stürmer*, about the J&S Kahn Co. after Karl Grimm had taken over the business. I was not able to read the article for myself until 2005, when I asked an American friend of ours who lives in Mannheim to research it. Joan Robinson sent me the front page and the article, and wrote that she was aghast and disturbed at the hateful publication of April 1939. The appendix pages contain the article and translation (exhibit 8.15) followed by a copy of the original front page (exhibit 8.16) and translations of the headlines.

In the following days and weeks, Dad and Mom had the opportunity to visit and converse with all the relatives in Luxembourg and give them an idea of how terrible and desperate their existence was and what it was like to be persecuted by the German people. They gave details and described specific events of how they were robbed of not only their dignity, but also their business, investments, and all money in banks. With the exception of some money that Mom and Dad had been able to bring from Germany to Luxembourg during visits years before, they were now penniless. They told of Dad's arrest and transport to Dachau concentration camp. Everything sounded so absurd and terrible that people's first reaction was to think that the stories were exaggerated or embellished. Sadly, they were not.

Yes, the truth was so horrible to listen to that it all sounded unbelievable, perhaps like fiction. And now, no one could project how long our artificial freedom would last. Luxembourg, one of the smallest countries in Europe had only 200 soldiers, and their purpose was of a ceremonial nature, serving the Duke and Duchess as palace guards and royal receptions.

Newspapers and broadcasts by the London BBC and Radio Luxembourg continually addressed concerns of a German invasion of Luxembourg and also neighboring countries of Belgium, Holland, and France. The two radio stations, and sometimes ones from America, were broadcast in numerous languages all over Europe. However, in Germany it was unlawful to listen to any foreign broadcasts, and if anyone was caught, severe penalties were imposed which usually meant being tried for treason and stripped of all personal freedoms usually at concentration camps. The rhetoric was always very speculative and not at all what freedom-loving people wanted to hear. Opa had no radio in Luxembourg, so I had to go to a neighbor's home to listen to the news.

The handwriting was on the wall even though the Allied countries, particularly England, France, and to some extent Belgium, bragged about their military strength and their numerical and technological advantage in manpower and weaponry including air and naval power. As we and the world found out later, most of these assertions were purely propaganda and fiction, hiding behind their military shortcomings while trying feverishly to beef up their defenses.

At the same time, Germany was gearing up its military strength with breakneck speed and had already proven its military strength and ruthless tactics. The Nazis had already militarized the Rhineland in 1936, occupied the free city of Danzig in 1937, Austria in 1938, and overrun Czechoslovakia just a few month previous. They also intervened in the Spanish Civil War from 1936-1939, sending troops and the latest fighter aircraft, the "Stuka" dive-bombers into action. All the guarantees and treaties that Hitler had signed were not worth the paper on which they were written. In fact he made his intentions to invade and conquer Eastern Europe clearer each day. His designs with regard to Western Europe were not as clear. Britain, France, and Belgium reasoned that the Germans considered the Maginot Line and the Prince Albert Line impregnable fortifications and, therefore, would not be attacked. Across from the Maginot Line and all along its entire western border, Germany had erected the Siegfried Line fortification also known as the West Wall. From there the Germans and French and Belgian forces had already been eyeballing each other for months across mutual borders with only minor sporadic skirmishes. This particular phase of non-engagement was referred to as "Phony War," or *Sitz Krieg*, sitting war, while the armies on both sides lay in readiness awaiting an attack by the other.

Luxembourg newspapers like the *Luxemburger Wort* and the *Luxembourger Zeitung* printed much detailed information on this quasi-border war as well as up-to-date information from all corners of the world. Much additional information came from travelers from different parts of Europe at the gare, and rumors circulated from there constantly. For us the news was mostly bleak, and the only hope on the horizon was that America would exert its political, economic, and military power openly and lift its immigration restrictions for us who were without a permanent home or country and in fear for our lives. In spite of all the gloom around us, our hopes were high especially when we read that FDR had presented a budget to Congress with over one billion dollars for defense and had also approved the sale of U.S. war planes to France. On the other side of the ledger was the news that the German American Bund organization was staging large pro-Germany, pro-Nazi, and Jew hating rallies in New York praising Hitler's conquests. Anti-Hitler regime rallies were also taking place in New York and elsewhere with equal fervor. These rallies were staged as a means of drawing attention to the world aggressors and to persuade the U.S. State Department and the White House to change its isolationist foreign policy.

Back in Luxembourg at Feidert, a very unusual and important Grand Duché government contract was received. It was for the construction and installation of armored vehicle road barricades. They would be steel and concrete reinforced structures to be installed on strategic roads at the borders of Luxembourg with Germany, France, and Belgium. Each of these obstacles was approximately twenty feet long, six feet high, and one foot wide. Inside each tank barricade, at approximately eighteen-inch intervals, were concrete filled teeth designed to be released and dropped into twelve-inch deep openings in the roadbed. They would provide an anchor for the barriers so that it would be impossible to remove them. The plan was to place these barricades along what was known as the Schusterline, named after its designer, a road where the terrain would make it nearly impossible for armored vehicles such as tanks to skirt around them. Heavily hinged on one side, the barricade would have to be manually closed and the weights released in the event of a military incursion by an army.

Upon completion, the tank barricades were loaded onto the largest and heaviest truck beds available and transported to their border destinations. Near the border with France they were placed near the towns of Petanges, Dudelange, and Rodange. Toward the Belgium border, they were placed near Gaichel, near the Belgium city of Arlon, Martelange, Longville, and along the road connecting Buderscheid with Bastogne, Belgium. Toward the border with Germany, the barriers were installed near Remich, Grevenmacher, Rosport, Bollendorf, and Vianden. There may have been other sites, but I cannot recall them. I was involved with the fabrication and installation of these barriers.

This huge undertaking for Feidert seemed like a good deterrent against motorized military columns, but no one had illusions that these monster barricades would totally stop any military force for long. Nevertheless, it was an attempt by this small neutral country to show its neighbors and the world that it wanted to maintain neutrality and did not welcome any foreign encroachment. The true Luxemburgers in their Letzeburger dialect used the slogan, "*Mir woelle bleiwen wat mir sin,*" "We want to remain what we are." It was part of their national anthem.

In spite of the often-distressing working conditions at Feidert Iron Works, I learned a lot about myself, and more importantly, I learned something new about the metal working trade every day. It was the latter that kept me from quitting my apprenticeship there. I took a liking to working in the blacksmith shop even though it was very hard and demanding on my strength and endurance. There was something mysterious and awesome about the glowing coal on the forge, which had to be re-energized with air periodically by manipulating the bellows. In spite of the heat I wore a long, heavy, leather apron, goggles, and a felt cap to keep flying cinders and red-hot steel pieces from burning my chest, legs, eyes, and hair. My shoes, in particular, took a beating from the hot metal.

The peculiar high-pitched clanging of the hammer as it struck the metal and then the anvil still rings in my ears. The cooling of the metal in water with its distinct sizzle and rising steam made me feel like a sorcerer or perhaps an alchemist. Wielding the hammer and beating the white-hot metal in one hand held by the long-handled tongs in the other, gave me the mastery to shape the material any way I desired. This shaping had to be done quickly before the metal turned dark red again. I learned to fuse two pieces of metal together or twist round metal bars and flat metals into distinctive and beautiful shapes, often using chrome clad alloy rods and those of copper alloys in combination with steel.

In the beginning I only assisted an accomplished blacksmith, but later, on my own, I crafted the most modern and stylish entrance doors, gates, fences, and balcony railings. The individual jobs had to be done according to drawings and exact measurements supplied to me, but I had considerable license for the artistic and ornate design. At certain times the customer was asked to view the work in progress and give an opinion on his or my prevailing ideas. At the time I didn't think to admire my own handiwork or consider myself an artisan. However, some years ago after World War II when I was able to visit Luxembourg, by choice I walked several streets that exhibited entrance doors I had created to residences that I remembered. Indeed, my hands had made them and they bore my artistic designs. It was only then that I choked-up momentarily while at the same time was overcome with a feeling of great pride for my craft. These ornamental, modernistic creations in front of opaque designer glass still had an aura of elegance, warmth, and functionality. Hopefully they will grace the residences for many years to come and bring satisfaction to the families that live on Rue Wilson and Rue des Etats-Unis (Street of America), and elsewhere not far from Rue d' Anvers 69 (Antwerpenerstrasse), where I had fashioned them at Feidert.

In the meantime my parents had persuaded Opa to have a lavatory and water line connected to their bedroom upstairs (but no toilet) so that they would not have to carry cold water up and down spiral stairs. They still had to carry hot water that had to be heated on the kitchen coal stove since there was no hot water heater in the house. However, the water line was a big help and I benefited as well. My parents were able to pay for this remodeling with money they had given Opa some years before for safe keeping.

It took some convincing for Opa to agree with the lavatory installation since he was used to washing himself downstairs in the kitchen sink, and Anna, the maid, washed herself in the annex to the house where the slop was heated for the livestock. Anna thought of this installation as extravagant and unnecessary, and she started to needle and agitate my parents whenever she had the chance. Her actions affected Opa who was now in the middle of this squabbling and getting upset over it. He needed Anna and started taking her side.

While Dad and Mom made the best of acclimating themselves to living in somewhat peculiar and antiquated surroundings, this unexpected disharmony between them and Anna added an unnecessary discomfort and at times resulted in verbal spats between father and daughter. At times it was hard for my dad and me to stay out of the fray, and we also became victims of Anna's never-ending goading. This was particularly uncomfortable since we all ate together, at the least, in the evening. I felt really bad about this deteriorating situation and so did Mother especially when she and Anna tried to decide how and what to cook. For years Opa had been satisfied each day of the week with a plate of quartered, boiled *grumbeeren*, potatoes, soup meat, and a soup made from the meat with some vegetables boiled in it. Mom, on the other hand, wanted to prepare different menus for more variety. We had a lot of milk and cottage cheese thanks to the livestock. My dad hated cottage cheese with a passion. Since I was at work on weekdays, except for lunch and supper, I was spared some of the verbal un-pleasantries.

It was a breath of fresh air when Irene came to visit us during her summer vacation in 1939. We had not seen her for almost three years, and she had grown into a pretty eighteen-year-old young lady. The separation from us was difficult for her at times, and her grades in school were beginning to suffer because of constant worries about our well-being. Of course, we worried about her also, but we knew she was in good hands and not being exposed to persecution.

Since Dad was unable to obtain a Luxembourg government work permit, it was hard for him not to be able to earn money. However, he contributed to the cost of the household from the money he had given Opa for safe keeping some years before. While Mom helped with the household chores, Dad spent many hours at the Jewish Consistory, a body governing the Jewish congregations of a province, the offices of what we referred to as the Jewish Federation of

EXHIBIT 8.17 My sister, Irene, at the Lycée Lille, France; second row from top, fifth from left.

Luxembourg. It was there that Jews, particularly immigrants, came day in and day out to learn the latest news and which country was issuing visas for Jewish refugees. Most of them were refugees like us who had fled Germany, Austria, and elsewhere and were now stranded.

Much was learned there by conversing with different individuals about their plights, contacts they had made, successes and failures, the paper work necessary to apply for visas at different consulates, and travel to other cities where specific consulates were located. There were bulletin boards with a multitude of information gleaned from news reports and other sources. The Consistory and the ESRA relief agency were places where hopes were nourished and despair shared with those present. The organization, ESRA or EZRA, is named after the biblical figure who, in approximately 458 BCE, led Judean exiles living in Babylon back to Jerusalem. Also there was a small paid and volunteer staff to assist anyone having questions or language problems when reading information from other countries, or needed help typing applications, etc. By and large, the approximately 900 Jews who were Luxembourg citizens looked upon all of the more than 1,600 refugees with some disdain because most of them had no means of support and received financial aid as well as housing and food support through their and other agencies' generosity.

Although they did not work there, the board members of the Consistory included Uncle Bernard Joseph and the "Grand Rabin," the Grand Rabbi Dr. Robert

Serebrenik. Uncle Berny was also on the board of *Societe des Malades*, Society for the Sick, as was Mom's cousin, Bruno Salomon. As far as I knew, neither my uncle nor my cousin were able to help us in any way and Dad had never asked them personally for any favors.

Basically, the countries that were looked upon at the time as possible safe havens for refugees in Luxembourg were America, South American countries, and Shanghai, China, in spite of its Japanese occupation. Palestine was not an option from Luxembourg, although as an ardent Zionist, I would have liked my chances there. Much of the information available was in the form of rumors that were difficult to substantiate. According to rumored news, on one day, applications for visas were being accepted for one country, and on other days, they were rejected. Still on other days, visas that had already been granted were suddenly cancelled. Hopes were raised one day and dashed the next.

Immigration to America depended on the application number assigned for the visa. Ours was high, meaning that based on the annual quota allowed to enter by Congress of approximately 25,000 for German refugees, we would have to wait until 1942 or later. Only after the war did I find out that these quotas were never filled. All of this vague information led to much confusion, anxiety, and disillusionment as I could tell from what Dad told us after coming back from a day at ESRA. My dad told us that some ships carrying passengers were still leaving from Italy, France, England, Spain, and Portugal to various destinations. But how would we get there, and what assurances would we have to be accepted by the country for which the ship was destined? We heard that several ships with refugees had been sent back to their port of origin. However, all of us, especially my parents and I, were resolute in our aim to save ourselves and Irene by trying to be calm, patient, and watchful for the one chance to start a new life somewhere. Realistically, it would take money. However, the Nazis had made certain that before any Jew left Germany each one had turned over all of their savings and left as a pauper.

Time marched on and we read about the New York World's Fair that had opened April 1939. The official theme was "Progress and Peace," and yet we sat on a powder keg of war. I was excited to hear and read that the British Parliament had approved the independence of Palestine in ten years with a division between Jews and Arabs. I wondered, "Why not sooner?" In the meantime the German Reich was registering everyone between the ages of fifteen and seventy in preparation for wartime assignments and had sent more than fifteen U-boats (submarines) into the North Atlantic.

The rumors and jitters of all-out war were becoming louder as Poland rushed troops to its border facing Germany, while Great Britain reassured Poland it would help if Poland were attacked. Americans everywhere on the European continent were hastily returning to America. At the same time Belgium proclaimed its neutrality as France and Holland began to mobilize its forces.

If all of this news was not scary and confusing enough, Russia and Germany signed a so-called "Non Aggression Pact" on August 23, 1939 and President Roosevelt ordered $85 million for the immediate design and production of bombers. All of this was too little and too late because on September 1, 1939, the Nazi forces invaded Poland, and with lightning speed, Blitzkrieg conquered and divided Poland between Russia and Germany, both countries having attacked simultaneously. There had not been a declaration of war. England and France issued an ultimatum to Germany, and when it was ignored, both countries declared war on Germany on September 3, 1939. It was a tumultuous month, and when my sixteenth birthday arrived, there was no joy in my heart, and no celebration. Hitler's prophesies of conquest had materialized, and the world could not stop the might of the German onslaught. Their armies and air forces were brutal, and the carnage of Polish soldiers and civilians was needless and catastrophic.

There was panic everywhere, but especially among the people of Western Europe, still free but wondering for how long. Jews in Luxembourg and elsewhere realized that Germany had left the ranks of the world's civilized nations, and were now frightened of what might come next before getting the chance to flee to some country and save themselves from further persecution.

Dad renewed his almost desperate efforts to obtain the necessary visas to America and any other country that would accept applications. Our survival was at stake, and while I was working hard during the day and coming home exhausted, there were hand-wringing discussions with family and friends in the evening. But none of that solved anything and it only contributed to many agonizing, sleepless nights. Newspapers and the radio were full of stories attesting to the barbarism of the fifty-six German military divisions, nine of which were armored divisions, and the Luftwaffe, which destroyed civilian as well as military targets in Polish cities. Warsaw surrendered to keep itself from being totally destroyed. Not only did the Nazi forces destroy cities and towns, but they mercilessly decimated its people with the most modern stuka dive bombers, tanks, artillery, and firing squads called Einsetztruppen.

News from our friends left behind in Mannheim and from family elsewhere in Germany was vague, very cryptic, and almost meaningless. The writers and callers knew that the mail or telephone calls by Jews to a foreign country like Luxembourg were being intercepted and monitored by the Gestapo. We knew that persecutions by means of concentration camps, physical abuse, and secret executions were taking place, but we did not know that they were very extensive. A curtain of disguise and silence had evolved, and we had become victims of this tragic charade.

It was a big, happy surprise when we heard from Aunt Helene and Uncle Max that they had arrived in Luxembourg after several attempts to obtain the necessary approvals to leave Germany from the German bureaucracy in Cologne (Köln). There had been no problems raised by the Luxembourg government since Aunt Helene, my Mother's sister, had also been born in Luxembourg. We learned that the Nazis had tried to extort money from them, but when that failed, they accepted Aunt Helene's valuable jewelry. I'm not sure exactly when they arrived, but I believe it was August 1939. Their arrival was a happy blip amid all the bad news around us.

Some years earlier, Uncle Max Cohen had bought Belgium bonds that the Germans were unable to get their hands on because they were in a safe deposit box in a Luxembourg bank. Now some of the interest from those bonds came in handy to rent an apartment in a suburb of Luxembourg called Walferdange, the French pronunciation, or Walferdingen, the German pronunciation. It was a fairly small, rural community about ten kilometers north from where we lived with Opa. Earlier they had shipped some of their furniture and possessions to Luxembourg as well, and thus were able to furnish their apartment very comfortably. Of course the main thing was that they were away from the clutches of the Nazis, at least for the present. I visited them often on weekends, and I remember the easy bicycle ride going there and the harder, longer trip back because of the steep and lengthy hills I had to travel.

Luxembourg was a fascinating, storybook jewel of a country with medieval chateaus, castles, and sleepy, quaint villages abounded. Three of us, Heinz Alkan, Leon Grossvogel, and I started to take bicycle excursions on weekends to different areas of the country. Sometimes my cousin, Georges joined us. Except for snow, the country could easily be called an image of Switzerland. The capital, also named Luxembourg, was equally beautiful, historic, and scenic, as I described somewhat at the beginning of this chapter. Several times we made our trips along the Luxembourg border with Germany where we observed the military positions of the "Wehrmacht," and their heavily camouflaged fortifications, equipment, armored vehicles and observation towers. Started already in 1938, known as the Siegfried Line and later the West Wall, we could see the concrete *Drachen Zähne*, the dragon teeth to ward off tanks at a depth of several kilometers. We also observed trenches, mine fields with barbed wire entanglement, and pill boxes where heavy artillery was located. Often we were so close to the soldiers we could hear them sing, play music, laugh, and shout commands. They were not bashful about showing off their modern equipment during localized maneuvers and exercises, and they delighted in speaking loudly to Luxembourgers working in their fields, whistling at girls, women, and even us as we rode along on our bicycles. We dared not speak to them and thought better of telling them what we really had on our minds. It was an awesome feeling, and watching them gave us goose pimples. We knew that sooner or later they would cross the border.

On one of the local holiday weekends we made a bicycle trip all along the borders of Luxembourg and Germany to the East and Northeast, Belgium to the Northwest, and France due West and Southwest. It was approximately 300 kilometers (186 miles) and took us three days. I always took my Hohner harmonica along and played it whenever we stopped for a rest of picnic. Leon played his guitar and we harmonized and sang along. For a while, but only for a while, we left all worldly problems behind. Bicycling was the primary mode of transportation of the local population, and their interest and participation in bicycle racing in the Duchy and adjacent countries, including the Tour de France, was phenomenal.

One of my fondest memories was a ride and visit to Echternach, the oldest Grand Duché's town, near the border with Germany. Traveling through the Müllerthal, a region with picturesque rock formations, waterfalls, and heavily wooded mountains and valleys was exciting. The town itself dated back to the 7th century including its ancient abbey and Gothic town hall. More relaxing was a modern swimming pool just outside the city of Luxembourg known as *Gantebein's Mühle*, where we cavorted with girls and had fun.

One memory from early childhood visits was the Hämmelsmarch. In late August the shepherds from afar led a procession through the city with all of their

EXHIBIT 8.19 Me and my best friend Harry Alkan at Gantebein Mühle swimming pool. Harry was the one we took with us when we finally fled for America. P.S. We didn't know that there was such a thing as an athletic supporter.

EXHIBIT 8.20 The "Hämmelsmarch," a rite where sheep dressed with ribbons are paraded through the streets with music by local shepherds.

sheep accompanied by musicians. It was a sight to see with each sheep adorned with colorful ribbons around their body. I have been told that this tradition began in 1340, when a shepherd's market was held in the city.

In more recent years, when I lived there as a young man, it had developed into a fun-filled fair and festival, the Schoberfouer, in the dialect referred to as *Kirmes*. Uncle Berny, Aunt Marthe, and Cousin Georges took me along to the fair but never treated me to any of the rides and food delicacies that they and their son enjoyed, even though they knew too well that I had very little, if any, spending money. It made me wonder and feel sad. However, I never let on and held no grudge. It was at this fair that I was first introduced to *pommes frites*, which we now buy at McDonalds and elsewhere – good old French fries.

I became very fond of Uncle Eduard and Aunt Julie Salomon, the sister of my Opa Raphael. They were kind people living near the Grand Palais of the Duke and Duchess of Luxembourg. He operated a barber shop by himself and in his window displayed postage stamps for sale to collectors. He always cut my hair for free while Aunt Julie offered me a glass of *framboise*, known in German as "Himbeersaft," and in English it was raspberry syrup stirred into water. It was a way of showing hospitality. I always enjoyed it, and in recent times have introduced Himbeersaft to our children. Our grandchildren especially liked it and would not have a soft drink or anything else except Himbeersaft when they came to our house for a visit.

The Salomons lived at Rue Lavandier 4, and their living quarters were behind and above the barbershop. Besides the one-man barbershop, I never got to see any other room than a small living room and the kitchen. The immediate proximity of the shop to the building that housed the Chamber of Deputies, similar to our House of Representatives, plus the fact that Uncle Eduard was a likeable man, meant that he received calls at all hours of the day to cut hair or provide a shave for one or the other officials. Benny, their son, was considerably older than I, and I saw him and his wife Estelle only occasionally.

Several of my mother's cousins lived in Luxembourg City. They were Frida (née Ehrlich), her husband Bruno Salomon and daughter, Solange. Fridel, as she called herself, was the sister of Uncle Charles Ehrlich in Lille France, with whom my sister

EXHIBIT 8.21 Uncle ("Moni") Eduard Salomon and his wife, Aunt ("Tata") Julie, sister of Raphael Joseph.

EXHIBIT 8.22 Cousin Bruno Salomon and wife Friedel. She loved to write poetry and we shared the same birthday.

EXHIBIT 8.23 Friedel and her daughter Solange.

lived. Fernand Ehrlich, a brother of Uncle Charles, lived in Paris and was a masseur and freelance landscape artist who painted in oils. Some of his paintings are displayed in my study. Of interest to me, and a historical oddity, was the strange fact that Uncle Charles served in the German Army during World War I because he lived in Herlisheim Alsace-Lorraine, north of Strassbourg, which at the time was a German territory. His brother, Fernand, had moved to France and fought with French forces against the Germans. In other words, two brothers fought against each other. Bruno Salomon's brother, Marcel, married Rosette (née Braun), and lived in the same modern double house at 17 Val Ste. Croix-Kreuzgruendchen in a fairly new suburb of Luxembourg known as "Bel Air." Their daughter, Monique, born in 1935, was only a toddler at the time.

I became somewhat fond of another of my mother's cousins and family who resided in a small town, Roodt sur-Syre, approximately 20 kilometers in a Northeast direction from the city. The Syre was a small river that fed into the river Mosel. Sally Kahn and Gabriella (née Hannaux) were my mother's first cousins, and I always called them Uncle Sally and Aunt Gaby, as she was known to everyone. They were hardworking, wonderful people who had two sons, Roger and Marcel. Part of their large house was a bakery with large ovens and other customary bakery equipment. With additional help they worked from early to late baking various types of breads, rolls, cakes, pies, and cookies and sold them in their store and delivered them to nearby towns. Because of their excellent reputation, they often delivered to the Palace of the Duke and Duchess. Whenever we visited, as children, and again when we lived in Luxembourg, it was always a treat to be with them. Without fail, we were treated to coffee, cake, torts, and cookies. No matter what time of the day, Aunt Gaby was a gracious hostess and we loved her for it. Behind their house was a wonderful garden where they grew vegetables, berries, and other fruit. Along with Roger, who was a year younger than I, and Marcel, four years younger, we played together and got along well.

Now and then in talking to refugees who recently fled or who were smuggled over the border from Germany, we listened to all sorts of rumors, which we later found to be true. We heard that decrees had been issued that no Jew could own any land or real estate. All objects made of gold, silver, and other precious minerals, as well as all jewelry had to be turned in to the Nazi authorities. All published or unpublished Jewish literature, books, and research papers had to be turned in to local libraries. All grants, foundations and the like had to be dissolved. All Jewish organizations had to cease. Jews were restricted to buying groceries only in a few designated stores and at certain hours. Jews were being evicted from apartments or buildings belonging to Aryans. Jews were forbidden to leave their homes after dusk. Radios and other listening or transmitting devises owned or used by Jews were confiscated. To prove to the world its sinister and inhumane deeds, the Nazis decreed that no Jew would be admitted to air raid shelters in the event of air attacks by the Allies. Finally, and worst of all, we heard in late fall 1939 of deportations of Jews from the eastern territories occupied by Germany. What was to come next?

Many times, a few fellows and I met at the upstairs apartment of Leon Grossvogel's parents in the downtown center of Luxembourg City and discussed local and international events. Leon had two older sisters who were musicians. They also participated in our weekend discussions and afternoon get-togethers. Among other things we talked about running away from home and attempting to cross over the border to France or Belgium and, perhaps, from there into Switzerland where we felt we would be much safer in the long run. In the end we concluded that we would hurt our parents immeasurably if we did so, additionally success was not assured, and therefore shelved the idea, but it was one of many ideas that kept returning. When the weather was nice we walked to one of many scenic spots near town. My favorite place was the fortress *Trois Glands* (*Drei Eicheln*, in German, and "Three Acorns" in English). It was named such because of the three round domed towers that had been built for the Austrian Army in the 18th century.

Another site that we sometimes frequented on Shabbat, Saturday or Sunday afternoons was *Place d'Armes* in the center of the old City. It was a large city square with an area of large trees in the center. A military style band played at the bandstand for the people who sat outside of cafes, restaurants, and fancy bakeries wiling away the time. It was very relaxing and eventually one would see friends and neighbors stroll by. It was on those occasions, outings, etc., that I bonded with friends, primarily Heinz Alkan and Leon Grossvogel.

Winter came and work at Feidert Iron Works became more demanding, often exhausting, and temporarily intolerable. All of the workers were inundated with work because Monsieur Feidert's son, Jean Pierre (also nicknamed Jemp), an engineer, brought in many more jobs. Sometimes I had to go into town by myself to pick up angle iron shapes, rods, flat steel, or pipes that were twelve to fourteen feet in length. I carried them at least a mile and a half back to the shop. The weight and length of the steel gave me sores and blisters on my shoulders even with padding under my overalls. People on the street looked at me and shook their heads, but old man Feidert knew what he was doing in order to save the cost of having the materials delivered. I hated that part of my job but I didn't complain because I knew that Feidert would only cuss me out and make my working relationship worse. The so-called shop steward was in Feidert's pocket and a convenient fixture. The good side of the job, however, was that I learned a valuable trade and found out that I had unbelievable strength and endurance for my age. I was not afraid to work hard and long when necessary. I revealed none of this drudgery to my parents who were having their own problems coping with their less than desirable environment.

On some clear days we were able to see the vapor trails of high-flying fighter planes, both German and British. We didn't know what vapor trails were then, but thought perhaps they were smoke screens. Many nights I stood outside Opa's house in Hollerich or at my open window and listen to the roar of British Blenheim and Lancaster bombers coming from the Northwest and flying in the direction of Germany. After all, Britain and France were at war with Germany. I liked the sound and hoped that there would be more raids and heavy destruction on German military targets and factories. Later on those nights or during the early morning hours, I heard the bombers returning from the opposite direction. Unfortunately, at times the returning roar was not as loud, meaning some of the bombers did not make it back. The following day German radio broadcasts bragged about the number of enemy bombers shot down and attested to missed targets and minor-to-no damage at all. Of course, when we listened to the BBC news, were heard opposite reports. The war propaganda was in high gear causing the desired effects on both sides. We refugees wanted to believe the newspapers and radio broadcasts from the Allied side because it gave us hope that the war would be over soon.

The local, French, and Belgian newspapers as well as local and free world radio broadcasts carried stories of German submarines sinking British war and merchant ships with heavy losses. One of those ships was the British battleship, *Royal Oak*, with 800 sailors lost. Travelers coming from Germany and elsewhere sadly told about cruelties against Jews and conditions beyond belief in concentration camps. There were also unconfirmed reports that the French and British had shot down German planes. There were constant reports of night raids by the Royal Air Force on strategic German cities, incursions by the Germans along the

French border, and forays by the French into the Siegfried Line. One of the highlights was that the darling of the German fleet, "the invincible pocket battleship", *Graf Spee,* had been scuttled and sunk by its own crew after being cornered by the British Navy December 1939 at Montevideo, Uruguay.

All of this terrible news and uncertainty contrasted with the easy-going, peace-loving, and good-natured lifestyle of the Letzeburgers. In restaurants, taverns, open-air concerts, and at home people were still trying to enjoy their freedoms. They continued to eat, dance, and sing to the melodies of the French crooner, Tino Rossi, with such love songs as, "J'attendrai D'amour," and "La Vien Rose." Winter came and went, and with the ushering in of 1940 eventually came hints of spring. The signs of war were always on our minds. By now Finland had capitulated to Russia and in April, Hitler's armies and navies invaded Denmark and Norway.

Early in the morning of May 10 it happened. Since I slept with my windows open, I heard noises coming from the street, people running around, an unusual amount of bicycle and automobile traffic, and planes overhead. Then I heard someone holler, *Die Prüsse kommen*! "The Germans are coming!" It was 4:45 a.m., and Mom and Dad were still asleep. I woke Mom and Dad; Opa and Anna were already up, and I told all of them the news. I telephoned Uncle Berney and Aunt Marthe, but no one answered. I found out later when I rode to their house on my bike that, according to the workers at their store, they had filled their car with suitcases and boxes and left. I thought that Uncle Berney would have called his father, Pop, or my mother, his sister, to say good-bye, but they fled in such a hurry that, apparently, there was no time for niceties or to ask any of us to come along. It was at that point that I realized self-preservation became more important to them than family.

When Opa, Mom, and Dad heard about Uncle Berny fleeing, there were raised eyebrows, unfavorable remarks, and some tears. Why hadn't they told us? They had to have planned their leaving in advance. Is this what our lives had come to? Selfishly leaving loved ones behind? It was not long before we found out that other mishpocha had also left. Among them were Uncle Eduard and Aunt Julie Salomon, their son Benny and his wife, Estelle, cousins Marcel Salomon, his wife Rosette and their small child, Monique, as well as Bruno Salomon, his wife, Friedel, and daughter, Solange. We also learned that many of our friends, including some of mine, had also fled overnight. After a while telephones were inoperative. I did not go to work because I did not know what was going to happen, and I wanted to be of help and comfort to Opa and my parents. The whole neighborhood was on the street exchanging information, rumors, what they had heard on the radio or at the gare. Some of our Christian as well as Jewish neighbors had also fled in panic. Most of them had left for France hoping that they would be able to wait for the war to end with France victorious. Then, they could come home in a few weeks or no later than a month or two, or so they thought. How wrong they were!

In spite of the fact that Great Britain had formally guaranteed Luxembourg's neutrality, Nazi German troops were invading without provocation. Grand Duchess Charlotte, her family, and finally most of the ministers had fled. By way of France, Spain, and Portugal they reached London where they continued as best they could to look after the welfare of their country as a government in exile. By mid-morning we knew that not only Luxembourg but Belgium, Holland, and France were simultaneously under attack. Because these countries had armies, navies, and air forces, Hitler hit them immediately with bombers, then paratroopers, and finally with ground forces. It was about 2:00 p.m. when we saw the first German infantry in the distance coming down Hollericherstrasse toward us. The shortest distance from Germany to Luxembourg City was about fourteen miles. Everyone went into their houses and locked the doors. There was no one waving flags to welcome them. We were frightened and huddled in the house peering out from behind the curtains.

Soldiers approached on both sides of the street, full field packs, helmets, rifles at the ready. They were drenched with perspiration and visibly tired. Their commanding officers on horseback shouted for everyone to put out water and wine for the troops. We saw many of the soldiers pouring water into their faces, over their heads, and onto their gray uniform shirts. Wine bottles disappeared into their backpacks, pockets, or in to the horse drawn wagons that came down the center of the road with ammo, guns, and other supplies. Some of the soldiers smashed individual wine bottles and poured the liquid over themselves after drinking a few swallows. The wagons veered to either side of the street to allow the horses to drink water. Anna had opened the door, and before we knew what happened, a German officer on horseback rode through the doorway into the hallway of the house with pistol drawn, and ordered us to put water into a tub and place it outside immediately or else. It was really scary especially when he shouted, *Das is ein Befehl*! ("This is an order!") It took several hours before the soldiers passed, but in the meantime everyone living on the street was busy setting out water and wine. A small neighborhood grocery store a few houses away from our house also put out bottled soft drinks and beer. Even today I can still visualize and hear the boisterous German officer riding through the stone floor entrance hallway into Opa's house, the iron horseshoes making crunching noises and creating sparks. It was an unforgettable and frightening sight. What all of us had feared was now happening, yet we were still stunned that it was reality. We were trapped again under the boots of the Germans.

After five days of useless resistance, the Dutch surrendered on May 15, and on May 28, Belgium capitulated in spite of the help from expeditionary forces from Great Britain and France, which had been pushed back against the North

Sea at Dunkirk, France. On May 14 the attack on France through Belgium had been a huge German success, and on June 14, Paris fell to the Germans. With an almost complete military disaster inflicted upon the Allies, the only flicker of success was the battle around Dunkirk. There, about 340,000 Belgian, French, and primarily British soldiers were rescued through an enormous evacuation by sea back to England. On June 22, France surrendered. The armistice established a German occupied France that included the entire French coastline and an unoccupied southern France, with a French puppet regime, bordering on Spain. A veil of darkness and utter silence had fallen over Europe, and disillusion, fear, and anxiety had become a painful and incurable disease among its inhabitants.

German ingenuity, determination, and their strategy known as Blitzkrieg, had proven all of the Allied military experts wrong. A relatively small group of German paratroopers had surprised and conquered the thought of impenetrable Belgian Eben Emael fortifications and bypassed the French Maginot Line which was then attacked from the rear. The French armored divisions, although superior in numbers, were no match against German tactics, their most modern equipment, and aerial bombardment techniques. The rhetoric and propaganda through the French, British, Belgian, and Dutch government, press, and radio had misled the people of the world, including us. This may have been one of the major reasons why Germany's Jews, along with Jews elsewhere in Europe, assumed that Hitler's armies would not be able to conquer Europe, and so, at first, made only feeble attempts to leave the continent. Instead, like us, thousands settled temporarily in other European countries.

In the days following the German occupation of Luxembourg, all of us tried to get back to some normalcy in our lives. In the meantime, the German High Command issued a declaration that Luxembourg was considered enemy territory, and the remaining government of Luxembourg would no longer be recognized. The decree was signed by "Oberfeldkommandant Gullmann, General Major." We were under military rule. The other shoe fell in July when German military authority was terminated and Gustav Simon was designated as *Gauleiter*, chief of the civilian administration of the Luxembourg occupied territory. This was followed by a series of decrees according to which Gustav Simon declared, "The age of democracy has come to an end." Next came a decree that terminated all Luxembourg laws and instituted German laws in their place. Again, we were under total dictatorship, as was all of Luxembourg.

Simon, however, did not stop there. He announced that his mandate entailed the preparation for the annexation of Luxembourg, a return to its *Mutterland*, motherland Germany, and the destruction of Luxembourg as an independent, sovereign country. His pronouncements were iron fisted, swift, and ruthless.

During the early morning hours of the invasion, thousands of the Luxembourg population fled; almost one thousand Jews, most of them Luxembourg citizens, were among them. Because of the ensuing confusion, lack of communication, surveillance by the Gestapo, and sheer fright, we did not know immediately what had happened to our neighbors, friends, and relatives, most of whom had fled. Earlier in this chapter, I wrote about Uncle Sally, Aunt Gaby, and their sons, Marcel and Roger who lived in Roodt. Even though Roodt was only a short distance from Luxembourg City, we were unable to communicate with them, and each time I telephoned, a German voice answered. I knew then that something was wrong. Only later did I find out what.

Since Roodt was only six miles from the German border, German troops had occupied the small town immediately. Because the Kahns operated a large bakery, a sentry was placed in front of the house and business. Next, two German soldiers were assigned quarters at their home and determined immediately that the owners were Jews. A new baker was brought in by the German occupiers and Kahn's bakery ceased to exist. All of the Kahns were then confined in their own house to a few rooms downstairs. Their bank account was controlled, and they had to pay rent to the German occupiers for living in their own home. In addition to daily insults, chicanery, and occasional beatings, the Kahns were ordered to vacate the premises and move in with another Jewish family named Bonem in the nearby town of Grevenmacher. Marcel and Roger's grandfather, Raphael Kahn, had lived with the family for years. He was ninety-three years old and could not understand why he and the rest of his family had to leave the home he loved and had lived in for so long. Distraught and confused by all of the events around him, Raphael Kahn passed away several days before the move. On the day that they were to leave their home, *Hitler Jugend*, Hitler Youth, appeared in front of the home and sang, "Cut their throats that way they don't come back home." This information was gleaned from a written account that Marcel had sent me in 2005.

Peace and freedom-loving Letzeburgers were very upset with this and other events, and tried, as useless as it seemed, to make known their love for their Cinderella-like country and their loathing of their Nazi occupiers. Luxembourg's colors of red, white, and blue started to appear from private homes and businesses everywhere. Slogans such as, *Mir woelle bleiwe wat mir sin* ("We want to remain what we are") and others more antagonistic suddenly were painted on walls, sidewalks, shop windows, bridges, placards and billboards, and on handbills that were available everywhere. Although poorly organized, a large underground resistance movement fueled this strong national feeling. Many students and other young men fled across the border to join the French Foreign Legion or the French resistance movement known as the *Maquis*. Workers who had belonged to labor unions, primarily in mining enterprises, went on strike.

Gustav Simon, Gauleiter, Chief of the German civil administration, employed the Gestapo, the German Secret Police, and German collaborators living in Luxembourg to identify the so-called culprits. Whenever they were caught, they

EXHIBIT 8.24 Postcard of the "Gëlle Fra" World War I memorial on Place de la Constitution, which was destroyed by the German occupiers. Image at right shows detail of the top of the memorial.

were sentenced without trial and then assigned to hard labor work details, put into prison, or worse, sent to concentration camps. From time to time, there were spontaneous demonstrations at the Place de la Constitution, where the National monument, *Gëlle Fra*, the "Golden Lady," stood. Over the years this sculpture of the golden lady holding a wreath of olive branches in both hands to denote peace and victory had become a symbol of Luxembourg's independence, solidarity, and pride. It had been erected for the 3,700 Luxembourg nationals who served in the French Army during the Great War and of whom, 2,000 died. Now it was a rallying symbol of resistance. It did not take the Nazis long before they tore down the monument on October 21, 1940.

Anyone caught at an anti-German demonstration was then at the mercy of the Nazis. They were usually taken to Villa Pauly, the Gestapo headquarters for interrogation, beatings, and torture (see exhibit 8.25 in appendix). Whenever we walked to synagogue, we always stayed on the opposite side of Boulevard de la Petrusse #57 where the Villa Pauly stood. At times going past that villa one could hear muffled shouts and screams. At other times it was just an overactive imagination. Either way, it was scary! Due to intimidation and harsh punishment opposing parties to the German civil administration had to go underground. Now under control, it became a negligible force after several months.

Working at Feidert became somewhat more difficult for me because the man to whom I had been assigned to for training and who everyone knew to be a German citizen turned out to be a staunch supporter of the Nazis and was an official organizer for the SA (brown shirts), youth HJ (Hitler Youth), and BDM (Hitler Girls). Often he came to work in uniform and changed into his work clothes. Everyone, especially me, was fearful and very careful not to say anything that could be misconstrued as being against the German administration or him personally, or sympathetic toward the Allies. I was in a precarious position since I had no idea whether he knew that I was a Jew. However, I was under no illusion that sooner or later he would find out. Now and then he threw his weight around and openly solicited everyone to join the Nazi Party. The big boss, Monsieur Feidert, did not dare interfere in these internal activities. He was more concerned with his own safety.

Speaking French was no longer allowed by law, and all street names or names of places with a French name were changed to German names and the wearing of berets was considered a sign of defiance. Our get-togethers on weekends at Leon Grossvogel's apartment became more restrictive and more cautious. We heard the rumor that two convoys, a total of one hundred Jews, had been able to leave for Portugal and Spain. Also, a few Jewish butchers had to close, and in August of 1940, a series of anti-Jewish laws were introduced. Jews were removed from public service, as were doctors, dentists, attorneys, and judges. All of the Nuremburg Laws that had been enforced since 1935 in Germany, were now enforced here. We found ourselves further enslaved. On September 24, 1940, Order #2 decreed that all furniture and real estate belonging to Jews were placed under severe restrictions, and all real estate and financial transactions by Jews were unlawful. All cash, stocks, bonds, and other financial assets like insurance policies of Jews in Luxembourg had to be deposited into special accounts where they were frozen. If that were not enough, during the same month the Jewish Consistory Council was served with an order expelling all Jews within two weeks from Luxembourg.

Rabbi Robert Serebrenik played an ever-increasing role of importance by being able to negotiate with the Gestapo at the highest level, even making a trip to Berlin. He persuaded them to cancel the existing order and agree to an evacuation process over a number of months whereby about 500 Jews with some sort of visa would emigrate to Cuba or some other country. They were to be escorted by bus and train through occupied France to the Spanish and Portuguese border. There, however, additional frustrating negotiations with authorities of these countries took place. Many of these families were never able to reach their promised destinations and were swallowed up in French camps of Vichy, France, and later transported to the death camps in Eastern Europe. At the time all we knew was that some people were able to leave. We were envious that they had been selected, but had no idea of their often-tragic fate.

We lived in a fishbowl with sharks, and there seemed to be no escape. Dad was writing more letters and sending telegrams to his two brothers, Ernst and Herman, and sister, Bella, in America, pleading for action to obtain visas for America. At this point we were so desperate that my Dad tried every possible country for even a temporary visa or permit to travel through a country just so we could escape the daily trauma being inflicted on us. In the meantime, the indignities and harassment became almost unbearable for us. We all had to turn in radios, bicycles, cameras, typewriters, and binoculars. Since I no longer had a bike, I could only visit Uncle Max and Aunt Helene at their apartment in Walferdingen by bus. The winter of 1940-41 was particularly hard on us because of the food rationing. We were fortunate to have milk and cheese from Opa's cows, and we were able to harvest potatoes, beans, carrots, and cabbage from his small garden, which helped tremendously.

The indignities did not stop there. An order was published and put into effect immediately confiscating all of the belongings left behind by Jews who had fled Luxembourg at the time of the German invasion. The man in charge of this effort was Herr Brauchman, who used to deliver milk door to door in the area where he lived. Now he was a Nazi big shot.

In February 1941, an attempt was made by the Nazis to torch the synagogue. Except for some minor damage, the attempt failed. Often, people, including Rabbi Serebrenik, were jostled, harangued, and beaten by Nazi thugs on their way to or from the synagogue. Then, on March 15, I received a huge shock. I was called upstairs into the office of Feidert and told, apologetically, that because I was a Jew I could no longer work there. Mr. Feidert gave me a letter of release and recommendation (see exhibit 8.26 in the appendix), shook my hand, and in his gruff voice said good-bye and good luck. His wife, Mariechen, who seldom came to the office, stood behind him and cried. It was as if someone had stuck a dagger into my heart. I picked up my tools, said good-bye to a few workers in the vicinity, and left. No one knew why I was leaving.

On May 9, 1941, as I was going to Shabbat evening services at the synagogue, a group of Nazi hoodlums obstructed the steps to its entrance. I left the scene, went to an adjacent street and warned people going to services to go back home to avoid confrontation. Other boys also gave out the word. It was no longer safe to go to the house of worship and pray.

After my release from work, I had plenty of idle time and spent many hours at the Jewish Consistory, specifically the organization ESRA. There I met Ingrid, a girl about my age who was a Jewish immigrant from Austria. I do not remember her last name. We spent many hours together talking about our fate, and making lofty unrealistic plans for the future, although we wondered whether there would be a future for us at all. This was not an ordinary friendship or love affair. It was an affair of love all right, not with each other, but a love for hope of a future and serenity. Sometimes we just sat in a field of wildflowers and looked at the clouds in the sky dreaming of a rosy ending to our captivity. Our favorite place was off Rue Merkels near a pedestrian bridge crossing the Petrusse River. There we hid behind the realities of the moment and lived just for a while in a make-believe world that was at peace and harmony. All of our tragedies, pain, worries, and shattered dreams dissipated behind white or dark clouds and we imagined the splendor of being free from torment and persecution. I remember those hallucinations. Both of us derived comfort and a momentary end to loneliness and despair. I have often wondered what happened to her and hoped that her dreams came true as mine eventually did.

There were additional transports of Jews expelled from Luxembourg to Vichy France, where their fate became precarious. Later, they were again rounded up for the Final Solution and transported to the east. Only a few transports managed to enter Portugal, and some convoys were turned back to Vichy where the refugees were interned.

Our family wanted to prevent the confiscation of our belongings by the Nazis. My mother was still very friendly with a woman with whom she had gone to school in Luxembourg many years before. Mom made arrangements with the woman's family to store most of our furniture, paintings, crystal, figurines, china, and linens and remains from her trousseau stored in a large steamer trunk. Fortunately, Arend Wirtz lived at 104 Rue de Strassbourg, only a short distance from where Opa lived. Still, it was very dangerous to move all of our belongings without being noticed and being reported to the Gestapo. Over several weeks, at two or three in the morning, with the complete cooperation of the Wirtz family, we managed to move our belongings in a small commercial moving van on different nights to their basement for storage. We all took a great risk, but the moves were successful. There were a few neighbors who asked questions. We told them that the Nazis had confiscated our belongings, picking them up during the night in order to avoid any commotion. The original furniture belonging to Opa, which had been rearranged to make room for ours, was now moved back into its original places.

Opa Raphael Joseph understood the scheme and no longer cared that the Nazis would eventually come and take his furniture and things away. He was now almost eighty-one years old, and he no longer had that certain sparkle in his eyes, and his zest for life had markedly diminished. He had become an old man concerned only about his children, including my mother, my father, and me to be saved from harm.

If it was the purpose of the German oppressors to break our will through insults, humiliation, physical and spiritual torture, which it certainly was, then they

EXHIBIT 8.27 & 8.28 Opa Raphael was resigned to whatever happened. One could tell that his will to live had diminished.

were certainly on the right track. On May 16, 1941, the heartless dictator Gustav Simon ordered the synagogue at Luxembourg City destroyed. After searching for a willing contractor, so the rumors indicated, the synagogue was dynamited. It hurt me so deeply that I was unable to go there and look at what had been a beautiful structure. This holy, magnificent edifice, built around 1894, had been of beautiful Moorish architecture. Its main sanctuary had been covered with a large ornate, bulbous dome capped with a tall spire. There had been two smaller dome structures on each side of the roof facing the entrance, several still smaller ones on each side, and the stained glass windows had been an arabesque geometric design of unbelievable beauty. By now, I had seen three synagogues desecrated and destroyed by the Nazis, too many for anyone's lifetime, let alone for a seventeen year old boy.

I was stunned, hurt, frustrated, but not disillusioned. As a matter of fact, now more than ever before, I saw a purpose for being strong, to continue to live so that some day when the opportunity arose, I could fight back, destroy those who wore the mask of the devil, and bring dignity and pride back to my family and me, freedom-loving people everywhere, and all Jews. My anger had turned into a resolve, and I swore to myself to find a way of revenging everyone who had suffered and despaired under the ruthless Nazi barbarians. So help me G'd! If that meant wiping Germany of the map, so be it!

EXHIBIT 8.29 This holy edifice, the synagogue, professionally dynamited on May 16, 1941 by Nazi occupation forces.

CHAPTER NINE

Precarious Journey

After more than seven decades it is still very difficult, if not nearly impossible, to put into words how the immediate family, including me, felt and coped with the unbelievable conditions foisted upon us, the Jews. Deprived of everything including our dignity, it was impossible to live a life resembling any kind of normalcy. Helplessness and despair alternated with thoughts of hope and liberation from the Nazis.

Opa, the elder member of the family, seemed almost resigned to whatever fate would bring him. His morning prayers started with the ritual of tefillin, a symbol using mind, heart, and body for good not evil. He and Anna looked after the livestock, which diminished to two cows. It was obvious that for him the joy of this work had disappeared. He no longer cared and for the most part Anna had taken over. Since she was a Christian, she had nothing to worry about except the political stigma, namely working for a Jew.

Mom and Dad had lost their robust demeanor. They tried to console as well as cheer each other, Opa, and me. Generally our conversations were full of gloom as there were few signs of hope. Most of the time I hid my feelings and tried not to fall in to an aura of hopelessness and desperation. Occasionally I went upstairs

EXHIBIT 9.1 Mom and Dad with a smile that deceived their true state of despondency.

to my room and played my harmonica, but that was only a front to momentarily deceive myself from the real world.

Every morning Dad walked to the office of ESRA where Jews congregated to hear about more deportations, individuals and families obtaining visas or travel papers, and other happenings. One day, May 29, 1941, I remember very well. Dad came home smiling, holding a folded piece of paper in his hand. After he assembled Mom, Opa, and me in the tiny, dreary living room, he was out of breath and had to sit down. After a minute or so, which seemed like forever, he unfolded the paper and told us that we had received permission from the Spanish Consulate to immigrate to America on a Spanish quota. Dad received this information after he had visited the American Consulate in Luxembourg. Dad's visa number was 8395, Mom's 8396, and mine was 8397. There was one stipulation, a big one: we had to leave from Spain. Nevertheless, we were so happy that Mom cried, and Opa had tears in his now bloodshot eyes. He hoped that we could save ourselves, but was also sad because we would leave him behind. The point needs to be made that there was no chance whatsoever that any country in the world would allow him into their country at his advanced age. All of a sudden the room became very quiet. Each of us looked at the others with questions, but none of us asked because we knew that there were no immediate answers.

Dad cautioned us to not broadcast the news for fear that unknown difficulties might result if the wrong person received the information. We did, however, inform Uncle Max and Aunt Helene, some of my parents' friends, and the few remaining friends of mine.

My friend, Heinz Alkan, was particularly envious. His mother became so emotional when I told her the news that she pleaded with me, and later my parents, to take Heinz along in spite of the fact that he had no valid papers to emigrate. When I told my girlfriend, Ingrid, she became very emotional, her whole body shaking as she sobbed without letup and I could not find any words to comfort her. She knew I would be leaving, and in all probability we would never see each other again. Sadly she was right!

Dad had to send our German passports to the Spanish Consulate for the appropriate certification. Meanwhile we waited and worried about getting them back. Because of the war, the mail was no longer reliable, especially mail sent by Jews or addressed to Jews. While we waited for the return of our passports, we heard about Nazis harassing Jews on the border between occupied France, Spain, and Portugal. Some had to return to their cities of origin; others were picked up and sent to concentration camps. Some Jews tried to escape to Vichy, France, which was not occupied. There, too, they faced an uncertain and precarious future. Some were in hiding; others were caught and sent to camps, first in France and later to the death camps in Eastern Europe. In late June 1941, Rabbi Robert Serebrenik, the Chief Rabbi of Luxembourg, was able to leave for Portugal while

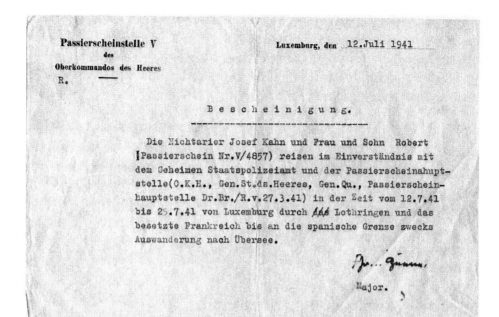

EXHIBIT 9.2 Original forged safe conduct and travel pass
(read the translation in the appendix, exhibit 9.2).

chaperoning a convoy of sixtysix Jews. Now he was not only a rabbi; overnight he had become a hero, perhaps even an angel!

Unbeknown to me and perhaps Mom, Dad was able to secure a forged certificate to give us safe passage through occupied France to the Spanish border. This safe conduct pass, dated July 12, 1941, supposedly executed by the German Army High Command (*Oberkommando des Heeres*), and signed by a Major whose name I cannot decipher, stated that our travel had been coordinated and agreed to by the Secret Police Headquarters (*Geheimen Staatspolizeiamt*). Dad wanted to increase our chances of being able to travel through France, and this document was an ace in the hole if needed. He never divulged to me or anyone else who had supplied him with this forgery or what it had cost.

Each day was suspenseful as we waited for the mailman. Finally in early July a large envelope arrived from the Spanish Consulate in Düsseldorf, Germany with the precious passports, desired transit, and visa certification. Dad had a good understanding of the documents' meanings and ramifications. Neither Mom nor I really understood what was involved. Dad lived with these matters for what seemed like twentyfour hours a day, and we left all decisions to him. Dad's passport number was 637, Mom's 638, and mine 639. All three of us readied one suitcase each for the journey, not an easy task. Packing became a daily and time consuming task as we tried to get everything we thought we would need into one suitcase that was limited to no more than fifty pounds. We knew from others that this weight was about maximum for anyone to carry for a reasonable period of time. Our suitcases were smaller and therefore held less than the maximum weight allowed. Suitcases did not have rollers then as they do today. We practiced carrying them. It would not be easy, particularly for Mom. Mom and Dad looked over my suitcase many times, taking things out and putting clothing items in. Finally Dad insisted that I take out my Chumesh, my Bible, which Rabbi Grünewald had presented to me at my bar mitzvah. I was also to leave behind my tallit. Space and weight were Dad's concern, but after a day or so I sneaked both items back into my suitcase. Even though Dad considered those items a liability, I thought they were an important part of my young life and was not willing to leave them behind. It was one of the rare times that I did not follow my dad's wishes, and I hoped that I would not come to regret it.

Because of our uncertain relationship with Anna, we kept much of our plans from her. Basically she knew that we were going away and leaving her master behind. We noticed a certain amount of her resentment, and Opa's depression increased more each day. I could tell by his red eyes and his nearby handkerchief that he had been crying, although not in my presence. My parents and I were very sad to see him that way, but we made every effort to reassure him that he had another daughter and son-in-law, Helene and Max Cohen, nearby to look after him. However, they were also trying everything possible to escape the clutches of the Nazis.

In the meantime, Heinz Alkan had received a visa for America, but his mother had not. Also he did not possess a safe conduct travel pass through occupied France nor a transit visa for travel through Spain. Finally Dad told me that we would take the gamble and take Heinz with us, although his decision was fraught with great uncertainties and risks to us all. Heinz promised his mother and my dad that he would obey him throughout the journey and assist us in every way possible. The addition of Heinz to our group was good news for me. Heinz's father had already managed to escape to Switzerland, and so this was a tough decision for Mrs. Alkan to make. Perhaps she may have had premonitions of what the future would bring for the remaining Jews. I didn't realize that saying goodbye to Aunt Helene, Uncle Max, and my few remaining friends would be so hard. On the surface, they were all happy for me, but I felt anguish and a certain amount of regret leaving them behind in uncertainty. We all said and hoped we would see each other somehow, somewhere, sometime, and we would then celebrate and continue our friendships forever. Of all the friends I left behind, only three girls would survive the Holocaust; the rest of my friends all died heroic and undeserved deaths.

Because of the severe restrictions and censorship on Jews regarding communication by mail or telephone, in June and July of 1941 we did not know that eight months earlier, on October 22 and 23, 1940, all Jews who had remained in the Rhineland (Baden) and the Palatinate (Pfalz) had been deported. A total

EXHIBIT 9.3 My friend Heinz Alkan and me. Note my knickerbockers which would be very important later.

of 6,504 people were forcefully expelled having only several hours or less to pack some of their belongings. Approximately, two thousand of them were from Mannheim alone. Age or health did not make a difference. The area was to be *Judenrein*, free of Jews. It was to be another triumph for Hitler. Years later we learned nine trains transported these hopeless people. This was the beginning of the end for many, but first they were delivered to their interim destination after a train ride of four days and three nights. Their destination was Camp Gurs, in the region known as Pyrenees-Atlantiques. The camp was located in the village of Gurs located in the Southwest corner of the unoccupied part of Vichy, France between the small towns of Oloron and Navarrenx, not too far from Bayonne near the Atlantic coast. The Pyrenees Mountains and Spain lay to the south, an area that was to have great significance to me later. My wife Gertrude's eighty-year-old grandmother, Ida Wolff, lived in Mannheim at the time, and did not survive the catastrophic conditions of the camp. Some of my parents' friends also suffered the same fate. We did not know! We did not know! It was an especially sad chapter in the tragic history of our friends and relatives. Those who survived Gurs were later transported to death camps. They are among the six million for whom we mourn forever.

July 14, 1941, was the date set for our departure from Luxembourg. I lay awake the night before listening to English bombers flying toward their targets, praying and fantasizing that in the morning, Germany would have surrendered and the war would be over and we could stay. Each of us, including Heinz, had a backpack full of clothes, extra shoes, soap, etc., a set of metal dinnerware and utensils, a half loaf of bread, some hard salami, cheese, and a thermos bottle which would be filled with hot tea. By 5:00 a.m we were ready, even though the truck for which Dad had made arrangements would not arrive until 7:00 a.m. We spend time with Opa, hugging and consoling him, saying things we hoped for but knew would not happen. What I didn't know that our embraces and kisses with him were to be our last. Then the truck came and backed up into the courtyard. The driver talked and argued with Dad, wanting the money in advance, not at the end of the trip. Dad gave in; he had no choice.

The driver opened the doors to the back of the truck and unloaded several rows of baled straw. Now I could see what looked like a big container with a lengthwise board that was to be our seats. The space was not very high, perhaps 4 feet wide, and we would have to crouch to get into it, and were crowded onto the makeshift bench. There was enough room in front of us to place the suitcases with backpacks on top. I thought that's what a casket would be like, but thought better of saying that. The space for us was just big enough so that we would touch each other's elbows. There was a curtain behind the bench where I later found a chair with a hole cut in the middle of the seat with a bucket underneath: a makeshift toilet. Overhead was a low wattage light bulb and several pipes for air in the ceiling. After the driver closed and locked the double doors, I was glad those pipes were there. As the truck began to move, more air came down through those pipes. I began to realize that this truck was camouflaged giving the appearance of carrying bales of straw and had probably transported others before us to safety over the same route. Smuggling refugees was a business, albeit a very dangerous one. Only years later did I find out that Heinz's mother, Uncle Max, and Opa had given Dad money to finance our escape. Mom sobbed as Dad told us that the driver was taking us to Paris where we would then take the train to Hendaye at the French border with Spain. That was when I became aware of the grand scheme. Heinz and I had never been to Paris, and in a way we were looking forward to it. The truck didn't seem to be going fast enough, and when it stopped, we did not know whether we were at a normal traffic stop or at a German checkpoint. We were glad and relieved when the vehicle started moving again. Several times the stops were longer, and once the double doors opened we heard German voices; the Germans only saw bales of straw. We held our breaths and then let out large sighs of relief when the doors closed again.

Dad didn't know how long the trip to Paris would take, but we must have been in the truck for about four hours when it finally stopped and the driver opened the doors, removed the bales that hid us and began talking with Dad very animatedly. Dad was visibly excited and spoke in a somewhat raised voice. Then he turned to us and said, "The driver will not take us to Paris; it would be too dangerous. We have to take the train from here to Paris." Here turned out to be the railroad station of Reims about halfway between Luxembourg and Paris. There was nothing else we could do. The driver had our money, and he was literally "in the driver's seat." He helped us out of the truck even carrying Mom's suitcase. We entered the railroad station from a side door, and even though Mom, Heinz, and I wore berets and Dad wore a customary hat, we felt conspicuous, as if we were criminals.

The driver told us to wait and came back in a few minutes later with tickets to Paris. All of us were relieved. Apparently the driver had purchased the tickets from the money Dad had originally paid him. The Reims station was not very busy, and so we sat on a bench and drank tea from our thermoses. Heinz and I shared a sandwich, constantly on guard that someone might become suspicious of us. The loudspeaker announced our train's departure, and so we walked to the platform from which it would leave. Dad suggested that Heinz and I should sit in a separate compartment from Mom and him. Heinz had packed a deck of cards in his backpack and we played for a while. Every now and then Dad walked past our compartment, and we did the same just to have something else to do, and to check on each other.

Earlier at Reims we had decided that if anyone spoke to us in French, Mom or Heinz would respond since both spoke fluent French while Dad and I could not. Because the train was not an express, we would be making various stops. Once a conductor came through to check our tickets. He said nothing other than *"bonjour, billet,"* upon which we showed him our tickets. I kept thinking about my inability to speak fluent French and also the fact that none of us spoke Spanish. Under certain conditions this handicap could give away our status as Jews fleeing the country, and give cause to French gendarmes or German occupiers to pick us up and send us to a camp as had already happened to so many others. These thoughts were worrisome even though Dad had procured a forged but authentic looking safe passage document from the German High Command of the German Army. What if someone figured out it was a forgery?

All of a sudden I had an idea. Initially I dismissed it, but the more I batted it around in my mind, the more plausible it appeared. Why not pretend to be deaf and mute if a difficult situation arose? All I had to do was act the part, make some hand gestures and some unintelligible sounds. Heinz was amused when I told him and then demonstrated my act, but after a while he thought it could be worth a try. As a matter of fact he tried it out himself, just in case, but neither of us told Mom or Dad.

As we looked out the window, we realized that we were approaching Paris. The rail traffic had become heavier, and our train moved more slowly with occasional short stops. Finally we pulled into the station, and the train stopped. Once again Dad told us to walk separately from Mom and him so as not to create attention, but to maintain eye contact. Strangely, I felt like a criminal on the run. The station was very noisy, smoky, and full of people including French soldiers, German soldiers, and the feared SS troops. Suddenly Heinz and I became alarmed when we saw a man in civilian clothing approach Mom and Dad. Then he spoke to them and kissed them on both cheeks, as was the French custom.

Immediately I felt a sense of relief. Moving closer I recognized him as Moni (how we referred to uncle at that time), Uncle Fernand Ehrlich, the brother of Charles Ehrlich of Lille, with whom Irene had been living. He was small of stature with a shorttrimmed handlebar mustache. He was a freelance landscape painter who also did some portrait work. He was not married, had no children and did not travel often outside of France. Due to the latter, our side of the family did not know him very well. Dad had called him before we left Luxembourg and told him about our planned arrival in Paris. Fernand told us later that he had been hanging around the station expecting us to show up hours earlier before our continued travel to Spain, but he was not surprised when Mom and Dad told him about the truck driver letting us off at Reims.

Moni Fernand took us to a quieter outoftheway area of the station where we had a late picnic-style lunch from our backpacks and then replenished them with a bag of foodstuffs he had brought for us. Bringing us food was not a simple task for him because food was rationed and could not be purchased without assigned ration books. Obtaining extra food meant resorting to the black market. He was born in Alsace where everyone spoke German, and so we had no problem understanding him. He told us that since so many Jews were fleeing from adjacent countries to France, and through France on the way to Portugal or Spain, the French authorities had become very concerned and disagreeable with the influx of homeless people. Most of them had no proper papers or money to sustain themselves and no money to continue their escape from the Nazis. They had become fugitives and were spotted easily, resulting in their apprehension and deportation to camps. The German occupiers assisted and encouraged the efforts to round up transient Jews and had found a willing partner in the French authorities to do their dirty work.

EXHIBIT 9.4 Uncle Fernand Ehrlich, who met us at the railroad station in Paris.

Now we readily understood the dangers facing us and listened intently to everything Uncle Fernand said and to every piece of advice he gave us. He told us that our plight would become more dangerous as we approached the French/Spanish border area. This was an area along the Atlantic coast under strict heavy German control and surveillance because of fears from an Allied invasion. He told us to do everything to avoid suspicion and to assume the role of casual travelers especially in the Bayonne and Hendaye areas. There, he said, people had been taken off of trains and then simply disappeared. While it was impossible for us to trust anyone, there were *passeurs*, smugglers, who would take people into Spain for money while others would do it out of the goodness of their hearts. Some of them were known as Maquis, members of the French underground fighters who were interested in enlisting people into their cause. There were others pretending to be sympathetic and helpful, but instead they were informers and turned the unsuspected into the Nazis.

Moni Fernand suggested that we take an overnight train that left Paris around 5:30 p.m., thinking that the controls and surveillance of passengers would not be as stringent at night. Dad agreed and both of them proceeded to buy the necessary tickets while Heinz and I kept Mom company. Next we placed our luggage and backpacks into lockers for convenience and to maintain a lower profile. Heinz and I said goodbye to Moni Fernand and then told Dad that we wanted to take a walk. Then we did something we never should have done. We went sightseeing in Paris. When we returned from our escapade, Dad was furious and read us the riot act. We never considered how worried he and Mom had been not knowing where we were or what happened to us.

It was only a short while before we boarded the train, and Dad had been worried that Heinz and I would not be back in time. We boarded the train and again split up into different, but back-to-back compartments, *coupe*, as they were called where there were only seats on each side for four people. We stored our luggage in a rack above. Dad gave us the last good piece of advice; when other passengers or anyone else entered, we should pretend to be asleep. That way we could avoid having to talk to anyone unless it was in an official capacity. In addition Heinz and I spread ourselves out almost horizontally to make it less inviting for others to share our coupe. When the train moved out of the station, no one joined us and the glass door leading to the outside corridor was closed. So far the strategy was working.

Again it was not an express train and there were many stops, too many to remember them all. I do remember stopping at Le Mans, Nantes, and later during the night, Bordeaux. We had no idea when we would arrive at the border town of Hendaye and were afraid to ask. It had been a long, strenuous, unforgettable day, and we found ourselves sleeping for short intervals, waking when the train made a stop and began to move again. We placed our tickets in clasps near the door so that the conductor didn't have to wake us up to check and punch holes in them. Several times someone opened the door selling drinks or soup, but we continued to sleep ever so lightly or pretended to sleep. When daybreak rose, we saw the Atlantic, military vehicles, occasional gun emplacements and other military activity. German soldiers dressed in various gear stood in the train's corridors, having arrived sometime during the night.

Dad came into our compartment and laid out his plans for the next chapter in our lives. He made Heinz and me promise that we would follow his instructions. From this point on, Dad felt that from Hendaye it would be too dangerous for the four of us to travel together into Irun on the Spanish side of the border, especially since Heinz did not have a Spanish visa. He told us to look for a passeur or a Maquis to help us over the border; Dad would stay with Mom hoping to enter Spain with the papers on hand. We were to separate and meet up again in Barcelona, where our ship would depart. There was over 500km between Irun and Barcelona that we'd have to navigate on our own. After giving each of us an envelope that contained large bills of French currency (francs) along with some cryptic handwritten instructions, he embraced and kissed me, bade us both good luck, and expressed that although he thought that this was the safest thing to do he wished we could all stay together. We walked to the next coupe to say goodbye to Mom who was in shock with tears streaming down her face. Dad's last words were, "We'll see you in Barcelona."

Suddenly we were alone in the world with only ourselves to rely on for decisions. We had stopped briefly at Bayonne near the resort of Biarritz, and now from the signs and the conductor's shouts, Hendaye was not far away. Heinz and I were very curious to read the instructions Dad had put into the envelopes. Each contained ten one thousand French franc bills. The instructions told us to head for Barcelona and upon arrival check in at the JDC (Jewish Joint Distribution Committee) Office. There we would receive information how to get in touch with Mom and Dad again. After Heinz and I read the note, we tore it up. The instructions would be easy to remember, we hoped! Except for one bill we hid all the other money in our shoes for safety.

As the train slowed, we saw the Atlantic Ocean close by. When the train finally stopped, we decided to wait a few minutes until the train platform was crowded with people including Mom and Dad. Some distance from our coupe we saw lines forming at a control station where passports, destinations, and personal effects were checked. It was only a few kilometers to the Spanish passport control of Irun, where my parents were headed. This would be a danger point for us. While I was really concerned about my parents, Heinz and I were also frightened as to what to do next. Heinz suggested that we go in the opposite direction than the other passengers and cross the tracks behind the railroad station. I agreed.

We walked at a normal pace then crossed the tracks and saw what looked like a lake or bay not far away. Evidentially, we were not headed for Irun, Spain. As we came closer, we saw a beautiful bay with numerous colorfully painted fishing boats plying the smooth water. I suggested that we talk to one of the French fishermen and ask him what was on the other side of the bay. We learned that Spain and the city of Hondarribia lay just across the Bay of Txingudi. We had never heard of the town, or the bay, but were told that it was a few kilometers north of Irun. The bay is also known by the French name La Bidasoa, I learned later. As the conversation between Heinz and the fisherman continued, I could tell that it entailed a negotiation to take us across to Hondarribia.

Suddenly the fisherman walked away, and we were afraid that we had hit a snag. He talked with another fisherman a few boats away, and then they both returned. As we suspected, there was a hitch. The official border was past the middle of the bay, and said they could not cross during daylight hours knowing we were fugitives. They agreed to take us separately in two boats at night for the cost of 2000 francs each. We shook hands, and sealed the deal, realizing that they asked for a lot of money. The pipesmoking fishermen then loaded our luggage into their respective boats that were about 18 feet in length. There were no more questions as their preparations continued. Heinz and I were both physically and emotionally exhausted, and soon fell asleep in the dirty, smelly boats.

When I awoke, I could not see the fishermen anywhere. Heinz noticed my alarm and reassured me that they were just taking their daily siestas. Finally they returned around mid-afternoon and asked us to help with some of the chores on board. We had many questions, and Heinz, conversing in French, was able to get more information for us. The fishermen discouraged us from going due east because of the Pyrenees Mountains, even though it was summer. The afternoon dragged on, and I thought and prayed that Mom and Dad had been able to cross easily into Spain via Irun, and take the train to Barcelona.

The thought crossed my mind several times that Dad had made a wrong decision by splitting us up, but he knew more than we did. The fishermen told us that German soldiers in civilian clothes along with the Gestapo, often recognizable by their long trench coats, had infiltrated and were all over Spain's larger cities looking for French resistance fighters and British spies who were using Spain as a staging and hiding area. All young men, like ourselves, who should have been serving in German, French, or Spanish armies were under immediate suspicion by German soldiers. Once rounded up, these young men were incarcerated, sent to camps, or worse. We had to be on our guard. The sun finally set and the two men waited for total darkness before starting our journey. Heinz and I tried to figure things out and anticipate our next move since we would be traveling separately across the bay. Heinz questioned the fishermen on how to best get to Barcelona. Neither of them had ever been there, but they were reasonably sure that if we wanted to travel by train it would have to be from Irun or for sure from Pamplona, a place neither of us were familiar with. From previous conversations Heinz and I felt that we should try to get to Pamplona and take a train to Barcelona from there since the Spanish border town of Irun would probably be heavily controlled to apprehend illegals.

It had been pretty warm all day, perhaps 80 degrees and we had taken off our shirts to look just like the fishermen. The time came to shove the boats fully into the water, and within a few minutes we raised a small sail and silently glided toward the opposite shore. I was asked to hand over the two thousand francs before we reached the Spanish shore, a trip that would take about twenty minutes. Heinz's boat was behind us, and once we were safely on shore, the two boats turned around immediately for the return trip. With our backpacks and suitcases in hand we started walking toward dim lights in the near distance. The time was around 11:00 p.m. Except for small slits in car headlight covers, lights everywhere were blacked out to keep light at a minimum so that Allied aircraft could not easily locate and identify towns and other sites. Homes and other buildings had blackout curtains over their windows for the same purpose. This was already a requirement by the authorities in Luxembourg, France, and here in the Spanish border area.

We had talked before about the necessity to acquire bicycles to continue our journey, but did not know where or how. We passed some houses on a dirt road leading away from the town but did not see any bikes. Our luck changed when we came to a tavern. We saw many bikes, some in racks and others leading against the side of the building. Heinz nudged me. Quickly I looked them over and then took one that seemed to be in the best condition based on frame and tires. And that was that! I had already taken off my belt to secure the suitcase to the luggage carrier and then took off in the same direction we had been walking. I was very scared. This was the first time I had ever stolen anything, and I worried that I would be caught. Then it occurred to me that if I were caught, even without the bike I would be in serious trouble. I arrived at a crossroad with a sign and arrows pointing toward towns, one being Irun. My idea was to avoid all towns if possible, but the opposite direction would be okay. I was passed by a few cars and motorcycles and often turned my head to see if Heinz was catching up with me, but there was no sign of him. I pondered whether I should take a break and wait for him, but anxiety and fear spurred me on. After a while I was so tired that I looked for a place away from the roadside to spend the rest of the night. I tried to make myself comfortable behind a clump of trees and bushes where I could still see the road, hoping that Heinz would come along soon. What if he hadn't taken the same route, or even worse, what if he had been caught?

As tired as I was, my mind was heavy with concern for my parents, Opa left behind in Luxembourg, Irene somewhere in France, and even for myself. From my backpack I took out some bread, cheese, and my thermos and gulped down everything without enjoying a bit of it. I took the only coat I had from my suitcase and used it to cover myself, and used the backpack as my pillow. Before I knew it, I was asleep. I would have slept longer had I not awakened to someone pulling on the backpack under my head. Startled, I quickly got to my feet only to see that the culprit was a white sheep dog that must have been attracted by the smell of the salami inside my backpack. After I scared him away, I realized that it was morning, time to put my things together and continue on my trek. In the daylight I was able to view the unfamiliar surroundings with people walking and riding bicycles, trucks going by in both directions, horsedrawn wagons, herds of sheep, and more. When I passed someone I pulled my beret down further on my face hoping that no one would speak to me other than a short greeting to which I responded with similar but unintelligible sound. The terrain was fairly flat, but after I oriented myself by the sun, I could see a mountain range rising toward the northeast. I passed road signs pointing to Irun 15km, and San Sebastian 30km, both cities that I wanted to avoid. I saw a sign on the side of a shed that read

Pamplona 100 km. I was somewhat relieved, figuring that I could easily make that distance in no more than two days. I badly miscalculated.

Little did I know that the mountain range I had seen was the Pyrenees and that the highest peaks were to the northeast. The next five days, which it took me to reach Pamplona, were to be the most treacherous, unpredictable, and demanding I had ever experienced. Heinz was not with me, and I had to continue by myself. It was hard having no one to talk to. The roads were becoming steep, at first covered with gravel, and later by snowdrifts. For the first three days I had to push the bike uphill, and it snowed intermittently. Heavy fog arrived in late afternoon and lingered until late in the morning. I made little progress since I had to push my bike, instead of riding it much of the time. The temperatures during midday were bearable, but during the night they fell into the low 30 degrees. I started to wear long johns, two shirts, a heavy sweater, two pairs of socks, gloves, and my overcoat. I never knew how even moderately low temperatures could affect a person over long periods. Sleeping on the ground was also very trying and distressing. I feared that I would freeze to death. The second night was dreadful. When I awoke in the morning I seemed to be frozen stiff and could barely move. I urinated into my hands and that helped. Then I applied the warmth from my hands to my face and massaged my cheeks and my ears until I felt more comfortable. It was a terrible feeling knowing what I had done that I have never forgotten and never talked about. I still remember praying and reciting the *shema*, the highest Jewish prayer. To make things worse, while riding on a short but steep downward stretch, I slipped and fell from my bike. Except for the scare I was not hurt, but the front wheel rim was badly bent to such an extent that the bike was now useless. Instead of abandoning it, I used it as a cart for the suitcase and backpack so that I did not have to carry both. I must have looked like an escaped convict; my clothes were dirty and I was unshaven. No vehicle going in either direction stopped for me. On the other hand I was glad that no one stopped for me because of my language difficulty that could have led to more problems.

As I proceeded into the foothills of the Pyrenees, walking almost southeast, the daytime temperatures became warmer. I pushed the bicycle into what appeared to be a large town, Leitza. Signs indicated that it was 48km to San Sebastian, the approximate distance I had already traveled in three days and three nights since I left Hendaye, France. There was still no sign of Heinz. I was hungry and thirsty. I had no food left in my backpack, and the fall from my bike had broken my thermos bottle. I had to buy food and maybe a bike to be able to continue on to Pamplona. This was Basque country, and many of the men wore berets, much larger than the one I wore, and drawn down over their right ears, a local custom. I still had some French money but knew I would have difficulty buying anything without local currency. I looked for a place where I could exchange the francs for pesetas in the village I went through.

Now the test of pretending to be mute and deaf came into play so that I wouldn't give myself away as a foreigner on the run. I didn't want someone in a bank to become suspicious and call the police. After mustering enough courage to walk into a bank, I laid the eight one thousand franc bills on the counter and wrote the word PESETAS on a piece of paper. The man looked at me, uttered a few words in Spanish that I didn't understand, and walked away with my money. Immediately I was worried. After a minute or so that seemed like an hour he returned with a stack of bills, spoke a few words and handed me the money. I walked away with a sigh of relief. My act had worked!

I was so hungry and thirsty that I settled for a nearby tavern whose aromas of food and wine called to me as I passed by. I unleashed my suitcase from the bike and walked inside seating myself at a corner table. I was becoming more confident. When the waitress came over I went through my hand motions, first to my mouth and next to my ears. She seemed to understand my sign language and brought me a menu. I looked it over carefully, uncertain of what it said, and picked out what I thought was a meal. When she brought a carafe of red wine, I pointed to an item on the menu and that was that. Soon she brought me a big plate of goat meat, potatoes, and bread. I devoured everything in short order and drank a glass of wine. I paid with a few bills and then left without waiting for change.

Next I looked for a shop that repaired bicycles, of which there were several. I stopped at an open market repair stand and pointed to the bent front wheel. Again I went through my silent language routine while the man tried to explain what could be done. He took one of the many wheels from a rack and motioned it as a replacement. Next he wrote the price on a piece of paper, and I gladly agreed. When he finished exchanging the front wheel, I paid him and rode off. Tired, dirty, and very uncomfortable, I pedaled to the entrance of an old and dirty-looking inn and walked inside with my bike. I held both hands to one ear signifying sleep; the clerk gave me a register to sign, then a key, and off I went to look for my room. The dreary room had a bed, chest of drawers, a chair, washbasin, a mirror, and window. The toilet was down the hall and shared with other guests. After what I had been through the past few days, I did not care about the slight inconvenience. After washing and shaving I went to bed and slept until the sun came through the window the next morning. I felt as if I had been given a new lease on life. It was time to leave for Pamplona. After I paid for the night, I noticed a fairly large map on the wall of the hotel lobby. The distance of about 50km to Pamplona was one I could easily travel by evening assuming hilly but not too mountainous terrain. I stopped to buy a loaf of bread, several bottles of sparkling water, and some grapes before setting off on the next leg of my journey.

The ride was easy and for the first time since leaving Hendaye I pulled out my harmonica and played it for myself after making my first rest stop along the road. I was more at ease hoping that by evening I would be sitting on a train to Barcelona. I envisioned being reunited with my parents and Heinz and putting the agony of the past few days behind me. This was the best day since I had left Luxembourg, but the uncertainty of the future still nagged at me. I reached the outskirts of Pamplona by early evening and started to look for signs of a railroad station. There were many signs but I was unable to read most of them, and could not decipher any Spanish words that looked like "train station." The town was large with people and traffic everywhere. I approached a nicely dressed man wearing a French beret like mine, hoping he was not a Spaniard. "*Pardon Monsieur, où se trouve la gare?*" I was in luck. He understood and pointed in the direction of the station, not far away. As I pushed my bike up a few steps to the station entrance, I encountered a uniformed man, probably a policeman. He waved his finger indicating that I had to leave my bike outside. I placed the bike into one of many racks, unfastened the suitcase and backpack, and proceeded into the station filled with people, noise, and smoke.

I learned years later that I was in one of the larger Spanish cities famous for its annual event, the running of the bulls, which had apparently concluded before my arrival. There were posters and advertisements on the walls with pictures of running bulls with people also running in front of and behind them. I thought they were advertisements for bull fights. However this yearly running of the bulls was probably a good thing for me. There were many tourists in Pamplona, and I was able to blend right in with them. Inside the station I noticed the area where freight was dispatched. I went outside to retrieve my bike and return to the area for its shipment to Barcelona. As I searched up and down the many racks I realized that it was not there. The bicycle that had brought me here, the one to which I owed my recent life, had been stolen in a fashion similar to what I had done just days ago. At first I was upset and angry but then tried to rationalize that I might not be able to use it in Barcelona anyway. Nevertheless it was a shock and another one of many disappointments to come.

Again at the ticket counter I wrote the word "Barcelona" on a piece of paper and used my hand gestures to convey that I wanted a oneway ticket. I laid some bills on the counter and received change in return. The ticket listed the departure time several hours later. Even though it was late evening, the terminal was hot and reeked of smoke and other unpleasant smells. I went outside again to search for my bike in the dim light of the racks, but to no avail. I sat on the steps and opened my backpack for something to eat and drink. I used the bathroom to clean up even though the facilities were primitive and dirty. I then boarded the train, which was filled to capacity. I found a space in the nonsmoking section, but after a while, to my disgust, several people started to smoke, but I was unable to object. Then the conductor came into our compartment, checked all tickets, and punched holes in them. The train traveled slowly through many tunnels. The ride was rough and the train stopped at every town along the way. In between stops I tried to catnap. Passengers in our compartment got up and walked into the corridors to retrieve things from their luggage or to look out the window. At some stops passengers got off the train, and others boarded taking their places. This activity continued for several hours until most of them went to sleep. Thank goodness there had been a minimum of conversation.

While there were signs at every stop, the only one I remember was Zaragoza. Finally the train picked up speed. As we approached Barcelona, daylight was beginning to break and I became very nervous and anxious. My mind seemed to be going faster than the train. Trains passed us from the other direction, and I could see roads with columns of military vehicles. After passing buildings and bridges in various states of disrepair, I remembered that there had been a bitterly fought civil war that had come to an end only recently. As we continued I could see more and more destruction caused by this war.

The train finally came to a stop around eight or nine o'clock in the morning. I saw signs all over that read "Barcelona." I had made it! I learned later that the trip by train from Pamplona was 400 plus kilometers. In my mind it had taken forever. The station as I remember it was huge, and it took me a long time going up and down stairs to get to the lobby that had been partially destroyed. In the bathroom I shaved, changed my shirt, put on a pair of knickerbocker trousers, and a clean pair of shoes, hoping to look halfway presentable. I found a German language newspaper in the trashcan and was anxious to find out what was going on in the world. As I quickly learned, German armies had made rapid advances in Russia; Germans and Italians were dividing Yugoslavia; German bombers were attacking Moscow; Japan had invaded Cambodia and Thailand; Spain had promised Hitler one army division to fight with the Germans on the Russian front. The war news was not good for the Allies or me.

During my many hours on the train to Barcelona, my mind dwelled on many things, but I never gave any thought as to how I would find the JDC, the socalled "Joint" office, when I got there. That was where I was supposed to find out where my parents were, if indeed, they had arrived. I walked out of the rail station, my backpack over my shoulder and carrying the heavy beatup suitcase. I did not have the faintest idea where to go or to whom I could turn. People were everywhere, among them men in differently colored military uniforms, riding bicycles or motorcycles. There were no cars because of the gasoline shortage. I felt hopelessly lost in a sea of humanity. I remember sitting down on the sidewalk next to a doorway just staring into space. I had come so far and now had no idea what to do.

I walked across the street to a telephone booth and looked in the phone book for such words as JDC, synagogue, *Juif* (French for Jew), and other combinations of words, but to no avail. I didn't know the Spanish word for Jew and felt that I was back to square one. I just started to walk and walk. Suddenly, as if lightning had struck, I saw a man with *payess*, side curls, a full beard, and wearing a large black hat and a long black caftan coat. There was no doubt in my mind that he was an orthodox Jew. I rushed up to him and said, "*Shalom*," Hebrew for hello and also peace. I must have said it several times before he stopped and acknowledged me by saying, *Alechem Sholom*, meaning, "and unto you peace." He seemed to be as surprised as I was. He began speaking Spanish, and when that didn't work he tried what I assumed was Polish. When he realized that I understood neither, he started speaking Yiddish, and I understood it to some extent. He pulled me by my arm and I began walking with him. He was sent by G'd; he must have been an angel!

As we walked I said "JDC" repeatedly, but he did not react. I motioned to him that I wanted to write. He stopped, and pulled out a pencil and paper on which I wrote the three letters JDC. His reaction indicated that he understood and we began walking rapidly in another direction. We walked for a long time; I was tired and shifted my suitcase frequently from one hand to another. He noticed my fatigue and helped me carry it. Where was he taking me? Soon I had my answer. We climbed the stairs of a hotellike building and there on one of the doors, barely recognizable, was a small Star of David. We walked in. It took only seconds for me to realize where I was! This was the JDC, the Jewish Joint Distribution Committee, a loose network of welfare institutions dedicated to helping Jewish refugees. I later found out that much of their funding came from American Jewish organizations. The Chasidic pious one motioned for me to sit down. Several times I said, *Vielen Dank*, "thank you," and reached out to shake his hand, but he refused. He then walked out of the office and I never saw him again. I was happy, confused, bewildered, and exhausted, but I had found the JDC, one of many of my interim destinations.

I walked to a desk where a middleaged lady sat and pulled out my various identification papers. She observed that the papers were in German, and so began speaking German to me. She asked whether I was hungry and motioned for me to come with her into another room. Dozens of people sat at tables eating, talking, napping, reading, writing, or smoking. I sat down at a table by myself, and it was not long before a Spanish lady brought me a large bowl of hot soup that I devoured with great enjoyment. It almost felt like home. After I had recovered a bit, I returned to the other room and asked the lady at the desk about Joseph and Martha Kahn and Heinz Alkan. She looked through several ledgers filled with names and finally said, "I have a Joseph Kahn. He is staying at Hotel Navarra, Rambla de Catalunya, not far from here. Heinz Alkan is there also." I could have jumped for joy as my eyes became moist. If my memory is correct, the JDC was located in or adjacent to a Hotel Bristol.

The lady asked me to sign various papers mostly in Spanish, which I did not understand, but I signed them without a moment's hesitation because I knew I was in good hands. She gave me an envelope containing pesetas bills, an official looking card that I was to give to the clerk at the hotel, and a sketch with directions to Hotel Navarra. Then she wished me good luck. I left immediately, eager to get there. I followed the directions and found the hotel with ease. It was an old building, poorly maintained, an understatement at best. A sign on the elevator pointed to a staircase, and I got the message. The second floor lobby was crowded with people on every couch and chair. All of a sudden I heard someone yell, "Robert!" It was Heinz, and within a split second two friends blended into one. There were no words; neither of us could speak. After a minute or so he left abruptly and disappeared only to return with my mom and dad. It was the first time I had ever seen my mother run! There was such a commotion of hugging and kissing, and as always, when Mom was overjoyed, she cried. It was a very emotional scene that I can still feel and see now as I write about it. We were finally reunited! It was a miracle to be sure.

I went to the desk clerk, gave him the card, and was assigned to Heinz's room. There was no key for me, but I didn't mind sharing with Heinz. The room was dingy with a tiny window and had a low wattage bulb in a ceiling fan. The room was very warm, but the fan made it bearable. Although it was only early afternoon, I was exhausted and went to bed, missed supper, and slept until Heinz woke me the next morning. We went to breakfast in a large dining hall on the next floor. About forty people including a few children were there, mostly Jewish refugees from various countries. Their outward appearance and demeanor gave me the impression that I was looking at a mausoleum for the living.

We each received chicory coffee or tea, one slice of bread, and a few grapes. Heinz explained that many foods including bread, milk, meat, butter, and eggs were rationed and could only be obtained with an official ration card furnished to Spanish citizens. Otherwise food had to be obtained on the black market, and severe punishment was imposed on anyone who was caught. I still had some bread, salami, and goat cheese left from my purchase in Pamplona and gladly shared it with Heinz that evening after a meager meal of soup, a spoonful of green beans, and a small potato. Drinking water was also scarce and was treated as if it were expensive champagne. Dad asked me to go for a walk with him, a pretense so that he could talk with me. He took his seventeen-year-old son by the hand, something he had not done for many years, and poured his heart out. He was sorry that he had told Heinz and me to make our own way from Hendaye to Barcelona fearing for our lives at crossing the border from France into Spain. With tears in his eyes he explained that, in retrospect, it was a wrong decision and that there may not have been any problem if we had all stayed together. He needed to apologize, and said that he had no idea what a terrible time we had getting to Barcelona. And then he really shocked me when he asked, practically begging me, to promise Mom and him never to reveal to anyone his erroneous decision or our hairraising journey that could possibly have cost us our lives. He had asked Heinz to

EXHIBIT 9.5 The four waitresses at Hotel Navarra, on the right is Lucy, who gave us additional bread and sometimes potatoes.

make that same promise. I had no problem agreeing; I was just happy that the nightmarish journey was behind me and I was reunited with my family, except for my sister Irene. I gave that promise and kept it until long after Mom and Dad had passed away. Even then I discussed my hellish journey from Hendaye to Barcelona with only a few people here in America. I never mentioned it specifically when the Spielberg Visual History Foundation interviewed Gert and me on January 26, 1996. I have never held Mom and Dad's decision against them. On the contrary, I feel that they made their decision out of love for me, a love I hope that I adequately returned.

Heinz arrived in Barcelona one day before I did. After we had crossed into Spain and became separated he continued in a southwesterly direction, in the vicinity of San Sebastian, before turning southeast toward Pamplona, avoiding the Pyrenees Mountains. Unfortunately I had proceeded in a southeasterly direction into the foothills of the Pyrenees Mountains before turning south. Neither of us had contemplated that part of the journey, and we were both unbelievably lucky to have made it unharmed. The most formidable and immediate problem now, aside from the heat, was the scarcity of food. Dad had never gained back his full strength since he had returned from Dachau Concentration Camp, and he was now losing additional weight, as was Mom. Heinz and I weren't faring much better. We were always hungry in spite of the fact that a nice relationship with a young, pretty waitress resulted in her leaving us extra slices of bread and potatoes. We shared these extras with Mom and Dad, but it was still not enough, and so we started buying food items on the black market. Knickerbocker trousers came in handy because we were able to hide black market purchases in them. Police and undercover agents randomly stopped people carrying packages to make sure they were not selling or buying things illegally. These things included not just food but also gasoline, kerosene, tires for cars and bicycles, shoes, and other wearing apparel.

One day I had in my trousers a link of sausages I had bought. As I walked along I heard several dogs yapping behind me. About five or six dogs had picked up on the scent of the meat in my trousers. Immediately I turned in to a store and waited for them to leave before continuing. The incident seems funny today, but it was not then. Instead of trying to speak Spanish, Heinz also imitated my deaf and mute hand signals since they had worked well for me. Because buying on the black market was extremely expensive, our money was unfortunately dwindling rapidly. The JDC office paid for our lodging, but that was all. Dad wanted us to save the money we had left for later, unsure of how long we would have to stay in Barcelona. Flirting with our waitresses didn't produce much more food nor did they accept money because they were afraid of being caught.

Through the JDC office Dad had been able to contact his brother Ernst in Chicago via telegrams. He asked for a loan of money and to have it transferred to the office so that it would be available to pay for our ship passage, if and when that became possible. Dad went to the JDC office every day pleading with the people there to find a way for us all to leave for America. Hundreds of other refugees were also looking to escape, most of them no longer caring what country or island would take them. Every day people disappeared from Hotel Navarra, and others took their place. At every morning or evening meal (there was no lunch), I looked around the dining room to see who was missing and who was new. The absence of those who had left was sad, and yet I was envious of them because they were going somewhere, finally free. I ask myself today, what happened to them? Did they make it? Many did not.

Cigarettes were in very high demand since it seemed that every Spaniard smoked, including women, like our waitresses, and even some children. Rationing had made them priceless. That fact triggered my idea to recycle cigarette butts. At first I scoured the streets and picked up butts wherever I could find them. At the end of the day I emptied the tobacco from the collected butts and rolled it into cigarette paper to sell the next day on the black market. I sold one or several at a time. This venture was very profitable, the only drawback was the constant bending down and being careful not to get caught. My ingenuity came in handy when I decided to put a nail through the heel of my shoe in order to spear the butts on the ground. Then I would quickly raise my foot and strip the butt from the nail and put it into a bag. It took some practice but this was faster, less fatiguing, and I was able to increase my sales per day by about fifty percent. Even though I had to tip toe on the foot on which the shoe had the nail sticking out. Sometimes I bartered cigarettes for bread or other food items or things we needed, like for instance pieces of shoe leather or socks. As you may remember in his early days, Dad had learned the shoemaker trade and applied it here for us and others with some tools loaned from hotel maintenance. Heinz made money legally, but made far less than I did. He caught crabs as they climbed up the harbor dock walls. He used a long pole with a snare at the end made out of gut, like a violin string. When the crab touched the snare with its claws, Heinz jerked on the pole and the snare tightened around the claws. That was it! The money we made from selling cigarettes and live crabs was our lifeline. Even though these endeavors were exhausting and not enjoyable, we were able to keep our family from going to bed hungry on a starvation diet.

While I was not too interested in sightseeing, I did take notice of a large amount of destruction caused by the civil war that had ended in April 1939 with a victory for the Nationalists and Generalissimo Franco. The Metro subway was inoperative due to heavy damage, harbor installations were damaged or destroyed, and only smaller ships could come to the dock. Many of the once beautiful churches and cathedrals were in shambles, yet the city still had earmarks of having been very beautiful.

Dictator Franco and Hitler were staunch allies. Hitler provided support for the civil war, specifically men, materials, and active aerial attacks by the "Condor" Luftwaffe on the revolutionary forces, and were largely responsible for the Nationalist's victory. Franco owed Hitler much, and he repaid him partially by giving Hitler access to the Mediterranean Sea where Hitler could conduct clandestine operations primarily by resupplying German submarines. Along the coastal area, and especially noticeable in Barcelona, was the presence of German soldiers, sailors, and the Gestapo, all incognito without military uniforms. We feared the Gestapo the most because one of their missions was to continue to terrorize Jews, and pick them up and ship them back to concentration camps in France, Germany, Poland, and elsewhere. Young boys of military age, like us, were very vulnerable. It was one way people disappeared, and no one knew what had happened to them. Unfortunately, while Franco's soldiers and the police did not cooperate in those efforts, they ignored the kidnappings and looked the other way.

We were constantly on guard and were doubly careful when we saw men wearing leather coats or jackets and hats. In all the heat, it was a sure sign they were Nazis. My parents and all others had to stay at the hotel most of the time like they were under house arrest. This was very frustrating for them, and impacted their moods more and more. Mother had frequent crying spells over the seeming hopelessness of our situation. The never-ending heat, scarcity of food, the worry that I might be caught by the Nazis, and the uncertainty of our future were all contributing factors to her depression. Dad and I tried as best we could to reassure her that help was on the way. Even Heinz talked optimistically about tomorrow. Now and then I tried to cheer everyone up by playing the harmonica, but it was only a temporary fix. Mom, Dad, Heinz, and I often succumbed to self-denial of our tragic situation.

We were already isolated from the rest of the world, torn from all of our family and friends. Each day Dad wrote letters and postcards to Luxembourg, Germany, and to Irene in France hoping to receive a reply that all was well. He sent other letters to America hoping that our family there would become aware of our urgent plight and do everything they could to help us and also obtain visas for Uncle Max and Aunt Helene who were still in Luxembourg. For Opa there was no hope. He had repeatedly been denied a visa to America because of his age. These were desperate times of war, and lives were expendable.

Days passed and each of us settled into a routine of sorts. We supported each other with words of courage while fearing for our lives and hoping for a miracle. One day I returned from cigarette butt scavenging with a loaf of bread in each pant leg, and Dad waved a piece of yellow paper in front of my face saying, "*Es ist angekommen! Es ist angekommen!*" "It has arrived! It has arrived!" A telegram from Uncle Ernst, Dad's brother in Chicago, indicated that he had dispatched $1,272 to the JDC office in Barcelona for passage of the three of us by ship. Elated as we all were, I immediately thought, "What about Heinz?" I was not about to leave my friend behind. Later that evening during supper in the dining room I told him the news. He said that he had also written a distant relative in America for passage money and was hoping to hear from him any day now. I was momentarily relieved, but not totally.

The JDC would tell us when and on what ship we would leave after determining the availability of the ship and finding out the safety of the shipping lanes at the time. The radio and newspapers were full of successful German submarine attacks on Allied ships in the Mediterranean and the Atlantic Ocean. Even though we were in a socalled neutral country, not every captain wanted to risk his ship because of the special human cargo on board, namely we Jews. We had no idea what was in store for us. We just wanted to leave, hopefully for America.

As time went by it seemed as if the days became longer and our anxieties increased by the hour. One afternoon as I was collecting cigarette butts, a Spanish policeman stopped me and frisked me. I played deaf and mute using hand gestures, but was relieved of all the cigarette butts I had that day. I was very scared, but the officer seemed sympathetic of my perceived affliction and let me go with what I thought was a warning. I told Heinz but not my parents. They had enough to worry about. Finally Heinz received word that this relative in America had deposited money for his passage also. What a relief for both of us!

Next, Dad told us that we had to go to the JDC office the next morning for a briefing regarding our passage to America. Heinz and I were so excited that we awoke at one o'clock in the morning ready to go. After breakfast we walked to the JDC. To avoid suspicion I walked with Mom, Dad walked alone, and Heinz followed a small distance behind. It was too dangerous to walk together as a family. When we arrived, we assembled in a room with about forty other people. From the many questions asked, I determined that most of them were German. We learned that we would be boarding the ship by the end of July and would receive only a half-day's notice. Information about the ship was rather vague. We did learn that the ship was under the administration of the Norddeutsche Lloyd (which had offices in Bremen, Germany), a wellknown and respected firm. Everyone thought that this fact could be an advantage for us traveling through the Atlantic that was infested with German U-boats. The four of us were encouraged by the news, and we returned to the hotel, a little more upbeat, walking separately, but united in mind as one strongwilled family.

The news came not a day too early. We had been without money for about a week and were buying food with Heinz's meager legal income from selling crabs and from the money I made selling cigarettes on the black market. We were living hand to mouth so to speak, supplementing our meager food portions at the hotel with whatever Heinz and I could buy or barter on the black market. We were on the cusp of poverty and slowly on the road to starvation. I could tell because when I awoke during the night my stomach was making some odd rumblings, and Heinz complained to me similarly. They were hunger pangs!

The war news that we heard by the biased Spanish press was not encouraging. The German armies were thrusting into Russia on all fronts stretching from the far north of the Arctic Ocean 2000 miles south to the Black Sea. The German tanks, motorized infantry and Air Force was overwhelming the Russians everywhere, and bombings of civilians in cities were heralded as great successes. How and when would it all end? Could the Allied forces eventually be victorious?

Finally, we received word that we would be picked up by truck around midnight on August 1. We were scheduled for the second of three trips the truck would make to the pier. Nervous and somewhat scared, we loaded into the open truck about 2:00 a.m. The trip proved uneventful, and I even pulled out my trusted harmonica and softly played a tune. We stopped in front of a ship that didn't look like a passenger liner, more like a freighter, but there was no larger vessel in the vicinity. We unloaded our backpacks and several suitcases. Spanish speaking sailors, who appeared to be having a good time, assisted us. The name painted on the bow of the ship said, *Ciudad de Sevilla*. There was already quite a bit of commotion from those who had arrived on the first truck pick up, and soon there would be more. We thought that our baggage was being stored below deck in what looked like a large cargo area, but soon found out that this was to be our living and sleeping quarters. Bunk beds with blankets and pillows lined three of the walls and center of the cargo hole. These were for the men. Females were directed to a similar area opposite from our so called cabin area. Makeshift curtain sheets provided privacy, and luggage, backpacks, and our only worldly possessions would be stored under the bunks or hung up on rusty nails in wooden planks rising perpendicular from the bunk beds. Bitter complaints arose from passengers who expected transport meant for humans, not cargo, along with curses and the shouting of obscenities directed at the JDC and the ship's captain. People became unruly. The ship's captain used the loudspeaker to make an apology and explain that all ships carrying emigrants from European ports were similar to this one, and he assured us that we would be given the best of care. Then he made a suggestion that in retrospect sounded like a disguised ultimatum. Anyone not satisfied with the ship's accommodations would be free to leave the ship. Despite his offer, I did not see anyone take him up on it. We were willing to put up with the unexpected, crowded, and primitive conditions as long as our lives were saved and we reached the shores of America. However, the grumbling and angry voices from others went on and on.

A door from our cargo/living quarters opened to a large area with two flush toilets and five large steel tubs for personal washing. Although not pretty or sanitary, it was functional. What no one was accustomed to was the lack of privacy except for the two toilets.

It was morning before everyone settled in. Most of the passengers were tired from the ordeal and slept or rested in their bunks. I was sound asleep when a bell rang signaling breakfast. We climbed stairs to the deck above where tables and benches were set up under tarpaulins. Sailors stood by to assist with the food that consisted of either tea, coffee, milk, two slices of bread, jam, and watermelon. There were two choices: Take it or leave it! The four of us sat together, grateful that we had made it through the night. We acquainted ourselves with people sitting next to us and began to relax somewhat. After all, we were all "in the same boat!" The sun rose gradually along with the rising temperature under the tarpaulin. A thermometer mounted on one of the beams indicated thirty-two degrees Celsius, almost ninety degrees Fahrenheit.

Where to go to stay cool became the problem, and air conditioning did not exist in Europe in 1941. There were no fans on board, at least not in the converted cargo compartment where we were quartered. The temperature rose even higher in the afternoon. Men walked around without shirts, some without undershirts. I rolled up my pant legs. Women walked with blouses open, and some even took them off and sat around just in brassieres. It was miserable. Some thought of going barefoot but then found out that the deck was so hot that it burned their feet. Most passengers never thought of bringing bathing suits, nor did we. We hoped that once the ship set sail that there would be a breeze to help us. So far there were no signs that we were going anywhere.

All of a sudden a sense of panic arose among the passengers. Rumor spread that a truck had pulled up and a dozen or more police had boarded the ship. Then the captain announced that all passengers were to come on deck with proper identification, evidence of paid passage, and visas. Now what? Was this some kind of hitch or just a routine check by the Spanish government? The answer came quickly. Fortytwo passengers lined up on deck under the brutally hot sun. Three policeman each sat behind a table, and a man in civilian clothes wearing a typical German hat sat behind a fourth. He was German, probably a Gestapo. Each one of the police examined different types of identification and proof papers. The man in civvies looked at everything again and in some instances asked questions in German. We found out later that the rest of the police were searching the ship, in particular our quarters, for contraband among our meager belongings.

Everything seemed to be going smoothly until some raised voices were heard from the fourth desk where the Gestapo sat. Outcries and loud voices from a woman and a man were aimed at the Gestapo. The Gestapo stood, pointed to the police and ordered, "*Verhaften sie diese zwei Leute!*" "Arrest these two people!" The police did as they were told and led the screaming couple away from the rest of us. It was a terrible and tragic sight to see and to hear the crying and pleading of the two. None of us ever found out who they were, why they were taken off the ship, or what happened to them. We could only assume, and those assumptions did not foretell anything good. We were all relieved to be waived on by the man in the hat. Perspiring from head to toe, we hoped that the ship would depart soon. We tried to sweet talk different sailors, but either they knew and wouldn't tell us, or they honestly didn't know.

Lunch was the same food as breakfast, and dinner turned out to be more of the same, coffee, tea, bread, jam, and watermelon. Some passengers complained, but the sailors who had set up the buffet table and served had nothing to do with the menu, but intimated that the captain would be informed. In the meantime some of the passengers were becoming sick from a combination of heat, watermelon, and unfiltered warm water. Today we know not to drink anything but bottled water in countries such as Spain. There was no ship doctor, but luckily almost everyone had brought various medications from home, and there was one doctor among the passengers.

Finally the next morning before dawn we heard the anchor being raised, and then with many saying "Thank God" we moved ever so slowly out of the harbor. I have no idea how fast the ship was moving except that we could now feel the ship rolling from

EXHIBIT 9.6 Our ship the *Ciudad de Sevilla*.

side to side and the bow moving up and down. In addition to illnesses from heat and food, some passengers were now becoming seasick. People ran to toilets or washtubs while others "fed the fish" while hanging over the railing. Heinz and I familiarized ourselves with the layout of the ship and met a few passengers who were our age, including two girls. We also found a small shady place at the bow of the ship where our group of six new friends met at random. On the wheelhouse where the captain steered the course a small copper plaque read, "Transmediteromea Compania, 1927, 6,279 Tonelaje," or 6,279 tons. Compared with today's cruise ships, our *Ciudad de Sevilla* was the size of a sardine can. The captain's name was also on the door, but I did not write it down.

There were other signs and regulations posted in several languages, some of which we already knew. For example, men had to vacate the women's quarters by 9:00 p.m. The women had similar restrictions posted regarding men's quarters. As small as the freighter was, there were "DO NOT ENTER" signs posted everywhere. We moved south along the Spanish coast, and although we did not understand the sailors, when one of them pointed to land and said "Valencia," we had a clue as to where we were. Most of the passengers, including Mom and Dad, were not as restless as they had been only a day ago. After all, nothing could be done, at least for now. An impromptu committee formed that was comprised of one man and one woman, who made an appointment to meet with the captain to discuss passengers' grievances. After their meeting they reported back that the captain would make an effort to purchase more food as soon as we reached a non-Spanish port.

The information gave everyone new hope and some satisfaction that their concerns were being heard and addressed. In the meantime we ate loads of bread, drank plenty of tea, and had as much watermelon as we could stomach. The committee also found out that the freighter's cargo consisted primarily of watermelon, hence no shortage of that item.

The following day, after I was also seasick for a while, we saw more ships including several British war ships. We signaled back and forth with high beam lights, primarily for identification purposes, I supposed. Our freighter flew a yellow flag bordered by red stripes top and bottom. The smoke stack was painted with the same colors of Spain. Hopefully that would keep the German U-boats from torpedoing us as Spain was a German ally. Even though the ship's movement provided a breeze, it was still very hot, but I had to wear a shirt so I wouldn't burn. Most of the passengers stayed in their assigned quarters sitting or lying on their bunks. Some men and women played cards; others read books that they had brought along. Occasionally, Heinz and I met at the bow with the other four new friends. We talked, joked, and played cards. I played my harmonica and we sang. Basically, we tried to while away the time as best we could. Best of all, since there were no restrictions, we stayed there until late at night and even slept there. It was a little like camping out. Dad worried at first when we were not in our bunks, but that was straightened out when we explained.

The next day things became more exciting. As early morning ship traffic increased and continued to increase all day, the captain made an announcement that we were approaching the Fortress of Gibraltar. Not only did we see ships, but now we saw airplanes. Some circled so low that we could see the British insignia on the fuselage, a red, white, and blue circle. We waved our hands, shirts, and handkerchiefs, and shouted words of jubilation. Unfortunately, the wind and the drone of the aircraft engines swallowed up our words. Momentarily, and for the first time since we had boarded, we felt that we had escaped the clutches of the madman, Hitler. We were now under British protection. Sometime past midafternoon a British patrol boat pulled up alongside our ship and ordered the captain to follow. For security reasons all passengers had to go below so that we could not see the minefields, Uboat nets, warships in the harbor, and the fortifications in the harbor and on the "Rock."

We must have been in our hole for several hours when the announcement came that our confinement had been lifted. The sight on deck was unbelievable. Still a good distance from the "Rock," it was an impressive sight to see hundreds of ships of all types and sizes. They were from many countries, anchored or on the move, as far as the eye could see. We were also at anchor. A British patrol had come on board to check our papers, the cargo, the ship itself, the sailors on board, and who knows what else. We were anxious to talk to the Brits and learn what was going on in the world. We pleaded with them to bring us additional food for our continued voyage. Later that evening a barge loaded with food staples was uploaded to the *Ciudad de Sevilla*. It was like receiving a birthday or Chanukkah present. That evening after four days on the ship we had butter, fresh eggs, and potatoes. I remember that our group went to the wheel house and sang, "*Hoch soll er leben, hoch soll er leben, drei mal hoch!*" It meant, "He should live a long life, he should live a long life, three times his present age." The captain came out smiling and gave each of us a piece of chocolate. One, two, three, it was gone!

Later that evening Heinz and I, somewhat foolishly, decided to go for a swim now that the ship was anchored. It was very hot and there was no discernable breeze. Also, we were under British protection and had nothing to fear, and there was nothing posted that forbade us to do so. We had cut off our trousers above the knee as a makeshift swim suit. Surely the water would cool us off. We dove in head first from the lower deck and soon had numerous passengers cheering us on. While we were enjoying the experience, a bunch of the sailors threw lifesavers attached to ropes to us and motioned for us to grab hold of them. They pulled us up on deck, and although we didn't understand what they were saying, we realized that we were being scolded in no uncertain terms. Mom and Dad had come to see the spectacle and were not amused either. They severely gave us a piece of their minds. We were called everything under the sun while we stood there smiling, having enjoyed our little swim escapade. It was not until the next morning when British sailors came on board that we learned that the waters there were infested with sharks that loved to feast on human flesh.

The patrol boat led us out of the harbor so that we would not run into mines or submarine nets. It appeared that we were headed for open sea. But that was not to be. Instead we headed across the Strait of Gibraltar to the port of Tangier. We did not dock, but anchored in the harbor where hundreds of ships were coming and going. A large barge approached and refueled our ship. In spite of near intolerable conditions, life on board ship settled down into daily routines. Passengers resigned themselves to endure the abnormal temporary conditions to be able to lead a new life in America free from persecution. We talked a lot about what to expect once we arrived in America, dreamed out loud about jobs, apartments, cars, and ice cream. We stayed in Tangier until the next morning when the ship's engines again began to churn, heading us into what we assumed was the open Atlantic. Our meals began to vary as we received an occasional hardboiled egg, a potato, and a small slice of sausage. In addition to watermelon we received a banana, an orange, or a few dates. All of it was still a far cry from a homecooked meal.

After several hours we started wondering where we were headed because we could see land on the starboard side of the ship. We were perplexed and got no answers from the crew. Evidently we were not headed out into the open sea. Day and night passed and we were no closer to an answer. On the other hand cruising in close proximity to land kept us safer from predatory submarines. In midafternoon we spotted a seaplane approaching, circle, and fly away. Its wings and rudder were red and green, and we had no idea what country it represented. Then about two hours later we saw a large rock with large letters, "Lisboa." Now we were really confused, assuming that we were near Lisbon, Portugal. Everyone was guessing and speculation ran rampant. If we had traveled from Tangier to Lisbon that meant that our ship had taken a north by northwest course which seemed like backtracking not on course to America. What actually happened was that after we left Tangier, we sailed around the entire Atlantic coast of Spain only to end up in Lisbon, Portugal! But why?

The harbor was huge, and I remember the city with its whitewashed houses rising above it. We docked right at a pier, and to our surprise, the captain announced that the following morning everyone could go ashore as long we were all back on board no later than 5:00 p.m., local time. It was an announcement from heaven. I believe it was still Shabbat, and we were making havdalah, without the usual wine, candle, or the spice box. I had learned earlier, and now found it to be true, that praying can be done anywhere especially under dire and unusual circumstances. We prayed for a safe journey, and included special blessings for

EXHIBIT 9.7 Our Journey: Luxembourg, through Paris to Barcelona, Spain, then by ship around the coast to Tangier, North Morocco and then north to Lisbon, Portugal.

those left behind as well as the allusive captain and crew on board. All of the passengers were exhausted from the strain of the journey so far, the heat, and loneliness. However, at that moment most of us were happy and watched the beautiful sunset as if it were a special signal from America. A good omen, perhaps?

Before we went to sleep that night, we young ones decided to go ashore together in the morning. Portugal was one of the few countries in Europe that had stayed neutral in the war, and since Lisbon was an important seaport, many disenfranchised Jews had fled there to wait out the war or to use the city as a springboard to freedom. It turned out that the Jewish community there had been alerted to the arrival of our ship. As the passengers set foot on the deck the next morning, local Jews greeted us and offered to take us to town. The six of us joined a group of other boys and girls greeting us on the dock and went with them through the terraced paths and elevators up to the city. They bought us ice cream that we devoured with gusto. Next they took us to a tennis tournament. Had I known as much about tennis then as I do now, I could have enjoyed it more. As it turned out, the only ones who really enjoyed the matches were the local boys and girls. Later they treated us to some sandwiches from a street vendor and then brought us back to the ship.

The day had been nice, but an awkward reprieve from what we had been experiencing on the ship. Conversation with our young hosts had been difficult due to the language barrier, and from what I could tell, they came from affluent Jewish homes and none of them had ever been exposed to violent anti-Semitism. My parents had also enjoyed the day with people of a similar age group, but interestingly enough, they had also formed the same impressions. On board ship nothing had changed except for taking on additional supplies.

When I awoke the next morning, we were again underway. Judging from the larger waves and the increased rocking of the ship we seemed to be out in the open Atlantic. Some of the passengers were seasick, including my Mom. The next two days went by uneventfully except that we now had more and better food. Ironically, none of us felt like eating much for fear of getting seasick. No matter how hard we tried to avoid being sick, eventually Heinz and I both succumbed. It was a painful ordeal. On the third day out from Lisbon we approached land. It was almost nightfall when we docked at Tenerife, one of the Canary Islands. Most passengers, including myself, had never heard of the Canary Islands, but a few seemed to think that we were somewhere off the coast of Africa.

We were not told why we were there, but the next day we refueled, took on additional supplies, and rested our sore stomachs. Our twopassenger committee had made an appointment to meet with the captain. He explained that the reason for taking a detour to the Canary Islands was to avoid heavy storms brewing in the Atlantic in the area of our planned route. He did not want to subject the passengers or the ship to the danger of the storm's magnitude. What he said seemed to make sense, but there was still doubt as to whether we could believe him. Finally we all agreed that we had no choice, and it was best to hope for the best. Was our next stop America?

The boat left the island and sailed in a westerly direction. Accidentally we found a place near the deckhands' quarters where we heard music from a radio, but as time went on all we heard was crackling sounds and finally nothing at all. The days were long and monotonous until the sky darkened and heavy rains and whistling winds signaled a huge storm. Conditions worsened, and rain and waves washing overboard created a small lake in our cargo hole. We moved belongings from the floor onto our bunks to keep things dry. We could hardly walk without holding on to something or somebody. The waves lifted the bow of the ship ten to fifteen feet high or more. Then the bow slammed down and the stern rose up exposing the propeller. When that happened the propeller increased its high-pitched speed making the whole ship shake. The ship rolled and pitched, and we had to be careful not to be thrown from our bunks when lying down on our luggage. The storm was terrible and there seemed to be no let up.

Earlier I had looked about the ship and found only thirty-eight passenger lifeboats and one small covered boat with an engine, probably for the captain's use. In case of an emergency there were not enough lifeboats for passengers and crew. But then the ship was not designed to carry passengers either. I did not dare tell anyone what I had noticed. The lack of fresh air in our hole and the stench of vomit were almost unbearable. Some of the passengers, including my mother, prayed saying the *shema*. I did some praying myself. After two days and three nights the weather began to slowly calm down.

Everyone was so relieved, and most of the passengers came up on deck to enjoy the sunshine even though it was really penetrating. The ship had covered less distance due to the storm, but at least everyone was fine, and we started to eat again. We were all anxious to get this voyage over with, and I often walked by the crew's quarters to see if I could hear the radio. Our little group met again in our little hideaway and talked about cowboys and our futures in the land of milk and honey, and then smoked a cigarette left over from my black market days in Barcelona. It was wonderful to air and exchange our fantasies, and this sharing took our minds off of reality. Now and then we saw a ship in the distance or at least a funnel of smoke, but no land. Even though we knew that German U-boats were prowling around, we weren't too concerned since our ship was flying the colors of Spain. Then one evening as I walked by the crew's quarters I heard a kind of music I had never heard before. It was jazz from America. I called my friends and even though the music faded in and out we listened in astonishment. Then we heard the announcer say something we didn't understand except for the words, "New York City."

We didn't sleep that night. Instead we listened to dance music and couldn't get enough of it. Two of the girls began to dance, and even though I had never learned to dance, I did now, and we all had a ball. By sunrise land was visible, and I went to wake up Mom and Dad. A few hours later after breakfast it seemed that all of the passengers were standing at the starboard deck railing anxious to debark. It was a chilly morning but no one seemed to mind. As we entered the New York port area, we gravitated to the port side of the ship as the Statue of Liberty came into view. It was the most beautiful sight I had ever seen. Even though I had seen pictures of her in books, I was still awed at her magnificence and at the deep meaning the statue conveyed. The thirty-eight immigrants on board were almost delirious as we all waved and shouted frantically to the welcoming lady, even though our voices were drowned by the ship's incessant horn blasts.

In this jubilant mood someone started to sing the "Hatikvah," the Hope, and everyone joined in. We had finally arrived and it was unbelievable. A dream, one of utter desperation, had come true. After docking at Columbus Pier on August 20, 1941, we said goodbye and good luck to our friends and then debarked with our meager belongings. Our nightmarish voyage was over. After leaving our ship, our walking gait returned quickly as we went through the immigration process with pertaining documents. Outside that large hall, Uncle Simon and his wife, Aunt Hilde, awaited us. It was a homecoming of sorts, but not yet a home. America was to be our new adopted home. We all had a sweet and emotional reunion with tears on every face. Heinz looked for his mother's cousin whom he did not know, but then a sign with the name "Heinz" on it brought the two together. After he expressed his thanks and said goodbye to my parents, it was our turn to say so long to each other. We exchanged addresses and then tore away from each other's embrace. We didn't know, but our lives were going in different directions from this point on. I took one last look at our sardine can, the cargo vessel that had brought us here to New York and shook my head in disbelief. Another miracle had happened.

CHAPTER TEN

The New World of Hope

Aunt Hilde, Uncle Simon, and their children, Ernst and Walter had left Mannheim June 21, 1938 and had arrived in New York July 2 after boarding the well-appointed liner President Harding in Hamburg Germany. Having left three years earlier than us spared them untold anxiety and agony, and we were glad for them.

Aunt Hilde and Uncle Simon looked good although they had lost some weight. Their apartment on Sutter Avenue in Brooklyn was modest but very comfortable. It was only a few blocks from the lady's hat shop which they operated on 539 Sutter Avenue, appropriately named "Hilda's Hat Shoppe." Hilde had not worked in Germany, but now in America it had become a necessity. We stayed with a family at a nearby apartment since Uncle and Aunt Hilde's apartment could not accommodate the four of them plus the three of us. My cousins Ernst (whose name now was Ernest) and Walter had grown quite a bit since I saw them last, and were going to public school, and then had homework. Therefore they could not spend much time with me.

It had always been our intention to move on to Chicago where another brother of Dad's, Uncle Ernst, had promised Dad a job in his business. After getting in touch with him, he sent us bus fare to travel to Chicago. We rested up from the strenuous past journey and therefore did not see much of New York. But my thoughts and those of Mom and Dad dealt with the future, in particular how we would learn the new language. The English lessons I took in Mannheim were like a pebble on the beach. Then came the day of leaving for Chicago on a Greyhound bus. We said good bye and were on our way. The countryside was interesting and different from what I had expected, but then it was America. We had left New York around noon and traveled during the night. It became foggy and I fell asleep. I awoke toward morning when the bus came to an abrupt halt and all the passengers were on their feet, some of them screaming. The windshield had been broken and the bus driver was standing there with a flashlight. The bus had hit a horse that tried to cross the road. It took several hours before another bus came so we could continue our trip. It was quite exciting, and somewhat nerve-wracking.

When we arrived at the Greyhound bus station in Chicago, Dad's two other brothers, Ernst and Herman were waiting. I had never met them since they came to America as teenagers before World War I broke out. After an emotional greeting, especially since the three brothers hadn't seen each other in many, many years, our few suitcases and backpacks were loaded into Uncle Ernst's car and we drove to Aunt Bella's house at 6728 Clyde Avenue, on the South side of Chicago, where our luggage was unloaded. Here, in short order, I had become acquainted with two of Dad's brothers and sister Aunt Bella, who married Alfred Danziger, and their 16 year old daughter Alice. It was kind of difficult at first to remember all the names and connect them in my mind. However, there were more relatives to meet as I would find out soon.

Let me transgress for a couple paragraphs and tell you a little more about Aunt Bella, her husband Uncle Alfred, and daughter, cousin Alice. Bella and Alfred were married May 4, 1922 in Germany. He was born in Chersk, today Belarus, then Prussia, December 13, 1880, one of seven children. He served in World War I as a German soldier, afterwards becoming a salesman for imported men's suit material. He had been a widower with two teenage daughters, Luci and Herta, when Bella met him. After getting married the four of them lived together in Berlin. Alice was born February 3, 1925 a healthy baby. Spoiled by her two step-sisters and the Danziger cousins, Alice loved to sing, dance and play cards. Alice told me that she had two cousins, Margot and Bernie Joseph, who were one and five years older than her, and a girlfriend, Ulla Schaeffer, who lived in the same apartment building as them in Berlin. On Sundays, her father Alfred took her to a café where he would read foreign newspapers while she ate apple strudel with whip cream. Alice went to public school in Berlin until 1935, and thereafter to a Jewish school where she participated in gymnastics, other sports activities, and competed against other Jewish Schools at the Jewish Sports Palace in the Grünewald area of Berlin. Her parents shielded her as much as possible from the political upheaval by the Hitler regime, as most parents did. In December 1937,

EXHIBIT 10.1 Aunt Bella, my dad's sister, and her husband Alfred Danziger. To whom we are most grateful for giving us refugees a home and love when we arrived in Chicago.

EXHIBIT 10.2 Uncle Herman, one of Dad's brothers, and his son Richard.

after Uncle Ernst furnished affidavits, Alfred, Bella, and Alice left on a ship from Le Havre France to America, leaving behind her two step-sisters who had gotten married in the meantime. Her oldest sister Luci died in 1938, leaving behind her husband Alfons Victor and two children, Gunther age 7 and Ingrid age 4. The other sister Herta, was married to Albert Levy.

When the Danzigers arrived in New York, they were met by Alfred's cousins, Joseph and Edith Schachno, who had lived in Brooklyn since 1934. He was a physician. On December 22, the Danzigers' took the popular *Pacemaker* train to Chicago. There, Uncle Ernst and Aunt Leone had rented and furnished for them (and Uncle Herman), the large apartment on 6728 Clyde Avenue. Uncle Herman, who had been divorced and would never marry again, had a son Richard who lived in Detroit, Michigan. Alice told me that she was very unhappy going to O'Keefe Grammar School since she had trouble with learning the English language. Later she went to Hyde Park High School where she was treated as an outsider, as an immigrant, and was not accepted by other Jewish children. She went to Sunday school at Temple Sinai where she was later confirmed.

Now that I gave a little background about the Danziger family, you can better understand what 6728 Clyde Avenue meant for us since that's where we would stay for the time being. The apartment had literally been a wonderful halfway house for most of the Kahn families and other mischpocha as they arrived from Germany in the late 1930s and early 1940s. Much of my thanks and gratitude goes to Uncle Ernst and a cousin of my Dad, Sidney Levy, who made the immigration to America of most of the Kahn tribe possible. It was Sidney's father, Simon Levy, who many years earlier brought Uncles Ernst and Herman to America. (Simon came to America sometime before the turn of the century and was the brother of both my grandmothers, Hannchen and Malchen.) After the Danzigers and Uncle Herman had settled in the apartment on Clyde Avenue, it was not long thereafter that cousin Norbert Isaak, who had been brought to America somewhat earlier, moved in, after first living with Uncle Ernst and Aunt Leone. Norbert, the son of Julius and Ida Isaak (née Kahn), had lived with his brother Helmut and sister Ilse in Aschaffenburg, Germany. Following Norbert's arrival, Otto Hertz, the husband of my cousin, Ilse, arrived from Havana, Cuba and stayed with Aunt Bella and Uncle Alfred. After that came Fred Berney and later his wife Rosel, both of whom slept on the enclosed back porch of the apartment where I was also assigned to sleep. When Ilse Hertz and her mother, my father's sister, Ida Isaak arrived from Germany, they, and son Norbert and Otto were invited to stay at Sidney Levy's house, in order that Aunt Martha (née Kahn) Lerner, another sister of Dad's, and her daughter Hannelore could move in, after they too had lived with Aunt Leone and Uncle Ernst initially. Uncle Herman, who traveled extensively for his brother Ernst's business, had in the meantime rented a room nearby.

By the time Mom, Dad and I had arrived at Aunt Bella's apartment, Martha and Hannelore had moved out to a small apartment a few blocks away at 6825 Paxton Avenue, awaiting the arrival of husband/father Julius, who had been incarcerated at concentration camp Sachsechausen. Hannelore would later Americanize her name to Lorie. It was amazing how, during all that many months past, everybody that had stayed with Aunt Bella and Uncle Alfred got along well with each other, so that, according to Alice, everything was very harmonious. Nothing would change after we had arrived. Mom and Dad had one bedroom, while I used and slept on the enclosed back porch. I did not remember Uncle Alfred, Aunt Bella nor Alice too well prior to Chicago, as we had not gotten together often in Germany. It did not take long for us to settle in, become comfortable, and become an integral of the household. Aunt Bella was an amazingly smart, helpful, and kind woman, and I learned to respect and love her at the same time. She ruled the household with a firm but very gentle hand and gave us good advice and encouragement. One example of her good advice was not to speak German if at all possible.

This first day of arrival in Chicago, was truly an exciting one. We had barely settled in and were kind of resting up when Aunt Leone came to greet us and invite us to their apartment for supper. And so that evening the three of us, Mom, Dad and I went to 6819 Merrill Avenue, very close to where we stayed. We ate in the dining room and were served by a maid. My cousins Lawrence, the younger son, was not at home and Herbert, the older son, stayed in his room, not even coming out to greet us. There was a lot of conversation about what had been transpiring in Europe, but soon the conversation shifted to what we should do to become Americanized. We were urged by both Uncle Ernst and Aunt Leone never to say out loud "*Bei uns Daheim*" – "this is the way it was at home." Americans, we were told, don't like that comparison! "You are here as Jewish refugees and should be

EXHIBIT 10.3 (L to R): Hannelore Lerner, Rosel Berney, and Alice Danziger.

EXHIBIT 10.4 Martha Lerner (on right), sister of Dad, and her daughter, Hannelore, age 13, Americanized as Lorie.

EXHIBIT 10.5 Julius Lerner died September 8, 1942 in Chicago after being incarcerated at Camp Sachsenhausen.

EXHIBIT 10.6 Uncle Ernst, dad's brother, and his wife Leone, who sent us passage money without which we could not have come to America.

thankful that we brought you over," we were told. Furthermore, "you have to go to night school to learn English and in the meantime speak English as best as you can. No more German speaking, from now on!" It was good advice and we took it to heart. But it would not be easy.

EXHIBIT 10.7 Cousins Lawrence and Herbert, sons of Uncle Ernst and wife Leone (photo taken many years later).

After dinner I went to see Herbert in his room who was no more interested in his somewhat older cousin than the moon. He was on the phone talking to a girl, no other than Sylvia Greenwald, who some years later became his wife. The record player was blaring out songs of that time, and after a minute or so having acknowledged my presence with a "Hi, Cousin Robert," I went back to the dining room where Uncle Ernst and Dad were shrouded in smoke and enjoying a cigar, and the two ladies were talking in another corner. Aunt Leone, having emigrated with her parents and two sisters from Remschid Germany in 1892, knew enough German to converse with us. Uncle Ernst indicated that he would pick up Dad and me tomorrow morning and drive us to his business, Chicago Specialty Box Company, near downtown at 20 East Kinzie Street. All three brothers: Uncle Ernst, Uncle Herman and soon my Dad, would work at the business together. Uncle Ernst would then take me around to some of his business friends who most certainly would have a job for me. It sounded good and my hopes were high. We were tired, physically and mentally exhausted, and returned to Aunt Bella's flat and shortly thereafter went to bed. Except for the occasional noise sleeping on the porch, it didn't bother me since it was summer.

To my surprise, Aunt Bella woke me and had made me breakfast, consisting of a bowl of Cornflakes which I had never tasted before. There would come many things I did not know of before but soon got used to it and never questioned it or made any comments about except to Mom and Dad. Dad and I were ready when Uncle Ernst picked us up. We drove along Lake Michigan and soon arrived at his business downtown, which resembled a warehouse. After Uncle Ernst showed Dad what merchandise needed to get ready for shipping and where packing materials were, he was on his own. Dad, in effect, became a shipping clerk. Now it was my turn to find a job with one of Uncle Ernst's business acquaintances. That morning and part of the afternoon Uncle had driven me to five different businesses were we were cordially received. Uncle Ernst told the same background story about me to everyone, and while everyone was interested and sympathetic that I was a newly arrived immigrant refugee needing a job, the answer was basically the same. Sorry we don't have an opening, no job. Uncle was visibly disappointed, and my original hopes were shattered.

On the way back to Aunt Bella's apartment not a lot of conversation took place. Dad could sense what had happened but said nothing. Uncle Ernst did not offer to try taking me again the next time or any time. He realized that finding a job for me would not be as easy as he had envisioned. Aunt Bella consoled me and said that tomorrow is another day. After a while, Uncle Herman who had driven home with us, Uncle Alfred who was a hardworking, door to door Fuller Brush salesman, and Dad were sitting in the front living room talking and each smoking a cigar. Mother was helping Aunt Bella in the kitchen and Alice had set the table. It was wonderful to sit with my new family at the dinner table and not have to worry about food or being in jeopardy. Everyone commented on how they fared that day, and each gave me, Mom, and Dad words of encouragement.

After dinner we sat in the parlor, the men smoking and all of us listening to the news of the day on the radio, in particular the progress of the war. Everyone one of us listened intently hoping to hear some glimmer of news that would indicate the defeat or retreat of the German Army on the Russian front. However, some of the news sounded contradictory and not hopeful. Alice was doing her homework and had a girlfriend Edith Monsen, also a refugee several years earlier, who lived in an apartment upstairs, drop in. We could hear their singing and laughing, something I had not heard in several years.

The next morning after I woke up and had breakfast, Aunt Bella pulled up a chair and sat down next to me with the previous Sunday's newspaper open to the wanted ads. We studied the ads; Aunt Bella explaining some of the words. We noticed that some of the places advertising for help were located on Western Avenue and so both of us thought it would be a good idea for me to look for a job in that vicinity. On a map she showed me where Western Avenue was and how I had to take a streetcar on 67th Street to that intersection. I made notes of all the major intersections from the map and got ready for my first American job expedition. I was uncomfortable and fearful that I could get lost and not find my way back to the flat, which is what apartments were called. Without asking, Aunt Bella gave me some change for the streetcar and off I went. Even so I had been a stranger in different countries before and then under constant threat of being picked up and incarcerated, this was still a daunting task.

After getting off at Western Avenue, which the streetcar conductor obligingly shouted out, the struggle began. On both sides of the boulevard were commercial buildings and factories. I looked at a piece of paper on which, with my Aunt's help, I had written some English sentences. Some places had a sign "Employment Office." I entered, each time repeating: "Do you have a job?" The answers varied but they all meant the same. No. Several places gave me an application of which I could only understand a few headings, filled it out as best I could and went to the next place. Some places asked me questions I could not understand, but my answer was always the same: "I can do!" Each time I left my disappointment became greater, yet I did not give up. Then I came to a place with a big sign that read "New City Iron Works," at 5401 Western Avenue. When I said that I was a machinist, the man behind a screened enclosure asked me where I had learned my trade. Reluctant to say Germany because Germans during war time were not kindly regarded, I said "at Luxembourg, Europe." Again, I had to fill out an application as best I could, upon without looking at it, the man said: "I can use you!" I had a job and felt like a giant. I remember walking out but then went back to ask: "How much?" "When start?" The answer to the first question was "forty five cents," and to the second, "tomorrow at seven." The streetcar didn't go fast enough for me as I went back to 67th Street and Clyde Avenue. When I rang the doorbell and Aunt Bella opened the door she could tell without my saying anything that I had found a job. Somehow it felt to me like a miracle had happened. Shortly thereafter, Mom accompanied by Aunt Martha, came home. The latter had taken my Mom to a ladies undergarment factory called Formfit Co. where she worked on the assembly line. Through the connection with her forelady, as her supervisor was referred to, Martha had gotten Mom a job there. Now all three of us had a job and were happy, in spite of the fact that Dad's job as a shipping clerk working for his brothers would be hard work and somewhat demeaning after having owned his own business in Germany. Mom, having never had a job for pay, was now supposed to stitch corsets with a sewing machine, somewhat unbecoming, never having been subjected to factory work. It was sad for them to start their life all over again at the bottom rung. As for me, I had a job, not knowing what kind of work I would have to perform tomorrow for $0.45 an hour. In spite of the fact that a new and hard cycle had begun in our lives, we felt good about what was to be and every one of the mischpocha congratulated us and wished us good luck on our new undertaking.

    I was not quite 18 years old, had missed out on most of my education, primarily high school, and was wondering how and when to catch up with the learning a boy of my age should have. But under the current circumstances, I had a full time job and there was no way to go to school and have my parents struggle alone to make a living. My parents surely must have thought about it but never openly discussed it with me. I saved them any embarrassment by having made up my own mind. None of us had any illusion about our situation. We had come as refugees without a penny to our name. We had to start from scratch and build our lives up from the very bottom. It would be hard, with many unknown obstacles and challenges ahead. Uncle Herman and Uncle Alfred started talking to us about signing up for evening English classes as soon as possible so we could make ourselves understood to other Americans. Mom and Dad tried to explain the necessity of finding out the situation of our loved ones who were left behind in Germany, France and Luxembourg, and to take whatever action necessary to bring them to safety. What had happened to my sister Irene? Aunt Irma, Uncle Charles and the children in Lille, France, where she had been staying? My mom's father, my Opa, who could not come with us? Uncle Max and Helene in Luxembourg and the many relatives left in Germany? It appeared that there were so many questions, and urgencies for us here, that it was impossible to cope with others than the immediate problems of our own, at least in the immediate days to come. We pleaded with Uncle Ernst and everyone else to take every conceivable action necessary to grant all those relatives affidavits, obtain visas for all of them as quickly as possible, and assist with paying their passage. Dad assured him his help in every way possible to expedite the paperwork, and spent untold hours furnishing him with the necessary detailed information. But even with the best intention, the bureaucracy at the State Department and elsewhere, intentional or not, could not be persuaded that this was a matter of extreme urgency as many precious lives were at stake. The bureaucracy's stonewalling was at its best and no pleading helped. And the National Council of Jewish Women and the National Refugee Service, Inc., were helpless to overcome the State Department's red tape. Exhibits 10.8 through 10.15 included the appendix will bear out the heart-breaking obstructions to rescue those whose existence was hopeless.

To be at my job the first day, Aunt Bella got me up around five o'clock in the morning. Of course I was excited, not knowing what to expect. It was still a good walk from 67th and Western Avenue to my place of work. After a few days I took a streetcar transfer from 67th onto Western Avenue and got there quicker. Even under the best circumstances it would take between 30 and 40 minutes, not to mention the wait time for the streetcar, which always took another 10 minutes. After arriving I received instructions to report to my foreman who could speak German but was a Pole. He assigned me a locker, showed me the time clock, then showed me through the shop and next gave me a job at a punch press. We had a 15- minute break in the morning and in the afternoon as well as a half hour period for lunch. Aunt Bella had made me a sandwich and given me a small bottle of milk for lunch. We were done around 4 p.m. then washed up and I was at home around 5 p.m. As far as I could determine the plant made structural steel products for buildings including high rises, bridges, cranes and other specialty structures. In the meantime, Aunt Bella had bought me a lunch bucket and a set of overalls. I also needed a cap for head protection, which I made from cutting out of an old felt hat from Uncle Alfred. Chicago at that time was a very dirty and dusty city, with awful smells emanating from the stockyard slaughter houses, and heavy pollutants from the steel mills in South Chicago and Calumet.

It was a long day for me being on the go for essentially eleven hours, including travel time. The longer I worked there, more demands were made on me, and was very tired in the evening, especially since I started to go to evening English classes for immigrants. I became acquainted with more people in the shop and found that most of them were immigrants originally from Poland, Germany, Italy, Hungary and other European countries. Thus I had no trouble making myself understood or understanding others. There was no union, and the company paid low wages even for overtime, which I was asked to do. Initially it didn't bother me because I wanted to work as many hours possible. How proud I was to bring home the first paycheck! I do remember one weekend when Dad, Mom, and I had all our first paychecks. We added them up and decided that from now on, one fourth would go to Aunt Bella and Uncle Alfred for room and board, one fourth to pay Uncle Ernst back toward the ship passage money he sent us, one fourth for our own maintenance expenses, and one fourth into a savings account. It was a lot of money for us and were proud of what we earned and how we would manage to pay back our benefactors who had come to our aid when we depended on them.

In the evening after supper, we would listen to news broadcasts and do some catching up on news, which we had not heard before since it was suppressed by the Nazi propaganda machine. For example, we did not know about the defection of Rudolf Hess, a very trusted friend of Hitler, to Scotland the previous May. Nor did we have any clue how huge the Lend-Lease Program to England and Russia was. Isolationism was being attacked by Roosevelt and others in Congress until in 1941, the Lend-Lease Act appropriated billions of dollars to the president to assist the Allies with ships, including older out of commissioned warships, and material. Since Japan had become an ally of Germany, America had restricted export of petroleum and other raw materials, especially since Japan had invaded what was then Indochina. America had become neutral in name only. At the same time there were groups and voices heard not only against the U.S. getting into the war, but the American Nazi Party under the leadership by Fritz Kuhn, and a vocal anti-Semitic priest by the name of Charles Coughlin, held rallies all over the country stirring up discontent, political confusion and pro-German sentiments.

Finally the Germans were tasting the bitterness of defeat here and there. The unsinkable German battleship *Bismark* was sunk by the British Navy. Yet German submarine U-boats were still sinking hundreds of merchant vessels trying to bring war materials to England in spite of the convoys being escorted by American or British naval vessels. The battle of Britain by the German Luftwaffe had all but failed after inflicting heavy losses and creating panic all over England. The Royal Air Force had heroically withstood the onslaught of the Nazi aggressor. However, German General Rommel's campaign in North Africa was still going strong. A glimmer of hope for the Allies was the Eastern front where Russian Armies had slowed the German offensive to a standstill at tremendous losses for the German Army divisions. And so our ears were glued most evening to the radio news and commentary by Gabriel Heatter, Walter Winchell on weekends, Edward R. Murrow broadcasting from London, and H.V. Kaltenborn, hoping to hear encouraging news of German defeats and the collapse of the German war machine.

On the lighter side, we would also listen to the comedy of Burns and Allen, Fibber McGee and Molly, and of course to the Jack Benny Show. While Aunt Bella, Uncle Alfred, Cousin Alice, and Uncle Herman were laughing and enjoying the comedy dialogues, we the newcomers had a hard time understanding the plot, trying to figure out what was so hilarious. Listening to the radio often was very valuable to me in gaining a better understanding of conversational English. Sometimes, going to the movie theater on 71st Street was another method of learning the language vocabulary by putting words and action together. Reading the newspaper was another method of learning, with the exception of the cartoons, the funnies, which I did not understand and after while simply ignored. Going to English classes in the evening, designed primarily for immigrants, three times a week was very strenuous for me, and I often started to doze off during class. When I worked longer hours I went there in my overalls since I didn't have time to change, and was particularly tired and didn't get a chance to have supper until about nine-thirty or later. Numerous times I was so exhausted on the way home that I fell asleep on the streetcar and rode to the end of the line, 67th Street and South Shore Drive and the conductor had to wake me up.

At work, more demands were made on me as time went on and I routinely worked 50 hours a week. Frequently I had to work on high rise buildings, putting beams into place and riveting them together. Walking on steel beams at different heights was scary enough. Catching red hot rivets from below in a metal container required the coordination of a juggler and the agility of a cat. It was dangerous and several times I made missteps which could have led to serious injury and possible death. The Windy City added its own hazardous windy dimension to the danger, especially in freezing temperatures when I was dressed like an Eskimo. For overtime work, I was paid an additional 5 cents more and for working outside on building construction, and an additional 5 cents hazard pay, for a total of 10 cents. While I hated to work outside on high rise buildings, the additional nickel an hour made me glad, but only afterwards.

As a German Jewish immigrant I had to endure much ribbing and was made fun of very often. Situations were always embarrassing, caused a temporary inferiority complex and raised questions whether I would ever become Americanized. I remember that one day my foreman asked "Luxi," (that was my name because I told everyone that I came from Luxembourg): "Go to the tool room and get a box of ambition." Of course the tool room manager was in on the joke. When I got there, the manager asked me what size box of ambition I needed. I didn't know and had to go back to ask the foreman. He told me to get a large box. I went back to the tool room manager and told him. He then asked whether I knew what color box of ambition I was to pick up. I didn't, and went back to my foreman to find out. Whereupon I went back to the tool room to request a large red box of ambition. The tool room manager gave me a wheel-barrow and hoisted a large red painted, very heavy machine gear into the wheel-barrow, which I then wheeled into the shop area where my boss and all the other workmen stood, laughed and whistled. I felt like an idiot, was terribly embarrassed and didn't think it was funny. There were many other instances, some of which were so bewildering, like the one where they suggested I order "hair pie" (which I did not know was vulgar slang for female genitalia) next time I take my date to a nice restaurant, which was so humiliating, and shameful for me, that I decided not to include more details herein.

One day in November 1941, I was called to the office. Scared, not knowing why I was to appear, I hoped that I would not get fired. When I got there, an office girl gave me a large heavy bag in a large cardboard box, and in it was something that looked like a large carcass of a dead animal. Upon which she said: "Have a nice Thanksgiving." To me none of this made much sense. I knew nothing about Thanksgiving and had no idea what I was supposed to do with that dead animal in the bag. I thought that this must be another joke on me and was about to throw the bag and its content into the trash container when I noticed other workers with similar bags. I was very uncomfortable on the streetcar on the way home having a dead animal in a box on my lap. That afternoon when I came home to Aunt Bella's house, the whole mystery was explained to me and everyone including myself had a good laugh. She was very glad that I had brought home a turkey, as it was the first Thanksgiving holiday that Mom, Dad, and I celebrated in the new country. We enjoyed eating the turkey, and even sweet potatoes, cranberries, and pumpkin pie, none of which I had ever tasted before. We gave thanks for many things and said some prayers around the table, out loud and in silence, for our loved ones still suffering in the old country.

Because of the war, it was not possible for anyone in Germany, nor from any of the German-occupied countries, to write or communicate by any other means with persons in any hostile considered country. Nazi Germany considered America one of those countries. Yet there were news fragments and rumors of all sorts often commingled that one could not discern the true facts. Much of these bits of information were revealed by congregants at Habonim, a synagogue established in the Hyde Park area of South East side of Chicago by German Jewish refugee immigrants who had come over a few years before us. Most German immigrants were members there, and so were we, the Kahns, the Danzigers and all of recent immigrant relatives. The other Kahns and longtime American Jews on the South Side went to the Temple Sinai, which was reformed to the extent that when I was invited to go there on a Shabbat evening I thought it was a theater at which a play was being performed. I thought that was the only time I would go there. Having said that, Cousin Alice nevertheless was confirmed there at the urging of Aunt Leone when she became sweet sixteen, in spite the fact that as a refugee she was snubbed and excluded from temple teen social groups.

From Fritz Dreifuss, the father of Erich and Herbert with whom I had been friends in Mannheim and who were now living in Chicago, Dad heard the terrible news that on October 22, 1940, already a year ago, all Jews still residing in Mannheim had been arrested and deported with only two-hours notification. They were abducted and transported on special trains through the unoccupied area of France to the French Concentration Camp Gurs in southwest France, near the Pyrenees Mountains. At first the news seemed unbelievable, but as time went by, more information became available that confirmed the horrible happenings. A total of 6,500 Jews, men, women, and children, the sick and old from all parts of the area known as Baden, Saar, and Pfalz, including 1,972 individuals from Mannheim. The details of that unbelievable deportation which led to many suicides is covered by various books and pamphlets issued by the City of Mannheim in recent years. Yet I cannot pass up the opportunity to make an attempt to translate the words from an eye witness and schoolmate, 15 year old Kurt Bergheimer, who was two years younger than I. He was among those deported and able to escape from Gurs to Switzerland, while his parents, like so many others, were later re-deported only to be murdered at Auschwitz extermination camp in Poland by the Nazi brutes:

Already on the street began our suffering. Heavily burdened with our suitcases, we were being escorted (to the railroad station) by Hitler Youth who had been excused from school for the event. It serves no purpose to mention that they did not spare us from curses, insults, and dirty tricks. They mocked us, hurled dirt on us and had us run regularly through gauntlets. We could not and were not allowed to defend ourselves. The Nazi youth, trained in brutalizing others, were in their element. It was good practical training for them to commit atrocities later.

That was only the beginning. Camp Gurs was erected in 1939 by the French government to intern former fighters of the Spanish civil war who had crossed over into France. The Jews were now behind barbed wire in barracks which were falling apart, had no heat, no sanitary facilities, no water, no bedding excepting straw, and no light unless it came in through the doors as there were no windows. Every day more transports arrived that the situation for the individuals became more precarious each day. Men, women and children were separated in different "Ilots," which were barracks. Since there were no paved streets, torrential rains had turned the entire camp into knee deep mud that made it almost impossible to walk or even bury people. The bad and insufficient nourishment coupled with the other unsanitary conditions led to an average of 20 deaths every day. So it was that my wife Gertrude's grandmother, Ida Wolff, who had been living in Mannheim, Hebelstrasse 20, died at Camp Gurs at age 80, after much pain, anguish and suffering. Her children and grandchildren, including Gertrude, had been able to save themselves in America. We heard of other camps in France with names like Masseube, Vernet, Noe, Recebedou, Nexon, and Drancy from where most of them were eventually transported to their last station, namely Auschwitz. More than 50 people, among them friends of mine, and friends of my parents all of whom I also knew, were among those deported, and beastly murdered by the Germans.

To think that we were in Luxembourg until mid-July 1941 and did not find out until now, a year later that all remaining Jews in Mannheim were deported, is proof of German secrecy, scheming and complicity of the German people, in spite of their play acting and lying after the war that **"We didn't know!"** Of course they knew, and as long as they thought that they were the Master Race, they gleefully participated, or were bystanders in Hitler's aim to destroy all Jews wherever they were found.

I remember that one time I went to Temple Sinai in Chicago's South Side, I had been invited by a female member congregant to stay after services for an Oneg Shabbat, a social. She introduced me to several people as a recent refugee from Germany, whereupon I was asked many questions about my own experiences, the Nazis, and the treatment of Jews there. They seemed to be very curious, and the more I opened up with details the more they wanted to know. There was quite a group of people around me, occasionally shaking their heads in disbelief, when all of a sudden the hostess broke into the conversation by saying "Bob, please don't talk about these unpleasant matters anymore! You are spoiling the evening for all these people!" I can still hear her words today. I was flabbergasted, deeply hurt, and in no time found myself standing alone, almost in tears. I highlight this episode because it demonstrated the overwhelming attitude of most Americans at the time and of American Jews who looked down at us as interlopers. They were not friendly, not very sympathetic, and more concerned with their cars, their minks and furs, other worldly goods and luxuries, and moreover they distrusted our eye witness accounts. There was no helping hand, no pat on the back, not an offer of help, no advice, never an offer for a ride home, or an invitation to their home. We were tolerated but shunned, excluded from the same people who once were immigrants themselves or whose parents had come before them as we did. Yet, in spite of this unpleasant situation, I found no time to dwell on it. I had to establish my own life amidst a society that was new to me. However, from that day on, I decided not to talk about my experiences or those of others in the country that had expelled me, and for which I had developed a great hatred.

There was one newspaper that every Jewish German immigrant would subscribe to, or if he or she could not afford the subscription, would share with someone who could. That paper was known as the *Aufbau*, literally translated, Reconstruction. It was a German language newspaper published in New York as a division of the New World Club Inc., and appeared bi-weekly. At its peak it had a circulation of approximately 50,000 in over 30 countries and was read in all probability by at least twice that many in my estimation. It was true to its name by serving as a platform for anything and everything a typical Jewish refugee would want to know or needed to know about establishing his life either in America or some other country. It dealt with what was known about Jews in Europe, dealt with the war, assimilation in America, religion, finding jobs, existing agencies of help, ads dealing with searches for missing loved ones, births, deaths. It was a paper that dealt with cultural issues of the time, carried want ads, carried jokes, and much more. It was a paper that tried to teach us to be better American Jews than being German Jews. Sadly enough the paper ceased their New York operations in 2004, having accomplished what it set out to do, subscriptions having dwindled to unsustainable levels. It is now printed in Zurich on a smaller scale.

It was through this paper that my dad noticed the address of the former rabbi of Luxembourg, Dr. Robert Serebrenik now living in New York City, who was continuing to act in behalf of all Jews exiled from Luxembourg. After Dad and other former Luxembourg immigrants living in Chicago got in touch with Serebrenik, all sort of news about those having been left behind became available. None of the news in general or about certain individuals was good. Shortly after we left Luxembourg, on August 11, 1941, twenty-five able bodied Jews were taken to a large former convent near the Luxembourg town of Cinqfontaines, also known as Fünfbrunnen and Ulflingen in German, to prepare the building to house many more Jews as a so called mini-ghetto. Then on September 4, ninety-seven Jews were forced to do hard manual labor in stone quarries at Nenning Germany, operated by Paul Wurth, for the completion of a highway through the Eiffel area, and on October 14, 1941, all Luxembourg Jews were forced to wear a Jewish star on the left side of their clothing. In the meantime all remaining Jews were transported to Cinqfontaines for incarceration, or were under house arrest. On October 16, 331 Jews were transported to the East in the direction of Litzmanstadt, known as Lodz, Poland. All our efforts to obtain visas and passage for anyone appeared too late and fruitless, especially since the U.S. State Department Visa division would not issue visas unless clear evidence could be shown that passage had been booked. Almost an impossibility. Yet Dad kept on prodding Uncle Ernst, and took it upon himself to write to HIAS, Hebrew Immigrant Aid Association, sending them money for visa applications, and to the State Department pleading with them to expedite the paperwork for Opa Raphael Joseph, Aunt Helene and Uncle Max Cohen, as well as for Uncle Berny, Aunt Marthe and Cousin Georges Joseph who had fled to Nice, France before it became occupied by the Germans. For them and others like Aunt Gerda, Uncle Manfred Ackerman, Cousin Kurt Strauss and his father Uncle Leo, still in Germany, there was no hope anymore.

In the meantime I was in touch with my friend Heinz Alkan, who had also found work as a machinist in New York, and had Americanized his name to Harry. He had been getting mail from his mother in Luxembourg through some very roundabout routing through willing intermediaries, and had been able to write to her the same way. He sent me various letters written by his mother Karoline, with a line or two by his father, Adolf Alkan. The letters were always signed Mami and Papi, and were heartbreaking to read. They were censored by the German authorities and yet were revealing of their life at the converted convent, at Cinqfontaines.

According to the Alkans, the first arrivals to the convent had claim on the largest and best situated rooms. Later arrivals were assigned rooms that were smaller, less desirable, and as more Jews arrived not only from Luxembourg but other countries, people were assigned rooms that were no bigger than prison cells and closets. Soon, larger rooms became the living quarters of four or more people. After a while, a constant rotation of people was in order as people were deported and transported against their will for unknown destinations in Poland, while new arrivals were brought to the convent. Karoline Alkan's letters were void of complaints, though she was bed ridden most of the time. She was more concerned about other inmates, and her son Harry now in the U.S., than about her own lot. Her letters told about her trust in G'd and her hope that the almighty will come to the rescue. She briefly mentioned my Opa Raphael Joseph being there, and how proud he was of me being in America having a job. She also mentioned my Uncle Max and Helene Cohen "visiting" as if the place was a resort. She never gave the impression of despair, whether this was for the benefit of her son Harry, whether it was to get the letter past the Nazi censor, or whether it was a sign of resignation to events she knew would come. As for myself, I was wringing my hands wondering whether my G'd, the G'd of my fathers and forefathers was leading his chosen children to a path of complete annihilation. Was our G'd testing our faith in him by subjecting untold thousands of his followers to cruelties never experienced by any civilization? Where was his comforting hand now in dire time of peril?

There were no answers, and the miracles of which the Bible has so many, did not happen now to save them who have followed his Commandments. I was becoming a doubter in my G'd and did not know whether this was a temporary or a permanent notion. I was in mental agony, and only my exhausting work on the job kept me from having sleepless nights. It did not, however, keep me from having nightmares.

Life nevertheless went on. There were a few Sunday afternoon family picnics in Jackson Park, with some of the American mishpocha and most of the refugee newcomers present. It was always enjoyable and relaxing and gave everyone an opportunity to talk about happenings in their life, and certainly not all of it a bed of roses. None of them knew what had happened to my cousin Kurt Strauss, who had been incarcerated by the Nazis for his political views and Zionist activities. Nor had anyone heard anything about his father, Leo, who last lived in Frankfurt

EXHIBIT 10.15 Playing "skat" in Jackson Park, Chicago. On left, standing, mother and Aunt Leone. From left sitting, dad, Uncle Ernst, Aunt Bella, Uncle Alfred.

EXHIBIT 10.16 Dad and Mom relaxing in the shade of Jackson Park.

at the River Main. The same discussion surrounded Aunt Gerda and Manfred Ackerman, formerly living in Bad Schwalbach, and last living also in Frankfurt. While no one had the answer, most of them had thoughts based on news and reported happenings of the day. Why could they have not immigrated when there was still time?

Mom's job at Formfit was not always pleasant and the pay for piece work was hard earned when production quotas were increased but not the pay. Many companies took advantage of the refugees who had no recourse. But jobs for women were hard to find and so she continued as best she knew how. When Uncle Ernst and Uncle Herman realized that Dad had a good knowledge of bookkeeping, they offered him the bookkeeping job and a raise in pay. Yet, he also continued his original work as a shipping clerk. It was strenuous work, but he felt it was worth the extra income. I, too, thought that the boss at New City Iron Works was taking advantage of me, on one hand because of the sluggish employment situation and the fact that with all of my immigrant handicaps, there weren't too many places that would hire me. I took every opportunity to make a few more dollars whenever I could by working overtime, working on outside high-rise construction jobs or both. On weekends I would earn some additional change by collecting empty 5-gallon water bottles from neighbors, filling them at a nearby water filtration station about three blocks away, and returning them for 25 cents apiece. The water from the sink faucets was just not as well filtered since it came directly from a pump station in the lake. It was customary in that area to obtain water from the local filtration station, and folks came in cars to fill up their bottles at no charge. I used one of those red wagons children used and was able to stack five bottles by laying them horizontally. It was a hard and time consuming job.

The place for shopping, bowling, going to movies, banks, restaurants, or just walking and passing the time or meeting people was at 71st Street. There was also a Walgreens Drugstore which was an amazing hangout for Hyde Park High School teenagers. The drugstore had a long soda fountain usually occupied by boys and girls after school, in the evening, and on weekends, eating all sorts of ice cream concoctions, sipping milk shakes, and cokes. Others were clustered behind them gossiping, making dates, and just having fun. Outside were other groups of teens, some with bicycles, and others honking horns from the cars borrowed from their parents. It was the place to be and be seen.

Early on, Cousin Alice and her friend Edith Monsen while showing me the neighborhood, had introduced me to 71st Street and of course Walgreens. Sometimes on weekends I would go there to buy a few groceries, see a movie, pick up dry-cleaning, loiter at a bowling alley, or buy an early edition *Sunday Tribune* newspaper late Saturday evening. This is where I made my first acquaintance of other Jewish boys and girls of similar age. One girl, a few years younger than I, who didn't mind being seen with a refugee boy was Joy Schless. She introduced me to other boys and girls, and so my circle of acquaintances slowly became larger than a dot. Joy invited me to her Sweet Sixteen party at the Chez Paree, the most famous nightclub in downtown Chicago, with perhaps 25 or more of her friends. It was a very expensive, chic, and glamorous club where they served food the likes I had never seen. That's where I saw my first and wonderful floor show with top entertainers and an orchestra for dancing. Most of the boys had their dad's car and drove with their dates there. I had no date, no car, and very little money. After Alice tried to teach me a few dance steps, I took the suburban train downtown and walked the rest of the way to 610 N. Fairbanks Court. I felt out of place but learned how the well-to-do, rich, and famous lived, and was happy to have been included. Over time I became friendly with Gil Cohen who lived on Clyde Avenue, and who had an older sister who was a knockout. I also made friends with Don Con, Sheldon Heiman, Elaine Kaplan, Shirley Rice, and Francine Travis. There were a few others but do not recall their names, all who lived within a few blocks of Aunt Bella's apartment. They knew my background, but never made me feel uncomfortable. Ever since the time that I was admonished by that outspoken hostess at Temple Sinai, that I was "spoiling the congregants' fun evening," I decided not to talk about that subject anymore. America's Jews wanted to know the exciting details of what was happening to their brothers and sisters in Europe, but then were embarrassed and ashamed at not having cared or done more to help when there was still time.

Early on a Sunday morning, as on previous Sunday mornings, I could hear the paper delivery boys throw the paper to the different back porches of all the floors of our apartment building and others around ours. I was used to this particular noise, but not to the shouting that went with it that morning. "Japan bombed Pearl Harbor!" "Japan bombed Pearl Harbor!" It was December 7, 1941, a day I will never forget. As in the case of so many people, I had never heard of Pearl Harbor and did not realize the significance of the news until later in the day, when more details came over the radio. More than 300 Japanese aircraft from several carriers had smashed the Army and Naval installations on the Hawaiian Island killing thousands in this surprise attack. As the day went on we heard that we had lost five battleships and other warships, anchored in the harbor, as well as almost all aircraft on the ground, with only light losses to the Japanese aircraft. The news could not have been worse and everyone was stunned. Congress declared war on Japan the next day, while President Roosevelt reassured the Nation that America will win this war. Two days later the U.S. declared war on Italy and Germany, since they were allied with Japan and must have known about the attack. World War II had begun in earnest for America. Now, war was no longer confined to Europe, Africa and the North Atlantic, but war would be waged in Asia, the Pacific, on land and on the oceans.

Between all the more detailed news on the radio from Hawaii, there was music from the bands of Artie Shaw, Glenn Miller, Harry James, Count Basie and others. It was reassuring that life in the USA had not halted, but was going strong. In the days to come we listened to the comedians Abbott and Costello, and remember seeing a movie *The Maltese Falcon*. I can't say "those were the good old days," as those were just extraordinary times with all three of us working very hard, making all the money we could at what seems now very low wages. However, when one thinks that you could buy a loaf of bread for 10 cents, butter for 38 cents a pound, a sirloin steak for the same price, and 50 cents for a dozen eggs, it all makes more sense. Clothing on Stoney Island or on 63rd Street was $30 for a suit, and slightly dressy shoes for $8-10. I remember buying a tie for a buck and buying Webster cigars for Dad at a price of a nickel and a package of cigarettes for 15 cents. Living was relatively cheap, but America's unemployment was still fairly high. With our commitment to pay Aunt Bella rent and reimburse Uncle Ernst for passage, there was little left for what we needed ourselves.

Chicago winter was a type we had never experienced in Europe, plus the fact that all three of us had a long distance to our respective jobs. It was good that the family gave us hand-me-downs such as heavy coats, hats, boots, sweaters, socks and other items. It saved us a good bit of money and was very much appreciated. The worst part for me was not the walk to the streetcar stop, but the wait for the streetcar with the wind from Lake Michigan less than a mile away howling around me. It was always good to come home where it was warm. In the meantime Hong Kong had fallen to the Japs, as we called them, and in the Philippines, American and Philippine troops under General Douglas MacArthur were in retreat from Manila to the Bataan peninsula. British troops surrendered Singapore and Borneo, while Nazi General Rommel in North Africa pushed British forces back toward Egypt. The Axis powers were redrawing maps all over the world. To counter these successes, President Roosevelt called for the approval of a $59 billion budget, the largest ever, of which $52 billion was earmarked to fight the war. All aliens were required to register, and all Japanese Americans living on the West Coast were interned. A bright star shone in Europe as Russia launched counter-attacks with high German losses, and British bombers attacked German cities. In essence there was so much war news each day that it was impossible to keep up with or formulate any specific conclusions. Here, we were just gearing up war production and converting the big automobile plants and shipyards, stopping all civilian automobile and other goods production.

It was March 19, 1942 when I quit my job because New City Iron Works would not agree to give me a raise in pay. As I was clearing out my locker, one of the managers started to shout and curse me as being an ungrateful immigrant, and unless I would change my mind he would send the FBI after me. But my mind was made up and I left. The very next day, after having applied at different machine shops, I started to work at a new job making 65 cents an hour at Ajax Engineering Co. located 2451 S. La Salle Street, Chicago. There was no outside work and I operated various turret lathes and different types of precision bench lathes. The hours were from 8 a.m. to 5 p.m. The only hitch was that I had to furnish my own tools, gages, micrometers and the like. After my first pay check I bought not only some of the required tools but also a tool chest in which I could lock the tools up at the end of the day. It was a big investment for me but it was something I would perhaps need in the future. The company made precision instruments for the Navy, such as sextants, binoculars, and "alidades"-- a telescope which would be used in conjunction with a gunsight on board ship. It was made of a special type of brass and bronze alloy that was hard to machine and had to be very precise.

It was around April 1942 that a one bedroom apartment became available at 2109 East 68th Street, only a block away from Uncle Alfred and Aunt Bella's apartment, and Mom and Dad thought we could now afford the rent. Shortly thereafter, having bought a few essential pieces of used furniture we moved in. We paid $40 for a four-piece mahogany bedroom set, a couch and easy chair for the living room, a day bed for me, a kitchen table and refrigerator from the people that lived there, for another $125. The most essential kitchen utensils were hand-me down gifts from our dear relatives, although as time went on we had to supplement. It was a start, and were very happy as well as proud of our hard earned accomplishments. My day bed was narrow and not comfortable, but I did not complain. It was one hundred percent better than sleeping on the enclosed porch where I was very uncomfortable in winter weather. When summer came, our apartment became very hot and there were many nights when the temperature was above 90° F degrees and a high humidity. It was very difficult to sleep, even though we kept all windows and the back door to the porch from the kitchen open to make some cross ventilation. I was lucky that Mr. Heineman, I don't remember his first name, who lived a few blocks away, picked me up with his car and drove me to work since he also worked there. We also drove home together unless he or I worked overtime which happened often. He refused payment for the ride, which saved me streetcar fare and time and was really appreciated.

As the war dragged on and successes of the Allied forces were at least spotty, Americans everywhere became angrier about the Nazis and the Japs. War production was speeding up and more men were drafted into the Army and Navy every day, although thousands volunteered, including women. Without Mom and Dad's knowledge or approval, I went to the recruiting office on 71st Street to volunteer. I was told that classified as an "Enemy Alien," I was prohibited to serve in the U.S. Army. It was the first time that I heard myself being called an Enemy Alien because of my German background. It made no difference that I had more, and more than anyone else, good reasons for fighting in this war, particularly against the Germans. I was distraught and disturbed. While America was still smarting from the blow at Pearl Harbor, a huge mobilization of its industrial might was under way; the work week was extended, more shifts added, and in many instances doubled to produce ships, tanks and aircraft as if they were cookies. Women filled the ranks of men in factories, and the name as well as the song "Rosie the Riveter" was heard on the radio. The fighting spirit had been aroused and any isolationist feelings had disappeared. We finally had something to crow about when Colonel James Doolittle launched a series of B-25 bombers from a carrier 700 miles off Tokyo to bomb that city. The balance of power seemed to have shifted after the battle of Midway Island, in the Pacific of June 1942.

American patriotism could be seen on posters everywhere, even so Nazi U-boat wolfpacks were sinking hundreds of allied ships in the Atlantic loaded with war material for England and Russia. After while our shipyards were able to replace the lost tonnage and add to it, but not the lost lives. Liberty Ships, 10,000 tons each were built in six weeks, record time. To pay for the war taxes were increased and everyone was encouraged to buy War Bonds and War Stamps. Then we were asked to make sacrifices through the issuances of ration stamps whereby limits were put on gasoline, butter, meat, textiles, cigarettes, tires, nylon stockings, shoes, electrical appliances, cars, and more. Mr. Heineman was able to obtain a limited amount of gas because he and I worked in a designated defense plant. The support by the American people in spite of some hardships was astonishing. Non-essential jobs were vacated and exchanged with jobs in factories producing products needed by the troops. Mom no longer worked on corsets and brassieres, but on nylon parachutes.

Times were also scary, especially when eight German spies were caught on the East Coast after landing by a German submarine. There were air raid drills, and blackouts were ordered along the eastern seaboard. Propaganda films were made by Hollywood in which American troops, the Navy, and the Army Air Corps always won. Then there came the film *Casablanca* with Humphry Bogart and Lauren Bacall, which I and thousands of others could not get out of their minds. In the windows of apartment houses, more and more little white flags with blue stars which indicated someone being in the military service, and more and more with gold stars, indicating those who had lost their life, became more visible.

Things were also changing at Ajax. More military contracts were received, more machines were installed and more people hired to operate them, including women. Among the latter was Lucille Mazzola, a girl from an Italian background with whom I had made friends and dated. She liked to dance and so we would occasionally go to the Trianon or Aragon-Ballrooms on weekends, where some of the big bands played. I would pay for the cover charge, she for the food, drinks and transportation. She was loads of fun, lived in Cicero, on the West side of Chicago, and didn't mind riding the streetcars. Francine Travis, a Jewish girl, was more straight-laced, somewhat more serious, and wanted to go on more formal dates, preferably in style with a car that I didn't have. It always cost me much more money going out with Francine, often taking a cab. However, she lived closer to me which was a big advantage time-wise, although she was never ready when I went to pick her up and had to wait for her in the parlor. Both girls came from an entirely different family background and religion, a diversity which I enjoyed and appreciated.

Because many of the Navy contracts were highly classified, I was no longer able to work in certain departments and as often the company tried to get me qualified for a security clearance, the investigating agencies would not furnish the necessary clearance because I was categorized as an "Enemy Alien." Mom knew a Fred Gilson in Luxembourg, who since had been appointed by the exiled Government of Luxembourg as Chancellor of the Consulate of Luxembourg in

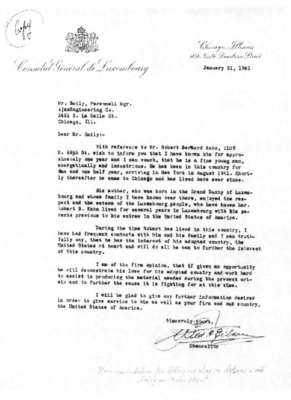

EXHIBIT 10.17 Recommendation for letting me stay on defense work despite being an "Enemy Alien" written by Fred Gilson. Larger version in appendix, exhibit 10.17.

Chicago. In our endeavors to maintain contact with our loved ones left behind, not only in Luxembourg, but also France, and Germany, Mr. Gilson had been very helpful, since through his diplomatic pouch and connections he was able to obtain inside information not otherwise available. We had been to his office and on several occasions to his home socially. He had gotten to know me and therefore I approached him to write a letter to Ajax Engineering to vouch for my character and my unconditional support and allegiance to America. However, despite his efforts, the ingrained bureaucracy of the War Department was not persuaded to give me the necessary security clearance. Yet, Ajax Engineering was very satisfied with my work and diligence on the job, and kept on trying to keep me. In the meantime they had me working in areas where I did not require a security clearance.

As time went on, the company had to shift me around, but the areas not requiring security clearance became fewer. Finally, I was put on the night shift from 12 o'clock midnight until 8 in the morning and saw my parents only in the evening since they had already left for work when I came home from the job in the morning. It was hard to get used to it but was able to adjust after a while. I slept until noon then went to the 67th Street beach and enjoyed the sun and fresh air. After a few weeks of this I signed up with the Chicago Park District for an afternoon shift as a lifeguard. The pay was very meager but the benefits, i.e. of being able to ogle the bathing beauties and being ogled by them in return because I had a good physique as well as some minor authorities, was worth it. It was fun! I also had lifeguard duty on weekends, when I could attend some exciting and sometimes wild parties in the evening with bonfires, food, drink and broads. Yes, broads who we took on exotic "snipe hunting" expeditions after dark.

EXHIBIT 10.19 Not a bad looking lifeguard!

EXHIBIT 10.20 Lifeguard with cousin Lorie Lerner.

As more men volunteered or were drafted for the military service, manpower became scarcer in factories, shipyards, steel mills, railroads, and everywhere else. Unemployment which was about 15% nationally when we arrived in America, was now almost non-existent. Everywhere were signs "Now Hiring Men & Women," and "Help the War Effort," and "Do Your Duty for Uncle Sam." The demand for new recruits in the military service was so acute that the War Department now decided to draft immigrants, referred until then as "Enemy Aliens." It was soon thereafter that I received a postcard from the Selective Service Board No.12, 1809 East 71st Street, Chicago Ill., that I had been classified as 1A, requiring me by law to carry this card at all times (see appendix exhibit 10.23). The card was dated April 23, 1943. I was fully aware now that sooner or later I would be called for the Service.

Paradoxically, during the last hour of my shift on January 8, 1943, totally unexpected, Mr. Smiley, the personnel manager at Ajax, called me to his office and told me that the Navy had requested to let me go, while apologizing over and over again. I had been fired for the first time in my life and for the wrong reasons. All because I had been labeled an "Enemy Alien!" (see exhibit 10.24 in the appendix for a copy of this letter). Disappointed, but confident that I would find another job until Uncle Sam would call me to join the military, I took my tool box and went home. After I had composed myself, I picked out several ads in the paper's help wanted section and made several phone calls. After going in person to Arens Controls Inc., 2253 S. Halstead Str., Chicago, for an interview and filling out the usual application, I was informed that I could start immediately, at 75 cents an hour. That was more than my prior job, which pleased me very much! Wages were going up as the pool of specialty workers became smaller. I had been fired and hired again on another job the same day without my parents knowing anything about either, since when I came home in the morning they had already left for their day job. They were surprised to hear the entire story that day at supper time, and glad that I had found another job.

The next day when I arrived at Arens Controls, the engineer of the department had a long talk with me about the products they were manufacturing, testing, and developing. He wanted me to be an Experimental Machinist, which meant to develop and test so called push-pull manual controls to activate certain flight and engine parameters of single and dual engine aircraft, as well as certain controls in small boats, cars, and buses. It would become interesting and challenging work. It was clear to me that in time this Company would provide controls for the Army Air Corps and Naval applications.

By now the war against the Axis, Germany, Italy, and Japan had unfolded in all its furor. It had spread over all of Europe, North Africa, Asia, the Pacific, and all oceans. The Germans were in retreat on the Russian front, British and American bombers were attacking industrial cities in Germany, Guadalcanal was recaptured from the Japs, and FDR received a war budget of $100 billion. Rationing of canned goods, shoes, and leather was added to many commodities already rationed. The entire world was involved in this war, but the Allies are making progress at heavy losses against enemies suffering far greater losses in manpower and equipment.

The news from concentration camps and ghettos was terrible and incomprehensible. Thousands of Jews and other so-called undesirables were being murdered every day. A heroic uprising by Jews in the Warsaw ghetto, begun on the eve of the Passover Festival came to end May 16, 1943 after battling German elite SS battalions for almost a month. Four thousand Jews were killed, and General Jurgen Stroop declared proudly that there were no survivors. We no longer heard from our relatives, nor from my sister Irene, in Europe. I feared the worst, but hung on with stubborn, and perhaps unreasonable optimism, hoping for miracles. Was there nothing the world could do to stop the monster Adolf Hitler and his henchmen to slaughter innocent Jews and other so-called *Minderwertigen*, inferior people, like Jews? Fighting went on all over the world and there was no priority in anyone's war plans to save the Jews from being slaughtered. I was angry, mad, and ready to join in the fight to destroy the Hitler regime, and all the German soldiers and people who so willingly supported the atrocities. Within me had developed a terrible desire to lay my life on the line to seek revenge, even if it meant swimming in the blood of Germans. And believe me, I was a good swimmer!

Yet, life in America went on with very little change. The zoot suit with baggy pants, a long jacket, long chains, crazy looking hats, became the rage of young men that had not been drafted yet or were classified "4F" unfit to serve, and in Boston a nightclub fire killed 300 people. The Jitterbug dance craze was in full swing. Movies were turned out by the dozen in Hollywood, and the stage play *Oklahoma*, made its premier on Broadway. However, signs of war could also be seen. People were standing in line at stores for groceries and other merchandise, ration coupon books in hand. Victory gardens were tended by school children and adults in an effort to relieve food shortages, since by now America was feeding not only its own, but also the allied soldiers all over the world. The Pentagon office building was built in Arlington, Virginia to house the administration for all military services.

Mom and Dad hardly ever went out for relaxation, the movies, or a restaurant. They were tired from working their job and then taking care of washing, ironing, making sandwiches for each of us to take along, breakfast, dinner, taking care of dishes, beds, going grocery shopping, and a host of other things. Of course I helped all I could, and was glad when there was a little relaxation on weekends, perhaps going for a stroll in the park, or along the lake. Now and then there was a picnic in nearby Jackson Park. In addition, all three of us were forever concerned about saving as much of our hard earned money and spending it wisely. All of our income was pooled, and I got to keep $5 dollars a week to take care of my expenses, which included entertainment. It was a challenge and we were determined to meet it. We gladly paid our debt to Uncle Ernst and even saved some money.

At work, someone was leaving practically every day to go into the military service. A cake was served, a short farewell speech was given hurriedly, and then he was gone. My turn would come soon. And so it was that I received notice from Uncle Sam to appear on October 2, 1943, two days after my 20th birthday for induction into the Army. I was glad, but not happy, because I knew that leaving behind Mom and Dad, already worrying about their daughter Irene and other family left to uncertainty, was an additional burden and worry for them. However, I knew that I had to get into the fight against the Nazi beast, and was determined to serve my adopted country proudly. The next farewell party at Arens Controls Inc. was for me, with the usual farewell cake, a short speech, handshakes, and good luck wishes. It had become a company tradition.

EXHIBIT 10.23 Mom and Dad, October 2 1943.

CHAPTER ELEVEN

Caught Up in the War Again

Saying goodbye is never easy especially when it involves friends. It is even more difficult when it involves loved ones like your mother and father. In the past years we had been torn apart from each other under several tragic circumstances. Thus, I knew it would be a very difficult situation having to leave my parents once again, only this time I was going to fight in a war. While my mind was made up, and it didn't bother me to put my life on the line, my parents and in particular my mother saw this from an entirely different perspective. For days before I had to say the final goodbye, she would wipe her tears whenever she saw me, but would not say anything. Yet I could read her mind; not knowing what had happened to her daughter Irene, now she could not be certain what was going to happen to her only son.

My male friends didn't take it too hard. There was a lot of kidding around, a handshake, a hug, and a promise to write. That was it. My female friends became a little more emotional and during one on one good bye sessions, there were some tender moments, embraces, a few kisses on the cheeks or on the lips, good luck wishes, and then it was over. Still for me it was an overwhelming experience.

Mom wanted to accompany me and Dad to the railroad station where I was to meet up with other inductees, but Dad convinced her otherwise. Saying goodbye to my parents first at home and then to Dad at the train station was sheer agony for me and for them that I will not attempt to further describe it. I don't remember which station I had to go to, only that we were to bring no suitcase or anything else, except our official orders to report. There were at least several hundred men. We were taken to the train platform and ordered, no commanded to "get on the train." The train ride was the most comfort I would be exposed to for months to come. It was my transition from civilian to military life, but had no idea what to expect. I looked out the window and realized that this was my first train ride in America and it was free, compliments of Uncle Sam. It was not too long that the train slowed down and I could see advertising billboards of Rockford, Illinois. I found out later that this was the nearby town near the army camp we were headed for. Finally, there were signs "Camp Grant," and "Welcome to Camp Grant." The train stopped. We were there! It was October 2, 1943, a very important day in my life.

As we alighted from the train, whistles were sounding and men in uniform were shouting at us "fall in," and "on the double." Neither one of those commands were meaningful to me and most of the other recruits. However, it didn't take long to find out what we were supposed to do. We didn't do it very fast, nor did we do it very gracefully. Before we knew what it meant there was "roll call" to make sure everyone was "present and accounted for." We had to shout "here" when our name was called. Next, while the man with the whistle in uniform would holler "left, right, left, right," we were marched at double time, a running pace, toward a large number of white two story buildings in front of which signs read Area D. The buildings also had large signs with numbers. We had to count off and 120 of us were assigned to each barrack. Ours was Brk 121. Inside we were told to stand in front of two tier bunks. Whoever got there after the lower bunks were taken had to be satisfied with an upper bunk. Speedy me had a lower bunk on the first floor. There were 30 bunks on each side, with an aisle in the center and the same number upstairs. I found out later that the sergeant in charge of the barrack had a room for himself near the entrance of the barrack. Thus, the saying: Rank has its privilege.

No sooner did we take possession of our bunk, whistles blew reinforced by shouting. We assembled around one bunk and were shown how to make a GI bunk bed. The sheets, blanket and pillow had to be laid out and folded in a specific manner, the Army way. We had to make our beds accordingly and then they were inspected. If the bed was not made according to "Army regulation," the inspecting corporal would tear it apart again and again until it was right. Some guys had probably never made a bed before and had to try many times before it was acceptable. We were forbidden to laugh at this seemingly comical procedure, and were told that this was serious Army business and infractions of any sort would be punished. Despite the seriousness, from then on, our bunk beds were referred to as "fart sacks."

Next, we had to "fall out," and in double time, and were taken to a nearby barrack with a Red Cross marking. There we had to quickly strip naked for a medical examination. We were thrown a fabric bag to put our civilian clothes in. It was an assembly line examination, performed by two medical doctors and perhaps ten or more Medical Corps GIs. At the end of the line each of us received a shot in the arm, and naked as we were, moved to an adjacent building and were thrown a "barracks bag." It was a large grey/green bag made of very heavy, strong material, about three feet long and about eighteen inches in diameter. On top was a draw string and a flap. We were rushed down the line, and were thrown khaki underwear and socks to put on immediately, next dress shirt, trousers, a tie, hat, fatigues, (clothes to wear when on base and training), belt, boots, shoe shine kit, dubbing to make the boots water proof, a mess kit, including knife, spoon, fork, and a canteen. Everything had to be stuffed into the barrack's bag we were given earlier. Next we were thrown a set of handkerchiefs, soap, toothbrush, toothpaste, razor, shaving soap, washcloth, a large and small towel, a comb and small brush. There was no time to try anything on and no one asked our size; the GI's behind the counter simply sized us up, and told us if it does not fit to come back for an exchange. It was the Army's way of doing things and I had quickly been initiated to become part of it. All of a sudden it occurred to a recruit that something was missing. He asked one of the GIs behind the counter: "What about pajamas? Don't we get any pajamas?" He was laughed at and all of us standing close by knew the answer without being told. Yes, we were required to sleep in our underwear! There was no privacy, no place for modesty.

After we had been ordered to put our "fatigues" on, we were marched at double time, barracks bags on our shoulder, back to the barrack. Nobody dared to lay down on the fartsack for fear that the bed would not look neat. The whistle blew again and we were ordered to "grab" our mess kit with knife, fork, and spoon and fall out again. I was exhausted and so was everyone else, but the noncoms, as the noncommissioned officers were called didn't care. They were hollering, "on the double," and "get the lead out." By now I knew what the first exclamation was but not the second. It didn't matter. Off, at double time we were marched with mess kits making all sort of tinny noises.

After standing in line in front of what came to be known as Mess Hall, we finally reached the point where a big fat mess sergeant, uttered some strange but loud words and proceeded to hit my mess kit with a spoon full of stuff that didn't look very appetizing. Into the other side of the mess kit another GI plunked something down like yellow shaving cream covered with peaches. My canteen cup was filled with some cloudy liquid, and with that plus two slices of white bread we proceeded to the tables. There another GI made sure that not a seat on the benches was left open and I moved to the next open seat on a long table where ten men sat on each side. Talking was not allowed. What had been served was spaghetti and meat sauce and didn't taste as bad as it looked. The other stuff was lemon meringue with peaches, but no pie crust. My drink was supposed to be lemonade, but looked like dish water and tasted like it. I was very hungry and left very little on my plate. On the way out, we were directed to two large containers marked "Edible Garbage," and "Inedible Garbage." I scraped whatever was left into the Edible Garbage container including my drink, and wondered who in their right mind would eat that garbage. Some weeks later I found out that this was for pigs on nearby farms, which the farmers picked up. I was relieved!

To clean the eating utensils there were two barrels, one with hot soapy water, the other with cold water. With the help of a brush, knife, fork, spoon and cup hanging on the handle of the mess kit, I scrubbed, immersed all in the hot soapy water, and next rinsed in the cold. It was simple and seemingly efficient. With mess kits clattering, we double timed back to the barrack where the sergeant instructed us on how to send all our civilian clothes and other non-essential items home in the bag given us in the morning. Mom kept the bag for some reason and I still have it. The cloth bag, 24 inches long and 14 inches wide was fabricated by the Werthan Bag Corp. Known as a Werthy Mailing Bag, it had a postage guaranteed mailing label. My address was now Private Robert B. Kahn, Area D, Brk D 121, 1610 - RRC - US Army, Camp Grant, Illinois.

No sooner had we packed our civilian clothes, attached a mailing tag and dumped them in a pile in front of our barrack that the order came again to "fall out." As our names were called we had to run to a small table were we were handed our individual metal identification tags on a chain. They were affectionately referred to from here on as "dog tags." And to go with the dog tags we were addressed as "dog face." We were instructed to wear the tags around our neck and never ever remove them. Imprinted on the tag was my name and my ID# 36691224T43. Also an "O" for my blood type and a "J" for my religion were stamped on it (see exhibit 11.1 in the appendix).

Next we were marched to a building with a big sign which read "Barbershop." I didn't need a haircut but I got one anyhow. Everyone got his hair shaved to one inch length. It took each barber, or should I call him a butcher, no more than perhaps two minutes per soldier. My curly blond hair was gone forever. It was a good thing my mother wasn't with me. She would have screamed. I had a hard time recognizing myself when I looked in the mirror and immediately covered my head with my fatigue cap, somewhat dismayed.

I hoped we could rest for a while, but no luck. At double time, we were marched to another building where we had to take a written IQ and aptitude tests. For me the tests were very uncomfortable because I could not understand a great number of questions because of my deficiencies in English and therefore could not pick out the right answers. Other parts of the tests where mathematical and technical problems, and trying to understand the question caused me to take too much time. I fell way behind and could not finish any of the tests in the time allocated. This was very upsetting to me and realized that even so I had been able to learn English sufficiently for basic every day communication, it was far below that expected from a young man of my age. Not only had I been unable to obtain a normal education in Germany because of restrictions imposed by the Nazi regime, but because I had to make a living for myself and help Mom and Dad once in America, there was no time to continue my education and complete high school.

Regardless of how badly I did on those tests, the Army was hard up for recruits and would take every warm body. I wondered what type of assignment would I get based on the low scores that I had achieved? Next, there were many forms to be filled out for a GI $10,000 life insurance, beneficiaries, pay and allotments. The pay was $76 per month, of which I arranged $50 to be sent to Mom and Dad for their use. Over the next few days we learned how to stand at attention, how to salute and whom. To my surprise we were allowed to leave camp one evening and go to Rockford, ever mindful that I would not forget to salute any officers. There was really nothing to do but walk around unless you went to a tavern and was sure to be back in camp by 11 p.m. The next few days were filled with being marched around and seeing several training films on security, personal health, and how to recognize the enemy. After a while, it was kind of boring. The best part of going to see the training films was that while we were waiting for the theater to be filled by other GIs some entertaining boogie woogie music was played over the loudspeakers and we could relax a bit and clap our hands to the beat of the music. After being in the Army just a few days I began to realize that I had lost my individualism and was being treated as part of a bunch. I had become an Army rookie among thousands of others. My 20th birthday came and went. Except for a birthday card from home, nobody cared.

New to me was the bugle call in the morning, reveille, which meant get up on the double and the bugle call at sundown, retreat, when the camp flag was lowered. Everything had to be done according to Army tradition and according to Army rules. Nothing was done that required individual thinking. Nor was there any time for it. We had become kind of robots. It was on October 10, 1943 that during our morning roll call formation names were called for trans-shipment to other destinations. We stood in groups and were given a destination number. After morning chow, we were ordered to pack everything issued to us into our duffel bags and report in front of the barrack next to sign 4. We were then marched to the train while other GIs sweeping the dock area shouted: "You'll be sorry!" Yes we felt sorry for ourselves not knowing where we were being shipped.

There were several hundred men on our train which soon went under way. It took the train about seven hours to our destination. We traveled through Illinois, Ohio, West Virginia, and parts of Virginia. Everyone was trying to guess where we were headed. We were able to talk to each other and become somewhat acquainted, although I couldn't understand some of their dialects and they certainly couldn't understand my peculiar accent. The last hour or so I saw the earth alongside the tracks was almost a deep red. I had never seen anything like it and didn't realize that I would see much more of this red clay during the next weeks. Finally as the train slowed down we could see thousands of barracks and other buildings, soldiers everywhere. Signs greeted us: Welcome to Camp Lee, Virginia. I had never heard of that camp before, but would soon find out its history. The camp was surrounded by Civil War battlefields on practically all sides between the nearby towns of Petersburg to the south and Hopewell to the northeast. The larger city of Richmond was about 20 miles due North of the camp. I knew nothing about the Civil War between the states, but was to hear more about it as time went on.

After the usual bureaucracy prescribed by the Army, I found myself assigned to the 12th QM (Quartermaster) Training Regiment at barrack #382. Our basic training would begin immediately. At the usual double time we marched to the supply room where each one of us "sad sacks" was issued a helmet with liner and

EXHIBIT 11.2 12th Quartermaster Regiment at Camp Lee.

EXHIBIT 11.3 In my dress uniform.

assigned our personal 30 caliber M1 rifle and bayonet. The rifle was rather heavy, weighing about ten pounds being about 43 inches long. It was semi-automatic and had clips of eight bullets. For the first several weeks we didn't fire the rifle. We trained with the rifle so we could stack them in the rifle rack in the barrack and make sure that we would retrieve the rifle assigned to each of us. We learned how to carry the rifle, switch shoulders, present arms, clean the rifle bore, load the breech, twirl the rifle, and do it a hundred times. Anyone who dropped his rifle was required to sleep with it. It was an exercise very uncomfortable in our small bunk. How do I know?

If I thought that Army life was tough at Camp Grant, here at Camp Lee I learned what basic training was really about. We were always on the go from early morning, noon and even at night. Drill instructors would wake us up during the night screaming expletives and having us dress in seconds, grab our rifles and "fall out" only to be run around at the parade ground for the next hour. We were issued gas masks and then had to go through actual tests by being ordered into a gas chamber where we had to put the mask on in split second time or risk being overcome by the gas. Afterwards we had to double time while counting loud, in cadence, and holler: one, two, three, four, and then very quickly one, two, three, four. We were issued field backpacks and were instructed what to put in it and how to wear that heavy 20 pound monster according to regulation. Next we had to watch training films from subjects on how to fix bayonets onto the rifle to how

EXHIBIT 11.4 Casual with a sweater bought at the PX, Post Exchange.

EXHIBIT 11.5 With full field pack and rifle in front of the barrack.

to prevent sexually transmitted diseases about which I knew nothing, never having had intercourse.

There was not a minute where we were not told what to do and how. Not why! More often we were ordered to do something we didn't want to do but had to do it anyhow. Any one mouthing off or disobeying orders was taken to the guard house jail. I had K.P. (kitchen police) duty in the mess hall like everyone else, latrine duty, guard duty, and fireman's duty. The latter required looking after the furnace and water heater in our furnace room with wood and coal.

Then there were the obstacle courses which we had to run with full field backpack, rifle and helmet. Even I who was in good physical condition had a hard time with 50 pounds of equipment to make all the obstacles like climb high walls on ropes, jump down and crawl under barbed wire while a machine gun fired over our heads. The one I dreaded most was the 20 foot vertical wall climbing. Coming down on the other side holding on to a rope net ladder there was a 3 foot wide water ditch. You get the idea. It was exhausting, but no one cared. This training which would last for six weeks was like nothing I ever imagined. The training personnel were rigid in their routines and had absolute control over every minute of our lives. Our 1st lieutenant watched from the sidelines as we suffered from stress, fatigue or succumbed as some men did. Some of the training, crawling for a long distance on our belly and making all day forced marches seemed almost sadistic. We were told that this would condition us to survive against a formidable enemy. As I found out later while overseas, they were correct. There were also so-called "night problems" where we split up into red and blue combat units and were assigned a certain area to defend while the others were ordered to attack. On several such maneuvers I decided to find a place in the woods to hide and sleep until the bugle sounded for assembly. If caught I could have gotten court-martialed.

Among the most important training sessions were the days we spent on the rifle range where we fired our M1 Garand rifle at targets simulating enemy soldiers at 100, 250, and 500 yards distance. We fired from a standing position, also in a prone, sitting and kneeling position. We

EXHIBIT 11.6 Going through one of the obstacle courses.

were also required to fire several rounds at rapid fire. We had to adjust the windage on the rifle to become more accurate. It was the rifle that I would take if I became involved in combat and therefore its accuracy was of utmost importance. We learned to take the rifle apart and back together and do it in the dark and do it quickly. Everyone had to fire the weapon at the same time after which the targets were pulled and read so that we would know how accurate our shots were. Mastering the squeezing of the trigger without moving the rifle was not easy. According to the recorded score we qualified as marksman or sharpshooter. I qualified as marksman and was later presented with a metal Marksman insignia. There were some men that flunked out and were reassigned to a non-combat position. We did not know this until later, or else many a slacker would have taken advantage of this situation by purposely failing on the firing range.

So far I haven't mentioned our bathroom, which was referred to as the latrine. You can't imagine what it was like for 120 men using a common bathroom facility. Ten toilets without dividing partitions, a twenty foot long urinal, a shower enclosure for 20 men to be used for four minutes maximum, a twenty foot wall with mirrors and washbasins for washing, shaving, and tooth brushing. By the way, there were recruits that had never taken a shower or brushed their teeth before. The supervisory non-com made sure that they learned quickly.

There are a few anecdotes I must tell to depict the lighter or more bizarre nature of the Army as I experienced it. We each had a foot locker, a wooden container, in front of our bunk. In it were almost all of our Army issued clothing and toiletries. The latter were in a tray on top of everything else. Each of us had been given a chart according to which every item of socks, underwear, and toiletries in the foot locker had to be arranged. On late Friday afternoons there was inspection of the barracks by an officer of the regiment. Every bit of the barrack had to be spic and span, windows without finger prints or smudges, floors had to be scrubbed and polished, clothing had to hang in accordance with instructions, and of course beds had to be made perfect so that a silver quarter would bounce when dropped on the blanket.

The latrine was always suspect because all of had to use it and it was difficult to keep all the metal and mirrors polished etc. If for some reason the inspecting officer found anything that was not the way it was prescribed, all men were restricted to the barrack for the evening or the weekend. Therefore, everyone had to be on his toes to assure that we all passed inspection. If we were restricted to the barrack because of a certain trainee not having done his utmost, he was physically punished by the rest of us. Thus it became a highly collaborative undertaking to get ready for that once a week event.

This particular inspection was performed by an officer very much disliked because of his testy character. As he came into the barrack, the sergeant called us to attention. While we stood at attention, the lieutenant put on a pair of white gloves. He then asked one of the rookies to close his foot locker, all of which had been open for inspection, and ordered him to push same in the center of the aisle. Below the ceiling was an aluminum heating duct which ran the entire length of the barrack and was prone to dust. In an effort to check the duct for dust, the officer proceeded to climb on top of the foot locker, stretched his arm, and just as he touched the duct the lid of the footlocker broke and he fell into the foot locker. His trousers and shoes were covered with toothpaste, which he had stepped on. He was embarrassed, but it was so hilarious to us that we stood there laughing at the funny spectacle. The lieutenant extricated himself from the foot locker and mumbling expletives left the barrack while we laughed and enjoyed ourselves.

"Policing the area" was another Army requirement whereby everyone had to cover a certain area around the barrack and pick up any trash or anything that didn't belong there. This was ordered each morning at 0630 before being marched to the mess hall for chow. The time allowed for this ritual was about ten minutes and since it was still dark in the mornings, this being cold November, we were lucky to find much. Nevertheless that was what the Army required and therefore it had to be done rain, snow or shine. When the sergeant blew his whistle we could come back into the barrack after we passed by him showing what and how much each of us individuals had picked up. Those of us that didn't have much in their hands were shouted and cussed at and admonished to do better the next day. Sometimes we had to do 25 push-ups. Everybody had their eyes to the ground hoping to find stuff, except me. I had figured out a system. Every morning when it was time to police the area, I was always the last one out. On the way out I would reach into the trash can and pick out a few little things including a few cigarette butts from the butt can. When it was time to come back in I would show my "find" to the sergeant and was invariably complimented for my thoroughness. Yes, there is always a wise guy and in this case it was me! I could go on and tell you some other stories but that would take too many pages.

Whenever we did get a six hour pass to go off camp, either to Petersburg or Hopewell, I would go to a movie and have some family type restaurant food in lieu of the slop we were fed at the mess hall. I remember seeing the movies *Bataan*, *Song of Russia* and some others I don't recall. Most of my buddies preferred to visit bars, drink, drink, and drink all evening since no alcohol was permitted on camp. Others tried to pick up women. Because these two options didn't interest me, I almost never had a companion when I went to town on a pass.

The first time I had a weekend pass, which didn't happen too often, I decided to take a bus to Richmond. Once there, I didn't know what to do and decided to take a bus just to ride around and see the city. The bus traveled from downtown, through residential, light industrial and apartment neighborhoods. There were many monuments. It gave me some idea of what the city was like. When the bus came to another stop, a black woman with two shopping bags struggled to get on. I got up, went to the door and helped her up the steps to get on. Immediately, the bus driver/ conductor as well as passengers started to shout as they were coming at me very angry with physical gestures, which were not at all friendly. From all the shouting I understood only the words "Yankee nigger lover!" This went on for several minutes and I decided it best to get off the bus since it looked like the crowd would get physical with me.

When the bus got under way again, I could still see and hear the conductor and the passengers angrily shouting and shaking their fists at me as they passed. I was flabbergasted and could not figure out what I had done wrong. Moreover there was no one I could ask. When I got back to camp I was too embarrassed to ask. Some knew that I was an immigrant, but everyone called me "Luxi," the nickname acquired when I was working in Chicago. It took several weeks before I realized that there was a racial issue involved and customs that were prevalent only in the Southern States. Even then I had only a vague notion of the circumstances that caused all that commotion and I could see nothing wrong in having helped that black lady onto the bus.

All 240 of us trainees graduated basic training about mid-November 1943. The graduation was reason enough for many in my Company to get drunk off base and were brought to the guard house jail by the MPs, Military Police. It just so happened that I had guard duty at the Guard house and for the first time saw one drunken soldier give another one a "hot foot." This is when one smears a lot of shoe polish on the other soldier's boot soles, and then sets the shoe polish on fire with matches. It can be very painful until the soldier can get his boots off. It caused a lot of hollering and turmoil behind the vertical bars, and I was flabbergasted having been introduced to this uncommon and dangerous prank.

One of the last things before graduation was a minor change in the spelling of my name. There was always loads of confusion in the Orderly Room where records were kept because of the spelling of my middle name, Bernhard. I was called to the Orderly Room several times because they wanted to be sure that the "h" in my middle name was not a mistake. The 1st Sgt. suggested that I drop the "h" and drew up some papers to make it legal. I signed and henceforth my middle name was "Bernard."

The next several months were spent in a Quarter Master (QM) maintenance and repair machine shop facility where I learned to repair everything from hand guns, machine guns, artillery pieces, tanks etc. It was interesting work and not as strenuous as the training routine months prior. Some evenings I would walk to the Service Club where there was music, entertainment, and sometimes dancing since members from the Women Auxiliary Army Corps (WACS) would frequent there. Most of the time I just wrote a letter home, which I had done at least once a week since arriving at Camp Lee, or I would buy a milkshake and read the newspaper to catch up with the news particularly the war news. Several times during the week, I would get mail from home always with a reminder to take care of myself—a message indicating their great concern for my welfare

The war in North Africa was going well for the Allies, and the Nazis were in retreat. Mussolini had abdicated and was under arrest by his own party. U.S. Flying Fortresses and British, as well as Canadian, planes attacked and decimated German industrial cities including Mannheim, even so they incurred heavy bomber losses. In Mannheim alone, one of the heaviest bombing took place in September with almost 400 dead (predominately civilian), 3,000 wounded, and one third of the city in ruin. To me it seemed like retribution, although I did not gloat. Sicily had been captured by British troops and Russian troops were gaining against elite German divisions on the Eastern Front. Landings in Italy had been successful even so with stubborn resistance by the Krauts. The news from the Pacific theater told about heavy fighting on land on the islands of Rabaul and New Guinea with stubborn resistance by the Japanse, but making progress. The Navy in the Pacific however was inflicting heavy damage to the Japanese supply and war ships. I became upset reading about American soldiers captured and tortured by the Japanese in the Philippines. The leaders of Russia, United States and Great Britain met in Tehran to discuss strategy, which meant that more Allied soldiers would die.

I couldn't understand why football, basketball, and other sports, as well as Broadway plays, horse racing, boxing and all forms of entertainment were still going full blast in all American cities while the war was going on, and men were dying everywhere. Perhaps this was good to keep the morale of the American people high. It just didn't seem right to me, when their sons were losing their lives on all fronts.

The theater on camp grounds showed the movie *Casablanca* and I enjoyed it immensely. Later in my life and even today when it is shown on TV, Gertrude and I watch it. Both of us love the theme song, "You must remember this, a kiss is still a kiss..." and hold it very dear because of the memories it brings back to us. We have probably seen it fifteen or more times. It is a classic. I still remember that we saw the film Casablanca for the first time with color dubbed in on cable television January 6, 1995.

It was always exciting to get mail from home. Mom and Dad wrote about working every day, and on Saturdays both would do their shopping on 71st Street. It took much longer now since certain foods and household articles were rationed. Dad told me razor blades were hard to buy and he had a leather strap with which he was able to sharpen the blades as was customarily done in Europe. Dad also wrote about having a hard time finding shoes since they too were rationed. Both thanked me for the allotment of $50.00 each month from my pay, which they were giving Uncle Ernst and Aunt Leone to pay back the amount owed for the ship passage for the three of us from Barcelona to America. They also wrote about being worried about becoming ill, having to take time off from work and therefore not earning any money, or worse having to go to the doctor since they could not afford insurance. I always included them in my prayers, as well as my sister Irene and all the other relatives in Europe who were in great danger. Mom and Dad had not heard any specific news about them for many months and hoped that they were still alive. According to rumors, all of the people including my grandfather Raphael Joseph, my Uncle Max Cohen and his wife Aunt Helene, my mother's sister were deported to Poland. The uncertainties were always on their minds. We did not find out that they and many other relatives and friends were murdered by the Nazis until after the war had ended. Mom and Dad went to evening English classes and their letters to me were mostly in English. Despite their problems including their worries about me, their letters always ended on a cheerful note. Yet I, too, worried about them.

There were times I felt lonely and homesick but never as much as on Jewish High Holidays. I did not ask for special passes to go to a synagogue either in Petersburg, Hopewell, or Richmond where surely I would have found one. Nor did I see anything in the local camp paper that special services would be conducted at a chapel. Basically I considered myself a soldier, alone and cut off from the outside world. However, on December 2, 1943, something very meaningful, significant and exciting happened. A call from the Orderly Room ordered me immediately to report in my class A dress uniform. I was out of breath by the time I got there and was immediately commanded to climb into a truck which already held about 15 more GIs, all in class A uniforms as well. It all was a mystery. When the truck departed there were about 25 of us seated in the truck. We could see the signs of Richmond and finally stopped in front of an impressive building on which a sign read: U.S. District Court. What had we done? What were we being accused of? We were ushered into a large room asked to stand at attention, cap in our belt. The judge made a short statement in which he indicated that we were to become American citizens! With right hand raised, we were asked to say the "Pledge of Allegiance to the United States of America." The judge then swore us in as American citizens, congratulated us and asked us to shake hands with each other. All of a sudden I was not only an American soldier, but had become officially an American! I was proud and could have jumped to the ceiling. My naturalization certificate from the U.S. District Court for the Eastern District of Virginia was #5829818. There was just one thing wrong with the certificate, my middle name was spelled with an "h" after it had legally been changed. After the war I finally received a duplicate certificate with my corrected middle name, certificate numbered #0900-8824 dated June 10, 1946.

In the meantime it had become 1944, and I thought about my past and present life and wondered what would become of me. In terms of money from September 1941, when I took my first job in the U.S., to the end of the year I had earned $495.90. In 1942, I earned $2,629.26, and in 1943, until I went into the service, I earned $2,258.23. But my accomplishments were much more than monetary. I had become an American citizen, a person free of persecution, an American soldier, with a commitment to fight Hitler's Wehrmacht with all the strength G'd would provide me. As soon as my president, the commander in chief, ordered the invasion. There was no doubt in my mind that the evil empire of this mad dog Hitler would be crushed and all his henchmen and collaborators would be punished for the misery they caused for millions of people.

Lately I would shun going to the small nearby towns of Hopewell and Petersburg because of their depressing business attitudes and their shabby treatment of service men. Richmond, although a greater distance away, was more hospitable by virtue of a "USO" a United Services Organization established by private organizations. As I found out later the USOs were also functioning in larger cities throughout the United States to provide helpful services and recreation to servicemen on leave. They also arranged for various types of entertainment on the premises. Basically USOs were designed to provide GIs with a more home-like atmosphere. The mostly female volunteers, of all ages, greeted every soldier, sailor or marine with a smile and words of comfort. They served food and drink other than alcohol. Areas were set aside for relaxation, reading, listen to music, play ping pong, cards, bingo, to talk to someone or just sit. The USO I had visited several times before was located downtown Richmond at the corner of Second and Grace Streets. I would go there on a Saturday morning stay the entire afternoon and evening and sleep there on a couch overnight. Later on Sunday afternoon I would take the bus back to camp. The few times I went were always pleasant and relaxing.

It was sometime in February of 1945 that I decided to visit the USO in Richmond again. It was very cold and wore my regulation overcoat, a muffler, and gloves. The USO ladies, some of them old enough to be my mother, while others were younger, and many junior hostesses made me feel at ease and offered me home baked cake and a good brew of hot chocolate. For a while I read the newspaper and took it easy. I also wrote a letter to my folks in Chicago. Toward evening we were offered sandwiches and soft drinks. Soon, I heard popular music being played and overheard that dancing was under way in one of the larger rooms. While I was not good at the Jitterbug, I enjoyed the slower and more conventional dance steps. I liked music by Artie Shaw like "Star Dust," "You Made Me Love You" by Harry James, "Blues In The Night" played by Woody Herman, and "Moonlight Becomes You" sung by Bing Crosby. In particular I liked big band music by the orchestras of Glenn Miller, Benny Goodman, Duke Ellington, Les Brown and a few others.

In any event I sat on one of the chairs placed along the wall with other GIs and hostesses when my eye caught sight of a young very petite hostess on the dance floor who was a "knockout." She wore a pleated skirt, pretty blouse, saddle shoes, and twirled around with the prettiest face and smile. Her curly hair was sort of brownish blond, but to me it looked golden. I was so taken in by this stunning, cute hostess that I didn't immediately realize that she was dancing with a sailor. When I did, it bothered me so much that I became jealous, got up, rushed onto the dance floor, and tapped him on the shoulder, which was the signal that I was cutting in.

Gertrude Wolff was her name, and during that dance and several others she found out quickly about my background after she detected my accent. I held her in my arms to the dream music of "Sentimental Journey" vocalized by Doris Day, and what became our favorite to this day, the theme song from the movie "Casablanca." To my surprise I learned that she too was immigrant refugee, namely from Neustadt Germany, which is only 20 kilometers from Mannheim. A girl friend of hers, Liselotte Boehm, from a nearby village of Lampertsmühle, was my distant cousin. But that was just the beginning. Both of us were so surprised and intoxicated by our happenstance meeting that we decided to meet later at a nearby drugstore for some ice cream. Back then most drugstores had soda fountains where you could sit and enjoy refreshments. While USO hostesses were forbidden to fraternize with GIs off the premises, for now and for Gertrude, those were just idle words. Gertrude had graduated Punchard High School in Andover,

Massachusetts on June 9, 1942, with a substantial scholarship from Erskine College, a private Christian college in Due West, South Carolina. But she had to turn it down because of her parent's inability to meet the remainder of financial college obligations. She then worked at the retail store of Marum's Knitting Mill, at the nearby town of Lawrence, before moving to Richmond to join her sister, Ilse, and took a nursemaid job with a family who had two young children, ages two and four. All of this was discussed later over a dish of ice cream. There was another revelation, namely that my Dad and her Uncle Alfred Marum who had owned and operated a large knitting mill in Sobernheim, did business together for many years in Germany. All of this was so astounding to the two of us that it was like magnetism that drew us together. We were excited and happy to have met each other. It got late and Gertrude had to go back to the Parrish family on Matoka Road. Our goodbye was a long one while waiting in the cold for the last bus. We gave each other a hug and then the bus took her away, but not before she gave me her address and phone number. The excitement of the evening had enveloped me such that walking in the freezing cold weather, and then waiting for my bus back to camp didn't bother me one bit. It was like a dream, and became the beginning of a long friendship that would eventually lead to our lives together.

It was March, still a cold winter and my training in the maintenance and repair shops continued. I couldn't get back to the barracks fast enough in the afternoon, shower, get dressed, and hoof over to the Service Club to make a phone call to Gertrude. I called almost every evening and we talked until I ran out of nickels and quarters because it was long distance. When that would happen, I would give Gertrude my number at the phone booth and she would call me back. I would also call Mom and Dad in Chicago once a week or so, but postage was free for those of us in the service. Then one afternoon as I got back to the barrack, I found a note on my bunk to be ready in the morning in full combat gear, field pack and all to go on maneuver.

We were loaded on trucks which drove for about 90 minutes until we saw a sign Bowling Green, Caroline County, Virginia. We continued on as the terrain became more hilly and rugged. We had arrived at A.P. Hill Army Reservation. We got off the trucks and were immediately ordered to pitch two man tents, for which the shelter half in our backpack, as they were called, came in handy. The tent pegs were hard to get into the frozen ground and my trench tool (a type of shovel) did wonders. We went immediately on a forced march of approximately 16 miles with constant attacks from an assumed enemy, requiring us at a given signal to fan out, take prone positions behind trees, in ditches, behind bushes etc. and take up defensive firing positions. There were mock air attacks mimicking gas deployment, which required the donning of our gas masks. Then we would have to double time for a mile with steel helmet, rifle, ammo, field pack and all other equipment weighing about 45-50 pounds. Next, we had to march while singing

"Roll Out The Barrel" and other typical Army songs. Those that would quit because of exhaustion were left to catch up with us later and were punished, known as remedial assignments. At one point several tanks were spotted and we were ordered to dig in. The tanks passed while we lay down a smoke screen. With my winter coat on, I was perspiring profusely and hoped that the day would come to an end. We finally passed a small chapel and after a short distance, we got back to our bivouac area.

That evening we ate canned rations for the first time. The only part of the ration I liked was a

EXHIBIT 11.7 AP Hill on maneuver--chow during a lull.

small candy bar. My buddy and I fell asleep in our pup tent immediately. When I woke up freezing during the night, I decided to try something. I took my blanket and walked through the woods to where I had seen the chapel. I entered and found a fire in a steel barrel in front of the altar. That's where I remained and slept until morning, appreciating the warmth of the fire. I did that all week long, kept warm and no one said a thing to me except my tent buddy from whom I could not hide the truth. As a result he joined me in the chapel each night thereafter.

A.P. Hill is named after the Confederate General who fought in a heroic Civil War battle in that area. The reservation is 35 miles north of Richmond and consists of 77,000 acres. Today, A.P. Hill is the permanent site of the Boy Scouts of America National Jamboree, which is held every four years. In 2004, 44,000 Boy Scouts, Leaders and staff attended.

After a week of strenuous maneuvers and training, we returned on trucks to Camp Lee and were glad it was all over. The time spent on A.P. Hill was a personal challenge, and gave me additional confidence in my physical and mental strength and willpower of being able to do whatever it would take. A few days

EXHIBIT 11.8 We learned how to climb trees, bayonet at the ready.

later we had more training, but under simulated battle conditions, whereby we had to tackle an obstacle course in full battle gear with our rifle. Toward the end of the course, we had to crawl under 200 yards of barbed wire while real machine guns were fired just above our heads. It was very scary! We were told that soon we would get our orders for assignment elsewhere, and so I mentioned this to Gertrude in one of our telephone conversations. Both of us wanted to see each other again and so she invited me to come and visit her at the home where she was employed. After talking

EXHIBIT 11.9 We learned how to set up gun emplacements in the ground.

to her employer, she told me what evening was convenient and I was excited to go there.

It was during the week, and had to be back at camp later in the evening before the curfew. It was a hurried up visit, but a very memorable one. We sat in front of a wood burning fireplace, looked at a photo album, and talked about many topics. The photos were particularly interesting to me since they showed Gertrude and her family living in Neustadt, Germany and other relatives who lived in nearby Sobernheim. Actually, it was fun to look at the pictures and gave me a better understanding of how their lives had changed since they came to America. The evening was kind of romantic, but only when we said goodbye to each other did we embrace and kiss. It was the second and last time that we saw each other before I was shipped out, but not before we had promised each other to write and stay in touch. It was a whirlwind meeting with romantic overtones. How long would it last? I had a strange never experienced before feeling, and was wondering whether I had fallen in love. Moreover, I was not certain whether Gertrude was harboring similar feelings or whether this was just the beginning of an ordinary friendship. I did not ask whether she had a boyfriend, nor did she ask whether I had a girlfriend. I was too timid and time was just too short to pursue those types of questions. My mind was on overdrive, my heart was beating ever so fast, and my head was spinning. I was smitten by her. I had met a most wonderful girl and did not know whether I would ever see her again.

EXHIBIT 11.10 The hostess at the USO Richmond, Virginia. Gertrude Wolff, who became the love of my life. It was love at first sight.

A few days later I received my orders to report to Camp Beale, California and a week's furlough at Chicago en route. Included in my orders was a daily subsis-

EXHIBIT 11.11 This is the photo of Gertrude, now "Gertie" or "goldfish," which I carried with me overseas. She was my "pin up girl" wherever I went— and was always a part of me, like my dog tags.

tence allowance of $2.95, which was to take care of food and shelter. It was late March 1944 when I had the most wonderful reunion with my parents. I took a cab from the train station at 63rd Street to their apartment on 67th Steet, I and whistled a certain seven note melody well-known to Mom and Dad. It was from an aria of a popular opera, called *"Gern habe ich die Frauen geküsst"* which translated to "With delight did I kiss women." It did not take long for Mom to pull the curtains to the side behind the window and wave to me. She had taken leave from her job for the day since she knew I was coming. I could hear Mom saying words of welcome and crying as I came up the stairs with my heavy duffel bag. Mom would always cry when she was happy and when she was sad. It was part of her natural makeup. Yet one could easily tell whether the tears were for happiness or sadness. She gave me a big hug and a long lasting kiss before I could set my duffel bag down. It was a wonderful moment. At last I was at home again and the aroma from the kitchen told me that she had been baking and cooking all morning, and perhaps for days before.

Later that afternoon Dad came home and the greeting scene repeated itself. He had a gleam in his eyes when he said, "I am proud of you being an American soldier." Since I had been relaxing, without tie, shirt open and shoes off, he asked whether I minded to get dressed so he could see me in full uniform. So I did. He said that I reminded him of the time that he was a soldier, albeit in the German Army. Strange twist, however that in this war I would fight the German Army that he had defended some thirty years earlier for what he thought was for a good cause. For supper, we had a meal that for six months I had longed for. Not only was it a home cooked meal but it was one of my favorite meals, namely *Sauerbraten* and potato dumplings. The festival was festively set with flowers and candles, as if on Shabbat. This was one of many ways Mother showed her love and I returned that love by thanking her, complimenting her and then eating like the house was on fire. It was just what the doctor had ordered, though it was truly a well-enjoyed last supper.

EXHIBIT 11.12 How I missed and longed for her. A living doll.

Over the next few days, and the weekend especially, there were visits from relatives and friends who lived nearby, which I enjoyed. There were people in our building that came to say hello, among them Mr. and Mrs. Koslowitz, and the Howards. From the relatives, I heard that cousin Norbert Isaak was in the U.S. Army 82nd Airborne unit, and his brother Helmut, who had managed to emigrate from Germany to Palestine, had volunteered and was serving in the British Army Air Corps. Cousin Ernest Kahn was in the Navy and Fred Berney in the U.S. Army Tank Corps. It seemed that at this point the "Kahn clan" was adequately represented in the struggle against the demons of the world, and several others still too young would join if the war would continue a few more years. As for my local male friends, they all had deferments for one reason or other. I guess they weren't as anxious, nor as motivated, as I was and easily found legal ways to stay home. Actually I was surprised to find out that they were draft dodgers.

Outwardly there were very few indications that a war was going on. There were many Victory Gardens in almost every empty plot in the area, meant to produce local food because much of the food raised on farms or processed in factories went to Army and Navy kitchens, or was sent overseas to our own troops or Allies. There were a lot of new dehydrated foods on the market which could be kept indefinitely. There were dried soups, mashed potatoes, dried pudding mixes, powdered milk, powdered eggs, and a list of others. However, as I learned later none of these dehydrated products had the taste as the fresh foods. There was now margarine instead of butter, and newly invented cellophane wrap kept food fresher. Women bemoaned the shortage of nylon stockings, and when a store had some for sale, lines would form hours before the store opened. Above all, there

EXHIBIT 11.13 Mom's festive dinner table on my furlough before being shipped out to go overseas, March 1943.

was not as much automobile traffic since gasoline and tires were rationed and everyone was carpooling.

Reading the local *Tribune* newspaper I could tell that the nightlife, and life in general, had not been much affected. Good times were had by every civilian, except for the Japanese Americans who had been interned as potential saboteurs. Unemployment was virtually wiped out since every eligible man and woman was now employed producing something for the war effort. New agencies sprung up in Washington, D.C. because of the war, among them the War Production Board (WPB) and the new Pentagon employed 40,000 Army personnel and civilians. There were big posters everywhere from proclaiming "Loose lips sink ships," praising "Rosie the Riveter," and encouraging all to "Join Navy," "Enlist in the Army," "Be a Civil Defense Warden," and many others. What came to my mind is that we had no black soldiers in our company. Black soldiers were segregated to form all black companies. This segregation, the poor treatment of black soldiers, was one of the reasons why defections and trouble broke out among them now and then at military bases. Yet the war gave Negroes new opportunities in military service as well as farms, factories, and elsewhere. This entire "black race problem" was confusing to me since it did not exist in Europe. I had never seen any black people in Germany to observe others' judgment firsthand; I had trouble understanding the situation here in America, especially when race riots broke out a year earlier in Detroit and 25 blacks and 10 whites were killed.

The war in Europe was making progress against the German barbarians. Soviet divisions were crossing the eastern borders of Poland, and taking huge numbers of German prisoners along the entire front. Big American and British air armadas bombed Berlin and numerous industrial cities in Germany, which caused heavy damage without heavy losses themselves. In the Pacific, the war on different islands and surrounding areas I had never heard of went on, and General MacArthur's strategy of "island leapfrogging" seemed to be successful. The Navy under Admiral Nimitz supported the operations and intercepted Japanese resupply convoys and sank many ships. However in Italy, the Germans halted Allied advances near the Anzio beachhead. What really got my attention was to hear radio broadcasts about thousands of American prisoners being held captive in the Philippines by the Japanese. They had been mistreated through torture, starvation, and killing during and since the Bataan death march. Will this be an example of events to come in that far-off war?

When I asked Dad or Mom whether they heard anything about our relatives in Europe including my dear sister Irene, there were only hesitant, incomplete, and unsatisfactory answers. From Aunt Bella, Uncles Alfred, Herman, Ernst and Aunt Martha, I also received seemingly evasive answers. It appeared as if there was a conspiracy of silence. Yet from the latest news and confirmed rumors it was clear that the plight of Jews in all countries occupied by German forces was near hopeless. Only bits and pieces of information of their transport to ghettos and camps primarily in Eastern Europe surfaced, and the details of their existence, torture and the mass killings were too horrible to comprehend and believe. Following more prodding, I could tell from my parents' body language and facial expressions how concerned and grieved they were that I decided not to pursue the subject further. One could only hope that the war would be won as quickly as possible and in that manner as many poor and innocent souls could be saved from the ultimate tragedy. With our traditional daily blessings, and on Shabbat we prayed for our loved ones, all suffering humanity, and the soldiers and airmen that were taking the fight to the enemy. It was all we could do, now that all other avenues to save those we loved were closed.

One evening during my furlough, most of my friends and I went to the bowling alley on 71st Street, where I had been many times but never bowled because I didn't want to spend my hard earned money. We bowled for a good hour and I really had a good time after getting the hang of it. Then Gil Cohn, Don Con, Sheldon Heiman, Elaine Kaplan, Joy Schless, and I went to Walgreens Drugstore, sat in a booth and had a soda or something similar. The good part was that they all treated me, since their parents gave them weekly allowances. I saw a few other acquaintances and we all cut up as in former days. Of course, I was the only one in uniform and the star attraction of the evening. I also telephoned Francine Travis and Lucille Mazzola, but made no effort to see them with the excuse that I was in Chicago only another day. They said they would write to me if I would write to them and wished me good luck, which I appreciated. After all, I needed all the luck provided the "All Mighty" had any to spare. Naturally I called Gertrude in the evenings, and told Mom and Dad at length about her and how we met. Both of them listened intently once they realized that she was special.

Then came the day I had to leave, which was particularly hard for Mom and Dad. After all, I was their only son and their hope was that the little flag with the silver star hanging in the window would not turn into a gold star, indicating a son lost in the war. I took a last look at the comfortable apartment and several large model fighter planes I had assembled, hanging from the ceiling, and went down the stairs, hearing the sobs from my dear Mom. I waived briefly to Mom and Dad standing at the window and got into the cab which would take me to the train station. In a way I was glad to quickly get into the taxi because it was ever so hard to see Mom in tears and Dad holding them back while always consoling her. It seemed that this was his job as a good husband and father. In recent years he had gotten good practice along those lines. Life for them under Nazi rule had come to a tragic end and now to establish a new life in America was very hard, while constantly worrying about their daughter and now their son. I loved them both very much and hoped that one day I could become a man like my father and perhaps have a wife that would embrace some of the wonderful qualities of my Mother. At this point I was only twenty years old and a long time away, so I thought, from assuming that posture and practicing their traits.

When I arrived at the train stop on 63rd Street, there where hundreds of soldiers, sailors, and marines, all wanting to get on the same train going to California. The train which had originated somewhere in the East was already filled to capacity so that no seats were available and the corridors normally used to get from one car to the other was crowded by servicemen standing or sitting everywhere. I stood for a while then sat on my duffel bag, though I was jostled around as the train would speed up, go around curves, come to a standstill to let other trains go by, or abruptly put on the brakes. I had never been on a troop train, but this was the closest to it. There were civilians on board, most of them having reserved seats. The air was stifling with foul and smoky air. The only air-conditioning, so I found out later, was in the dining car which I never saw from the inside. Civilians had made reservations there and it was off limits for us GIs. There were long lines to use the toilets such that you had to get in line well before you had the urge to go. It was an almost chaotic situation. However, nobody complained, after all there was a war going on. The train moved at a slow pace, a conductor snaking himself through the mass of passengers, and when the train came to the first scheduled stop there were ladies in their USO hats waving to us and handing out sandwiches and soft drinks through the lowered windows for all GIs on the train. They also handed out writing tablets, pencils and reading material. It gave me a big lift and I felt appreciated. Others felt the same way. It was patriotism that showed the broad support by the American people for the war and us uprooted GIs in particular. When the train moved again

I fell asleep to the rhythm of the clickety-clack of the rails, atop of my duffel bag.

When I woke up having slid to the floor, I noticed that someone had placed something soft under my head. It was a fur coat. No sooner had I noticed the fur, a young lady came over to me and invited me to sit in her seat while she would go to the dining room. I accepted her offer without hesitation. She slipped away while getting a lot of whistles from the other servicemen. She came back shortly, and as I got up to let her sit down she motioned that there was enough room for both of us. She snuggled up to me and got real cozy, an experience totally new to me, but did not struggle against it. When we stopped at St. Louis, the reception from the USO ladies on the station platform was more grandiose than at the previous stop. There must have been fifty or more of them in their special caps and patriotic costumes waiting for us with hot dog carts from which they served hot sandwiches, hot dogs, soup in little metal cups which they wanted back, candy bars and what not. I got two sandwiches and shared one with my new friend. We also shared the seat during the first night and was glad I could sleep on a seat, a soft fur coat and more. Finally when we got to Denver my lady friend got off and suggested that I get off too and continue on the next train. That was too much for me and so we parted ways, but not before she hugged and kissed me and had our picture taken with my camera.

EXHIBIT 11.14 The lady on the train with the fur coat.

I had next to no idea where Camp Beale was except in California which by looking at a map in Chicago was on the side of the Pacific Ocean. The longer I rode on this train the more I realized how huge and beautiful America was. We had traveled through fairly hilly, then flat and now mountainous terrain with snow in the distance at higher elevations. The telephone poles spaced at like intervals made it somewhat monotonous and the train whistle from time to time gave me a lonesome feeling. When I had gotten briefly off the train back in Denver, I had counted twelve passenger cars plus a number of freight cars, with two diesel engines in front and one at the rear of the train. I had never seen a passenger train that long and that crowded. Time went very slow and I thought about different things, but primarily the war. What would my next camp be like? How long would I be there? When would I go overseas? When would the war be over? Would I be wounded or worse? Would I see my sister again, my parents, my relatives, friends? Gertrude? But then there would be a distraction like entering a tunnel and everything got dark on the train and my thoughts changed to another subject. As night came again, lights could be seen in the distance while others closer seemed to whiz by. Some soldiers played cards, and I would now and then take my harmonica from my pocket and softly play a tune as other GIs in the immediate vicinity would sing or hum along.

Finally the train stopped at Marysville, California and I had to get off. But I was not the only one. There were hundreds like me looking around in this unfamiliar place. Strangely enough there were no townspeople greeting and welcoming us as at other previous stops. There was no way they could, as there were hundreds of us coming and going all day and night long. There was a long line of grey green buses which took us to Camp Beale about twenty minutes away. I was assigned to a barrack just like the one at Camp Lee and made myself at home. For the next number of days I was required to attend orientation with lectures, demonstrations and movies. Much was about personal survival under hostile conditions. I had to report to the dispensary for varies inoculations, turn in all my heavy olive green uniforms and receive new lighter weight khaki ones. There were numerous drills and parades. The latter I enjoyed because there was always a military band behind us when we marched. We had to see many actual "official" combat footage of the fighting against the Japs and the Germans in Italy. The purpose of showing us this footage, I suppose, was to condition us to the serious and gruesome nature of this war and the type of situations we were to encounter and deal with. At the time I could not find a U.S. map to orient myself. Locations of camps and bases were purposely not printed on maps, only the towns and cities nearby. Ever since Pearl Harbor there was considerable hysteria regarding the possibility of attacks on the American mainland from the Atlantic and the Pacific; everything that had to do with troops, deployment, troop shipments, training, camps, military strength, weapons as well as airplanes, and ships had to be kept secret. There was also considerable fear of sabotage: one of the reasons that Japanese people living on the West Coast were confined to special camps.

Camp Beale was located about 70 miles due west of Lake Tahoe, and 40 miles north of Sacramento in the Sacramento Valley, part of Yuba County. I was told that the area supposedly has 300 days of clear weather each year and that the entire installation consisted of roughly 40,000 acres. The 81st Wildcat Infantry

Division was trained here but had shipped out by the time I got there. Only later did I find out that this division participated in the invasion of the Pacific island of Peleliu, part of the Palau Island group, which is so small and unimportant today that you have a hard time finding it on a map. Nearby Camp Beale was a small hick town, Marysville, which thrived and profited by the influx of soldiers to the area. There were not many stores and I mostly remember having a professional portrait taken so I could send a copy home to close relatives in Chicago, New York, San Francisco, and to Gertrude, who by now had become a weekly pen pal. If you look at the map of California you will agree that the camp was in the boonies and very isolated. Today it is known as Beale Air Force Base.

On Easter weekend I was granted a three day pass and decided to hitchhike to San Francisco about 140 miles southwest of camp. I remember hiking on a Thursday late afternoon to the road leading to Sacramento. It was my first hitchhiking experience in uniform. There was no passenger automobile traffic and I had to depend on trucks going that way. The sun was setting and I was worried about my chances. Yet a truck finally pulled over and I got on board. I was in luck, the driver was going to San Francisco with a load of vegetables and fruit. He had been on the road for many hours and so pulled into filling station to tank up. Thereafter, we went into a small diner adjacent to the filling station where we had soup and sandwich; and to my surprise he paid for us both. Because it was late at night, we made ourselves comfortable at one of the diner tables on opposite wooden benches and went to sleep. It was not too comfortable, but by now I was used more to discomfort than comfort. We probably slept a good four hours and then continued toward San Francisco after washing up in the restroom.

Since my trip to San Francisco was unplanned, I had been unable to contact my cousins Ilse and her husband Otto Hertz earlier. I hoped that they would be at home, and would not be offended by my dropping in unannounced. While I had their address, I did not have their phone number. Anyhow, I asked the truck driver to let me off at a San Francisco bus terminal from where I took a cab to their home at 2727 Ortega Avenue. You cannot imagine how surprised and happy my cousin Otto and my Aunt Ida were to see me. Ilse was still at work as a welder at the shipyard, and came home later and greeted me with the same enthusiasm. More surprised were their twin girls, Judy and Joan, who were not quite two years old. Without a doubt, they were the most beautiful curly haired darling children I ever saw. I immediately started to fuss over them. When they were not asleep I would play with them, tell them stories while each sat on my knee, and took them proudly for walks in their side-by-side stroller. It was a big change and relief from my soldiering duties and I enjoyed the twins royally. I had never met Otto and so in becoming acquainted, he told me how after he and Ilse (née Isaak) were hastily married in Germany they had to separate. He came to the United States via Cuba. I remember Ilse coming to Mannheim to say good bye to us prior to her leaving for America.

EXHIBIT 11.16 The twins-- Judy right, Joan left.

EXHIBIT 11.17 Joan and Judy with their Uncle Bob.

It was in Mannheim where Ilse took her driver's lessons since she came often to play in handball tournaments with a Jewish team, perhaps called "Hakoah"…or at least that is the name that comes to mind. She was always very active in sports, as were her two brothers Helmut and Norbert, both of whom played team soccer. Helmut had immigrated to Palestine and enlisted in the British Air Force when the war in North Africa looked very bad for the British, having been thrown back by the Germans into Egypt. L.A.C. Leading Aircraftman, his official military designation, Helmut Isaak was part of the 462nd Squadron R.A.F. (Royal Air Force), Middle East Command, North Africa.. His brother Norbert, a Sergeant of the 29th T.C. Squadron, 313 TCQ U.S. Air Corps later participated in the invasion of France.

EXHIBIT 11.15 Holding Joan is Otto Hertz, next to me is Aunt Ida, holding Judy, with me in the middle.

Back to cousin Ilse; even so she had very young twin girls, she worked patriotically in a shipyard as a journeyman electrician. Her mother Ida, my

Dad's sister, was happily taking care of the little girls while Otto was establishing a business selling spices and nuts. Saturday morning Ilse showed me a few of the San Francisco sights. In the afternoon all of us went to the Golden Gate Park and enjoyed the wonderful flowers, varieties of trees and other vegetation. However, the Japanese gardens were closed for the duration of the war for obvious reasons. I became very attached to Judy and Joan, and enjoyed their happy demeanor. It was a short visit and had to hitch hike back to camp Sunday afternoon. It turned out to be my last days in civilization because a few days later, I got my orders for overseas embarkation.

EXHIBIT 11.18 Aunt Ida Isaak (née Kahn), a sister of my dad.

From here on, everything pertaining to shipping out, no matter what we thought was inconsequential information or detail, was secret and could not be divulged to anyone. To make sure of that, we were restricted to camp and no more passes were issued. What bothered me most that while being able to call Mom and Dad, I was unable to tell them that I was going overseas and that they would not hear from me for a little while. Then on May 27, 1944, without notice, we were awoken at 2 a.m., herded on trucks headed for the Camp Stoneman staging area. The camp was located in Contra Costa County close to the city of Pittsburg, California, approximately 40 milesnortheast of San Francisco. The camp of about 800 barracks could accommodate 20,000 Army personnel at one time. After several days of processing, including all sort of inoculations, we were assigned additional equipment, exchanged our heavy winter clothing for light weight clothing needed in hot climates and finally boarded the ship USS *Corsi*. We were assigned to Casual Company 83 and an APO (Army Post Office) overseas number #7843. These numbers made it easier for the post office to sort and deliver mail, except for the fact that in all instances the specific locations could not be revealed to anyone back home. We were on our way!

I had no idea how many GIs were on board except that it was very crowded in the "hole," the cargo hole that is, were all of us were bunked. However, I would estimate that there were about three hundred of us. That part was somewhat reminiscent of the set up on the *Ciudad de Sevilla*, the boat I came on to America. At least this was a much bigger ship. It was similar to the Liberty ships being assembled at the Kaiser Shipyards in Richmond, California. In fact it could have

EXHIBIT 11.19 Camp Beale CA May 1944: knowing that I would be shipped overseas to fight the enemy, I thought it would be good to have a portrait made in the nearby town of Marysville, CA and mail it to my parents and all my uncles and aunts so they would remember me in case I would not return.

been a Liberty ship, but I have since been unable to find the name on a website register. As far as I could tell, the *Corsi* was about 450 feet long and about 55 feet wide and had a 10,000 pound tonnage. She was driven by a steam engine, which according to a plaque mounted somewhere produced 2,500 horsepower with a top speed of 11 knots. At that speed she could barely outrun a canoe. There were a total of five cargo holds and the deck served to carry large vehicles, self-propelled guns, all covered with camouflage tarpaulins. There was a Navy crew of about fifty men, who had far better quarters than we, and as we found out, were served better food.

No sooner did we leave port, we were indoctrinated in the drills that we had to follow each routine day and in the event of various types of emergencies, including enemy attacks from the sea and from the air. Life preservers issued had to be carried with us all the time, but not necessarily worn. There were numerous guns on deck, the largest one, a 5" was mounted at the stern. A 3" gun was mounted at the bow, with two 37mm anti-aircraft guns in the same general area. Then there were six 20mm rapid fire air cooled machine guns mounted in specially designed tubs, three each on port and starboard side of the ship.

The Navy crew was trained as gunners. After a day or so at roll call, names were called to be trained on the different guns. My assignment was a 20mm anti-aircraft gun tub port side. The training was intense but I didn't mind. Unless you had some sort of assignment there was nothing to do except to play cards, or some other game, read, sleep, stare into the Pacific Ocean, write letters, although the mail would go nowhere until we reached a port or our destination. Who knew when that would be?

There was also a roster which additionally assigned each one of us to a watch of a given radius of the ocean at certain places on the ship, including a look out up on the crow's nest, the highest point on the vessel to watch for other ships, including feared submarines. There were two GQs, General Quarters each day, when everyone on board ship had to proceed at top speed to their assigned battle station. I had to strap myself into a halter of the 20mm gun, so I would not fall when the gun was raised, lowered, or turned to aim at a target. I also had to put my earphones on so I could listen to the commands from the bridge. Another fellow had to supply an ammunition magazine, and with a torque wrench give it the right feed tension, then slide same into the barrel. Next he would ready another magazine. The ammo magazines which were heavy came by conveyer belt from below deck. In the meantime I was searching the sky and water for my assigned field of 90 degrees radius. At times we had practice firing whereby each gun was firing at targets set on the water at varying distances or balloons released from aboard ship. When several guns were fired including the 37mm, the 3" and the 5", the noise was deafening. Depending on whether all the guns were fired from port or starboard, the ship would roll and list dangerously toward the opposite side. Being strapped to the gun was then a big advantage otherwise I could have fallen out of the gun tub. Those of us who were assigned on a rotating basis to a night watch had to wear polarized goggles four hours in advance so we would be conditioned to the darkness when we would go on duty.

Once we were on watch duty, having good binoculars at our disposal, whether night or day, anything we saw in the air or ocean had to be reported to the bridge. This included birds, floating garbage, leaves, paper, oil slicks, smoke, pieces of wood, strange reflections in the sky, etc., in other words anything and everything. There was a real threat of enemy ships, submarines, mines, torpedoes, and enemy aircraft. This became more acute the farther we were from our home base. For that reason our ship all of a sudden proceeded in a zig zag pattern which was changed at random, but at least every hour, and made it impossible for anyone of us to know or guess where we were or where we were headed for. Of course this maneuver slowed the progress of our ship further, yet it was noticeable that as the days went by the weather became warmer and after about a week out, the days became hot. Our CO, Commanding Officer having obtained permission from the ship's Captain, announced that all of us could remove our undershirts, after which many came down with sun and wind burns. I wore my plastic helmet liner which protected my face somewhat and my khaki undershirt. It was impossible to walk barefoot because the steel deck was so hot that it would burn your feet.

In my spare time I read a few old magazines and the latest newspaper available from San Francisco. I was particularly interested in what was happening in the Pacific since that's apparently where we were headed. There was a small article about Jews from Hungary being shipped and murdered at Auschwitz. In France, the Maquis resistance movement was fighting the Germans, but they had large losses of poorly armed volunteers. However, the SS murdered many innocent French civilians as reprisals for attacks on the German occupiers. The Russian Army was making mincemeat of the Germans on the Eastern Front. General MacArthur had initiated a big offensive in Dutch New Guinea and taken the town of Hollandia, while the bulk of the Japanese forces had been bypassed and was still to be reckoned with. Admiral Nimitz had provided a softening up process by naval bombardment from a large task force and provided aerial support from several carriers. Also the island of Biak, off the coast of New Guinea, was taken by American forces. This collaboration between ground, naval forces, and aircraft was a good sign, although I didn't have the foggiest idea where these places were and what their significance was in the Pacific Theater of war. Little did I know that I was to find out very soon.

In the meantime in Europe, American and British fighter aircraft had achieved air superiority over Germany, making relentless attacks on German cities by Allied bombers possible, in spite of heavy losses from ground anti-aircraft. At home, meat rationing was rescinded, also a good sign. And finally it seemed that the Allied forces were on the verge of liberating Rome, Italy. The news looked pretty good, and somehow I hoped that perhaps the war would come to a victorious end soon. But that was just a dream, wishful thinking at best.

With all the regimen on board ship, the days were mostly monotonous, hot, uncomfortable, and often scary. The nights, with many alarm interruptions, were distressing and lonely. Not knowing what the future would bring added to my inner restlessness and worry. The food onboard was at best lousy. The use of fresh water for washing ourselves and our clothes was curtailed so we would have enough drinking water. There was no entertainment of any kind except that which we would muster among ourselves. There would be occasional telling of jokes, playing card or board games, reading, me playing the harmonica, and a few others strumming a guitar, while those in the vicinity would sing along or hum. The longer we were confined on this tub, the shorter the tempers would be, and arguments were abound with occasional fights among the troops. By mid-May, all of us looked like shipwrecks. Most of us, except me, no longer shaved, our hair was long and was not kempt, our body was tanned, sun burned, with crusts forming everywhere from the salty sea breezes. Our uniforms consisted of tattered shorts, cut off boots without socks and those who still wore them, tattered undershirts. It was between mid or late June that preparations were made onboard ship by Navy personnel, who by the way had many more conveniences and privileges than us soldiers, to get ready to cross the equator, and with it all the ceremonial activities. Most of us doughboys had never heard about these ceremonies and were dumbfounded when we were required to bow to all navy personnel whenever and wherever we met, and additionally shine their shoes. However that was just the beginning and in advance of the crossing, when we the "pollywogs," were told the ritual of initiation would take place. That was just the beginning.

The hoopla all started when we actually crossed the equator and we were to be transformed from dirty, cowardly, shameful pollywogs into capable, seasoned and trustworthy "shellbacks." Each one of us Army "dog faces" were taken, one at a time, hands tied behind our backs, and blindfolded before his royal highness "King Neptune's Court." There, we had to kneel on the hot steel deck planks and asked many self-incriminating questions by his assistant, who went by the name of Davy Jones. After we gave whatever answer, we were beaten on our backs with heavy wet ropes, kicked, accused of crimes we had not committed and asked to perform certain acts of repentance, some of which were too gross to elaborate here. I had to kiss the Royal Baby's ass, which was covered with a terrible mixture of stinky, smelly, nauseating material and hair. I never found out whose ass I had kissed, and no one ever told me. Next I had to show King Neptune and his court of trusty shellbacks that I could swim. I was made to lie face down on the burning hot deck and perform the breaststroke until the hair on my chest and stomach, not to mention the skin, was singed. I was in pain. Additionally, my hair was cut, and a large "V" for Victory was shaved into the scalp of my head. Before my turn came, I had heard that anyone who resisted was particularly singled out for special consequences. I cooperated, and yet it was a terrible ordeal while the shellbacks had a good time and were enjoying the whole thing. After all, they apparently had to go through a similar initiation on their first crossing. I could go on with detailing the consequences others had to perform, enough that they were brutal, but carried out with the consent of the skipper of the ship. There were no exceptions because of rank, even if you were an officer.

That afternoon I went to sick bay for the first time, but had to wait for over two hours because others had come for medical attention before me. Some had to stay in sick bay for days because of what they were made to swallow, drink, or hurt from some other indignation. Later that evening I was given a certificate with the seal and signature of "Neptunus Rex," ruler of the Raging Main, that I would henceforth be a trusted shellback after having been duly initiated into the "Solemn Mysteries of the Ancient Order of the Deep." For whatever it is worth, it was not until 1980 that the Department of Defense issued orders to restrict this hazing to something less barbaric.

Our daily call to battle stations took place on the day of the crossing, and as usual they came unannounced. However, the time it took for everyone to get to their assigned battle station and call in to the bridge took much longer than normal and caused a good chewing out by the Captain of the ship. Therefore, the following day we had to "swab" wash the deck, which in the grueling heat was no picnic. Now and then in the days and weeks to come, we would encounter some isolated ships near the horizon and each time the alarm to man battle stations was sounded. Fortunately, they were U.S. ships patrolling the sea. We were told that we had passed in the vicinity of the Gilbert Islands, which nobody, including myself knew anything about. We were now over one month on this ship without knowing our destination and becoming increasingly concerned and restless. The routine in the morning, lining up to be thrown one yellow Atabrine pill into our open mouth to counter the effects of malaria, we were told, was getting to us. The majority of our company, including myself, were beginning to have a somewhat yellowish-colored face on top of our sunburned look. We were getting nervous and restless. One day we were told that we were close to the New Hebrides Islands, and the Captain would go on land for a meeting. Also, he was looking for volunteers to put new camouflage paint on the side of the ship. Because of boredom I volunteered with a dozen others, and as a reward that evening at "chow," dinner, all of us volunteers were permitted to eat at the crew mess, where we had a good steak and trimmings. Upon return, the Captain announced that he had received his final SECRET and SEALED orders, and that we should ready ourselves, our weapons and other equipment in preparation for a landing. Not knowing when and where the landing would take place, we worked feverishly to examine and clean everything, so that on short notice we would be prepared.

Until now we had been traveling south by southwest, but now we noticed, even so we were still following a random zig zag course, that we were moving west by northwest, almost in the opposite direction, without the slightest clue as to where this would take us. I was beginning to get homesick and scared, in addition to which I had developed a funny feeling in the bottom of my stomach and became seasick for the first time on this journey. Uncertainty had become the best of me. Training films had shown footage of how the Japanese had brutally killed civilians and soldiers in Shanghai and in Nanking. The enemy was fearless and merciless as demanded by the emperor, and as shown at Pearl Harbor, and after the surrender at Corregidor. What would become of us, me, if the Japs didn't abide by the Geneva Convention? More in jest, but still a reminder, we were handed a "Jap Hunting License" signed earlier by Uncle Sam to let us know what we were here for. See exhibit 11.21 in the appendix for the Jap Hunting License. See exhibit 11.20 in the appendix for certificate.

CHAPTER TWELVE

Modern Warfare Among a Stone Age Civilization

Wars have been fought for many reasons but none to teach the combatants something about geography. After having been on our ship for thirty-three days we only knew that we were headed for the South West Pacific. We had not the slightest clue where we were headed for specifically. All the speculation, of which there was a goodly amount, had created in us more anxiety, more uncertainty, and less confidence. The razor blade which I had magnetized already at Camp Beale, California, and which I floated on the water surface of my canteen cup did not help much. It only showed that we were changing course now and then, and that the predominant direction of our ship was South by South West. Not even the permanent Navy personnel knew where the ship was headed. The Captain of the ship had been given secret orders which were undoubtedly changed many times before the ultimate landing spot was definitive.

June 29, 1944, after sighting islands and larger land masses as well as several small patrol boats and aircraft, we were ordered to man our battle stations. Finally, after many confusing, drastic and erratic maneuvers we seemed to be headed for land. The word got around quickly: New Guinea. While we were headed toward what appeared to be a small temporary pier jutting out from the beach, I tried to focus on the scenery before us. With my binoculars loaned to me by the Navy, I could see a debris covered beach followed by bare trunks and stumps of palm trees as far as I could see. The palm trees were void of most of its foliage, and the trunks looked like large tooth picks of all sizes and heights. Many of the trunks were splintered apparently as shells had hit them, some charred black, and a few of them still smoldering. There was no other sign of life except for us. Approximately three hundred men strong, the 5th Replacement Battalion, 6th Army was about to land.

New Guinea is the second largest island in the world, extending 1600 miles east to west and is approximately 450 miles across at its widest point. The island contains more than a 300,000 square mile area of which a major portion was then, and is still today, largely unexplored because of the high mountains, impenetrable jungle, swamps and disease infested interior areas. Some of the mountains are snow covered, the highest peak being 15,000 plus feet. Big rivers cross the terrain and form large lakes before flowing into the Pacific Ocean. The tropical heat, as we found out, was extremely humid and stifling in a narrow range of at least 92°F every day and often exceeding 100°F except in the mountains where

EXHIBIT 12.1
The remnants of battle.

EXHIBIT 12.2 The eastern part of New Guinea, showing "Morobe" where we landed as well as other landmarks mentioned in this chapter. The entire island of New Guinea is shaped like a dragon, and the end where we landed was the tail of that dragon.

the temperature can be less but not the humidity. The humidity was always high in a range of eighty-five percent and higher.

There was a monsoon and rainy season with a rainfall of over 100 inches per year and in some parts of New Guinea upward of 300 hundred inches. There were many unusual animals not seen in other parts of the world. Those which bothered and scared me most during my duty there were huge rats, giant bats, wild pigs and dogs. Crocodiles, 10 feet long and longer, were a menace in the swamps as well as many species of snakes, some of which were venomous. I considered them all venomous since I didn't know one from the other. The most dangerous and often deadly were the insects like the malaria carrying mosquito, as I experienced later. Now and then we would hear strange shrill noises that came from birds, including the most beautifully plumed Birds of Paradise, parrots, also from monkeys, wild turkeys, and an assortment of rodents and large insects. However, as we would find out very quickly, our Japanese enemies would often imitate such noises to signal each other since other means of communication were not suitable in jungle warfare. Now and then we would come across beautiful flowers including orchids. But beware! There were many instances where flowers, trees and other vegetation were booby trapped, maiming or killing the unsuspecting GI.

Finally, but most importantly, were the primitive people of this huge and largely unexplored island. They lived in the mountains, valleys, along the coastal areas, even in huts built on stilts in lakes, rivers and bays and in relatively small tribal units. Their skin was dark and their hair was bushy. While most of them were of medium stature, we came across some pygmy tribes, which contrary to their small size, were every bit as fierce and yet as primitive as other tribesmen. Strangely enough, each tribe had a different language only understood by that particular tribe. Most of the natives, as we referred to them, knew nothing about the white man's civilization. We also referred to them in our GI lingo as "Fuzzy Wuzzies." Their tools and weapons, primarily spears, with tips made of stone, clubs, blow guns, bows and poison arrows with which to hunt, were primitive and seemingly of Stone Age vintage. I was told later by the Aussies that there are probably more than a thousand different aboriginal tribes, some of them so well hidden in the back country of the island, that even as of this writing, no one knows or has been in contact with them.

All tribes had their unique secrets, spirits, customs, special traditions and rituals for birth and death, coming of age, marriage, and especially for warfare. In case of the latter, as we found out, that the victorious tribe indulged in cannibalism of the other tribes' dead, wounded, and captured. All males and females were decked out in various types of body and face paint and in some instances tattoos, as well as facial decoration of bones imbedded in their lips and noses. They believe in the existence of all sorts of spirits who control their destiny. Their chieftains wear grotesque, but elaborate and often beautiful headdresses for ceremonies or when on the war path.

Women's breasts were not covered, and since they let baby animals, such as piglets, suckle their breasts, in addition to their own children, they were large and disgusting to look at. Women and girls wore bracelets and necklaces made of colorful shells and feathers, their faces often painted, and their private parts covered with ferns. Most of them looked repulsive and even the young girls were ugly. This made such a nauseating impression on me that, in one of my letters home, I wrote that I never wanted to see another woman naked again. I changed my mind since!

The natives were basically shy vis à vis us American soldiers. Perhaps they were scared and cautious based on earlier encounters with Japanese soldiers who had been on the island a year prior to American and Australian troops who

EXHIBIT 12.3 Often we encountered fierce looking tribesmen.

EXHIBIT 12.4 Ugly, frightening, and smelly women were disgusting.

forced them out of their original positions. I also observed that different tribes would cover their body with ashes or mud while others covered their body and hair with oily substances derived from plants. Later we noticed that they would use discarded engine and transmission fluid from vehicles including airplanes for their hair and body.

I expected none of this and found a world that was mysterious and frightening in every aspect. There was vegetation and animals, including insects I had never seen, and a civilization that I would have presumed extinct, yet lived here as man lived thousands of years ago. I was not the only one aghast and terrified when we came across their villages by happenstance, only to see bleached-out human skulls on stakes, reminding us that after all, that they were head hunters and cannibals. While they would supplement their food by hunting animals, they would also eat fruit from trees, coconuts, bananas, plant leaves and roots and something that looked like sweet potatoes or yams, and fish. Uncle Sam who had so meticulously trained us to become soldiers, never told us what to expect in New Guinea, and I am not yet talking about our enemy, the Japanese. Besides, having come from Europe, I most certainly expected Uncle Sam to be smart enough to take advantage of my background and motivation and send me to the European theater of war. There, I had an axe to grind and could not comprehend why I was sent here.

What little I knew about New Guinea came from the time I collected postage stamps as a teenager. When Germany assumed the North Eastern part of New Guinea as a Protectorate, and Britain the South Eastern part of the island in 1884, it issued regular size and horizontal stamps on which was printed "Deutsch Neu-Guinea." All stamps depicted the German Kaiser's yacht named *Hohenzollern*. After Germany had been defeated during the First World War in 1918, the German protectorate of New Guinea and the area Britain controlled passed to Australia as a trusteeship. The Western part of New Guinea was then ruled by the Dutch. None of these political divisions of the island made any difference to me. It all looked all the same to me. The longer I was on this G'd forsaken island the more I detested being there. Eventually I thought of this place and referred to it as (forgive my crude language) the "asshole of the world," and have not changed my mind since. Of the six hundred smaller and larger islands surrounding the Northern and North West coast of New Guinea, none are much different. To the contrary, most are even more desolate, isolated from civilization and uninviting, as our armies found out in recapturing many of them from the Japanese.

Our ship did not get close to the makeshift pier as we thought, and we were all relieved from our battle stations while the permanent Navy contingent took over the guns. Instead, anchor was dropped several hundred yards away from land and we were ordered to climb down the landing nets, essentially heavy rope ladders, which had been lowered over the sides and were free swinging. This was a very difficult and exhausting task since we had to carry our duffel bags and the rest of our individual gear, including rifle, ammo, machete, trenching spade, gas mask, hand grenades, rations, first aid kit, canteen, steel helmet, all weighing perhaps eighty pounds and feeling like a hundred. Although we had practiced similar descends during basic training, I had much more gear now. The high temperature and humidity coupled with fright and anxiety added to the laborious task. Luckily for us we were not under enemy fire. However, I was so exhausted from the climb down the rope ladder that I skipped the last four or five rungs and was glad when I hit the water fully clothed and found myself shoulder deep in water. Others, unable to hold on to the rope ladders fell from greater heights. With all my gear soaking wet, I stumbled and crawled onto the beach, prone in the sand, exhausted, and thankful that I had made it, so far.

After a while a number of "Amphibious Ducks" (DUKW), vehicles approximately thirty feet long, which can drive on land and maneuver in the water, appeared from the tree line. About twenty of us were loaded and taken through the jungle for approximately one half mile. Everywhere were signs of earlier battles with remnants and twisted pieces of airplane wreckage, mortars, various types of machine guns, howitzers, expended ammo shells of all calibers, and an array of personal equipment such as gas masks, belts, caps, shirts, shoes and so on. This was left over from recent American, Australian, and Japanese battle carnage. The Ducks halted at a fortified camp area bristling with soldiers and we were immediately ordered to set up six men tents including foxholes. In addition, we were cautioned to be on guard and make as little noise as possible. While the initial battles were over, we were informed that the enemy would conduct probing skirmishes and brief but deadly harassment attacks at any time, but especially during the night.

The heat, humidity, soft ground, and having to be on constant alert with our firearms in close proximity was responsible for our slow progress. Resting periodically and drinking warm water, first from our canteen and then from Lister bags filled with stale water to which chemicals had been added, provided additional discomfort. It had been an eventful and very tiring day, but this was war and nobody was sympathetic to our lot.

All around us were battle worn GIs, none of whom we knew and none of them knew us. They were quiet, in a defensive mode, watching us and the jungle around us. Now and then we heard nearby or distant gun fire, an explosion noise from a hand grenade and peculiar noises from above and other directions. Between being exhausted and scared we finished our tent and individual foxholes, as others from our ship also had done or were still completing. Word got around that we were, at least for the time being, dependent on canned "C" rations. For the first time I opened a small can of Vienna sausages, eight, I believe, to a can. They were so tightly packed that they were square as I pulled them out and looked disgusting. When I asked one of our "host" comrades where and how to heat up the ugly looking meat sticks, he told me to make a small fire in the bottom of the

EXHIBIT 12.5 The swamp.

EXHIBIT 12.6 The jungle was a perfect hiding place.

foxhole under my helmet. After my lukewarm gourmet meal, I climbed or rather stumbled onto my cot, tugged my mosquito net under me and was quickly asleep, my bolt action M-1 rifle snuggled uncomfortably next to me.

I was suddenly awaken by the pounding noise on the tent canvas, which turned out to be a downpour of rain accompanied by terrifying thunder and lightning. It was an awesome display of natural forces. During a sustained lightning bolt I could see the rain water running through the tent, and all five of my buddies were also sitting up, not knowing what to expect. Shortly thereafter it happened! Someone was giving the alarm signal with a portable siren and all hell broke out around us. The Japs were attacking.

Grabbing my metal ammunition box, grenades, and rifle, I jumped instinctively into the foxhole next to my cot and found the bottom of the former filled with water almost up to my knee. I realized that I was barefoot, in my briefs, and without my helmet. I reached up to get a hold of my bayonet on my cartridge belt and fixed same to my rifle. I also carried my own six inch hunting knife on my belt, which I bought prior to going overseas. It was a "Cattaraugus 225Q," and surprisingly, it is still in my possession today. After a few days I strapped that knife to my left leg since I was a southpaw copying other GIs, except that most had their knife or bayonet strapped to their right leg. It was pitch dark with enemy fire coming from basically two directions. Flares from the Japs lit up some of our positions, and flares fired from our side attempted to shed visibility onto the attackers in the thick of the jungle. The enemy was so close that we could hear but not understand their shouting of commands. The noise from machine gun

EXHIBIT 12.7 Airplane wreckage, machine gun emplacements and other fighting remnants greeted us.

and rifle fire, the screaming and whistling noises of bullets, mortar shells, and exploding hand grenades were deafening.

I was soaking wet from the continuing downpour and the water in the foxhole. My body was full of mud and had no poncho or raincoat. None had been issued to us. The rain had mixed with my perspiration and I was shivering. Yet as hard as I tried to penetrate the darkness to detect any approaching enemy, I saw only the high jungle grass, bushes and leaves move and thought momentarily that they were silhouettes. They weren't. I was scared but had no time to dwell on it. After about an hour the all clear signal was given. For now it was over, but for how long? All six of us climbed out from our respective foxholes. We looked like coal miners, grease monkeys, and mud wrestlers all in one. Briefly we stared at each other and let out a brief laugh. But the laugh was hollow. For the next several hours we cleaned ourselves and our khaki underwear in the rain water, too

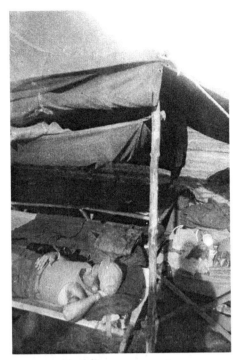

EXHIBIT 12.8 The tent, cot, and mosquito nets above.

excited to go back to sleep. We had come through the baptism of fire without a scratch and without firing a shot.

In the morning we went for chow, food consisting of cold scrambled powdered eggs, lukewarm grits, stale bread, but hot black coffee which calmed my stomach somewhat. A handwritten note posted on a tent pole indicated that the Battalion had lost two men and eight wounded during last night's skirmish. During brief conversation with several "old timers" here I found out finally where on this G'd forsaken island we were. The location, Morobe Bay. Now that I knew, what difference did it really make? One of the coconut tree stumps bore a number of wooden signs and most pointing in one general direction. Frisco 6,500 miles, Chicago 8,400 miles, New York 9,500 miles, and a sign pointing in an almost opposite direction read Tokyo 4,400 miles. It gave us greenhorns much food for thought. None of it good!

So here I was at Morobe Bay, pretty much toward the North Eastern tip of New Guinea. The Japanese forces had landed sometime in 1942 and occupied all of the North side over the entire length of New Guinea, all of the Solomon Islands, Island of New Britain, the Caroline Islands, the Gilbert Islands, the Marshall Islands, the Marianas Islands, all of the Netherlands East Indies, Thailand, and Burma. But the biggest loss of all were the strategic Philippines. The United States, Great Britain, France, and the Netherlands had not only lost big chunks of their empires or territorial possessions, but also irreplaceable raw material resource and thousands of soldiers killed or taken prisoner. Lost also was valuable equipment, commercial transports and large convoys of ships, as well as a significant armada of warships sunk and their crews, captured or killed.

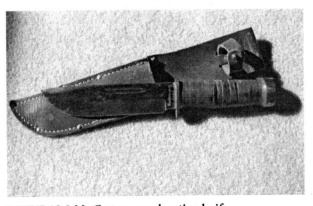

EXHIBIT 12.9 My Cattarangus hunting knife.

The United States and Great Britain had been brought to their knees from the savage blows and naval disasters brought about by the Japanese. In Europe at that time, Hitler's armies were still a tremendous threat, and the fighting by the Allied forces was very grim. The overwhelming majority of people at home did not realize the gravity of the situation.

From what I was told and later witnessed myself, the Japanese soldiers had been so confident of victory that they came ashore nonchalant in New Guinea at Buna, July 21, 1942, wearing sandals, carrying only their personal weapons, burlap bags of rice for sustenance, and "sake" for drinking enjoyment. They knew then that there would be no opposition. Their intention was to invade Australia next. They moved with all their heavy equipment and monumental effort across heretofore impenetrable and uncharted jungle over the Owen Stanley mountain range intent to capture Port Moresby and hence Port Darwin on the continent of Australia. The Japanese Air Force had air superiority since American and allied aircraft had almost completely been destroyed on the ground during 1941/1942 air attacks. When the Japanese naval invasion fleet was intercepted in the Coral Sea, May 1942, by an American Naval Task force and had to withdraw, it was the beginning of an important turning point in the battle for Australia and New Guinea. General MacArthur had taken over the South Pacific Command and developed an island leapfrogging strategy which in retrospect was successful. The battle of Midway, June 3, 1942 helped significantly in forcing Japan to alter its grand scheme war blueprint strategy. This was followed up with the invasion by U.S. Marines of Guadalcanal in the Solomon Islands, August of 1942 and the brutal fighting which lasted for another eight months. During roughly that same period the Jap forces were forced back over the Owen Stanley Mountains in New Guinea by a monumental effort of Australian, U.S. forces and air support. Japan's dream of taking Port Moresby and invading Australia was shattered.

By the time we had landed at Morobe Bay the Japanese forces were stubbornly holding on to the interior areas West of the Buna/Gona region of New Guinea where we engaged them time and time again. We now had

EXHIBIT 12.10 New Guinea woman carrying fruit and a Japanese vintage container.

EXHIBIT 12.11 Australian soldiers, or Aussies as they were known, were tremendously helpful. They knew the jungle and some knew the pidgen English some tribesmen understood.

Aussie military advisors who were very knowledgeable with jungle warfare, and showed us how to hack our way through the bush, and how to make bamboo ladders, bamboo stretchers, and rope bridges over rivers, among other things. They also made us aware of tricks by Japanese scouts or snipers in trees, hiding in brush and man high "Kunai" grass, and how to recognize booby traps that looked like valuable souvenirs. In addition to referring to the Australian soldiers as "Aussies," we also called them "Diggers," but don't remember why.

It was refreshing for me to engage the Aussies in conversation because they knew every jungle survival skill and were able to communicate in "pidgin" language with some of the native tribesmen. I remember several bushmen pointing at me calling me "Grismin" (for "grease man") when they saw me changing the oil on a "Higgins" amphibious assault vehicle, also known as a LCVP short for Landing Craft Vehicle, Personnel. They wanted the dirty oil to put on their body and hair in exchange for pretty ocean shells. I obliged and still have a few those shells that look like cat eyes.

A note on the photographs in this and future chapters: While taking photographs was no problem elsewhere, here it was a huge problem. It began when we landed at Morobe Bay when the half-dozen rolls of film I carried with me were spoiled wading through the water. It took several months before I was able to obtain replacement film cartridges from home. In the meantime, I was able to share copies of photos taken by some of my buddies, some of which were taken with a Japanese camera and with odd film developed in nearby medical facilities. Humidity was the biggest culprit for film spoilage. Once film was available to me, and I was able to once again take photos, I made good use of Uncle Sam's supplies of condoms, which were readily available for Army personnel, and were an excellent resource to protect the film from the humidity. Later, I would give the exposed cartridge to the Aussie contingent who would have them developed in Australia and in turn I would give them copies. It was a system that was not very efficient, but it worked. Finally, I was able to obtain several "official" photos from an Army cameraman in trade for several Jap souvenirs.

For the Japanese armed forces, the supply lines were considerably shorter than ours since they received supplies and reinforcements from nearby Rabaul and New Britain. In contrast, we lost many supply ships with their badly needed cargo to enemy aircraft, Japanese submarines and other warships. Yet, somehow important supplies got through and we were able to clear the enemy from that region by inflicting heavy casualties, usually with finality. Our casualties were many, and seeing their suffering made us more determined. The Japs were well dug in, often connecting their well-fortified caves with tunnels. We had to bring in flame throwers to flush them out of their bunkers. I had not seen flame throwers in action before, but I can tell you that their results are effective with gruesome results. Only in very isolated instances were we able take any prisoners since the Japs preferred to commit *hari kiri*, a ritualistic suicide required by the then Hirohito Emperor of Japan. It was performed ritualistically with their own sword if they were officers, or with a bayonet or inverted rifle, if they were not. If for some reason there was no time to apply these methods, we had no other choice than to kill them. All of the enemy had been brain washed, had an unbelievable fighting spirit and were not afraid to die, since they believed to die was to honor the Emperor.

Seeing, and hearing the enemy soldiers holler while they were being incinerated alive was the most gruesome thing I ever experienced and the most nauseating stench of burned flesh. Yet, it was a fight to the death, them or us. Sometimes I felt as if I was insane and found myself vomiting as close man-to-man combat continued. But no one stopped fighting, driven primarily by self-preservation; we did what we had to do, instinctively, until everything around us became quiet. Only then did we bow our heads in silent prayer and with thanks. The stifling heat and humidity, and soon the smell of dead, grotesque looking, decomposing bodies with maggots and other insects feeding on them is still indescribable today.

Snakes, scorpions, exhaustion, and disease became one of our major concerns. It was the first time in my life that I had seen dead people, not to mention soldiers, severely wounded or dead, torn apart by gunfire, grenades, shrapnel, explosive force, or bayonet. Later that day or the next, those on our side, wounded or killed, were just listed as missing when their names were read during the usual roll call. We didn't see them again and didn't know what had happened to them. They had become casualties, and that's how familiar faces disappeared almost daily. All of this was becoming very impersonal. They had become a statistic, and of interest only to the burial detail. We paid the nearby villagers, if there were any, with cigarettes to carry our wonded on handmade stretchers to Battalion First Aid, where life and death decisions were made by doctors and nurses. What we valued most beyond our own lives and some safe rest, were our ponchos and our knee high leggings. The former protected us from almost often constant rain, the latter from insect bites and the dreaded "Jungle Rot," a devastating fast spreading fungi which many of my comrades contracted. The infection inflamed large areas of the body and caused painful decay of the skin. Despite all of the precautions, I became afflicted with it some months later. Drinking water, while often not available, was seldom a big problem. When it rained, a helmet would fill up quite rapidly. For me it was impossible to determine when the monsoon season ended and the rainy season started. Disease was rampant among my comrades. In addition to those already mentioned, dysentery, yellow jaundice, and typhus were rampant. To ward off malaria we took "atabrine" tablets every morning, a yellow pill which when taken for several weeks and months, made your skin turn yellow. Yet most of us kept taking the pill whenever we could, realizing the alternative consequences. Whenever I had a scratch, a sore, or open wound I applied "sulfanilamide" a recently developed miracle powder (to treat bacterial infections) in small packets which I carried in my First Aid kit. The Medics used it extensively to treat the wounded.

The importance of the New Guinea campaign, and for that matter, the entire South Pacific War is pretty much ignored today, if not almost forgotten. There are no excursions to the bloody battlefields like Normandy, no cemeteries to visit. The struggles, heroic sacrifices and significant battles, by all the soldiers, sailors, marines, airmen and others, have taken a back seat to the glitzy and glamorous fighting in Europe. There are no big reunions, no large memorials, no reenactment of landings or invasions as there are at Normandy, France. Yet, the battles here in the Pacific theater constitute the most ferociously and the most strategic ever fought by Americans, with enormous casualties.

While originally there were small native settlements along the coast, most of them had been abandoned for safer areas in the interior because of the Japanese invasion and later because of the incursions by American and Australian forces. Further inland, where the Japs made their stand, the jungle clad ridges and ravines were so dense that we were quickly swallowed up by the underbrush. This was a tremendous advantage for the fortified enemy since it was impossible to deploy a large concentrated attack force. Nor did this quite swampy terrain lend itself for bringing up heavy tanks, trucks, or heavy artillery. Sometimes offshore gun batteries from naval forces and artillery stationed along the beaches would be called upon to soften up the enemy positions. Thereafter, we would attack with light tanks followed by small fragmented units consisting of ten men squads.

Often the enemy would fortify their positions behind insect and snake infested swamp areas and difficult terrain where we would easily become disoriented and bogged down. I remember this being the scenario in one instance. The enemy was able to mow us down as we were trying to cross the swamp. Luckily for me, by the time my squad reached the swamp, the earlier remnant waves of our men were already on the other side of the swamp. Creeping through the swamp, I felt something on my legs and quickly realized that leeches had attached themselves to my skin. Some of my buddies felt them too. While seeking out the enemy and dodging bullets there was no time to do anything about them and I was unsuccessful in pulling them off. Much later when there was a brief lull in the skirmish and mopping up operation, I took my machete and literally scraped them off my skin, killing most of them in the process. We had to do this to each other, especially where the leeches were sucking on our backs. It was a painful and disgusting procedure, but had to be done before the leeches would sap our strength.

This jungle fight was bloody and savage. Our enemy was deceptive and cunning, and used every trick from their book. We learned how to camouflage using only products from the natural surroundings. We learned about men, each other, enemy equipment, booby traps fashioned by the Japs from shiny mother-of-pearl like objects, snipers lashed to tree trunks or branches, and enemy soldiers who imitated the noises of wild birds or other animals as signals or to confuse us. We learned the hard way about the difference of slimy foul smelling mud and that of decomposing bodies; theirs and ours. But the worst for me was seeing my comrades wounded and bloodied, dead bodies bent into grotesque shapes, often with severed legs, arms, heads, with entrails oozing from the corpse. Some were covered already with flies, scorpions and worse, feasting on what was once a wonderful human being. It made all of us ill, but awakened our most base instincts and our determination to kill them so we would live - a paradox of the most insane choices. At first I fought with my own conscience, trying to achieve, at least in my mind, an equation between the value of the life of an enemy soldier, and being under orders to kill him. Yet, luckily for me, when the time came, I could not hesitate nor ponder the question. It was kill or be killed!

Again we had been unable to take many prisoners, and those that didn't escape had been killed in their fortified earth bunkers and tunnels. We had to collect all remaining enemy weapons, carbines with fold out bayonets, the first I ever saw, go through their belongings to pick up anything worthy of examination by our intelligence officer, like maps, letters, photographs etc., always being mindful of the unexpected. We collected Japanese pistols, rifles, carbines, machine guns with exchangeable barrels and all sorts of ammunition. I remember the rifles and pistols having an imperial chrysanthemum flower insignia engraved. We also picked up Samurai swords with beautifully decorated handles, but could not keep them as souvenirs. Later, these soldiers were usually bulldozed into the ground.

Our casualties in comparison with theirs where relatively light, but still too many of ours dead. Our wounded were put on stretchers waiting for the natives, who had fled during the fighting, to reappear. For two cigarettes they would carry the wounded on makeshift bamboo stretchers to the Battalion first aid station where a decision was made by doctors and nurses whether they could be successfully treated there. If not, an evacuation to the nearest field hospital would take place since there were better facilities, doctors, and nurses available. The dead awaited another fate after their dog tags were collected. As a rule I had nothing to do with the onsite burial, and a bugler playing "Taps" was not always available. Stateside, "Taps" the best known of all bugle calls was used at all military installations to indicate "lights out" and at military funerals. Especially then it was a very melancholy and serene series of sounds. I loved and hated it, but I will never forget it. For those that died in battle it was "lights out" forever.

The daily sporadic downpours and constant rains turned creeks into fast flowing rivers and the ground into a sea of mud that made the movement of men and equipment come to a standstill. Roads of any kind were nonexistent. There were no railroads and improvised airfields were usually far away. Friendly natives were coaxed to help us find our way, and trails used one day were overgrown the next and no longer visible or passable.

Our leaders, officers, had no detailed maps. Maps were simply nonexistent, and orders to engage the enemy were at best vague and often ambiguous. Intelligence information was based on hour-by-hour visual sightings from the ground and less frequently, but very much welcomed, from the air. The P-38 Lightning were twin boom fighter bombers produced by Lockheed, fitted with aerial cameras as well as machine guns, performed invaluable aerial reconnaissance to determine enemy strength and precise location. This two engine aircraft was far superior in speed, maneuverability and firepower over Japanese fighter aircraft, the Zero and Tony. Less frequently would we see our carrier-based Hellcat, Corsair, or the two-man Avenger torpedo bomber since they had a shorter range. However, both the P-51 Mustang, although not as fast as the P-38, but with seemingly greater maneuverability, as well as the Royal Australian Air Force Boomerang fighters and Kittyhawk fighter bombers would keep Japanese aircraft off our backs. Now and then we would receive air support from Douglas A-20 Havoc attack bombers. They were stationed primarily in Australia and later, on improvised airstrips in New Guinea and the Philippines, and could be called upon to soften up enemy fortifications and known troop concentrations. The natives who had never seen airplanes before referred to them as "canoes of the spirits."

More than once did we see aerial dog fights in the distance or almost above us. Each time I would hold my breath, hoping that our pilots would triumph. Unfortunately that was not always the case. Once I saw one of our fighter planes being shot down, the pilot had bailed out, the parachute had opened while the plane in flames spiraled into the ocean with a big splash. The enemy Zero fighter plane circled the U.S. pilot hanging in the parachute and fired glowing tracer bullets into his silk chute until it caught on fire and disintegrated while the pilot fell thousands of feet into the ocean. I was horrified, never having expected that kind of brutality. It made me very angry. We were hearing news about other more terrible and sickening Japanese atrocities having taking place during the invasion of the Philippines, during the fighting at Guadalcanal, Iwo Jima, and other places. While I tried to discount some of the stories as exaggerations I hoped and prayed that I would survive not seriously wounded and not become a prisoner of the enemy. Occasionally, we were able with our field radio to tune in on shortwave radio to broadcasts from Japan to hear a 15 minute news and propaganda program by "Tokyo Rose," directed to us GIs, designed to demoralize us. It always made us very angry, yet we laughed at the lies and her weird stories.

It was my lucky day when I was able to trade my heavy, inefficient M-1 rifle for a carbine. It was lighter, and used cartridge clips that no longer required a noisy bolt activation. Yet, just carrying my own essential combat equipment in foot-deep mud was exhausting and made me feel like a stumbling or drunk fool, especially when we had to additionally carry disassembled mortars, machine guns, bazookas, grenade launchers, pertaining ammo, flame throwers and their napalm mixture. I thought the enemy was very smart, tenacious, and at times courageous. They goaded us to attack in stifling 90-plus degree heat, while they preferred to attack with noisy suicide charges during darkness. The jungle conditions made every attempt for us to apply military tactics impossible and laughable. In the final analysis every man was for himself and did the best to stay alive while hoping to take out as many of the enemy as he could. Yes, to some extent we had acquired an almost wild animal instinct. It was exhausting and often somewhat demoralizing.

As we advanced toward the west of the island, villages like Buna, Salamaua, Lae, which was about 60 miles west of Finchhafen, next Madang, Wewak, Atappe, and finally Hollandia were for me just points on the map. Their existence as a village or town was not visible except for temporary harbor and dock installations built by the Navy construction battalions known as the "Seabees." Evidence of their all-important work was at Hollandia where they had constructed air strips with thousands of interconnected metal landing strip mats. They were also building some essential roads, repair facilities, fuel and ammunition storage sites as well as field hospitals. With their heavy construction equipment they were capable of providing many critical facilities in record time, sometimes it seemed overnight. Our successes of overwhelming and sometimes burying our enemy in heavily fortified bunkers were frequently credited to Seabees who used several of their monster size tractors and motorized shovels ahead of or in conjunction with medium size tanks and infantry, sometimes in combination with air support. The Japanese soldiers who had landed at New Guinea many months earlier had plenty of time to build these fortifications and thought them invincible. They were not, but caused us many casualties.

At times the jungle was so dense that our field of vision was limited to ten yards or less. Here, nature had become a formidable enemy. Clearing an area around our encampment and defensive positions for increased security could take days or longer, and surprise banzai attacks with their accompanying screams could come from any direction and always caused initial chaos. In a fluid search and destroy mission it could happen that we and the Jap elements would circle each other without knowing the other was near because of the dense jungle and individual camouflage. Under these conditions I witnessed the incomparable courage of soldiers around me, sometimes driven by sheer guts and desperation.

Reinforcements, supplies including ammunition, rations, and first aid supplies were lagging more often than not. In desperate situations, aerial drops would be made by C-47 transports which flew very low and therefore at great risk of being damaged or shot down by enemy fire. The shortages were due in part because of unavailability, lack of coordination, inaccessibility to our location, perhaps our precise position was not known, or some other bureaucratic screw-up. Because of the desolation, I sometimes had the feeling that we were the only fighting group on this G'd forsaken island and no one knew or cared that we were here. I was acquainted with loneliness escaping the Nazis in Europe. But this was a different kind of loneliness; a loneliness among comrades. Seeing tribesmen nearby with spears as well as bows and arrows and hearing them communicate with each other by different drum beats brought me quickly back to reality.

Without any sanitary facilities, Spam and Vienna sausages from rusting metal cans filled with awful tasting greasy Australian mutton were eaten mostly cold or at best, lukewarm. Most of the time we could not heat the contents at all or insufficiently. The war always had a priority over food. We had plenty of cigarettes and matches, the latter were kept in specially designed waterproof metal containers, and sometimes we had cans of beer, if you liked warm beer. Stowed away in the wrong place and exposed to the merciless sun, the beer cans would explode and scare the wits out of us plus giving our exact location away to the enemy. Since I had not lost my prize possession namely my pipe, I would strip the tobacco from cigarettes and smoke it. This was one of my few pleasures, which unfortunately never lasted long enough. We yearned for very simple things like a hamburger, a slice of pie of any kind, a cold drink, perhaps a milk shake, or a soft bed, but to no avail. There were no ice machines, and consequently, no ice.

While we lived like civilized savages, I tried as best to keep clean and stay healthy. However, it was not to be and I came down with a case of hepatitis which manifested itself by severe stomach cramps, tremendous headaches and vomiting of any and all food. These symptoms were accompanied by great weakness that I was finally unable to go on my own to the first aid tent. At last several of my tent buddies, realizing how sick I was, helped me to the first aid tent. The medics there determined that I had a very high fever and decided to have me transported to the nearest Field Hospital. Once there, I was told that the white of my eyes had turned yellow, a sure sign of jaundice. My second hospital stay was caused by severe Jungle Rot on both legs, a tropical disease about which heretofore not much was known nor a cure. It is an infection of tissue of unknown origin that infects succeeding layers of the skin while spreading in size and depth to the bone. It was extremely painful, accompanied by chills and fever. I saw hundreds of cases much worse than mine where the sores were on hands, face, other parts of the body, or all over the body. The next time I was hospitalized was caused by the most dreadful disease malaria. This in spite of all the precautions of taking atabrine tablets every day and sleeping under a mosquito net whenever possible, which was most of the time, not the case. However, the Anopheles mosquitoes attacked in spite of my precautions and produced temperatures of 103-plus degrees until I was delirious. I didn't realize how debilitating and more often fatal malaria could be. The disease was rampant among my comrades and in the entire South Pacific theater and resisted the drugs available to us. The malaria carrying mosquito breeds enormously in this humid and wet climate, and we were constantly in danger. Although we had been issued mosquito netting we often tore them up since we found the netting more advantageous as a medium for camouflaging ourselves and our positions.

As terrible as these diseases were with the attendant trauma, there was also a bright side: the hospital. These field hospitals were away from the immediate combat zone and were configured as long large tents, open on all sides. Each wounded or ill soldier had a cot with two blankets, a mosquito net, and a wooden box serving as sort of a nightstand for medication and water, the lower part for our personal belongings, of which we didn't have many left. There were also Army doctors and young nurses as well as something resembling a PX (Post Exchange) where I could buy pipe tobacco, and believe it or not, candy bars, ice cold Coca Cola, newspapers that were a month or two old, playing cards and other miscellaneous items including limited wearing apparel. We wore hospital gowns, had clean towels, were able to take showers and had the first warm edible food in months. Most important in my case to bring the temperature down or make me feel more comfortable was the availability of an ice machine. Also, there were decent toilet facilities, which I had not seen since on board ship. If that wasn't already like heaven in New Guinea, the American Red Cross was also represented by sympathetic volunteer ladies. They had paperback books, stationary, phonograph records and movies that would be shown several times a week in the tent. One of the Red Cross Volunteers was a Lois Ellman who said she would get in touch with me after the war.

This hospitalization was in Hollandia, once an important town in the Dutch part of New Guinea, now part of Indonesia, about a thousand miles west of our original landing site. It had a large deep harbor for ships to come close in and a large airstrip with steel plate-reinforced runways, mainly for B-25 Mitchel bombers, P-38 Lightning, and P-51 Mustang fighter planes, as well as C-47 transport planes affectionately referred to as "Gooney Birds". Hollandia became a huge forward supply base for every conceivable item of war material required. There were warehouses and storage areas for every type and caliber of ammunition, construction material, equipment, fuel, trucks, jeeps, half tracks, cement, artillery pieces, medium and heavy size tanks, medical supplies, on and on. This base was so important that the somewhat arrogant, corncob-pipe smoking, always debonairly dressed Commander General Douglas MacArthur, had his Headquarters built in the hills overlooking the base, the harbor and beyond. It was built by our standards sturdy, with building material from the US, not from local lumber. The Seabees had constructed a special road up to this mountain retreat, the longest and while not paved, the only all-weather road in the area. The GIs, Marines, and Seabees fumed because of the extravagance at their expense. Since in former days he had been appointed Field Marshall of the Philippine Army, he wore a distinguished looking cap, a showroom looking pressed uniform, and shirts of which the pockets brimmed with several fountain pens. The General was never seen without wearing large imposing sunglasses. While we gave him credit for his brilliant strategy of "island leapfrogging," nobody seemed to like his snooty manner and arrogance. I never saw him personally.

Here in the hospital I was nursed back to health, and at least I was once more sane and safe. I swapped experiences with others who were sick from bush typhus, dengue fever, malaria or the badly wounded. I found out that most of them had gone through far worse conditions and situations than I had. I also learned what had or what was happening in other parts of the South West Pacific area. The big naval battle of the Bismarck Sea had taken place where the 5th Air Force commanded by General Kenny had sunk or disabled a dozen of the Emperor's biggest war ships, all troop transports with thousands of human replacements and most Japanese fighter planes in aerial combat. Large enemy naval forces were intercepted and sunk by our Navy commanded by Admiral Nimitz with heavy support by our air power. This denied the Japanese forces on most of the occupied islands, of which there were many, of urgently needed supplies and prevented evacuation of their starving soldiers on some of the smaller Pacific islands. Still, the Japanese Army forced us into bloody battles on islands never heard of before. Their names show up today only in books of the Pacific War history, for example New Georgia, Treasury Islands, Bougainville, Iwo Jima, Rabaul, Tarawa and others. Yet it seemed that the U.S. and its allies were making slowly progress, albeit at a great cost of life and material.

Reading some of the way out of date newspapers gave additional clues as to the progress of the war. I was astonished to read that 40% of the American casualties in the S.W. Pacific were due to tropical diseases, illness, and infections from cuts by coral and a variety of accidents. That was one of the main reasons that the casualties we incurred decimated our ranks and when replacements arrived directly from basic training stateside, they were inexperienced "green" soldiers without much help to us. In fact they were as green as we were when we landed.

As I was recuperating from malaria, a young Army nurse befriended me and we went out for short walks and swims. This was heaven compared with the life back at my battalion. Her name was Janet Bushee, from a suburb of Boston, Massachusetts. While fraternization between nurses and GIs was against Army rules, she did not seem to care and neither did I. Besides she was kind of pretty.

EXHIBIT 12.29 Nurse Jane Bushee.

Being in the 4th General Hospital APO 322 gave me much time to think about many things. My morale and that of others around me was rather low, mostly because we felt somewhat betrayed by our Government for sending us here insufficiently trained, ill equipped, poorly supplied, and insufficiently supported with weapons for jungle warfare. On the other hand, our enemy's morale was high, well-trained and equipped for this terrain and climate, indoctrinated to fight to the death. That's why our advances were so very painstakingly slow and tough. My morale was also negatively affected because I felt right along that my cause to put my life on the line was to fight the Nazi Germans. My enthusiasm to fight the Imperial Majesty's forces had been replaced by a strong will not to become a dead hero in this unforgiving hell hole!

News from my dear parents, friends and acquaintances on V-Mail (Victory Mail) stationary was infrequent and usually came in bunches, six and more com-

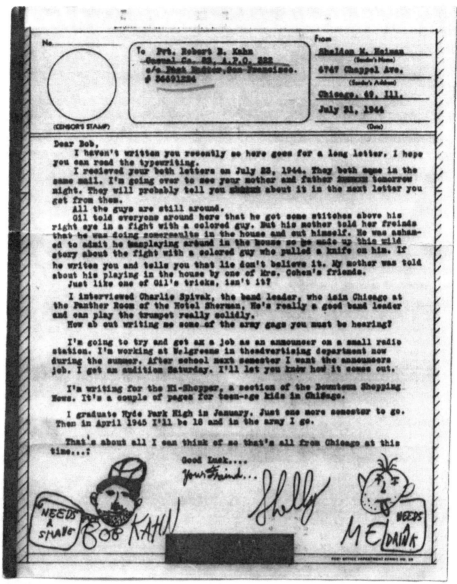

EXHIBIT 12.30 A typical V-mail letter. This one is from my draft dodger friend, Sheldon Heiman, Chicago.

munications at a time. There were two types of mail service from here, airmail, provided I had a six cent Airmail envelope or an Airmail stamp, or V-Mail, which was free for us and went by slow boat. Air Mail was preferred, but it was almost impossible to keep the envelopes from being ruined in the prevailing stinking humidity, rain and ever present mud when I couldn't even keep my shoes and socks dry. The envelope flaps would be stuck to the envelope and the stamps would stick together or stick to something else. That's why I had to use V-Mail most of the time. After the one page form was filled with whatever message,

EXHIBIT 12.31 All letters from us went through censorship so we could never write where we were or what was happening.

address and return address, I had to fold it and place it into a box at the Company orderly room tent for mailing. Somewhere at a central remote field post office, the letter with all others was censored, then photographically reduced to 4" x 5", stuffed (after I had folded it the letter) into a special 4-½" x 3-¾" envelope and marked Official Business. Mail Call, as it was known at our level, happened infrequently. The more time elapsed between mail calls, mostly a month or longer, the more letters I would get at one time. Much of the mail I sent to the mainland and the other way around, especially the "care packages" from home or from relatives and friends never got to me. My parents and others worried because I never mentioned receipt or thanked them. On the other hand they wouldn't hear from me for a month and often longer. Mail was sent by ships which perhaps were sunk, were diverted to a different APO (Army Post Office numbered addresses overseas), or the mail bag simply got lost.

While I was always glad to hear from Mom and Dad, knowing without them telling me how they struggled to make a living in Chicago, it pained me not knowing what may have happened to my sister Irene in Lille, France now under German occupation. I was also anxious and concerned about the many relatives and friends left behind in Germany, Luxembourg and wherever they had been transported, so called resettled, in Eastern Europe by the Nazis. After all, by the time I was shipped overseas there were unconfirmed and confirmed news stories about concentration labor and death camps as well as ghettos where Jews had been banished. Of course I knew and often saw with my own eyes what atrocities and despicable acts the Germans were capable of while I was still in Mannheim and later at Luxembourg. While I suspected that the worst could happen to them, I fervently hoped and silently prayed that even against poor odds, they would survive.

I was always glad to hear from my latest flame Gertrude Wolff, and with somewhat less anticipation from my Chicago friends Francine Travis, and Ille, whose last name I have forgotten, Shirley Rice, and Elaine Kaplan, as well as my draft dodger buddies, or should I say draft rejects also from Chicago including Sheldon Heiman, Don Con, Gil Cohen and others. When I wrote to my parents I tried not worry them with details about myself or my circumstances. Therefore I would give them always a subdued or rosier picture of my activities and never mentioned the frustrations of the day, the infernal hell of the jungle or the savage fighting. Besides, I was always aware of the censor. What was noticeably strange that none of the letters I received told me anything about their own frustrations, nor how they felt the war was progressing in Europe, North Africa, Russia and elsewhere. It is my guess that they too didn't want to worry me. Perhaps they were right. And so, both I and my parents played a similar game. Generally, news of elsewhere on sea, land, or air was scarce. We did not learn about allied or axis successes and setbacks until months later. Some of the details did not become known to me until I came home from the war, in September 1945. As a matter of U.S. government policy our own military failures and setbacks were hardly ever reported, including those in our theater of operations. Occasionally we saw a copy of the *Stars and Stripes*, Army newspaper which was light on the war coverage but heavy on cartoons, funny stories, jokes and sport events back home.

After being discharged from the hospital my orders were to report to the Hollandia airbase, approximately 1000 miles from Morobe Bay where we first landed. Upon arrival I was integrated into a unit that was assigned to repair all physical damage to incoming aircraft. This was not regular maintenance work. We had several large metal shops under oversized camouflage tents which we called hangars. They were equipped with medium size metal cutting, bending, drilling, riveting, and welding equipment also a small blacksmith shop. With my excellent background in metal fabrication, I was well suited for this work, although it was quite different from anything I had done before. Additionally the work required ingenuity, inventiveness and imagination. There were no blueprints or repair manuals to fix the damage to the airplanes from Flak anti-aircraft guns, machine gun damage from enemy fighter, etc. Sometimes I wondered how some planes could make it back with big holes in the fuselage, wings, stabilizers or some other structural parts. Often there was equipment failure as a result of enemy fire and planes came in on fire, black smoke trailing, pilot or crew badly wounded. It was only through sheer determination, courage and good luck that some planes were able to land. Other planes were so badly damaged that that they had to be junked and used for spare parts. Sadly, many fighter planes as well as B-25 two engine fighter bombers and C-47 transports went down somewhere in that huge unforgiving jungle or Pacific Ocean. There was a song, "Coming in On a Wing and a Prayer," by the Song Spinners. It was a pretty tune and the words so true and fitting our situation.

It was good duty, even so we worked from dawn to dusk, a minimum of ten sometimes twelve hours a day, seven days a week. The personal reward and perceived contribution to the success of missions flown was incalculable. It was months after Hollandia was captured from the Japs late April 1944, and we were safe, except at night when one or two Japanese bombers dubbed "Betty" would give the harbor and other installations including the airbase a look while dropping a few flares, and now and then a few bombs. Never too accurate with their bombs, our Flak wasn't very successful either in bringing them down. Its two engines had such a distinguishable roar that the "Betty" could be identified by sound alone. Because there was no ground fighting in our area my mood was more relaxed. The food in the outdoor mess consisting of powdered eggs, spam, toast and hot coffee (see exhibit 12.34 in the appendix) was a monumental improvement and so were our accommodations. Still in tents with mosquito nets and cots, but with wood floors and electric lights operated from generators. There were even movies in the evening with the screen set up inside a truck to preclude being spotted too easily by enemy reconnaissance planes. One time we even had a USO show with Hollywood celebrities including Frances Langford. We laughed, cried and let go with whistles and wolf calls every time a pretty girl came on stage. Of course everything was under the open sky, and we, hundreds of men, were sitting on the ground or wooden boxes, our prize possession.

The newspaper *Stars and Stripes* for our consumption was more up to date here and we had a little more time to read and put girly pictures, "pinups" on the walls of our tent. A beautiful photo of Gertrude was among mine. Some GIs whiled away their free time away by gambling or just playing cards. Others succeeded in concocting and drinking a brew known as "torpedo juice," so called because part of the brew came from torpedo alcohol or "jungle juice," which consisted primarily of fermented coconut milk. Both had horrible side effects, one of them being temporary blindness. There were graffiti images of popular cartoon characters of "Sad Sack" and "Kilroy Was Here" on every latrine wall and everywhere else where there was space to draw or carve these peculiar images. The Sad Sack character was from a comic strip cartoon from the "Yank" magazine. The term "Kilroy" is said to refer to a shipyard inspector in Massachusetts who would acknowledge his approval by signing "Kilroy was here" on the pertaining structure of the vessel. The big nosed character peeking over a wall is believed to be a British character named "Mr.Chad." During the early part of the war the two characters apparently merged and the fad was born.

We read news about U.S. Marines overwhelming the Imperial Japanese Armies on islands we never had heard of, sustaining heavy casualties in spite of prior heavy US naval bombardment and aerial support. Nevertheless, joint operations caused U.S. victory on islands of Noemfoor, Saipan, Tinian, Guam, Gilbert, Biak, Truk, Rabaul, Peleliu, Morotai, and Wakde, an island not too far from Hollandia. The Japanese losses during these island leapfrog operations were staggering beyond belief since they defended their positions until they were wiped out to the last man. Still today these islands are difficult to find on a map unless it is highly detailed.

I will digress for a moment since an incident comes to my mind which is worth sharing. One very hot and sweaty afternoon, being caught up with my repair work, I checked out a Jeep from the motor pool. Driving along the shoreline of Hollandia's Humboldt Bay I looked for a shallow beach free of sharp coral where I could take a swim. After parking the jeep in the shade under the tree line I took a nice refreshing swim in my khaki colored shorts. Thereafter I rested on my khaki towel until I was dry. When I got back to the Jeep I donned my fatigue pants and under shirt, when I heard an odd hissing sound above me. As I looked up I was startled by a huge snake slithering slowly down the tree. It was a python about eight feet above me. In my near panic I grabbed a .45 caliber automatic pistol stored in the door of the Jeep, released the safety and point blank fired at the monster. As the bullets hit, it was like a bubble bursting on a pancake in a skillet, and still the snake was coming down the tree. I fired several more shots and then remembered that I also had a machete with me. Instinctively I dropped the pistol, swung the machete and severed the head of the snake. The head fell into the Jeep while the body about 6 inches in diameter kept on squirming for several minutes before falling to the ground. It took another five minute or longer before the wiggling ceased. After I had composed myself, I measured the python with my stride and estimated its length at 15 ft without the head. I had already seen larger snakes. They kill by strangling animals as big as wild boars, crocodiles, mules, ponies and other large game. When I saw the first native on my way back to camp I let him have the head and pointed in the direction where he could find the remainder.

When the Japanese forces landed at Buna, the North coast of New Guinea, July 1942, they intended to cross the heretofore impenetrable Owen Stanley mountain range to Port Moresby and hence invade Australia. To achieve this goal they had brought with them hundreds of pack mules. Not realizing the unknown difficulties to overcome, many of the mules died through sheer exhaustion, disease, injuries, and from Aussie and American attacks. However, many pack mules died also from venomous snake bites or choking by boa constrictors, pythons and others. My encounter with the python near the beach was a scary experience I can never forget.

While I was patching up battle damaged aircraft I met many pilots and crew members. One of the P-51 fighter pilots, a very young happy go lucky fellow, always mocked me because on some mornings or evenings I would go to the interdenominational chapel to pray. My prayers to Elohim–G'd, were for my parents, my sister, all my relatives friends left behind in Europe, for the U.S. and Allied troops everywhere, and finally for myself. He, on the other hand, was an outspoken atheist with a devil-may-care attitude. But fate had caught up with him one day when he landed badly wounded. When I went to see him in the field hospital before he died from his wounds, he handed me a piece of paper. I didn't look at it until I got back to my tent villa. One of the Red Cross ladies typed it for me before I sent it home. My dear mother kept many things over the years, photographs, letters, etc. Among them she kept the letter which contained what my pilot friend had given me. It is reproduced here because it reveals the frailties, psychological stress, and internal conflict on one hand, and courage as well as heroism on the other. The poem also attests to the fact that when the final veil came down, he started to believe in G'd having premonitions of his death. Everyone changed his outlook out here.

With A Friend

Look, God, I have never spoken to you,
But now I want to say, "How do you do."
You see they told me you did not exist
And like a fool I believed all this.

Last night from a shell hole I saw the sky,
And then decided they had told me a lie.
Had I taken time to see the things you made
I'd have known they weren't calling a spade a spade.

I wonder if you would shake my hand,
Somehow I feel you will understand
I had come to this hellish place,
Before I had time to see your face.

Well, there isn't much more to say,
But I am glad that I met you today.
The zero hour may soon be here;
I am not afraid since I know you are near.

There is the signal, so I must go.
I like you a lot I want you to know.
Look now, this is a horrible fight,
And I may come to your house tonight.
Though I wasn't friendly to you before,
I wonder if you'd want me at your door?

Look, I am crying! Me, shedding tears!
I wish I had known you through the years;

I must go now so, God, goodbye,
Since I have met you, I am not afraid to die.

By September 1944, activities at the Hollandia air base had increased fourfold and so had the number of aircraft arriving. More of the jungle had to be cleared to make room for aircraft parking and junked planes. Never had I seen so many airplanes in one place. It was awesome (see exhibits 12.32 and 12.33 in the appendix). In the meantime U.S .troops had landed on the Island of Morotai, 300 miles North West of New Guinea without much resistance. We now worked around the clock in shifts as we were ordered to make modifications on P-51 Mustangs to accommodate an external fuel tank increasing its range by about 40%. They were designed so they could be released and dropped from the aircraft when empty or if involved in a dog fight to give the plane greater speed and maneuverability. Our maintenance crews had also received instructions to install retarding fuses in certain types of bombs. This would permit very low flying aircraft to drop bombs on targets with great accuracy, while giving the aircraft and crew sufficient time to leave the target area safely prior to the explosion. P-51, P-38 fighter aircraft, B-25 medium bombers and C-47 transports camouflaged and sitting on aprons off the runway were too numerous to count. Rumors circulated that heavy bombers from the 14th and 20th Air Force, primarily B-29 Super Fortress, were now attacking the Japanese mainland from Saipan, Guam and other heavy bomber bases. Our Hollandia harbor was bristling with hundreds of ships including destroyers, troopships, cargo ships, large barges, LSTs (Landing Ship Troops) a few PT fast attack torpedo boats around a tender, several escort aircraft carriers, as well as a cruiser. Most of the other captured islands had harbors and airstrips, some of which had been constructed by the enemy as advance supply and support bases, and after repair were now used for forthcoming advances toward Japan.

CHAPTER THIRTEEN

Invasion of the Philippines

We could sense that a major amphibious attack landing by our combined U.S. Forces was in the making but had no idea of the target nor when it would take place. We were finally placed on a standby alert, and with that our anxiety started. I wrote a few letters home not knowing what to expect and spent time cleaning my equipment, packed, and waited. One by one different units in the area were called up and loaded on ships of all types and descriptions. I counted well over one hundred vessels in the harbor and a series of PBY sea planes. The call for me didn't come, and when I looked down into the bay in the early morning of October 16, 1944, as I would do every day, all but a few ships had left. While the Japanese High Command expected an invasion of the Philippines which consisted of more than 7000 islands of different sizes, they did not expect landings at the island of Leyte on October 20, under the protection of the U.S. Third and Seventh Fleet with over 150 warships and more than 1000 carrier launched aircraft. In spite of brutal naval battles during which the Japanese employed Kamikaze suicide aircraft attacks on our ships, our landings were successful. General Douglas MacArthur triumphantly waded ashore at Red Beach with his troops on Leyte near the town of Palo. Shortly thereafter the capitol of Leyte, Tacloban fell into our hands and with it the all-important airport.

On or about November 15, my call finally came and I reported to the given numbered dock where my ship, a relatively small supply ship, was waiting. It was crowded, had no bunks, and we wound up sitting and sleeping on deck wherever there was an empty spot. There were no toilets, and our needs had to be discharged into buckets which we then emptied into the Pacific Ocean. It was not very graceful, rather it was disgusting. We ate our own rations which tasted as horrible as always, especially after we had gotten used to edible food at Hollandia. Soon I became seasick and had to use a bucket or the rails like many others. When we left San Francisco, I was part of the 6th Army under General Walter Krueger. The Army Air Corps out here was commanded by General George Kenney. It was a strenuous and unpleasant voyage. It rained hard for more than a day and the sea was angry. The next morning I noticed that we were part of a convoy of about twenty other merchant ships and transports with several fast destroyer escorts on our flanks.

We had crossed the Equator again but this time heading north. There were no celebrations or initiations as was the case when we crossed the Equator steaming south from San Francisco. The convoy traveled North by North West passing Mindanao, still in Japanese hands. Now, more often we were visited by our P-51 Mustang and the twin fuselage P-38 planes, as well as Navy Avenger torpedo bombers, launched from carriers. We did not see the carriers since they were beyond the horizon. I was thankful that we did not encounter any Japanese aircraft or ships for very good reasons. The Third and Seventh Fleet had sunk or put out of commission at least twenty of the Emperor's capital warships, the greater part of the Japanese Navy, including about seven hundred carrier based planes. Their defeat came during the largest naval battle ever, the Battle of the Leyte Gulf, around October 26, 1944. However, the U.S. Navy did not come away without the loss of a number of ships and their crews, primarily from very effective Kamikaze suicide attacks whereby young devoted Japanese pilots crashed their aircraft with a heavy bomb into one of our capital ships. The losses of several of our aircraft carriers, and other large warships as well as a huge number of personnel was not revealed to the Nation until much later. While America had a great ability for replacing and adding to our war arsenal of ships, planes, guns and munitions, regrettably there were no scientific methods to bring back to life those soldiers, sailors, marines and others whose life was snuffed out.

We came closer to land every minute and were told to prepare for debarkation and to expect enemy "harassment." In the distance on the starboard side was the Philippine island of Samar. Closer on port side was the island of Leyte, about one hundred miles in length. Several ships in our convoy were ahead, some behind us, and others had left the convoy for other destinations. We docked at a wooden pier and were told later near the town of Palo, the East side of Leyte, where our Commander, General MacArthur waded ashore uttering the famous words: "I have returned!" We were loaded on different trucks based on our specific order document, whereby my destination was the airstrip near the city of Tacloban, on the same side of the island.

To my great surprise there were roads, even though they were primarily mud with deep tire tracks. Riding in the rear of the truck was worse than being on board ship at stormy sea. Along the way we saw U.S. troops and Philippine armed guerrillas known as Huks, securing our flanks against sporadic attacks by remnants of Japanese forces. Although the Huks were ill-equipped soldiers, most wore no shoes, but had great enthusiasm and stamina. As we drove in a westerly direction through relatively hilly country, destroyed or wrecked Japanese tanks, armored vehicles, trucks, artillery pieces and some of ours had been pushed off to the side of the road. Now and then we had to pull over to the right or left of the road and stop, either because small motorized convoys were coming from the opposite direction or U.S. soldiers were probing for land mines the Japs had left. We traveled it seemed about 20 miles in about two hours and were kind of shook up and tired because of the poor, bumpy and at times muddy road conditions and having a very tiresome sea journey behind us. Now and then I saw dirty looking barefoot peasants and barrios, rural villages in which they lived. They consisted of small grass-thatched dwellings built on wooden stilts, similar but far better constructed than those in New Guinea. All of this made me feel better compared with the primitive fuzzy wuzzies of New Guinea. After all, I was glad to see some form, a glimmer of civilization. The people that I saw at least wore clothing, although ragged.

We finally arrived at what appeared to be a very busy airbase, significantly enlarged by the Japanese Air Force after their occupation of the Philippines with much larger and longer runways than Hollandia. There were large Quonset huts, permanent and semi-permanent structures including a well-equipped control tower. Although there were aircraft of all types, the airstrip was not suitable for our heavy bombers such as the B-17 and B-29 because of the soft ground. Even the steel mats which were added after we recaptured the base would not compensate for this geological situation. After reporting to the Orderly Room for housing and duty assignment, I settled down in a tent with four cots and three new "roommates," mosquito netting, but no electricity and no wood floors. My assignment would be similar to that at Hollandia, except that there was a big backlog of aircraft needing structural repair before they would be airworthy again. Also, there was an assortment of Japanese aircraft wreckage which later became a great curiosity for me and many others.

After settling into my new surroundings my new tent buddies asked me to come along on a weekend evening to the town of Tacloban. I accepted figuring that a change of pace and scenery would do me some good. On the outskirts of town, the shacks that people lived in were abominable. The town itself, at least from what I saw, consisted of one and two story buildings that looked like relics of the past, and the dirt streets were still covered with rainwater filled mud holes that were difficult to avoid. The noise, a combination of music, people laughing and singing, came from the second story of a nearby building. That's where we were headed after parking our Jeep. The place was crowded with boisterous GIs and screaming Philippine girls and woman. There was beer and liquor, as well as many drunk Army personnel, sailors, seabees, and a few marines. My comrades ordered drinks paying with Pesos, the local currency. It was not a place to my liking. The cigarette and cigar smoke was so heavy that everybody, including myself was coughing. Had I known how to get back to the base, I would have left by myself. As it was, I tried to endure the appalling situation.

It was not long until a fight broke out between a number of GIs, and before I knew what had happened, the entire place was involved in a colossal brawl the likes I had never experienced. MPs, Military Police who were posted at the entrance of this sleazy "night club," as we came in, tried their best to break it up but it was to no avail. I knew then that it was time to save myself from harm and looked for an exit. Being close to the windows I saw a large metal sign outside at a right angle to the building several feet below. I reached for the rod on which the sign hung, pulled my body out the window and let my entire weight hang on the sign. The rod on which the sign hung bent downward, pulled away from the wall, and before I knew I was on the ground, the sign advertising the club in my hands.

A crowd of locals and GIs watching were standing there laughing while I was safe but embarrassed by my high wire act. My immediate goal achieved, I waited for my three musketeers and was glad when we got back to our unpretentious abode. My first brush with civilization was just that, a brush!

Our air activities in support of troops in the northern and southern parts of Leyte and the island of Samar were enormous, and I was busier than ever repairing and patching up aircraft. Special efforts were on the way here too, to fit special bombs with retarding fuses and others with parachutes to delay the explosions where low level strafing was necessary. Like in New Guinea, the rains were incessant and the weather unpredictable. On or about December 13, 1944 we experienced the forces of a very powerful typhoon coming from the Leyte Gulf. The tropical winds were so violent and of such long durations that the tents, including ours, were ripped to shreds and its contents soaked. In the midst of this terrifying storm all personnel on base, including myself, were ordered to provide additional moorings to the aircraft on the tarmac. The winds were so strong that time and again I had to kneel and crawl in order not to be blown over. In spite of our efforts there was considerable damage everywhere, including heavy damages to several aircraft which had come loose from their moorings. We had received over 20 inches of rain in a 24-hour period. To me it seemed that the end of the world had come. It was only later that we heard that the typhoon sank three U.S. destroyers with 800 sailors on board, not to mention heavy damage to other ships and installations. Everything in my duffel bag was soaking wet and had to be replaced. I hoped that my film could be salvaged.

The news from all fronts in Europe was good and encouraging. I was always hoping to hear some good news about my sister, but letters from Mom and Dad written six and eight weeks earlier did not mention anything. It saddened me very much and there was not much else to do for me than to hope and pray. Then, all of a sudden, my prayers were answered. It was sometime in January 1945 when during mail call I received several letters from home that were over a month and a half old. In the oldest of their letters they wrote that Lille, the French city where Irene had lived since 1934, had been liberated by British troops on September 3, 1944, and had news that Irene, Aunt Irma, as well as Uncle Charles and children Claude and Eliane were safe. This news had been conveyed to them in a letter mailed from a U.S. soldier, Karl J. Loewenstein, dated September 19, 1944, confirmed shortly thereafter through Walter Cohen, a nephew of my Uncle Max Cohen, who was serving in the U.S. Army in Europe as an interpreter. Being somewhere in France he went on an "unofficial mission" to Lille in October 1944 to locate my sister. Shortly thereafter, my first cousin Norbert Isaak, paratrooper with the 82nd Airborne unit and the invasion forces in France, also came to visit her in November 1944 during a lull in the fighting, while his Airborne unit was located not far from Paris. By the time it was possible for the news to be written, mailed and transported from the French battle zone to Chicago, weeks had gone by. Thereafter, it took many weeks before the news by letter would arrive at my base at Leyte. This delay was lengthed because of my recent relocation and the time it took for my parents to receive my latest address change.

EXHIBIT 13.1 Sister Irene didn't have my parents address thus the letter went to dad's brother Ernest. Nevertheless it was a letter sent from heaven to learn that she and the family Ehrlich were alive and well.

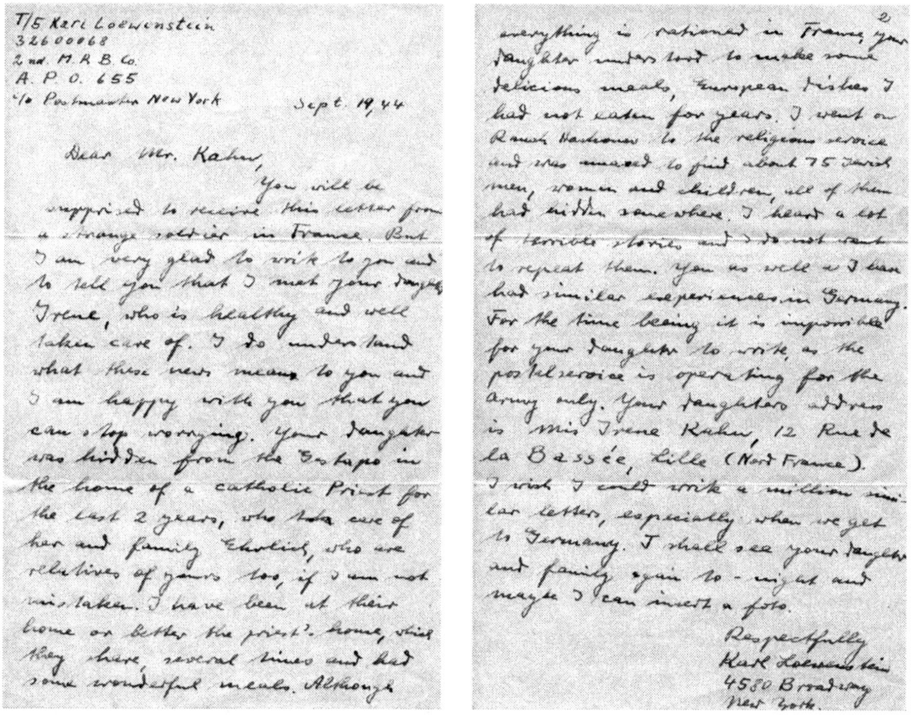

EXHIBIT 13.2 The letter from American soldier, Karl Loewenstein, with news to Chicago that my sister Irene is alive. Larger image of the letter in the appendix, exhibit 13.2.

T/5 Karl Loewenstein
32600068
2nd M.R.B. Co.
A.P.O. 655
c/o Postmaster New York   Sept. 19, 44

Dear Mr. Kahn,

    You will be surprised to receive this letter from a strange soldier in France. But I am very glad to write to you and to tell you that I met your daughter Irene, who is healthy and well taken care of. I do understand what these news means to you and I am happy with you that you can stop worrying. Your daughter was hidden from the Gestapo in the home of a catholic priest for the last 2 years, who had taken care of her and family Ehrlich, who are relatives of yours too, if I am not mistaken, I have been at their home, or better the priest's home, and had some wonderful meals. Although everything is rationed in France, your daughter understood to make some delicious meals, European dishes I had not eaten for years. I went on Rosh Hashana to the religious service and was amazed to find about 75 Jewish men, women and children, all of them had hidden somewhere. I heard a lot of horrible stories and I do not wish to repeat them. You as well as I have had similar experiences in Germany. For the time being it is impossible for your daughter to write, as the postal service is operating for the army only. Your daughter's address is: Miss Irene Kahn, 12 Rue de la Bassée, Lille (north France). I wish I could write a million similar letters, especially when we get to Germany. I shall see your daughter and family to-night again maybe I can insert a foto [sic].

Respectfully,
Karl Loewenstein
4580 Broadway
New York

    Irene's sign of life was the best news I could have ever expected, except perhaps that the war was over and we could all go home and be reunited with our families. But from here it did not look that peace was imminent. Nevertheless, I needed wonderful news like this to keep me from being further disillusioned. It was almost like having received a blood transfusion. I sat down immediately and wrote to Irene, having so much to convey to her and a thousand questions to ask. However, I asked that she channel her reply to me via Chicago, through our parents, a more indirect but a more reliable route. Somehow Irene had become acquainted with Morris A. Sandhaus, a major in the U.S. Army, who served as a Jewish Chaplain with the troops. It was through him at first that letters from her and the Ehrlichs were funneled to the U.S. and vice versa, including care packages from our parents. My letters to her likewise went through Major Sandhaus (see exhibit 13.3 in the appendix). This was necessary at the time because it was not possible for anyone but U.S. military personnel from Europe to communicate with civilians back home in America and the other way around. Likewise, I could not communicate with Irene directly. One of the letters from Major Sandhaus written from France to Mom and Dad in Chicago on February 13, 1945 arrived March 17, at the Fort Dearborn Post Office, Chicago, and was delivered to our parents April 20, in other words five weeks later.

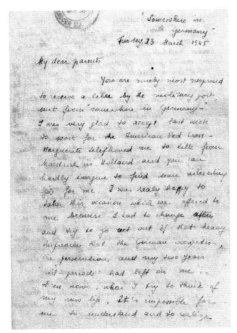

EXHIBIT 13.4 Letter from Irene to my parents, forwarded to me. She wrote in English because that's the language our parents and I spoke now as Americans. Full letter and transcript in the appendix, exhibit 13.4.

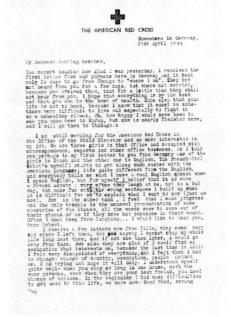

EXHIBIT 13.5 Letter from my sister Irene. Full letter in the appendix, exhibit 13.5.

For many years I did not know Irene's story in detail, only that she was in hiding facilitated by a Catholic priest, Abbe Vancourt and his niece Raymonde Lombard. Now and then some additional details were revealed by Irene after the war and after she managed to come to the United States. From an account which Irene wrote April 21, 1973 for an oral presentation to an interested organization, it became abundantly clear to me what exactly had happened and why there was so much pain for her to talk about the past. For the sake of carrying on her new life in America and maintaining her sanity, it was important for her not to dwell on her memories and suppress the past as much as possible. Quoted below are the salient parts of her talk, her thoughts, and an overview of what actually happened:

CIRCUMSTANCES OF MY LIFE LEADING TO THE RESCUE

I was born in Germany, where I lived with my parents and brother until April 1934. Fellow students had been making anti-Semitic statements and teachers were actively discriminating against Jewish students. Our house was searched, and my father's business was marked with a huge yellow star poster. My parents finally agreed to let me leave and stay with my mother's sister and family in Lille, France and go to school there. From then on I saw my parents only during summer vacation and could not comprehend why they would stay there. Finally, when I was taken off the train at Aachen, Germany in 1937, which was to take me back to Lille, I was fortunate that same day to obtain permission through some Nazi Authority to leave Germany. I vowed that I would never return even if it meant never to see my parents again.

Uncle Charles, Aunt Irma and their two children with whom I stayed were orthodox Jews and observed a strict kosher household, which I had to get used to. Mom and Dad did not maintain a household in strictly orthodox fashion since they practiced a more conservative Judaism. However, nothing "trayf" (food which according to Jewish ritual law should not be eaten) was ever served. Nor did Mom bring dairy foods and meat dishes on the table at the same time or immediately afterwards, because this too is forbidden by ritual laws. What I did not know was that according to orthodox customs there should be a different mustard with dairy food "milchig," than with meat dishes "flayshig." This got me into trouble because I brought the milchig mustard on the table while flayshig food was being served. It got me so upset that I wept.

Like many others, my father was taken to Dachau, November 9, 1938. Released, the family finally left for Luxembourg in 1939, a short time before the war broke out. I saw them there for a few days. France was at war with Germany and as a German I was severely scrutinized by the French Security before they let me return to the Lycée (school) to finish my last year before the second part of the Baccalaureate (Bachelor Degree). Persecuted by the Germans, I was technically the "enemy" in France, except that I had many friends by now, including the teaching staff of the Lycée.

The invasion of France in May 1940 put me again face to face with the Germans, and the French asked me many times to act as interpreter for them and intercede for whatever "war crimes" the peasants were charged for: withholding crops, hiding chickens and rabbits, or cutting transmission wires while Hitler made a victory announcement.

My studies were naturally interrupted. I learned office skills and took a job at a Peugeot garage translating orders and bills, and tutoring children in English and German from 1941 to 1942. Lille was under military law from Brussels

EXHIBIT 13.6 Eliane, Aunt Irma, Claude and Uncle Charles.

(capital of Belgium). I knew that my parents had left Luxembourg for the USA. My family, Mr. Charles Ehrlich, his wife Irma and their two children, Claude, 13, and Eliane, 8, watched with terror as the Germans marched up and down in our street. In spring of 1942, a letter arrived from Luxembourg with information that another Aunt and Uncle (Helene and Max Cohen) would be deported to Poland.

The fear of being trapped grew in me again. A few days later, orders were issued for Jews to wear the yellow star. I can't remember how they were distributed, but I recall sewing it on my coat and watching people as they walked by me, smiling and encouraging me. I was even proud but for a short while only. I came to my senses when somehow a rumor was circulated that at Brussels orders were issued to arrest all "foreign Jews" in Belgium, Holland and France, and that meant me. The lists were provided by the respective police departments where all foreigners were duly registered.

Within a couple of days I arranged with the family of the children I was tutoring to leave on vacation with them as their governess. And so I spent a few rather quiet weeks in one of the Loire castles trying to figure out if there was a way that I could get into (unoccupied) "Free France," and then over the Pyrenees (mountains) into Spain. None of the people there (at the Loire) knew or cared that I was Jewish, since traditionally French people are oblivious to that aspect of a person. It just doesn't matter, so they never asked.

One day I received a phone call to meet Madame Pattine, a friend and neighbor of the Ehrlich family, at a village inn. It was the second day of Rosh Hashanah. She came to tell me that the Gestapo had searched the Ehrlich's home looking for me to arrest me. They had threatened Claude, the 14 year old son, if my Aunt would not tell them where I was hiding. The poor women told them and dispatched Mme. Pattine immediately to inform me of the imminent disaster, if I was to stay in the chateau (castle). Mme. Pattine also offered to seek a place to hide me, if I should come back to Lille. A phone call to her husband in Paris the following day arranged for me to return to Lille where Mlle. (Mademoiselle) Marie Louise Siauve, a teacher I had at the Lycée, would pick me up at the Lille railroad station, arriving late in the evening.

By streetcar I was taken to a part of town unknown to me, and we hardly spoke. We walked a short while in the dark since there was a complete black out, stopped at a house near a hospital and entered a dim lit hall. Once the door was shut more lights went on and found myself facing a tall man in priest garb. Standing near him was a young woman. I had been brought to the home of Mr. l'Abbe Raymond Vancourt and his niece Mademoiselle Raymonde Lombard. I remember very little of the first evening or the next few days. Actually I was rather exhausted from the tension and became very ill on Yom Kippur and then took to bed for several days. It was like a nervous breakdown and the cardiologist who was called suggested that I get up and find something of interest to keep my mind and body going. Then Mr. l'Abbe sat with me and asked me to help him translate some German into French. He insisted that he needed to have whole chapters translated since he worked on a translation of M. Nicolai Hartmann's book "GRUNDZÜGE EINER METAPHISIK DER ERKENNTNIS," which was published 1945 in French.

EXHIBIT 13.7 L'Abbe Vancourt. The heroines, Raymonde Lombard (left) and Marie-Louise Siauve (right) 1942/1943.

Mr. l'Abbee Vancourt lived at 12 rue de la Bassee, next to la Clinique St. Catherine, where he was the official chaplain, officiating daily for the sisters and bringing comfort to the patients. He was also Professor of Philosophy at the University Catholique de Lille and Professor of Theology at the Catholic Seminary of Lille, a rather busy schedule. Raymonde, who was of my age, was taking care of the house and also managed to take courses at the University, planning to be a teacher. Her studies

EXHIBIT 13.8 The priest's niece, and on right, Irene.

often suffered because of the lack of time to devote to them. When I arrived the possibility existed that I would be going to a monastery or other hiding place, but suddenly I was asked if I wanted to stay, take over all the household responsibilities and help with the translation. No one saw me come in and I would not go out. People who would visit would be told that I was a friend of Raymonde, and that I was stuck here.

A new lease on life, I made the most of every minute that I spent in the care of these extraordinary people. Mr. l'Abbe gave me his master bedroom and we shared the whole house. Everything was open and available to me as if I was a member of the family. It was a three story house with loads of woodwork to polish, floors to keep clean, cooking and washing to be done. Through friends, Mr. l'Abbe obtained false identification papers for me having a different name and birthday, none of which I can remember. Mine were buried in a sack of flour. It was even then hard to remember the new identity. Additional food stamps were obtained with these false papers through Mlle. LeRoy, an elderly friend in the neighborhood. The sisters of the hospital provided extra food and Mr l'Abbe's family and friends from the country helped generously to provide for a good table. Guests from the Sorbonne (University) came to lecture in Lille and stayed at the house regularly. Sometimes the story about me had to be changed to fit the situation, and there came a time when I was uncertain how I had explained my identity previously. When I asked Raymonde: "Who am I?" she thought for a second that I had lost my mind, and we both burst out laughing. Yes, we did laugh, sing and joke!

She shared her study interests with me, her fears and her doubts. Often one of us would read aloud, while the other sewed, knitted, or puttered around in the kitchen. Both of them obtained much knitting yarn for me, and I remember a glove pattern by heart. I made sweaters and pullovers as presents for friends and family of my new home. After trying to get some fresh air at night I discontinued it since I was too afraid to get caught. A couple of bicycle trips had to be stopped also.

I never opened the door to anyone ringing the bell and never went to the window while the curtains were open. The seasons came and went, and I could tell by the leaves on the trees sprouting, turning green, then brown and falling in the chilly wind (what season it was). I became a whiz at lighting a fire with only one match, a few bits of paper, and shredded wood early in the wintery mornings, and stretching the food supplies into tasty dishes.

At night I often lay in bed hearing the sound of boots outside coming nearer and stopping, and with it my heart would almost stop also. Then the boots would stomp the sidewalk again and my heart would race ahead of my breath while lying in a cold sweat. Often it was a nightmare, and maybe the two (dreams and reality) got mixed up. A few times the bell would ring and Mr. l'Abbe would go to the door. Sometimes it was German soldiers, and politely he would direct them away from the house. He would tower over them, determined, sure of himself, and probably praying with every fiber of his being. But he would never let me know.

Mlle. Siauve, my teacher, would come to visit and bring me news from the Ehrlich family. Then she would return there to reassure them that I was safe without telling them that I was right here in Lille. Sometimes we listened to the BBC (British Broadcast Co.) when it was not too garbled. For a few weeks our house was giving shelter to two young teenage girls, also Jewish, who spent all their time embroidering delicate hankies and crying a lot. I never knew all about their background and parents. They were taken to a monastery as a safe place. Somehow I found out after the war that they were found out and deported.

Bombardments by the British and Americans started in 1943. We took refuge in the air raid shelter of the hospital (next door). I had nightmares of noise, fear, and confusion. After a few times, one would sit in a corner and whimper. Fear of getting killed, fear of being found out, fear of living without hope. Mr. l'Abbe emerged from all these crises as a tower of strength and confidence in the future. Then one day he let my aunt come to see me, and shortly thereafter he made the entire Ehrlich family of four move into his house. He had given them warning of immediate danger so that they would leave without luggage and without being noticed by the neighbors. The next day, so we were told, the Gestapo knocked the door down to deport them all. In their fury of having been outwitted, they ransacked the whole house. Yes, the French Jews too were arrested and taken away. Who would have believed it?

Now the house was really crowded, beds and cots were found, additional food was obtained, and the children now 15 and 11 years old had to be kept busy and quiet. No one saw them come to the house. They were not to go outside in spite of the 1944 spring weather. My Uncle Charles suffered from depression and Mr. l'Abbe kept him busy rebinding his much worn books. I suffered from an outbreak of boils and stomach pains. My Aunt Irma accidentally punctured an eye and had to be hospitalized, and was nursed to health by Sister Bertille. She had a heart of gold and kept her lips sealed to keep the truth secret. I had an infected finger which had to be lanced by a doctor who came to the house. All these people had to be trusted.

We had many bombardments, slept with part of our clothes on, ready to run into the cellars. All cellars on the block had been connected by a crawl through opening, connecting all the houses to the St. Catherine Hospital air raid shelter. Soon after came the V-1 and V-2 German flying bombs which sometimes misfired and fell back into Northern France, pretty close. Much "student" activity was going on at the house. A young man by the name of Jean Lecanuet came to seek refuge after blowing up some bridges and committing other violent sabotage acts. [Note from editor: He would later become a well-known French politician, even becoming the mayor of Rouen, Minister of Justice, and Minister of State among several other prestigious positions.]

By now, Liberation Armies were approaching, house to house searches were made by the Germans, and we were spending time and even sleeping at St. Catherine. Nothing made sense to me and we did not dare ask any questions. Mr. l'Abbe's teaching and study schedule was interrupted by students seeking counsel. He was home when he should have been at the University. The streets were deserted one fall morning of 1944, a German tank was standing ready to blow everything up, machine gun fire was heard, but the tank did not respond because he had no ammo. People started to come to 12 Rue de la Bassee. The door stood wide open and I stood in the hall watching this extraordinary sight of Mr. l'Abbe giving information, instructions, organizing groups (of men), and directing them to specific tasks. Jean Lecanuet was among them like many other students I had seen before. To this day (April 21 1973) I do not know Mr. l'Abbe's involvement in the Resistance, but I know, and I am here to prove it, that he saved my life and that of Mr. and Madame Charles Ehrlich and their two children. He did it with the help and devotion, sharing the risk with his niece Mademoiselle Raymonde Lombard. It is now Mr. le Chanoine Raymond Vancourt. He and Mlle Raymonde Lombard still live at 12 rue de la Bassee, Lille France. May the world and G'd know of their deeds."

Not withstanding the exiting and wonderful news that my dear sister Irene was alive and well, the war in Europe and in the Pacific continued unabated. The Filipino people seemed very industrious, and they farmed using domesticated water buffalos and tended to their rice paddies. Fishing in the Canabato and San Pedro Bay is also important in this area.

The Philippine guerrillas in large and small groups were visible everywhere. Armed to their teeth with weapons now supplied by the U.S. Army or leftover from the defeated Japanese, they were fearless men. They lived off the land, supported primarily by their own people, and very successful in ferreting out, cutting off, or by passing enemy bands of Japanese Army stragglers hidden in the jungle. I heard about them bringing in a live Japanese prisoner on rare occasions, for which the U.S. Army paid them a handsome bounty. As a rule of honor, the

Japanese would rather be killed than be captured. (See exhibits 13.9-13.19, and 13.30 in the appendix for additional photos)

Now and then I became a quasi-observer on an aircraft, especially one I had worked on, to ferry parts, supplies, and special ammo to our airfield near the town of San Jose on the Island of Mindoro, not to be confused with the town of San Jose near the airstrip on Leyte where I was stationed. This particular base and other installations on that Philippine island were used for the buildup of the planned invasion of the Island of Luzon, the most important and largest of the Philippines. The flight as I remember was about 300 miles one way as the crow flies. Although designated as "observer," to check the repairs made to the aircraft during flight, in other words its air worthiness, I usually filled in or doubled up as a quasi-crew member and took whatever position I was assigned. Because we were in a combat area, regulations were often loosely adhered to, giving way to whatever was expedient and deemed necessary during the circumstances. Individuals like myself had very little to say and did what they were told. It was a way to maintain my sanity and hopefully stay alive. Thus I flew many non-combat support missions on B-25, or B-24, the latter known as the flying coffin, as well as C-47 planes.

The flights were never easy. Weather was always threatening and unpredictable. Fog, monsoon rains, strong winds and thunderstorms often delayed or prevented take-off or landings on either end. Sometimes we were waiting uncomfortably for hours until the pilot received the take-off signal. Once in the air, flying over high mountains, through mountain passes or around mountains, the pilot always tried to avoid isolated enemy anti-aircraft fire from land or while flying over the Visayan and South China Sea. At higher altitudes, in non-pressurized aircraft, temporary earaches, headaches and nausea were to be reckoned with although we had uncomfortable oxygen masks. We never knew what to expect. The flights were generally very bumpy, with sudden altitude drops when incurring downdrafts and abrupt rising of the aircraft when encountering updrafts. All of this, in combination with tremendous yawing, in other words sideway motions, produced most uncomfortable physical reactions often resulting in vomiting. I was often scared, wondering when it would all end, and the prayer of the *shema* was always on my mind and lips.

On a few occasions, depending on our load and mission, the pilot would go after a target of opportunity if only for intelligence information, unless we were flying a C-47 cargo aircraft not equipped with offensive or for that matter defensive weapons. With B-25 and B-24 bombers it was a different matter. Always the pilots and co-pilots were briefed before takeoff from Tacloban Airbase where to look or avoid hotspots, and load appropriate ammo or chaff, to confuse enemy radar and sometimes even leaflets. It was always a big relief for me when we prepared for return to base. Getting some sleep afterwards and a few hours of relaxation was the right medicine for me.

EXHIBIT 13.20 Here's looking at you! Me sitting in cockpit of B-24 with pin-up.

EXHIBIT 13.21 I'm standing next to a B-24 bomber. Notice the steel landing mats.

Many times there were close calls, at least that's the way it seemed to me. Later on the pilot assured the crew that we were never in "great" danger. But in danger we were all the time. While in the air I was always glad to hear the crew's and pilot's voices over the intercom headphones, and learned all about the "Roger Wilco" expression. Roger meant "received" or "OK," while "Wilco" denoted "understand, will comply." One time, I believe it was in June, just as we were returning from a so-called airworthiness check out mission, someone noticed that an incendiary bomb that had inadvertently been left on board had jammed in the bomb bay. The arming wire had been sheared and the arming vane was exposed and rotating in the airflow. By the time a visual inspection was possible, the situation had worsened and hot phosphorous material was spewing out causing a dangerous fire hazard. Luxi, which had remained my nickname, was close by and proceeded to pry the bomb loose. While attempting to kick the bomb free I exposed my left foot and lower leg to the tremendous heat. Luckily I succeeded, but had some burns on the inside of my calf since some of the incendiary had burned through my trousers which I cut away, and my leather boot. A lucky star had been with me and we landed without further incident. The burns were dressed at the Quonset hut first aid station and had healed completely after a few weeks.

EXHIBIT 13.22 Bob also known as "Luxi."

On one of my scavenger trips to the aircraft wreckage boneyard to find a piece of cable, I stumbled across a small metal box. Inside was some Japanese invasion money, and a variety of Japanese postcards and personal photos, which I kept as souvenirs and mailed them to my parents in Chicago.

On the island of Leyte, all organized ground fighting by the Japanese forces had in the meantime ceased around Christmastime 1944; however there were isolated attacks of enemy aircraft. The stubborn enemy had incurred amazing high losses while in comparison ours were light. Like in New Guinea, thousands of Japanese soldiers had retreated into the mountains or jungle after having survived mopping up operations and did not surrender. Now and then here in the Philippines they would manage to infiltrate our bases and steal from our warehouses, especially food since they were completely cut off from resupply. Sometimes their intrusions were with armed force and caused much confusion and a few casualties. The islands of Guam, Tinian, and Saipan were now under American control and served as launching bases for our long range B-29 Bombers to soften up the enemy everywhere including Japan proper.

EXHIBIT 13.23
In this vicinity of the aircraft wreckage boneyard, I found the small metal box of Japanese vintage.

Next came the invasion of Luzon on January 9, 1945 with landings in the Lingayan Gulf, in spite of incessant Japanese kamikaze attacks. Once the important and huge airbase Clark Field, approximately 50 miles northwest of Manila, had been secured by the end of January, we were able to fly supplies and reinforcements with C-47 transports, while hundreds of ships brought much needed supplies and equipment.

As in the past, the news didn't catch up with us until later. I was therefore shocked and saddened to find out that my revered President, Commander in Chief, Franklin Delano Roosevelt had suddenly died on April 12, 1945. Although I felt he could have done more to help European Jews to immigrate to the United States of America and thus save their lives, I was convinced that he did what he could, having to deal with an obstinate, isolationistic, and anti-immigration Congress. I also credited him for supplying the European Allies, including Russia, with large amounts of war material including fifty destroyers on a "Lend-Lease" basis, long before Pearl Harbor happened. While he was able to relish successes of U.S. and Allied Forces in the European and Pacific theaters of operation, he would be deprived of witnessing the unconditional surrender and victory over Germany May 8, VE-Day, less than a month after his death.

There was general excitement and relief when word got around that Adolf Hitler had committed suicide on April 30, and Berlin had fallen to the Russians. Hitler and Roosevelt had both come to power in 1933, and both were dead within a few weeks of each other. Hitler was despised and hated by the world, Roosevelt was loved and revered. Was there a message or was it sheer coincidence? As for me, Hitler's demise felt like a personal triumph and brought great momentary joy and relief to my heart. However, the unbelievably horrifying conditions out here had made our senses numb, and our responses to joy and sadness somewhat insensitive. Good or bad did not affect our emotions greatly, and then only momentarily. I had learned the hard way, that every victory, whether here or elsewhere on these G'd forsaken islands, had its price in precious human lives. I was not off the hook either.

On a flight to bring supplies to Clark Air Base, we encountered one of the worst monsoons accompanied by ferocious continuous lightning and extremely high sheering winds. After being battered around for a while and losing altitude, the C-47 transport suddenly went down in a terrifying noise. That was the last thing I remembered of the event. The next thing I recollect was coming back to consciousness surrounded by Filipino tribesmen, some smoking long stemmed pipes, the likes and fierceness I had not seen. They were quietly sitting at a respectable distance from me, some with bows, arrows, and long bamboo blow guns. If that wasn't enough of a shock and being scared, there were no signs of the rest of the crew or of the plane. Bewilderment, anxiety, and pain were the last things I remember before I lost consciousness again. Later I would learn the plane had evidently gone down in a remote area and I never found out what happened to the rest of the crew, or the aircraft.

When I opened my eyes again I was in a hospital tent, and a Philippine nurse's aide dressed in white was fanning me through the mosquito net surrounding the bed. I was startled and tried to speak but couldn't. I tried to sit up but to no avail. Anguish hit me, not knowing whether all of this was just a bad dream or reality. It was toward the end of June 1945, the heat and humidity were stifling, and the torrential rain incessant. As much as I could make out, I was in a long tent with flaps open on both sides, and very uncomfortable. The noise of the rain beating on the canvas was like a constant drum roll, and the water flowed into a deep drainage ditch which ran along both sides of the tent and about four feet from my bed. Some of the rain water would trickle through onto the tent floor making everything around me muddy. The white uniforms and clog-type sandals of the Philippine nurse aides, as well as the khaki uniforms of the Army nurses, were mostly splattered with soil from mud puddles that were everywhere. As for me,

EXHIBIT 13.24 The hospital tent.

I didn't have to go anywhere and couldn't unassisted. It was a nightmare to live through at the time and difficult to write about now.

There were about fifteen beds on each side of the tent, most of them occupied. From what I was given to understand by medical staff, I had a concussion which was impairing my nerve system and produced a partial paralysis of my arms and legs. No one, including the Army doctors told me what medication was administered, why a spinal tap was performed, or what the results and diagnosis was. Military physicians had an entirely different relationship vis-a-vis their soldier-patient than a private physician with regard to a private patient. During the weeks of stay at this field hospital, the Philippine nurse's aide to whom I was assigned was Virginia Songco. She made me feel comfortable and took good, if not special, care of me. Every morning she would bring me a bunch of wild flowers picked on the way from the tents where the local workforce was housed. She'd put them in a plastic cup and placed them on the wooden box next to my bed, a so-called night stand.

One day when she brought her daily bouquet she mentioned that in the mountains where she and her family lived, there grew orchids of all colors including a black variety. Jokingly I told her not to bring me any more of those common garden variety flowers, but to bring from now on just black orchids. The following day she did not show up for work, and I was deprived of her caring attention. The heavens had opened up during the night and rain was coming down relentlessly. Later that afternoon, about the time the aides would normally leave for the day, I saw a figure clad in white, long black hair flowing below the shoulders nearing the tent. As the figure came closer I noticed that the woman was barefoot, carrying her sandals in one hand and in the other some flowers. You guessed it! It was Virginia, her bare feet and legs covered with mud, her clothing and herself dripping wet. She carried her wooden sandals because in the deep mud they are of no use and only get stuck. In the other hand she held several black orchids. I was so moved and touched by this extraordinary gesture and unheard sincerity that for the first time since I went into the Army I had tears in my eyes. They were tears of happiness, surprise, and awe, as well as tears of embarrassment for making this supposedly innocent remark about the flowers two days earlier. From that

EXHIBIT 13.25 Inside the hospital tent.

EXHIBIT 13.26 First aid and operating area.

day until I was evacuated, she continued to bring me flowers and photographs of herself and her family. I think she had taken a liking to me.

Prior to being evacuated by air to Manila, doctors here subjected me to treatment with sodium pentothol, a muscle relaxant and hypnotic stimulant to alleviate post trauma anxiety. During this treatment, the doctors told me afterwards, they were able to piece together not only what happened to me when the aircraft went down but also some significant and less important happenings during my adolescent years, but didn't tell me what. In the days following there began a noticeable improvement in my arm and leg reflexes, and gradually I obtained use of my legs and improved dexterity in my arms and hands. It was very encouraging and gave me hope for recovery.

It was not too long afterwards that several patients including myself were told to pack whatever belongings we had and get ready for evacuation. We were not told what that meant specifically, except that we would not go back to our military units. Instead, we were going to be "shipped out" to another hospital for recuperation. It was very vague indeed and made me very uneasy. Finally the day came when I said goodbye to all the sick and wounded I would leave behind, as well as the nurses, and aides. Among them was Virginia Songco, who with tears in her eyes pressed a piece of paper into my hands with her permanent mailing address, pleading with me to write to her as I nodded my head.

We were carried on stretchers to Army ambulances some of which got stuck several times in the deep mud on the way to the nearby airstrip and had to be pulled out by other vehicles equipped with a winch. It was a very bumpy ride and I would have been better off sitting than lying on a stretcher. This was my first,

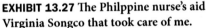
EXHIBIT 13.29 Virginia and me in my hospital attire outside the tent.

EXHIBIT 13.27 The Philppine nurse's aid Virginia Songco that took care of me.

EXHIBIT 13.28 The black orchids she brought me.

and hopefully the last, ride in an ambulance. I was unable to see where we were going since there were no windows. Finally, arriving at an airstrip unknown to me, we were loaded onto a transport aircraft with large Red Cross markings. The flight was rather uneventful, being cared for by two WAC (Women Army Corps) nurses and several corpsmen. As we landed, already in the flight pass approach, I was able to recognize certain features of the important Air Base, Clark Field. Again, there were a number of ambulances waiting, and we didn't know where they would take us. The rumors among us "casualties" were rampant. The one I liked best was that we were homeward bound. But then that was too good to be true, and yet each one of us hoped it would be. This thought faded rapidly after riding for about an hour in what we affectionately called the "meat wagon."

Finally the suspense eased when we arrived at the outskirts of Manila. Being allowed to sit up, I was able to see the city's devastation through the driver's windshield. It was in this general vicinity that the invasion of the major Philippine Island of Luzon began January 9, 1945, whereby General Krueger's Sixth Army, of which I was a part, encountered its fiercest resistance. Glad I missed it!

While the advances of our troops after landing from the Lingayen Gulf were fraught with many surprises and great obstacles, the drive southward toward Manila, after capturing Clark Field, became stiffened and American casualties high. The capture of Manila, the capital of the Philippines, was important for many strategic and political reasons, not the least of which was the concern for as many as four thousand American prisoners held by the Japanese at Santa Tomas University. You cannot imagine therefore how shocked I was when the ambulance doors opened to discharge us, and on the building we were to enter, the inscription above hewn in stone read "Santa Tomas." Was it coincidence, or was it destiny?

Santa Tomas, prior to the capture of Manila by the Japanese, was the largest and best known private university in the Philippines. Thereafter it became a prison for Americans whose lives then became very precarious under the unpredictable treatment by the Japanese military guards. The liberation of Santa Tomas and its inmates was celebrated by stories of unbelievable heroism by the prisoners, as well as by the U.S. Army columns spearheaded by tanks and guided by Philippine guerrillas. After its liberation in early February 1945, Santa Tomas was converted into a hospital and recuperation center and now became my temporary home. During my stay, I became well enough and able to leave the hospital for short outings to see the city and its surroundings. Like many cities ravished by war, the structures which once defined the capital city of the Philippines were now nothing but heaps of rubble and twisted metal. The Japanese defenders had converted every building into elaborate above and underground fortifications, bunkers and heavy gun emplacements. In the final assault by American troops, they had to be destroyed from ground, air, and even naval batteries, especially since the inner city walls, remainders of centuries earlier built fortifications, were often 20 feet high and up to 30 feet thick. While Santa Tomas was liberated first, the rest of the city itself was not secured until a month later, namely March 3, after fierce hand to hand combat for every building.

At Santa Tomas I was sheltered from the actual participation in the war, but mentally the horrors of the war were with me vividly every moment. The more leisure time was available, the more concerned I became as to what happened to the men I left behind, and my loved ones in the CONUS, i.e. the Continental United States, and moreover all my dear relatives and friends in Europe. No longer did I have to worry about "C" and "K" combat food rations with its SPAM in metal cans containing a mixture of potatoes, ham and pork. Only under dire circumstances did I ever eat that concoction because of my religious dietary restrictions, and traded the cans with one my buddies for something else. The few packages received out of the many sent by my parents and friends in Chicago contained, as I remember, hard to get film for my camera, hard salami, fruitcake, and argyle socks sent from Massachusetts, which Gertrude had knitted herself. She still worked in the retail store of the Marum Knitting Mill, in Lawrence, Massachusetts. The socks, by the way, were G'd sent because they helped keep my feet dry. There were other things I received like recent photographs and newspaper articles. One photograph in particular, a portrait off Gertrude which I had received months earlier, turned out to be one of my most valuable possessions. On a few occasions I managed to send a package home with some combat souvenirs taken from dead Japanese soldiers, some sea shells and trinkets I made from Australian coins etc. I also made a metal sculpture depicting a P-38 twin fuselage fighter from various spent brass shell casings and sent it home disassembled in a wooden box. In the year 2001, I had the base of the sculpture appropriately engraved and gave it to my grandson, Sam Rapoport, as a remembrance.

Now I had plenty of time to write V-mail letters and regular airmail to catch up with my correspondence, and delved eagerly into available reading material at the hospital. Basically there were months-old magazines, old newspapers, and pocket editions of books. In the meantime I was examined, re-examined and treated for battle fatigue and stress, besides undergoing some physical therapy. By listening to the radio in the recreation room, I was catching up with the war's progress news in Europe, Asia, China and of course the South West Pacific. Other patients played cards, made sketches, painted with water colors, or hung up photos on their beds and nearby walls of wives, girlfriends, film stars and pin-up girls, girls in discreet or more accurately said "glamorous" poses. All advertisements in magazines of products for civilian consumption were scrutinized by me with great interest and awe, since I had been out of touch with civilization for several years. I also read the details about the successes of the Allied Forces after the invasion of Normandy on D-Day, and the brilliant advances through France, Belgium, Holland, Luxembourg and Germany.

Hitler's decision months earlier to launch V-1 and V-2 pilotless flying bombs toward England, where they caused much damage and great panic, did not change the course of the war's predictable outcome. Hitler's cowardly suicide, the fall of Berlin to the Russians, was one of the final nails into the coffin of Hitler's dream for a 1000 year Nazi German Reich. Earlier, the elite army of the "Super Race" had been defeated in North Africa and everywhere else. Italy had made a separate peace with the Allies. Based on all of these military achievements, it came as no surprise that Victory in Europe, V-E Day, on May 8, 1945 had become a reality, and Hitler's self-professed invincible armies and criminal regime had been eradicated from this planet forever. However there were no big celebrations here since the empire of the rising sun, Japan, still had to be subdued and there was no sign that they would give up easily.

Once again the mail had caught up with me at Santa Tomas. But instead of getting a few letters, I received perhaps a dozen or more at one time, each being from six to eight weeks old. Hungry for news from loved ones, I read each letter time and time again making sure I didn't miss anything. Newspaper clippings were enclosed in several letters giving me some idea what was going on at home. My references to "home" now herein mostly means America, although I made my home for several years in Luxembourg, and was banned forever from my birthplace Mannheim, Germany. Bits and pieces of news from Europe over the shortwave radio at the hospital were shocking. While most of my fellow GIs were not too concerned or interested, the horrible findings and conditions at the liberated Nazi concentration, death, and labor camps made me sick to my stomach, madder than hell, and very, very sad. The details were still fragmentary and yet the descriptions of atrocities performed by the Nazis on Jews and other prisoners, the extermination methods in gas chambers, cold blooded executions, and the eye witness reports by barely existing survivors was enough to make my blood boil. These ruthless and beastly treatments of defenseless and innocent men, women, and children fanned my feelings of hatred of Nazis, and momentarily called for merciless revenge on all German perpetrators and so called bystanders and helpers. It brought me back to my earlier realization and bitterness that I had been sent to fight the wrong enemy. My rightful place should have been with the conquering and liberating armies in Western Europe and Germany. My role of responsibility was not here, but on the other side of the world. That's where I felt my rightful place should have been. My role in history was turned upside down by the most misdirected decision of the U.S. Army.

Time went by very slow here at Santa Tomas, although there were many activities patients could participate in. I thought much about the near and not so near past and contemplated my very uncertain future. In the meantime there had been many amphibious operations to clear the Japanese armed remnants from hundreds of Philippine islands with substantial support from Huk guerrillas. The toughest and most stubborn resistance was experienced on the island of Mindanao. There was much less news and less coverage of the fighting going on in Borneo, India, Burma and China. Perhaps, that was because the war was fought in a different part of Asia and primarily under the Command of the British, although Australian, Indian, American, and armies from other countries supported those operations with men and material. Military operations there against the Japanese invaders were also successful, and the invincibility of the Japanese Armies and Navies was being unmasked more each day. The end of Japan's quest for domination of that part of the world was in sight.

CHAPTER FOURTEEN

Japan Surrenders – I'm Going Home

By now it was August 1945 and still no news regarding most of my relatives and friends left behind in Germany, Luxembourg, France and elsewhere. If they were not subjected to concentration camps there was hope, otherwise their fate was much more uncertain. These thoughts, to which I had no ready answer, nagged and haunted me more and more as time passed. There was no one here that I could share my thoughts with. I did not know anyone here well enough to assume they would have an understanding for my concerns and apprehension. All the more urgent were my daily silent prayers for them in which I uttered all their names and tried to visualize their likeness. Would the prayers help? G'd had saved me so far. Perhaps he had been able to save them as well.

Meanwhile I was told that I was slated to go back to the States "when my turn came," but not a single clue when that would be. If anyone was ready, I was, and my new duffel bag would be packed within ten minutes. As more and more bombing attacks were made on Japan proper by B-29 Superfortresses, the name of cigar smoking General Curtis LeMay, who was in charge of the Heavy Bomber Command in the Pacific Theater, became more prominent. He was credited with crippling Japanese cities, their industries, and weakened the fanatic will of their people. Next came the news that an "atomic bomb," the first time I had ever heard that term, had been released by B-29's over the cities of Hiroshima, August 6, and Nagasaki, August 9. 1945. Apparently, the atomic explosions destroyed and incinerated everything and everybody within several miles of ground zero. The use of terms such as "shock waves," "radiation," "fireball," and "mushroom cloud," were new to my vocabulary and increased my curiosity.

A few days later on August 15, I will never forget the moment an announcement came over the loudspeaker in the mess hall, as I was having lunch, "Emperor Hirohito has unconditionally accepted the Allied surrender terms!" It was repeated several times. Within seconds several hundred patients and hospital cadre climbed on benches, tables, cheering, shouting, applauding, whistling, beating their mess kits and throwing into the air whatever was not nailed down. Being caught up in this unexpected, unrehearsed pandemonium, I embraced and hugged the fellow next to me, whom I did not know. We messed each other's hair up as if we were little kids, or bigger kids having gone off their rocker. We heard shots and salvo after salvo being fired outside, nearby, and in the distance. From the direction of Manila Bay, not too far away, we could hear salvos being fired from

DAILY PACIFICAN Extra

The Army Newspaper in the Western Pacific

Vol. 1 No. 62 Tuesday, 14 August 1945

DOMEI SAYS:

JAPAN ACCEPTS

SAN FRANCISCO, (UP) – Aug. 13. An Imperial message accepting the Potsdam proclamation is forthcoming soon, the Japanese official news agency Domei reported in a Tokyo broadcast intercepted here tonight (Tuesday afternoon Manila).

"Immediately upon receipt of the Allied reply yesterday the Japanese government started deliberation upon its terms, which created a very serious problem for the Japanese people.

"The cabinet has been in continuous session until late Monday night. It is understood the government reply will be available as soon as legal procedure is completed."

There has been no confirmation from Washington.

EXHIBIT 14.1 Terms of surrender accepted by Japan's Cabinet.

anti-aircraft guns, and seeing colorful red and green tracer ammunition as well as signal flares going into the air. Euphoria claimed the rest of the day while being glued to the crackling sound of the short wave radio and listening to rumors that nobody could substantiate. Was the war with Japan over or were there more surprises to come? Tokyo Rose was no longer broadcasting Japan's victories, U.S. Army's defeats, and other lies. It was a good sign.

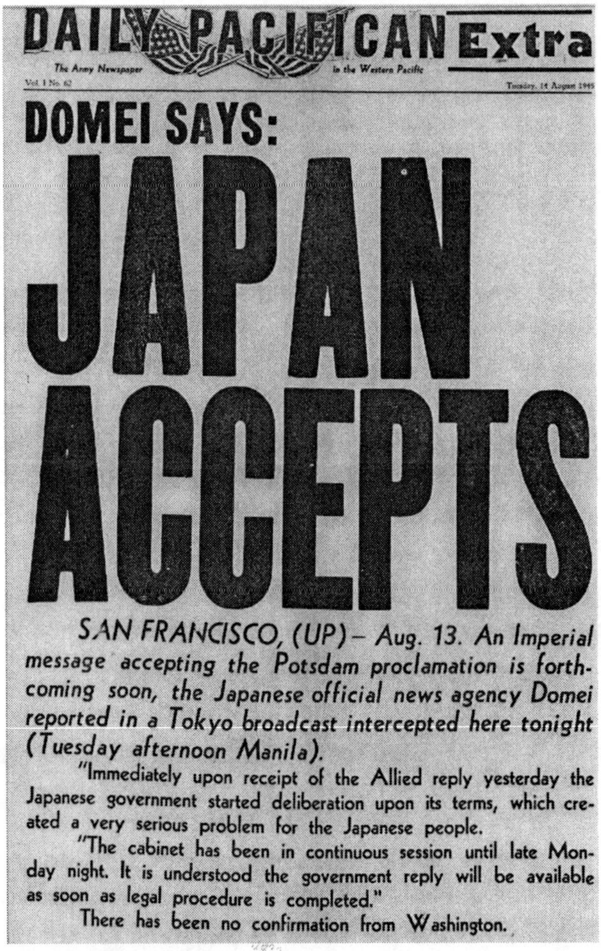

Finally on September 2, Japan's fate was sealed when its ministers, generals, and admirals signed the surrender documents on the Battleship Missouri which had steamed into Tokyo Bay. At that time I was already on board of the hospital ship *Monterey* as it was navigating out of Manila Bay. The signing of the surrender documents made this "VJ Day," Victory over Japan and "VP Day" Victory in the Pacific. I was just settling in on this liner which had been converted into a hospital ship. As I found out much later, this ship was once known as the luxury liner *Monterey*. In other words it had been an elegant cruise ship. During the war it was converted and became a U.S.A.T., a U.S. Army Transport. It was 632 feet long and had a beam of 79 feet, with a displacement of 26,000 tons. Its design speed was 23 knots when carrying 700 passengers. The ship was not large by the standards of today's cruise ships, but then it was a refuge and a welcome sight, certainly the biggest ship I had ever been on. As a troop transport she had carried no less than 6,200 soldiers. She had served in the Mediterranean as well as in the Pacific and had distinguished itself during various U-boat convoy attacks by rescuing hundreds of survivors. The *Monterey* was caught once in a

EXHIBIT 14.1 Victory is ours.

volcanic eruption off the East Coast of New Guinea whereby all troops she carried had to abandon ship. Finally, the U.S.A.T. *Monterey* transported enemy prisoners of war, first Italian and German prisoners from North Africa, and later allied prisoners held by the Japanese in the Philippine internment camps including Santa Tomas where I had been hospitalized. Now she was home to hundreds of sick and wounded soldiers going back to the USA.

The cabin to which I had been assigned had three bunks on top of each other on one side. I can't remember whether by choice or not I had the upper bunk. There was barely enough room between my bunk bed and the ceiling that I could sit only in a Turk position. There were two additional bunks on the other side of the cabin. The five of us considered ourselves somewhat as shipwrecks. The ship had two large smokestacks, was loaded with sick, wounded and a large number of personnel to take care of them. We could see daylight through two portholes, side by side, through which we could see that the ship was moving rather slowly. We took turns looking through the portholes, even so for days on end there was nothing to see except ocean waves. Standing there when we opened the portholes gave us a chance for fresh air since the only air circulation was produced by a small rotating fan on the wall. Considering that we didn't know each other and the crowded condition in the cabin with only one bathroom, we got along fine. Conversations about baseball and the forthcoming World Series were boring to me since I knew absolutely nothing about the game and could therefore not participate in the discussions. Baseball was not played anywhere in Europe and I never had the opportunity to attend a game once I had arrived in the U.S. After all, I had to work long, 10 to 12 hard hours to help the family make ends meet, went to evening school three times a week to learn English and American history, and on the weekends

I earned some money by getting water for neighbors at the filtration station. The classes in American history were deemed necessary to prepare myself for the required citizenship examination, which as fate would have it, I never had to take.

Time went by very slow and was monotonous. I found it strange that none of the five of us had the desire to talk about our recent war experiences. I guess none of us wanted to be reminded of the cruel, savage slaughter, and the suffering of men on both sides now that the war was over. I read the few magazines we shared among us. Not only would I read every article, but I also scrutinized each and every advertisement regardless of subject. As in the past there was a routine of quasi-military discipline on board ship. At six a.m. a recorded bugle sounded reveille over the loudspeaker to get us up. Next came mess or chow call at seven. By 8:30 a.m. we had to have our bunks made up ready for inspection and rounds by the medics. Basically, my cabin inmates, including myself, didn't require any special medical attention, but the system made no allowance for that.

In the next cabin, one of the patients always screamed when the medics would come in. A few times when I visited him he was as calm as a cucumber and told me that he was held in a Japanese prisoner camp and often beaten by guards in white coats. I put two and two together and suggested that the doctors when making their rounds in that cabin remove their white coats. It was worth a try, and to my surprise and the doctors, it worked. That convinced me that the physical abuse and psychological trauma had affected that soldier's mind. Being together 24-hours a day, we, the five shipwrecks, developed a casual comradery and a very peculiar sense of humor. We had not laughed in so many months that any whimsical remark or joke would only produce a change in our facial expression, but not necessarily loud laughter. That I guessed we all had to learn again.

If I thought the days were long, the nights were even longer. Almost every night I had nightmares and my cabin mates would wake me up when the screaming and talking would keep them awake. The other cabin mates had similar problems even during daytime that we had to wake the individual up and calm him down. Sometimes at night I would look out the porthole, stare at the clouds, the moon or the stars making up the Constellation Southern Cross, and immediately my mind would carry me somewhere else. It was so peaceful. The war, the war to end all wars, had ended. And yet there was a feeling that the wherewithal required to win this war had caused so much pain and suffering for those of us that remained alive, that it would probably take years, a lifetime, perhaps a century to recover from this manmade insanity.

Having lost my fountain pen, I wrote long letters with pencil. I had completely forgotten that the letters I wrote would not go anyplace until the ship made port. How dumb of me. Weeks passed and we hoped each day that we would see land, but no such luck. It was the beginning of the third week that we were told that we would be home any day now. After months of different promises by Army personnel, those words sounded good but had a hollow ring. Yet, early on September 21, I noticed unusual activity onboard ship. It began when at the mess hall eating my breakfast I saw that doctors, nurses, corpsmen, and other Army and Navy personnel, not in their usual white coats, fatigues, or work uniforms. Most wore their dress uniforms. The cooks and servers were friendlier and the music over the loudspeaker came unmistakable from a San Francisco radio station. I ate my breakfast in a hurry and rushed back to my cabin where I packed everything into my duffel bag and made certain that I was the first at one of the portholes. For the first time I realized how small the porthole opening was compared to my head, not to mention for the five of us with only two openings to look through.

The excitement mounted when we finally saw land. We were not able to recognize where we were, although it most certainly was the West Coast of America. To my greatest surprise, over the loudspeaker came an announcement, inviting all assigned to certain cabins on deck #3 to don their robes and appear on top deck. I couldn't get there fast enough and was immediately immersed in a mass of GIs who wanted a long awaited peek at home turf. After climbing on a higher deck structure I could see a mass of military uniforms of all types and colors, including those of us in blue lightweight robes. In spite of the fog which came in large sheets over the ship, I could see for the first time how large the ship *Monterey* was. There were huge red crosses painted on deck, on the stacks, and I imagine on the side of the ship, and therefore supposedly immune from enemy action. Of course the war was officially over and worries about our safety on the way home from the Philippines had all been removed from our minds. In all of this excitement on deck I had not noticed that there were several Coast Guard Cutters and harbor patrol boats on the starboard and port sides, some spewing streams of water in the air, others tooting their whistles and foghorns. Another had a large banner the length of the cutter, "Welcome Home!" What a contrast! When we departed for our overseas mission, everything was shrouded in secrecy plus a natural fog. There were no tooting escorts, good byes or other acknowledgments.

Now there was an ocean going welcoming party and jubilation among us. My throat had become so dry from excitement that I could not speak to anyone around me. I could clearly see people waving their arms to us from much smaller vessels, while others were waving flags with stars and stripes, holding signs that read "Well Done," "You Did It," and "Thank You." If I could have held up a sign it would have read, "Back Alive in '45!" The *Monterey* would also let loose with some loud blasts in succession. In short, all of us returnees were on an unbelievable high and with it a certain amount of pride overcame me, a feeling I had not experienced before. Indeed, even so only in a minute measure, I had certainly contributed to the defeat of the "Axis Powers."

EXHIBIT 14.2 Alcatraz and a famous bridge--we are back from where we started.

As our transport vessel was moving slower and slower, I caught my first glimpses of the Golden Gate Bridge. Still the bridge was too far away, shrouded in haze and fog that only portions of this enormous structure were visible. It seemed to float in air as if it were a mirage. Finally, we came close enough that I could see the entire span of the Golden Gate, so aptly named. To me it was more than golden, it seemed as if it was made of red rubies that shone upon us. I could see cars and trucks driving across the bridge, not camouflaged drab Army vehicles, but beautiful looking automobiles. At last I knew that I was back in the land whose precious freedoms I had learned to love and had protected. When the loudspeaker announced for everyone to return to their duty stations and cabins, I still had my Army issued olive colored handkerchief in my hand and it was moist. As the hoopla of having returned to mainland USA had subsided, the ship finally docked and most of us were taken by buses to Letterman Army Hospital located in the Golden Gate Park near the famous Presidio of San Francisco. On a more somber note the San Francisco National Cemetery was close by.

Routinely I underwent all sorts of examinations, tests, and interviews. Based on the results I was categorized for certain treatment. There were so many sick and wounded received each day that their disposition and treatment was decided practically on a production line basis. Doctors and nurses seemed so overwhelmed that they had no time to give me any explanations or answers, although I tried to ask. There was no discussion, not even a little comment regarding the diagnosis of my condition or treatment plan, and not a word of encouragement. For me the nightmare of war was over, but another nightmare, namely uncertainty of my future and a certain feeling of loneliness and detachment became an ever growing monster.

What a pronounced difference it made to be back on terra firma. Almost every day some "Gray Ladies," volunteers who wore gray uniforms, came around bringing books, magazines and writing material, and all important smiles. I wrote to Mom and Dad immediately, letting them know where I was and that I was safe. Since I could not use the telephone, I also wrote to cousin Ilse and Otto Hertz who were living in San Francisco, hoping that they would come and visit me with their cute twin daughters Judy and Joan. But as chance would have it, by the time they received my letter and came to visit, I had been relocated to an Army hospital in Danville, Kentucky. Of course they had been very disappointed and naturally so was I. Whether it was because of my condition, medication, or lapse of memory, I do not remember anything about being "shipped," as it was called then, from Letterman Hospital to Danville, Kentucky. My arrival there was September 29, 1945, just one day before my 22nd birthday. As it turned out, not surprisingly under the circumstances, there was no birthday cake and no celebration. The exact name was Darnall General Hospital, named after Civil War Brigadier General Carl Rogers Darnall, and was activated in December 1941. It was one of sixty-six general and convalescent Army Hospitals in the U.S.

EXHIBIT 14.3 Postcard of Darnall General Hospital.

to take care of sick and wounded soldiers during World War II from all theaters of operation.

After a few days I managed to orient myself better and noticed a big lake toward the rear of the hospital. The town of Danville, so I was told, was about five miles down the road and Harrodsburg was eight miles. Lexington, a much larger city, was about forty miles to the north. In the hospital were men and some women suffering from wounds, sickness, mental trauma, or a combination of them. After many exhausting examinations, I was shifted from isolation to a private open room. For the first time in two years of Army life I was able to obtain quality rest and fairly good food, a combination that would take me hopefully to the road of recovery. In the meantime an official letter was sent by the hospital on October 2, 1945 to my parents advising them of my admittance to the hospital, and requesting a summary of my family health history. Having been advised that they could come to visit me, Dad and Mom immediately filed an "Application for Travel of Enemy Nationalities." This was certainly a shameful requirement for my parents. Not only were they considered "Enemy Aliens," but had to submit five copies of this insulting application to visit their son, who as an American soldier was hospitalized. On October 12, the application for their travel was approved by the United States Department of Justice to depart October 19, by train and return October 21, 1945. The approved application further stipulated that "An alien of enemy nationality shall not travel from any locality to another except as herein provided." These bureaucratic requirements were certainly an affront to me as a U.S. Army soldier, seeing my parents treated worse than common criminals. How must they have felt?

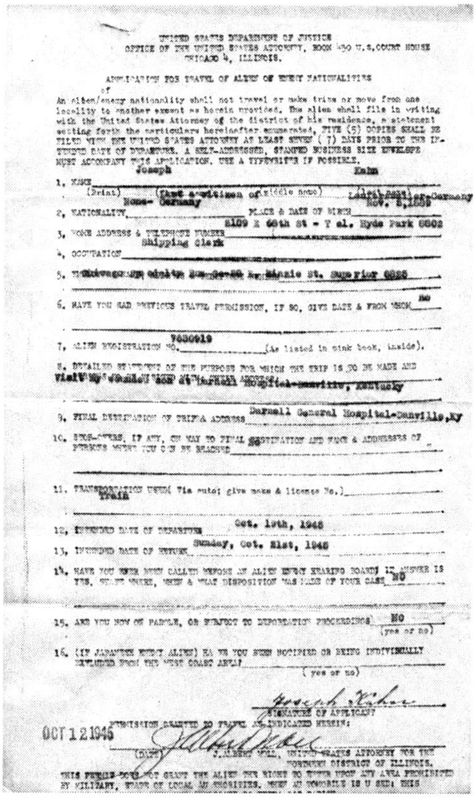

After being at my "Sweet Kentucky Home" for about a week or so, I noticed German Prisoners of War (POWs) working around the hospital. They wore light gray fatigues with a large PW printed on their back. All wore their former uniform cap minus all official German Army insignia. One day as I was resting in bed, I noticed a ladder being moved in front of the door to my room which led to a hallway. A German PW with a pail of paint and a brush, ready to paint started to climb the ladder. At first I was startled, but then hollered as loud as I could, and in my best German command: *Was machst du da?* ("What are you doing there?") I had no idea of the reaction of the German PW. There was no vocal response, but his body language said it all. At first he jumped down from the second rung of the ladder, put the pail with the brush on the floor, clicked his heels, stood at attention facing me, then with a stern face raised his arm and gave me a snappy German Army salute. It was a most peculiar and unexpected response, and while it took me by complete surprise, I enjoyed every moment of the episode. Only later that afternoon did I realize what affect my four German words had on the rest of the PWs. All afternoon at various intervals, numerous individual PWs came to the entrance of my room clicked their heels and saluted. It was an unexpected repeat performance, somewhat hilarious to me, yet puzzling. To think that even as captive prisoners of war, after Germany's defeat and unconditional surrender, these men had not lost their military discipline and respect for each other and their officers. How ironic, for one whole afternoon a despised Jew, mistakenly, was honored as one of their officers.

EXHIBIT 14.4 Application for Travel. Both applications are in the appendix, exhibits 14.4 and 14.5.

In the meantime I received several care packages from Mom and Dad containing recent letters they had received from Irene and others. Of course I enjoyed reading them. Also, as I had requested, one of the packages contained a pair of comfortable shoes, candy, shaving cream, and some good cigars. Mail and packages were delivered to me personally by lady Red Cross volunteers. These "Grey Ladies" not only augmented the military medical care, but provided other important services which the staff was not prepared to render. They were friendly, good listeners, helpful, and understanding. They were the closest thing to family.

There were various planned activities during the day and different types of entertainment in the evening, such as BINGO, live music, movies, and dances. All of this contributed to our so-called readjustment from hellish overseas experiences to a civilian life transition. There were handicraft programs and some moderate work assignments. What I liked best were the parties and dances, and open house evenings when girls from nearby towns made us forget, even if only for a while, our deep-seated memories. There were also USO planned professional variety shows in an attractive theater that gave the feeling of a big club atmosphere. The Post Exchange carried a variety of merchandise and a soda fountain where, if one had money, you could purchase a milkshake, soda, or ice cream. While all that reminded me of civilian life, I was always on my toes, as we were instructed, to remember that I was still a member of the U.S. Army and subject to its rules and discipline.

Mom and Dad who had plans to visit me never did. It may have been that I told them of my imminent discharge from the Army and therefore there would be no point to visit me, especially since the trip requiring several train changes would be rather strenuous and expensive. I remember vaguely that my cousin, Alfred Berney, who was stationed at the time at Fort Knox, Kentucky, visited me and certainly must have given my parents an uplifting report. From one of the German prisoners, I bartered a very nice water color painting of a typical Tyrolean Alp house with mountains in the background. Mom and Dad had it framed later. It hung in their living room over the couch in apartment 2109 E. 68th Street Chicago. It cost me eight packages of Camel cigarettes. After being stored for many years in our attic in Dayton, Ohio, we sold it at our neighbor's garage sale in 2004. I also exchanged several packets of cigars for two promotional letters signed by General Sperrle and one from Field Marshall Herman Goering.

On October 26, 1945, two years after I was inducted into the United States Army, I received my "Honorable Discharge." The certificate reads in part "... this is to certify that Robert B. Kahn 36691224 Private QMC, Co. 5th Camp Bn. Army of the United States is hereby discharged from the military service of the United States of America. This certificate is awarded as a testimonial of Honest and Faithful service to this country." It further reads: "Given at Darnall General Hospital, Danville Kentucky. Date, 26 October 1945." It is signed by Frank H. Dixon Colonel, Medical Corps Commanding. In addition I received a "Certificate of Disability for Discharge" Section I AR 615-361.

Hurrah! By the stroke of a pen I had become a civilian again. There were no ceremonies, no fanfares, not even a thank you. I was handed my mustering out pay of $100 in cash plus $20.30 travel pay, a new uniform, cap and GI shoes, a duffel bag, as well as a one way rail ticket to Chicago. For them it was routine, for me it was a big event in my life. Once I was on the train, full of people, I still felt very lonely and disoriented. There I sat in my new Army dress uniform, bedecked with all sort of ribbons, insignias, and medals. No one engaged me in conversation. What would they say anyhow? I felt very uncomfortable among all of these strangers. I had to change trains in Cincinnati and was trying to visualize the reception with my parents at the La Salle Station in Chicago.

The scenery, fields, farms, and towns just flew by as I looked out the window. I contrasted that with what I saw in New Guinea and the Philippines. What I saw here was absolutely beautiful. I filled my pipe with tobacco, put a match to it and watched the smoke

EXHIBIT 14.6 I am going home. My honorable discharge certificate, exhibit 14.17, is shown in the appendix.

at first linger and then disappear. Finally the train pulled into the station and came to a stop. Quickly I found myself in the arms of my father, who as always wore a hat as was customary in those days. The embrace was silent, neither one of us who had so much to say and ask each other could say anything. We kissed each other, holding on to one another as if there would be no tomorrow. People stopped walking and stared. I am sure they could tell that a son had come home from the war to his beloved father.

Mother had stayed at home at the apartment to make last minute arrangements for my arrival and to prepare the "Henkersmahlzeit." Literally translated, a meal a prisoner could request before he was to be hanged. In other words, she was preparing my most favorite meal. When the taxi which Dad had hired stopped in front of our apartment house, I could not get out of the car fast enough. I stood below our first floor apartment and used several particular whistling sounds, which in prior years had always announced me to the family. It was my so to speak trademark. The short whistling sounds were no less a few notes from one of the popular arias of Verdi's opera, *Rigoletto*. Hearing that familiar whistle, Mom pulled the drape aside and waved to me while at the same time removing her apron. I ignored Dad for a minute, opened the entrance door and heard the buzzer to the security door. Opening that door quickly, I ran up one flight of stairs and fell into the arms of Mother, her tears of joy running down my face as we locked in a jubilant embrace. Mother, like her Mom, could shed tears on any occasion whether happy or sad, but these tears were extra special, although they spotted the collar of my olive Army shirt. Her son, her boy, who had fought for his new country, and helped win the war, had returned safely. For a long moment there was tranquility around us as if the universe and its planets therein stood still.

Mom knocked on the door of our next door neighbor and yelled to our neighbors upstairs to tell them the good news and show me off while I was still in uniform. But as soon as I had been greeted by Mr. and Mrs. Koslowitz, and the Howards upstairs, I took that "monkey suit" off and got into some of my more comfortable civvies which were a little too large and baggy, but I didn't care. For me the dining room would at night again become my bedroom. The daybed had already been made up with clean smelling linens. Everything looked so familiar, everything exactly the same way and in the same place as it was before I left for the war. It was as if I had never left.

Reality set in when I noticed a little white flag with a blue star hanging in the front window, a sign that a beloved member of that household was in the military service. It had served its purpose, and asked Dad to take it down. On two of the windows across from our apartment were more small flags with blue stars and one with a gold star, denoting that a member of the family had made the ultimate sacrifice for our country. Mom let Dad and me know that dinner was being served by ringing a small brass bell. By now it was about 2:30 p.m. and I was very hungry. Usually dinner was eaten around 6:30 p.m., but then this was a special circumstance, a celebration of sorts. Dad came to the table with his hat on. Realizing that he was about to say a special brocha, a blessing to fit this special occasion, I, too, donned my uniform hat. Dad said the blessing for the wine, then for the bread, and uttered some appropriate words of thanks to "Elohim," our G'd for shielding and protecting me during my overseas duty and hopefully soon reuniting us with their daughter, my sister Irene.

It was very festive and solemn although there were only three people at the table. Next with great fanfare, Mother served matzo ball soup, followed by *kartoffel schalet* for which there is no good translation because it is strictly a Jewish dish for which there as many recipes as there are Jewish households. It is similar in taste as a potato latke, or perhaps a potato pancake, which we eat on the festival of Chanukkah. Except, the schalet is much bigger. Baked in a 9 or 10" round iron skillet or Pyrex dish, 2-3" high, it feeds 5-6 people with leftovers for another day.

Here is the recipe as Gert and I remember it:

Ingredients:

3 lbs. potatoes, peeled and grated
2 medium onions finely grated
2 day old rolls, or 4 slices of white bread soaked briefly in water
3 eggs

1/4 cup of flour

2 pinch of salt, pepper, nutmeg or ginger

3-4 tablespoons of chicken fat, any other fat or oil

Directions:

Pour enough fat or oil into iron baking skillet so that bottom and sides are greased. Combine all ingredients and stir well until mixture is smooth, then stir in eggs. Pour mixture into baking skillet and bake at 400°F degrees in oven until a solid brown crust has formed on top and bottom of skillet; when done, Schalet can be removed unto a larger plate without falling apart; cut in pie size slices and serve hot with apple sauce or any type of fruit.

Try this recipe and you will love it (but it is high in cholesterol)!

As an aside, for hundreds of years, Jews in Alsace and adjacent regions of France, Belgium, Luxembourg, and parts of the Rhine and Mosel Valley, considered Shabbat without the traditional schalet like having erev Shabbat Kiddush without candles, wine, or challah. On Passover, the same recipe was always prepared with matzo instead of rolls or bread. Heinrich Heine, the well-known German poet referred to the schalet as *wonnebrot des paradies*, bread of paradise, because it was a simple, wholesome down to earth food dish.

No need to reveal here that I enjoyed the schalet immensely and would have eaten a second portion if Mom hadn't reminded me that another of my favorite dishes would be served next. How I salivated when Mother brought sauerbraten and klösse potato dumplings, and a large saucer of sweet and sour gravy to the table. What a feast, and what a wonderful with love prepared homecoming dinner. But it was not over yet, dessert was still to come. The aroma from the kitchen preceded the dessert as Mom opened the baking oven to deliver my favorite pie for slicing. I had not smelled that unusual scent for years and realized how I had yearned for a piece of *zwetchgenkuchen*, or purple plum pie. In Europe purple plums were grown everywhere and during the season it was common to bake zwetchgenkuchen, or simply eating the plums as you would any other fruit.

I was so absorbed with the enjoyment of eating that our conversation centered naturally on the delicious meal and not on the uninspiring canned or dehydrated stuff we had to eat overseas. It was good that way since I was in no mood to talk about the war or anything connected with it. In fact, I had promised myself not to talk about that horrible past ever again. But would that be realistically possible? After Dad helped Mom clean the table, I retreated to the daybed situated against the wall, removed the bolster pillows and was ready for a well-deserved nap. The swinging door between the dining room and the kitchen muffled any noise and I fell quickly asleep as if I had never slept before.

EXHIBIT 14.8 Certificate from State of Illinois Service Recognition Certificate signed by the Governor of Illinois.

When I awoke it was the next morning, the sun shone through the blinds and curtains. Both Mom and Dad had already left for work. Mom still had her job in the corset factory, and Dad had gone to his brother's bottler supply business where he worked as a shipping clerk and bookkeeper. Both had breakfast in the kitchen before they left, but the noise had not awakened me. There were several notes from them on the dining room table with loving messages ranging from "good morning" to what's available for breakfast and lunch. It was sort of odd but nice. For the first time in several years I was alone, at home, still somewhat bewildered, but finally at peace. My new life had begun! It began when the mailman brought, among other things, a large envelope for me with a certificate of recognition for my service signed by the Governor of Illinois, David Green.

CHAPTER FIFTEEN

Life After Victory

All of a sudden our three room apartment had again become my headquarters from where I could develop ideas and perhaps plans for my future life. But first I had an urge to catch up with the news of the world which passed me by while I was in the military service. In addition I wanted to get together with my friends with whom I had been in contact from time to time but had not seen for some time. None of them had been in the war because of deferments, going to college or having some medical reason. They were the lucky ones! Then there were also relatives whom I wanted to visit and become reacquainted. Also, I wanted to become reacquainted with myself since for several years I had been someone else.

Mom and Dad had saved for me all sort of letters to read and copies of LIFE magazines which back then were published bi-weekly and were very popular and informative. They had also put aside newspaper articles and clippings for me dealing with matters they thought of interest. I was very anxious to go through all of that material in several boxes and see what I had missed or forgotten, and spent much time doing so. At least for me, some of the more significant happenings that I had not become aware of were that:

- Four million men, equal to about 28 Army divisions had been inducted in the U.S. since 1943 and required the call up of almost 12,000 men a day, between the ages of 18 and 38.
- British Prime Minister, Winston Churchill had told the House of Commons of a "complete plan of action" to "make the enemy burn and bleed in every way." The plan was adopted at the Casablanca Conference by President Roosevelt, Winston Churchill, and French General Charles de Gaulle, January 1943.
- The 69th Kentucky Derby took place with attendance restricted to residents of the Louisville area. Later, January 1945, the War Mobilization Board placed a ban on all horse and dog racing.
- The captured Doolittle fliers were executed by Japanese firing squads after they had dropped their bombs on Japan.
- Clark Gable, the great film star, had become a U.S. Army Air Corps Captain assigned to a bombardment squadron in England.
- Torpedo Boat PT 109 under command of John F. Kennedy, who in later years became our President, was rammed by a Japanese destroyer in the South West Pacific, but survived.
- October 1943, Italy declared war on its one time Axis partner and former Ally Germany, after Italy had surrendered to the Allied Armies. Sure surprised me!

- Four clergymen, military chaplains no less, gave their lives by drowning in the Atlantic Ocean. They were on a large troop transport when the ship was torpedoed by a German submarine. As the ship, the *Dorchester* was sinking they gave their own life preservers to the soldiers. A noble, unselfish and heroic act. Their names, Reverend George L. Fox, Rabbi Alexander D. Goode, Reverend Clark J. Poling, and Reverend John P. Washington.
- The bloody 5 months battle for Stalingrad Russia, ended with 91,000 German soldiers captured including 24 Generals, 100,000 German soldiers killed in battle.
- Cologne (Köln) was raided by Allied bombers 112 times.
- Errol Flynn, a good looking Hollywood film star age 33, who was physically unfit to serve in the military, was acquitted of three charges of statutory rape.
- February 1944, Income Tax Withholding was established, and in June of same year Germany launched the V-1 flying bombs on Britain.
- Nazi officers tried to assassinate Hitler but failed.
- Anne Frank was arrested in her Amsterdam attic where she and her family were hiding.
- The sound barrier was broken in a Bell X-1 rocket propelled aircraft flown by a U.S. pilot at 659 miles per hour.
- Famous band leader Glenn Miller disappeared in a flight over the English Channel. I loved his wonderful music and still do today.
- Grand Rapids Michigan became the first U.S. city to fluoridate its drinking water, January 1945.
- Benito Mussolini was hanged by Italian partisans at Lake Como Italy, and Adolf Hitler committed suicide in his Berlin bunker, April 30, 1945. The world shed no tears!
- Four hundred B-29 bombers attacked Tokyo with a multitude of different bombs. It happened in May 1945 while I was still overseas, and just read about it now. Strange!
- Heinrich Himmler, the master mind behind establishing the death camps had committed suicide at war's end.
- The first long playing record was demonstrated in the U.S., and the UN Charter was signed at San Francisco.
- July 1945, Allied leaders met at Potsdam Germany to decide on how to divide and occupy Germany among the victorious Armies.

I would not have been aware of most of the above cited information all these years had my dear parents not preserved clippings and newspaper articles in a cardboard box beginning when I went into military service. This material had turned somewhat yellow and brittle, had outlasted its usefulness, and finally found its rightful place in the trash recycling bin.

What disturbed, shocked, and saddened me more than anything else at the time were reports of the worst kind of persecution, the incarceration and barbaric extermination of Jews from all over Europe (see exhibit 15.1 in the appendix). There was now (in 1945) absolute proof that more than two million innocent Jews had been murdered since 1939, by the German occupation forces in the Eastern territories, and that perhaps five million more Jews from all over Western Europe had experienced the same fate. All in all, Hitler's beastly killers had murdered eleven million people, the majority Jews, including a million and a half young children and babies.

If anything made me feel a little better was the fact that in many instances Jews aggressively defended themselves in many ghettos, camps and elsewhere with homemade and smuggled in weapons. In April 1943, at the Warsaw Ghetto, Poland, 48,000 surviving Jews resisted their deportation to the death camps by orchestrating an uprising involving fierce and heroic combat with every conceivable type of weapon at their disposal. During a month long battle against an overwhelming German Army, referred to as the "Warsaw Ghetto Uprising," 4,000 Jewish fighters were killed, and the remaining 44,000 captured went to their death in the camps. Germany's inhumanity and genocidal activities affected me deeply. But there was more detail to come, and made my blood boil. The unbelievable methods of wholesale slaughter of Jews and the calculated devilish techniques were yet to be fully told. More details, photographs, and eye witness accounts were published daily. The average American and people the world over couldn't believe what they were told and shown in photographs, as revealed during the Nuremberg trials.

From the 1996 book, *Hitler's Willing Executioners* by Daniel Jonah Goldhagen, we know that "941 forced labor camps (were) designated especially for Jews within the borders of just (today's) Poland. An additional 230 special camps for Hungarian Jews were set up on the Austrian border. The Germans created 399 ghettos in Poland, 34 in East Galicia, 16 in small Lithuania. So just the known forced labor camps designated especially for Jews totaled over 1,600. In addition to these, there were 52 main concentration camps." The enormity of this genocidal killing apparatus is incomprehensible by any imagination.

One of the first orders of the Allied Control Council was the dissolution of the German Nazi Party. Hurrah! The above, were just some of the thousands of news items I combed through over the next weeks at home, looking with amazement at the exceptional photography in *LIFE Magazine* and newspapers. It may seem hard to understand, but it seemed as if I had been in a deep long sleep similar to a fairy tale that had lasted several years. I was playing catch up.

One aspect of the war years I was not keenly aware of was the massive rationing program under which people even in the United States had to live. Some of the rationing was already in place before I donned my Army uniform, but restrictions were tightened up quite a bit as time went on. Yet, most people did not complain too much. Winning the war was a first priority for them. Items that had been taken for granted most of their lives had to be purchased now in much smaller quantities and at longer intervals. Bare shelves in grocery stores were the norm. People had to curtail their purchases of items such as meat, butter, cheese, coffee, sugar, cigars, cigarettes, gasoline, tires, shoes and many textile items and could only be purchased with ration card stamps. But there had been a host of other items not rationed which were just as hard to find in stores. Although the war had been officially concluded tire rationing did not end until December 1945, and except for sugar, which continued to be rationed until June 1947, most items had come off the rationing list much earlier.

Dad told me that one ration point used to qualify for the purchase of a 6 oz. can of fruit juice. Seven points allowed for the purchase of one pound of hamburger meat, 16 ration points were needed to buy one pound of butter, and 18 points for a 16 oz. can of peaches if and when any of these items where available. The ration points consisted of small postage size pieces of paper that were made available to each household in small booklets. There was a lot of good natured stamp trading among people. Human nature what it is lead to some hoarding of scarce goods which would later be sold on a black market at a much higher price. People that could afford to pay under the table took advantage of these opportunities, although the Office of Price Administration had put a price ceiling on most products. My parents and all other immigrants who had fled the European Continent knew that the effects of rationing were far worse there. At least in the U.S. no one had to suffer or die from malnutrition too.

Here in America when motorists were caught violating any of the rationing laws, some were forced to surrender their gasoline ration books because they were using counterfeit or stolen gas coupons. Of those, 32,000 were taken to court and convicted. I am reminded that today we still use the expression, "this is the greatest thing since sliced bread." This expression originated during World War II because loaves of bread had to be sold un-sliced, which saved labor from hours of slicing, the hours to produce the slicing machines, and to use the metal from those machines for other war-time equipment.

For a while I was trying to relax, although somehow I just couldn't make an immediate transition from the rugged regimented Army life to a life of comfort and leisure. I could not get used to sleeping on my soft converted daybed and felt much more relaxed and comfortable sleeping on the lightly carpeted parquet floor. Some nights Dad would wake me up when he and Mom would hear me having nightmares. Fortunately they were just that! Yet they seemed so real that I awoke covered with perspiration, reliving the torment and hardships I had experienced and thousands others with me, day and night.

Somehow it was hard to get used to the idea of being back home, and for hours I took refuge listening to the radio with its periodic local, national and international news. Mostly I enjoyed the music of which I could not get enough. The "Hit Parade" songs, those that were weekly selected by the program of the same name, were played over and over again so that after while I had memorized not only the melody but also the lyrics. A few of my favorites were "Rum and Coca Cola," by the wonderful harmonizing Andrews Sisters, and "Sentimental Journey" by the swing and dance band of Les Brown accompanied by his singing lady Doris Day. Then there was a real snappy tune "Tampico" by the band of Stan Kenton and singer June Christy. How fondly I remember "On the Atchison, Topeka and Santa Fe" by the crooner Johnny Mercer.

Listening to music was good for me. It kept my mind from re-hearing the tattering noises of guns, the whistling of mortar shells, bombs, and other horrible sounds of men screaming, attacking, dying, and the lingering stench of mayhem amidst constant rain and humidity. Other tunes I had become fond of were, "You Belong to My Heart," sung beautifully by Bing Crosby accompanied by the Xavier Cugat band with a Latin beat. Perry Como sang "Till the End of Time." I could mention some more but all of them soothed the ex-warrior's heart. The sound quality of the radio had much improved in the few years since I had been gone and so had the programming.

During the day I was all alone while Mom and Dad had gone to work, and I had plenty time to think. Always there was the nagging realization that I would have to rearrange my life in basically two areas. One was to overcome the physical and psychological trauma left over from the war. The other was to create a life for myself that would be productive and meaningful. To achieve both of these goals would require consideration of many factors, including my past, over which I had no control, and of my future over which I certainly had some influence but not total control either. I knew that I had to make the best of both hands dealt to me and adapt myself as best I could to the post-war changes in the prevailing economic environment. These were very difficult times for me that I could not describe or share with anyone, least of all with my dear parents. Reliving the war sometimes even during the day caused periods of anxiety, moods, and feeling depressed. Sometimes I became irritable and argumentative with family and friends, which occasionally lead to outbursts of anger. Other times I felt alone and isolated, but most of all I suffered from a lack of concentration, particularly of numbers. There was no one that I could confide in with these innermost thoughts that troubled me and no one I thought that would understand and give me good advice.

After much thought I came to the conclusion that returning to my last job, entailing the work of an experimental machinist, was not the way I wanted to spend the rest of my life. According to the law I could have gone back to Arens Controls and claim my veteran's job rights. But I did not. On the other hand, I realized that going in a different direction would require making up for the education I was deprived of in Europe because of Nazi restrictions on Jews, plus four additional years without any additional education since arriving in America. Here I was, just having turned 22 years old, and not having completed a high school equivalent education. How far would that get me in today's (1945) world? That was my dilemma! Somehow while making a living I would have to catch up with my education. A formidable problem and task indeed.

So many other problems, ideas, and questions came across my mind all at once that at times it became very disturbing and confusing. One of the questions that constantly nagged me only my parents would have the answer. It was the question of what happened to our loved ones who had been left behind in Europe and were trapped there during the horrible war years. I could tell by their self-imposed silence that they did not want to talk to me about this subject willingly. In a way fearing the worst, I had been reluctant to ask up to now. Yet it bothered me so terribly that I had to know. On Saturdays, Dad worked only half a day while Mom, not having to work Saturdays, did some shopping on 71st Street and some chores around the apartment. It was mid-afternoon, Dad was smoking a cigar and had taken his traditional "Shabbes" Shabbat nap, and I thought the time had come to broach that subject.

Mom had baked a *streusel kuchen*, a crumble topping cake that I loved, and proceeded to make us comfortable at the kitchen table with a cup of coffee. It was all very pleasant and tranquil until I mentioned a few names. Mom's eyes started to become glossy while Dad was trying to hide his emotions by attempting to light his earlier not finished cigar with a second and then a third match. "So tell me what happened to our loved ones at Laufersweiler, where you were born?" I asked. Hesitant he explained that all Jews that had remained in that small community were deported to "Konzentrationslagern," concentration camps and only two people, Josef Heimann and Johanna Rauner, had survived the camps. When on July 27, 1942 the last fifteen Jews were deported, the town's many eye witnesses described that the Jewish men, women, and children were assembled in a courtyard. There, for all of the town's people to see, in desperation, kneeling, others in a prone position, crying, they were begging their Nazi tormentors to let them stay. All the pleading was of no avail. They were deported, and according to a local report "probably killed." As Mom openly sobbed and Dad fidgeted with his cigar, my blood was boiling with anger, and shaking as I listened to more details as they unfolded. All of the reports I had read and photographs I had seen all of a sudden took on the faces not of unknown others, but the faces of my own family, relatives and friends. I was shocked! An instant unsurmountable disgust of the Nazi

> Die Gemeinde Laufersweiler gedenkt ihrer ehemaligen Jüdischen Mitbürger die von 1933–1945 wegen ihres Glaubens verfolgt, gequält und ermordet wurden.
>
> Hermann Fain,
> Fanny Frank, Isaac Frank
> Mayer Frank,
> Elisabeth Frank
> Albert Hanau, Hilda Hanau
> Gertrud Hanau-Selig
> Gertrude Joseph
> Ruth Joseph
> Magdalena Loeser
> Josef Marx
> Bernhard Mayer
> Paula Mayer, Eva Mayer
> Gerd Mayer, Kurt Mayer
> Sally Mayer, Rosa Mayer
> Emma Scholem
> Ludwig Scholem
> Bernhard Josef Strauss
> Moses Tenzer-Seiden
> Klara Tenzer-Seiden
> Zacharias Weiler
>
> Laufersweiler den 31. Januar 1988

EXHIBIT 15.2 The tablets commemorating Jews of Laufersweiler The synagogue of Laufersweiler which has been restored on the outside, serves today primarily as a museum. Inside are two tablets with the names of the 25 Jews from Laufersweiler who were murdered by the Nazis. Among them are some of our relatives: Albert and Hilda Hanau, her mother, Magdalena Löser, and their daughter Gertrude. The tablets introduce the names by stating "the Community of Laufersweiler commemorates the former Jewish fellow citizens who from 1933-1945 were persecuted and tormented because of their faith and were murdered." Lauferseweiler, 31 January 1988. See exhibit 15.3 in the appendix for more on this memorial.

animals including the German people came over me. They, for reasons of Aryan and world supremacy as well as blind hatred, had murdered these innocent, helpless and peaceful people.

Although I had always addressed Isaak and Lenchen Löser affectionately as Uncle and Aunt, they were actually my great uncle and great aunt. Lenchen was the sister of both my grandmothers, Malchen Joseph in Luxembourg and of Hannchen Kahn of Laufersweiler. I was saddened when Dad told me that Uncle Isaak died (presumably) of natural causes June 15, 1942 at age 79, in Laufersweiler. It was especially painful for me when Dad told me that Isaak's wife, my Aunt Lenchen, age 79, was also deported from Laufersweiler on the same day as the others to the concentration camp Theresienstadt (Terezin) where she perished shortly after incarceration. Of the children of Uncle Isaak and Aunt Lenchen, my dad's first cousins, only cousin Hugo Löser, living in Mulhouse France, survived.

None of their three married daughters, Hilde Hanau, Karolina "Lina" Berney, and Else, nor their husbands and children survived the Holocaust.

By this time the coffee Mom had poured was cold and the streusel kuchen remained untouched. I had lost my appetite and my desire for cake and coffee. Dad continued to share this sad tale with me as the three of us agonized at every word.

Hilde Löser (born March 15, 1892 at Laufersweiler) married Albert Hanau (born February 28, 1885), and both were deported to their certain death from Laufersweiler where they lived on the same day as the others. Albert was a butcher, and the meat and sausages derived from his trade used to be sold at the Löser's grocery store. Their daughter Gertrude "Trude" who was born May 4, 1922 in Laufersweiler, was always a playmate when I vacationed there. She was deported from the German city of Wiesbaden to a camp near Riga, Latvia, which was under German occupation, shortly after being married. Her life was snuffed out by the Nazi imbeciles at the young age of 20. Her brother, Heinz Jacob Hanau (born July 16, 1923) in Turkismuehle, also located in the Hunsrück, had miraculously survived. As elsewhere reported herein, he and I always managed to have a good time when we were together at Laufersweiler and managed many pranks which I have not forgotten to this day.

Heinz wound up fighting the Germans in a very extraordinary fashion. Sometime after the so-called Kristallnacht his parents Hilde and Albert managed to send Heinz to her brother, Uncle Hugo Löser (born in Laufersweiler February 11, 1898) who was living in Mulhouse, France. From there, Heinz managed to get to Switzerland where he worked for a while as a farm hand, but later joined the FFI, also known as the Maquis, the French Resistance. These outnumbered and relatively poorly armed but highly motivated patriotic groups were merged into the Free French forces, FFL, after the Allied invasion 1944, at Normandy. When Heinz established that his parents and sister were murdered by the Nazis, he enlisted in the French Foreign Legion hoping in that manner to have the opportunity to avenge his family. He was wounded in battle near the town of Hagenau in the Alsace region of France, and was decorated for his valor.

It was only in 1947 that he was able to come to America where he married a childhood acquaintance Renate Alice Joseph also born in Laufersweiler (June 11, 1930). While her parents went into hiding during the war at a farm in Limoges and Brives-la Gaillarde, France, Renate was hidden by nuns at a convent. Heinz, who adopted the name Henry, and Renate, who preferred her middle name Alice, settled eventually in Waukegan, Illinois where they raised their children Marc and Helen. Henry died unexpectedly March 18, 2000. Uncle Hugo Löser is survived by two sons Roger and Herbert living in France, presumably in Muehlhausen. Alice was born to Laura née Lippman and Isidor Joseph. Her mother Laura was first married to Moritz Baum of Laufersweiler who died at an early age. Two sons Alex and Marcel stem from the first marriage and were living in California.

EXHIBIT 15.4 Heinz Hanau, now Henry, in America after the war.

Memories of the wonderful and happy childhood and early teenage visits and vacations in Laufersweiler paled quickly in front of me like an old Charlie Chaplin silent movie clip. All of a sudden as these tragedies unfolded it had become warm, smoky, and uncomfortable in our kitchen, but there was more tragedy unfolding as if this was not enough already. Both, Karolina "Lina" Löser (born in Laufersweiler May 30, 1890) and her husband Heinrich Berney (born April 22, 1888) lived in Wiesbaden, Germany after their marriage. They too, as well as their daughter Beate did not survive the brutality of the concentration camps. However, their son Alfred, a third cousin of mine, escaped his parents' and sister's fate by being able to come to America with his wife Rosa (née Cohn). Rosel and Fred, as they preferred to be called, settled in Chicago and remained good friends of my parents and my sister Irene. Fred served in the U.S. Army during World War II, as did 80% of all Jewish immigrants of military age and in acceptable physical condition. He visited me at Darnall General Army Hospital in Kentucky while he was stationed not too far away at Fort Knox with an armored tank battalion. Their children, Margaret Florence was born June 18, 1942, and Howard Don, May 5, 1951. No other information has become available to this date regarding the demise of Else Löser, Isaak and Lenchen's third daughter, who at the time lived in Wiesbaden Germany, presumably she was murdered by the Nazis.

Jacob Hanau, the father of Albert Hanau, was born 1859 in Bosan, Hunsrück, and married local girl Matilde Sender (born March 4, 1861). Their six children were all born in Bosan: Albert, Leo, Berta, Selma, Lina, and Frieda (who was born August 20, 1897). Frieda married Alfred Boehm, a Christian (born July 24, 1896 in Eger, Czechoslovakia) and moved to Kaiserslautern, in the Palatinate of Germany. There, my distant relative and playmate at Laufersweiler, mentioned earlier herein, Lieselotte Boehm, was born October 21, 1923. Her father had become the director of "Spinnerei, Weberei, Lampertsmühle," a textile spinning and weaving mill. They lived in a large, beautiful estate, which my parents and I visited on occasion. Gertrude (my beloved wife) and Lieselotte met by coincidence and became friends in 1937 at the Goldschmidt Schule, a private Jewish boarding school located at Berlin-Grünewald, Hohenzollerndamm 110. What must be considered more of an astounding coincidence, that when Gertrude and I first met as complete strangers, both of us were surprised that we had a mutual friend and relative, namely Lieselotte Boehm. The connection between that unique trio seemed like a good omen and brought us immediately closer.

While the mixed marriage between Frieda Hanau and Alfred Boehm raised some eyebrows, it turned out to be a life saver for all three of them. Not until late 1944/45 did the Nazi regime deport children of mixed marriages. Lieselotte was eventually deported March 8, 1945, although the fortunes of war had turned against Germany. She was liberated by American troops from camp Theresienstadt (Terezin), Czechoslovakia, now Slovakia, on May 9, 1945. Because of her typhoid condition she was not evacuated until a month later. In 1950, she was able to come to the U.S. living in Andover Massachusetts. Her mother Frieda followed her to Andover after Alfred had died in Germany.

This was one of the few tragic stories told by my Dad and Mom that ended on a happier note, but I could tell from their demeanor that more family tragedy was in the offing. I remember it being a dreary afternoon with rain and periodic thunderstorms that had created its own gloominess and crescendo.

The name of another who was destroyed by the Nazis was my cousin Kurt, the son of Leo and Jenny (née Kahn) Strauss, sister to my Dad. Uncle Leo and Aunt Jenny lived in Frankfurt, Main. Jenny had died December 11, 1930 at the young age of 51. Cousin Kurt who espoused to socialism and was an ardent Zionist, died of a lie concocted by the Nazis, called *körperschwäche* (body weakness) or malnutrition, at Camp Sachsenhausen at 3:15 p.m. on April 5, 1940, according to the death certificate discovered by me during research after the turn of the century. His death came after several earlier incarcerations by the Nazis for his political views. Other information indicates that an urn of his remains sent to his father was buried alongside his mother's grave on June 5, 1940 at the new Frankfurt cemetery. However, I have not been able to substantiate the latter information. Additional information obtained through the International Red Cross indicates that Uncle Leo died in a concentration camp. Only in recent years was it revealed that urns sent to the families indeed did not contain the ashes of their loved ones, but consisted of other materials. What a fiendish mockery on top of murder. Kurt was only 22 years old when his life was ruthlessly terminated. Quoted from a German pamphlet published in Germany 1996, "over 200,000 people were imprisoned in the Sachsenhausen Concentration Camp until its liberation. Tens of thousands of people died there of starvation, disease, forced labor and mistreatment or were victims of the systematic extermination operations of the SS." Less than half of the incarcerated survived. Photographs of the camp indicate the location of the gallows, the sites of the crematorium and extermination operations, execution trenches with bullet catch bins and "automated gallows," as well as other terrible torture facilities. Now, the coffee was cold and Mom put the untouched cake back into the refrigerator.

And then I asked what they had heard from or about Uncle Manfred Ackerman and Aunt Gerda (Gertrude), with whom I had spent wonderful vacations at Bad Schwalbach. There was a long pause and a long sigh by both Mom and Dad. My father was visibly affected by my continued questioning and fidgeted with his cigar in the ash tray. Aunt Gerda was one of his dear sisters, and he proceeded to tell me that both, she and Uncle Manfred had been deported in September 1942 to Camp Theresienstadt where they perished, likely meaning that they were starved, or died from other torturous causes with which we are now all familiar with. She was 51, and Uncle Manfred 52 years old. Today, his name, but not the name of his wife, is engraved on the wall of the "Ermordeten" of the murdered in the city of Frankfurt.

I wished that our dreadful conversation that afternoon could have come to an end, yet I had to find out what happened to the rest of our family. What other horrible news would I find out? Was there a better time? And yet, it was a terrible strain on me and far more agonizing to my parents since their relationship to the deceased was in most instances a much closer and endearing one than mine. Dad started to complain of stomach pain (ulcer), something he would experience from time to time as a result of his World War I typhoid and other illnesses, but especially when he was in a state of stress and excitement. Yet I needed to know.

When I asked about Opa, Mom's dad, she started to weep uncontrollably raising both arms toward the ceiling as if expecting an answer from high above. It was a sight of despair I hoped never to see again. As explained in an earlier chapter, we had to leave Opa behind in Luxembourg because we were unable to obtain a visa because of his age. No country wanted to be burdened with an old man even so it would have saved his live.

Already in March 1941, unbeknown to us because we had not yet left Luxembourg, the Gestapo had their eyes on the former Convent at Cinqfontaines, also known in German as Fünfbrunnenen, outside the town of Ulflingen. The Nazi plan was to convert this somewhat isolated convent located in northern Luxembourg into a "mini ghetto," for all the remaining Jews of this small country. On August 11, 1941, after our escape from Luxembourg, 25 Jews were forcibly taken there to make preparations and repairs of sanitary and heating installations pending the eventual arrival of 674 additional Jews who were rounded up daily for weeks and months to be interned at this former convent which had a normal occupancy for one hundred Catholic seminary students.

Among those interned in August or early September 1941 was Raphael Joseph, my Mom's father, my beloved Opa, age 81 years. However, Uncle Max Cohen and his wife Helene (née Joseph), a sister of my Mother, who had fled from the city of Cologne, Germany and had settled in the small community of Walferdingen

(Walferdange in French), not far from the city of Luxembourg, had not been taken there. As a matter of fact they came to visit Opa at least once. Yet, their fate in the end was no different from the rest, as described shortly. They had been reluctant, as so many others, to make arrangements to leave Europe until it was too late. They, as well as my parents and thousands of others, thought that fleeing to Luxembourg, or to some other Western European country, would give them and us a temporary safe haven until Germany was defeated.

On September 4, 1941, 97 able bodied Jewish men were picked up and forced to do hard manual labor for the Paul Wurth Co. in the stone quarries of Nennig in the Eifel district of Germany for the construction of a highway. And on October 14 of the same year, Jews in Luxembourg had to wear the Jewish star, the Star of David "clearly visible" on their clothing.

Soon, the conditions at Convent Cinqfontaines were becoming over-crowded with four and five people assigned to a small room originally designed for one student or nun. At first, each person could bring a few belongings and several pieces of furniture. Later, as the rooms became more crowded, the only thing that remained was perhaps one bed or a chair. All others had to sleep on mattresses on the floor. Food was prepared by the interned and served by them in a dining hall. The sick were looked after by incarcerated Jewish doctors and other inmates. On top of this unjustified and inhuman incarceration the prisoners had to pay for food and lodging.

From lists that became available to me during years of research, I recognized very many good friends and acquaintances had also been in residence at Cinqfontaines. Among them were the two girls and their mother who lived in the house next to Opa; Denise Levy, the youngest daughter a good friend of mine, was born March 8 1923, and her sister, Edith had been born several years earlier. Also, housed at this place were the parents of my traveling companion to America, Heinz's parents Adolf Alkan and Karoline Alkan. It is from many letters that Mrs. Alkan wrote to her son Heinz, who in turn sent the letters to me, that I gleaned some of the details of their ordeal at the mini ghetto convent. All of those letters were censored by the Gestapo and each expressed time and time again her hopes and innermost prayers that G'd would protect and take care of them. Already on October 16, 1941, a few months after we escaped, the first transport of 331 unfortunate Jews from all over Luxembourg, including 20 from the Convent, were loaded on closed freight cars on a railroad spur almost directly in front of the Convent. Several suicides are recorded. Their destination was the Ghetto "Litzmannstadt," the German name for Lodz, the second largest city of Poland. Only 11 people survived. It was on the second transport from Luxembourg destined for Izbica Lubelska, Poland on April 23, 1942, that my Aunt Helene and Uncle Max Cohen and 25 others were taken, fourteen of whom from the Convent. The town of Izbica had been cleared of all non-Jews and converted into a very primitive "transit ghetto," on a major railroad line, 145 kilometers from Lublin, and perhaps 50 kilometers from Belzic. Since transports arrived frequently, the ghetto became overcrowded that 10-20 people had to live in one room. Correspondence to the outside world was forbidden. Most of the inmates were taken to Belzec, known as a death camp, where they were gassed. There were no survivors.

Raphael Joseph, Mom's dear father was on the 5th transport from Convent Fünfbrunnen with 158 others to Theresienstadt on July 28, 1942. That's where on February 6, 1943, only six months later, the debilitated life of my beloved Opa came to an end. Records indicate that only 8 persons from that particular transport survived the horrible camp conditions; less than 1%. All of the deported Jews had been told that this was a resettlement (*eine Umsiedlung*). Lies which the Nazis had taken great pleasure to invent.

While Theresienstadt was not considered a death camp, malnutrition, starvation and disease were often the cause of death. Also the records show that a great number of inmates were sent to other camp destinations from which they did not survive. That was the case with Denise Levy who was on the sixth transport with her sister Edith. Both were transported April 6, 1943 from former Convent Fünfbrunnen to Theresienstadt. Denise was transshipped from there on August 9, 1944 to a destination unknown and did not survive. Her older sister Edith was married at Theresienstadt in a secret religious ceremony, sometime in 1943, to a Gert Edelstein. In September the couple was shipped with others to Camp Auschwitz from where she survived although she had contracted tuberculosis while performing slave labor in a cotton mill under very hot and humid conditions. Mr. and Mrs. Alkan were on the same transport to Theresienstadt. Adolf Alkan died May 20, 1944, while Karoline (née Meyer,) his wife survived. Ironically, on the same transport from Fünfbrunnen, Luxembourg was Berthold Lieben the proprietor of the leather business where my Dad was employed prior to World War I. He also died at Theresienstadt on December 3, 1943 at the age of 73.

A total of 674 men, women and some children were interned at Fünfbrunnen. Of those, only 43 survived the transports to the Eastern camps and ghettos. Already at Fünfbrunnen the inmates were harassed and tormented for the most ridiculous reasons. A guard found some cakes of soap which were not of the same type issued as part of their rations. As a result, 12 individuals were taken on January 29, 1942 to the Gestapo Headquarters, where they were interrogated, mistreated and severely beaten. They became part of the second transport to Izbica from which none survived. A Dr. Fritz Hartman, an official of the Gestapo in charge, constantly instituted more restrictions and harassments for the interned. For example: January 7, 1942, internees were allowed only one bar of soap in their possession; 2 pairs of underwear per person; not allowed outside the building; no smoking; no reading of newspapers, periodicals, or books; and no flashlights.

While the basic information about the individuals described above was part of the original discussion that afternoon with Mom and Dad, most other details surrounding the circumstances of the interned plight were pieced together from data I researched over many years and determined their authenticity. Unfortunately, Mom and Dad's revelations did not end there. They began describing what they knew about the whereabouts and happenings to Bernard Joseph's family including his wife Marthe, and son Georges. On the morning of May 10, 1940, when Germany invaded Luxembourg, Berny, my Mom's brother, had fled Luxembourg with his family by automobile to escape the Nazis. I don't know the details of their journey but they finally settled in Nice, France which remained unoccupied by the German Armies for some time. Nice is located at the Cote d'Azur, also known as the French Riviera about 15 km from Monaco and perhaps 20 km from the Italian border. My cousin Georges was enrolled there in a school studying art until about November 1942, when the Germans had infiltrated, occupied, and taken over administration of all of France with Gestapo and secret police being most feared.

By then information had become known as to what the Nazis were doing to Jews in the other occupied areas of Europe and especially in the countries of Luxembourg, Holland, Belgium, and the occupied areas France. It was no longer safe for Jews in Nice. For that reason Aunt Marthe rented a small apartment in an obscure part of town, while Uncle Berny and Cousin Georges, now 18 years old, fled into the Italian Alps where they hid, joined and fought with the partisans underground fighters of Piemont, known as the Maquis. These freedom fighters were named after a shrubby plant primarily growing in the Mediterranean area known to be good hiding places for fugitives. Georges was apprehended by the Italians "with weapons in his hands," in a nearby town of Demonte, and was turned over to the Germans. According to an e-mail confirmation from Alberto Valmaggia, the Mayor of Cuneo to whom I had written, Georges was shot by a German firing squad April 26, 1945, in the Italian city of Cuneo. Georges and seven named others were executed "under the fifth arch of the Ponte Nuovo" in that city. Cuneo is approximately 80 km NNW from Nice. The circumstances that surround his fighting, his capture and death are not known. However, I seem to recollect that his mother Aunt Marthe mentioned many years later that a jealous girl revealed his whereabouts. This could be true, because further research on my part showed that he and a girl by the name of Hortense Jeanne Ghislaine had opened a joint bank account in Switzerland. Tragically, Georges' life ended because of his selfless bravery against the German criminals at age 21. Fortunately, his mother and father survived, but lived out their lives in the shadow of their son's brutal death.

After the war when Uncle Berny and Aunt Marthe returned to 18 Rue de Strassbourg in Luxembourg, they found their apartment above their former business in ruin. The German civil administration, primarily the Gestapo, in their

EXHIBIT 15.5 How sad that beautiful and intelligent human being, Georges Joseph, my dear cousin, lost his life through bullets from a murderous firing squad. See exhibit 15.6 in the appendix for a copy of the email I received from the Mayor of Cuneo.

zeal to destroy the Jews, had taken most of the furniture and possessions in their apartment. When my parents received the news that they were alive, sadly minus their son, Mom and Dad wanted to help her brother and sister-in-law as much as possible to start a new life. My parents told them to contact Arendt Wirtz in Luxembourg, with whom we had stored most our belongings from Mannheim prior to fleeing to Luxembourg, and to take everything stored there to re-equip their empty apartment. The Wirtz family, who incidentally lived on the same street, cooperated fully and all our "things" had found a good home. It was a good deed that Uncle Berny and Aunt Marthe never forgot.

A first cousin of my Uncle Berny, also a cousin of mine, Marcel Salomon (born October 13, 1899 in Dudelange, Luxembourg) and his wife Rosette née Braun (born June 13, 1908 in Offenbach, Alsace), also fled Luxembourg May 10, 1940 to France with their young daughter Monique. Marcel and Rosette were deported without Monique from France with Convoy #72 April 29, 1944 to Auschwitz where they perished. The convoy consisted of 1004 Jews; 606 females and 398 males. There were 174 children under the age of 18. Only 50 from the entire convoy survived. When Monique returned to Luxembourg as an orphan, Uncle Berny and Aunt Marthe treated her as a daughter, adopted her officially and lived with them from age 13 until she became 23 years old. Monique was born March 13, 1935 and was only five years old when I lived in Luxembourg. Therefore I did not know her well. The Joseph's had lost a wonderful son, but had gained a new daughter whom they treated as if she was their son.

My other cousin, Bruno Joseph Salomon, was the brother of Marcel. He was married to Frieda (Friedel) Ehrlich, born in Herrlisheim, Alsace Lorraine. Since she was born September 30, 1899, the same day as me, we always enjoyed sending each other birthday greetings and wishes until she passed away at a residence for the aged in New York City August 16, 1986. She was a wonderful woman who had beautiful handwriting and loved poetry. The two brothers, Bruno and Marcel were partners in a small men's clothing manufacturing establishment on the first floor of the house where both families lived. Frieda and Bruno's daughter, Solange Sophie Salomon (born August 6, 1928) fled with her mother and father to Spain and fortunately was able to come to the U.S. and thus all three survived. After the war they returned to Luxembourg to see whether their earlier possessions and life could be salvaged. They lived there for a few years but decided to come back a second time to the U.S. in 1951, not being able to resume their interrupted lives. Solange changed her name to Sonya, is married to Ernest Hartog, born in Aachen, Germany and at present live in Florida. They have two married sons and five grandchildren. Lloyd and wife Erica live in Tarrytown, New York and, Marc and Cindy live in Westport, Connecticut.

As the afternoon turned into early evening we were still sitting in the kitchen unraveling the tragedies suffered by our mischpocha. The incessant rain outside, and the occasional lightning followed by thunder, set the tone for our macabre discussions. However, by now Mother's tears had subsided and Dad, who had tried to finish his cigar all afternoon, had given up and was now smoking a cigarette. I was overcome with sadness, disbelief, and helplessness as the ravages on each family member were detailed. It was Mom who reminded me that we had almost left out Uncle Sally Cohen, the only brother of Max Cohen. He, like his brother, had been born in Cologne (Köln) had never married and was somewhat of a loner. Eventually he was found out by the Nazis and deported to Theresienstadt in 1942 (exact date not known) where he died November 20, 1942. He was 47 years old.

Dad seemed to have regained his composure and abruptly exclaimed "enough already," or some words like that, and left the kitchen. And so it was that a devastating and numbing afternoon had come to an end. It had become one among many of the most dramatic days in my life. Unfortunately there had been some before and there were a few more to come.

Letters from Gertrude and occasional phone calls between us broke the otherwise uneventful and often gloomy days. I looked forward to her often lengthy letters and her sweet voice created an aura of contentment and yearning. These feelings were not unnoticed by my parents, and I made no effort to hide them. Eventually, I got around to making phone calls to my neighborhood pals including girl friends and met with them either at their apartments, or as we did long ago, at Walgreens Drugstore on 71st Street. Most of them wanted me to come over so their parents could welcome me back and talk about my experiences in this "glorious war," and the medals I earned as a hero. Several asked me to come over in my Army uniform so they could see how handsome I looked. However, they didn't realize that I wanted no part of this, and made short shrift of their probing questions during my visit. I had other things on my mind in particular the terrible fate of 19 of my relatives and millions of others that were butchered. But that was not their main interest or their immediate concern, and I could tell that they felt uncomfortable with the topic. As strange as it seemed, we had all gotten a few years older and somehow had developed different interests. My buddies were no longer the happy go lucky bunch I remembered and neither was I. We had all changed, perhaps matured in ways I cannot explain or describe.

I called Francine Travis who was enrolled in the University of Illinois at Champaign, Illinois, but who would come home some weekends. She was happy to hear from me and we decided to go out Saturday evening on a date. As usual she was not ready when I called on her. However, her father greeted me then ushered me into the parlor where Francine's mother was also waiting. At first they talked to me about the war. Then the subject shifted to how the years of war had affected his liquor store businesses because the alcohol rationing and the draft deprived him of dependable help and managers. Mr. Travis followed this line of conversation by saying something like this: "When Francine gets married, I will take my son-in-law into the business. Then I can retire and let him (son-in-law) take over the stores and the business." Right away I realized what he had said and to whom. Me! I was flabbergasted, and for a while didn't know what to make of this oblique proposal. There was a pause of silence, while Mrs. and Mr. Travis sat smiling and I realized that I had been offered a deal if I married their daughter.

I was surprised, shocked, and humiliated by this turn of events, but was careful not to show my disappointment and anger. There was a friendly embrace as Francine entered the room and we left after saying a polite good bye. Fran, as I had come to call her, and I had a nice evening having dinner at a restaurant on 71st Street, thereafter some ice cream at the soda fountain at Walgreens and then back to her apartment. Francine was a very nice, polite, and sincere person, of whom I was very fond. But all of that had changed now. Of course she had no knowledge of what her father had said and offered me in the presence of her mother. It was the last time I saw Francine and her parents, but it was perhaps better that way than for her to know what had happened that evening in the parlor.

To put my life back together and make up for the years I was in the military service plus the education I was deprived of since Hitler came to power added up to almost ten years. In practical terms I had never received a high school education. Without it I was doomed to spending my life as a failure, something I was not willing to do. Luckily for me as well as for several millions of other discharged U.S. veterans the "Servicemen's Readjustment Act of 1944," referred to by everyone as the GI Bill of Rights (Public Law 346) provided the opportunity to make up education while attending costs were to be paid by the U.S. Government. It was a well-deserved thank you from a grateful nation. This public law actually went farther to cover hospitalization, the purchase of homes and businesses by way of loans, and a string of other assistance programs, all geared to help home coming soldiers to make the adjustment back into civilian life.

While the far greater majority of ex-GIs enrolled in colleges and universities all over the country, I was one of the very few who enrolled in day classes at Parker High School in Chicago to earn a long overdue high school graduate equivalent. Books and fees were paid by the Veterans Administration. I received a $65 in monthly stipend and $22 for my service connected disability. Having been away from studying, and now doing so in the English language, it was hard for me to concentrate during classes and to study at home. For the first several weeks it was also embarrassing to walk into a classroom full of teenagers gawking at me, a 22 year old fellow, as if I were some sort of pre-historic oddity. I took on a heavy load: English, Civics and Social Studies, American History, and General Science.

Every weekday when I left the apartment for school Mom and Dad had already gone for work and I was home studying before they came back late afternoon, usually very tired. I started to feel as if I was a burden and somewhat ashamed that I was not contributing my share to meet the expenses of the household, as well as to repay Uncle Ernst for the ship passage on a weekly basis. With this in mind, I applied to the U.S. Postal Service for a part-time night job at the Main Post Office near downtown Chicago, and worked there from 6:30 p.m. to 10:45 p.m. with a 15-minute break. I learned to sort mail and earned 75 cents an hour. While my schedule was fairly strenuous now, considering I was also going to school, I felt more relieved and happy with myself not being a burden to Mom and Dad, and being able to turn over to them all my earnings, except what I needed for transportation and a few dollars for allowance.

We received letters from the Ehrlichs in Lille, France thanking Mom and Dad for the many packages of clothing and food staples sent to them. Upon return to their home in Lille, they saw the German SS had taken everything movable, and what they could not use they destroyed. Thus, Uncle Charles and Aunt Irma had to start from scratch at a time when just about everything in France was rationed or not available anywhere. Irene wrote relatively happy letters from different places in Western Germany since she was now working for the American Red Cross and moved her detachment wherever the 9th U.S. Army units needed support. Every letter ended with her prayers and hopes that she would be able to get her papers approved so she could come to America and be reunited with us. We could tell from reading between the lines that she was very homesick. I also longed for her. It had been almost eight years since we were together as a family. Eight long years where she didn't know if we were alive, or vice versa.

In the meantime, the world was trying to heal its wounds from this terrible war that had caused the suffering and death of approximately 70 million people. The trial, perhaps the most important trial of the century, began November 20, 1945 in Nuremberg, Germany. There 22 high ranking German officers and henchmen of Hitler were being tried for the most heinous of war crimes and crimes ever committed against humanity. The tribunal was made up from the four

EXHIBIT 15.7 Irene as an American Red Cross worker and her GI driver 1945.

victorious nations: the United States, France, Russia, and Great Britain. When the trial came to an end one year and one month later on October 9, 1946, only twelve officers were sentenced to death by hanging. To my regret and outrage, seven received lesser sentences and four were acquitted. However, investigations and trials of individual Nazis and collaborators continued in many localities and in many European countries. I asked myself, "Will the world be able to punish all those men and women responsible for the indescribable crimes they committed against defenseless people?" I was listening to the news on the radio and reading the newspaper for answers. Justice was served when I heard that the Nazi Gauleiter, civil administrator over Luxembourg, hangman Gustav Simon had committed suicide in prison December 18, 1945. Dr. Freitz Hartman, in charge of the Gestapo in Luxembourg, who created a living hell for Jews he incarcerated at the Convent Fünfbrunnen, was condemned to death and sixteen officers of the German secret police were found guilty and sentenced ten years of prison during other trials.

From my hometown Mannheim the news was sobering. What were the inhabitants' rewards for pursuing their vile activities and persecution of Jews which lead to the murder of at least 2,262 of their own Jewish Mannheim neighbors? What were the rewards for the people of Mannheim for clamoring and enthusiastically supporting a war of German world domination? What was their reward for having disowned and disenfranchised all of the city's Jews, and making an additional 4,300 of them exiles in other countries around the world? Did they, the Aryan superior race of Mannheim, think they could get away with their unworthy and despicable deeds? No, they did not get away with them, and their reward was nothing but a humiliating military defeat which cost them dearly. According to Mannheim's own chronology, their rewards were grim. They endured 151 heavy aerial bombardments during which a total of 2,000 civilians died. In addition 10,000 soldiers originally from Mannheim's families were killed on the front lines by Allied soldiers whose fighting ability they once had belittled. To this figure must be added thousands of wounded for whom I could not find a statistic. Nor could I determine how many German soldiers from Mannheim were taken prisoner, some of whom ended up in Russia, and did not return until 1955. It should be pointed out that there were 20,000 Allied prisoners of war and foreign laborers who were required to do whatever work needed to be done in and around Mannheim under the most difficult conditions and under inhumane treatment.

Hitler, realizing that he could no longer win the war, had given the order to institute a "scorched earth" policy. What American artillery and bombs did not destroy, German soldiers and civilians were encouraged to render useless. On March 22, 1945, the Mayor of Mannheim Carl Renninger who was responsible for the great Nazi Renaissance by making the life of defenseless Jews untenable, fled with his Nazi cohorts to Babstadt near Sinsheim hoping to escape judgement for their bigotry, evil deeds and misguided fanaticism. Unfortunately, Renniger was not convicted for his hate crimes. Too many of his cronies testified for his goodness, thereby saving their own skin. When the artillery was lobbing shells into the city, reality of their cowardly conduct had set in. Ironically, an American medical doctor, Captain Franz S. Steinitz, who fled Nazi Germany in 1937 for America, was instrumental in bringing about the surrender of Mannheim on March 29, 1945. Chronicled from accounts in Mannheim (freely translated): "When people came out of their basement and bunker, one could tell what they had experienced (during days and nights of bombing). Many were visibly emaciated looking very tired. The "Heil Hitler" greeting was gone (as if swept away). Several houses that once flew Swastika banners had white sheets on their flagpoles. Most of the Nazis no longer wanted to be reminded of their past. They were glad that they were left alone. Most of them pretended as if they had never been Nazis."

Not much of Mannheim, as I remembered it, was left. The relentless bombing of the city during the nights of September 5 and 6, 1943 and the heavy bombing September 3, 1944 and again March 1, 1945, totally destroyed 50% of the buildings including factories, communications and transportation infrastructure. The two buildings where we had once lived were heaps of rubble. Only 5,250 of the 21,000 buildings in Mannheim were nominally damaged and could be repaired. The inner city was a field of rubble. All of the physical destruction had added to the personal losses and the resulting suffering. The grief was not worth the twelve years of being the "master race." Their national anthem, *Deutschland, Deutschland Über Alles, Über Alles in der Welt*, "Germany, Germany greater than everything in the world," was no more! Of this German national hymn, only the third less controversial verse is heard and sung today.

EXHIBIT 15.8 Mannheim after the destruction by American and British air attacks; streets have already been cleared of rubble. See the appendix for photos of Mannheim's memorials to its murdered Jews, exhibits 15.9 and 15.10.

There was no glee in my heart, no happiness, nor was I jubilant finding out the physical damage that had happened to my former hometown, the city that I had once loved. Yes, I still have very fond recollections of the city of Mannheim, but not of the people that tormented me, my family and others. They, and all the Germans who participated in the crimes to humanity, deserved what they got in the end and more! Their excuses that they "did not know," or that they "had to follow orders" were bold faced lies that left me cold and totally unsympathetic. They had participated willingly, each trying to outdo the others. The final dark curtain had come down over Nazi Germany's armies of hatred and atrocities. In the end, they begged for their lives. It may have been the historical conclusion of the war and Holocaust, but for me there will never ever be an end or closure. Even when I die I will take the sad memories of the Holocaust with me into my grave!

October 1954 saw the installation of a memorial at the Jewish Cemetery in Mannheim, consisting of a huge urn standing on a pedestal with the engraved inscription (freely translated): "to them who found no burial." It took until November 2003 for a memorial sculpture to be erected at a prominent busy pedestrian spot in the heart of downtown Mannheim. It consists of a glass cube a few inches short of 10 feet by 10 feet by 10 feet, and bears the names of 2,240 Jews. They are the names, determined as of 2003, of those former Mannheim residents who perished (murdered) at the hands of the Nazis. My research determined that the number of those who perished was more in the neighborhood of 3,691.

I doubt whether it is ever possible to determine the exact number. Similar memorials were erected in cities and towns all over Germany and other European countries as testimonials of guilt of the German people, but do little to tell of the suffering and torment the Jewish people experienced.

Back in Chicago, my schoolwork plus my early night job became more strenuous as time went on. What must have taken a native born Chicago high school student one hour of homework, took me at least two to two-and-a-half hours. I did the best I could during the week and studied additional hours on weekends. I would take the South Shore suburban train each afternoon to Van Buren Street Station in downtown Chicago, from where I walked an additional six or seven blocks to the Main Chicago Post Office, now referred to as the "old post office building," a huge building by the river. Since 1996, the building with its 2.5 million square feet of space sits empty since a new post office building has been built. In winter it was a quite cold, windy and tiresome walk, which I had to walk twice each day. Sorting the mail for four hours was strenuous, but the break helped. I would always get myself a chocolate milkshake at the cafeteria to perk me up a little. At the end of my shift I was glad to get back to 71st street by train, walk another 3 long blocks home and hit my bed between 11:30 p.m. and midnight, exhausted from the day's activities. Mom and Dad were by that time asleep and so it was that some days I did not see them at all until the weekend because of our conflicting schedules. However, I made about $56 per month, less tax, which helped toward maintaining our household. After several weeks though, I began to realize that I could not continue this fatiguing schedule over a long period and looked in the paper for other job opportunities.

One day I saw a small ad in the paper: "GERMANS NEEDED. The Army Air Forces wants approximately 200 persons capable of translating scientific and technical information from captured German documents for work at headquarters Air Materiel Command, Wright Field Dayton, O. Veterans are preferred...report...13th floor 211 E. North Water, today or tomorrow." I had no idea where "Dayton, O." was and assumed it was

> **'Germans' needed**
> The Army Air Forces wants approximately 200 persons capable of translating scientific and technical information from captured German documents for work at headquarters, Air Materiel command, Wright field, Dayton, O. Veterans are preferred. There is no age limit. Applicants should report at Chicago Procurement field office, Air Materiel command, 13th floor, 211 E. North Water, today or tomorrow.

EXHIBIT 15.11

Oregon, Ohio, or Oklahoma. In any event, I went for the interview as soon as I could. It went well and I was asked to fill out an application "Form 57," which was then to be reviewed for my qualifications. After that I would be notified whether I was accepted for the job. I had no idea of the salary, but did find out that the job would be temporary. When I asked various questions during the interview, such as the availability of housing and how long the job would last, I was told that they did not have that information available. Now the wait for a reply began. When I researched information on Dayton, I seem to remember that it said to be a highly industrial city with a high percentage of owner occupied homes, and a population of 250,000. The big issue was whether I wanted to move away from my folks and whether this would become a hardship for them or me. On the other hand when Irene eventually would come to live with us, there would be some difficulties. Ours was only a one bedroom apartment, and I was sleeping most of the time on the floor in the dining room since I had a hard time getting used again to the soft daybed. We had talked about this matter and thought that Irene could sleep on a roll away bed in the living room. Additionally there would be a problem with only one bathroom for the four of us and insufficient closet space. Considering all those angles, it seemed that my moving out would be a good solution. However, I didn't have to make a decision yet since I had no job offer in my hand.

While Mom and Dad had a busy work schedule, there was not a day when they didn't buy things or pick up some food or clothing items from relatives and friends to send overseas to our loved ones in France and Luxembourg, including of course Irene. However, it was primarily on weekends that the actual buying, gathering, packing and mailing took place. Dad would also take clothing and food staples in bags to his place of work. He had boxes and wrapping material there since he was a shipping clerk and bookkeeper working for Uncle Ernst and Uncle Herman. Everything the Ehrlichs had in their home was gone when they returned from their temporary exile hiding at the priest's home, and the children Claude and Eliane had grown out of their clothes, which were difficult to buy. I remember that Mom and Dad had sent a boy's suit to Claude for his bar mitzvah. During the week our dining room table was crammed with stuff, and pieces of paper indicating who would be the recipient. Packages also went to Uncle Berny and Aunt Marthe, as well as Uncle Eduard and Aunt Julie and others. How wonderful it would it have been had we been able to send packages to other relatives, but they had not survived the murderous hands of the Nazis. Those agonizing thoughts were always with me.

Irene was doing all right in her American Red Cross job, attached to the Headquarters of the 9th Army. She had gotten most of the necessary papers together, including affidavits, birth certificates, and other certificates from the French Government, a visa from the American Consulate and money for the ship passage to come to the United States. Her Red Cross unit had followed the American troops as they advanced through France and into Germany. I was always looking forward to her letters and of course would always add a few lines to the letters that Mom and Dad wrote to her and the other surviving relatives.

Best of all were the letters I received from Gertrude, who would write at least once a week and so would I. Once a week, mostly on weekends, we would talk to each other on the phone which was always very exciting for me and I was looking forward to hearing her sweet voice. My guess is that I had fallen (madly) in love with her and hoped that she felt the same way. Gertrude had returned almost a year earlier from Richmond, Virginia and was back in Lawrence, Massachusetts, and living with her parents. She was working full time at the Marum Knitting Mill Retail Store, 15 Union Street in Lawrence, and her letters were full of details of her daily life. My letters to her at 57 Jackson Street likewise told about my daily routine, which in my opinion was rather monotonous and to some extent frustrating. At least she had graduated high school, whereas I was still a *Dummkopf*, a dummy, still trying to catch up.

EXHIBIT 15.12 Gert's mailman brought her a letter every week from me.

Of course there were other letters which Mom and Dad had kept for me to read. What interested me quite a bit was the fact all of my cousins, some of whom had managed to escape the clutches of Nazi Germany, others born in the U.S., had served heroically in the Armed Forces of our Allies and the United States. Herbert Isaak, who passed away at age 81 on November 18, 2001, the son of family friends Emil and Therese Meier Isaak of Mannheim, served as a field commissioned Second Lieutenant in Europe, and was present at the Nüremberg War Crimes Trial. He and his sister Lotte were immigrants from Mannheim. Herbert was together with my father at Concentration Camp Dachau. Another cousin, Helmut Isaak, the son of Ida Kahn Isaak and Julius Isaak, was fortunate to escape from Aschaffenburg and became a *chalutz*--a pioneer at a kibbutz in Palestine. He volunteered for the Royal Air Force (R.A.F.) and served in the North Africa and Mediterranean theater of war. He was a crew member of No. 614 bomber squadron when he suffered injuries during a flying accident and had to ditch the plane at sea. This occurred August 14, 1944, 20 miles off the coast, according to the official letter sent to his mother in San Francisco by Group Captain C. E. Maude. Helmut's brother Norbert had the opportunity to leave Germany and come to America in late 1937. He joined the Army Air Corps during the war in 1941 and served four years, participating in the liberation of Western Europe. He saw action at Casablanca, North Africa, the invasion of France as part of the Airborne troops, the battle of Bastogne, and wound up in Berlin. He was among one of the first to find my sister Irene in Lille, France and sent word to my parents that she had survived. He passed away late September 2001.

Henry Mayer, born as Heinz Mayer from Laufersweiler, is a cousin by marriage to Lorie (formerly Hannelore) Lerner, from Eberswalde, Germany. He was with the 2nd Engineer Combat Battalion and experienced the D-Day landing at Normandy, and the Battle of the Bulge. He died of cancer in the summer of 1998. Both of my American born cousins, Herbert and Lawrence Kahn, sons of my Uncle Ernst Kahn and Aunt Leone (née Freudenberg), served in the U.S. Army. Herbert was drafted in 1942, and received an injury during the fighting in the Hürtgen Forest, Germany. After hospitalization in England he went to OCS, Officers Candidate School, and served as a Lieutenant with a Graves Registration Unit until his discharge in 1946. Lawrence, being the younger brother served in the Army at the end of the war from 1946 to 1947. Luckily he was spared from overseas duty and the mental and physical agony connected therewith.

Richard Sinsheimer, American born and happily married to my cousin Alice (née Danziger), enlisted 1942 in the Army Air Corps and served as part of the ground crew as an electronic equipment specialist; He advanced with his squadron as a Tech Sergeant from North Africa to Italy and then France. Alfred Berney, formerly of Wiesbaden, Germany, who had been incarcerated in the Dachau concentration camp, was in the Army attached to a tank battalion. I don't know whether his unit went overseas. However, when I was in the Darnall General Army Hospital, Danville Kentucky, he came to visit me from Fort Knox, not too far away, where he was stationed.

My cousin, Ernest Kahn, the son of my Uncle Simon and Aunt Hilde who escaped Mannheim with his family in 1938, joined the Navy and saw action in the South West Pacific off the Philippine Islands. His ship was located at the Island of Samar while I was hospitalized in Manila, the capital of the Philippines. However, we were unable to meet. His brother Walter, who was several years

EXHIBIT 15.13 Henry Mayer and Lorie. Lorie is the daughter of Martha Lerner (née Kahn).

EXHIBIT 15.14 Herbert Kahn and his wife, Sylvia. Herbert is the son of my Uncle Ernst Kahn and Aunt Leone.

EXHIBIT 15.15 Lawrence Kahn and his wife, Bette. Lawrence is the son of my Uncle Ernst Kahn and Aunt Leone.

EXHIBIT 15.16 Richard Sinsheimer and his wife, Alice. Alice is the daughter of Aunt Bella (née Kahn) and Uncle Alfred Danziger.

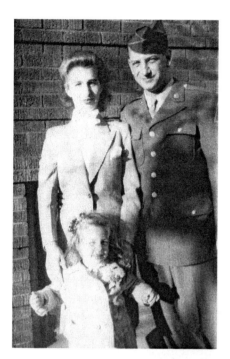

EXHIBIT 15.17 Alfred Berney wife Rosel and Marguerite.

EXHIBIT 15.18 Ernest Kahn and his wife, Marilyn. Ernest is the son of my Uncle Simon and Aunt Hilde Kahn.

EXHIBIT 15.19 Walter Kahn and his wife, Barbara. Walter is the son of my Uncle Simon and Aunt Hilde Kahn.

younger did not see military service because of his age. The military service of my cousin Henry Hanau, formerly Heinz, with the French Forces and the heroism of Georges Joseph with the partisans in Italy have been described earlier. Most of Gertrude's cousins also served, as well as both of my future brother's in law, Lester Salten, formerly Ludwig Strauss from Iserlohn, Germany who was married to Gertrude's sister Ilse (née Wolff), and Albert Poll, who would later marry my sister Irene. Lester went into the Army in 1943, received his basic training at Camp Lee, Virginia as I did, and his stationing there was the reason why Gertrude had come to Richmond, Virginia to see her sister. Lester served with an organization that was to become the military government of the occupied territories. First stationed in Birmingham, England, later after the invasion he was stationed somewhere in France and finally in Mainz, Germany. Lester passed away after a long illness in February 2002.

Irene was still working for the American Red Cross in one of their Field Service Sections. She had moved around quite a bit which turned out to be good experience, and as she put it, a real adventure. Her work was mostly to keep American soldiers informed, help to arrange emergency furloughs, loans, and deliver joy, grief and messages of sorrow to individual soldiers. Above all, she was able to improve her English. After traveling back and forth to the American Consulate in Paris, she got all her papers, including her affidavit, and was ready to come to America. Finally, she received a telegram with her visa from the State Department, in Washington D.C. This enabled her to board the troop ship, the SS *Washington* on February 17, 1946 at Le Havre, France with 7,000 American GIs on board. She and about fifty other civilians, mostly women, were restricted to their respective quarters for the journey for "safety" reasons. Too many men, very few women!

When the ship finally docked at Staten Island in the evening of February 21, George Washington's birthday, immigration officials made her pay port tax which she thought she had already paid. Since she didn't want to pay the high duty on a bottle of French liqueur, she poured the liquid out on the dock, but paid for the champagne she had brought along. Uncle Simon, my dad's brother, was there to welcome her and boarded her for the next three weeks at his and Aunt Hilde's apartment in Brooklyn. Cousin Walter showed her New York, while his older brother, Ernest, attended optometry school. She also visited friends and relatives she hadn't seen in many years, and contacted wives, and parents of GIs to convey personal messages.

In the meantime back in Chicago, Mom, Dad, and I were anxiously awaiting her arrival and to be reunited again as a family. Finally, on March 15, 1946 Irene arrived on board the Pacemaker train at La Salle Street Station. She wanted me to be there in my Army uniform, and I obliged, but never wore that uniform again. It was an emotional happy occasion, not having seen each other during seven

EXHIBIT 15.21 United once again a happy family with Irene. The painting on the wall, now framed, was bartered from a German POW at Darnall Army Hospital.

scary and eventful years, and having been separated since 1935, a long eleven years. Reporters from the *Chicago Times* took some photographs and interviewed Irene, and the story and pictures published in several newspaper editions (see exhibit 15.20 in the appendix). However, the story as it appeared had many of the facts wrong. Mom, who had stayed at home to prepare a good meal, cried as usual because of unbelievable happiness and excitement to have her daughter back, alive. It was so wonderful for our small family finally to be together again.

It had been a long day for all of us and preparations had to be made for Irene to sleep in the living room on a roll-away bed. It was kind of crowded but all of us were very happy and managed. Life went on as before while Irene became acclimated to life in Chicago. There were several weekend receptions with uncles, aunts, cousins and friends invited to meet Irene. Mom always went all out to bake, cook, make our small apartment hospitable and do so with great pleasure and etiquette. But, quoting Irene: "They all talked about the good life here, no one asking about my life under the Nazis, or how I survived. I spent much time in Mom and Dad's bedroom crying." I remember very well experiencing similar situations after we arrived in America five years earlier. While I too found it rather odd and somewhat puzzling that no one ever, not even until today, asked what we had experienced, I tried not to let it bother me. Perhaps our American relatives didn't realize that we had escaped a certain genocide that had awaited us which ultimately took the lives of nineteen of our loved ones and millions of others.

After a couple weeks, Irene got a job at the University of Chicago Press through the Jewish Vocational Service at a weekly salary of $28.00. In comparison, Irene had a much better grasp of the American language than I had upon my arrival in the U.S., as for eleven months she was employed by the American Red Cross in Europe, and she had an excellent opportunity to learn English by communicating with her superiors, other Red Cross workers, and most of all the GIs for whom she served. Finally I was receiving my first monthly check from the U.S. Veterans Administration of $57.50 for a 50% military Service connected disability. The money came in very handy to support our household and make payments to Uncle Ernst who had paid for our ship passage. The V.A. also offered me vocational rehabilitation which I did not accept since I did not want to pursue a trade or go back to work as a machinist or something similar.

Irene and I didn't get to talk to each other very much except on weekends, when the family and I were usually not tied to work schedules and I to morning and afternoon classes. By the time I would come home from my night post office job downtown, it was usually close to midnight, and everyone was already asleep. Even then I had to be very careful and silent to come into the apartment because the entrance door opened immediately into the living room where Irene slept.

EXHIBIT 15.22 Irene with helmet in Red Cross uniform on VE Day, May 8, 1945 and two of her fellow workers in American-occupied Germany.

I had almost given up on the government job I had applied for when to my surprise I received a letter notification from the War Department indicating that I should report on July 1, 1946 to the Headquarters AMC (Air Materiel Command), Wright Field, Dayton Ohio. The "position" was a Temporary Appointment at T-2 Intelligence, Air Documents Division as a Translator (Technical Data) CAF-7, at a salary of $3,397.20 per annum. A provision in my letter of appointment provided a travel authority and reimbursement of transportation costs. At first, I was surprised and stunned, but after a few minutes I realized that this could possibly be a first step out of my immediate predicament, perhaps on to a more normalized life, and the beginning of a brighter future. After sharing the news and engaged in a lengthy discussion with Dad, Mom and Irene, they all agreed reluctantly, especially Mom, that I should accept. I was glad that I had their blessings and was looking forward to my new venture in life.

Since I didn't have to report for another few weeks I kept on going to school and in the evening pursued my job at the post office. It was the night of June 5, 1946 as I was leaving the post office building that I heard the shrill noises of fire engines mingling with the drawn out sound from ambulances which seemed to come from all directions. Then I could smell acrid smoke, and as I looked into the sky I saw the big fingers of flood lights crossing each other and lighting up the dark clouds in the direction of La Salle and Madison Streets. Curious to determine where the fire was I headed in that direction and was aghast and frightened to see the rather old but luxurious La Salle Hotel ravaged by unbelievably hot flames. The hotel was well known for its sumptuous Blue Fountain room, which I had never seen, but had heard about. As a matter of fact, I had never been inside the hotel. While the area was cordoned off, I was still able to witness several people jumping from windows to their certain death. It was a horrible sight and later robbed me of a good night's sleep after coming home. The papers next day told of sixty one people who lost their lives, a tragedy no one could have foreseen. It left a lasting impression of Chicago before leaving for Ohio.

CHAPTER SIXTEEN

Away from Home and Marriage

The train that took me from Chicago to Dayton, Ohio stopped several places on route plus a half-hour layover at Indianapolis and an engine switch. Of course I was very anxious to get to my destination. However, it ultimately took seven hours for an estimated three hundred miles including the layover.

Union Station in Dayton where I arrived was not very impressive. I proceeded with my suitcase to the corner of 6th Street and Main where I hailed a cab; about 25 minutes later the cab delivered me to Headquarters Air Material Command, Wright Field. The reception area was a rather large wooden structure, more like a warehouse, where I had to fill out several forms and was given a map of the base and another one of the surrounding area. I had been assigned a shared room in the barracks area known as Skyway Lodge, room #142. An Army bus drove me to that particular building, one of several hundred that all looked alike, and all looked similar to the barracks I had lived in during my basic military training. It was referred to as a men's dormitory.

My room was perhaps 11' x 11', had a single bed on each side, a desk at the wall that was flanked by a window on each side, and a small closet for each of us. Not exactly what I had expected, but then, this was only my first day. A common bathroom was down the hall to be used by all men on the first floor. It had about ten toilet stalls, ten wash basins, and an equal number of shower stalls. Unlike in the Army barracks, there was some privacy. Also, there were a dozen or so ironing boards and irons for anyone's use. However, there was only one phone booth on each of the two floors in the building. If a phone call came in, a person in the vicinity at the time would answer the phone and had to walk to the particular room mentioned by the caller to get the individual on the phone. Those then were my living quarters for months to come. Oh yes, each room had its own key, and clean towels were delivered each week. After taking a little snooze, I went to find the cafeteria, which served meals that I considered just a few notches above regular Army grade. However, they served inexpensive warm meals. A few streets away was a small grocery store and a dry cleaner. For anything else I would have to take a public bus to the twin towns of Fairfield and Osborn, about 15 minutes away. I could never figure out which was which because the towns seemed to be intertwined. After a few years the residents decided to merge the two towns under one administration and Fairborn became the new name.

The next morning I reported to my place of work where I met my military and civilian supervisors, and was assigned a desk. Thereafter, I was briefed on security, security regulations, and the requirement for total secrecy about the type of work I would be required to perform, and with whom I was working. Now, after 70 years I suppose that I am no longer sworn to secrecy and can freely write about those years. The code word for the overall effort was "Project Paperclip," designed for the systematic importation into the U.S. of primarily (but not to the exclusion of other allies or adversaries') technology which had supported the Nazi Germany's war effort. It meant the examination and analysis of all their highly advanced research, production methods, and the testing and deployment of every type of military hardware. To this end a vast program had been set up to collect all types of records and patents from thousands of German companies, universities, research laboratories and manufacturers, including tests conducted on inmates of concentration camps. The Field Information Agency (FIAT) and the Office of Technical Services (OTS) were also involved.

To accomplish this huge secret undertaking, the U.S. military in the Pentagon had sent teams into all corners of Germany to entice (or where that was not possible, to grab) every German scientist, engineer, technician, doctor and industrialist and bring him to Wright Field, Dayton, Ohio, or to Huntsville, Alabama Space and Rocket Center, among other locations. These teams made great efforts to locate and confiscate any and all seemingly interesting or thought valuable equipment found in factories, research laboratories and proving grounds, pack it up and send it to the U.S. for analyses. At the same time, the Russians tried to similarly obtain scientific data, equipment, and the German scientists who had any knowledge about a given item or experiment. It became a race primarily between those two powers leading up to the Cold War, and it is hard to say today which side won.

There were about seventeen men and as I remember, three women in the office area in which I worked. Two of the men and one of the women were of Japanese descent. Later, I found out that there was also a requirement of Project Paperclip to review large boxes that contained captured Japanese documents, including microfilms containing information pertaining to their war effort and war material. There were also people with a Russian language background who worked on Russian language drawings, etc., captured first by the Germans and then again recaptured by American Forces.

After a few days, a meeting was held in a conference room where an Army Air Corps Colonel, Donald Putt, the man in charge of the entire Project Paperclip effort at Wright Patterson Air Base, and a Lt. Colonel, A. A. Arnhym, who had about a two-inch long dueling scar on his left cheek, spoke to us about the importance of our mission and the necessity of extreme secrecy. Arnhym, who had a very slight accent, must have been of German origin although I never found out.

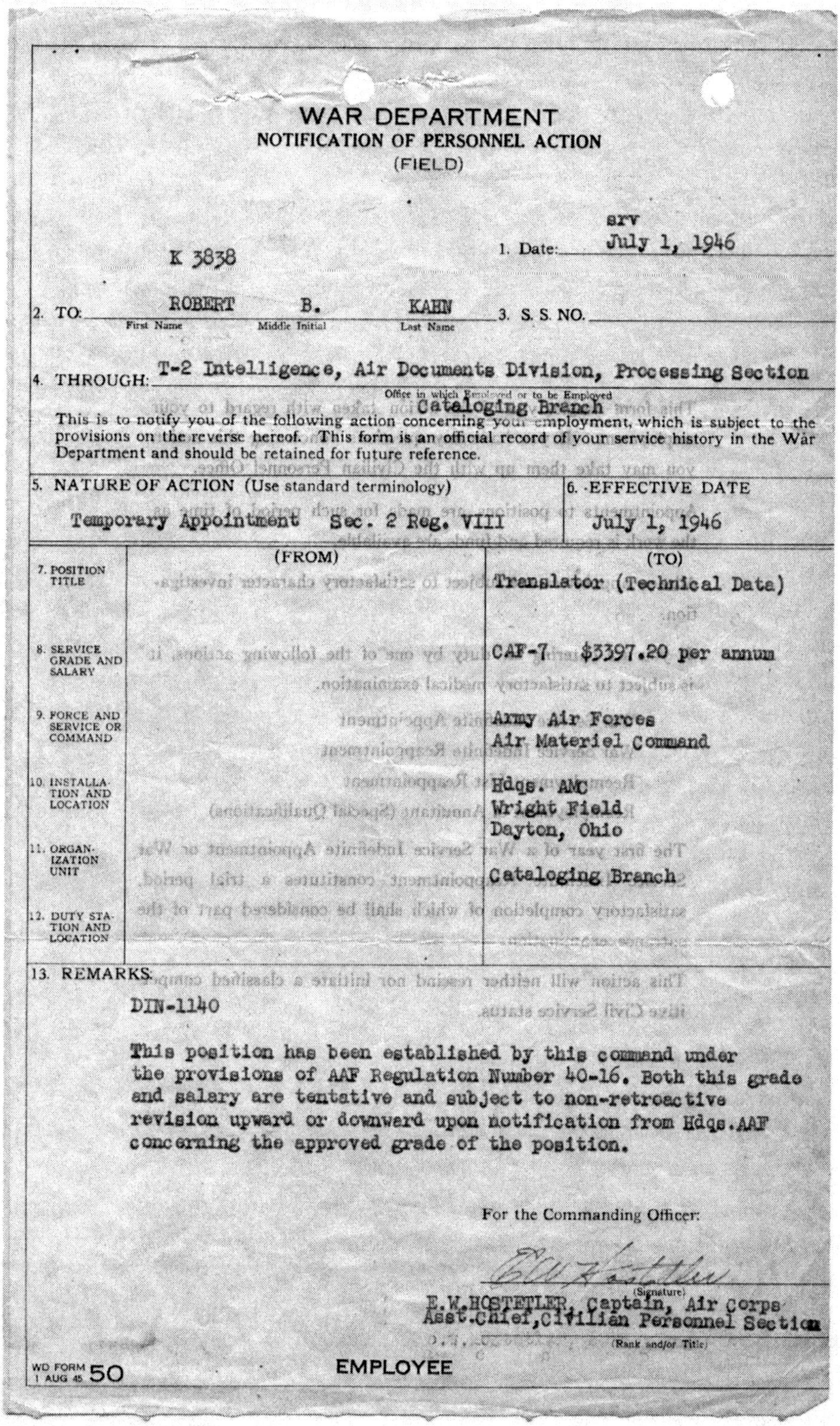

WAR DEPARTMENT
NOTIFICATION OF PERSONNEL ACTION
(FIELD)

srv

K 3838

1. Date: July 1, 1946

2. TO: ROBERT (First Name) B. (Middle Initial) KAHN (Last Name) 3. S. S. NO.

4. THROUGH: T-2 Intelligence, Air Documents Division, Processing Section Cataloging Branch
(Office in which Employed or to be Employed)

This is to notify you of the following action concerning your employment, which is subject to the provisions on the reverse hereof. This form is an official record of your service history in the War Department and should be retained for future reference.

5. NATURE OF ACTION (Use standard terminology)	6. EFFECTIVE DATE
Temporary Appointment Sec. 2 Reg. VIII	July 1, 1946

	(FROM)	(TO)
7. POSITION TITLE		Translator (Technical Data)
8. SERVICE GRADE AND SALARY		CAF-7 $3397.20 per annum
9. FORCE AND SERVICE OR COMMAND		Army Air Forces Air Materiel Command
10. INSTALLATION AND LOCATION		Hdqs. AMC Wright Field Dayton, Ohio
11. ORGANIZATION UNIT		Cataloging Branch
12. DUTY STATION AND LOCATION		

13. REMARKS:

DIN-1140

This position has been established by this command under the provisions of AAF Regulation Number 40-16. Both this grade and salary are tentative and subject to non-retroactive revision upward or downward upon notification from Hdqs.AAF concerning the approved grade of the position.

For the Commanding Officer:

(Signature)

E.W.HOSTETLER, Captain, Air Corps
Asst.Chief,Civilian Personnel Section
(Rank and/or Title)

WD FORM 1 AUG 45 50

EMPLOYEE

EXHIBIT 16.1 My employment contract.

While I resettled in Chicago, my correspondence to Gertrude had become one of the ritual highlights of my working day. In addition to writing each other just about every day, we called each other quite often. So I wouldn't have to have a pocket full of change to put in the telephone coin box at Skyway Lodge, Gertrude let me reverse charges, which really helped me a lot. We hadn't seen each other since we met in Richmond, Virginia before I went overseas, and we were itching to find a way to see each other again. But how? I assumed that I would be unable to take any time off since I had just started my job at Wright Field on Monday, July 1st. In just a few days, Thursday would be the July 4th, Independence Day, a National Holiday. If I could take Friday off from work, I would have a long weekend with the possibility of visiting Gertrude. I talked to my boss who explained that I could take Friday off without pay provided I would submit to him a request for leave on a certain form. I did, and he approved it.

Of course I had talked to Gertrude in advance about my plans to visit her in Lawrence, Massachusetts, and she was all excited that we would finally meet again after almost three years. There was only one big problem for me. I had sworn never to fly again after I had that airplane mishap in the Philippines. However, the flight from Dayton to Boston in a large commercial aircraft turned out to be a breeze compared with crouching in B-25 fighter bombers as I had been accustomed to fly in the South West Pacific. It was a plush and smooth flight that made me lose my prior fear and apprehension. Gertrude had given me information as to what train to take from Boston to Lawrence, but she hadn't told me that it would be a local train that would stop at every little hick town in between. I remember that all these stops made me kind of nervous and anxious. Finally I was there and Gertrude was waiting for me with open arms. It was a wonderful moment to see each other again, a very tender moment not very easily forgotten.

From the station it was a good walk but not too far from #57 Jackson Street, the address I had written at least several hundred times on envelopes over the past years. Gertrude's parents, Hedwig and Frederick were waiting to welcome me. Their small apartment was on the third floor of a building in which a doctor's

EXHIBIT 16.2 It was wonderful to see each other again.

EXHIBIT 16.3 Gertrude's parents: Frederick and Hedwig Wolff.

EXHIBIT 16.4 Uncle Richard Loeb and his wife, Florence.

office was on the ground floor. It was hot and there was no air-conditioning. Gertrude's sleeping quarters could not be considered a room but a cubbyhole, in the attic. There was only room for a bed and a chest of drawers, yet she had never complained to me or anyone else about this. I was appalled but said nothing. Through a friend of the Wolffs, I had a room in the adjacent house.

I could tell that the Wolffs lived very frugally. Mr. Wolff was employed at the Marum Knitting Mill, where he took care of time cards and made the payroll for approximately one hundred employees, while Mrs. Wolff repaired knitted socks at home, which had not passed inspection because of minor flaws. Only years later when I found out how little they were paid did I reach the conclusion that Mrs. Wolff's relatives who owned the mill probably took advantage of Mr. and Mrs. Wolff while they, the Marums lived high on the hog in mansions of nearby Andover.

Nonetheless, Gertrude and I had a wonderful time. We went for walks in the Commons, a park right across from where the Wolffs lived. We sat on a bench feeding the pigeons. We also walked to the mill and through the business section of town, where Gertrude introduced me to many of her friends and acquaintances. She also took me to the Italian owned Tripoli Bakery where they baked the best macaroons, and still do today. We had dinner at Fieldstone's restaurant with the Wolffs and Gertrude's Uncle Richard Loeb, a brother of Mrs. Wolff, and his wife Florence, who came especially from New York to meet me. The following day we took a bus to an amusement park at Canobie Lake, New Hampshire and had an afternoon of going on rides, eating ice cream and cotton candy, which I had never tasted before. We behaved as any two people madly in love. It was exciting and wonderful. Then on Sunday it was goodbye since I had to be at work again on Monday morning. It was a very short but an unforgettable, wonderful visit.

After about a week at my new job, I was summoned by my supervisor Mr. Bill Mintz and was told that I was to meet Theodore Zobel, a German jet aircraft specialist, in another building. My assignment was to record his research and experiments performed in Germany, some of which were on microfilm while others were on typed bound paper brochures. My job was not an easy one. The research accomplished by this man and another German engineer, Alexander Lippisch, was far beyond anything American aerodynamic engineers knew or were working on. Lippisch, whom I met briefly, had designed and tested delta wings, at the time something unknown here. One of the most difficult aspects of my assignment was that no equivalent technical English terminology existed to describe what Zobel and Lippisch had invented, tested, and perfected. I had to consult with aircraft designers at Wright Field to create an informal German English technical dictionary so I could convey the cutting edge aerodynamic and aeronautic achievements of these German scientists to our own engineers.

But there was a much larger problem, and it had impacted me personally in a way that I could not share with anyone else at the time. German engineers, of whom there was perhaps seventy-five or more at Wright Field at the time, were being viewed and treated by their American counterparts not as former adversaries, but as valuable pawns who could immediately contribute immensely to the advancement of the flying arsenal of the American Air Corps. After all, the Nazi Luftwaffe had shown itself far superior and far more advanced in aircraft design, performance, jet engine design, navigation, bombsight accuracy, aircraft crew rescue, survival equipment, as well as aerial photography. Even the German aircraft detection (radar) equipment, pilot-less reconnaissance vehicles and the manufacture of materials capable of absorbing electro-magnetic rays (radar) were new to the U.S. military. Most came too late to be implemented and was still in the experimental stage. However, I found out in due course that I was not the only one concerned about most, perhaps all of these scientists, who not so long ago had been ardent hard core Nazis, many also were wanted war criminals who had participated in human work exploitation, experimentation, and in some instances torture to achieve their scientific goals and production quotas.

The Office of Special Investigations (OSI) also had serious concerns about some of these imported Nazis sabotaging the very effort we were engaged in by giving us erroneous information and being intentionally uncooperative vis-a-vis interrogating personnel, like myself, or unsuspecting American scientific counterparts. Most of the so-called captured German engineers and scientists who were living in comfortable nearby off-base housing had not undergone the "de-nazification" process prescribed for all Germans by the American Joint Chiefs of Staff (JCS), and thus had escaped criminal prosecution through the court system set up for that purpose in occupied Germany. Here they were free, having slipped through the net of criminal justice while their criminal cases were still pending in Germany.

Because of these irregularities and my own intuition, I was naturally very suspicious, constantly on my guard, and really hated working with the German bastards. Yet, I told no one of my feelings. These thoughts did not develop in me over night, they developed after months working on this job under many varying conditions, working with different American and imported German mechanics, engineers, scientists, the latter with titles a mile long. Today we know that it was a tragedy when zealous Allied interrogation teams ignored the horrendous inhuman conditions at certain camps, test stations, production facilities, and laboratories run by the Nazi scientist henchman because it was deemed more important to acquire the know-how of Hitler's ingenious weapons, operating manuals, and the fiendish S.S. engineers behind them. We brought these callous men to Wright Field and other military bases in the U.S. and treated them like royalty, and for the most part, forgot or covered up their criminal past. Only years later were some of these men brought to justice, stripped of their American citizenship and deported back to Germany where they collected American social security each month.

I make no excuses: My original instincts were correct and hated their guts. How did all of this anger in me manifest itself? I will tell you a few episodes that got me in trouble with my bosses and resulted in my almost being fired from my job. One day, as I worked with one of the German scientists, his name I cannot remember, he proceeded to divert my attention to a letter he had just received which included several photos of his family back in Germany. "Herr Kahn, I want to show you pictures of my family." Having said that, he handed me the photos. Without looking at them I took the photos and tore them into pieces while telling him that our relationship was strictly confined to technical matters and nothing else! I He was surprised, became upset and reported the incidence to Col. Putt who called me on the carpet and read me the riot act.

It was Christmas 1946, and the Central Air Documents Office (CADO) organization of which I was a member had a party arranged at the Miami Hotel roof garden ballroom. The Miami, which was a beautiful hotel located at the corner of 2nd and Ludlow Streets, would later be imploded in 2001 to make room for what is now the Schuster Center, a beautiful theater for the performing arts. It was a dressy event and I had asked our office secretary, a girl by the name of Edna Bishop to be my date. We danced, drank, talked and ate. I had not realized that the German scientists with whom we worked were also invited. One of them, somewhat inebriated, put his arms around Edna, as she was sitting next to me, asking her to dance with him. She said no several times but he wanted none of that, and didn't leave her alone. I finally became angry. I got up from my chair, grabbed him by his shirt and started to beat him while using my pipe very effectively on his face and head. My immediate boss Bill Mintz, who was a big fellow, I estimate 6' 2", weighing about 225 pounds, finally broke up the fight. Again Col. Putt read me the riot act.

EXHIBIT 16.5 This, one of my favorite pipes, broke where the stem and bowl meet. Luckily it was repaired with a stainless steel band. It taught this "Kraut" a lesson in good manners he did not forget.

However since the incident happened off the military base, the Colonel had no jurisdiction and the case resulted only in a verbal reprimand. I still have the pipe which had been broken that evening in the fight as a souvenir of sorts. There would be other situations where I could not resist showing my disdain for these disguised Nazi criminals.

I am reminded of one other particular event, which took place in the base cafeteria at lunchtime. I had just sat down with my food tray at a table when three of my German scientist friends sat down at the same table, two places away from where I sat. At first I paid no attention until their loud German voices became annoying and I could understand what they were saying. Essentially, they were remarking how tasteless and badly prepared the American food was compared with the food they were accustomed to eat back home in good old Germany. The more detailed their discussions became the more they vocalized their criticism of the cafeteria and the food. I got really steamed and finally had enough of their arrogant nonsense. I got up from my chair, went over to where they were sitting, took their trays with the food and said in my best German: "If you don't like our food, you don't have to eat it!" Then I quickly took their food trays, and placed them on the conveyor where the food would go to the garbage cans and the dishwashers. My job was done! I had heard enough of their bitching and had helped them out of their misery. Again I was verbally reprimanded, except that both of my military bosses, Colonels Putt and Arnhym couldn't resist snickering as I walked out of their office.

With the arrival of mid-summer, the heat in my dorm room became often unbearable. There was no air-conditioning. However, there was always a letter from Mom and Dad, Gertrude, and sometimes from Irene, who had gotten herself a new job with higher pay at Time Magazine to answer subscriber complaints. She proudly told me of her $52 per week salary and excellent benefits.

The building in which the Skyway cafeteria was located had a lobby with chairs, a few couches and tables. Since it was comfortably air-conditioned, I would spend many lonely evenings there to write letters home and to Gertrude, who was still working at the Marum Mill retail store in Lawrence. We were getting paid every two weeks and my checks were $ 130.60, less $19.00 for federal tax. I sent $50.00 each month to Mom and Dad, the rest I needed to pay for my room, food, and a few miscellaneous things. I did my own laundry and ironed my own shirts. My weekly rent for my shared room was a reasonable $16.00. Most of my co-workers however had rooms off-base, somewhere else in Dayton. Of course they didn't send any money home, so they could afford the additional expense. Instead of taking the bus to and from the office, I took a shortcut through a large concrete culvert, which went underneath US Highway 444 and right into the base.

Some of the people I worked with, other than my supervisors, were Mr. and Mrs. Otto Fambacher, Dr. Patek, Miss Athenstadt, Miss Dorothy Berg, Mr. Leon Morokus, who spoke Russian, and Dr. Hausknecht, an eccentric who spoke primarily Russian, Polish, Rumanian and other Eastern European languages. He had been with President Roosevelt at the conference at Yalta, and lived at the Biltmore Hotel downtown Dayton. The ladies were primarily editing whatever I and others gathered together. Of course there were many other people in our office but their names are no longer in my memory.

I became friendly with at least four associates and would occasionally pal around with them on weekends. George Sonnenschein was a street philosopher of sorts; George Stark, who could not stay away from the booze; Michael Novak, who knew loads of jokes and years later became a chiropractor; and a fellow by the odd and funny name of Schimmelpfennig, who was an amateur magician. Each of them was single, and when we would go out on a weekend, we had a real good time, or should I say a blast. To get to the downtown area of Dayton, we had to take a bus or if we were all together we would take a cab and split the cost.

I liked Dayton with its wide streets and everything within walking distance. There were many restaurants, several very nice department stores, drug stores, banks, and many merchandise establishments. There were streetcars, or trolleys as they were called, going to different parts of town, making it easy to get around. There were also several movie theaters, nightclubs, and several elegant hotels. This was in real sense a "large small town," a far cry from the sprawling, dirty, and smelly metropolis of Chicago. There was a large firehouse at Monument and Main Street with a water fountain in front. Steel High School graced the same area with beautiful English architecture. Farther down Main Street was the ten story Rikes Department Store. If you couldn't find there what you were looking for, well, it just wasn't available. Other, but smaller department stores were Elder & Johnson, the Home Store, Adler & Child's, and a variety of ladies' fashion stores like Thal's, Donenfelds, and Zapoleon's. Then there was the Van Cleve Hotel with its elegant Mayflower dining room, the Miami Hotel with the Purple Cow restaurant, and the Biltmore Hotel. Restaurants I frequented on Main Street were the College Inn, the Esquire, the Green Mill, the Golden Pheasant, and the Seville on West Second Street.

I also enjoyed going to the five large movie theaters, the Lowes, the Keiths, the Colonial, State and Victoria theaters, all of which had variety shows in addition to first rate motion pictures. Most intriguing and enjoyable were visits to the Arcade, a big enclosed fresh food market under an enormous and beautified glass covered cupola, where one could buy fish, chicken, meat, vegetables, baked goods, on and on. I would often buy a sandwich or some Milwaukee hand cheese (*Handkäse*). I can still remember at least three Gallagher Drug Stores downtown, each with a sit down soda fountain. It was great to be downtown.

Friday or Saturday evenings when the four or five of us Musketeers went out on the town, our first stop would be at a Jewish delicatessen on Salem and Grand Avenues, the Brass Rail, where we would order creamed herring as an appetizer. We would then walk to the next corner to Sully's Tavern for a couple beers, then return to the Brass Rail for our deli supper. It was so much fun and it got our minds away from the drudgery of working with the *Kraut* scientists. Next, we would go across the street and catch a trolley back downtown and visit Lantze's Merry Go-Around night club, where we would order drinks, dance with the girls and have a rip snorting good time before going back to our respective abodes.

As of this writing, all of the above mentioned places have disappeared except for the Biltmore Hotel, which has been converted into a low cost housing facility, and the Victoria Theater, which was completely remodeled, and restored to its former ornate splendor. Today the latter functions as a beautiful intimate theater where Gert and I have been volunteer ushers for eleven years. There is very little activity downtown anymore, especially in the evening, and the majority of shops have been replaced by office towers. The Arcade is still there but it is closed and nobody knows what to do with it. Almost everything has moved into suburban malls including the wonderful department stores, drugstores, restaurants and movie theaters. They say it is the price we pay for progress. I often doubt it! In its place we have produced a far higher rate of crime. Progress? Ha! No way.

There was plenty going on around the world and in our own country. Gertrude Stein, the famous but controversial American author had died; large bloody riots occurred in Jerusalem over the British plan to partition Palestine; the bombing by the Jewish underground of the King David Hotel in Jerusalem that was housing the British Army Headquarters, killing almost one hundred British soldiers and civilians; riots in Calcutta over British plans for India's independence; war between Chinese Communists and Nationalists; Nazi Herman Goering, former Minister of the German Air Forces, committed suicide before his death sentence by hanging could be accomplished; Russia's first nuclear reactor site went operational; French President Charles de Gaulle was voted out of office; the U.S. Supreme Court ruled segregation on public transportation illegal; labor strikes paralyzed U.S. harbors; atomic bomb tests were conducted by America off the Bikini Atoll in the Pacific; and on the lighter side, the play *Annie Get Your Gun* premiered on Broadway.

It was on June 21, 1946 when Gertrude's parents became U.S. citizens. Coincidental, it was also Hedwig Wolff's birthday and the couple's wedding anniversary. An important day for them. On July 23, while at work I had a relapse of malaria symptoms, accompanied with very high temperature and was taken by ambulance to the Veterans Hospital where I was treated and released again August 1. It was the first such occurrence since I was overseas and was told that this could happen again.

Not a day would go by that I didn't think and dream about Gertrude. It was more than just puppy love. I had given serious thoughts about marrying her, but had never broached that subject in my letters, nor had I ever discussed it with her on the phone, or on my recent visit with her in Massachusetts. On the other hand I was afraid that she would turn me down if I raised the question. Somehow we would have to meet again, and at that point just perhaps I would have enough nerve to ask her that delicate question. The plan finally evolved that we would meet in Washington D.C. on November 11, 1946, what was then known as Armistice Day, today renamed as Veterans Day. To satisfy the etiquette of the time, arrangements had been made that we were to be chaperoned by no other than Gertrude's sister Ilse and brother-in-law Lester, who lived in Richmond, Virginia, not too far away.

In order to spend the most amount of time together, going by rail was not an alternative for me, and getting there by air posed another problem, namely I had only a limited amount of savings and wasn't sure I could meet all the additional costs for the trip, hotel, and other Washington stay expenses. Reluctantly I asked my sister Irene to telegraph me $100.00 through Western Union directly to the Lee Sheraton Hotel, where we had made our reservations for three separate rooms. Luckily, I had to pay for only one, namely my room.

When I checked in at the hotel the money order which Irene had sent was waiting and that was a big load of my mind. The message dispatched by Irene with the money read. "You stinker you. Love, Irene." Exactly what that meant I haven't figured out to this day, although I have a pretty good idea. There was, however, one additional big problem and that was a huge carbuncle, a boil in back of my neck, which had been festering for some time and was full of pus. It was painful and the hot water in the shower gave me some relief. I had not told Gertrude about it.

Gertrude arrived by train. She called my room to say that she was in the lobby and so I rushed downstairs to meet her. It felt so natural and wonderful when we embraced and kissed each other as if we had done this many times. Of course we hadn't. What a wonderful meeting, and she looked so beautiful and alluring. Next I got to meet her sister Ilse and husband Lester Salten who had come by car. She was as petite as Gertrude, and Lester made up for it by being short, but somewhat on the heavy side. He was a traveling salesman for ladies coats and another of so many former refugees who had escaped from his hometown, Iserlohn, Germany. Sadly enough, his parents and sister who were left behind were murdered by the Nazis.

EXHIBIT 16.6 Ilse, Gertrude's older sister, and husband, Lester Salten.

Shortly after our meeting and a brief rest in our respective rooms, Gertrude and I went into the beautiful dining room. We both ordered steak tartare, a delicacy which we both liked at the time and enjoyed. It was a very romantic evening with dinner music and later a dance band gave us the opportunity to dance into the wee hours of the night. In the morning the four of us had breakfast together, and then Gertrude and I went sight-seeing. The hotel was strategically located at 15th and L Street NW, and was in walking distance of the White House, the National Mall, Smithsonian Museums, the Capitol, and the many beautiful monuments.

During the two and a half days of our stay, we did loads of walking and also visited the National Arlington Cemetery where we saw the changing of the military guard at the Unknown Soldier's Monument. As we sat on a bench near the White House, we saw President Harry Truman drive by in a convertible limousine. Although the time flew by like a hurricane, we talked about the future and us but not about our combined future as Mr. and Mrs., although there were circular discussions which intimated such a possible event. Gertrude seemed to understand and her body language was encouraging.

Before departing on Monday afternoon, we agreed that our next meeting would be in Chicago so Gertrude could meet my family. Our relationship had warmly progressed and I was satisfied with the direction in which it was moving. When I got back to Dayton, my roommate had moved out and that was fine. The room was rather crowded for two people and I preferred to be by myself and have some privacy. Irene seemed to be fairly happy in Chicago, having met a nice student at the University of Chicago on a Shabbat evening at Hillel religious services. His name was Nathan, or Nate for short, Diament.

My parents seemed to be doing well and Dad surprised me by telling me that he had bought a used maroon color Packard sedan automobile which made it easier for him and Mom to get around. Also, they had made the last payment to Uncle Ernst to reimburse him for the ship passage, without which we could not have come to the U.S. It appeared as if everything was falling into place and their life was a little less complicated and somewhat more relaxing. Yet the memories of the past and the loss of all their loved ones through the gruesome murder by the Nazis was never far from their minds, nor mine. Dad had started to write letters to different agencies, both here and in Germany, to find out more details of the relative's demise, their belongings, our belongings left behind, our business that stolen from us and bank accounts confiscated. He had engaged an attorney in Mannheim to assist in these matters especially since all sort of German laws applied. The immigrant newspaper *Aufbau* kept everyone informed of so called restitution issues.

Winter had arrived and the heat in the barrack where I was housed was insufficient and the rooms were always cold. At times it was so unbearably cold that on weekends I went into town and rented a room at the Holden Hotel, one of the cheaper places next to the Union Station downtown. The wooden barracks were not built for comfort and were not insulated, and the windows leaked air like an open barn door. During the week, going to the cafeteria to keep warm was the only solution. However on weekends the cafeteria building was closed.

Every couple months I would take the train to Chicago to warm up in more ways than one and enjoy Mom's good cooking. It was on one of those trips that I talked to Mom and Dad, and of course Irene, about my intention to marry Gertrude and suggested that she come to Chicago to meet them, and at that time perhaps we would receive Mom and Dad's blessings. I had a feeling that my parents would like her and wanted to be prepared to announce our engagement at that time. Dad asked the father of Sylvia Greenwald, who was engaged to cousin Herbert Kahn, to come over with some samples of engagement rings since that was the business he was in. I selected a ring that I liked and more important, a ring I could afford. That same evening I phoned Gertrude and invited her to come to Chicago to meet the family. I said nothing about the ring or our probable engagement. That was to be my big surprise. The train ride back to Dayton was uneventful but there was excitement inside of me.

My work at Wright Field was not getting any easier and my rapport with the German scientists was, to say the least, very strained. It was incredible what the German war arsenal had in development and on the drawing board. Had those secret weapons been brought into service earlier during the war, greater Allied casualties would surely have been the result and the war would have been prolonged. For the first time I had to contemplate filing a tax return for the year 1946. I received a withholding statement from the Chicago Postmaster Ernest J. Kruetgen for having worked there part time at night. Total wages were $626.97 for approximately 6 months, minus $55.30 in federal tax. The income for the other 6 months spent working at Wright Field amounted to $1,421.15, less tax of $203.80. It was not much of an income, but I was satisfied, getting by on it, even with the money I kept sending home. On top of it, I managed to save a little. My yearly salary from the War Department being on a temporary appointment to T-2 Intelligence, as a "translator of technical data" Grade CAF 7, was $3,397.20. It was on December 19, 1946, I received a certification from the Civil Service Commission for a 10 point Veterans preference. This was to give me a slight edge on other Civil Service jobs over non-Veterans on future job openings provided I had the necessary qualifications.

There was a Civilian Club on the base and I would go there with a few of my workplace acquaintances on weekends. There was also a canteen, and in a ballroom they usually had an orchestra and dancing. I would have a beer, a hamburger, enjoyed my pipe and listened to the tunes of the moment. "Laughing on the outside, crying on the inside," "Doing What Comes Naturally," "Sioux City Sue," "Prisoner of Love," and "To Each His Own" are some of the tunes that still today come to my mind.

In the meantime Gertrude was still working full time at the Marum Knitting Mill retail store. Her pride and joy was on January 8, 1947 when she was naturalized and became a proud American after being sworn in at Superior Court, Lawrence Massachusetts. The date which Gertrude chose to visit Chicago was April 12, 1947, still a few months away. While we corresponded and telephoned each other, Gertrude made plans to accompany me back to Dayton after her visit to Chicago. The purpose was to get to know me and each other better, and take stock of the city (unspoken: in which she would live after we were married). It was a somewhat gutsy decision of Gertrude and I am sure her parents had some justified reservations.

But sure enough things did not develop without a hitch. Again, on January 29, 1947, I was admitted to Wright Field Station Hospital with a 103.6 temperature, and shortly thereafter was transferred to the local Veterans Hospital, where I was diagnosed as having another relapse of malaria. I was there for about ten days before being released again. It was very scary for me, and of course for Gertrude. Would these relapses of malaria continue? Nobody could tell me. Could this possibly detract from our plans to become married? I hoped not.

Wright Field where I worked was, and still is today, a huge air base as well as an enormous research and development complex. Size, approximately 8,000 acres plus with a payroll of $1.25 billion yearly and many major military units stationed there. Roughly 30,000 people including about 10,000 civilians were employed there. Two thousand housing units were on the premises, and a total of 850 permanent buildings connected by about 120 miles of roads. Of course there were numerous active runways to accommodate every conceivable type of aircraft with an estimated 40,000 takeoffs and landings per year.

Our organization moved several times since I came on board. One of the reasons was growth of the staff, but the main reason was to increase security of the operation. From building 16B, area B where we were located, we could see one of the runways and all sort of experimental airplanes, such as the twin fuselage P-51 fighter; the newly developed F-84 jet fighter; the H-13 Helicopter; the B-36, which was a 6 pusher type turboprop engine experimental bomber. There were remote controlled B17 bombers with no crew aboard; and pilot ejector seats were also tested in jet aircraft over the runway. Then there was the flying and testing of all types of captured German and Japanese aircraft. Certainly, there was never a dull moment. At times it was pretty noisy, but I got used to it. For Daytonians', so I found out, it was a desirable place to work and everyone was jealous and curious of what was going on there.

For me it was a somewhat lonely life. Now and then, because of my terrible war time experiences, and the agonizing aftermath of the Holocaust, I still had some horrible nightmares, which is why several people who roomed with me had moved out. Then again I had some good dreams dealing with utopia, where a world was at peace with no nations at war, and people of all races and religions getting along with each other. I dreamt that diseases were under control and no one anywhere on earth was starving. It was the most wonderful feeling when I awoke after such dreams, not in a deep sweat, and not horrified as in other dreams that were nightmares.

At the office, going through reams of microfilm, journals, photographs and drawings, I learned that thousands of innocent people were murdered at Dachau concentration camp and other places in the name of science, while being used as guinea pigs. Some were purposefully infected with diseases while others were force fed with seawater to determine their rate of survival. Other experiments were conducted on "subjects" with oxygen starvation to simulate high altitude survivability. Many "test subjects" were exposed to high wind forces in open aircraft cockpits to determine their survivability. There were many records of people being submerged in sub-zero temperature seawater until they lost consciousness. And the list goes on, attesting to the Nazi bestiality. However, none of the German scientist bastards I worked with like Theodor Zobel, a jet aircraft specialist, nor Ernst Eckert, a jet fighter expert, or Theodor Knack, a parachute designer, admitted to knowing about any of such experiments with or on concentration camp inmates. They attested to have used volunteers supplied to them from prisons and hospitals without any coercion having been applied to them. I did not believe their stories but was not permitted to pursue that matter any further and to prove them to be liars. I was not privileged to read their dossiers although I asked for them since they were originally prepared by "Project Paperclip" recruiters.

Working with these war criminals bothered me much and was constantly on my mind. What infuriated me was that they complained about their imagined substandard treatment here in America and claimed that the barracks where they were housed were not fit to live in by people of their high standing. However, they had privileges in stores established only for military families, the so-called PX. At first, after their arrival at Wright Field, they were escorted into downtown Dayton to boost their morale. Later they were permitted to go unescorted. They had no shame or remorse for what they had done in Nazi Germany and ignored the fact that they, the German super race, had lost the war.

In the meantime, the news of the German Scientists at Wright Field spread like wildfire in the Dayton community through investigative newspaper articles. The results were picketers with signs at entrances to Wright Field, as well as small demonstrations by war veterans, Jews and Gentiles in downtown Dayton. Because of my job I could not become involved but was a silent sympathizer. Suffice it to state that the U.S. intelligence agents who brought them secretly to America, also suppressed their heinous past. Years later the Justice Department investigated many of these German Scientists and stripped them of their American Citizenship, which they had obtained by falsifying their background information. In other words they had lied about their Nazi past and specific criminal activities and involvement which over time had been brought to light.

In the evening hours and on weekends, I tried to leave my thoughts about work behind and occupied myself with correspondence and matters of my future life, which I hoped to soon change. My preoccupation concerned my forthcoming engagement to Gert and her coming back with me to Dayton. It raised all sort of questions for which there were no immediate answers or too many multiple answers. Where would she live? What would she do during the time until we decide to get married? When and where would we become married? Where in Dayton would we live afterwards? Would we be able to afford living as man and wife? Would our marriage succeed? These and many others questions were spinning around in my head.

After coming to America I had very little time to devote to my spiritual needs and seldom went to synagogue services, except on Jewish high holidays. During the war years in the military, there were only rare occasions when I could practice Judaism. Later, when I was confronted with the nightmarish happenings of the Holocaust and the terrible fate of nineteen of my loved ones, I became embittered and forsook the G'd who had forsaken them and millions of others. The horrible events of that period had made me skeptical that there was indeed a G'd, and I shunned the prayers which I learned well during my childhood and during my formative years. I had not set foot in a synagogue since I had arrived in Dayton. True, it was an impulsive response to the Holocaust and anger against the world. Now, with the beginning of a new chapter in my life, I felt that I had to reexamine my current attitude and the struggle toward my faith. Gertrude, on the other hand, was not raised by her parents with Jewish values, and knew very little of Judaism until she continued her education at the "Goldschmidt Schule," a private Jewish school in Berlin (it was unlawful for her to attend public school in her hometown of Neustadt). It was there that she went to a synagogue for the first time. I reasoned that because of her lack of traditional Judaism it would be fairly simple for both of us to decide on the extent to which we would dedicate our spiritual commitment.

These considerations were very important, especially if we would decide to raise a family. The latter was another mysterious point since I knew nothing about procreating, had never engaged in sex, and did not know whether Gertrude was better informed of the subject. Propagation of a family in those days was still treated as somewhat sacred, and not with gusto as it is today.

With utter excitement I took the train to Chicago having made reservations at a nearby hotel where Gertrude would stay since there was no room at Mom and Dad's one bedroom apartment. The latter was already crowded with Irene staying there, and me temporarily during my visit. When I picked Gertrude up at the railroad station, my pulse rate had increased very noticeably. She looked as adorable as ever and her smile was angelic. After arriving at the apartment Gertrude hugged my Mother as if she had known her a long time. In a way that was true because of my constant mentioning Mother and matters that had involved my family for almost the past four years we had known each other.

After Gertrude had rested up a bit she went into the kitchen where Mom was cooking a special, but typical Shabbat dinner. She stayed in there a long time and obviously the two of them got along very well. After while Gertrude, helped Mother set the festive Shabbat table with candles, the challah, and wine glasses. When Dad and Irene came home, we all sat in the living room and schmoozed so that everybody became better acquainted with each other. I was taking it all in, and was proud of Gertrude who was sitting there like a living doll.

All along I had the gift box with the engagement ring within eyesight. Earlier when I had asked Mom for the appropriate moment to present the ring, she suggested after the meal and before the dessert was being served, while I was itching to give her the ring right now. After the traditional prayers and customs for the occasion, the meal was served and everyone enjoyed themselves while eating and talking. I went out in the kitchen, asking Mom whether she liked Gertrude and whether she thought she was the right girl for me to marry. Without hesitation and a certain gleam in her eyes she kissed me and said "You have my blessings!" That's what I wanted to hear, and went back into the dining room. No, I floated back to the dining room. I was on cloud nine.

EXHIBIT 16.7 Gertrude is getting acquainted with Mom, Dad, and Irene over a game of cards.

Now it was time for dessert and Dad went to get a cigar. I went after him and asked him what he thought of Gertrude. His answer was a question: "Do you love each other?" I said yes! Upon which he said: "Then give her the ring!" It was tantamount to him saying yes. At least that's the way I interpreted it. You have no idea how emotional and thrilled Gertrude was as she slowly unwrapped the gift box with the seventy-point carat diamond engagement ring. She was very much surprised, elated, and before I knew what was happening, she put her arms around me and kissed me. It was the first time we kissed in front of my parents. If that was not enough pandemonium, Mom embraced Gertrude and so did Irene. Then, Gertrude gave Dad a hug, but making sure she wouldn't get burned by the cigar he was smoking.

The ring looked good and sparkled on Gertrude's finger. She turned her hand from side to side still somewhat shocked by the surprise, while she beamed like a child with a new toy. I had never seen her like that before and it made me very happy. Irene, Dad and Mom wished Gertrude *mazel tov*, good luck.

While having dessert all of us talked about various times of our past, celebrated the present with several toasts and the clanging of wine glasses, and the two of us talked a little about our uncertain plans for the immediate future. We both realized that it would be an unscripted adventure, but we were willing and strong willed to succeed. After chanting and singing the prayers after the meal, Gertrude made a call to her parents in Lawrence and conveyed very excitedly the news of our engagement. There were congratulations forth and back until everybody, including myself had a chance to get on the phone. The pitch of the conversation was high and the blood pressure of all of us was running above normal. I could tell that the Wolffs' were as excited and happy as we were. It was an evening vividly in my memory. Mother had spread the word about Gertrude's visit and asked the entire mischpocha and friends to drop in Sunday afternoon to meet her. It was nice to see everyone and to show off my fiancée and her ring. There were a lot of questions about Gert's family and Neustadt where Gert was born and raised. Of course I was asked about my job with the U.S. Government and told them basically that I was translating some German documents, but was careful not to mention anything about the true nature of my work, nor the German scientists with whom I was working since all of that was to be kept a "Secret."

During all the time I had worked with these unsavory Nazi characters I had never mentioned anything to Gert about them or about my utter contempt for them. After all, even the name "Project Paperclip" was highly classified, and I could not let my feelings interfere with my obligation not to reveal any details of my assignment. Everyone visiting that afternoon eventually gravitated to the dining room table where Mom had set up a wonderful variety of cakes, tortes, cookies, coffee and punch. She was an excellent baker and had always enjoyed entertaining. I relaxed and smoked my pipe with a highly aromatic "Whitehall" brand of tobacco which Mom always enjoyed. If that was not enough smoke, Dad, as well as Uncles Ernst, Herman, and Alfred were smoking their cigars. No one knew then for certain how bad smoking was on the lungs and how it would shorten their life expectancy. It was fashionable to smoke and we all enjoyed it.

I also met Irene's friend, Nathan Diament, a very intelligent and reserved individual who came from an Orthodox family background. He was a student at the University of Chicago, working on his Master degree in Business Administration.

The next day it was good bye to my parents, Irene, and Chicago, at least for a while. Dad drove us with his treasured maroon Packard automobile to the 63rd Street Station from where we took the train to Dayton. [

Both of us were exhausted from the whirlwind events of the past weekend and tried to relax. We ate sandwiches Mom had prepared for us and had fun with the conductor with whom on previous trips I had always asked whether it was more correct to say "the train slows up," or "the train slows down." It was kind of silly. But it was a good time to be silly. It was a long ride and I read a magazine which covered some of the important national and world news. The previous November, President Truman had abolished all wartime price controls and let supply and demand regulate the economy; a nation-wide coal miner strike was called off after the Supreme Court fined the Union millions of dollars while a nationwide strike by the telephone workers was crippling America's communication service; General Ike Eisenhower had become spokesperson for a nationwide drive to raise funds from the general public for the relief of the remaining Jews in European countries who had survived the Holocaust; in Germany, the U.S.

and British occupation governments arrested several hundred Nazi underground organizers; the war between the Nationalists and the Communists in China raged on; and because of attacks by the Jewish Irgun underground fighters on British soldiers and establishments, martial law was declared on Palestine's Jewish population;. Those were some of the major happenings in the United States and elsewhere.

When we arrived in Dayton I took Gert to the Holden Hotel where I thought she could stay until more permanent housing for her could be found. The hotel was right next to the Union Station, and not too expensive. However, those were the only advantages. The Holden was a second rate hotel and I was glad when the next day Gert moved to the YWCA. While I had to pursue my job, Gert went looking for a more permanent place to stay, and look for a job downtown at one of the stores. Researching in the local newspaper, she found a suitable room with kitchen privileges in a private home in the Belmont area, only a block away from the trolley stop. An elderly lady, Mrs. Earl Kinney, a widow, owned the one story Cape Cod type home on 2416 Mundale Avenue. One of the first priorities for Gert and me was to earn a sufficient income to pay for our living expenses and save enough to have a cushion for expenses that we would certainly have in the future. As much as I hated to do it, I wrote a letter to my parents that said with our plans to marry in the foreseeable future, I could no longer send money home from each of my paychecks as I had done in the past. Dad and Mom were very understanding and the matter was settled. In the meantime Gert had been hired at Donenfelds, one of the high-end ladies fashion stores downtown, 35-37 S. Main Street. She was happy, but had to work hard since she worked on sales commission. Getting together at her rented space was not always easy since first I had to take the bus downtown and from there, transfer to a trolley that would stop near her place. It would take me over an hour and a half. Coming back late in the evening or weekends would take longer since fewer trolleys and buses were scheduled. Often it meant that I didn't get much sleep and had a hard time staying awake on the job the next day.

EXHIBIT 16.8 Nate Irene's new friend, Nathan Diament.

May 13, 1947 was a big day for my mom and dad. They gave an oath to the United States of America and became very proud American citizens. June 15 was

EXHIBIT 16.9 Dad's humongous Packard.

an even bigger day for my parents because it was on this day that their daughter, my sister Irene, and Nathan Diament became married. Gert and I took the train to Chicago to attend the wedding. For me it was the first wedding I ever attended, and I kept my eyes open to see whether there was something that could be copied for ours. The wedding ceremony officiated by Rabbi Bernard Wecksberg and the festivities that followed were performed according to Jewish Orthodox traditions. Mr. and Mrs. Diament, the parents of Nate, as everyone called him, had arranged most of the wedding details at a South Side Chicago Hotel, including a small band which played the usual Jewish melodies. I was happy for Irene and for my parents. It was wonderful to see the newlyweds in their glory and the two sets of parents being proud and happy for their children. Afterwards Gert and I took the train back to Dayton.

Pretty much our routine, Gertrude and I would write a letter to each of our parents every week, and it was nice to receive mail from them and an occasional phone call. The Wolffs sent a number of packages with Gert's clothes to her new address since she had brought only what she could fit into a suitcase. She also had to work on Saturdays, whereas I did not. I would do my washing and ironing in the morning, and then meet her for lunch downtown, do some shopping for her and myself, and meet her later after the stores closed. Frequently we would see a movie or have supper someplace. The situation was anything but ideal, since we didn't have a car it was difficult to get around. Often we would not see each other during the week and our only communication was over the phone. A car was definitely on our mind, but it also had to fit our pocketbook.

There were a number of problems with buying a car. During the war years, cars were not manufactured for civilian use. Thereafter, it took months before conversion of production lines from tanks, airplanes, ships and other war material to passenger cars could be accomplished. By then, because of the pent-up demand, dealerships were taking names for delivery in six to nine months. This created a bonanza for car dealers who took money under the table to deliver a car earlier to the highest bidder. We of course could not afford that and so we looked for a used car. Since no cars were made during the war that meant that we had to look for a pre-war car, perhaps one of 1941 vintage. The other problem was that I knew nothing about cars, had never owned or driven one, except a jeep overseas in the jungle of New Guinea and the Philippines. Besides, I had no driver's license and could not test drive a car that we were considering to buy. We looked at many cars but could not afford the asking price. Finally we located a car for which the used car dealer wanted $750. It was a gray color 1941 Plymouth two door Club Coupe. Basically it was a two-passenger car with two very uncomfortable foldout seats in the back, which locked into place by putting a metal post into the floor of the car. In those days cars came with a manual floor shift, no power steering or power brakes, a lousy AM radio, a very poor heater and no air conditioning. A fellow at the office, Paul Cavenaugh, whom I had befriended came along, drove the car and thought it was okay. In short we bought the car for $ 725, a lot of money in those days and especially for us. We had about an equal sum left at Winters National Bank, which had a branch at Wright Field. Winters National Bank eventually, became Bank One, and in recent years merged with J. P. Morgan Chase Bank. Paul drove our new car back to my dormitory and parked it in front and soon thereafter I took out an automobile insurance policy.

EXHIBIT 16.10 Just Married: Nathan and Irene Diament.

The following Saturday and Sunday when most civilian activities were closed at Wright Field, I drove the car into the base and taught myself to drive and park. The next day I went to a registrar's office in Dayton to take a driving test so I could obtain my license. I was not surprised, just a little disappointed that I flunked the test based on my inability to park correctly and do it right the first time. What to do? The following day I drove to the registrar in Fairborn, which was at the police station. There the officer asked me numerous questions, and whether I was an ex-GI. I answered in the affirmative, then he asked whether I had driven any vehicles while in the military service, to which I replied that I had indeed. He said: "That

EXHIBIT 16.11 Our first major purchase, a 1941 Plymouth Club Coupe which we affectionately dubbed, "Junior."

EXHIBIT 16.12 Proud and happy.

will save me a lot of time and bother!" He then issued me a driver's license without having to take a driving test, and that was that. Still I was not sure of my driving ability and was very careful.

Now my life became somewhat easier. I was able to drive to see Gert almost every evening without wasting many hours taking buses and trolleys between my place and hers. The more practice I had driving, the more confident I became. With more practice I also became a much better driver. In addition I learned more about the mechanics of a car, the battery, the cooling system, the tires, and the oil. Yes, the oil became very important because as I found out, the engine burned a quart of oil just about every hundred miles. Occasionally on weekends, Gert would prepare a picnic basket and we would drive to Eastwood Park, not far from Wright Field, where they had a public swimming pool. We swam, sunned ourselves, relaxed and sometimes washed and polished "Junior." That's what we had named the car. Among the things that Gert's parents had sent was her portable radio which we also enjoyed listening to. Often we talked about our future and discussed an appropriate date for our wedding. Gert wanted the wedding to take place in Massachusetts and that was fine with me. Of course all of this had to be coordinated first with her parents then with mine. Making all the detailed arrangements over long distance by letter and telephone took a lot of time and effort for Gert but she didn't mind. The date was finally set for September 7, 1947 and slowly every detail fell into place.

Now with Gert being in Dayton, we had become acquainted with several other nice married couples, and others more or less in a similar situation as us. Having the car made it so much easier to meet some place, have dinner together, see a movie, or meet at someone's apartment to play cards. One of our favorite eating places was the Hungarian Village, a restaurant with good food and of course Hungarian violin music and singing. It was located on West Main Street, in a primarily black neighborhood, commonly known as the West Side. Yet during that period of time it was safe to go there. Not so anymore today. Among our acquaintances was Paul Frankfurt who worked nearby in my office. He was engaged to be married to a local, in my opinion and shared by others, very ugly girl named Isabelle. Then there was George Sonnenschein, single who also worked in my office, Lou Herz, married living in a small house in Dayton View, and several others whose names I don't remember. It was our first adventure at socializing as an engaged couple and it was fun.

Not knowing too much about the car, nothing about fixing anything, and worried about a possible breakdown, I decided to join the American Automobile Association better known as the AAA. They were located at the time on the second floor of the Gibbons Hotel, now the Dayton Grand Hotel, on the S.W. corner of Ludlow and Main Street. They also provided maps and created the best routing to wherever members wanted to drive to. This was essential for our upcoming journey to Massachusetts by car to become husband and wife. Of course there were loads of preparations, purchase of bridal gown, dresses, a suit and shoes for me, and many other apparel items for our trip, the wedding and of course our honeymoon.

I had already bought a wedding band for Gert in Chicago at the time when I bought her engagement ring, but there was no wedding band for me. I had an idea for my wedding ring and Gert was only too anxious to have one specially made for me with the design I had indicated. It was to be a gold band with both of our names cut out of the material. When it was finished it read BOB & GERT on a band about half inch wide. Even so the ring was reinforced on the inside it turned out later that the gold metal was too soft to withstand every day stresses. Therefore, after wearing the ring for about eight months after our wedding I decided to put this beautiful ring aside for fear that it would develop a crack. However, I would wear it on social occasions and for religious holidays. Gert had picked out another nice, but simple wedding band which I would wear instead.

A few days before we were to go on our trip the fellows in our office decided to give both Paul Frankfurt, also getting married around the same time, and me a so-called "Bachelor Stag" party. It was arranged to take place after working hours at Huffman Dam Park, just off US Route 4. There was food, a keg of beer, and everyone made sure that Paul and I never had an empty glass. At first it seemed like a fun party, but that didn't last too long. Every one of the fellows gave an impromptu speech and toast requiring the two of us to drink more beer. By design, both of us had become somewhat inebriated. The party became rough when the fellows ganged up on the two of us, stripped us of our pants and underwear, and with a red solution of Mercurochrome (an antiseptic) swabbed our private parts, although we resisted. I had gone through an ordeal that had never happened to me before and hope no one else will have to. It was degrading for me and Paul but the others had a good time. Despite being under the influence, I still managed to drive to Mundale Avenue where Gert roomed. She was appalled when she saw me in the inebriated condition I was in and stumbling around. Of course she had no idea what had happened. She brought me a cup of coffee which I promptly dropped on the living room floor making a big mess. I was embarrassed, deeply ashamed and apologized a hundred times for my behavior. It was the first time I had seen Gert angry at me and she had every right.

Finally she threw me out, told me to go back to Skyway Lodge and sober up. The next day I called, told her the entire sequence of events at the previous day's party, promised that it would never happen again, and asked for forgiveness. It took a few days, but she finally forgave me. All these years of marriage I kept my promise and have never been in that drunk condition again, nor did I drink again except on social occasions.

It was a difficult and time consuming job trying to remove the red stains left from the Mercurochrome on my skin and I stood in the shower for hours on end trying to rid myself of the discoloration. I drove to a drugstore in Fairborn, but even the pharmacist had no suggestion how to remove the awful red color. It came off very gradually and for days I spent more time under the shower and used more soap than I ever did in my life. My clothing and underwear, which had also been soiled had to be discarded since the stains would not disappear by using the most powerful detergents. At the office I pretended as if nothing had happened, although now and then the culprits tried to bait me with all sort of questions and remarks. I pretended as if nothing had happened. Paul Frankfurt however, chose to do otherwise and fell into the trap of being ridiculed and made fun of.

As our date for the trip east came closer, I equipped myself with maps and Trip Ticks put together by the AAA and studied them for hours. It seemed as if we were going on an expedition. Indeed it would be an arduous and exciting experience that neither Gert nor I have ever forgotten. There were no interstate highways and the AAA routed us on US highways and state routes all the way. Gert had prepared numerous individually packed sandwiches, a bag of fruit in season, a couple thermos jugs, and we loaded Junior up and left Dayton before sunrise in order to make the trip of an estimated 950 miles hopefully in two days.

We took US 40 toward Columbus, US 42 toward Cleveland, and US 20 along Lake Erie, passing Buffalo, New York, past the Five Finger Lakes area toward Albany and Troy. We stopped numerous times to stretch and rest a few minutes. A number of times we pulled into a filling station to obtain gas at 24 cents a gallon. The price included a complete check under the hood by the attendant who filled up the oil with one of the quart cans stored in my trunk. He also checked the air in the tires, wiped the windshield while Gert and I alternately went to the restroom. How things have changed over time. Today, I pay almost $3.00 a gallon and there is no longer an attendant. He has been replaced by a cashier and the credit card. The filling station of yesteryear, which also had mechanics that could do all sorts of repair work, has been replaced by do it yourself stations that are part of a large convenience store.

Automobile traffic was amazingly light compared with what it is today, and trucks were of much smaller size and did not dominate the roads. Driving in general was far more relaxing, enjoyable and driving at a top speed of 50 mph (where possible) took the strain out of driving. We drove through small towns and saw the rural life unfold in front of us. We pulled off the road several times, spread out a blanket, and had an improvised picnic. There were no state roadside parks and that worked out fine too. Now and then we were treated with unique poetry usually on six small red signs placed at perhaps hundred foot intervals along the side of the road. They sported white writing from the Burma Shave Company that manufactured brushless shaving cream products for men. They displayed very fascinating and humorous jingles in five parts, ending with a last sign concluding "Burma Shave." I wrote a few verses down years ago and stashed the paper away until today: Past /schoolhouses / take it slow / let the little /shavers grow / Burma Shave. And another one: Within this veil / of toil / and sin / your head grows bald / but not your chin / Burma Shave. The last one I wrote down: He played a Sax / had no B.O. / but his whiskers scratched / so she let him go / Burma Shave. Sometimes when we were driving near a city that had a radio transmitter we could listen to some music on the car radio. There was no FM program yet. Most of the time the radio would just crackle and after a while would fade out completely. The most exasperating part of the trip was driving through Albany and Troy, N.Y. because of the congestion through both cities while trying to find State Route 2, which would take us through the Berkshires to Massachusetts. With maps in hand, watching traffic and signs, we finally got onto NY Route 2 and into very twisting mountainous terrain which I had not experienced before. Constantly shifting into second and first gear to go up hill and likewise shifting while descending was hectic but the scenery made up for it.

We were now on the then celebrated and famous "Taconic and Mohawk Trail." Soon we passed the towns of Graven and then Petersburgh on the border between the States of New York and Massachusetts. It displayed some of the most picturesque views I had ever seen. We were at several thousand feet altitude and at every turn in the road a new more spectacular view of valleys with farms, churches and bridges unfolded, creating paintings of nature.

After we passed the picturesque town of Willamstown, we came to North Adams, and passed Mt. Greylock, 3,500 ft. high. It was late afternoon and we were tired, worn out by the driving, the unending beauty of the area, and thinking about where to stay overnight. Not until we had passed the famous "Hairpin Turn," did we notice a small motel at the Whitcomb Summit appropriately named after the Summit. It was fantastically located; a number of small cabins with a sign reading "Cabins for Rent." As I am writing this, Gert reminded me, not that I had forgotten, that we rented two separate cabin rooms, each costing $15.00. We unpacked the few things needed for our overnight stay and settled down in our separate cabins in the sky. Together, we finished up the last of our sandwiches, some fruit and cookies, sat on a couple of rocking chairs in front of our cabin and watched the sun set. Next we walked briefly to a nearby gift shop with a large tepee and totem pole, bought a few postcards and then turned in for a well-deserved night's sleep in our separate rooms.

We both awoke early and after I checked the car's radiator water, tires and engine oil, left for the final leg to Lawrence. Near Charlemont we stopped at a diner for breakfast, tanked up with gas, added another quart of oil to the engine and drove on, past colorful old houses, barns, old schoolhouses, and churches. We crossed quaint looking bridges and small creeks meandering into the valley below and enjoyed the magnificent views. The remainder of the trip was no less spectacular, but as we drove on the road became less mountainous and curvy passing and going through small and large towns, their names I had never heard off. We arrived shortly after noon at our destination, 57 Jackson Street, Lawrence and were happy that our long but beautiful trip had ended without a hitch, thanks to the one above and our car "Junior" which had done very well!

Is there such a thing as euphoria so overwhelming that partial amnesia sets in, making a recall of certain details impossible? Well, it happened around the time of our wedding. For instance I can't remember where I stayed overnight that weekend, although I know that I didn't stay with my future inlaws since they had only a one bedroom apartment. I do remember (as verified by Gert) that she stayed at Herta and Jülle Stern's house at 3 Kensington Street, Andover where we were to be married. Herta (née Marum) was a first cousin of Gert's. She stayed there because after Jewish tradition, we were not supposed to see each other until the ceremony. Gert had lived with the Sterns' some years ago when she went to Punchard High School and in return looked after the three Sterns' children,

Peter, Eva, and George. For that she got a small weekly allowance, learned to cook and received 10 cents an hour when she baby sat for other people, 15 cents after midnight!

I assume that I stayed at Shawsheen Manor at Andover where my father, my mother, my cousins Ernest Kahn and Steffi Zimmern, short for Stephanie, also stayed. Both had also emmigrated from Mannheim. While most Jewish weddings take place in a Synagogue, ours did not, partially because the Wolffs were not affiliated and because they could not afford the additional expense. My sister Irene and her husband Nate, to my surprise and sorrow, would not attend. Irene was unable to take time off from her job and Nate was studying for his Master examinations at the University of Chicago. Besides, the expenses to travel from Chicago plus hotel accommodations in all probability were too much for a couple that was just starting out. As mentioned earlier, they had gotten married in June, had to pay for a small apartment, and lived only on Irene's salary.

In the morning of our wedding day, Sunday, September 7, 1947, I got ready and all of a sudden realized that I had left behind a new black pair of shoes in Dayton. What to do? I telephoned Gert who made arrangements with a friend, Curt Kalmer, to bring me a pair of shoes. We met somewhere on the road to Andover and he gave me a box with the shoes. There was only one problem. When I finally put the shoes on and walked on them I felt a nail sticking out from the sole which I was finally able to hammer down so it would not bother me. It was an unnerving episode that in retrospect was kind of funny.

The wedding was beautiful. The chuppah, the wedding canopy, under which the ceremony took place was held high with four poles by cousin Arnold Marum, as well as Ernst Krakauer, Jülle Stern, Gert's cousins by marriage and Lester Salten, Gert's brotherin law. A large fireplace with flowers on each side formed the background. Betty Young, a good friend of Gert, wearing a lovely pink dress, was maid of honor. My cousin Ernest Kahn had the honor of being best man. Mother wore a pretty rose color dress and my mother inlaw, Hedwig Wolff, wore a teal blue dress. The men wore dark suits and, as was customary in those years, hats. I was the exception. I wore a traditional kippah, a small embroidered skull cap also known as a yarmulka. George Stern, about 5 years old and wearing a sailor suit, was our flower boy.

The large living room and the adjacent rooms and hall were overflowing with people when Rabbi Herschel Levin of Temple Emanuel, Lawrence, was ready to start the service. (Years later a new synagogue was built in Andover). At the first sounds of appropriate wedding music coming from a wind up Victrola record player, Gert, appeared like a queen at the top of the stairs. She was wearing a long light blue gown with accordion pleats from the waist down, with matching color elegant lace gloves up to the elbow. Her head was covered with a beautiful light blue colored veil, and she came slowly down the spiral staircase holding in her

EXHIBIT 16.13 Here Comes the Bride.

hand a beautiful bouquet of twelve white roses. It was a sight equal to the most beautiful sunrise, one not lightly forgotten, and I have not to this day. The rabbi recited several benedictions and blessings over the wine. After both of us drank from the same cup, each of us recited our marriage vows while I slipped a wedding band onto Gert's finger and she slipped that unique wedding band onto mine.

The rabbi read the socalled marriage deed, the *ketubah*, a written marriage commitment to which each of us responded in Hebrew and English. It was followed by numerous benedictions over a second cup of wine. The ceremony was almost concluded when I had to crush a drinking glass wrapped into a dinner napkin which had been placed under my foot, symbolic of the destruction of the Temple in Jerusalem. Finally Rabbi Levin pronounced us bride and groom and said: "You may now kiss the bride." I did! This was followed by applause and everyone in the room shouting "Mazel Tov! Best wishes! The best of luck! Le Chaim, to life!" We were now legally husband and wife.

There was a lot of hugging and kissing while my father inlaw's barber took a few more photographs and Harvey Lebow, Gert's cousin by marriage and Julius (Jülle) Stern signed the certificate of marriage as witnesses.

Later, shortly after noon the entire wedding party and relatives were invited to the Shawsheen Inn for a reception and luncheon, which Gert and I enjoyed with much excitement and considerable relief that our most important day went off perfectly. After a while we excused ourselves. Gert changed into a going away suit and I likewise changed into something more casual so we could leave for our honeymoon. When we loaded Junior, we noticed writing on the rear window

EXHIBIT 16.14 The Happy Couple.

EXHIBIT 16.15 The Wedding Party. From the left: Ernest Kahn, Betty Young, Hedwig Wolff, Frederick Wolff, Gertrude Wolff Kahn, Me, Martha Kahn, Joseph Kahn, and the flower boy, George Stern.

Gertrude Wolff, Collegiate Shop, married **Robert B. Kahn**, September 7, in a charming ceremony performed by Rabbi Hershel Levin at Andover, Massachusetts. The bride wore a pastel blue gown with a high, round neckline, lace mitts, a fingertip veil of blue illusion, and carried white roses. Her maid of honor, Betty Young, wore a pink gown; Ernest Kahn, New York City, was best man, and Frederick Wolff, father of the bride, gave her away. After a reception, the couple left for a honeymoon trip, which included Canada and Niagara Falls, before returning to Dayton. **Mr. Kahn** is in the Intelligence Division, Wright Field.

Mr. and Mrs. Robert Kahn

EXHIBIT 16.16

EXHIBIT 16.17 Junior is being decorated with cans by our flower boy, George Stern. No recollection what happened to the car's fender. Gert and I looking on.

"Just Married," and loads of cans tied with string unto the rear bumper. All of this was new to us, but we enjoyed the notoriety and fuss everyone made over us. After we had gone back into the dining room to say goodbye, everyone accompanied us to the Shawsheen Inn entrance where we received a shower of rice as we walked to our car. As we drove off with the cans hanging from the bumper making all sort of clanging noises, everyone was waving their handkerchiefs, an old German custom. We were finally on our way, filled with so many kinds of emotions that Gert had tears in her eyes. I had to keep my eyes on the road and on my map as we headed north toward the White Mountains and Canada.

We took State Route 28 through Manchester and Concord, New Hampshire, skirting Lake Winnipesaukee. It was in that general area that we lost the last can tied to our bumper. Then came Route 16, a beautiful mountainous road winding past Mt. Shaw, and the town of Conway with its famous Conway Scenic Railroad and ski resorts. We were getting very tired and started to look around for a place to spend the night. In those days there were no motels as we know them today; only privately operated tourist homes, inns, some of which had a restaurant, and cabins.

We came to Echo Lake State Park at an elevation of about 3000 ft., and saw signs directing us to an area with cabins. Since they appeared very inviting we stopped and were able to rent one for the night. The cabin was rustic, equipped with a pot belly stove and firewood, which came in handy the next morning to take the chill out of the air. I do remember carrying Gert over the threshold, which was funny to both of us, brought in our small suitcase and shortly thereafter "cuddled up" for the night. Don't ask what color nightgown Gert wore, the lights were out and it was dark. But I would almost bet that it was light blue and matched her wedding gown. I do remember that I still wore pajamas my mother had made for me in Europe. The color, I don't remember. But so that you the reader may get a laugh out of it, there was no fly in front of my pajama pants. It is my guess that it was less time consuming to make them that way. Gert and I still chuckle about this today.

The next morning we wanted to leave early but had to wait until the fog had cleared. At the town of Glen we took US 302 past Mt. Parker, 3000 ft. elevation. Mt. Washington, the highest mountain at 4700 ft. in New Hampshire, could be seen in the distance. The view and scenery were spectacular to say the least. On through the historically famous town of Bretton Woods, backtracking on US 3 to Franconia Notch until we came to a lookout where we could see the then famous granite stone profile of the "Old Man of the Mountains." The sight was very impressive and a thrill to see. It was the natural pride of New Hampshire and thousands of tourists like us would come to see this natural weathered phenomenon each day. In 1955, the U.S. Mint printed a 3 cent postage stamp featuring the Old Man of the Mountains. Unfortunately, the popular granite profile collapsed on May 3, 2003 after having weathered millions of years, and is now only a memory for those who traveled the area in prior years. More recently, in the year 2000, a quarter coin was minted honoring the lovely state of New Hampshire with the profile of the Old Man of the Mountains engraved on the reverse side.

Next we drove through Vermont and upper New York State, until we came to the St. Lawrence River, which we then followed northward along the scenic area designated as "Land of the Thousand Islands." After finally crossing into Canada, the engine having consumed about 14 quarts of oil since leaving Dayton, we arrived at our destination, Montreal. We stayed at a small hotel downtown and for breakfast the next morning I ordered steak, while Gert had an approving smile on her face. After breakfast we went sightseeing. Just as we had stepped off the curb on the corner of one of the main streets downtown after the traffic lights had changed to green, a car came around the corner at an excessive speed, brushing against me, spinning me around and continuing on. I ran after the car and told the driver off when she had to come to a stop at the next traffic light. A policeman who stood in the intersection came over to see what was going on. I told him what had happened and he proceeded to admonish the driver. In the meantime I thought better and left, meeting up with Gert again. It was not the time nor the place to become further involved.

We did a lot of walking and navigated some narrow uphill cobblestone streets where the sidewalks had steps like a stairway. We enjoyed window shopping the many different stores until we came to the plaza leading to the NotreDame Basilica. The resemblance to the cathedral of the same name in Paris, France was striking from the distance. As I recall, the interior was enormous, almost shocking: old gilding everywhere and beautiful stained windows. Behind the main alter was a fairly large wedding chapel. Had we only known a few days earlier! But then again we were not Catholics. The peaceful and beautiful architecture everywhere was one of the highlights of our one day of sightseeing in Montreal, although much too short. In the evening we were taken for dinner by one of Gert's second cousins, the Liebels. A couple by the name of Goetzel, originally from Mannheim and friends of my inlaws, joined us. We ate at a nice Chinese restaurant where to our amazement, the Chinese waiter spoke a few words of Yiddish.

The next morning we checked out of our hotel and were on our way to Niagara Falls via the charming city of Ottawa. We were lucky with the weather and had no particular problems with the car. As we passed through the city of Ottawa we noticed that some of the more prominent buildings had copper roofs which had oxidized over the years and looked impressively green, but we did not stop to admire them closer. We drove on past Toronto and finally reached Niagara Falls, staying overnight on the Canadian side. What a shame that we didn't have more time to sightsee all of the attractions. Neither one of us had been allowed more time for a socalled vacation, or should I say honeymoon, from our place of work. In addition, we had very limited funds and surely would have run out of money. Credit cards and ATMs had not been established until many years later and everything was more or less on a cash basis. Fortunately, I had several American Express travelers checks left. With some of the money we decided to buy a souvenir, a very colorful porcelain candy dish which we still use today. The pattern name on its backside reads 'Trellis Rose" and was made by James Keat Ltd., in London, England. The Falls were spectacular and the views from every angle very dramatic. At the time, seeing the falls was the "in thing" for newlyweds and for us it was very romantic. Today couples go elsewhere and Niagara Falls is no longer revered as it was then. After staying for two nights, which gave us a full day to admire the rushing water, the rainbow over the foam, the mist, and the beautiful flowers of the surrounding grounds, we were on our last leg back to Dayton. It would take another two days of hard but enjoyable driving.

We had experienced a lot, and seen wonderful parts of our great country, during an all too short whirlwind tour, which we have never forgotten. Best of all was that Gert and I had tied the knot for a bright future and a bond of love and happiness that would be unshakeable and wonderful. Our marriage had given our lives a new meaning, renewed hope for a future which we were clamoring to shape into something special and beautiful. If we couldn't reshape the entire world into harmony, peace and happiness, we could certainly try to build that kind of world immediately around us. There was no other option in our mind than to succeed. And today, as I write this and reminisce about the past, I feel that together we have accomplished and perhaps even exceeded our lofty goals.

CHAPTER SEVENTEEN

New Branches for the Family Tree

Everything must come to an end. Dad used to say, "even the Wurst, the sausage comes to an end!" True, after you eat it! The honeymoon was over and now the reality of our marriage was coming to the foreground. I was looking forward to continuing our love affair and our combined lives like a man lost in a dark tunnel finally seeing sunlight in the far distance. Our one bedroom with only a single bed, which Gert had rented when she came to Dayton, was no longer an option for two people. I had no problem sleeping on the floor with a blanket and a pillow. I was used to sleeping on hard surfaces while in the Army. However, I was not prepared to live like that for too long. Gert's landlady, Mrs. Kinney, had given me permission to move in and stay there until we could find something more suitable. In addition, the three of us now shared one bathroom, the kitchen, and the wash tubs in the basement. It was to say the least very awkward and uncomfortable, but we made it work and were very happy newlyweds.

Upon my return to the office at Wright Field, I found out that there were big reorganizations in the works. This all on account of the U.S. Congress decision to eliminate the Army Air Corps and create a separate military service, namely the "United States Air Force," under the direction of General Carl Spaatz. The Corps had finally been recognized for its enormous contribution to the victory of World War II, and for its significance to the future of air warfare. The Air Corps had finally evolved into its own.

Rosh Hashanah, the Jewish New Year, and Yom Kippur, the holiday for atonement and fasting were approaching and that seemed like a good time to begin my spiritual homecoming and the beginning of a religious awakening for Gert. There were three congregations in the city of Dayton. One ritualistic orthodox, Beth Jacob on Kumler Avenue, the other conservative, Beth Abraham on Wayne Avenue, with a new home under construction on the corner of Salem Avenue and Cornell Drive, and a reform synagogue, Temple Israel at Emerson Avenue. We decided to visit Temple Israel. Although I had been brought up with conservative religious values, I thought that it would be more acceptable to Gert who had very little background in Judaism and could not read nor understand Hebrew. While everything about the synagogue and the congregation was new to both of us, we found everyone very hospitable and warm toward us newcomers. We introduced ourselves to Rabbi Selwyn D. Ruslander and developed an immediate rapport given to his friendly countenance, and who displayed a sincere interest in us as newlywed newcomers to the city and Temple Israel. We decided we would give Temple Israel a try provided we could afford the dues. In retrospect we made a wise decision and have not regretted it since.

At the end of 1947 we had to file an income tax for the first time as a couple, and it was fairly simple since none of us had a complicated income scenario. My income from Headquarters Air Materiel Command, its official designation, was $3,644.48, minus $546.80 federal tax withheld. Gert had to report her income from Elder & Johnston Co. $1,637.69 and $234.17 taxes withheld. In other words our combined net income was $4,501.20 and even with that we were able to put some money in our joint savings account. Hard to imagine that with that meager income we were able to pay for food, rent, clothing, automobile and health insurance, and some limited entertainment. We lived like proverbial misers, but were very happy.

It was February 4, 1948 when I presented my "Certificate of Eligibility and Entitlement, under the GI Bill to continue my education to Mr. Thompson, Principal of Parker High School of Dayton, located across from Memorial Hall on East Second Street. It has since been torn down. Before coming to Dayton I had earned a total of 9 high school credits from attending school in Chicago, and needed 7 additional credits to earn the equivalent of a high school diploma. You may remember from previous chapters that the Nazis deprived me as a Jew the opportunity to finish my secondary education in Europe and had no chance until after being discharged from the Army to start playing catch up. Now 24 years old, married and working full-time, I started again going to high school twice a week in the evening. It was tiresome considering that I had to study and take tests like any other full-time high school student. It was hard and often overwhelming, especially in winter time with driving in the snow and icy roads, often coming home around eleven p.m. dog tired.

From the very beginning of World War II, all industries in the Dayton area were cranked up to produce war material. Since Dayton was a highly industrialized city, being the home of National Cash Register (NCR), Fridgidaire, several GM plants, numerous tool and die shops, foundries, meat processing facilities, and of course the Air Base of Wright Patterson, it had attracted thousands of workers from surrounding cities and States needed to fill the many newly created defense jobs. NCR had been converted to produce aircraft parts and the effective Colt .45 revolver; the Dayton-Wright Airplane Company produced the DeHaviland-4 airplane; and the General Motors plants produced over two million M-30 machine guns.

Dayton, after the war was known as having a very high percentage of owner occupied homes and a very small number of apartment or rental units. No new houses could be built during the war years, and a tremendous scarcity of rental units or just rooms was the result. Because of this unbelievable housing shortage there were almost no for rent ads in the newspaper. Whenever an ad appeared, people would stand in line in front of the building to be sure they would get the first chance to rent. Prices were sky high and deals to snag a unit were often made under the table. Our chances were as good as everyone else's, but we had to move faster than everyone else.

One early morning in April 1948, I had gone to the corner to buy a newspaper as usual, and saw an ad for a two room apartment in an area that was convenient to Wright Patterson and transportation for Gert to get downtown where she worked. By seven o'clock the same morning, we rang the bell at an old two-story home at 1233 Huffman Avenue. Mrs. Hapner, a widow who lived there with her five children, showed us the rooms which were upstairs. The furnished bedroom was spacious and faced the street. The other room had a beat up sink, an old fashioned gas oven, refrigerator, a steel wall cabinet, a chrome table and two non-matching chairs, a closet and enough room to make it a combination kitchen and living area. The bathroom, which we would have to share at times with the family was off the hall, between our two rooms which were not adjacent. There was another bathroom downstairs which the family would use most of the time. It certainly was not an ideal setup, but it was an improvement over where we were living. We paid our rent for the week in advance and were relieved that we had finally found a more suitable place to live after struggling for six months in very cramped quarters.

We bought fumigation canisters for each of the two rooms, closed the windows and let the chemicals do their work. Next, Gert and I cleaned the rooms from top to bottom, bought sheets, pillow cases, and a blanket for the bed so we would be able to sleep for the first time in comfort. We didn't have much stuff to move and that was certainly an advantage. Over the weekend Gert bought some cute curtains for the windows of our "kitchen-great room" combination and bought two cheap wicker chairs with colorful back and seat pillows. At the grocery store, we found two wooden orange crates which Gert uniquely covered on all sides with some material that kind of blended in with the wicker chairs. They became nice accessories to store a few books, my pipe and tobacco, Gert's cigarettes and other things for which there was no other room. The free standing sink was kind of an eyesore. My own interior decorator Gert, sewed a skirt and attached it to three sides of the sink so that the pipes under the sink were no longer visible. A disgustingly blah looking kitchen and sitting area had been transformed into a room that looked sort of cute, and we were pleased with our very humble and rather austere surroundings.

As we sat there one evening relaxing from the pressures of our respective jobs, I saw a mouse running from under the closet door along the wall of the kitchen. I took a broom and chased that poor animal, probably as surprised as I was, around the room along the baseboard. After an exciting chase I had finally immobilized and killed our little unwelcome friend. I don't remember whether Gert was cheering me on or whether she was making shrieking noises for other reasons. In any case it was an evening both of us have not forgotten.

Back in December 1947, Gert had to look for another job since there was a reduction of sales personnel at the department store and she was let go. Fortunately, with her experience in sales, she was hired at Thal's Ladies Fashion, 35-37 South Main Street.

Housekeeping as a married couple was relatively new to both of us, but we managed very nicely. Whatever we needed during the week I could easily pick up from the nearby grocery store on the way home, and still be home half an hour to forty five minutes earlier than Gert. She would normally give me some instructions on what to start preparing for supper, and would give the meal its final touches when she got home. However, there were many awkward culinary moments, one of which stands out in my mind. I was to heat up the soup, a meat dish as well as a can of sauerkraut. We were not as completely set up in the kitchen with the necessary cooking utensils dinner and tableware as we are today. When I looked for a large long handled spoon to stir the sauerkraut I only found a large salad spoon made of red plastic. After stirring the kraut, I sat down and read the paper, not realizing what would happen to a plastic spoon when left in hot food. When Gert came home and the two of us finally sat down to eat, we complimented each other on a delicious tasting dinner. Only several days later when Gert could only find the salad fork but not the spoon, did I realize that I had left it in the hot sauerkraut and it had melted. Both of us were very concerned, but then laughed aloud wondering whether we now had a plastic lining in our stomach. We are still wondering today! Luckily we did not get sick on account of my stupidity.

Several weeks after we had moved into our new place on Huffman Avenue, Gert was informed by the employment office at Wright Field that her earlier job application was approved and to report for work on a specified date. Both of us were extremely happy because now we could drive to and from work together. Besides, Gert's pay would be somewhat more than what she was receiving at the fashion store downtown where she earned a small salary and worked on commission. Her new job title was "Bilingual Clerk" and her place of work would be at the Technical Library Area B, within a short distance from the building in which I was working. It was a win-win situation.

During the previous winter and now during spring months, I had various appointments at the local Veterans Hospital where different doctors reviewed my progress against the post-traumatic stress disorder left over from my war time experiences, and illnesses, superimposed on my traumatic experiences and the aftermath of the Holocaust. I always dreaded these interviews because basically the doctors seemed to have no clue as how to help me or anyone else with similar conditions. They would ask loads of questions, record them as well as my answers, and that was that. Ever so slowly I was adjusting to a more satisfying life, yet the wartime memories lingered on and the nightmares became a bit less frequent. Although it would scare Gert when I screamed, shook or talked in my sleep. My happy marriage had become an important factor in my state of recovery.

With all the things we had to do to keep our small household afloat and other things we had obligated ourselves to do, there were very few evenings that we could sit, relax, and listen together to news and music on Gert's portable radio. It was standing on top one of the orange crates transformed by Gert into a piece of furniture. Gert would relax with an occasional cigarette, and I would smoke my pipe. She would write one letter a week to her folks and to mine as well. Sometimes I would add a few lines but not all the time. Our parents would respond in kind. Occasionally I would see Gert read from a book with a red cover. For a while I didn't know what she was reading, but one day nosey me looked, only to find out that its title was "Marriage & Sex." It became a very important book for both of us because we wanted a child and had to find out all about it and the how.

The world was still suffering from the war's aftermath but the Marshall Plan pumped American financial aid into the European countries for their recovery, and was very effective. The Dead Sea Scrolls discovered in Palestine in caves near the Dead Sea had become great news and a big mystery. Also at that time, the entire country was on edge hearing about the sightings of several extraterrestrial flying objects dubbed "flying saucers." Congress had debated and now ridiculed the continued usefulness of the so called "Spruce Goose," a gigantic wooden seaplane capable of carrying several hundred fully armed soldiers, and did all but cancel the contract with the Hughes Aircraft Co. in Culver City, California. The aircraft, the Hercules H-4 was the brain child of millionaire and eccentric Howard Hughes. It had eight engines, was 79' high, 218' long, with a wingspan of 320'. Hughes took the colossus on a short but successful test flight of about two km on November 1947, too late for deployment in World War II. Although one of the greatest disasters of the century had taken place while we were on our honeymoon, there were still many questions and investigations regarding the fire and chain-reaction explosions which had killed seven hundred people aboard ships and nearby oil storage facilities at the Port of Texas City, Texas.

There was however one unbelievable great joyous moment for Gert and me, as well as for Jews in the entire world, when on May 14, 1948 we heard the news on our radio that the Jewish State of Israel had been born in the land of our forefathers. A homeland had finally been established for all Jews and especially those who had become homeless and displaced persons because of the war and persecution by the Nazis. A dream of a thousand years had become reality. The Zionists had fought hard for this miracle to happen. I, Irene, my parents, my ancestors, and Jews everywhere had prayed for and expressed every year at Passover Seder in unison and with a loud voice: "Next Year in Jerusalem!" Our prayers had finally been heard and answered. Praised be the lord, Elohim!

Gert had started her new job at Wright Field in April at a CAF-4 rating with an annual salary of $2,394. Since our working hours were the same we were able to drive to work together and come home together. It simplified our daily routine. In front of the library building where Gert worked was a small water fountain and goldfish pond with a few benches on each side. Since we packed our lunches, we would meet there at noon and eat our lunch, provided the weather gave us that opportunity. In short it was an ideal situation.

It was on a hot July weekend when Gert's sister Ilse, and her husband Lester visited us from Richmond, Virginia. Since he was a traveling salesman for a ladies coat manufacturer, he had to have a large car to carry his sample line. Plus, his Lincoln model had air conditioning, something our car didn't have. We showed them our so-called two room apartment and could tell from their body language that they were not very impressed. We went with them for a ride to show them the town, had a bite to eat out and said goodbye to each other. We really enjoyed their brief visit.

Whenever we had some leisure time we read the newspapers or recent magazines. I also had some studying to do so I could earn my remaining credits toward my high school diploma. As usual there was a lot going on in our own country and the world over. The free world still bemoaned the assassination of the respected Mahatma Gandhi of India. On the scientific front was the development of the first transistor, which would later play a much greater role than ever anticipated. There were two other outstanding events which come to my mind. The first was the enormous Allied airlift to West Berlin, which was under a blockade by the Russians who let no food or other essential supplies into the Allied controlled zone. Beginning in the latter part of June, hundreds of Allied planes landed each day to deliver more than 8,000 tons of supplies needed by West Berliners to sustain their livelihood. The Airlift would last 15 months and at its peak landed almost 600 planes per day. The other event of great impact and importance was the decree by President Harry Truman to end all segregation and shameful discrimination in the military services. This executive order issued with much opposition would set the tone for other equality and civil rights laws in years to come and are a credit to President Truman as a true visionary statesman. Both Gert and I voted for him in November 1948 and he became our President for another four years.

We enjoyed our car and made our first trip to Chicago. It took us 11 hours since most of the way we were on two lane roads which at best could not be traveled at more than 50 miles per hour, even though the average speed was more like 40 mph. It would not be for another ten years before the interstate highways would be started. We made many rest stops along the way. It was a very exhausting trip although the AAA had furnished me with detailed routing information. Of course everyone was glad to see us and we enjoyed showing off "Junior," our car, which by now was approximately seven years old. In those days cars needed a lot of attention. The metal was beginning to rust and we decided to have the car repainted. It was a cheap process but it would last through a few more seasons, especially winter. Every thousand miles the car required oil and filter change as well as the lubrication of many fittings. Before winter, the radiator had to be drained and filled with a mixture of antifreeze and water, and snow tires or chains were required when it snowed a few inches. Batteries were not made to last and had to be checked periodically. Yes, driving a car was convenient, but also required much time consuming maintenance, especially when the car was not housed in a garage, which ours was not.

On weekends Gert and I would sometimes go for a ride in the car to while the time away, not really having a destination in mind. A few times we would drive to Cincinnati, which took a good afternoon, going through many small villages. Now and then we pulled off the road, spread a blanket and relaxed for a while admiring the quiet countryside. The pace of living was certainly much slower and less complicated than what it is now. It was peaceful and it felt great!

Mrs. Hapner, our landlady, had to take care of her five school age children. We never asked about her husband. In the morning, before she send the children to school, they all had popcorn and milk for breakfast. Bologna was another key food they would eat often at noon or supper. It was cheap food but not too nourishing. She may have been poor, but she was religious. On several occasions when we came home in the evening, entering from the front door into her living room, there were prayer meetings with many others present. We had to go through her living room in order to reach the stairway to our two room grandiose apartment. It was in those instances that we thought about and had dreams being in our own private apartment or house. We had been reading about Levittown, on Long Island where a Mr. Levitt was building hundreds of 750 sq. ft Cape Cod style homes for about $8,000. We were envious.

We heard from Dad that Berta Katz (Bertha, American spelling) née Cohen, a sister of my Uncles Max Cohen and Sally Cohen, had taken her own life on October 25, 1948. She and her husband Karl Katz were living at the time in New York. It was hard to understand that after surviving the Holocaust someone would choose this course. However, some people could not cope with their own family tragedies of the past, their own persecution, and the problems of their new life in America. Her brothers Max and Sally, and Max's wife Helene, my mother's sister, had been murdered by the Nazis. For the next few days it was much harder for me to work with the German engineer war criminals at the base. I hope that you the reader will understand that my wounded heart and soul had not healed by then nor have the psychological scars healed to this day. I hated their guts!

Sometime earlier I had written a letter to Mr. Brinkman in Mannheim at our old address. He was the caretaker of our apartment house then. I asked him whether he had found a violin in its case wrapped in a red bedspread. For a long time I did not hear from him. However, one day I received a large wooden crate through the mail. In it was my violin in its case still wrapped in that red bedspread just as I had hidden it in our attic hoping to save it from destruction by the Nazis. When I opened the crate I first was in shock momentarily and then in tears! The strings had all broken. The fine white hairs of the bow had separated at one end, showing the signs of neglect for many years. The bridge had fallen into the violin case, and the rosin was in two chunks. At last my long lost friend had come home! However, it was not a happy homecoming.

Whenever we went out for a bite to eat alone or with other couples we enjoyed the juke boxes which were installed in every neighborhood restaurant or tavern. For a nickel or dime you could select the latest tune from a great number of records stored in the machine. We had a gramophone machine, a big piece of furniture in our bedroom, which played 78 rpm recordings after it was wound up with a hand crank. Each record would play for approximately four minutes. Now and then Gert or I would stop in McGrory's five and dime store downtown, and pick out a new classical, semi-classical, or a big band record. Our favorite tunes then were, "Some Enchanted Evening" and "Bali Ha'i" by Perry Como, "Riders In The Sky," by Vaughn Monroe, and "Mule Train," by Frankie Lane. This was one of our pleasures and a genuine treat. In general we were very thrifty and tried to save as much as we could. It was not hard. Both of us had been brought up that way.

Combining our yearly incomes, my, $4,009, Gert's $1,657 plus $416 from the store downtown where she worked through spring, we had been able to save $800. We thought that was pretty good. Before the year's end I converted my $10,000 GI term life insurance to 20 year life. Which meant that on December 4, 1968 my insurance would be all paid up provided I would pay my premium each year on time.

Early on in 1949, Gert started to feel kind of physically odd and Doctor Philip Champion, located then at #1040 of the Fidelity Bldg. downtown, confirmed that she was pregnant. Both of us were very happy and so were our respective parents. We realized however, that our lives as parents would definitely change and as a first priority we would have to find a more suitable apartment. Fortunately we had time in our favor.

In the meantime the new Beth Abraham Synagogue building, at the corner of Salem Avenue and Cornell Drive, had been dedicated and since the service was a conservative, we had gone there on several occasions. The synagogue itself was modern and beautiful inside, with the most colorful stained glass windows

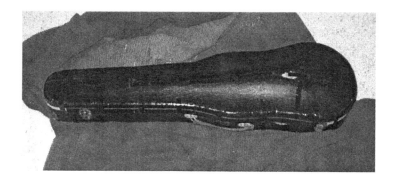
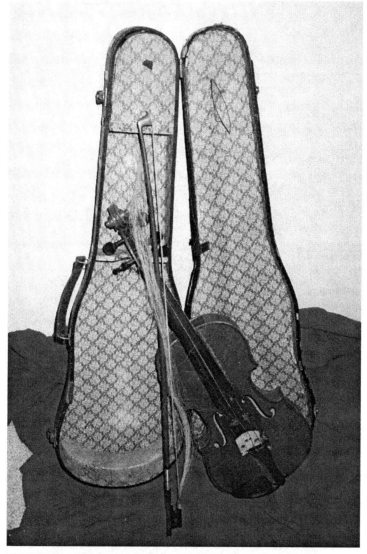

EXHIBIT 17.1 My dearest violin as I received it. Still in the red bedspread I covered and hid it in the attic November 10, 1938. Only many years later did I donate my violin to the United States Air Force Museum in Dayton, as part of a permanent Holocaust exhibit.

My Violated Violin

A package arrived of an odd shape
Held together with loads of tape

From Mannheim Germany it was sent
where I had suffered much torment

I opened it with apprehension and concern
While my fingers quivered, my face burned

A familiar black case stared me in the eye
Wrapped in a red bed spread with washed out dye

Gently, I opened the battered case and held my breath
My violin lay there, having died a thousand deaths

I lifted it from the worn out and mangled case
A look of great sadness came over my face

Tears rolled down my cheek, as I held it under my chin
My beloved, treasured, old, and time worn violin

The bow's white hairs detached, strings broken and unwound
The violin incapable of bringing forth any sound

Memories of the past came back to me
When I could play a beautiful melody

The amber colored rosin, somewhat pale
Stared up at me as if in agony and in dismay

The memories of that terrible day came back to me, as if lightning had hit
I put the violin back in its case, and tenderly closed the lid

Reminded of Kristallnacht brutality and terror, was sheer agony
Forced by Nazi Storm Troopers to serenade them, with my violin from the balcony

Below, in the yard, most of our belongings had been thrown and set on fire
My Dad was being badly beaten, while my mother was loudly crying

The crowd was cheering, our belongings gone up in flames
While I was playing the violin, as if in a trance

My father and I were herded through the city
Past the smoldering Synagogue, what a pity

Father was taken to Dachau concentration camp
Where thousands of other Jewish men were sent

After more than sixty years, hidden in attics and never sold
To me, the violin is worth more than all the gold

When my idea of creating a Holocaust exhibit came to fruition
It did not take long for me to make a tough decision

The once beautiful violin rests now peacefully in a glass case
So viewers can learn about Nazi cruelty, brutality, and unheard rage

The US Air Force Museum has given my violin a place of honor and dignity
Safeguarding our Holocaust legacy so we can teach its history

When you view the glass case housing my beat up violin
Listen quietly, and you will hear it sing

That day of shame and horror the violin will always remember
Long after I am gone, those days in November

a poetic eulogy of sorts by Robert B. Kahn, author

surrounding the sanctuary. It was through Otto and Selma Farnbacher, both of whom German refugees also working at Wright Patterson Base, that we met another German refugee couple, Julius and Bertel Sender. Through them we met other refugee couples, namely Henry and Friedel Schlesinger, as well as Walter and Helen Leopold. All of them were much older than Gert and me, and had been in America years longer than us. The men seemed to have good paying jobs and businesses, lived in nice apartments or owned homes. Yet they were kind enough to befriend and include us into their social circle in spite of the fact we were unable to reciprocate.

We were often invited to Senders' or Schlesingers' homes on Saturday evenings for dinner and card playing thereafter. It was always enjoyable and relaxing to be among people that had similar backgrounds and so much in common with each other, yet were economically on a more solid footing than the two of us. The two young cute Sender girls, Sharon and Miriam, were always a delight. It was good for Gert and me to be able to pick up the phone and ask our new found friends for advice on different matters. The Senders had only recently moved into their very own home located on the corner of Kumler and Princeton Drive. Julius was working at Duberstein's, one of the largest metal scrap dealers in the area. Walter had a supervisory job at Sucher's Meat Packing Co., no longer in existence, and Henry operated a successful grocery store on the near west side of town. Next to the Sucher Meat Packing Company was a small ballpark, on which certain days was converted into a wrestling ring arena. Gert and I would go there sometimes in the evening to watch the wrestling matches. It was fun and exciting.

Our association with our new friends and their advice prompted us to consider buying a building lot in the general area where they lived. It led to the purchase of a lot #46438 right across from Beth Jacob Synagogue on Kumler Avenue, which had been vacated for their new and beautiful home on North Main Street where it is still located today. Several additional major considerations went into our decision to build. First, because of the apartment scarcity, we didn't think that we could find a decent one in a good location and that was affordable. And second, as a veteran I was certain that I could get enough of a low cost loan under the GI Bill to pay for the construction. We started looking at ready made plans for a small bungalow.

Throughout spring and summer I would drive Gert downtown to the Fidelity Building to be checked over by Dr. Champion and everything was coming along fine. Then in late June we drove to Massachusetts to visit Gert's mom and dad and were back in Dayton by July 6. Gert didn't have a driver's license yet so I had to do all the driving. Not that I minded, to the contrary, I enjoyed the driving and above all taking in the wonderful scenery. A few weeks later I became very ill. I had a high fever, pain and severe swelling of my eyes, profuse sweating, chills, weakness and chest pain. We could not get a doctor to come to see me and I was unable to be seen by them. Finally, I was hospitalized at the Veterans Hospital from the end of July for a month. I was diagnosed by Dr. Samuel Maimon as having a case of trichinosis, which is a food borne disease caused by a microscopic parasite mostly embedded in pork. What? A Jewish boy having trichinosis? Eating pork? Gert and I never did, except when I was overseas and there was nothing else. So what is the explanation? Afterwards Gert and I did some detective work. We found that the grocery where we also bought our meat had only one meat grinder. Every kind of meat would be ground in it. Here was the culprit! They never cleaned the machine after they ground pork before a slab of beef would be ground for hamburger. Therein lies the unfortunate evidence.

While I was in the hospital, Gert visited me almost every day. It was a long and tedious trip to get from the east end of town to the VA Hospital on the far west side of town. But she did in the heat of the summer, even so she was pregnant, having worked an eight hour day, and traveling by streetcar. She was devoted as no other, and I have never forgotten and hopefully repaid her with my own loyalty for more than 69 years. Not too many years before, persecution and beastly hatred by the Nazis had almost destroyed our lives. Now, and in later years, our love for each other, and our determination rebuilt our then fragile lives. Later that summer when I went for additional examinations by Dr Maimon, it was determined that I had a "right bundle branch blockage," which could sooner or later affect the heart with unknown consequences. Whether this was a condition brought about by my former illness was never established.

My sister Irene and her husband Nate, who had moved to Huntington, West Virginia had their first child Marc, born last February 5, 1948. Nate had accepted a teaching position there at Marshall College, now Marshall University. On October 19, 1949 Irene became a proud American citizen. It was a big day for her at which time she gave a talk to show her appreciation for her adopted country. Both Irene and Nate were proud of their achievements and so were both of their parents in Chicago, Hammond, Indiana and Gert and me here in Dayton.

Then something very unnerving happened that caused us to change some of our plans. During one of the summer nights while we were asleep, our bedroom door opened and in came the oldest boy of our landlady. He jumped on our bed and right on top of Gertrude. She screamed, and with that the intruder ran out of the room. Gert and I were both so terrified that we didn't know what to do. After everyone in the house was awakened by the commotion Mrs. Hapner, our landlady came to apologize and so did the son. The teenage boy apparently did not know what he did in his sleep. When we related this episode to our friends they advised us to move out as soon as possible. They told us about a four unit apartment house being built at 915 Kumler Avenue, almost at the corner of Superior Avenue, by Glen R. Smith Realty. I immediately called and gave all the personal information they wanted. Next I followed up with a letter and was pleasantly surprised when they accepted us as tenants in a one bedroom apartment on the second floor. We were elated. It was in early October that we moved in with our few belongings, hauled there with our Plymouth club coupe, making just two trips. There was a drawback, and that was that driving to work would take me at least 45 minutes while from our other place it was only fifteen. However, I gladly lived with that inconvenience and looked only at the pluses.

EXHIBIT 17.2 Our one bedroom upstairs apartment, 915 Kumler Avenue, Dayton.

The apartment was new, small, and not fancy. I estimate that it was no larger than 450 sq. ft., plus a few closets. The kitchen had a range and a refrigerator but there was no dishwasher, and microwave units had not been invented yet. At one end of the kitchen was space for a small dinette table and chairs. The living room and bedroom were relatively large and light. A washing machine was in the basement as were some clotheslines to hang clothes up to dry. Also, there was a nice bathroom with tub. We were thrilled even so we had no furniture, other than two wicker chairs and a radio. Again, our friends the Senders came to our rescue. They knew of a furniture store in nearby Lebanon, where the owner would give us a price break. It was called Fred's Furniture. We bought a double bed set with mattress, two chests of drawers, and two night stands all in limed oak. I don't know whether that store is in still in existence, but the bedroom set still is after some 67 years, although with some modifications. After we had moved into our present home on Haverstraw Avenue, we converted the double bed into a queen size, bought a larger mattress set and had all the other pieces stripped and refinished in a dark oak. It still looks very nice and may someday become an antique. We also bought a hideaway couch in a medium green color for the living room, so if the Omas and Opas would visit, which they were expected to do, we would have a place for them to sit and sleep. In addition we bought an oblong cocktail table with glass cover and two small tables for each side of the couch so we could place some lamps on them…when we found some we liked and had the money to pay for them. These additional pieces were also limed oak, a finish which was in style at the time. Everything was all so new and wonderful and we couldn't wait for the furniture, our own, to be delivered. The arrangement was that we would pay for everything in ninety days and had made only a down payment.

The world again had been good to us, and there was a lot going on out there in the world. Dr. Chaim Weizmann had become the first President of the State of Israel. The North Atlantic Treaty Organization, a collective defense alliance better known today as NATO was founded, while on the other side of the world Mao Zedong ordered the Chinese armies to liberate all of China from the Nationalists. The Federal Republic of Germany was born with Konrad Adenauer at its helm, after the Blockade of Berlin by Russia had come to an end. Of great significance was the vote at the U.N. which made Israel a member of that body although the delegates of five Arab Nations walked out in protest. Chilling was the news that Russia had developed and exploded its own atomic bomb. Other news, without much political flavor was, that actress Ingrid Bergman quit her marriage because of her romantic involvement with the Italian film producer Roberto Rossellini. Rita Hayworth, another film star married Aly Khan, an Indian playboy billionaire. Too bad they transposed the letter "h" in his last name. RCA-Victor introduced the seven inch 45 speed records, with a possibility of eventually replacing 33 long playing records developed by Columbia Records. It happened after a couple years. President Truman created the Department of Defense, a very important decision that affected me personally and the future of the three Armed Services in later years. Also, Harry Truman raised the minimum wage per hour from 40 cents to 74 cents, a measure long overdue. When I was hired on my first job in America, August 1941, I started with 35 cents an hour.

Shortly after we had moved into our apartment, the doctor recommended that Gert stop working since it was getting close to the time when the baby would be due. We didn't know whether it would be a boy or a girl. The equipment to facilitate that information had not yet been perfected. We would be happy with either one and hopefully healthy. Every day I would call Gert from work, and she would do likewise, to make sure she was OK. She was getting the apartment lovingly ready for the newcomer. Then in the afternoon of November 13, 1949 I received an excited call from Gert that she was having labor pains and that the doctor told her to get to Good Samaritan Hospital immediately. Only the day before, Gert had washed and cleaned the 25 steps which led up to our apartment. She was then, and has been ever since, very meticulous in keeping everything neat and clean.

It was no different then, as I suppose it is today. The expecting father is ushered to a waiting room where he uncomfortably waits, now and then chews his fingernails, goes into the hallway to stop every nurse and everyone in a white garb, including doctors, asking how the wife is doing. At least that's what I was doing while I imagined the ordeal that Gert was undergoing. The afternoon turned into evening, then night, and at 7 a.m., Dr. Philip Champion came in to the waiting room, his mask hanging around his neck. I rushed toward him and before I could say a word he said "Congratulations, it's a boy. Mother and infant are fine." I would have liked to dance a jig, but all I could say was "Thank you!"

Ronald Stephen Kahn was born 6:50 a.m., November 14, 1949 weighing in at 7 pounds, and 12 ounces. It was a shining moment in my life and a moment too exciting to ever put out of my mind. Of course there were hugs and kisses when I saw Gert holding Ronald, "the first born." And of course there were flowers from me and Western Union telegrams with congratulations from the folks in Chicago and Lawrence.

We talked about having a *b'rith milah*, the traditional circumcision. It is a sign of the covenant between G'd and the Jewish people. Therefore it is a tradition that goes back to Abraham of the Bible. Since Ishmael, the son of Abraham is also regarded as the father of Islam, Muslims also circumcise their boys, but at the age of thirteen. In the Jewish tradition it would require a *mohel*, a Jew who specializes in this medical procedure. It is done on the eights day after birth in the presence of a rabbi and gives rise to a gathering of relatives and friends ending in the offering of food and drink sponsored by the parents. The parents also decide on a Hebrew name for the baby which is conferred by the rabbi with prayers and blessings.

There were a number of reasons why we decided not to have a b'rith m'ilah ceremony. First, it was impractical and too costly for both sides of our parents, sisters and husbands to come on the spur of the moment, plus staying at a hotel. For us to pay for a rabbi and a mohel, food and drink was also financially imprudent. Therefore, we asked Dr. Champion to perform the circumcision at Good Samaritan Hospital before Gert and the baby were discharged.

Gert had already bought diapers, diaper bag, sleeveless cotton shirts, long cotton night gowns, bibs, and booties she had knitted herself. We had to buy bottles, nipples, bottle brushes, measuring spoons, and a sterilizer. The bassinet, a baby crib, some toys and some baby clothes were gifts from both Omas and Opas. We also bought large and small cotton towels, wash cloths, sponges, powder, oil, swabs, a scale, room and water thermometers, baby blankets, a tiered metal serving cart, many cans of Similac and a whole bunch of other stuff that I can't remember. It all added up in cost. We still have and use the red serving cart after 60 years.

Next we made arrangements with Rabbi Ruslander of Temple Israel to bring baby Ronald to synagogue on a Shabbat evening so he could bless Ronald and convey proudly to him the Hebrew name from the bima, being "Joseph ben Baer," after my father and me, since my name in Hebrew is Baer. It was a memorable Shabbat evening. Gert already knew how to change diapers since in earlier years she took care of babies. For me that was something new. I got used to doing it but sometimes wished that I had three hands so I could hold my nose with the third hand. We had a diaper pail for the dirty diapers and Gert washed them. We had no diaper service until Karen was born years later. For Chanukah 1949 we bought ourselves a nice present, namely a "Dormeyer" mixmaster. Gert used it until 1995, in other words for 46 years, when I bought her an up-to-date "Kitchen

Aid" mixmaster for her 70th birthday. We gave the old one to Karen since she didn't have one.

One of the tenants downstairs and another neighbor in the house next door had television sets and sometimes we would visit them to watch a special program. Sometimes there was a program about the Holocaust only to learn more details about what happened and how the murders were accomplished. Too many family members, friends of our parents, and ours were among them. For me, until today, there has only been a partial conclusion to that period. Unfortunately, there will never be an end!

One of the few luxuries we enjoyed was the delivery of half a dozen hard rolls every Sunday morning from the Cincinnati Bakery on Salem Avenue. We looked forward to their delivery and would often have a soft boiled egg to start the morning. The money came partially from my monthly veteran's disability compensation which had been raised to $85.00 because of our new acquired dependent. That federal compensation helped considerably since Gert no longer had an income and we were dependent on my income alone. The year 1950 was an eventful and busy one. One of the worst blizzards hit us early on and again toward the end of the year, making the driving to and from the Airbase very treacherous and time consuming. Since we didn't have a garage, cleaning the car of snow and ice while the wind was blistering cold was no picnic. The snow would settle again on the windshield as soon I could brush it off. Heaters and defrosters were very inefficient and took a long time to produce any significant results, plus the fact that I was still driving a ten year old car.

Oma and Opa Wolff visited us in February and stayed with us five days before they took the train to Richmond, Virginia to visit the Saltens. In April, my sister Irene, her husband Nate and their young son Marc came from Huntington, West Virginia to visit, and later that month, Gert's sister Ilse and husband Lester came for a brief stay. Our small apartment became kind of crowded. The guests slept in the living room on the pull out coach, and all of us shared the one bathroom. But it all worked out and we enjoyed it. All of a sudden Ronald had become the center of attention and we loved it. Then in June we decided to make a return visit to Richmond by car to be with the Saltens and meet our new niece Peggy. In the heat of July, we decided to drive to Chicago to visit Oma and Opa Kahn. The trip was strenuous with baby Ronald in a basket in the rear compartment of the car. We made frequent stops for feeding, diaper changes and a little relaxation for us the parents. Of course the grandparents and other relatives were happy to see us. It brightened their day and for a while all their problems, of which there were many, were left behind.

Every Friday evening, Julius Sender would pick up Gert with his car and drive to Henry's Market, operated by our friends Henry and Frida Schlesinger. There, Gert would conveniently do her shopping while I took care of Ronald. It was a nice, but not a large neighborhood store, a good mile or more from where we lived. Large grocery stores as we know them today were not in the area at the time.

We finally decided that we could afford a television set and not impose any more on some of our neighbors whenever we wanted to watch a program. It was a large piece of limed oak furniture with a 9" viewing tube. We placed the Motorola make set on one of the limed oak end tables in the living room and enjoyed programs in black and white, like *The Show of Shows*. Once a week we watched this program on NBC starring Sid Caesar, Imogene Coca, and Carl Reiner. It was a very funny show with all sort of skits that had us in stitches laughing. Of course there was the *Howdy Doody* show for children but baby Ronald was too little to watch it yet. It was quite a ritual to turn on the TV, wait for about five minutes for the set to warm up and then fool around with the rabbit ear antenna to obtain the best picture possible. Even the best picture was grainy, but we thought it was great and the sound was usually good. Programs were not on all day and night as they are now. There were only a few stations and they would broadcast for a few hours in the morning and then in the evening. Before each broadcast a test pattern came on and you could try to adjust the set so the pattern was crisp. Now and then I had to replace the electronic tubes in the set after taking them to a store to be tested. Reliability was not built into any of the TV sets. It was a real nuisance, but it was state of the art and enjoyable when it worked.

The year 1950 also had its political ups and downs. President Truman requested the Atomic Energy Commission to build a hydrogen bomb, and Senator Joseph McCarthy started a long congressional investigation of suspected Communists in the Federal Government. It turned into a "witch hunt" of over 200 State Department employees and others and interesting when the procedures were televised. North Korea invaded South Korea and the United States military forces became involved on the side of the South Koreans under the direction of General Douglas MacArthur, who was my commanding General in the Pacific theater during WWII. Because of the dire situation in Korea, President Truman declared a National State of Emergency, including price and wage controls. Finally, and most significant was a thwarted attack by two Puerto Ricans intent to assassinate President Harry Truman by shooting their way into the White House. On a lighter note, "bobbysoxers," girls so-called because they wore long white socks followed singer Frank Sinatra and screamed wherever he appeared with the Tommy Dorsey band. Locally, the villages of Fairfield and Osborn merged into one town named Fairborn.

When I filed my 1950 Federal Income Tax forms I reported total income from Wright Patterson Air Force Base as $4,643.21. Not much of an income compared with salaries of today. However, we lived very modestly and saved every penny we could. On March 1, 1951 we sold lot #46438, 1377 Kumler Avenue for $1,950 to Harry E. Wurtz after we realized that building a house would entail considerable time consuming details, contractual and legal matters, and possibly unforeseen risks at additional cost. I also discussed all of this with people who had experienced building homes, and obtained advice from friends and several acquaintances. Taking this information under advisement, Gert and I decided not to pursue building since there would be too many uncertainties and things that could go wrong. It would be less complicated to look for a ready built home, and so we started to look around.

We met a very nice young Jewish couple living a few houses from our apartment on Kumler Avenue. Their names were Bess and Joe Kanter. After their first daughter Andria was born a few months after our son Ronald, Gert and Bess would go for walks together with the two infants in their respective baby carriages except when it rained. Occasionally we would hire a babysitter, but only after someone recommended the person to us. We considered this a very responsible job and did not trust a person without beforehand determining her trustworthiness.

Ronald progressed very nicely and periodically we would take him to the pediatrician nearby on Lexington Avenue. Dr. Julius Ohlman, also a Jewish German emigrant, had his practice in his home where his wife Alice served as his nurse. When we visited with Dr. Ohlman, Ronald would immediately start to cry and wouldn't stop until we left. For that reason and because we ourselves never felt too comfortable with Ohlman's mannerisms, we switched to Dr. Cohn, another pediatrician located on Salem Avenue across from Good Samaritan Hospital. Shortly thereafter we had a discussion with our family physician, Dr. Morris M. Groban, after which we decided to take Ronald also to him for routine evaluations and treatment if that became necessary. In retrospect this turned out to be a wise and practical decision for which we were never sorry. Morris Groban, who was located 1246 South Wayne Avenue, became almost like part of the family. He was always available when we needed him and made us feel comfortable regardless what situation arose. Ronald liked and learned to trust him. Likewise, our two later born daughters, Susan and Karen. We would still be his patient today had it not been for his retirement and untimely demise.

While working at Wright Patterson Air Force Base it was very convenient to open a savings account at the local Credit Union, known as the Wright Field Credit Union, which had offices in different buildings. Interest rates were higher than at local banks and that was an inducement. Gert and I watched the newspaper especially on weekends to see what houses were for sale, knowing that we had about $8,500.00 saved up, some of which could be used as a down payment. The housing market in 1951 was still very tight because of the great demand buildup after the war. New homes were either too expensive for us or were being built in the wrong area. Besides, certain areas were restricted to Jews, like in Oakwood. Finally, we located a nice bungalow in the upper Dayton View area, located on 2320 Rustic Rd. It was a charming Cape Cod-style, two bedroom brick and frame home. It had a basement with an old coal furnace converted to gas, and a partially finished upstairs with possibilities for one or two additional rooms. There was one feature which in those days only new and more expensive homes sported. Namely, a clothes chute in the bathroom which transported the dirty clothes to the laundry in the basement. It alleviated that Gert or I would have to carry a basket precariously down the stairs and was somewhat magical.

EXHIBIT 17.3 Our new home, no, our Castle: 2320 Rustic Road.

There was a detached garage, a covered front porch, an attached breezeway with a built in stone and brick barbeque grill and a nice fenced in yard. The entire living area including a small dinette on the first level was approximately 700 sq. ft. The partially finished upstairs was perhaps another 400 sq. ft. and included a nice dormer. The living room also had a wood burning fireplace with a large mirror above it. All the rooms were small but to us it was like a castle. Although Gert and I would seldom speak German, we would say: "*Klein aber mein:* Small but mine". On March 14, 1951 we signed the purchase agreement with the seller, Patricia O. Karch for the amount of $ 16,400. Gert and I were in our glory having made the purchase of our first home.

A few days later came the big surprise when I went to the Credit Union office to deposit some money. A sign at the office read "Closed Until Further Notice by order of State of Ohio Examiners." There were a few other people standing around but no one knew anything further. Only the next day while reading the local newspaper did I find out that the State Examiners had found fund shortages of more than $50,000. Additional newspaper articles appearing the following day raised the shortage to approximately $ 250,000 and blamed the Secretary of the Credit Union who was also its Treasurer for embezzlement. The Credit Union, which was chartered in 1932, had never anything happen like this before. Mrs. Bernice Emerick, a young-looking grandmother aged 49 years was blamed for the crime. She was known as living a luxurious lifestyle, giving lavish parties, wearing expensive jewelry and clothes. However, no one suspected any wrong doing. Luckily, we had taken out sufficient funds earlier for the down payment on the house. However, there were still several thousand dollars in our account that had been saved the hard way, and we didn't want to lose them. In the meantime we had applied for a $9,000 20 year FHA loan, and knew that it would take several weeks to obtain the necessary approvals through Homestead Savings & Loan Association, in the first block of East Third Street. The loan was finally approved at a 4½ % interest rate. How proud we were to go downtown at the end of the month to have our payment recorded in our "Pass Book."

I contacted Byron Holzfaster, an attorney who had advised the CU in the past years. He indicated that in all probability the Credit Union would have to declare bankruptcy since more than $250,000 of $5 million on deposits had been embezzled and the reserves were insufficient to cover that amount. The bankruptcy proceedings could take months and could be tied up in the courts for years. By that time the cost and fees of accountants and attorneys could easily double the estimated amount embezzled. In other words, the depositors would stand to lose far more if bankruptcy would result. The only way for the losses not to materialize immediately, according to Mr. Holzfaster, would be to go through a CU reorganization process with a promise to the current shareholders to repay the account shortages over time. This seemed to me the best course of action to take and I proceeded to establish a committee of interested shareholders to look into the ramifications.

We moved into our new home on April 1, no April fool's joke, and had to hire a moving van since we had acquired quite a bit of furniture living in our apartment on Kumler Avenue. But it was all worth it and we loved our little "chalet." For the first time Ronald had his own little room. Of course there was a lot of decorating to be done, but that would have to wait until we had replenished some of our savings and the reorganization of the CU was accomplished. Meetings were held at our new home with about a dozen or so affected shareholders and the attorney. We discussed the pros and cons and decided to reorganize rather than bankruptcy. Next we arranged an open meeting at the Civilian Club of the Air Base for all Credit Union shareholders at which time the situation as well as alternatives were explained, and a draft of the CU reorganization charter presented for adoption. The vote was positive, and after the State of Ohio gave its approval a Board of Directors, of which I became part, hired a new CU office staff to start cleaning up the books and operating the business again under the name "Dayton Federal Employees Credit Union." We also separated the jobs of Secretary and Treasurer to have better control. It turned out to be a win-win situation. After several years of operation, many meetings and much consternation, all the money lost through the embezzlement had been recouped and all of the shareholders were repaid in full. It was my first experience with finance and running a Credit Union.

In the evening after all the chores at home had been completed and Ronald was asleep, we would relax, read and listen to the Hit Parade on the radio with tunes like "In the Cool, Cool, Cool of the Evening" by Bing Crosby and Jane Wyman, "Jezebel" by Frankie Lane, "How High the Moon" by Les Paul and Mary Ford, and one that is still somewhat popular today "On Top of Old Smoky" by the Weavers. It was on one of those leisurely evenings that Gert called my attention to an article in the Reader's Digest that linked smoking to cancer, while I was sitting there smoking my pipe. It was a warning that we paid attention to from then on, but didn't take it too seriously at the time. I also remember going to the movie downtown to see *The African Queen*, starring Katherine Hepburn and Humphry Bogart. It is still a classic today and have watched it on television several times since.

My job had changed considerably. I had been assigned to the Army-Navy-Air Force Central Air Documents Office, and promoted to serve as Chief, Translation Branch, Foreign Documents Section, Production Division. I was now part of the Air Research and Development Command, located at Baltimore, Maryland. Because of space requirements the office was moved from the Airbase to the Hulman Building, downtown Dayton at 4th and Main Street. It was a promotion to grade 10 which now paid $5,500 per year. My duties were to plan, organize and direct the work of a staff of 15 people divided into an East European and a West European unit. In turn their assignment was to write abstracts, digests and translate foreign technical and scientific data, gathered through various Intelligence channels. Of course everything was classified as Top Secret which posed a real problem when someone would ask me what kind of work I was doing. No longer did I come in contact with German scientists, and that was a big relief for me.

In the morning I would walk about three city blocks to take the bus downtown. As a rule, if the weather was good, Gert with Ronald in the stroller would wait for me in the afternoon at the bus stop on the corner of Catalpa and Hillcrest Avenue. Sometimes she would combine picking me up with grocery shopping at Knives Market, which was also at that corner. It was always a happy meeting as we would walk home together.

Oma and Opa Wolff came to visit us for a week in June that year and Oma and Opa Kahn visited us later in August. You can imagine how excited and proud we were to show them our new home, which was now sporting new drapes in every room. All enjoyed sitting in our backyard where we had planted an assortment of flowers. Of course our parents loved to play with Ronald who relished all the attention he was getting. We also had cookouts in our built-in Bar B-Que grill in the breezeway and enjoyed the outdoors. One thing that had not changed and that was that our guests, as before in our apartment, still had to sleep in the living room on the Simmons Hide-a-Bed and all of us still had to share one bathroom. Our parents were happy to see us happy, and we were happy that they were! It was their vacation and we wanted them to get a good rest.

In the meantime, the embezzler Bernice Emerick had skipped Dayton on July 3, according to the newspaper and was arrested August 4 in Los Angeles by the FBI in connection for her crime. Eleven days earlier she had married a Dell Lyman, 34 years old in Las Vegas, who didn't know of her crime nor that she was

EXHIBIT 17.4 Oma and Opa Wolff enjoying Ronald.

EXHIBIT 17.5 Oma and Opa Kahn visiting. Ronald with Gertrude standing in the middle.

already married and had grandchildren. Who knows what would have happened had the Wright Field Credit Union declared bankruptcy? As of 2015, the Wright-Patt Credit Union as it is known today serves over 150,000 members and has assets of $16 billion. To think that perhaps I had something to do with its survival is short of fantastic.

In other parts of the world, Chancellor Konrad Adenauer in a speech to the West German Parliament at the time, had thanked that body for unanimously voting to pay reparations to the Jewish people for the unspeakable crimes committed by the former Germany. Many millions of German Marks have been paid since then, primarily to the State of Israel to take care of those that survived the *Shoah* (Holocaust). No amount of money can bring back those loved ones of our families who were brutalized, exiled, or murdered. Gert and I each received $1,000 after we applied for having being deprived our education in Germany by the Nazi regime. We used the money wisely to rebuild our lives that were so painfully interrupted and almost destroyed.

In England King George VI had died and Princess Elizabeth II became queen. Wernher von Braun, the German ex-Nazi rocket scientist, now in the U.S. heading up the Army missile program, suggested building rockets that transport people to Mars. Armistice talks with North Korea were continuing with little progress. The musical *The King and I* opened on Broadway and our radio would feature some of its tantalizing songs like "Getting To Know You." On TV we watched *The Honeymooners* with Jackie Gleason, Art Carney, and Audrey Meadows. The program was a riot and we saw to it that we didn't miss it too often.

Compared with today's prices the cost of living in 1952 seems cheap. Yet, on my salary of $5,428 per annum, we could not be extravagant. Gasoline was $0.27 per gallon, a loaf of bread cost $0.16, milk was $0.96 per gallon, postage was $0.03, and a Pepsi Cola $0.08. We also had a mortgage on the house, and life, home, and car insurances. Health as well as retirement insurance was deducted from my biweekly paycheck. What we did not realize until we sat down and figured out a monthly budget that the expenses for Ronald alone exceeded what we spend on ourselves. We knew that we had to live very frugally, and yet we had to do things that were comfortable for us and perhaps expected of us. Therefore Gert and Ronald still went to visit Oma and Opa Wolff in Massachusetts in March. They took the train, the *Jeffersonian*, which stopped at the Penn Station in New York briefly where, as prearranged, Uncle Richard, the brother of Oma Wolff and his wife Florence, greeted Gert and little Ronald. They had to change trains there to Boston, and once in Boston, change to another train that went to Lawrence were the Wolff's lived. It was an exhausting trip for Gert and a two and a half year toddler. She and Ronald stayed with her parents for two weeks and showed off Ronald to all relatives and acquaintances. It was a long two weeks for me and I missed them. Ronald missed me more.

Gert phoned me and mentioned that Ronald seemed rather unhappy and missed his Daddy reading him bedtime stories and could not be separated from his puppet, Mr. Mike. Oma Kahn in Chicago had made this stuffed toy-like puppet from white, red and black material. It had kind of a round face, a skinny body, unusually long floppy arms and legs. From what both Gert and I remember it was about 15" long overall. We gave the toy puppet the name Mr. Mike and it stuck. Ronald was so cranky and upset at missing his Daddy that Gert had to take him to a doctor because he had developed a slight temperature. While at the end of

EXHIBIT 17.6 Uncle Berny and Aunt Marthe from Luxembourg visit us. For a change I am in the picture, with Ronald.

their trip they both had a good time, all three of us were happy reuniting upon their return home. Here, he had all his familiar toys most of them stashed in a one foot cube toy box which I had made for him from plywood, stained and decorated with happy decals. It was so sturdy that it outlasted his childhood. We gave the toy box to him a few years ago as a keepsake. One toy he enjoyed very much was a beautifully colored stuffed rocking horse made of very strong material. It was about one foot tall so he could comfortably sit and rock on it and often he would sit on it and watch the *Howdy Doody* children's program on television. For us, we watched the *Liberace Show*, the showman clad in glitter who played the grand piano.

To our surprise, Uncle Berny, Mom's only brother and his wife, Aunt Marthe, from Luxembourg decided to visit America. They arrived on June 1 in Chicago where they had a grand reunion with my parents, all our relatives, and especially with Irene, Nate and their two children Marc and Faye. What surprised us even more was that they decided to visit us here in Dayton and we were thrilled to have them with us for a few days. Both still grieved for their son, my cousin Georges, who was so brutally executed by the Germans in Cuneo, Italy with seven other partisans. It was on the same day the German occupation forces were retreating from the area. It was their final act. Although they had adopted Monique Nina Salomon, also a cousin from Luxembourg, who had been orphaned since both her parents had been murdered by the Nazis, she was never able to take the place of Georges. We rolled out the red carpet for them. Among other things we treated them to a dinner at the swanky Van Cleve Hotel, where live music was played for the pleasure of diners and for dancing. Today the Van Cleve, which used to stand at the corner of First and Ludlow Streets, has given way to a parking garage.

Ronald turned out to be a fussy eater, sometimes spitting out more than he swallowed. When this continued, Dr. Groban suggested giving him a Hershey's candy bar so he would drink his milk. Don't you know, it worked!

The summer was enjoyable, as Gert tended the flowers in the garden and I mowed the lawn with a push type lawnmower. Anne Frank's diary had been published revealing the nightmarish life of her and family under the brutality of the Nazis in Holland and at the concentration camp. The name Anne Frank became instantly recognizable and is still today in the annals of the Holocaust literature, and a mandatory read in many schools.

Now, while everything was going smoothly in the daily Kahn routine, out of the blue sky came trouble. I received a letter from the Wright Air Development Center Headquarters that various phases of work were being curtailed, and my job was to be eliminated as of December 12, 1952. Whoever thought Government jobs were permanent was dead wrong. Nothing it seems has a status of permanency. It was almost Chanukah time and we had planned for the candle lighting, the singing and the gifting. Gert and I had already gone through so much in our young years that we did not let this notification dampen our spirit. Self-confidence after all was and is still today one of my greatest assets. Chanukah came and Ronald received some additional track and several cars for his wind up train layout which he had gotten for his November 14 birthday. We had decorated the living room and for eight days Ronald got presents from us and from the entire mishpocha. We likewise had bought, wrapped and mailed presents to our little nephews, nieces and not to forget to our parents.

Regarding my job, I began to realize that there was no predictable future in the foreign documentation field and therefore should look for a suitable job in some other area. With my background required in foreign technology, although limited, I applied for three different job specialties with the Civil Service Board, namely: Industrial Specialist; Production Specialist; and Commodity Industry Analyst. I qualified for the first two but not for the last. I was finally offered a position as an Industrial Specialist with the Department of the Air Force at Wright Patterson but at a lower grade pay. It was a hard decision to make, but looking at other choices, which could have involved leaving Dayton, I decided to bet on the future and therefore accepted the job offer.

The "Cold War," a term denoting the belligerent state between the two great world powers of Russia and the United States had turned into frenzy of spying, espionage, mistrust, an arms race, anti-Communist hysteria, and now a general fear among the American people of invasion, bombings, war, atomic and nuclear warfare, on and on. Therefore I was not surprised when my new job showed some elements of this fear even in official government circles. My job involved establishing plans to prevent or minimize production delays due to a direct attack, sabotage, or other potential enemy action either external or internal in nature, also the establishment of plans for quickest resumption of production. This is just the gist of what I was to be working on. But I am sure you get the idea. I was glad to again have a job without interruption of pay. Besides, Gertrude was pregnant again and was expecting in another month.

In the existing international and political turmoil, Dwight D. Eisenhower was elected President by defeating the man I liked much better, Adlai Stevenson. The first successful sex operation had changed George Jorgenson to a woman named Christine Jorgenson. The German murderers of 650 French civilians in Oradour-sur-Glane, France were tried and sentenced. The former Soviet leader Joseph Stalin had died, and a polio vaccine developed in the U.S. appeared to be a success. Most important to most of us were the talks that seemed to be nearing an armistice between North Korea and the US. All of these events appeared as good omens for the beginning of 1953.

Happiness had another beginning when on January 16, 1953 a beautiful little girl was born to Gert and me. Born at Good Samaritan Hospital at 2:45 p.m., we named her Susan Marilyn and her Hebrew name would be Emunah. We were overjoyed that the baby was apparently healthy, mother had no special complications, and Ronald had a sister. As for me, I could not have been happier, a proud father in seventh heaven. All of a sudden things in our home became a hustle and bustle and the clothes chute in the bathroom was working overtime. When Gert was feeding Susan a bottle of milk Ron wanted something to drink also. Gert figured it out and poured him a cup of milk at the same time so she didn't have to stop while feeding Susan.

Up to now Gert was able to get along with doing the diapers herself and hung up the clothes after they came out of the washing machine either on clothes lines strung in the basement or outside behind the house weather permitting. To make it easier on her and less time consuming, we bought a dryer. Taking care of two infants had become a full time job for Gert, not to mention the other household chores that needed to be done also. I helped as much as I could especially when I came home from the office in the late afternoon and on weekends, and still had to take time to study for my high school diploma. Yet, we made the best of the little free time available to us. We were happy and proud of our family, each other, and our day-to-day accomplishments.

The Babee Tenda crib which we had bought for Ronald a year ago came in real handy since he could be left in it safely to play while Gert or I attended to some other chores and Susan was in her basket and later in her crib. It was a table two feet square, about 20" high with height adjustable legs, much more versatile and safer than a high chair with no possibility of the infant being able to climb, fall, or slide out. It had a padded seat and backrest, its table top made of Formica where suction cup toys and other toys could be placed. Feeding in the Tenda was a snap, often while we were also eating at the adjacent dinette table. Another good feature was that it could be folded somewhat similar to a card table. Thus we could carry it downstairs or outside into our little garden or take it with us in the car. Ronald was a happy child and enjoyed when I would read to him and tell him a "hunkle dunkle" story, stories I made up as I went along before he would go to sleep. My stories would mostly deal with animals, including elephants. Either Gert or I would take turns reading to him from one of the "Golden Books." He enjoyed that very much and he remembered the stories word for word. He would let us know in no uncertain terms when we left out a word, a sentence, or worse if we tried to skip a page.

Two days after Susan was born, and Gert was still in the hospital recuperating another important event took place. The new sanctuary of Temple Israel was dedicated and consecrated. It had taken many years of debate, planning and constant fund raising that had finally come to fruition. The ornate marble entrance to the new sanctuary was from Salem Avenue. The former sanctuary in the Ruslander Building with its entrance from Emerson Avenue had been converted to a social hall with the Sunday school rooms, library, and the temple administrative offices remaining similar to before. Because of our blessed event we could not attend. However, the blessing of Susan by Rabbi Selwyn D. Ruslander several weeks later made it possible for us to admire the beauty of the new edifice. The new sanctuary was simply stunning. (See exhibit 17.7 in the appendix)

Soon after we had moved into our own new home on Rustic Road, we decided to join Phillip's Swimming Pool located on Leo Street, almost at the North East corner of Keowee Street. It was a large clean pool, well managed, surrounded with grass areas for sunning, playing or just relaxing. A number of other Jewish families were also members, which gave Gert and me an opportunity to meet others and engage in conversation. Since Gert did not have a driver's license we made use of the pool mostly on weekends. Economics and other reasons were responsible for the closure of the pool in August 2007.

We had some nice neighbors, which made us feel good and somewhat more secure. A nice elderly couple, Mr. and Mrs. Meier, lived next door from us. She made bean bag dolls for Susan and Ronald, which they enjoyed very much. Several houses up the street from us lived Ruth and Irv Nieman and their twin daughters, Bonnie and Eileen, a few years older than our children. Many years later we became very close friends with Irv and Ruth, but as fate would have it, both passed away years ago. Down the street from us lived the Guerras. Rus Guerra was very well known throughout the city as the "Flying Cop." Being a member of the police force, he had the distinction of reporting over the radio on the traffic each day from a helicopter. It was an important service for the commuting population, and I listened to him each morning before I set out to drive to the base. Later, as their son and ours became older, they became friends and played together. Behind our house, we shared a common fence with Judge Jackson. While I did not know him better than just as a neighbor, some years later he fixed a parking ticket for me. I guess it's always good to know a Judge with whom you share a back yard fence when you need a favor.

EXHIBIT 17.8 Opa and Oma Kahn's first visit with Susan.

Oma and Opa Wolff visited us in June, and Oma and Opa Kahn later in August. They met Susan for the first time. Although we had sent them photos, they could not get over how pretty she was. Both Opas enjoyed holding and playing with her, while admiring Ronald who had grown a lot since they saw him last. Both Omas relished giving Susan her bottle and taking her for walks in the carriage while Ronald helped to push. They also enjoyed having the children on their knees and singing to them children songs in German like: "*Hoppe Hoppe Reiter, wenn er fällt dann schreit er, fällt er in den Graben da fressen ihn die Raben*"! All the time bouncing either Susan or Ronald up and down, at the end opening their knees and letting the child fall but not all the way to the floor. The kids loved it. There were other children songs: "*Wie das Fähnchen auf dem Turm*," during which Oma Wolff would turn her hand as if it was a flag in the wind. Oma Kahn would sing: "*Kommt ein Vogel geflogen*" and "*Rudy, Rudy Lalala!*" Neither Susan nor Ronald ever got tired of the games and the singing. It was the grandparents' vacation and we did everything to make their vacation enjoyable and fun. Since my Dad was more of a handyman than Opa Wolff, I discussed with him my ideas of transforming part of the basement into a recreation room. It was something that I wanted to do so we could entertain a few of our friends and otherwise use it for ourselves, especially making it more attractive for the little ones to play.

With the new job at the base I had to drive to work again and realized that slowly but surely our car, the 1941 two door Plymouth Club Coupe, now 12 years old was requiring more maintenance and frequent costly repairs. Gert and I came to the conclusion that it was time to look around to buy a new car. With the growing family and anticipating frequent trips to Chicago, Lawrence, and other places, in addition to going back and forth every day to work, we decided to purchase a light gray/green four door 1953 De Soto at Krieger Motor Sales on North Main Street, not far from what was then Frankie's Forest Park. We sold our car to a private party and thought that we got a fairly good deal. What a difference in cars in operation, and what a big difference in driving and riding! We had a radio with push buttons for different stations, and comfortable seats. I immediately bought seat covers for front and back which was customary in those days. Today nobody buys seat covers anymore because the material is cleanable.

Now with a larger and more modern car and to compensate for the higher cost of insurance, I tried to find two or three people in the general area that were interested in riding with me to and from work. I hung up a sign on the bulletin board at work and soon had three people that I would pick up in the morning and drop off in the evening. Of course the driving time took a little longer but it was worth it since each passenger paid me a certain fee for the days they rode. In addition, I enjoyed listening to their conversation which made the 45 minute driving time a bit less monotonous.

I was always a very careful and considerate driver and could not understand why on July 22 of that year I was pulled over by Base Police on US Route 4, on the way home from Wright Patterson AF Base, for reckless driving. Normally the traffic was very heavy since people left the base every half hour. I admit having changed lanes several times, but not in a manner to endanger other vehicles or at high speed. In any event I was summoned into Federal Court located then in downtown Dayton at the Old Post Office Building on West Third Street between Ludlow and Wilkinson streets. The Federal Court had jurisdiction since that section of Route 4, where I was stopped by Base Police runs through Federal property. I had drawn up an affidavit signed by the three persons riding in the car, properly notarized, and attesting that no reckless driving occurred. When I pleaded my case in front of the judge, I wanted to submit this affidavit. The Judge did not want to see it and fined me thirty five dollars. I was naturally disappointed and upset because the judge did not want to hear my side of the story. I learned a bitter lesson, namely to stay out of court if at all possible because little people like me don't stand a chance!

That year my income from Wright Patterson was $5,781 less deductions for health and retirement insurances. It was a salary that barely covered our expenses and yet gave us the opportunity to set a small amount of savings aside. To protect the family in case something would happen to me, I had taken out an Ordinary Life, 20 year Family Income Contract with Aetna Company, in the amount of $4,248. It was not much, but I also had retained my $10,000 National Service, so called GI life insurance for which I was paying $251.00 per annum until 1968, at which time the policy would be paid up. Additionally I was still drawing a monthly check for a 50% military service connected disability for which I was examined at least once a year. I received a check each month from the Veterans Administration in the amount of $113 which came in very handy although I didn't think that I was still 50% disabled.

After much consideration and planning I started to convert our dreary basement into a play and so-called recreation room. First I partitioned off the storage room, the furnace, and the laundry area from the rest of the basement. The lower part of the installed frame walls were solid while the upper part was vertical slats set at an angle so no one could see what was behind and yet air, particularly warm air could circulate. It was beginning to look very nice. All the while Ronald would enjoy helping me and using his toy tool set. Next I built shelves for the children's toys and more shelves for glasses, dishes, and other items for entertaining, so we would have less stuff to carry up and down when having friends over on occasional party. Next, I installed a floor alternating black and green asphalt tiles. I had an electrician install a battery of fluorescent lights and then I finished the ceiling with white acoustic tiles. With the addition of some inexpensive couches, chairs, and a tables, voila, we had a great place for the children to play and for entertaining friends. At the time it was a lot of work but in the end it was well worth the effort and the investment.

Now and then when it would rain for a day or so, we would get water seepage through one of the walls in our new playroom, even after I applied several coatings of "Thorough Seal" cement. Since the walls were constructed with hollow cinder blocks, water would seep in from the outside. Then when the water pressure became too strong the water broke through. Eventually I remedied the situation and reduced the water pressure buildup by running a small diameter copper pipe from one of the cinder blocks into the floor drain by the wash tubs and washing machine. Satisfied that there would be no more water leaks, I covered the walls with wood panels and stained them. A dreary basement had been fashioned into a nice looking and comfortable family room.

There were a number of trips each year to Chicago and one trip to Lawrence. Susan was not a good traveler since she often became car sick and we had to stop until she would settle down. Besides, she resisted going to strange toilets and thus we had to take her potty chair along from home. At first Susan didn't like baby food and spit it out. When she woke up from her nap, she would call one of us letting us know that she wanted to get out of her crib. On our car trips Ronald would enjoy waving to truckers and truckers would either toot their horn, blink their lights, or both. In those years there was only an occasional truck, not like today. A crib mattress placed on the floor of the rear of the car provided a convenient sleeping arrangement for either and at times for both.

On April 30, 1954 we drove to Chicago. Many roads in Indiana were flooded and we had to take several detours, which were very tedious and took several hours longer. Trips to Chicago were always difficult and cumbersome through the industrial areas of Gary, East Chicago, and Calumet City, Indiana. Heavy traffic, railroad crossings, lousy road maintenance, and above all the smell of the air was always putrid. The kids would complain of not being able to breathe, having stomach aches, or needing to vomit. For Gert and me, it was equally uncomfortable. In those years there were no "clean air standards," and we were glad after passing that general area. The Chicago toll road avoids this area today all together.

This time we stayed with my sister Irene and her husband Nate who lived in a nice rented double house on 9935 Forest Ave. Marc and Faye got along very well with Ronald and Susan and it was a pleasure for the two families to be together. Visiting with Opa and Oma Kahn was always one of the main reasons for making the trips. However there were other relatives that we had to see otherwise they would feel slighted and convey their hurt feelings to Mom and Dad, who then would feel bad too, and pass it on to us. You guessed right, we then would also feel bad too. At the time, there was Aunt Bella and Uncle Alfred, Aunt Leone and Uncle Ernst, and Aunt Martha, all of them living not too far from each other so stopping in for a brief visit was not too difficult. However, we always managed to do some neat things while in Chicago since there are some excellent museums and walking along the lake front was always exciting for the children and we enjoyed it with them.

My mom had gotten older and so had my dad. The strain of the past years, first being persecuted in Germany, being exiled temporarily to Luxembourg, then being uprooted again fleeing to save their lives and coming to America, all that had not settled just in their clothes. They had lost everything they had worked for. In Chicago, Mom had to work in a factory, Dad had become a shipping clerk to make a living. They had been separated from their daughter who miraculously survived in France. Their son, me, had been in harms way in the South West Pacific. Then, after all that, finding out that eighteen of their loved ones and almost all of their friends had not survived the Holocaust. Talking to them and looking at them, I could tell that all of this had left them with a burden that was causing constant pain, deteriorating health, and premature aging. Our visits to see them and their visits to be with us, our children and Irene's, gave them brief pauses from their heartaches. Their daily life was hard and their leisure hours were few and lonely.

EXHIBIT 17.9 Oma and Opa holding Susan. Ronald, Marc and Faye holding hands.

Dad was constantly researching what had happened to all his loved ones. He was writing to people he knew in European cities where they had lived and had hired attorneys in New York and overseas to obtain more specific information, including how to go about obtaining restitution from Germany for the loss of their lives, his business, and all else. Every step of the way, and whatever information he obtained brought him and Mom more grief and more obstacles. He would show me his many files of handwritten and some typed correspondence including letters he received from individuals, Banks, German courts, lawyers and many other sources. Mom's father, Raphael Joseph, had succumbed in the nightmarish hell of Camp Theresienstadt. She lived with that horrible news day and night. I swore to myself in silence, that someday in the future I would continue Dad's painstaking work and hopefully bring it to some form of respectable completion. I did just that after my dad passed away years later. A respectable completion, yes, but by no means a satisfactory ending!

A month earlier namely in March 1954, I was persuaded and gladly joined Post 587 of the Jewish War Veterans in Dayton, and paid my dues to the Post Treasurer Max Bundman. Still today, at this writing, I am still a proud dues paying member but have never clamored to be an officer of the Post. There are no meetings as such. However, sometimes a delegation of members goes to the local Veterans Hospital to play Bingo with wounded Veterans. Also, at various times of the year, for example around Chanukah, there is a latke, a traditional potato pancake, dinner for member families in combination with the lighting of the Menorah and singing of Chanukah songs. At other times there is an elaborate Sunday morning brunch, lately held at one of the local hotels, at which time there is usually a speaker or some other form of entertainment. On the National level the organization lobbies the Veterans Administration and Congress for improvement of Veterans Hospitals, treatments, and other benefits for discharged and disabled Veterans.

For some time now we have had an occasional baby sitter for Ronald and Susan so we could go to a movie, concert or other events now and then, or attend social invitations at some of our friends' homes. One such reliable teenage sitter was Delora Paul. In August, after we had visits from both sides of our parents, we drove with the children to Miami Beach, Florida, taking Delora along to look after the children. We treated her as part of the family and all of us spent a delightful vacation at the Seabrook Hotel and Apartments, located right at the beach on North Collins Avenue. We had rented a lovely apartment with all the amenities needed to make the five of us comfortable and safe. Perhaps half a mile from us was the Kenilworth Hotel, owned by Arthur Godfrey who at the time was a famous American radio and television broadcaster and entertainer with a dubious rumored streak of anti-Semitism, supposedly having a sign at the hotel reading, NO DOGS or JEWS ALLOWED. It took us almost three full days to get to Miami but we did some sightseeing at Silver Springs, and I heeded the speed limits and drove carefully with many stops for roadside picnics and the usual pit stops. In those years there were no rest areas as we know them today, but now and then there was a picnic bench or several in a shaded area along the road. At other times we would simply pull off the road spread a blanket, bring out our picnic container and enjoy some of its contents. Besides, it gave me a break from driving and the children an opportunity to run around a little. Of course we had to stop twice at a motel overnight. The first night was just before Knoxville. Ronald and Susan liked the little soap packages in the bathrooms. It was the beginning of a "soapy" collection, to which I added whenever I had to go on an official business trip. Still today I have a shoe box full of "soapy."

While in Miami one evening, Gert and I went to a very exclusive and expensive night club to see and hear Tony Bennett, famous for singing "I Left My Heart In San Francisco." I remember as we were being seated, the maître d' stuck his hand out for a tip, but instead I shook his hand. Of course I had no idea at the time that tipping was customary and expected. How was an immigrant country hick like me supposed to know? Everybody enjoyed visiting the "Parrot Jungle," and on the return trip we visited "Cypress Gardens," and saw the mermaids as well as a spectacular water ski show.

Back in Dayton, having some time ago amassed sufficient credits to become a high school graduate, I had enrolled for evening courses at the University of Dayton. So far I had taken: English Composition; Effective Speaking and Writing; Applied Psychology; Mental Hygiene; and Industrial Resources and Production. For all of these courses so far I had earned 15 college credits, and was now enrolled in an Introduction to Business course. It was anything but easy to have a demanding day at the office, rush home for supper, spend a little time with Gert and the kids then go to class at UD, not to mention homework assignments, all of which took precious time away from family. However, Gert was very supportive and my bosses at work were very understanding.

I took my work at the office very seriously and was eager to sharpen my skills to compete with my co-workers. In my annual performance appraisal my boss put the following in writing: "Most aggressive employee in the Unit. Likewise the only one who presents new suggestions and ideas…Of considerable assistance in the preparation of speeches, presentations, etc…Employee should be promoted." Of course it was the last comment I liked best. My work over more than a year's time culminated in my writing of an extensive 105 page booklet entitled "Industry Guide to Planning for Restoration of Production." It was found of substantial value and importance that it was published by the Department Of Defense and sold by the US Government Printing Office for a measly $0.35. For all the work I put into it I thought that it should have been sold at least for a $ 2.35. The printing alone cost the government at least fifty cents; a very bad business practice indeed. As a result of being the author of this guide, I now had to travel more to give talks and got my name into letters, meeting agendas and the newspapers. I also suggested the making of a movie on the possibility of a major industrial catastrophe by virtue of an enemy attack or other causes, to be shown to industrial management. The movie was approved and I became the Technical Advisor for SFP Project # 368 Title: "It's Your Decision." It was to be in animation and color. Being the TA, I had to travel many times to Orlando Air Force Base, Florida where the film was scripted and animated, and later to New York where the film was produced. It was a tough assignment but very challenging and enormously interesting. The opposite side of the coin was having to be away, not attending classes at UD, away from the family which was a real hardship for Gert, the children and of course tough on me. Ronald and Susan were always happy when I returned from a trip with "soapy" for their collection.

All the while, Paul H. Packard, the civilian Deputy Chief of the Directorate of Procurement and Production, had become my mentor and considered friend. He had taken notice of my exemplary work and fervor and challenged me to continue my studies at UD and accomplish my assignments at the highest possible level of my abilities.

1954 was a good year for family Kahn yet the world had its ups and downs. Here are some of the more satisfying happenings: *Cat on a Hot Tin the Tin Roof* by Tennessee Williams premiered on Broadway; the book *The Lord of the Flies* was published; the baseball great Joe Di Maggio and Marilyn Monroe were married; the first color 12" TV set produced for the public by Westinghouse Co., was selling, get this, for $1,100; frozen food items were becoming more plentiful; the first children were inoculated with polio vaccines; and the High Court banned racial segregation in public schools. More of concern was the news that Germany was permitted to re-arm with certain limitations; the first American nuclear submarine, the USS NAUTILIS, was launched; the U.S. exploded the first hydrogen bomb; and President Dwight Eisenhower ordered the construction of the Distant Early Warning line of radars (DEW) to warn of a Soviet attack. The entire country was scared of Russian overt designs on the US and other countries particularly in Europe. It had become a vicious circle of political maneuvering and military upmanship between them and us. There was an enormous sense of urgency and my job was driven by this climate in the direction of "industrial preparedness" just in case. The nation had become somewhat panic struck and the possibility of a missile attack was considerable.

Our home life was very little affected by all this posturing, except momentarily when we watched the national news on television, listened on the radio or had discussions with some of our friends at social gatherings. Our focus was the family, Gert and me and the children. Ronald and Susan had become the center of our universe and both of us made sure that they were safe, healthy and happy. While there was talk about building above and below ground bomb shelters, our love for each other had no bounds and we did not let our tragic past or the tumultuous happenings in the world of today interfere. Besides, I had visions to create and live a successful and happy life. Without this dream I could not have approached the challenges that presented themselves in the past and present. Surely, without this dream I would not have been able to meet the challenges of the present and certainly not of the future.

Attending religious services on Shabbat, High Holidays and on other occasions was always rewarding. The worship services and the meaningful sermons by our beloved Rabbi Selwyn Ruslander always strengthened our resolve to live a meaningful, productive, and righteous life. One day a photographer with a pony came up Rustic Road offering to take photographs of children on the pony in cowboy attire. Gert decided this would make a nice souvenir and surprise for me. She told Ronald not to say anything about it to me since it would be a birthday present for me. Guess what the first thing Ronald said to me that afternoon when I came home? You guessed it. "Daddy! Horsey came to my house today!"

As far as I could find out Dayton's first Jewish settlers arrived in the year 1842. Temple Israel had its beginnings in Dayton at a bank building in 1850. A Baptist church was converted into a house of worship in 1863, and in 1873 the congregation joined other congregations to form a Union of Hebrew Congregations. In 1892 a new Temple was built at First Street and Jefferson Street. Thereafter, a community house was built in 1925 on Salem and Emerson, with entrance on Emerson Avenue which also served as the spiritual home for conducting services until January 18, 1953 when a new sanctuary with entrance on Salem Avenue was dedicated.

Time goes by very fast when you are busy. We were busy with all the chores that needed to be done. Since Gert didn't drive, many errands had to be taken care of when I was at home or whenever I could take a few hours leave from work. That however changed after Gert realized that she had to learn to drive so she didn't have to rely on me, which was time consuming and always tied up two people, and most of the children. Rather than me trying to teach her, we hired a driving instructor. Eventually she went for her driver's test. Her instructor, a Mr. Wirshing, suggested that all his students take the test in Xenia, about 20 miles from Dayton in Greene County. He claimed that the test conditions there were easier than in Montgomery County. She went there, had passed the driving test and the examiner was doing the paperwork, when Gert backed the car over the curb. Noticing that, the examiner told her that she had flunked the test, and said she would have to come back. When she came back the second time for the driver's exam she passed and received her license. Hurrah! After driving with me a number of times, it was time for her to drive solo. She decided to do so on a Sunday morning while I was taking care of the children. She drove to the home of Werner and Ruth Roman, friends of ours who lived on Earlham Drive. I was on pins and needles until she drove up the driveway, while I was standing on the porch patiently waiting.

We all had the usual colds and other worrisome illnesses, especially in the wintertime. Dr. Groban came to the house and told us that the air was too dry, and that we needed a humidifier. We had one installed and that alleviated the health problems. Today doctors don't make house calls anymore, which at the time was taken for granted. We also had metal awnings installed at all of our bedroom windows so in summertime we could leave the windows open when it rained, since home air-conditioning was not yet in vogue. I installed a three speed 30" exhaust fan in one of the upstairs windows, which helped keep the house more comfortable in hot days and hot nights. And to make Gert's work easier, we bought a canister type Electrolux vacuum cleaner. I still remember the salesman coming to our home one evening to demonstrate the various models and then explaining how we could pay for it on a monthly basis. For us every large dollar purchase required much thought and consideration of affordability. We didn't want to go into debt. As it turned out the vacuum cleaner was a great toy for Ronald and Susan. Whenever Gert would clean the house either Ronald or Susan would sit and ride on the canister while Gert would vacuum. Sometimes both of them would sit on it. It was their idea of having fun, but the cleaning took longer.

Friday afternoon, May 25, 1955 I came home from work, helped Gert pack the car, got the kids ready and drove to Chicago to visit my parents. In order that I would not get too tired and sleepy while driving I took an over-the-counter "No Doze" caffeine tablet. On June 9, we left for a longer trip to see Oma and Opa Wolff in Massachusetts. Taking the Pennsylvania Turnpike for the first time was a new experience for us. It was much easier driving and I could maintain a fairly constant speed of 50 miles per hour. Also for the first time we saw island rest stops with filling stations and restaurants. There were also toll booths where you paid for the privilege of the road and tunnels built at a high cost. In general, even driving to Chicago, we noticed a lot of road construction and road improvements which saved me some of the laborious and tiresome driving of previous travels. During our stay in Massachusetts we went to Hampton Beach and all of us enjoyed the fresh air, the sun and the water. Later that August, Mom and Dad visited us. They usually came by train which was convenient for them, and as always we had an enjoyable time together.

Time did not stand still and already Ronald started public kindergarten at E. J. Brown School on Willow Wood Drive and Fairview. It was a quarter of a mile walk from our house on Rustic Road to the school. At first Gert would take him in the morning and pick him up. There were no buses. After while we trusted Ronald to walk to and from school with specific boys and girls who lived in the neighborhood. One of them was Michelle Bender who lived few houses up the street from us. Quite a difference from today where we wouldn't do that anymore because of the huge increase of abductions and the high crime rate. It was also exciting to see him consecrated at Temple Israel in October, *erev* (evening before a holiday) Simchat Torah with 32 other boys and girls all around 6 years old. The ceremony at the synagogue marked the beginning of a somewhat more formal Jewish education that the children were to receive from this day on (see exhibit 17.10 in the appendix). As a symbol of that special day in their life, each child was given a miniature replica of a Torah, and all children received a special blessing by Rabbi Selwyn D. Ruslander. Susan took it all in and was rather proud of her "Brodie," short for brother. Of course there were times that Ronald or Susan had to be disciplined. Occasionally, Ronald was relegated to the closed detached garage. But that didn't faze Ronald for long. We found him after while riding his tricycle having a good time. Soon Susan would be doing the same and copying her brother.

EXHIBIT 17.11 The conductor Ronald and his electric train.

Finally President Dwight Eisenhower instituted the construction of the National System of Interstate Highways (in 1956) which would eventually encompass approximately 47,000 miles: the largest highway system in the world. It would crisscross America and would take many years to complete. However, major east-west and north-south routes would be completed in just a few years. It was a monumental undertaking but a great boost to interstate commerce and opened this beautiful country up to the general public in particular the National Parks.

It was a nice spring and our tulips and narcissus were blooming beautifully when we received a phone call with the terrifying news that Irene's husband Nate had been in a fatal auto accident. On April 10, driving home from Joliet Arsenal where he was employed as a training specialist, he was hit by an Illinois Central train at a rail crossing. It happened in the town of Peotone Illinois, in Will County. The cause of death was "traumatic brain injury caused by skull fracture." He was buried April 12, 1956 at Jewish Waldheim Cemetery, in Forest Park

Illinois. I made the sad trip to attend the funeral of Nate Frank Diament and wished that I could forget the agony, the crying of his parents, the hysteria of Irene and the tears and sadness of Marc and Faye. Nate's mother had to be held back from throwing herself into the pit where the casket was being lowered. It was a funeral according to orthodox tradition which added to the heart wrenching atmosphere. Irene and the children were devastated and sat *shiva* for a week and said *kaddish* as prescribed by Jewish tradition each morning and evening for an entire year. A young and beautiful family had been robbed of husband and father at a time when he was needed most.

Each year as usual Oma and Opa Wolff visited us, this time in late June. On July 26, we drove to Atlanta and stayed overnight with the Saltens. Though Ilse was pregnant with their second child, Lester was restless and wanted to drive someplace. After several days he decided to show us the mountains and so we followed Lester, Ilse and Peggy to Gatlinburg, Tennessee where all of us stayed overnight. The Smoky Mountains were beautiful. Thereafter we drove back to Dayton and they returned to Atlanta.

Upon our return from our trip I had received a letter from the Veterans Administration advising me that as a result of a recent physical examination, my physical condition had improved and my disability compensation was reduced to 30%. Essentially, as of October my monthly check of $113.75 would drop to $50. I reasoned that it was far more important to be blessed with good health than to receive a larger check and was happy with their decision and my improved health.

Since Ronald was almost seven years old, had a different school schedule, different toys and other interests than his sister, Gert and I decided to fix up the upstairs for him. So now each of them had their own room and would no longer interfere with each other. Both enjoyed their new found privacy. The upstairs was the largest room in the house with many built-in shelves and sliding doors ideal for Ronald to organize his precious toys and collections. He had grown from a wind up train to an electric train with a variety of cars, and several track switches set up on a large sheet of plywood. On birthdays and other occasions he would receive additional pieces to make the train layout more interesting and enjoyable. He would often occupy himself for hours while wearing an original railroad conductor's cap. Susan played with her collection of dolls, a doll house and a toy kitchen with loads of cute but noisy miniature utensils. She could play with them for hours.

To my surprise, I received an "Outstanding Performance Rating" from the Air Materiel Command Headquarters and was awarded a check for $300. It was also written up in the local newspaper. I was very proud of this achievement and received many handshakes from my supervisors and the people I worked with. I should mention at this point that I had been promoted to the next higher pay grade, GS-12, the previous November at a yearly salary of $7,570. The written substantiations which led to my nomination for the large monetary award, copies of which are still in my possession, are astounding as I read them today. I naively thought that I was doing just what my position required me to do.

Next we enjoyed a brief visit from my sister Irene who arrived by plane with Marc and Faye. It was their first trip by air and were very excited to tell us all about it. Irene had been doing well in coping with the loss of her husband, but her hurt was noticeable by her demeanor. After they had flown back to Chicago, Gert and I got ready for our own vacation which would take us and our sitter Delora for the second time to the Seabrook Hotel and Apartments at Miami Beach, Florida. The tranquility of our trip was interrupted briefly by a sudden and terribly painful toothache that I had developed. After Gert called around for me to be seen by a dentist immediately, I walked across Collins Avenue and a few more city blocks to a merciful dentist's office who had promised to see me right away. What a relief after he took care of me. It could not have been worse!

On our drive back to Dayton several unexpected events happened. We stayed at a Motel on US 41, the outskirts of Valdosta, Georgia. As I had done for many years, and learned while in the Army, I would always put my wallet under my pillow at night for security concerns when in strange surroundings including motels or hotels. There weren't any safes in the rooms as there are now. We left early in the morning and drove as far as Tifton, Georgia when I realized that I had not picked up the wallet under my pillow. I was in panic! What to do? We went to a nearby restaurant where I made a telephone call to the motel and asked them to retrieve my wallet in the room where we had stayed. They found it thank God! Then I asked them whether they knew if any of their overnight guests were driving North. A family was just checking out and said they were driving North on US 41 and would gladly bring the wallet to the restaurant. I was somewhat relieved and happy when after several hours this family stopped at the restaurant and returned my wallet. Now that I had money again I could pay for our own breakfast and also paid for theirs. It all had a happy ending.

The next happening was of an entirely different nature. Realizing that we had lost a little more than two hours, I was trying to make up some time and drove in excess of the posted speed limit. Many cars including ours were suddenly pulled over by the State Highway Patrol. An officer approached and asked me how fast I was driving. Upon hearing my admission he said, "You are the first driver I pulled over this morning who admitted driving above the speed limit. Therefore, I give you just a warning. Go on, but stay within the speed limit." I thanked him and drove on. It was my lucky day, and had learned some important lessons.

Because my work put me touch with major industries and defense contractors, I was invited to become a member of the "Industrial Security Institute," an organization determined to improve the professional and scientific knowledge of industrial security. Because of the many meetings I had to attend at locations all over the country and the variety of presentations and speeches I had to make, it was necessary to work many hours beyond normal working hours and I often brought work home with me during the week and on weekends. Not only did this affect time with the family, but also made me miss many classes I was scheduled to attend at UD. Yet, between June '53 and June '56, I had been able to complete the courses of Introduction to Business; Production Methods and Control; Principles of Economics; American Literature; Investments; and another course in Economics. With the evening courses I had already completed I now had a total of 33 college credit hours.

In spite of being very busy I still found time to play with the children, spend time with Gert and did work for the office and my studies many nights after the children and Gert had gone to sleep. My nagging ambitions provided the challenge that made me feel good about the progress I was making. There were personal sacrifices I had to make, but five hours of sleep did not seem to bother me. Enthusiasm for a good life was my greatest catalyst.

Sometime in spring 1956, I recall that I received a frantic phone call at the office before noon from Gert that there was a fire in the basement and the fire department was on the way. With that she hung up. Without a word to my supervisor, I ran out to the parking lot got into my car and drove home. When I arrived there was a fire truck, and police and firemen moving about rolling up water hoses. As I found out, the firemen used only portable fire extinguishers and the hoses were rolled out as a precautionary measure. According to Gert, both Ronald and Susan were downstairs playing. Susan in her playpen and Ronald playing with other toys. Gert was upstairs in the kitchen when she smelled something burning. She ran downstairs and followed the smoke and noticed some rags and paper burning. She lifted Susan from the playpen and shouted to Ronald to hurry upstairs and go out of the house. She ran with Susan to the next door neighbor and asked them to call the fire department and to look after Susan. Next she ran back into the house and called me at the office.

By the time I came home it was all over, except for the smell of smoke from the basement and the scare which had befallen both Gert and me. We looked for Ronald but he was not in or around the house. People who had gathered outside had seen him run up the street so the police and firemen started looking for him. When they found him he was hiding in some bushes; he was crying and was really scared. The fire chief talked to him briefly and asked that we bring him to the fire station next Saturday morning so he could talk to Ronald about fire safety. We did and as far as we know, Ronald never again played with matches. As for Susan, she took the whole thing in stride. It did not seemed to have bothered her in the least.

One evening when we had a party at our home, Al Yaross, Bob Feist and I talked about Wright Patterson where all three of us worked. We talked about many things and finally about the terrible photo on our identification passes. It was then as we circulated the passes among us that we noticed that all three of us had birthdays on the same day. Al was the oldest by two years and Bob Feist was one year younger than I. What an incredible coincidence! From that time on the three of us and family would have a birthday dinner or lunch together each year and as was the custom we would get a free desert and singing from the waitresses and waiters. It was fun. Bob Feist and I still subscribe to this yearly ritual although we miss Al, and his wife Gladys, who passed away several years ago. At Bill Knapp's Restaurant on Shiloh Springs Road and Salem Avenue we would each get a 5-inch chocolate cake after we showed our driver's licenses to verify the date.

EXHIBIT 17.12 The Three Musketeers on their identical birthday, September 30th. The youngest, on the left Bob Feist, the oldest in the middle, Al Yaross, and on the right, the other Bob.

It was November 1956 and the Jewish War Veterans Post #587 had their yearly Monte Carlo benefit night. Ruth Nieman, who lived up the street from us, was selling raffle tickets for the door prize. Gert bought one since it was for a good cause. Of course we never thought that we would have any chance to win. But to our great surprise we did, and won a large electric broiler rotisserie. We were so excited that when we came home we woke Susan and Ronald up to show them what we had won. Of course they had no idea what the rotisserie could do, but were as happy as we were. We still have the rotisserie as of this writing and use it several times a year but especially on Ron's birthday to make his favorite dinner consisting of a rolled beef rump roast on the spit and potato salad, which Gert prepares a la Oma Kahn's German recipe. Today, a similar broiler rotisserie would be fairly expensive although most of them are built in permanently in modern kitchen ovens.

On New Year's Eve of that year we had a party at our house. Our recreation room, as it was called, in the basement was decorated and tables and chairs were set up. It was very festive and the five couples, including us had a great time. There were the Bogins, Yarosses, Frankfurts, Feists and us. We played charades, had refreshments, woke Susan and Ronald up at midnight and let them enjoy the hats, noise makers and other favors before sending them back to bed. We served some food and then played cards. It was great fun and inexpensive.

EXHIBIT 17.13
New Year's Eve 1956 at the Kahn's. Gert performs.

EXHIBIT 17.14
Everybody has a good time at the Kahn's. Straight ahead, Julius and Bertl Sender, with Bess Kanter.

Some weeks later, an unfortunate accident happened to Gert. She bit into a slice of bread in which a small stone was embedded. As a consequence she incurred a fracture of the lower left molar. Since White Baking Company was not responsive to our report we engaged Asher Bogin to file a claim, which was settled basically for the cost of dental care and attorney fees.

After having been invited and attended several B'nai B'rith Lodge meetings, and determining that its members were doing many worthwhile community services locally as well as nationally, I decided to become a member of Eshcol Lodge # 55 April 1957. I received a very cordial welcoming letter from the local President William W. Goodman. Around the same time I received a merit award certificate from Morris Bernstein, Chairman of United Jewish Appeal for service and volunteer work for the organization. At the time I deemed it important to become active in the Jewish community in which I was living and where Gert and I were raising our young family.

We were looking forward to a visit from Opa and Oma Wolff who had made reservations to come by train to Dayton and then to Atlanta. Opa didn't like to fly. Then came the news that he had to have an operation to remove tumors on his brain. After Gert had made arrangements with a lady to stay at our house and take care of our two children, she flew to Boston to be at the side of her father and mother at North East Center Hospital where this delicate operation was to be performed. During the operation it was detected that there were tumors on both side of the brain that had to be removed. Unfortunately due to complications, Frederick Wolff died in the afternoon of June 28, 1957 / 29 Sivan 5717. He was only 67 years old. Upon being notified of this unexpected and shocking news, I requested emergency leave at my office and flew the next afternoon via TWA to Boston and from there took a train to Lawrence. We flew through a tremendous turbulent thunderstorm, the likes I had not experienced since I flew during typhoon conditions in the Philippines. It was so scary that the lady sitting next to me on the propeller aircraft asked if she could hold my hand. An odd request indeed. However, I saw no harm in granting it. When we landed in Boston, she let go of my hand and was embarrassed to see she had torn my watch from my wrist. Both of us were glad to be safe and sound on the ground and I did not pursue the incidence further.

The funeral was at the Jewish cemetery in the nearby town of Andover. It was a very sad day indeed and a tremendous loss for his wife, Hedwig, Gertrude, her sister Ilse and the entire family. No longer did the grandchildren have their Opa Wolff. It was an untimely loss which may have been prevented if the tumors had been detected earlier. The death certificate indicated cause of death was cerebrovascular insufficiency; bi frontal meningioma; and hypertensive heart disease.

During that same year, the beloved actor Humphrey Bogart, best known for his role in "Casablanca," died from cancer, as did the well-known French fashion designer Christian Dior and the acclaimed symphony conductor Arturo Toscanini. Their deaths however, were not as traumatic as the sudden death of my father-in-law. There also was some good news: John F. Kennedy, the Senator from Massachusetts, who later became our President, received the Pulitzer Prize for authoring "Profiles of Courage." Dwight Eisenhower was sworn in to a second term as our President. Not so good news was the finding that linked smoking to lung cancer and created health issues of monumental proportions for years to come. The governor of Arkansas ordered the State National Guard to Little Rock schools to prevent integration of black students into public schools in defiance of federal laws. In the field of science Russia surprised the world by launching the first satellite into orbit and around the world. Our space scientists were baffled because of their own launch failures. We referred to the Russian satellite as "Sputnik."

In my own orbit I had become busier than ever. My military bosses, very satisfied with my approaches to whatever assignments they gave me, sent me to more meetings, conferences, symposiums and schools either to solve problems, learn, participate, or speak. Letters which they received from industry management or other government agencies indicating satisfaction with my performance were also feathers in their cap, and so I was singled out for special assignments whenever the situation presented itself. It was very demanding on me since much travel was involved, usually out of a very disappointing Quonset type-hut out of metal constructed terminal near Vandalia, known at the time as Cox Municipal Airport. It looked more like a converted temporary military warehouse than a passenger terminal. For a city that prided itself as the home where the two inventors of flight, the Wright brothers, built and tested their airplane, this was a very sad first impression for visitors. The good part of my travels was that I became acquainted with things I did not know or did not know enough of, and a country I had not seen enough of. For Ronald and Susan I always managed to bring home more "soapy," once in a while a new toy or book, and for Gert an occasional surprise gift.

I must tell you about a trip that turned out quite embarrassing for me and others. At the conclusion of an industrial security conference in New York City a telephone message was waiting for me at the hotel I was staying. The Colonel back at the office at Wright Patterson, Dayton conveyed to me that certain type of ball bearings produced by a manufacturer in New Hampshire were urgently needed by one of our aircraft repair facilities. While the bearings were ready for shipment, a labor strike at the manufacturer's plant prevented the shipment. He requested that I travel to that facility in N.H. the next morning, instead of flying back to Dayton, to negotiate with the Labor Union in order that they would agree to ship the urgently required parts on an exception basis. I agreed in spite of the fact that my change in plans would require me to travel on a Saturday. After calling Gert to let her know that I would not be home as planned, I rented a car and was on my way early the next morning. It was mid-morning when I arrived at the plant, the name of which I don't remember. After I obtained permission to drive through the picket line by showing my Air Force credentials, I headed to the administration building where I was to meet with the Manager of Operations. He received me very politely and I told him the purpose of my visit. Upon which he proceeded in a completely different direction of conversation. He said: "Mr. Kahn are you Jewish?" Perplexed, I answered: "Yes." Upon which he said something to the effect that he was a stout Catholic and knowledgeable of the Jewish Sabbath. Therefore, he continued, it would be wrong for him to do any further business with me regardless of the urgency. He stood up, shook my hand and escorted me politely to the door. My head was spinning, I was not offended, but thoroughly embarrassed and a little ashamed. I called my boss at Dayton after going through the switchboard. He was surprised and told me to come back home. It was Sunday before I arrived back in Dayton still in a quandary as to what happened.

Monday morning at the office was the beginning of a very bad day. First I had to make several oral reports to various echelons of my military supervisors. That was embarrassing enough. I also had to file a lengthy written trip report which was read by many people and raised many eyebrows and many more questions which came back to me as formal memoranda, which again I had to answer. For me it was an incomprehensible event that had me wondering whether this was a moment of divine guidance and a reminder of my faith? I truly think so.

Around Easter vacation we visited Opa and Oma Kahn in Chicago and spent some time with Irene and her children. In August of that year Opa and Oma decided to take their vacation at Spring Mill State Park, Indiana and we joined them there. The park was and is still located in the South Central part of Indiana near the town of Mitchell with train service from Chicago. It was an ideal vacation spot for Mom and Dad: scenic, quiet, good accommodations in a rustic lodge, and wholesome locally prepared food. Ronald and Susan enjoyed it also since there was a restored village with a frontier trading post, a water driven grist mill, a lumber mill, and old time shops. There also was a lake and some caves. Instead of staying in the lodge we stayed in a nearby cabin, which was another fun experience for the kids. Ronald was now going into second grade at E. J. Brown School, room 104. He walked every day rain or shine about six city blocks accompanied by other boys and girls from his class that lived in our area. He enjoyed school and often had boys his age over to play. In addition to his train layout he enjoyed playing with all sorts of "Tonka" made dump trucks, tractors, cranes and others. By now Ronald had developed an enjoyment playing with glass marbles of all colors and sizes, some of which were known as "steelies." He guarded them jealously. Gertrude was pregnant again and we were expecting another child in spring of next year.

We realized that our present home would become too small for five of us and our family budget would become very strained, and so I decided to go to work at the Ewing Realty Co. at 2010 Salem Avenue in the hopes of pursuing the real estate trade some evenings and on weekends. The Ewings, who at the time were the largest real estate company in Dayton, had over one hundred sales people. Because of their size they had a training program which I had to attend twice a week in the evenings, plus I was scheduled to answer the phone for several hours on other evenings or on weekends. It was a hectic schedule with my work, school in the evenings twice a week, and now real estate, but I needed to have some additional income outside of my regular working job in order to pay for the expenses we knew were coming in the near future. Our income from Wright Patterson for the year 1957 was a total of $7,508, which was sufficient for now, but not a family of five.

For an indeterminable future period I had to defer my studies at the University of Dayton. There was no way I could possibly pursue the real estate business plus other studies. However, I had plenty to study in order to take and pass the State of Ohio Real Estate Board. I took the exam in November and received notification January 1958 that I had passed and my license issued. I now was a bonafide real estate salesman. At my suggestion Alan Yaross had also joined Ewing and passed the exam as well. While working at Ewing I met other salesmen and saleswomen, from whom I learned many of the fine points and legal issues of real estate. Often we collaborated on office hours or showing of homes when one of us was unavailable. During that time a fellow who worked with me at Wright Patt, (short for Wright Patterson), Orin Cohen, became a good friend. He and his wife Adelle had a home in the suburbs and were raising chickens. He would always bring fresh eggs to work and my coworkers and I would buy them. We would get together socially at their house or ours and always had a good time. She passed away many years ago and he married again. Although Gert and I were in touch with him all these years, he passed away June 2009 after his retirement and move to Florida.

Both Susan and Ronald were of good health and had become very enjoyable, well behaved children most of the time. They enjoyed TV which we let them watch certain hours of the day for their programs like *The Mickey Mouse Club*, *Howdy Doody*, *Captain Kangaroo*, and *Davy Crockett*. We also had our favorite shows like *The Show of Shows*, *The Ed Sullivan Show*, *The Honeymooners*, and *The $64,000 Question*. When I didn't have an open house or telephone duty on weekends, we would go for a leisurely drive, or a walk in one of the many parks around Dayton. It was also the time that the "Frisbee" was becoming popular and we would enjoy throwing it to each other, catching it, and throwing it again.

On one of those leisurely weekends we drove to Miamisburg, perhaps fifteen miles from Dayton, where we wanted to show the children the prehistoric remains that form the largest conical mound in Ohio and in which Indians used to bury their dead. The mound is approximately seventy feet high and covers a large area. When I explained that Indians had buried their dead in the mound, Ronald asked: "And who buried the last Indian, Daddy?" I was dumbfounded and to this day haven't been able to answer that question. As usual we spread out a blanket and had a nice restful picnic.

Today most people take Interstate highways and never see the interesting sites that Ohio and other states have to offer. Getting from one place to the other as fast as possible is the order of the day. Dayton and its surroundings still have a lot of charm for me, although much has changed. The beginnings of the city goes back to the 17th century when the Miami and Shawnee Indians lived in the area. In the latter half of the 18th century the area known as Dayton was the site of constant warfare between the French and the Indians. Finally, the fighting was ended with the treaty signed at Greenville, Ohio. This allowed settlers to move into the area of the Great Miami and the Little Miami rivers. A land prospector responsible for much of Ohio's settlement sold the land to several people in 1795, among whom was Jonathon Dayton. Settlers arrived in 1796 at the Dayton town site. By 1820 the population had grown to 2,950 and the Erie Canal between Dayton and Cincinnati was responsible for economic growth by providing good transportation of goods and people by boat. However, by the end of the Civil War, railroads had made the Canal obsolete. In 1886, John H. Patterson built the National Cash Register Co, later referred to as NCR, which produced cash registers for the entire world. Then the Wright brothers, Wilbur and Orville, invented, engineered and built their first airplane in Dayton. Edward Deeds and Charley Kettering built the Dayton Engineering Laboratories (DELCO), in 1910, to manufacture automobile ignition systems. The black poet and writer Paul Lawrence Dunbar also left his mark on Dayton with his literary genius. Not too well known is the great disaster that took Dayton by surprise in 1913, when after four days of tremendous rainfall, a flood hit the city. In certain areas, the water rose to 29' from ground level and more than three hundred people drowned. Since then Dayton has come a long way and has become a very modern city with much growth and opportunity, and a series of high dams have kept Dayton from being flooded.

Susan and Ronald were getting all the prescribed immunization shots including the polio vaccine and appropriate boosters. They came down with occasional colds and fever but were spared any of the major children illnesses. There were some minor calamities, like falling in the house or worse, outside on the driveway or on the concrete steps, or falling off the tricycle. There were plenty of band-aids or bandages, and the crying as well as the tears to go with it.

It was March 31, 1958 when the stork visited Gertrude again and brought us a precious little girl. Her name would be Karen Francine, and she was delivered at 3:09 a.m. to room #14 at Good Samaritan Hospital, Dayton. She weighed in at 7 pounds, 5 ounces, a lot for a stork to carry. We gave her the Hebrew name Miriam. Susan, Ronald and I would stand on the sidewalk outside the hospital and wave to mother and their newborn sister standing by the window. The children were of course very excited and anxious to have their new sister at home. We had engaged a lady to come for several weeks and perform somewhat like a practical nurse. After Gert and Karen were home for a number of weeks, Karen moved from our bedroom to Susan's who couldn't be happier to look after her little sister. However, our little dream house had reached its capacity and we started to feel a little crowded.

In July, Oma Wolff came to visit, the first time without her husband Frederick. Seeing Karen for the first time and how Susan and Ronald had grown helped to forget her grief if only for a while. Some evenings when the young ones had gone to sleep, the three of us would play Scrabble, which she won most of the time. She was really good at it and had brought us a scrabble set as a gift. During the day Oma would help Gertrude and play with the children or read to them. We also purchased a new 4-door De Soto auto for $2,439, which at the time seemed like loads of money when my income from the Air Force was only $8,614, plus a small income from selling houses. Being able to deduct all of my expenses connected with pursuing the real estate trade when filing my income tax return, in particular the car, helped considerably.

It was August when all five of us drove to Clifty Falls Park Indiana, a few miles from Madison, along the Ohio River. There, in a very comfortable lodge, Oma and Opa Kahn had spent part of their vacation. The park trails and the waterfall area were very scenic. We stayed for a while and all of us drove back to Dayton where they stayed with us for another week. It was first time they met Karen and were thrilled to have five wonderful grandchildren now. Opa and I played chess and checkers. Ronald already knew how to play checkers a little was anxious to have Opa teach him to play chess. Oma Kahn read to Susan and played the card game Old Maid with her. It was a *mechaieh*, a pleasure, to watch them.

The world had its lighter moments as well. The American Express credit card came into use. The Boeing 707 Jet engine passenger plane started trans-Atlantic service with Pan American Airways. The Lego plastic toy blocks were first marketed. The first integrated circuit was invented, as well as the Hula Hoop which became a sensation all over the world. Of course Susan and Ronald had to have one and practiced to become good at it. There were Hula Hoop contests everywhere, not only for teens but also for adults. It had turned into a craze for an entire generation. Popular tunes of the day on radio, television, and on the record player were: the "Purple People Eater," and as I remember, "Volare," with the refrain Nel Blue Dipinto Di Blue. Most people like myself didn't know what the words meant but they sounded good. And then there was the tune "Tequila." I knew what that was but never had it to drink.

At the end of the year I had listed three residences and sold one. The second was sold by a salesman of another real estate office and so we split the commission. The third was still for sale. Every week I received the listing pages and photographs from all sales agencies in town including notices of those that had sold. All of these had to be filed in two large notebooks by postal zones and old listings needed to be removed. I explained to Ronald how to sort and file them and he would help while both of us were sitting at a large desk in our recreation room downstairs.

On a somewhat different note, Elvis Presley was inducted into the Army. The motion picture *Vertigo* premiered and two powerful books were published, namely *Dr. Zhivago*, and the thriller *Exodus*. Both were later made into sensational film productions. And finally on a very tragic note, a large Atlanta, Georgia synagogue was destroyed by a bomb placed by an anti-Semitic terrorist. Fortunately there were no casualties. We celebrated the end of 1958 and rang in the year 1959 with a party at the Yaross's home on Vancouver Avenue. Their recreation room in the basement, which was customary then, was set up for the party, while their children, Carolyn, Wendy, and Danny, went to sleep shortly after we got there. It was a fun evening.

CHAPTER EIGHTEEN

The Tranquil Years – Part I and Part II

PART I

This is the first time since starting to write these memoirs that I was not sure how to title this particular chapter. For all of the previous chapters selecting a title was very clear, but for this one it was not. I want to continue to chronicle the evolvement of the Kahn family as I remember, and since there was no rush, I decided to review most of the previous chapters hoping to come up with a most fitting title.

During my review I realized suddenly, that over all the years described herein, I had undergone a dramatic transformation. While somehow I thought transformation was a chemical or at least a scientific phenomenon, I concluded that what I read about myself was something entirely different. Having survived years of persecution, gone through unbelievable suffering from the monstrosity of the Nazi cult, escaped, started a new life, served in the war, returned with years lost without much education, an immigrant without help from anyone. Then with a job, marriage, children, a home, a future! I am no longer the person I was, and have come from living within a barbaric society to living peacefully; from what seemed like a fictionalized world to a country that let me breathe and treated me with dignity. From a broken and empty soul I had morphed into an individual with a heart that was full of love, happiness, contentment, and most of all, full of ambition.

I reason now that my transformation was possible because of my upbringing to be resilient, because I valued tradition, the importance of family, as well as Judaism. Instead of continuing to live with hatred, bitterness, and anxiety, I had tamed these phantoms of the past. My struggle was between remembering the horrible past while reconstructing my future and that of our wonderful young family. I must also credit G'd because he appeared to me privately and in secret for giving me the will to live through Dante's Inferno and for the infectious spirit which has brought me to this juncture. And that is one of the many reasons why I selected the particular title for this the latest chapter.

The year 1959 brought greater demands on Gert at home and me at my job with the Air Force, and my part time job in the real estate business. I was required to travel often to the Pentagon in the Washington D.C. area and most of the time had reservations at Hotel Harrington or the Raleigh Hotel near downtown. Neither was luxurious, however the Government was granted special rates and therefore it was required that we stay there when on TDY (Temporary Duty). At the time, the Department of Defense had compiled a "Top Secret" list of key industrial facilities which had to be surveyed each year. To explain here the why, and how these surveys had to be conducted would entail considerable detail, some of which "secret," and therefore thought to be beyond the intent of my writings. Suffice it to say that I was responsible to the Department of the Air Force that these surveys, required by the Department of Defense, were professionally conducted by many specialists throughout the entire country.

In February I received advice through the Office of the Assistant Secretary of Defense that was highly complimentary for having completed 99.2% of the required program. These written compliments were passed on to my boss, Colonel Beverly Montgomery, who had endorsed the various memoranda to me and the Personnel Division. The memo read in part: "your sincere interest and intense desire to assure the complete accomplishment of this detailed task is particularly noteworthy. I am especially pleased to note that your efforts have been recognized and reflects great credit upon your capabilities, this Command and the Air Force."

In March we received a note from the Brown School nurse that a medical examination of Ronald, who was now in 3rd grade required further eye examination since his reading on the Snellen Chart revealed some deficiencies. We had noticed when Ronald would read to us that he would get letters mixed up, however we had no idea that it had something to do with his eyesight. We took him to an Optometrist who verified that his eye sight needed correction and recommended reading glasses. This helped him immensely as confirmed by his teacher.

It was early April when we decided to pack a few suitcases and other things, especially for the kids, and drove to Chicago to visit Oma and Opa Kahn. Since we left in the early afternoon, made numerous stops, we got to Chicago rather late in the evening, too late to drop in to see Oma and Opa. Instead we stopped at the Dunes Motel on the near South side, perhaps ten minutes driving time from their apartment to get a good night's sleep. As usual we had a good time with our folks and they had a delightful time with their growing grandchildren.

As an extension beyond the scope of my work, I had developed a keen interest in the prevailing political and military concerns and fears instilled by our government and the press dealing with the possibility of an unprovoked attack on the U.S. by air or sea from the Soviet Union. Therefore I decided to design a template that would enable the user to compute various vulnerability factors of probable target areas in the United States. After having worked on this idea for many months I submitted my invention to the Government Patents Board requesting the assignment of all rights and entitlements to me. I did so since I had some concerns that the nature of the invention could be determined to fall within the Executive Order 10096, which provides the patent policy for inventions made by government employees because of my employment by the Air Force. Finally, on April 23, 1959 I was advised by correspondence from Major General M. R. Tidwell USAF, Staff Judge Advocate, that "the entire right, title and interest in and to the invention shall be left to the inventor, subject to law." Now that I had acquired all rights to the invention I could have tried to market it which seemed to have good prospects. However, initial follow-up on costs to do so, and in addition to the time and financial constraints, made me decide not to pursue this course any further.

Because my Division Chief, Colonel Montgomery was being reassigned to a job in the Western U.S., he put one of his cars up for sale. It was a 1954 model De Soto that was very well taken care of. I drove it and came to the conclusion that it would make a good second car for me to drive to work, considering my two paying passengers. In that manner Gert could drive the newer 1958 Chrysler which she had been used to driving now and then. We bought my boss's car for $575, which was a good price since we had looked around to buy a second hand car anyhow.

Then in early June I was selected to attend a four day staff college course on Industry Defense and Mobilization at Battle Creek, Michigan under the auspices of the Executive Office of the President. I made several presentations that were well received. Upon my return to Dayton, Gert and I decided that we should buy Ronald a nice bicycle. He was about nine and a half years old, doing well in school, and other boys in the neighborhood also had bikes. It was an Evans make bike serial number E 09006 B24. For 50 cents from his own saved money he obtained his registration and license and was indeed proud of his first big possession. Now came the hard part, namely to teach him how to ride the bicycle. But before doing it I made some adjustments on the bike and added training wheels. In spite of these and other precautions there were some minor scrapes.

With children one can always expect surprises, and so it was that Susan, being six years old, wanted to know exactly what I was doing at work. Realizing that she was not old enough to understand it even if I made an attempt to explain, I resorted to simply saying that it was a secret and therefore couldn't go into details. Upon which she surprised me by asking: "Daddy, what do they do with the old secrets when there are new ones?" I was dumbfounded with that question and had to laugh, my tongue in cheek. "No," I said, "they don't throw the old ones away, they keep them." Susan turned out to be a smart and pretty girl admired by all the neighbors and our friends. One day Bill Patterson, a commercial photographer who lived a few houses up the street, asked us whether he could use Susan in some photographs. The resulting photos of Susan at a spinning wheel, in black and white, came out beautifully.

EXHIBIT 18.1 Susan and her new bike, her older brother, and her new sister Karen.

She always wanted to be dressed nicely, and one day when we were having a birthday party for her at the house she insisted on wearing white gloves. I guess that came from looking at magazines and perhaps watching television. You can imagine the joy Oma Wolff had with the children when she visited us in July. She couldn't get over how Susan, Ronald and Karen had grown and how mature they were for their age and enjoyed when Ronald would dress up in his cowboy regalia including gun holsters.

It was July 19 when I received word and substantiating papers indicating that I had been promoted to GS grade 13, now to receive $9,890. It was a thousand dollars more than I had previously been making and it felt great. On top of this promotion, I again received an additional check for $300.00 as an "Outstanding Performance Award." I may not have been on the top of the world but it certainly felt like it.

The following day we took Ronald to the YMCA downtown since Gert and I thought it would be good for him to spend a week with other boys at Camp Kern's Indian Village, located on 485 acres in the Miami River Valley of Southwest Ohio near Oregonia. Before we waived goodbye as they left on board a bus, Gert reminded him again when to change his underwear, his socks, his shirt, and brush his teeth. I had also given him fatherly advice since this was the first time he was going to be alone away from home. When we picked him up a week later with his little suitcase, he was full of smiles and told us that he had a great time. After we got home Gert opened his suitcase and realized that he had worn the same walking shorts, the same yellow and navy striped shirt he had on when he left, and the same socks all week. She wasn't sure of his underwear and it is too

EXHIBIT 18.2 Ron, off to Camp Kern Indian Village.

late and perhaps a little embarrassing to ask him now. In any event, he proudly showed us two First Place ribbons: one for underwater distance swim, the other for dead man's float. Regarding his socks, Gert had thrown out a pair of socks that had holes in them only to find out later that Ronald had retrieved them and was wearing them. After Gert pitched them a second time the same thing happened again. Later she found them hidden among his toys. He claimed those "holy" socks were his favorite and didn't care whether there were holes in them or not! He wanted to keep them.

When my sister Irene came to visit with Faye and Marc we had some great picnics and went on hikes to find fossils in the dried up lake bed at Englewood Dam. We used screwdrivers, a crowbar, and hammers to unearth the fossils and then took them home to scrub and clean them. It was great fun for all of the kids.

After our visitors had left, Gert and I decided to look around for a larger house because ours was decidedly too small now with three children. Since I had all the details and photographs of homes on the market for the Dayton metropolitan area, including lots and new homes that were being built, we were able to screen good information which saved us considerable amounts of time. Time had become very precious because of my second job in real estate, which demanded more hours than I had ever anticipated. It seemed that many young families were also looking to own their own home since apartment living was at best somewhat restrictive and there were hardly any apartments available and fewer yet were being built. We went south of town to look because a building boom had developed in an area where later the now prominent Dayton Mall was being developed. We saw a model home that we instantly liked and talked to Herb Simon

EXHIBIT 18.3 Uncle Bob with nephew Marc and niece Faye, and their cousins Susan and Ronald.

builder/realtor, who told us that his company was also considering building similar homes in the North West Dayton suburbs.

We investigated further and learned that in the proximity where these homes were being built would be the future Jewish Community Center and recreation area, including a swimming pool. We thought this would be an ideal location for us to live and raise our three children. In addition, we found out from salesman Arthur Peterman that he himself was building a home in that development, known as Northgate, and that other young Jewish couples had either signed a building contract or were very interested. Some of the people Art mentioned were Temple members whom we knew. After many other considerations, foremost financial, also schools, we decided to look into it more seriously. However, we wanted four bedrooms and the "Avalon" model had only three. I drew a sketch of the changes I thought necessary and let the architect Richard O'Rourke determine the feasibility. The resulting response was yes, and on August 24, 1959 we signed a contract with the Catalina Corporation for building a four bedroom ranch home.

Our new home, once built would have 1,800 sq. ft. of living space plus a two ½ car garage. The living space would be almost three times the space of our Rustic Road home, and all on one floor. It would have 2 ½ bathrooms, and a large 12 x 18 ft family room which we would use as an informal dining room since we had eliminated the formal dining room in favor of a 4th bedroom. Everything was modern, especially the 12 x 12 ft kitchen with built-in double oven and range, disposal, built-in food blender, loads of cabinets, and dishwasher. There was a radio and intercom throughout the house, a large patio and sufficient closet space. The lot was almost 100 x 75 ft and on flat land. The house would be located on Lot 66, Section III of Northgate Plat in Madison Township, with city gas, water, and sidewalks. The final cost after we added numerous changes and additions in 5 amendments to the contract was $26,463. We took out a loan which we hoped to pay off in 15 years. Now all we had to worry about was to sell our present home on Rustic Road. Not quite true, because as we found out, we had to check the work almost daily as the building progressed to make sure everything was done as in the contract and moreover that it was done right. The address of the new home would be 3639 Castano Drive, perhaps five miles from where we were living at that time. Our friends thought our new house was way out in the country, but we assured them it was not. All we had to do is drive North on Salem Avenue to Free Pike, go west until Denlinger Road and you were at the Plat. The Avalon model home was featured with photos in the November 1959 *House & Home* magazine as one of the twenty best designs in the country, which was reassuring to us. (See exhibits 18.4, 18.5, and 18.6 in the appendix)

When Oma and Opa Kahn visited us in early September we took them to the Northgate Plat to show them the model home and explained the major changes we had contracted for. They were impressed and happy for us. Opa would spend much time with Ronald, who was anxious to show him how he could ride his bike, and how well he did in school, and hoped he could beat Opa at checkers and chess. Oma spent more time with Susan and Karen. Susan was interested in making things with fabric and yarn and had a toy sewing machine. Oma had all sort of health issues, primarily with her kidneys, and did not look all that good. Opa, who would be 70 years old in November, was still working every day in Uncle Ernst's business downtown when he really should have been retired and enjoying his life. But, as you the reader knows, fate had not been kind to him, nor to Oma, and the years during the 1930s under the Nazi regime and beyond have left their marks on them physically and spiritually. Besides, Opa was still pursuing all avenues to determine the fate of all our loved ones left behind, and to obtain the money and other worldly goods left behind by Uncle Max and Aunt Helene, as recorded in their duly authenticated and certified will. Both were last known to been transported to Izbica Lubelska, Lublin Province. Poland, and exterminated or shot either in Belzec or Sobibor.

In the meantime my supervisors at Air Materiel Command decided to enroll me in a two months school conducted on Base. It was a concentrated course on Materiel Management offered by the Institute of Technology of the Air University, and the School of Logistics in cooperation with the Ohio State University. I completed the course October 30 1959. It didn't interfere much with my real estate business. However, I had to play catch up with my bread and butter job at the base, which meant bringing work home every evening and on weekends insofar it was not classified.

In the little spare time available to me I had become active in the Cub Scout Pack #65 sponsored by the Jewish Community Council of Dayton because we had enrolled Ronald. It was essentially a father and son activity program although each Pack was divided into Dens with Den Mothers in charge of meetings. Ronald enjoyed the activities and worked on different projects, which earned him the Maccabee Emblem of which he was very proud. Susan had completed a year of kindergarten at Brown School, and had been consecrated at Temple Israel by Rabbi Ruslander. It was really cute to see Ronald and Susan walking to school with other children of the neighborhood, each carrying their colorful lunch boxes. In the fall she would move up to first grade and Ronald into fourth. On Sunday mornings when Gert and I wanted to sleep a little longer one of us had to take both to Sunday school at Temple. Karen was coming along fine also. She was a very happy toddler. Time was just going by very fast and we the parents were very busy with the three children and our own pursuits.

Since we had contracted to have a new home built I talked to the Ewings, the owners of the real estate company where I worked, to let me sell our present home ourselves since we were the owners. I wanted to do so in order not to pay a sales commission. When they did not agree, I severed my relationship with the company and signed on with Harry L. Carter Real Estate Company on October 24, 1959, who had no objection to my endeavor. As soon as the "for sale" sign could be printed, I put it in the front yard. It read: "For Sale, by Robert Kahn, Harry L. Carter Realty." I kept my fingers crossed that we could sell it reasonably soon and at a decent price.

My dad's 70th birthday was on November 5th, so we drove to Chicago to celebrate that special day in his life. As usual it was an arduous drive but it was worth the effort. The folks had moved from 2109 East 68th Street to a nicer and larger apartment at 6958 Clyde Avenue. The Greenwalds, the jeweler who helped me buy Gert's engagement ring and whose daughter Sylvia who married my cousin Herbert Kahn, used to live there. The apartment was much closer to 71st Street where my mom and dad would do their shopping. Also the apartment had two bedrooms instead of one which made it possible for us to stay. Gert, Karen, and I would sleep in the guest bedroom where Dad had set up a borrowed crib, while Susan and Ronald slept in the living room in sleeping bags.

Karen got to meet her older cousins, Marc and Faye, and my sister. Irene told us that some time ago she had a big flood in the basement of her house. When that was all taken care off she rented out one of her bedrooms with kitchen privileges to an 80 year old lady for the summer to supplement her income. When Irene went to work and the children started to go back to school in fall, the lady became so lonesome that she moved out. Next Irene rented the bedroom to a woman with a child about Faye's age, and that didn't work out too well either.

I could see the strain on Irene to raise Marc and Faye, as well as manage her own life without her late husband Nate.

Oma had prepared an elaborate multi course dinner for Opa's 70th birthday and topped it off with a home baked bundt cake. We all sang happy birthday while Opa blew out the candles. Then we had coffee and cake, after which he lit one of his favorite cigars. It felt so good to see my parents in a happy mood, but also somewhat sad for me to see Mom for the first time walk with a cane. (See exhibit 18.7 in the appendix)

Back in Dayton, all parents were invited to attend the dedication of several building additions to E.J. Brown Elementary School including a new auditorium. It was held on November 10, 1959 with much pomp and ceremony. Thereafter, parents were invited to tour the building and meet the teachers. Of the dignitaries present I remember City Manager, Herbert Starick. The enrollment from kindergarten through eighth grade was 1,300 with a faculty of 40 teachers.

Before the year came to an end I was appointed Cubmaster for Pack 65 of the Boy Scouts of America, responsible for determining all activities and the well-being of the pack. My greatest pleasure was inducting new boys into the pack, awarding badges, ribbons and medals for various achievements the boys earned, including those for learning about Judaism. The pack was very active and had over fifty members, many of them still in the community, and are serving as role models. Some of the names I remember or had written down, other than Ronald are: Richard Block, Mike Cooper, Jim Finn, Jon Graubarth, Tom Insel, Jim Mayer, Charles Tiber, Jerry Baum, Marshall Beeber, Brad Donoff, David Fink, Ben Goldberg, Norman Goldman, Sandy Jacobson, Eddie Kress, Philip Levy, Walter Maimon, Roy Marokus, Bruce Mendelson, Irvin Moscowitz, Leon Muler, Craig and Teddy Ozer, Steven Sax, Steve Scheer, Michael Schlesinger, Larry Snyder, Bobby Tarsky, and many others. We always met at Temple Israel social hall downstairs when Temple was still located on Salem and Emerson Avenue. I have been active in scouting, and in particular, with Jewish Scouts, having served more than 50 years.

Each year every boy had to make gifts to be taken and given to children at Barney Convalescent Hospital, the Pediatric Department at Good Samaritan Hospital, and the Jewish Home for the Aged. I must give credit for leadership and guidance to the Den Mothers whose names are equally important: Leona Ozer, Mrs. Robert Goldman, Ann Zakem, Ruth Insel, Ruth Tiber, Bobby Graubarth, Bertha Goldberg, Harriet Moscowitz and Harriet Levy. Dick Insel, who had reached the rank of Life Scout, and many of the fathers were also very active, as was Lester Nelinson who at the time was Director of Jewish Community Activities.

When one raises children it is important that father and mother set good examples so that the children learn about good behavior and character. Gert and

I felt strongly about this matter and are still convinced today that it is never too early nor too late to instill in children good socially responsible attitudes and motivation for successful living.

Several enormously important events happened during the year, namely Alaska and Hawaii became the 49th and 50th State respectively. No less important was the completion and dedication of the St. Lawrence Seaway that connected the Great Lakes to the Atlantic Ocean and opened it to ships from all over the world. Less spectacular and more on the bizarre side was the embargo announced by the U.S. Postal Authority forbidding shipping of the book *Lady Chatterley's Lover* through the mail because of what they thought were writings of sexual details which their purist souls needed to be private. Memorable also was the movie *North by Northwest*, the thriller story by Alfred Hitchcock, and the tune "Mack the Knife" sung all day long on radio by Bobby Darin. And to note the scary, the forceful takeover of Cuba by the rebel leader Fidel Castro that seemed to destabilize the entire region.

We had some calls regarding the sale of our home on Rustic Road and had a few "open house" Sundays. Later in November, a couple by the name of Wayne and Frances Overholser, who had lived at Walton Avenue, had liked the house and made an offer. I negotiated the price and conditions with the result that they purchased it for $17,000. We were satisfied and I was pleased having been able to complete the entire contractual transaction, usually the job of the realtor. Then on January 2 1960, after we had met the required down payment and secured the loan, we received the signed warranty deed from the builder Herbert Simon for our new home at 3639 Castano Drive, Lot 66, Northgate Subdivision, Section 3, as recorded in Plat Book ZZ page 79. The final price, because of the many changes and additions we had made came to $27,000. While our home was being finished on the inside, I made daily inspections during my lunch break to make sure the final details were in accordance with our contractual specifications. However, the outside grounds could not be completed until early March because the ground was still frozen.

It was a momentous event and very exciting when in February 1960, Atlas Van Lines moved our furniture and other belongings to our new home. It was also a crowning achievement for Gert and me, having come to America as refugees with not much more than the clothes on our back. Inside of us we experienced a colossal pride that no one could see, but we could feel it inside ourselves with a sensation that is difficult to describe. Our new phone number was 277-3576 and its ring was like a sweet rhapsody to our ears. And finally we had an attached garage that could accommodate our two cars.

While all of the activities connected with the search for our new home, as well as marketing and selling ours, were now in the past, my work at Air Materiel Command, Wright Patterson Air Force Base in what was known as the area of

Supply and Logistics, went on. With all the high visibility assignments having come my way, I was now additionally directed to be a member of the Command Post, a very hush hush top secret facility located in a well-protected underground bunker from which operations in support of a war emergency could be conducted. There were regular duty as well as standby duty assignments, including requirements for standby after normal working hours at night and on weekends, which necessitated leaving a phone number where I could be reached at all times. Almost at the same time I received notification that I had been assigned to the Net (Net is abbreviation for Nuclear Threat) Evaluation Subcommittee of National Security Council.

Without revealing here the top secret details of the mission, I made the most comprehensive preparations deemed necessary and left for Washington D.C. on a T-39 Fighter trainer which took me to Andrews Air Force Base, Maryland. From there a staff car drove me to the so-called Old Executive Office Building (EOB) which was next to the White House West Wing, separated only by West Executive Avenue. It housed some of the White House staff, including speech writers and contained a large law library. The offices I worked in were in the West and Center Wing facing 17th Street N.W. It is my understanding that the building has since been occupied by every Vice President following Lyndon B. Johnson. Although I had to shuttle often to the Pentagon, this building is where most of my work was conducted while working with others on the National Security Council. Notwithstanding the plush and historic building I worked in, my overnight accommodations at the Harrington Hotel 436 11th Street N.W. were abominable. The building was ancient. The rooms were small and dreary. The soundproofing nonexistent. The mattress was lumpy, and the decor was pre-dinosaur. The air-conditioning was noisy, alas it worked. The only thing good about this dump was its location, with fairly decent restaurants in the area, transportation around the corner, and important venues for sightseeing within easy reach.

One evening, as I was going for a bite to eat nearby, I was hustled by a panhandler whom I gave a quarter since I was glad the day was over. No sooner had I done so and walked on, there was a tap on my shoulder. I stopped and turned around. It was the same beggar who proceeded to say. "Mister: This isn't enough to get me a bed at the Mission tonight!" He was very animated and held out his hand holding the quarter I gave him. His insolence got me little hot under the collar, so I grabbed the quarter out of his hand, said something to him like: "You ungrateful jerk," or worse, and walked away.

This particular assignment in Washington D.C. demanded that I work long hours including entire weekends and no one considered my family and the strain it put on them: Gert had to take care of our new home, the household chores, and the three children who missed their Daddy being at home, loving them, reading to them, and telling them "Hunkel Dunkel" stories before going to sleep at night.

As stressful the days must have been for Gert while I was away, she always carried on happily, without complaining, even if one or all of the children got sick. I know that because I telephoned her every day and listened to the problems of the day. Her admirable attitude helped to keep the family well, our marriage strong, successful, and confident. To her I owe much for our success in "making it," and surely she deserves a special medal if only someone could appropriately design one. Both of us had great confidence in each other and in our combined future because, and according to our marriage vows, we were going to spend the rest of our lives together.

Instead of Gert receiving letters of commendation, I received letters from the Assistant Secretary of Defense, the Department of the Air Force, and from Lieutenant General, Mark E. Bradley, Jr. for "the creditable duty performance of Mr. Robert Kahn of your Command have been noted with pleasure. Mr. Kahn has, through his significant contributions to the Net Evaluation Subcommittee of the National Security Council, reflected a great deal of credit upon your Headquarters as well as the entire Air Force." (See exhibits 18.8 and 18.9 in the appendix)

To be certain that our investment in our new home would be safeguarded, we had worked closely with our friend and attorney, Asher Bogin, who at the time was part of the law firm Goldman, Bogin & Fox, in the then American Building, 3rd & Main Street, Dayton. There were numerous items yet to be corrected, installed, repaired, or completed after we moved in. All of this took time since the contractor had to schedule the necessary work. For space and cost considerations we had eliminated a wood burning fireplace and air conditioning. Instead we had a 30-inch two speed exhaust fan installed in the hall ceiling, which worked well and saved us considerable electric cost in summer. For us it was an ideal house with the most modern amenities available and affordable. After all of our belongings had been placed into our new home we came to realize that additional furniture was needed to make the house a truly family home. And so we prioritized our needs and wants. From the interior decorator Francine Margolus we special ordered a kitchen/dining table with two extension leaves and six white Naugahyde covered chairs. When we entertained we moved this table from the center of the kitchen to the adjacent recreation room area and were able to seat up to twelve people easily. Ninety two inches long when extended, this Formica clad table has served us well. We are still using this table today. It still looks like new, and we can even use it for special occasions when we entertain casually or set up for a buffet, dinner, hors d'oeuvre, or dessert.

Next we ordered two long white Naugahyde couches for the family room and bought several unfinished dressers, which I stained for each of the children's rooms. Then came curtains and drapes and slowly our new house began to look like a home. The kids enjoyed having their own rooms and having a hand in decorating them. Now they shared their own bathroom while Gert and I had our own master bath. Since we had a much larger house than before everything seemed far better organized and simplified, especially since we had many more large closets. Soon more families occupied the adjacent homes and we became acquainted with the ones we didn't already know. Because the Jewish Community Center being build was a short walking distance away, many young Jewish families bought homes in the plat. On our street alone lived Fred and Doris Butler, Steve and Sybil Jaffee, Joe and Sis Litvin, Charles and Charlotte Fox, Jerry and Helen Jacobsen, Art and Elaine Peterman, Shep and Phyllis Rosen, Al and Gladys Yaross, Joe and Dorothy Berger, Mort and Phyllis Levin, Gert and Larry Jaffee, Perry and Evelyn Ross, Max and Ruth Sommer. Undoubtedly I left a few names out, after all it's been many years ago. We were friendly not only with all of them but also with our Christian neighbors, the Omlers, Tom and Liz Kenny, Taylors the Loebs and many others. Over time as other streets and homes were built we met many other families with whom we are still today good friends, such as Ron and Shirlee Gilbert, Chuck and Joyce Kardon, as well as Jane and Walter Bergman now in Florida. And of course we are still friends with families that lived on our street. They all had children and walked in small groups each day to Belle Haven elementary school, came home for lunch and walked back to school. Belle Haven was a good school with strict teachers and a strong Parent Teacher Association.

We had joined the Jewish Center and in the summer months Gert would take our kids, and often some of their friends, to the Center for swimming, fun, and relaxation. We allowed Ronald to go there on his bike and Susan once she was a little older, but always with another friend. It was an ideal place for the adults too, and many an acquaintance turned into more permanent friendships. Tennis courts were added. After a few years a large permanent Jewish Center facility with an indoor swimming pool, walking track, gym, library, social hall, racquet ball courts, and kindergarten facilities, was built and rounded out the Center complex. The facility was only one half a mile from our house and Denlinger Road, which at that time was not heavily traveled. Susan, Ronald, and Karen often walked there and I did likewise if the weather was decent. Karen had inherited Ronald's curly blond hair when he was her age and everybody admired her. She stood out in a crowd of kids her age. Susan had beautiful long brown braided hair that required lots of combing, especially after it had been washed. Ronald still had blond hair but it was cut and combed out, no more locks. It was exciting and a pleasure to see all three growing up smart and well behaved. Now and then it was necessary to discipline them, and usually Gert left that to me after I came home from work. If there was a need for more than discussion, a "persuader", namely a wooden spoon tucked away in a kitchen drawer was mentioned and occasionally, but very delicately, used. The persuader also found its place on the dashboard of the car when we were driving someplace. It was a constant reminder to keep things from becoming unruly in the passenger compartment.

EXHIBIT 18.10 Oma Wolff and Karen.

EXHIBIT 18.11 Ronald and Susan pose for a portrait.

Understandable, on longer trips, the three of them would get into each other's hair, literally, and that would be a distraction for me as the driver.

In Chicago my dad was pursuing various claims against the German Government according to the laws which had been formulated by them after the war. It meant that every claim had to be proven and substantiated to the satisfaction of their courts. Dad had finally obtained a sworn statement from a Sigismund Lennon, formerly of the Jewish Community Council at Luxembourg,

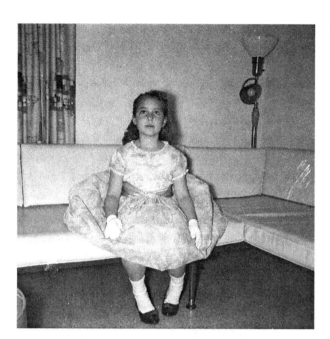

EXHIBIT 18.12 Susan dressed to go to a party with white gloves.

that all of the furniture and household effects that had remained with my Opa in the city of Luxembourg after we had fled, was indeed confiscated by the German Nazi occupation authorities. Furthermore, Lennon stated that everything left in Opa's home was taken to the Convent at the small town of Fünfbrunnen (also known as Cinquefontaine), Luxembourg, in 1942. At first, Jews, including my Opa Raphael Joseph were incarcerated there before being shipped to the death camps in Poland and elsewhere. The German Courts ruled that this sworn statement was not sufficient proof to warrant compensation. Only six years later when another witness, Josef Petri, gave a sworn statement to the court at Trier (Treves), Germany, that two truckloads of furniture from Opa's house were taken and stored in the basement of the Convent. Later after all Jews incarcerated had been forcefully shipped to other concentration camps in the East, the furniture was sold or distributed to people in Germany who had lost their belongings during Allied air raids. Only then did my dad receive a token payment from the German courts. These procedures were known as *Wiedergutmachung*, or restitution. Certainly a sinister way of attempting to right a catastrophic wrong for which no amount no matter how large could make up for the inhumane treatment the Nazis had inflicted on us Jews. No one can understand how my parents had suffered over the years and how their past and the loss of their loved ones was consuming them each day and each night.

I, too, had problems coping with the Holocaust years. However, only my love for life, my wife, my children, the challenges of my job, the fact that I had survived the Holocaust and a brutal war had kept me sane. Having conquered many of the odds against me, gave me the psychological strength to put the horrible past in a special compartment of my brain where it would lay dormant until recall. And so I began to ask myself when should I tell my children about my past during the Holocaust. Should I tell them anything at all, should I keep it a secret? Ronald was almost eleven years old, is he too young to know? The answer to all these questions was a loud "Yes." I wanted my children happy, not burdened with stuff of what I had put into that special compartment, no nightmares. Perhaps in Sunday school at Temple, perhaps in Belle Haven School there would be discussion, and they would have no idea that their father and mother had been in it and survived. That would be better, and so I let the subject rest. Yes, at the time I thought I did the right thing, however the subject was never far from my mind.

What was making me very uncomfortable and angry inside at that time was the rise of the so-called neo-Nazi movement all over Germany and in some of the other European countries. They not only denied that the Holocaust existed, but also vandalized and destroyed the remaining vestiges of the Jewish past where ever they had survived. Anti-Semitic crimes were not only on the increase but became more brazen as time went on. Attacks on Jews were infrequent since there were only a few that had returned from the camps, but defacing and destroying remaining cemeteries and remnants of synagogues were daily, or more appropriately said, nightly occurrences. When these hate groups couldn't find a better target they resorted to attack foreigners, in particular Turks, other Slavic minorities and more often Muslims who had immigrated.

There were also reports of clandestine operations having taken place for the evacuation of Nazi war criminals and collaborators disguised as Displaced Persons (DP's) primarily to South American countries and to a lesser degree to Canada and the United States. Although there had been Displaced Persons legislation enacted by the former President Harry S. Truman, directives issued thereafter were loosely interpreted or circumvented thus permitting proven war criminals from Germany, Latvia, Estonia, Croatia, like Ivan Demjanjuk to enter the United States. I agonized over this state of affairs but had no choice but to leave it to organizations like the Office of Special Investigations of the US Department of Justice (OSI), the Anti-Defamation League (ADL) and others agencies to ferret these criminals out and bring them to justice.

Sadly, there was no outcry by the Jewish immigrants of Dayton, nor were there any noticeable concerns voiced by the organized Jewish Community of Dayton. In this country too there was a noticeable increase of hate groups and with it the dissemination of hate literature. Requests for demonstrations, marches, and rallies by neo-Nazi skinheads at various cities and towns had to be granted under the Freedom of Speech Act and took place under the worrisome eyes of the local law enforcement agencies. Did we fight World War II for naught, or was this simply a blip of anti-Semitism in our history? We just had to wait and see.

Once a year Belle Haven School had a carnival as a fund-raiser sponsored by the Parent Teacher Association. We had become members and enthusiastically supported the effort by manning one of the many booth. It was fun and at the same time provided money to buy items needed by Belle Haven to make it a better school. At the very first carnival since we had moved into the area, Karen won several goldfish which she brought home very excited in a plastic bag filled with water. We put them in a glass bowl after the kids named them Flopsy and Mopsy. So that there would be no ownership disputes, the fish bowl was placed on the kitchen cabinet near the window where they resided for many years. They were inexpensive pets and were much fun to look at.

Because I had enjoyed collecting postage stamps, and once upon a time had a very nice collection which the Nazis took away from me on Kristallnacht in Mannheim, I tried to transfer that enjoyment to Ronald. I spent many hours with him sorting stamps from different countries, soaking them in water to remove the remnants of envelopes, drying them between pages of telephone books and finally affixing them to the correct pages in stamp albums. For several years Ronald devoted many hours of his free time to this hobby, through which he also learned about geography and history. Gert and I spent much time with Ronald and Susan helping them with their homework. It was always necessary and sometimes difficult to find a balance between play time and school and Sunday school home work. Although we made a rule that homework came first, Gert saw to it that there would be exceptions. In the long run homework and the necessary reading or brushing up for next day tests were always completed. Loosely knit rules about television watching were also in place, however there too exceptions were made if there was a special program we wanted the children to watch or they wanted to watch.

In the meantime, our lot was sodded and we planted a birch tree in front of the house, and another one in back. I didn't know that birch trees do not last long in this area. A small plat of flowers graced the entrance to our home. Karen and Susan were always willing helpers while Ronald was more inclined to do the heavier jobs like helping me with digging holes for the trees and bushes.

It was a peaceful and happy time. The newspaper was at the door every morning, and the milkman left glass bottles of milk in an insulated box by the front door. So did the Dunkers woman who brought us fresh country eggs each week and home baked goods if we ordered them. I left early to go to work after I picked up my riders in the neighborhood, Walter Bergman, Saul Hoch, and Benny Goldberg. We rotated the order of driving on a weekly basis unless a situation came up where that had to be changed. It was a time when the mailman came once in the morning and then again in the afternoon. Gert saved S&H Green Stamps given by merchants at time of a purchase, then they were pasted into small books and eventually redeemed for useful items at Green Stamp outlets.

There was penny candy which the kids coming home from Belle Haven School bought at a small grocery store on the corner of Brumbaugh Boulevard and Free Pike. A McDonald's hamburger was fifteen cents, and so was a cup of Coca Cola. Postage stamps were only five cents. Kids collected baseball cards and our two girls made chains from gum wrappers. Passenger trains stopped many times a day at Union Station terminal downtown and there were newspaper stands everywhere selling the local newspaper known as the *Journal Herald*. Also there was Goody-Goody restaurant on Salem Avenue, just a little North of Good Samaritan Hospital where our family would go for some eats only on very special occasions. They had the best hamburgers and the best french fries, and our kids loved to go there. It was also a hangout for teenagers after Friday night football games, and for grownups like us maybe after an evening at the movies. Sometimes we would go to Parkmoor restaurant also on Salem Avenue. But a special treat was when Mom and Dad decided to buy Arby's at the restaurant also on Salem Avenue. Ronald, Susan, and Karen would hear us say in German, *hingehen oder herholen*, which meant go there, or get some. Since Arby's sandwiches were loaded with sliced roast beef, we would buy three, bring them home, and made five out of them, with extra buns we usually had at home. It saved money and made it possible to buy Arby's roast beef sandwiches more often.

Yes, those were the tranquil years!

We couldn't wait for Oma Wolff and Oma and Opa Kahn to visit us so we could show off our prides and joys, our wonderful children first, and next the beautiful home we were now living in. Oma Wolff visited us in June and Oma and Opa Kahn in July. What a difference they thought from our first house on Rustic Road and compared it with their own apartments. We lived pretty much outside the city and had this aura of open space and fresh air. Whereas at our Kumler Avenue apartment and later at our Rustic Road home our guests slept on the Simmons Hide-Away couch in the living room, the arrangement was now reversed. Gert and I slept on the couch in the living room and we turned over the master bedroom and master bath to them. In this way it was much more comfortable for them and we didn't mind the little inconvenience.

We could not hide how proud we were of ourselves for what we had achieved and our parents were delighted and equally proud of us. We took them to the Jewish Center and spent several afternoons at the swimming pool, sitting in the shade under a huge concrete umbrella, while Susan, Karen and Ronald showed them their swimming and diving expertise. For a while all their troubles and worries were forgotten so it seemed, and their smiles and periodic laughter appeared to serve them better than the medication they had brought with them. We took photographs with our Kodak Brownie camera, and used blue flash bulbs for indoor shots. For a real treat we all went with Oma Wolff for dinner at the Tropics on North Main Street. The restaurant had an original Hawaiian decor outside and inside. Our children, who had never been there, fell in love with the place, not just because of the authentic decor but the food was also excellent. They had a live band, waitresses were dressed in Hawaiian sarongs and the owner Georgie Rudin was very personable making sure that his customers were treated like royalty. Therefore when my folks from Chicago came to visit our three children badgered Gert and me to take them also to what now was their "special occasion" restaurant, and we did. Of course my parents enjoyed it also.

Because we had so much to do in our new home inside as well as outside and because we had been visited earlier by both sides of grandparents, we decided not to make our usual summer trips to Chicago and Lawrence. Besides, we needed a little rest for ourselves too. We let Ronald go to Camp Kern for two weeks and he came home with a certificate of having "successfully participated in the springtype air riflery program." This time he made sure to change his clothes while he was there. His grades at Belle Haven School were good and so were his grades at Sunday school. In fall he would be starting 5th grade and Susan would start 2nd grade. According to her home room teacher, Mrs. Dorothy Hazlett, Susan received an "H" in all subjects for "High Standard of Achievement." In Sunday school at Temple Israel her teacher Mrs. Joanne Shaman thought that in the first quarter she "occasionally" talked a bit too much , but that improved in second and third quarter and did not keep her from being promoted to 2nd grade. And Karen, well she celebrated her second birthday in March with a big party of most of the younger kids in the new neighborhood. She was a handful and cute as a button!

As a father of a Cub Scout and also Cubmaster I helped Ronald to get ready for the Pinewood Derby taking place in fall. He learned to carve a race car out of a block of pinewood, no easy task for the Cub Scouts. It required loads of patience of me, of Ronald and the other boys in his Pack. When the day of the race came the cars were first judged for looks and then the race began down a specially designed inclined track. Each participant received a special ribbon, and the first three winners were awarded gift certificates for meals at Hasty Tasty restaurants. Occasionally on a Saturday or Sunday afternoon we would drive to the municipal airport restaurant, now Dayton International Airport, buy everyone an ice cream cone and watch airplanes land and take off. It was exciting and a good way to spend a few leisure hours together.

When Chanukah approached Gert baked loads of special cookies with designs of menorahs, dreidels, and the like. The best part of the preparation for Chanukah was decorating the home. Everybody helped. There were different garlands and other decorations all purchased at Temple Israel gift shop. It was fun for the entire family. Each of the kids brought home a small brass menorah from Sunday school adding to our family's more traditional menorah which had been gifted us by Lester Salten, my brother–in–law in Atlanta. We also had a few

45" records with traditional Chanukah songs. The last thing to prepare were the latkes (potato pancakes), and it was fun to see all five of us in aprons helping with mixing all the ingredients and finally frying them up in several iron skillets. Of course Gert and I made a big *tsimmes* (a big production) out of it. The kids learned the story of Chanukah at Sunday school and were told that it was different from Christmas, which is celebrated about the same time but only for one day and for different reasons.

It was easy for us to buy presents for the three children. They always needed clothes because they were outgrowing their apparel, but then came toys, books, additional pieces for Ronald's train layout, and for the girls some not too expensive jewelry. For us parents it was fairly easy to buy gifts for each other because we needed or could use so many things for the house and ourselves which we had deferred because of other priorities. The kids made small gift items in school, also at Cub Scout meetings, and could buy things at the Temple gift shop with money they had gotten from Oma Wolff and Opa and Oma Kahn. We also took them downtown to Rike's and Elder Department stores, as well as to Mc Crory's 5&10. Rike's always had beautifully decorated windows with animated winter scenes, Rudolf the red nosed reindeer, elves, angels, dwarfs, Santa, electric trains, dolls and appropriate sound effects. In the evening we drove downtown to admire the Christmas decorations especially at the NCR auditorium on South Main Street, which unfortunately is no more.

Gert and I had to wait until the children were asleep in the evening so we could wrap their presents. It was a big job because we not only had to wrap presents from us to them but also presents from the grandparents, from aunt Irene, aunt Ilse and uncle Lester, unless they were already wrapped. Next we had to wrap presents for our nieces, nephews, our respective parents and mail the packages so they would get there on time. It was quite a job but we enjoyed it. In the meantime Karen, Susan, and Ronald became more excited every day. We had sort of a countdown so the children would know how soon "Chanukah Man" would be coming. The name Chanukah Man was a holdover from the days Irene and I as children had Chanukah in Mannheim. The first night of Chanukah was the best of all the eight days of celebration.

We always found a way for the children to be out of the house early in the evening so Gert and I could bring out the gifts and place them for each on chairs, the couch, or on the floor. Interspersed were also small sacks with chocolate filled Chanukah *gelt* (chocolate coins wrapped in gold foil). Then when the kids came home we pretended as nothing had happened until one or the other found the surprise packages in the living room which had been left dark, while we were sitting in the family room reading or watching TV. After the initial pandemonium had subsided, all of us opened our gifts with hoopla, ahhs and ohhs. Next came the lighting of the menorahs, each of the children lighting their own colored

EXHIBIT 18.13 For Chanukah we sent this portrait to all our relatives. We were proud of our family.

candle with a little help from Mom and Dad, while I would chant the *brocha*, the blessing. The menorahs were all lined up on the marble sill of our eight foot panorama window with the curtains open, reflecting the flame of each candle on the glass larger than life, for the whole world to see. We proceeded to sing "*Mo'oz Tzur*" to the melody of "Rock of Ages" the children singing with us because they had learned it in Sunday school. The best was yet to come after I put the record player on. Susan and especially Karen danced happily to music of "Chanukah, Oh Chanukah, come light the Menorah," "*S'vivon, Sov, Sov, Sov*," and "I have a little Dreidel." Since the dreidel is spun around, Karen would turn and turn around until she became dizzy and sat or fell down on the carpeting.

All of this evoked vivid, fond but sad memories of my childhood because of the restraints put on our families at Chanukah because then we lived under the boots of the Nazis. I missed our very large brass menorah which the Nazi confiscated. It was good that neither Ronald, Karen, nor Susan knew anything about it and I have never discussed it since. Why spoil their fun.

After the children had spent time with their gifts and we with ours, Gert set the table and heated up the latkes, which we ate with applesauce, sour cream, and gusto. It was a delicacy served only once a year, a tradition that goes back probably hundreds of years. The celebration required one additional phase and that was the traditional spinning of the dreidel (top), according on which side the dreidel fell you either won some walnuts or you lost some. It was a fun game and we all loved it. For seven more days each child would receive at least one more gift, brought by Chanukah Man during the night, and the lighting of the menorah with one additional candle added each evening continued with the traditional singing and dancing. Chanukah celebrations were always the happiest and most memorable days of the year and are still today.

As the year 1960 ended we, the Kahn family, had much to be thankful for. Yet the world around us was restless and the whole country was concerned that the "Cold War" could at any minute ignite into a hot war while each side was posturing for that eventuality. Soviet leader Nikita Khrushchev made various outrageous accusations highlighted by hitting his shoe on the table during a UN General Assembly session, increasing that possibility. The rhetoric from all sides of the media was at a fever pitch scaring the entire population. Some Americans afraid of a "Doom's Day," and radiation from an enemy atomic or nuclear attack, built fallout shelters underground. There was even talk of evacuation routes from cities.

On the other hand we had great hopes that John F. Kennedy, our newly elected and admired to be President, would bring about a drastic de-escalation of international tensions. Here at home we had great internal unrest leading to racial rioting with some black and white people killed, protest marches in the South, and sit-ins at restaurants, as well as altercations between racial factions. It was the beginning of Negroes' struggle to bring an end to segregation. Susan was learning something about the history of Negroes in school and was eager to discuss with us the unfairness of treating Blacks as second class citizens. Even at her young age of seven she seemed to champion the cause of racial equality and felt grown-up in doing so.

And on a different level, a great feat was accomplished by the State of Israel when its secret agents captured and managed to smuggle out of Argentine the reviled Nazi henchman Adolf Eichmann, who was responsible for masterminding the almost successful genocide of all European Jews. Ricardo Clement, as he was known under his assumed name in Argentine, was flown to Israel for trial. Another trial was held in Moscow. There, Gary Powers was found guilty of spying by flying a U.S. U-2 spy plane over Soviet Union air space then being shot down by soviet missiles. His sentence: ten years prison. The 1960 Olympic Games in Rome Italy, and the passing of the great actor Clark Gable unfortunately were overshadowed by these and other world events.

On a less ominous note were some of the prevailing and captivating TV shows now considered classics: The Danny Thomas, and the Red Skelton comedy shows, and the series *Wagon Train* and *Gunsmoke*, which had become hits with the young ones. Hit songs I remember from that era by Elvis Presley were: "It's Now Or Never" and "Are You Lonesome Tonight," as well as the thriller motion picture *Psycho* produced by Alfred Hitchcock.

We ushered in the New Year of 1961 with great expectations; and in accordance Karen received a weekly allowance of 25 cents, 50 cents for Susan and $1.00 for Ronald providing he would help with outside chores. Of course we reminded all three that keeping their room in a neat fashion was part of obtaining the weekly allowance. They did pretty well, but needed some assistance and a gentle reminder on occasion.

We had a great Chanukah party for all the Cub Scouts and their families at the Social Hall of Temple Israel. Immediately after the flag ceremony, the boys, including Ronald, put on a nice Chanukah skit followed by menorah lighting, traditional singing and a social with special Chanukah refreshments. We also had a Boy Scout Troop #65, which under the direction of Mel Berko had expanded its activities including outdoor camping. As the Cubs became older they would eventually join that Troop. Each year we had a Blue and Gold Dinner. This year, 1961 we observed the 50th birthday of Scouting. I asked Leo Cooper to do the detail planning for the event at which time I inducted Stewart Brooks, Richard Frank, Ronnie Freemas, Alan Goldsmith, Michael Katz, Stephen Lindenbaum, Mark Sharfman, Howard Shuman, and Gary Zakem. Also, I started planning our participation in the Scout Sabbath which was held Shabbat evening February 12 at Beth Jacob Synagogue. (See exhibit 18.14 in the appendix)

At my job I was developing a "Directory of Mutual Aid Associations," to be used throughout the country. It was to include chapters on how to organize, descriptions of their functions, and legal implications. It was a fairly complicated assignment with a publication target date of April, which I eventually would meet and for which I received many verbal and written compliments, recognitions, and an Outstanding Performance Certificate and again a monetary award. (See exhbits 18.15 and 18.16 in the appendix)

On January 20, 1961 our newly elected President John F. Kennedy would be inaugurated in Washington D.C. This momentous event was something I clamored to witness in person because it was billed to become a great spectacle, and because of the great respect I had developed for this man who was preceded by expectations of presidential greatness. With all the business trips I had made to the Pentagon near D.C., I had to figure out how to arrange a TDY official Temporary Duty trip inclusive of January 20, which was a Government holiday for the District of Columbia and nearby Government Offices. With my co-worker William (Bill) Frost, we called our counterpart at the Pentagon, Mr. Thomas Baptist, a retired Army Colonel, to do us a favor and send a message to our front office at Wright Patterson requesting our attendance at an important all day meeting on the 19th of January.

This simple but ingeniously calculated skullduggery worked, and my military Chief informed me to prepare the necessary orders in compliance with the request from higher Headquarters. Since the 20th fell on a Saturday, we had our orders state the return trip to begin Sunday the 21st of January. The next problem was to find overnight accommodations since hotel rooms were heavily booked, and the few vacancies we found were $500 and more per night. Bill and I had both our secretaries make phone calls and they finally found a room at a Government Employee Housing facility in Alexandria Virginia, not too far from the Pentagon and near transportation. The location was ideal, and the rate was not hiked for that special weekend.

We left on Thursday early afternoon by TWA, Trans World Airlines and arrived at Washington National Airport (now Reagan International) in time to visit the Senate Office Building before the offices of Ohio Senators Stephen Young and Frank Lausche would close. We hoped to garner some free tickets for the inaugural weekend activities. We were able to get tickets for an inaugural concert for the following evening at the Armory, tickets for watching and listening to the swearing in ceremonies and the inaugural speech of the President, and tickets for bleacher seats on Pennsylvania Avenue to watch the inaugural Parade. We weren't able to get tickets for any of the inaugural balls, which were only for VIPs, but we were satisfied having done better than expected. Dog tired from all the walking we finally got to our abode and settled in for the night after having a snack and a drink from one of the automatic dispensers in the building.

In the morning we took local transportation to the Pentagon cafeteria. After breakfast we met our colleague Thomas Baptist who had arranged a meeting with several DOD, Department of Defense Officials. After a few hours we had reached agreements on several issues that were on the front burner. Low and behold looking out the window, it was snowing pretty hard. There were at least four inches of that white stuff on the ground already. We had lunch at the Executive Dining Room. That's where our high salaried DOD officials ate and invited us to join them. Then there came a surprise announcement over the loudspeaker that all of the Government offices in the area were closing at 2 p.m. because of the snowfall and more was predicted. That suited us fine, except we were not prepared for this kind of weather, the low temperature plus the high winds that accompanied. It took us more than an hour with surface transportation back to our quarters, a trip that had taken us only about fifteen minutes in the morning. We had no boots and neither of us had a hat, cap or earmuffs. We became very concerned about getting to the Armory for the concert that evening, and for the inaugural activities the next day.

We ordered a cab and told the dispatcher we would gladly pay double the rate because of the terrible driving conditions. The cab came forty five minutes late but we were more concerned about getting to the Armory. On the way we saw hundreds of stranded or abandoned cars along the road side, the snow being about six inches deep and drifts considerably higher. Besides, it was a terrible traffic jam, a nightmare to drive in it, and cars were stalled having run out of gas. Thanks to our driver we got to the Armory safe and sound and paid him handsomely. The concert was provided by several different orchestras, and a variety of bands including several military bands. More discerning was the exciting atmosphere and the jubilant crowd which drifted in late because of the terrible weather. We didn't wait for the concert to end so as not to get stuck in the huge crowd and managed to get back to our temporary residence after midnight with ice cold feet and other body parts.

On the way back we saw thousands of U.S. Army and District of Columbia personnel with dump trucks, snow plows, and shovels. What amazed Bill and I most were, believe it or not, Army Engineers using flamethrowers to melt snow and ice along the parade route which we had to cross. Thank G'd it had stopped snowing, the snow now being eight or more inches deep. Would it be possible to have the inauguration of the 35th United States President proceed as planned? We could only hope! Although we didn't get much sleep that night, we got up early knowing that it would take forever to get to the Capitol Plaza where the swearing-in ceremonies of the youngest President, forty-three year old John Fitzgerald Kennedy, would take place on the East Portico of the U.S. Capitol.

After I had stuffed a number of newspaper pages under my shirt to keep warn, something my Dad did to keep from freezing at the Dachau Concentration Camp, we took public transportation to the District where each of us bought a wool cap, gloves, and a scarf, but unfortunately boots were all sold out. After a long and tedious walk we were cleared by security, showed our passes and immediately were engulfed by a mass of humanity, who like us were anxious to see the promised spectacle. By now it was almost ten a.m., two hours away from the scheduled ceremony. Even so, we got there relatively early, and were standing perhaps 200 feet from the platforms erected for the dignitaries. Within minutes there was already a sea of people behind us. It was an awesome feeling and bitter cold. It was good that I was wearing two pairs of socks although as time passed it felt as if I was wearing none. The only consolation was that the thousands of people surrounding us suffered from the cold and wind just as we did.

Slowly the platforms in front of the Capitol were beginning to fill with public dignitaries, many I recognized as Senators, Congressmen, former Cabinet members, and other high Government Officials and their wives. Their names were often being whispered by spectators around us. Then there came military bands and numerous uniformed Officers that would escort the dignitaries to their assigned seats. Next came a large contingent of people in colorful long gowns, ostensibly a choir. Thereafter, Kennedy's newly appointed Cabinet members entered while their names were announced over loudspeakers. They were followed by former Presidents and Vice Presidents. Next we heard four ruffles and flourishes followed by the traditional sound of "Hail to the Chief." Kennedy with wife Jacqueline followed by V.P. elect Lyndon Baines Johnson and wife Lady Bird. The crowd went wild with applause and cheers which lasted several minutes.

I don't remember the exact order of events, but there was music, singing, the swearing in of Vice President Johnson by the Speaker of the House, Sam Rayburn, and finally President Kennedy by Chief Justice Earl Warren. The eminent poet Robert Frost recited two short poems, all the while I was trying to use my camera which had a frozen shutter. All of my efforts to warm the camera up in my coat pocket and everything else failed miserably. Darned!

Finally came the long expected inaugural speech by our new President. It conveyed to me and perhaps others, a real sense of purpose. There were many memorable phrases all of which resulted in jubilant applause. The one which impressed me the most was: "In your hands, my fellow citizens, more than mine, will rest the final success or failure of our course." There were others more like clichés. This inauguration speech warmed my heart and soul, but not my toes and feet which were like ice, and not the shutter of my camera which was still frozen in this 20 degree weather.

The inaugural part for the program was over except for a thunderous twenty-one gun salute from a battery of howitzers, the booms of which reverberated and reminded me briefly of the battle noises and worse, which I experienced during the war, except that this was not the noise of war but hopefully the ushering in of a peaceful era. As the platform emptied of dignitaries and guests, the people around us, who had willfully suffered the cold like Bill and I, started to leave in all directions. We had tickets for specifically numbered bleachers on Pennsylvania Avenue and therefore headed in that direction. On the way Bill and I found a building that was open and so we walked in to warm up while sitting on the carpeted stairway. I finally got the camera to work and was hoping to get some good shots during the parade.

It was an amazing sight to see the parade route as clean as a whistle from snow and ice while other main and side streets as well as sidewalks were still covered with snow and drifts. We had already walked perhaps 2 ½ miles getting to the Capitol and had added an additional two miles toward our viewing bleachers. So far this was a rather unusual day and we were stimulated to such an extent that all the walking and standing in snow and wind hadn't dampened our spirit. On the way we bought a couple souvenirs and a few bags of pretzels so we would be good for a few more hours. The bleachers were off the ground, which helped to keep our feet a little warmer and drier. Security was very tight with police and Army personnel being stationed every ten feet apart on both sides of the parade route, and all manhole covers along Pennsylvania Avenue having been sealed shut. Now came the wait. Suddenly the crowd came alive when at about 2:30 p.m. the flying wedges of motorcycles, their red lights blinking could be seen in the distance. Behind them in black armored Cadillacs came our long awaited President who now and then left the limousine and walked with Jacqueline a few minutes only to get back into the car, drive a short distance and repeat walking to the cheers of the onlookers.

We were lucky as both of them walked right by us to deafening cheers, waving, and applause of people in the immediate area. Then came a lull of perhaps twenty minutes to give the presidential caravan time to become situated in a specially constructed viewing pavilion. We were anxious but not disappointed to see military units of all types and all Services, including motorized units, armored vehicles, interspersed with colorful marching units, bands, floats, equestrian units, every State of the Union represented. There were so many highlights that you really had to be there to appreciate them. There was one unit that stands out in my mind still today and that was the replica true to size and all other features of PT Boat 109 which Kennedy captained during World War II, with the crew that had survived after a Japanese destroyer split the boat in two. These PT Boats were very fast and were deployed in the Pacific theater to attack enemy ships with torpedoes. The parade went on although it became dark and colder. Yet none of the spectators left until the last unit had passed which was about six thirty p.m. The entire event was a thrill of a lifetime and made me proud to be an American, having witnessed an unforgettable historical event. (See exhibit 18.17 in the appendix)

After I returned home Gert gave me the sad news that Uncle Berny, the only brother of my mother, had passed away January 21 vacationing at Nice, France, although he and Aunt Marthe had their permanent residence in Luxembourg City, Luxembourg. It was a great loss, particularly to my mother since now all three of her siblings were deceased. Her sister Irma Ehrlich, whose family first sheltered Irene in France, had died in 1948 from a rare skin disease called Pemphigus. My mother's other sister Helene, was murdered by the Nazis with her husband Max Cohen at Izbica, Poland nearby Belzic, or perhaps at Sobibor death camp. Now her brother had died and she was the sole survivor. This sad event added to her grief and already frail health which seemed to become worse as time went on.

That was not the only bad news. While I attended the Inauguration, all three children had come down with some type of flu. Dr. Morris Groban prescribed medical suppositories since none of the children could retain oral medication. When Ronald was little he referred to the suppositories as silver bullets because they were wrapped in aluminum foil, and resembled the silver bullets the "Lone Ranger" used in the TV program of the same name. All of the children had well recovered by the time Oma Wolff visited. As usual her visit was always enjoyable and she always brought small gifts along for her grandchildren. For us, and especially for me, she brought a box of macaroons with a cherry in the middle. They were always considered a delicacy since I bought the first ones at one of our many earlier visits to Lawrence. Baked by the Tripoli Bakery at 106 Common Street in Lawrence, we have bought many pounds of them and brought them back to Dayton where they were rationed so they would last for a while.

With all the regular and overtime hours I put in at work and at home, selling real estate, being a good father and husband, I still managed to do some volunteer work for Montgomery County for which I received a 100-hour Certificate of Recognition the second year in a row. Again my Commander, by request from the Department of Defense through Department of the Air Force, assigned me to a Task Force to participate in a "Nuclear Attack Assessment Study" in the

Pentagon. The specific task was to "evaluate the impact of the attack on Air Force production resources and supply schedules" for which a co-worker and I received several written commendations. One of the nicest compliments received on an internal Memo Routing Slip read by Charles Rush, my Unit supervisor: "Bob: I want to reiterate what is said in the attached letters (see exhibit 18.18 in appendix). To those of us who work with you it is just another illustration of the type of effort you constantly put out. This is why we have such a high opinion of you as a fellow worker." What no one knew nor realized was that, while I always did 110 % of what I was assigned to do, I hated this work, work that was always connected with war and weapons that kill people and things. No one knew, not my co-workers, supervisors or even Gert, and I didn't tell until after I retired and then only in strict confidence.

April 18, 19, and 20 of 1961, I participated and contributed to the fifth Annual Industrial Mutual Aid & Disaster Control Seminar in Houston, Texas. There were demonstrations along the Houston Ship channel to determine how best to protect highly vulnerable industrial facilities to avoid a possible repeat of the Texas City disaster of September 1947 which cost over 375 lives and injured more than 2000.

The spring of the year brought about a slew of events that in a way shaped America and the world. The first Intercontinental missile (ICBM) was launched in the Nevada Desert; the Peace Corps was established; the fiasco of a U.S. launched invasion of Cuba by about 1500 Cuban exiles, known as "The Bay of Pigs," was the first major political embarrassment of President Kennedy; the beloved film star great Gary Cooper had died; and a Russian cosmonaut beat U.S. Commander Alan Shepard into space by several weeks. More significant for women in America and eventually the world over was the recommended safe use of an oral contraceptive, a so-called birth control pill. It changed forever the way society lived and surely increased promiscuity.

It was June 7 when I was advised that my position would be transferred from the Air Force Logistics Command (AFLC) to Detachment #1 of the Air Force Systems Command (AFSC). Eventually, I was told that I was being considered for a permanent move to the Washington D.C. area, namely Andrews Air force Base, Maryland, where AFSC Headquarters were located. I was given the opportunity to visit the Maryland and D.C. area for four days with Gert, all expenses paid, to determine living cost differences, housing availability and cost, and other factors so Gert and I could make a decision whether to accept the potential relocation. Upon our return from the Washington area, and after long discussions and many considerations we decided against accepting a transfer, although the offer included a promotion to a higher grade salary. With our refugee background, both of us having been displaced from our homeland to many places before settling in Dayton, we just could not feel comfortable moving again. Here, we had finally established roots. To uproot us again did not look too appealing. We had made friends, the children were happy in school, we were enjoying our new home and our new surroundings. The grass may have looked greener on the other side, but we were happy with the shade of green on this side. The promised promotion and possibly higher grades in the future did not persuade us otherwise.

We had told our children the bare minimum about my reassignment and the possible transfer situation as not to cause them undo concern and worry. It was not a matter of keeping secrets, but it was a matter of keeping their well-being foremost in our mind. Most of our decisions, even those made on a daily basis and in later years, were always guided by that principle, and in retrospect was a good sign post to go by.

Sunday school for Susan and Ronald was becoming more meaningful and the studies had become more progressive. They learned Torah content, prayer and acts of kindness. They learned about the holidays and the attending celebrations and ceremonies. This was supplemented with learning of Hebrew, the State of Israel, and the obligation for "*Tsadakah*," giving to charity. Finally, a meeting was set up with Rabbi Ruslander to talk about Ronald's forthcoming bar mitzvah the following year and what we had to do to prepare himself for that momentous occasion. He suggested that we contact Mr. Hymie Chodos, who was the "Kabei," Torah reader at Beth Jacob Synagogue. Rabbi Ruslander set the date for the bar mitzvah, November 24, 1962 when Ronald would read "Chayye Sarah," from the book of Genesis, dealing with the death and burial of Sarah. Mr. Chodos agreed to teach Ronald to read, chant, and understand the Hebrew text and the significance of the Torah portion provided we bring Ronald once a week to his home on Lexington Avenue, in the Dayton View area, for one hour. Chodos was a pious man, and it took Ronald a while to lose his apprehension and actually begin to understand and like this man who practiced an orthodox life style.

Some of our friends had movie cameras and projectors and showed us various clips of what they had recorded. They were in color and we thought it would be nice if we could film some movies, take them along to Chicago and Massachusetts, and do a little bragging while showing them to the mischpocha, the relatives and friends. At the time it was too expensive for us to buy and we had other priorities. However, we determined that we were able to rent a movie camera at Malone's Camera store on East Second Street downtown, which was a lot cheaper in the short run. Besides I didn't know whether I could handle this new innovation. So, before we went on our vacation trip to Massachusetts in July I had a chance to experiment with the camera and the rented projector to familiarize myself with all the levers and buttons.

There were many opportunities as we drove along Lake Erie, and made many stops to shoot some funny action clips of the family on the way to Lawrence for a return visit to Oma Wolff. We had the 8mm film developed there and had fun showing that film and others of our new home on different occasions. I remember driving to Hampton Beach, a beach not too far away in New Hampshire, where Karen ran after seagulls shouting: "Come back birdie!" It was funny, and made us laugh when we saw it projected on the screen. Soon everyone had a movie camera and every year the cameras and projectors improved, except there was no sound. But even that could be added if one wanted to pay the price. Today, I have many boxes of regular and super 8mm film reels in the closet and hope someday (soon) I find the courage, time and money to have someone convert them to a mode that will enable our past come to life again on a TV or computer screen for those interested. As usual we had a good time, and visited some of Oma Wolff's relatives of which she had many. On the return trip we made a detour to New York where we stayed a couple nights. We took a boat tour around Manhattan and saw the magnificent Statue of Liberty. In addition we went to the top of the Empire State Building. Karen was a little scared at first, but we all enjoyed the sights and sounds of the big city.

The rest of the summer went fast. The family spent much time at the JCC pool and I joined after work and on weekends. Susan enjoyed reading and couldn't get enough books from the library. Her hair was beautiful and braiding it, while time consuming, made her look adorable. Karen's hair, like Ronald's when he was her age, was golden blond and curly, cute as a button. We all loved the fresh air, sun and naturally the water. Of course Ronald had a date every week with Mr. Chodos and he didn't mind studying and practicing at home. The vacation was a big relief for him since he had a very demanding and strict teacher at Belle Haven School by the name of Mrs. Gilbert. Although the summer days were hot, the big exhaust fan installed in the hall ceiling kept us comfortable during the day and especially during the nights. Our lawn and the flowers around the house had become a real delight and we spent much time tending the yard and relaxing in it. Ronald helped with mowing the lawn with a push type mower and the girls assisted in cleaning up.

Earlier in the year and on top of so many different assignments, I was given one additional top priority job as a result of a critical report rendered by the USAF Inspector General. The report had cited numerous deficiencies determined in "aircraft flight testing and acceptance procedures" of almost every aircraft being manufactured. A high level Committee of experts had been established in December 1960, however its chairman was reassigned and I had been delegated to become the new chairman. As you can imagine this put me in a somewhat peculiar position. Two other factors gave me considerable concern. One, I had become the chairman of a group of military and civilian experts, all of whom outranked me in position and professional stature. Second, I was totally unfamiliar with the technical matters underlying the subject. When I asked my military supervisor, all he would tell me is that I was assigned by order of the Commanding General. That was it! On my Committee were one Colonel, three Lt. Colonels, three Majors, and four civilians. All, except the civilians were proficient pilots.

You cannot imagine how this additional workload affected me initially. I spent one whole week, including many evening hours delving into the intricacies of the subject, next understanding the problem, and finally to decide on an approach on how best to analyze and come forth with solutions and feasible recommendations. The only good part for me was that after convening the first meeting to direct and redirect the effort with individual assignments, I delegated to the Committee members to furnish me a progress report each week and hold full day meetings every thirty days. In addition I would meet with one or several individuals on a need basis which required hasty trips to Air Force Bases and contractor facilities I had never been before.

On one of my trips to Kelly Air Force Base, Texas, I recalled a visit several years earlier with my then military chief Colonel Beverly Montgomery. He was invited by the Base Commander for dinner and insisted that I come along. The Commander, the name of whom I don't remember, was very hospitable, and as his charming wife served dinner I noticed that it was ham. Montgomery, who knew I was Jewish, mentioned that I had dietary restrictions and could not partake. Upon which the Base Commander's wife graciously fried me several eggs. Colonel Montgomery never mentioned one word about me being Jewish. He was indeed a true gentleman and above all a very correct human being. By speaking up for me he certainly saved me from considerable embarrassment. I also remember that, on this same trip, as we stood outside the San Antonio airport, a lanky Texan dressed in cowboy boots with spurs, flopping leather pants, and cowboy hat walked up to the blue uniformed Air Force Colonel, and in a loud voice while tipping his hat asked, "Are you the station master?" Montgomery, surprised, replied "no." Upon which the Texan cowboy tipped his hat again and left. Colonel Montgomery and I couldn't help laughing real hard.

It was the beginning of fall when we drove to Chicago to visit Oma and Opa Kahn. Since it was too much for us stay at their apartment on 6958 Clyde Avenue, we decided to stay for the next few nights at the Thunderbird Motel on Lakeshore Drive. We had taken a few sleeping bags and pillows along and were fairly comfortable. Oma cried for happiness when she saw us. It was one of her livelong trademarks to shed tears for happiness as well as sadness. She had a difficult time walking, walked with a cane, often with some help, and sat in a chair most of the time. It was sad for me, Gert, and the children, to see her deteriorating condition, but could not help. Her hair had turned snow white just as I remembered her mother (my Oma Malchen) in Luxembourg a few years before she died.

Irene had moved about a city block away from Mom and Dad. She had to sell her previous home because an expressway was being built and the land was needed. Her present house was a two flat, a building with an apartment for herself downstairs and one upstairs located at 6921 S. Merrill Avenue, immediately across from O'Keefe Elementary School. She was now working at the University of Chicago Hospital as a receptionist. Nephew Marc was studying for his bar mitzvah which was to take place the coming year, only eight months before Ronald's. Faye and Marc got along very well with our three hooligans. All of us spent a few very enjoyable and interesting hours at the Museum of Science and Industry where the kids watched chicks being hatched. Karen couldn't see enough of it and was excited. We also saw a special exhibit of an underground coal mine and watched how coal is mined and how miners descend into the mine via a shaft elevator and then are transported via motorized carts to the place where coal is mined with air hammers. A dangerous job. We also enjoyed the vintage car exhibit and were astounded to see a German submarine, the only one captured during World War II.

Dinner at Opa and Oma's apartment for all of us was enjoyable and special. Oma had always been a good cook, although now she needed help from Opa in the kitchen since it was difficult for her to get around. Afterwards, while the children were playing games, Dad showed me the massive files of handwritten and typed correspondence with lawyers and agencies in this country, Germany, and Luxembourg to obtain the inheritance funds left by Mom's sister Helene and husband Max Cohen after they had been killed during the Holocaust. Dad had received a copy of their last will and testament which was written and duly certified only days before they were carted off to Poland, never to be seen again. The correspondence was a nightmare. The German Government and courts, at that time located in Bonn, resorted to every legal maneuver possible to deny that the funds left in Luxembourg banks were confiscated by the German occupation forces and used for their own purposes. But Dad had no intention of giving up and appealed every decision made by the German courts. He also was in a legal battle to obtain compensation for the business which he had to "sell" under threat of his life, while he was in the concentration Camp Dachau. I could tell that his life's ordeals, and now with Mom being almost a semi invalid, had left him with visible aging scars. Yet, his and Mom's eyes would light up when playing with, talking or reading to their grandchildren. They were indeed their pride and joy.

With very few exceptions we always managed to visit Aunt Bella and Uncle Alfred (Danziger) as well as Aunt Leone and Uncle Ernst (Kahn). The latter had moved into a smaller apartment at the Eastend Park Hotel at Hyde Park Boulevard since both of their sons, my cousins, Herbie and Laurie had married. We didn't see them nor the other cousins, Alice and her husband Dick Sinsheimer, as well as Lorie and Henry Mayer, too often since they no longer lived nearby. Driving to Chicago was becoming somewhat easier every time we traveled because each time another stretch of interstate highway was finished. Still it was a drive that took us about nine hours, the worst stretch was around the industrial area of Calumet City, Indiana with all its smells and rail crossings.

Back in Dayton, Ronald studied hard in school as well as for his bar mitzvah and Mr. Chodos was satisfied with his progress. His fee for tutoring Ronald was $25 each week and well worth it. My Committee had almost completed its findings and I was putting together the final report when during the early morning hours of November 21 and 22, the Annex to the Headquarters Building, Air Force Logistics Command was gutted by fire. My office was in the basement of that building known as Building #262 Annex. Luckily this happened during off duty hours, else there could have been a large number of casualties. Two Base firemen were however killed. Luckily for me, I had much of the drafted report in typing at the adjacent building while other Committee members had duplicate copies of the draft to provide more input and or corrections. In addition, most of the backup data was in a fire proof safe. The Final Report which was published December 15 1961, was designated a "Privileged Document" and not releasable in whole or in part to persons or agencies outside the Air Force without express approval of the Secretary of the Air Force.

In summary, the adoption of certain recommendations which were approved by the Air Staff after several briefings would save 30% of the total flight test program cost for eleven aircraft types including the B-52 bomber, C-130 cargo, and F-105 fighter. For the KC-135 tanker a reduction of 61% in flight test and acceptance cost by both contractor and Air Force had already been achieved during tests by applying the recommended and approved changes. The AF Committee had done its job, and as Chairman, I received many accolades especially when making formal presentations at different levels of the Command and to the Air Staff at the Pentagon. I must admit, although I had made many official presentations at various levels of Air Force Commands and to the Secretaries at the Pentagon in the past, I was always uptight before, resulting in a mild form of upset stomach. To counter that, Dr. Groban had prescribed a pill for me to take an hour before to settle my stomach. Fortunately it worked well and relaxed me. I carried it with me all the time and still take it today when I am under stress and feel it in my stomach. (See exhibits 18.19 and 18.20 in the appendix)

It had been an important and exciting year for us. We could look back on the many important accomplishments at home, for which Gert deserves much of the credit. At the office, the work had become very demanding and hectic for me, although it was rewarding upon completion of the many special assignments. The free world however was still precariously struggling to keep the peace. It was only past October that American and Russian tanks faced each other at the border between West and East Berlin Germany. The Russians insisted on forcibly keeping the population in their zone of occupation and from migrating to the more prosperous and democratic West Berlin by building high concrete walls fortified with barbed wire and watch towers called the Berlin Wall. This however was not the only unrest in the world. There were rumblings of discontent in North Africa,

Vietnam, the Caribbean, and other areas of the globe, and Nazi henchman Adolf Eichman was sentenced by Israeli courts to die by hanging.

Here in our own country the Peace Corps was established by our President, and in science the X-15 rocket propelled craft reached speeds of 4000 miles per hour, while IBM was marketing the sensational so-called golf ball typewriter which changed the office routine everywhere. On the artistic side, the films of *West Side Story, Breakfast at Tiffany's,* and *Judgement at Nuremberg,* are still in my mind and have been revisited by Gert and me many times since on TV.

To ring out the old and ring in the New Year of 1962, Gert and I decided to throw a party and had invited six other couples from our new neighborhood and the old. It was loads of fun to plan for games, food, and decorations in every detail and got much help as well as ideas from Susan, Ronald and of course Karen. For one of the more exciting but somewhat risqué games we blindfolded one of the fellows and after turning him around several times he had to feel the legs of several girls (up to the knee only) until he determined the one that was his wife. It was hilarious and I still remember the fun and giggling the game generated. It was a wonderful evening with much hilarity, good food, drinks and many prizes. In a way it set the tone for our future social life.

THE TRANQUIL YEARS: PART II

Based on years of having lived through winters in Dayton the weather was not very predictable. Temperatures were mostly bearable although there came some days or a week when temperatures hovered around zero and we could count on minus zero weather on occasion. Snow was another matter and forecasts were not always reliable. Leaving the house in the morning was not the problem because the car was parked in the garage. It was a different story in case of snow over night when I first had to clear the driveway. Depending on driving conditions, I would pick my riders up 20 minutes earlier in the morning so we get to work on time. The parking lot at the base provided a more challenging problem at the end of the work day if there was a lot of snow on the ground, on the car, and the windshield was iced up. There were instances where we were let off work early in case the weather and driving conditions had worsened. And regardless of the weather, the children would walk to school in boots, coats, scarfs, hats and gloves. There were no buses for them since we did not meet the distance criterion for school bus service.

Notwithstanding the normal and sometimes not too normal hardships of winter, our home was warm and comfortable except for the dry air produced by the gas perimeter heat. Every home heated with gas has that problem since the gas flames of the furnace suck up the oxygen in the house thus reducing the humidity level. This created a substandard dryness and caused all of us to come down with dry throats, coughs and colds. I countered that situation with some success by pouring water into the perimeter conduits every evening before the children and we would go to sleep since this increased the humidity in the house and found we had fewer colds and sort throats problems. Of course, because of the weather, we spent more time at home which gave all of us more time to do other things. The children always liked when it snowed and were looking forward to making a snowman outside our patio. They had learned how to roll the snow so it would become an ever larger mass and could create a larger and taller statue. It was not uncommon that I had to bring a ladder to add the arms, neck, head, and then fit the tall figure with gloves, maybe a broom, charcoal eyes and mouth, a carrot for the nose, a scarf, hat and sometimes ear muffs. It was great fun for the whole family and we watched this colossus day after day until the warmer weather performed its melting trick.

One day we received a call from the janitor at Bell Haven School that he had caught Ronald in the schoolyard after a snowball had broken a window and Ronald was the only one there. When Ronald came home his story was that some of the kids had a snowball fight and they broke the window. They all ran away after the window was broken but Ronald didn't since he knew that he didn't break it. After all these many years of explaining, preaching and admonishing Ronald as well as Susan that they had nothing to fear as long as they told the truth. All of a sudden that advice had backfired. Ronald could not understand why he became the fall guy for the culprits who were responsible, even so he had nothing to do with it and was only a passive bystander. It took a while to explain to Ronald that there are circumstances where that rule that Mom and Dad, also teachers had repeatedly explained does not apply. To wit, when bad things happen it is not a good idea to stick around. It is certainly difficult to explain that to children when adults don't always understand how to react in similar situations. We paid for the replacement of the window and hoped that Ronald had learned something from this particular experience.

EXHIBIT 18.21 Marc Diament Bar Mitzvah portrait.

It was not a favorable time of the year to drive to Chicago but my nephew Marc's bar mitzvah on January 13, 1962 was a special event we did not want to miss. The roads were not bad but Chicago had still a lot of snow on the ground. That did not dampen the excitement that surrounded the event.

Marc did a terrific job in chanting his Torah and Haftorah (reading of the prophets) portion. He also conducted a part of the morning service at Congregation Habonim. One could see that his mother Irene, his sister Faye as well as Opa and Oma were delighted and very proud of him. Missing unfortunately was his beloved father Nate who six years earlier had befallen such a tragic death. The festivities were wonderful, yet not the same without him and this sentiment was on everyone's mind. Ronald took note and realized that in not too many months he would be called upon to do similarly.

Our trip would not have been complete without receiving from Irene a variety of different wattage light bulbs that customers could ask for, free of charge, when they paid their electric bill. Both Irene and my parents would save them for us, and with our new home in Dayton we always had bulbs burn out. On our drive home we stopped at Sarge Biltz on the outskirts of Lafayette, Indiana, the kids' favorite restaurant on route to and from Chicago. However, it would not be too long that progress with the Interstate Highway system led traffic around Lafayette that Sarge Biltz succumbed for lack of customers. While the Interstate Highway system would eventually become a boon to car and truck traffic, businesses that used to be on the left and right side of U.S. or State Highway roads went gradually out of business. Today, one has to exit the Interstate in order to find filling stations, restaurants, motels, hotels, and other businesses. Progress can be a boon to many, but for some it can be a bust. The Interstate Highway System lead to boredom at 60 mph and sadly eliminated adventures of the U.S. and State Highways at maximum 50 mph.

The day had been expected with much excitement for our astronaut Lt. Colonel John Glenn to attempt orbiting the earth in a Mercury spacecraft. After many weather and equipment caused delays, the spacecraft was launched February 20, 1962 from Cape Canaveral Florida. It was televised and watched by people all over the world including family Kahn. It was nerve wracking when various technical difficulties occurred during the capsule's descent, which appeared to jeopardize the mission and more importantly, Glenn's life. However the splashdown, while precarious, had a happy ending. I had mailed four envelopes with project Mercury stamps to Colonel Glenn several weeks earlier asking him to dedicate one to each of the children and me, and have the envelopes specially postmarked with the date of the flight. It was a long shot. I assumed that my request would in all probability be ignored and was completely surprised and amazed when about ten days after the flight a large envelope, supplied by me earlier, arrived with the four envelopes inside signed by Glenn as requested. Only in Chanukkah 2009 did I give each of the children the properly personalized envelope specially framed. Certainly a unique and historical gift which I had kept in a bank safety deposit box all these years.

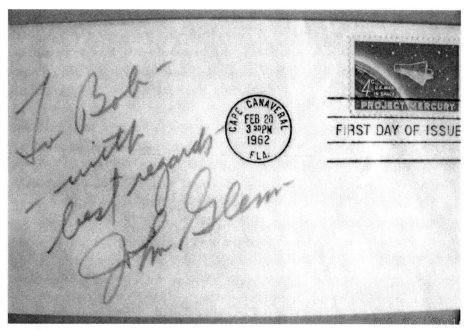

EXHIBIT 18.22: A souvenir of an historic event signed by the astronaut.

While some years earlier Susan and Ronald had attended public school kindergarten, we decided, for many different reasons, affordability being one, to enroll Karen in Mrs. Selden's nursery school operated by Mrs. Selden, a Jewish lady. This private nursery was located on Salem Avenue and came highly recommended. Because there was a much smaller group of children, Karen learned to socialize with others quickly and also obtained more individualized attention. One day I went there for a visit and with Mrs. Selden's permission, recorded the activities with my movie camera. The film clip turned out to be very funny and is almost hilarious when viewed today.

One evening Gert and I went downtown to see the several hours long movie *Lawrence of Arabia* on the wide screen. It was a marvelous and action packed flick which we have seen since many times on TV and always enjoyed it.

The Cold War was sparking everywhere. Berlin and Vietnam were heating up more each day, while Russia's Nikita Khrushchev made threats on all diplomatic fronts, and our President John F. Kennedy decreed to stop all imports from Cuba. Who would cry chicken first? It was an uncomfortable time for the American people who more than ever feared a nuclear threat. I could feel the pressure and uneasiness by the stepped up intensity of activities at the Air Force Base, with which I was sometimes involved. Thank G'd the children didn't know anything about the world crisis, and the birthday parties for Susan and Karen were happy days for them, their friends and us.

It was late February 1962 that at the annual Wright Patterson Credit Union meeting I was reelected to its Board of Directors for a two year term, an honor, but required a lot of work to restate procedures and policies to make sure that the Credit Union would operate in accordance with State and Federal laws, serve its membership and assure its continued growth. Later in March I was singled out to serve on a Command Subcontract Management Task Group which oversaw the unique problems inherent in delegating uniform authorities and procedures to prime contractors so they could effectively manage their subcontractors. The task required an enormous amount of travel, untold hours of work including evenings and weekends away from home. Much of what I learned found its way into a comprehensive report with recommendations for inclusion and changes in the Armed Services Procurement Regulations (ASPR). Letters of commendation attest to the value of my participation on this Task Group and its deliberations of which I am very proud.

My travels and the attending absences from home posed additional burdens on Gert and left the children longing for their Daddy and his nighty night "Hunkel Dunkel" stories at bed time. Nevertheless, the home comings were always happy and joyful reunions. Daddy always brought "soapy" back from his trip and often some gifts for Gert and trinkets or toys for the children. I remember bringing home a barking and walking dog operated with battery and a handheld controller with buttons that would make the dog's tail wag, its head move and eyes light up. Karen enjoyed playing with it and the rest of us had fun watching.

In the meantime my post war traumatic stress syndrome had eased to the point where upon my recent medical examination I received a letter dated April 17, that the Veterans Administration had reduced my disability compensation from 30% to 10. I was very glad to be doing well in life in spite of the fact that, even then, seventeen years after the war, the medical community still didn't have a clue how and why a soldier could be so seriously affected by the trauma of war, and furthermore had less of an idea how to deal and cure the symptoms.

Oma Wolff visited us over Memorial Day, and from here she flew to Atlanta to spend a few days with Lester and Ilse Salten and their children. She enjoyed flying and it saved us a long trip by car to visit her in Massachusetts.

Because I had Air Force business to attend to at the Pentagon, I decided to request permission to drive a few days earlier and take the family along. This gave us an opportunity to see some of the prominent and interesting sites in our Capital, Washington D.C. Before leaving Dayton I had obtained passes from Ohio Senator Frank Lausche to attend the 87th Congress, second session, in the Senate Chamber. We also had passes from Ohio Congressman Paul Schenk to attend the House of Representatives, both sessions convened in the Capitol Building. While I was at the Pentagon, Gert showed the children some of the other sites around the city including the Washington Monument, the Lincoln Memorial, the FBI Museum, and Arlington Cemetery. It was very educational for Susan and Ronald, Karen being somewhat too young to appreciate the significance of much of it.

Ron's good friend John Hamilton, who lived across the street from us on Castano, had moved to St. Louis, since his father, who was some type of manager with TWA, had been promoted. Ron was able to obtain a free airline ticket through John's father, and so that summer he visited. Ron had a busy summer. In addition to being tutored for his bar mitzvah he also started to play Little League softball sponsored by Kapnas Super Market located then 7600 North Main Street. He enjoyed sport activities and collected baseball cards. As if Gert wasn't busy enough she volunteered to be co-chairman with Dottie Hoch, wife of Saul with whom I car pooled, on "Operation Sukkot" the harvest festival for Temple Israel. Other ladies who worked on various committees to make arrangements for food, decorations, publicity, entertainment etc., were Selma Feigelson, Ruth Hochman, Elaine Peterman, Ruth Feist, Frieda Schlesinger, Joyce Maggied and Charlotte Bloom. It turned out to be a wonderful event and cemented friendly relationships between the participating families further.

On some weekends we went on interesting short hikes at Glen Helen Park near Yellow Springs, or Englewood, Taylorsville, or Huffman Dam's recreational areas. Five of these huge engineering marvels were constructed after a catastrophic flood destroyed much of Dayton in spring of 1913. They now regulate the flow of several area rivers, have protected the city of Dayton ever since, and play an important part for recreation. U.S. Route 40 crosses the top of Englewood Dam and provides beautiful views. Occasionally we went other places to visit a farm or wildlife refuge to watch some animals. We also went once to the Veterans Cemetery where thousands of Civil War, World War I and II soldiers are buried.

By coincidence, on my 39th birthday, Gert and I received our first Sabin oral polio vaccine from the local Montgomery County Medical Society, hoping that we would never contract the terrible debilitating disease from which our former President Roosevelt suffered. Our children had previously received polio shots, which had been developed by Dr. Salk.

Earlier in the month, an American U-2 spy plane was shot down over China. Of course this created additional anxieties that resulted in the activation and alert staffing of the Air Force underground Command Post at Wright Patterson AF Base to which I had been assigned certain daytime or nighttime shifts including weekends. The Soviets successfully developed highly advanced missiles and warheads, which were also now aimed at all of Europe and Great Britain. Their long range rockets were thought to have the capability of reaching the North American continent.

Since our humiliating defeat at the Bay of Pigs Cuba, the Soviet leader Khrushchev had secretly offered his sinister services to Cuban dictator Fidel Castro by suggesting he place missiles directed toward the U.S. on Cuban soil, to which Castro agreed. The country first sensed something was wrong when our Intelligence Services spotted an unusually large number of Russian vessels loaded with odd shaped equipment heading for Cuba. Finally, on Sunday, October 14, 1962 we received highly classified messages at the Command Post that a U-2 aircraft had photographed at least several dozen Russian medium range missiles and more than 13 longer range missiles on launch pads near San Cristobal, Cuba. All of them were directed toward the U.S. In addition, Russian MIG fighter aircraft and IL-28 jet bombers were identified on Cuban airfields. This ratcheted up the U.S. Armed Forces DEFCON (Defense Condition) alert status and readiness of all Forces. President Kennedy met in secret with his closest advisors and members of the National Security Council to determine the options available to counter this serious provocation. Reservists were called up for duty. It had become a national emergency.

To me and others in the know, a nuclear war was imminent but were sworn to secrecy that no one, not even our wives could be told what was happening. I came home at irregular hours, usually late evening, and pretended nothing was amiss. Of course Gert sensed something out of the ordinary was happening when one early evening the telephone rang. The caller, who identified himself as an officer from the base, asked where I was. She told him that I was getting a haircut at the barbershop at the Northtown Shopping Center and gave him the telephone number where I could be reached. Imagine my surprise, when sitting in the barber chair the barber handed me the phone, and the caller ordered me to immediately present myself at the underground Command Post. I paid the barber although he was not finished, and high-tailed to the base for duty. I was scared but had to keep my cool in spite of the fact that, according to our own secret intelligence sources, the American arsenal of nuclear missiles was far greater and more accurate than that of the Soviets'. To me it seemed that a strategic advantage by the U.S. would make little difference. Once the "nukes" were launched, regardless of who launched them, mankind would suffer a blow of untold proportions on both continents.

New messages that came across my desk concerned themselves with threats from the Soviets that would create two Germanies: an East and West Germany for good. Kennedy addressed the Nation on Monday October 22 and told us about the reckless brinkmanship caused by the Russians, his instruction as Commander in Chief for a naval and air blockade of Cuba, and also called for the immediate unconditional withdrawal of all Russian weapons from the island. Now the nation was stunned and full of anxiety realizing the gravity of a possible doomsday in the making. Kennedy's speech and demands avoided an immediate showdown and resulted in some high level diplomacy that I have no further knowledge of. Then we learned at the Command Post that one of our U-2 reconnaissance planes did not return from its mission over Cuba. People everywhere started hoarding food, looked for ways of survival by leaving industrial and population centers, while others hastily tried to build protective shelters.

The tension had escalated to a fever pitch and school children practiced air raid drills. Ronald and Susan were asking questions that Gert and I could not answer except for creating special prayers instead of telling them "Hunkel Dunkel" stories when I was not on duty at the Command Post. Finally, with many ups and downs in this war of nerves, an agreement was reached between the two powers on October 28 to the effect that all missiles would be dismantled and shipped back to Russia while America would lift its blockade of Cuba. It was a great relief for the American people and my duties at the Command Post became less demanding. While the worst was over, the crisis was kept at a low boil for many months while our nuclear strike bombers were in the air 24 hours a day, ready for any sudden eruptions or new escalations. It was not a time for celebration, but it was a tremendous relief for the entire country.

Now that the family was getting back to a state of normalcy, I could be at home in the evenings to help Susan and Ronald with their homework again, and assure the latter that his chanting of the portion for his bar mitzvah was fine. It was so much fun watching Karen again in the bathtub taking her bubble bath while blowing bubbles from her bubble pipe. It was so outrageously funny that I couldn't resist taking movies of her having the fun of her life, all so bubbly in the tub. There were also things that I was able to help Gert with and spend some quality time just the two of us, alone. There were always things to do that required me to sit at my desk which was in our bedroom and from which I did my real estate work that demanded many phone calls and other paperwork. Susan would often take care of the filing of listing pages in two large binders so that sales and homes for sale in Montgomery County and nearby counties were always up to date. While I was able to obtain new listings and make a sale now and then, it required loads of work, many hours making calls and showing properties that my free time to devote to the family became worrisome.

Many times Gert received real estate related calls at home which, if I was at the office, she relayed to me, sometimes requiring that I had to schedule appointments during my lunch time. Other times I had to stall a client to a time in the evening. Occasionally, I would lose a listing or a sale because I was out of town or unable to meet a client's schedule. The time had suddenly come for me to make a decision to go full time into the real estate business or stay on my job with the Federal Government. The decision was not an easy one. On one hand the job with the Air Force did not agree with my conscience because the nature of the work would result in the development, manufacture and deployment of devices for warfare, which I despised. On the other hand, I had established myself and felt that my job was relatively secure based on my excellent reputation. Looking at the real estate business I immediately realized that it was dependent on the economy, which would dictate whether I could make sufficient sales to provide an income to sustain my family's financial needs and wants; although, I would have more independence and perhaps less stress. The die was cast when on October

10, 1962 I formally resigned from Harry Carter Real Estate Company, and did not plan to renew my Ohio real estate license.

The one thing I realized was missing from my resume was a college degree, something that in all likelihood kept me from being considered for promotion to a higher grade position in the future. It had started to bother me since that type of information would always precede me whenever I would be considered or assigned to special projects or introduced at professional gatherings. It was also a considerate embarrassment at social gatherings because that topic would come up invariably in many different ways, and I had to be silent. How I could obtain a college degree and maintain my job at the same time became a perplexing question. I kept this question pretty much to myself. Education was not only a concern for myself but also for our children. To widen their horizon further with knowledge we decided to purchase a complete set of Compton Encyclopedias for $181.55 after looking at several others on the market. It turned out that all three kids, as well as Gert and I, used them quite a bit over the years and I use them still today although some of the information is outdated.

As the date for Ron's bar mitzvah came closer Gert and I met with Rabbi Ruslander to go over last minute details. I must digress briefly to mention that Selwyn D. Ruslander was a sweet man, very kind, understanding, loved by all of the congregants, and respected by all other congregations as well as the Dayton community at large. He was everyone's friend. Upon his death many years later, as Vice President of the local B'nai B'rith Lodge I recommended and succeeded in renaming of the Chapter, Ruslander Lodge in his honor. As the Rabbi talked to us we mentioned that Ron would like to wear a tallit in the synagogue for his bar mitzvah. He had no objection, although ours was a reformed congregation and the only ones wearing a tallit were the rabbis and cantor. Ronald would be the first congregant to don a prayer shawl. It was an honor for Ron and made him very happy.

The Salten family, including Fifi the dog, arrived Friday November 23 afternoon by car. We always called it a "pimp mobile" because it was a large Lincoln Town Car. They checked into the Holiday Inn. Oma Wolff, whom we picked up at the airport, stayed with us and so did my dad who always enjoyed the flight from Chicago, having a little glass of Schnapps (bourbon) served by a stewardess. In those years we were able to go out on the tarmac with a small bouquet of flowers for a cordial welcome. Unfortunately, my mother who had a minor stroke earlier was unable to come with him and was sadly missed during the festivities, as was my sister Irene and her two children. The latter were unable to come for several reasons. While Dad was here, Irene would take care of Mom during the night while an aide took care of her during the daytime. Also, Irene had only recently started a new job at the University of Chicago Lying-In Hospital as a receptionist and could not take time off.

All of us rested for a while and then sat down for a festive Shabbat dinner which Gert had lovingly prepared. Gert lit the Shabbat candles while Ronald, Susan, Karen and I said the various broches, benedictions, over the wine and the challah, a braided loaf of white bread. After we changed into our fineries, Ronald in his new suit, we proceeded to temple where services were scheduled to begin at 8 p.m. The ushers, Don Stotter, Dr. Richard Serbin, Milton Marks, and Vern Zimmerman greeted us and escorted my dad, Ronald, and me to be guests at the pulpit. It was a great honor for all of us, and there are not too many occasions were individuals are given that honor. My dad especially cherished that evening. Rabbis Ruslander and Allen Podet entered, greeting each of us cordially with a handshake and a few well-chosen words, as did Cantor David Dashman.

Rabbi Ruslander welcomed a large group of visitors from the United Church of Christ from Johnsville and the Congregational Christian Church of Covington, before services began with choir music by the talented organist Isidore Freed. A nod by Cantor Deshman gave rise for Gertrude and Susan to come forward to the bima where they had the *mitzvah*, the joyous honor, of lighting the Shabbat candles accompanied with the appropriate Hebrew blessings. To see Oma Wolff and Opa Kahn in their glory made Gert and me very happy. All of us were tired, and with an even bigger day coming up tomorrow we drove home and called it a night.

Although services Shabbat morning didn't begin until 11 o'clock, all of us were up early. Uncle Lester and Ilse, Gert's sister, as well as their children, Peggy, Roslyn, and Rita, met us at Temple. Dad and I, accompanying 13 year old Ronald, sat on the bima. The entire family was attentively waiting for Ron to read from the Torah portion, "Chayye Sarah", Chapter 23 of Genesis, dealing with the death and burial of Sarah, the first matriarch of Judaism. When the time came and the Torah scroll was opened, Ronald being a Cohen, just like his father and all of his ancestors before him, was the first called to the Torah by his Hebrew name, Joseph Ben Bear. A small wooden box was placed for him to stand on so it was easier for him to see and read the Hebrew text from the scroll. Proudly standing there wearing his tallit, he chanted his parsha aloud and without hesitation, while my dad and I stood next to him. Ronald next read the English translation of what he had read in Hebrew. Dad and I said the broches for the next Torah portions, both of us wearing tallits as well. I wore the one gifted to me by my father and mother at my bar mitzvah twenty six years earlier in Mannheim. It too had miraculously survived the terrible years of the Holocaust. Another mitzvah was given my brother-in-law Lester, and then Ronald gave a short sermon in which he addressed the rabbis, parents, relatives and friends in the congregation.

"There are two beautiful stories in today's Torah portion. The first story demonstrates Abraham's love and deep respect for his wife Sarah after she had died. Abraham did not want the customary burial place for Sarah, but a very special one."

Little did Ronald realize that many years later we would visit the city Kiriath-arba in Israel's West Bank, now better known as Hebron. Here, we saw the cave of Machpelah in which Sarah was buried. Later, Abraham, as well as Isaac, Rebecca, Leah and Jacob were also buried in this cave (Rachel is believed to have been buried near Bethlehem). A mosque was built on top of the cave in more recent times to protect and worship these patriarchs and matriarchs who are venerated by both Muslims and Jews as their ancestors.

Ronald continued: "The remaining part of the Torah portion deals with the second story, namely Abraham's love and concern for his son Isaak. The story is told that Abraham was old, and he asked one of his servants to swear to him that he would find a good wife for Isaak, just like Sarah was. Both of these stories have one thing in common which is very important today. When we use such phrases as "Love they Neighbor as Thyself," we often forget its true meaning. Love they Neighbor, is something that must be practiced first at home, as in the stories told in the Torah. It must be carried over into every activity and to each member of the family; – and only then will we be able to extend this practice to our fellow man next door, across town, in other cities,– and finally in all parts of the world. Only if all of us follow Abraham's example, can we as Jews live up to our responsibilities and make this a world where people understand and trust one another."

Ron then thanked the rabbis for their support and spiritual guidance, Mr. Chodes for preparing him for his bar mitzvah, his grandparents and relatives for honoring him with their presence and to all the congregants for worshiping with him. Last but most important he thanked Gert and me *"for all they have done for me. I hope that in years to come, I will be able to live up to their expectations."*

Rabbi Ruslander asked Oma Wolff, Opa Kahn, Susan, Karen, Gert and me to stand in front of him for G'd's blessing while he held both hands over our heads. A separate blessing came next for Ronald also in front of the open ark. Richard G. Shaman, the President of Temple Israel, proceeded to honor Ronald by congratulating him then presenting him with a Certificate of his bar mitzvah on this 27th Heshvan 5723 according to the Jewish calendar, and with a Kiddish cup, - a goblet for wine, as well as a Chumesh, - the Pentateuch and Haftorah. As the service was concluded everyone was invited to the social hall for a Kiddush, which we sponsored, followed by blessings over bread and wine. Several sweets tables had been set up with a specially prepared variety of cakes, torts, cookies, tarts, fruit, wine, coffee and punch. Everyone now had a chance to wish us the parents, relatives, Karen, Susan and of course Ronald a Mazel Tov, good luck and congratulations accompanied in many instances with hugs and kisses from our friends. And so ended the most wonderful formal part of Ron's bar mitzvah.

While in the afternoon the adults rested, our two girls had much fun getting reacquainted with their cousins from Atlanta. Ron, on the other hand, was trying out and showing off his new bike, a present from his parents, and other gifts from his friends in the neighborhood.

For the evening we had made reservations for the twelve of us at the "Tropics" for dinner. It was Ron's, as well as Susan's and Karen's, favorite place. We were greeted by a hostess dressed in authentic Hawaiian attire. At the table Ron picked out a huge high back fan-like South Sea Island bamboo chair which dwarfed him completely. We all enjoyed excellent food with wine, and a Shirley Temple for Karen. Georgie Rudin, the owner of the Tropics, came over and congratulated Ron. During the evening there were many toasts for the occasion by Oma, Opa, Uncle Lester, and myself. As usual, Opa Kahn smoked a cigar after dinner while Oma Wolff and other guest in the restaurant complimented Susan's and Karen's pretty dresses and shoes. There was good music and entertainment and all of us had a great time.

It was Thanksgiving weekend and as custom we continued the holiday by having a relaxing day while the young ones were looking forward to a prearranged bowling party at Trotwood Lanes in the afternoon. At other bar mitzvahs, parents would arrange lavish and costly dinner parties, primarily for their own friends and business acquaintances, at the best hotels or country clubs in town. We however decided to make this a fun afternoon only for Ron and his friends. He was allowed to invite a total of twenty boys and girls, plus his sisters and cousins from Atlanta. After a couple hours of bowling everyone went to the party room where hamburgers, french fries and drinks were served while I took some movies of the gang having a rip roaring time. I had also taken movies of other activities that weekend, including Ron's rehearsal of his Torah portion in the synagogue. As parents picked up their children at a prearranged time, Rabbi Ruslander, who picked up his daughter Judith, complimented us for having a party just for the young people, which he thought was "more to his liking."

Loaded down with the many presents he had received from his friends coupled with many gifts and money from family and our friends as well, it took Ron many hours to unravel all the gift-wrap and many more days and weeks to enjoy "the loot."

For him and for us, it was a weekend of excitement and fulfilling events that neither he nor the rest of his family could ever forget. It had truly been a weekend of Thanksgiving, and a time for giving thanks, a weekend that had filled us with much *naches*--- pleasure and contentment.

At the end of the school year, Susan and Ronald were awarded a Certificate of Merit from Belle Haven School for completing a year of studying German, a foreign language program sponsored by parents. The certificate was signed by their teacher, Ida Nisam and the school principal Francis M. Birt. There are a number of important stages in one's life, and education, we thought, was the most important. Probably all of the young couples who belonged to the Parent

Teacher Association believed so likewise. This is why we insisted that the elementary school curriculum be taught as a means of personal development rather than emphasis on memorization of subject matter. The exposure to a modern language seemed to be on the path of achieving this objective. Of course, both Susan and Ronald thought taking German would be a cinch since this was their parents' mother language, and they would surely help or do their homework. No such luck! We helped to the degree that we encouraged them to study and understand why.

As the year 1962 came to a close my concern and that of millions of others was our government's increasing involvement in Vietnam with both men and equipment. I could not see what we had to gain by our involvement nor what we had to lose by staying out of the fray. However, the defense industry, known as the Military Industrial Complex, managed to manipulate our lawmakers with their well-endowed lobbyists to keep the pot boiling, thus feathering their own nest with millions while the U.S. was keeping statistics on losses of our own brave men.

I continued to take evening classes at the University of Dayton, which I deemed pertinent to enhance my work at Wright Patt now that I had given up my time consuming real estate side line. Although I too had homework, I still had more time than before to spend with the family, especially on weekends. Also now that winter had arrived there were fewer outdoor chores except for snow removal on the driveway with which Ronald gave me a hand in the morning, and if it snowed during the day before I came home, the whole crew did the driveway so Daddy could drive into the garage. Then came income tax time and it was always good to have all the papers, receipts and figures together for a family of 5 in 1962.

While gasoline was only $0.31 per gallon, you didn't have to pump it yourself. There was an attendant who filled up the tank but also checked the oil, water in the radiator, cleaned the windshield, and checked your tire pressure, while addressing you politely as mister or madam, and not "you guys" as we are greeted everywhere today.

It was a very good and eventful year, one that stands out in importance for the Kahn family, and one in which Adolf Eichman, responsible for the murderer of millions of Jews, was sentenced by an Israel court, and hanged.

To make our living room more inviting for visitors we had selected and purchased through Eileen Phinick a long Thayer Coggin couch. It was covered in a medium brown cloth and complimented the other pull-out hide away couch. We had the Thayer Coggin couch until spring of 2012, although it had been recovered with an off white leatherette type material by then.

At my job I was still traveling quite a bit. In March of 1963, on a business trip to New York, Uncle Richard, who at that time was divorced, took me out for dinner. Unfortunately, it was the last time I saw him. On April 15, 1963 he passed away in his sleep. Earlier in March, I was again on TDY (temporary duty travel) with a task group representing different Command installations. It took us to Vandenberg Air Force Base, where we happened to witness a missile launch, and also visited numerous AF contractors in the greater Los Angeles area. Instead of flying me back to Dayton over the weekend, or the other members back to their respective home base and back out again, the officer in charge decided that we would stay put at the Mission Inn at Riverside and save the Air Force the expense of travel.

This historic and ornate Mission had been converted into a Hotel, which occupied a complete city block, dating back to 1876 and was originally under construction for about thirty years. It was so impressive with its Moorish Spanish architecture, its castle towers and minarets, catacombs, daunting hallways that it gave me a feeling of traveling back through time. As I walked around I came across an ornate chapel which had some original Tiffany stained glass windows. Everywhere you could spot bells of different sizes hanging in archways, towers, and steeples. All-in-all it was a beautiful atmosphere with elegance and historic charm. My room was very spacious and decorated with furniture of years gone by. It was quaint and yet very comfortable. It gave me the feeling as if I was in a huge ancient monastery.

The entire area was under a severe drought and water was rationed to the extent that we were offered soft drinks, beer or wine in the dining room since drinking water had to be trucked in and demand was at a premium. We worked until late Friday evening to prepare a draft report of our findings of government contractors we had investigated and had Saturday and Sunday to ourselves. Since we had acquired several Government cars from a local Air Force Base motor pool, several of us decided to do some sightseeing. I had a Government authorized driver's license and did the driving. We went to visit Disneyland in Anaheim which was loads of fun and full of amazement. Next we visited Knott's Berry Farm at Buena Park, not as well-known but very interesting. Basically it was a large 150 acres entertainment park with amusements, live shows, waterfalls, gardens, restaurants, rides, a ghost town, and a place for gold panning. On Sunday I drove with several of my coworkers to Marineland of the Pacific (closed in 1987) to see the water show with trained sea animals. It was very exciting and much fun. Last I drove to Palos Verdes to see the Wayfarers Chapel, a small but beautiful cathedral like church built primarily of glass supported by redwood beams anchored in stone. Surrounded by beautiful gardens, the chapel sat on a hill site overlooking the Pacific Ocean. It was an amazing and unforgettable structure, built by the son of the famous architect Frank Lloyd Wright in 1951. I promised myself that someday, G'd willing, we would be able to see all these sites as a family (See exhibit 18.23 in the appendix).

In May, while Oma Wolff visited the Saltens in Atlanta, she fell and broke her wrist. She still had her cast on when visiting us in Dayton. It didn't seem to bother

her very much and enjoyed being the focal point of conversation at the annual Temple Israel Sunday School picnic.

The children were doing well in school and Ron started to play baseball in the Senior League. He really enjoyed the game and we were excited watching him and the team play, win or lose. Susan had joined the Girl Scouts, made many new friends and had a good time at the meetings. One afternoon she went to Jill Levinson's house where they played and pretended to operate a beauty parlor. When she came home Gert noticed immediately that Susan's hair looked different. Guess what? Jill had cut Susan's bangs. Oh well, after a few weeks the hair had grown back. During summer vacation we let Susan go with her other Girl Scout friends to Camp Whip-Poor Will in Morrow, Ohio. In some ways the camp was somewhat primitive: at night, with flashlight in hand, the girls had to go from their tent to an outhouse toilet. When she came home from camp we heard her flush the toilet and say, "This is sweet music to my ears." As for Karen, she was always the leader at every activity at Mrs. Seldon's Kindergarten class. Later when we enrolled her at a dancing school she took an unrehearsed solo bow on stage although it was a group performance. Bashful? Not a chance!

Unfortunately, Gert had developed and suffered from frequent migraine headaches which were often so severe that it caused her to vomit or be so painful that she had to lie down, unable to function normally. Under this condition she would often feel faint. Although she would try many different types of prescribed medications this condition was not preventable nor was it cured. Sometimes we had to cancel different activities and social engagements which understandably was very embarrassing. Only over several years of suffering did the condition diminish in intensity and finally subside completely. It was a great relief for both of us.

Although Oma Kahn's general health condition had stabilized, it was still very difficult for her to walk as she visited us again. Of course it was wonderful for us to have both Oma and Opa at our house for a brief and restful vacation and the children added to their pleasure. Ronald was very proud of having made the Honor Roll in his 8th grade class at Belle Haven with a 3.5 average. So were we and his grandparents. It was well deserved because his teacher Harold Cassidy was very particular and strict and so was the school principal, Francis Birt.

While the days were long for both Gert at home and me being at work one thing was always a welcome relief, and that was when the mailman delivered the mail, once in the morning and then again in the afternoon. Often someone in the family, either from Massachusetts, Georgia, Illinois or from overseas would write. It was something Gert especially would look forward to and I would enjoy reading the mail when I would come home. One day in late October I received a call at the office from Gert and could sense some excitement in her voice. She told me that I had received in the mail a summons from the IRS for a desk audit of our

1962 income tax return. Of course I was not amused and had to get ready for the appointment on November 6, 1963. It turned out that the examiner was particularly interested in my real estate business deductions. Since we had purchased a new car the previous year, I had depreciated the old car on a yearly basis. I was told that I could not depreciate the car below its salvage value and therefore had to pay an additional $69.93 for this mistake. I paid and was glad to be off the hook since I did not cherish sparring with the IRS.

That episode behind us everything seemed to have settled into a fairly normal routine. But no, it was only the calm before the storm. The fateful day came on November 22, when at approximately 12:30 p.m. the news came to us in the office over the radio that an attempt had been made to assassinate President John F. Kennedy. The wire services confirmed that the President had been shot as he was riding in a motorcade in Dallas, Texas and was wounded as he was passing Dealey Plaza. The first reports coming in were sketchy, yet as the minutes went by there was confirmation that the gunman had wounded Kennedy seriously and was rushed off to the nearby Parkland Hospital. All activity at the office, and I am certain all over America, had stopped. It was as if the earth was standing still as the news revealed now that our beloved President had been killed by one of three bullets shot by the assassin, Lee Harvey Oswald, who had been holed up in the Texas schoolbook depository building overlooking Dealey Plaza. The man who had given America and the world great hope, who earlier had sent troops to Alabama to quell racial violence, who had given a divided Berlin new hope by his now famous speech at the Berlin Wall by professing *Ich bin ein Berliner*, was pronounced dead. Shortly thereafter, Vice President Lyndon Johnson was sworn in, but the grief for J.F.K. that was felt by the world lasted for weeks and months. It was one of those events in history that no one who was alive at that time would ever forget. And I have not! (See exhibit 18.24 in the appendix)

When I came home, I tried to explain what had happened to the children. I am not sure they grasped the enormity of the event. I went outside and raised the flag at half-mast. Neighbors did the same. Photographs draped in black of the President appeared in windows of homes and stores, and church bells rang from every church. Black streamers hung from the radio antennas on automobiles, and conversations dealt with the same somber subject. Gert and I watched TV more than ever before and saw how Jack Ruby shot the handcuffed assassin Harvey Oswald in the Dallas jail, the never ending lines of mourners paying their last respect to their president as he lay in the Capitol's East Rotunda, and finally the sad burial of a beloved President at Arlington Cemetery. Those days will stay forever in my memory. Kennedy was not in office long enough for history to judge him on the role he played in the political theater of the world nor on the plans he had for America. In my mind the purposes and establishment of Peace Corps was his greatest accomplishment and lasting legacy.

Early in 1964, I entered a relationship with the investment house Merrill Lynch Pierce Fenner & Smith by buying 20 shares each of General Telephone and Electric Corp. for $656.45 and U.S. Steel for $1,194.28. It seemed like a good investment and I believed that we should have some of our savings in the Stock Market. I added these to our shares of Midwest Realty Inc., ATT and Standard Oil of New Jersey, all of which paid good dividends.

After having received so many accolades, recognitions, and awards for my performance over the years on the job, something was missing to be considered for eventual promotion. I did not have a degree in higher education. My former boss, friend and mentor Paul Packard, had mentioned this to me often and urged me to seek a degree that would open the door to me for further advancement. I was looking for this opportunity but had not found a program with the right conditions until I talked to people from the University of Oklahoma that offered a degree of liberal studies through their College of Continuing Education, in Norman, Oklahoma. After reviewing the requirements for admission, reviewing the on and off-campus study requirements, I decided to submit my credentials for high school and college courses from the University of Dayton and government provided training. Next, I availed myself to a series of placement tests, such as the sequential tests of educational progress (STEP) and the school and college aptitude tests (SCAT) provided by Princeton University. There were requirements for being on campus for comprehensive examinations, residential seminars, inter-area studies, inter-area residential seminars and examinations. Three major areas of studies were required for the degree of Bachelor of Liberal Studies (BLS): biological sciences, earth sciences, and the physical sciences; economics, history, political science, geography, anthropology, psychology, and sociology; and last, literature, philosophy, religion, and the fine arts. It indicated a well-defined and tough program to tackle. As it turned out, it was a bear.

I estimated my cost including housing, meals, and transportation to and from Norman Oklahoma to approximate $4,500 per year. In retrospect, I never kept exact track of the total cost although I took deductions on my income tax. The process of obtaining consent and approval by my supervisors at all levels and finally the Personnel Office was tedious and time consuming. On one hand I had to substantiate to everyone's satisfaction that my periodic and often lengthy absences from my job, as well as time required for studying, would not interfere with my job assignments and responsibilities. Secondly, I had to assure my supervisors that I had enough leave saved up to allow me to be absent for weeks and months, and that all expenses were a burden to me and not the Air Force. It required much internal correspondence and approvals which I finally obtained June 1964. The most important and vexing question was can I, being now 41 years old, with family, tackle this undertaking and be successful without hurting my family or myself? I decided to throw caution into the wind and plunge myself into the unknown.

Long before then, I had long discussions many times with Gert to weigh these considerations. Of all people she needed to understand what I was proposing to involve myself in, and for her to understand that she was the one that had to make significant sacrifices. From the very beginning, she was supportive even if she didn't understand all the ramifications of being alone while I was away at the University of Oklahoma Campus. There were many things she had to do that normally I would, and at times she would be lonely. I explained it to Ronald and Susan, while Karen was sad that I wouldn't be around to tell her Hunkle Dunkle stories at bedtime. While a full time student could complete all requirements in four years, I found out the hard way that it would take me much longer to pursue academics while at the same time holding down my job. However, at the time this seemed to be the only way to accomplish my goal. I was adamant to do everything to succeed. Failure had heretofore never been in my vocabulary. Why introduce it now? Also, I wanted to set an example of perseverance, to reach goals, for our children.

Among all of these considerations, not an important one, yet one that I kept private was the fact that Oklahoma still had a big American Indian population, which consisted of many tribes that had originally settled there, and a number of existing reservations. With my fondness and curiosity for American Indians and their history, I thought of all I could learn there by being in the area about which I had read so much as a young boy. And so it was that when I filled out a questionnaire regarding my preference of a dorm roommate, my answer was easy. An American Indian, of course!

Meantime, my employment situation at Wright Patterson had become somewhat tumultuous because of a Department of Air Force wide reorganization aimed at improving effectiveness in view of external and technological changes that would affect any future war scenarios. There were consolidations and restructuring of organizations with mass transfer of personnel. Since I had turned down a physical transfer to Andrews Air Force Base, Washington D.C., I was fortunate to be reassigned to the Central Contract Management Region Headquarters, which was located at the Wright Patt. It entailed an entirely different type of work, but I was able to adjust quickly.

Now working as a Management Analyst one of my duties was to concern myself with Air Force contractors to determine whether they were meeting contractual schedules, and if not, ascertain any negative impacts on Air Force operations. As such I undertook a study of 73 high priority contracts which had become delinquent. The findings and recommendations were published and determined significant so the study was submitted for review at the next Commanders Conference. My presentation was well received.

While a year earlier I had been assigned Alternate TOP SECRET Control Officer, I was now appointed the primary TOP SECRET Control Officer for the organization (see exhibit 18.25 in the appendix). Remaining in Dayton was a big concern for the family and meant, among other things, that I did not have to resign my Directorship at the Wright Patt Credit Union and was able to attend their meetings as well as perform the necessary duties of its Committees. Since I relinquished my Ohio Real Estate License, I was able to devote some effort in behalf of the Jewish Federation by becoming active in the Jewish Campaign under the leadership of Robert Fitterman, Director, and Robert A. Shapiro, General Chairman. We had to make individual house calls, which was time consuming, tedious, and sometimes embarrassing. However it gave us solicitors an opportunity to explain the present goals and needs of the Jewish Federation and thus opened up pocket books (see exhibits 18.26 and 18.27 in the appendix).

A highlight for the entire family was a wonderful and exciting car trip to the New York World's Fair by way of Niagara Falls in July 1964. We stayed at a motel outside of New York City and visited the Fair by train which was much more convenient and less hectic. The theme "Peace Through Understanding" seemed perfect at the time. A 12-story high stainless steel globe model of the world, the Unisphere, dominated the grounds at Flushing Meadows, and is still there today. The Fair was an opportunity for all nations around the world to showcase their culture and technology. Ethnic food was available at most international pavilions, and live performances, stage shows, automated displays, and film presentations of all types kept adults and children especially interested and motivated.

Next we made a short visit to Gert's cousins Gerd and Erica Levy at Syosset, Long Island. From there, not to be outdone, we drove to Sharon, Massachusetts to visit my cousins Ernest and Marilyn Kahn. The entire vacation was a long and eventful trip with opportunity to take many movies, and I must say the children were well behaved. The big wooden spoon, the so-called persuader, was always on the dashboard but never used.

Before the summer was over we had a nice visit from Oma and Opa Kahn, while Karen learned to ride her bike without training wheels. All three children, especially the girls, as millions of others, had become obsessed by the antics and songs by the Beatles, especially when on TV. For me a bitter sweet day came when my former World War II Commander of the Pacific, General Douglas McArthur, a brilliant strategist, who led us to victory, passed away. All that overshadowed the Tokyo Olympics for which I had little interest.

While Vice President Lyndon B. Johnson was immediately sworn in after President Kennedy's assassination, the actual installation and official swearing in for his first term did not occur until January 20, 1965. Again I managed to be in Washington on official business a few days prior so I could attend some events, the spectacular inauguration and parade. However, for me it was not as memorable as the inauguration of President Kennedy. After all, President Johnson was not as charismatic as Kennedy. Also he must take the blame for getting the U.S.

involved in a full-fledged miserable no-win war in Vietnam which would last for years to come, with nothing to show, except for thousands of American and Vietnamese casualties.

While I had hoped to have been out of contention for being transferred to another location I was now being informed that my present job was being relocated to Arbor Vitae, California. However, the letter stated if I declined the move "you cannot be guaranteed another position, although effort will be made to place you." Of course I declined again, taking my chances as I had done before, banking on my known reputation throughout the Command, as documented additionally in my official personnel file.

No sooner had I been served with the transfer notice that the Commander of the Central Contract Management Region, Colonel Henry McDonald advised me of the award of a Presidential Citation by then President Lyndon B. Johnson for "Recognition of Significant Economy and Efficiency Achievements…" How timely this prestigious award was and how proud it made me feel is not difficult to understand (see exhibit 18.28 in the appendix). It was shortly thereafter, that I was offered and accepted as a last resort in order to stay in Dayton, a position at a one grade lower salary with the Department of Defense, AIMS System Program Management Office at the base. In addition to making less money was a minor inconvenience that this office was located several miles distant from where I had been working. The organization was responsible for the development, testing, certification, and operation of Air Traffic Control Beacon Systems i.e. an Identification Friend or Foe (IFF) system to be installed in aircraft, ships, and ground units. The system was known as Mark XII/XIIA. At the time there were too many, often unreliable systems in use by our Army, Navy, Air Force, and of our allies, as well as of commercial aircraft and ships, who were unable quickly to identify each other as friendly. The program was to develop and standardize a system that could rapidly and automatically, by means of a transponder, identify any flying aircraft, ship, or other kinds of flying objects. It entailed work that was entirely different than what I had been working on in past years. Yet I caught on quickly. It was developed, tested, and today is installed in most military and commercial aircraft and other vehicles.

It was March when we undertook a visit by car to Chicago to visit Oma and Opa Kahn and stayed at the Zanzibar Motel on South Lake Shore Drive. To our amazement there was still a lot of ice on Lake Michigan and very pretty to look at while walking all bundled up along the Lake front. Not long thereafter we celebrated Gert's 40th birthday. We presented her with a young Birch tree which we promptly planted and decorated with colored streamers. Unfortunately, the birch tree lasted only a few years since it became infested with borers. We didn't know that this area is not kind to birch trees and therefore you seldom see any grown Birch trees in this area.

Karen's dance recital came up fast and she was very excited wearing her new tutu. It was fun to watch the little girls go through their dance routines with much applause from the attending parents.

At Sunday Religious School, Ronald received a "Certificate of Honor" for Excellence in Studies, of which he and us parents were very pleased. Susan and Karen realized that there was something to strive for. Ronald had set a good example.

It was June 21, 1965 that we celebrated Oma Wolff"'s 70th birthday, topping it off with a wonderful evening and dinner at the highly rated Van Cleve Hotel at First and Ludlow Streets. Gert's sister, Ilse and husband Lester Salten with their children Rita, Peggy, and Roslyn had driven in from Atlanta to join the important milestone of their mother and Oma. I had prepared a special poem for the occasion, and everyone enjoyed the evening.

The Hotel has gone like so many stately others, but the sweet memories of many pleasant evenings have lingered. A month later all five of us packed our suitcases and drove to Andover Massachusetts to see Oma Wolff. After Opa passed away 1957, she gave up her third floor apartment at Jackson Street in Lawrence and bought a small, ground floor, one bedroom condominium in Andover, conveniently located within short walking distance from a shopping center. The condo was also close by where her sister, nieces, and nephew lived, and therefore could look in on her when she needed help. We stayed at the nearby Rolling Green Motel where we had nice accommodations and a beautiful swimming pool. Just what the kids, Gert and I really enjoyed. On the day we were leaving, Oma gave me Opa's valuable stamp collection and asked me to take good care of it. Opa Wolff had collected stamps in Germany and it was a miracle that Gertrude and her sister Ilse had been able to take them along on their way to England when they left Germany with the Kinder Transport. When we came back to Dayton, I promptly rented a safety deposit box at the bank to safeguard them.

Before school started we took a trip to Natural Bridge State Park, Kentucky. It was really located in the boonies, very isolated, but picturesque. The nearest town was called Slade and it had a post office and a grocery store. When we left to drive back home we encountered hundreds of turtles 8-10" in size covering the road, and had to be very careful not to drive over them, although many had been killed by other cars. It was exciting and we had never seen anything like it before or afterwards.

Years earlier when I came out of the military service I took out life insurance through the Veterans Administration and was surprised that now it had a $4,046.60 loan value. That was in addition to other commercial life insurance that I had taken out to protect the family in case something would happen to me. Thank G'd, nothing did happen to me while the family was young. Our real estate taxes for the year were $376.00, a far cry from what they are today. Already by the following year 1966 those taxes went up to $406.00. As long as the Government appetite becomes larger, we the citizens have to pay the bill.

In January 1966 I transferred from Eshcol Lodge of B'nai B'rith to Miami Valley Lodge #2254 where Steven Abrahams was President. All they wanted to do at Eshcol was to play cards without any interest in the purposes of B'nai B'rith. I was irked by that attitude of the members. In the final analysis, it was the lodge's downfall and years later the lodge went belly up.

Gert and I received 5000 Marks each from Germany, minus lawyer expenses. At the time that was approximately equal to $1,100 for each of us and constituted restitution for loss of our education under the Nazis. It was a pittance and could not buy the education we lost here in America. It was the second installment of a similar amount received by both of us in 1958. My studies at the University of Oklahoma had become very demanding and time consuming because of all the books I was required to read and study. From time to time I had to take tests on campus and always sweated out the results. On top of that, I had to write various essays and reviews, some of which I kept until today. It often meant staying up late and not getting too much sleep. My portable typewriter had become my good companion. In response to one of my written reviews of the book by Friedrich Hayek, "The Road to Serfdom," my Professor, W. E. Hollon wrote: "I wish that I had a chance to discuss these world shaking problems over a good bottle of bourbon. We still would not come up with the answers, but it would be fun."

A while back I noticed an ad in the Jewish Immigrant newspaper *Aufbau*, wherein the mayor of Mannheim, Dr. Hans Reschke asked the surviving Mannheimers to write about their experiences, there, and here. In my astonishment and relentless bitterness about the horrible past under the Nazis in Mannheim, I wrote a scathing letter to the Mayor assuming never to receive a reply. I was wrong, and an apologetic, yet straight forward response arrived which made me rethink and ponder my hate filled viewpoint. Here is a quote from the letter: "I may state that many Mannheimers feel the heavy debt the German people have loaded upon their shoulders by the cruel persecution of the Jews. We therefore consider it our duty to restore, to honor the disgraced name of our Jewish fellow-citizens." The letter was written in German and a second one in English, signed by a Dr. Watzinger, whom I later met when I visited my once hometown, but which no longer was my home.

Whenever Gert and I had some quiet time, usually after the children went to sleep, we watched one or the other of two shows on TV, namely *The I Love Lucy Show*, or *The Red Skelton Hour*. Both were funny and relaxing. Since we had radio intercom in every room some of the hits played over and over again were "Monday Monday" and "Winchester Cathedral." As a special treat the family went to see the Holiday on Ice Show at Hara Arena. It was magnificent with all the well-known skaters.

Sometimes we would go to Miracle Lane Shopping Center, especially to Garvin Furniture store since they primarily carried modern furniture. One day we saw a couple blue print chairs which we liked and bought both for a little more than a hundred dollars. We still use them today in our living room. For many years we were able to buy the same automobile license plate numbers, 756RK Ohio and 757RK Ohio, at the Waterveliet License Bureau in Belmont. The numbers and initials were easy to remember, and therefore convenient. Unfortunately, I was informed that I could no longer reserve the same numbers, and so a yearly ritual came to an end.

On May 25, 1966, the sixth of Sivan 5726, according to the Jewish calendar, Ronald and 32 other boys and girls were confirmed by Rabbis Selwyn D. Ruslander and Joseph S. Weizenbaum at Temple Israel. Also that same month I finished putting together after much research a comprehensive text for the Department Of Defense entitled: "Industrial Mutual Aid Association." It was distributed widely to industry since it explained how to organize such associations including its legal implications. Major General William W. Veal gave me several personal photographs as an appreciation of my work under his leadership. He was very fond of me and I had much respect for him (see exhibits 18.29 and 18.30 in the appendix).

During the summer vacation of the children we decided to take a trip to the Dearborn Village, Michigan, where we visited the Henry Ford Museum which exhibited the history of the automobile. Next Gert had arranged a meeting with Ruth Brooks nee Posner, living in Detroit, who were schoolmates in Berlin at the Jewish Goldschmidt School. It turned out to be a wonderful reunion, not having seen each other in over twenty eight years, there was plenty to talk about. From there we drove to Battle Creek, Michigan to explore the Bird Sanctuary, and last to Saugetauk Beach, Lake Michigan. It was a somewhat educational trip with time to relax and play.

Dayton was not spared the unrest and civil disobedience which the black community initiated all over the country to obtain their rights of equality. Late August 1966, I seem to remember, Lester Mitchell, a known bootlegger active in the black community, was shot supposedly by a gang of white men. The uneasiness, which already existed on the West Side of Dayton, set off a firestorm riot for two days which was only quelled when more than a thousand National Guard intervened. 130 people were arrested, and several city blocks of the West Side neighborhood was in shambles after the looting and destruction. It was scary for everyone because we feared that the rioting would spread to other parts of the city including our neighborhood.

November came and we took the holiday of Thanksgiving to spend with Oma and Opa Kahn and my sister Irene as well as Marc and Faye in Chicago. There we met also Irene's new husband Sidney Altman. My mother's turkey dinner was superb, and the five children couldn't get enough of Oma's good stuffing. Then in December Oma Wolff and family Salten came to spend Chanukkah with us in Dayton. It was a busy but exciting time to spend the festival of lighting candles, singing, and gift giving with us. It was also a busy time for Gert doing the cooking and the young ones, Peggy, Rita, Roslyn, Ronald, Susan, and Karen had a great time helping to make the latkes. In the wake of the Watts riots in California, African Americans also wanted to have their own festival, around Christmas and Chanukkah. They named it Kwanza. Using seven candles, that holiday was conceived to last seven days to begin each year on December 26.

We were all surprised and somewhat saddened that the company producing the shaving lather Burma Shave had decided to do away with its advertising signs bearing jingles along roads that had for years amused us and all other travelers. Progress seems to have a peculiar way of taking away those things we have learned to love.

CHAPTER NINETEEN

How We Won The West

The year 1967 turned out to be an exciting one. So let me tell something about it. Ronald was a senior at Meadowdale High School making good grades and enthusiastically playing Varsity tennis. He was inducted into the the National Honor Society. Often he asked me to go with him to the Jewish Center up the street to practice at the tennis court. At first all I did is pick up balls he served. Later, I became more interested, and bought myself a cheap racquet, then still made of wood, and taught myself the game with Ronald's assistance (see exhibit 19.1 in the appendix). Susan was a freshman at the same school and was an ardent cheerleader, always in practice or cheering on the Meadowdale Lion basketball and football teams. Karen was going to Belle Haven Elementary School, a good fifteen minute walk from our home. She was still taking private dance lessons and looking forward to her yearly dance recital, which were always a blast.

From traveling across the U.S. when I was in the military service and on the job for the Air Force, car trips to the University of Oklahoma at Norman, Chicago, Massachusetts, and of course our honeymoon, I came to realize how big and beautiful this country really is. I promised myself that before Ronald went to college, I would take the family on a trip to show them some of the beauty this country had to offer. For practically an entire year I planned, with the help of the Automobile Club, a trip by car that would take us across the United States to take in some of the most spectacular sights in America. I had saved up enough vacation time on my job that I was able to spend the 37 days it would take for the planned trip, provided that my boss would not object. He and other supervisors up the line were at first very skeptical to approve my request, asking that I convince them in writing my work would continue to be accomplished without detriment during my absence. Several months prior, I had briefed and instructed one of my coworkers how to assume all of my assigned responsibilities temporarily. I had done this for him once before although not for as long a period. Even with that, it was no easy task to convince all my civilian and military chiefs. In addition to submitting my detailed task paper it required a number of in depth discussions and pleading with each before I finally received their approval.

As time for our departure came closer, Gert and I talked to the children about the planned vacation who naturally became very excited and interested to learn where we were going and what to pack for such a long trip. About a week before leaving we had a rehearsal how to store everything in the trunk and on top of the car in the luggage rack. That accomplished, I drew a diagram of the storage plan which we would have to follow each day for the entire trip out West. It would be

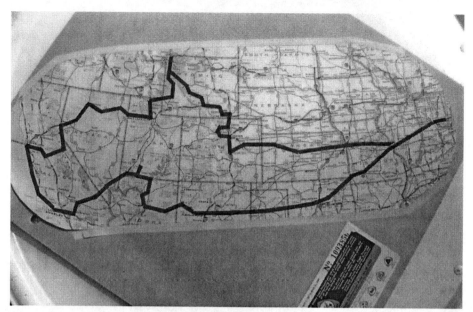

EXHIBIT 19.2 The route of our trip. See exhibit 19.3 in the appendix for the trunk and luggage rack diagram.

a trip of a lifetime, and in retrospect it was. Ronald, now 17 years old had taken drivers education, had his driver's license and was a careful driver when he practiced driving our Chrysler 4-door sedan. We had decided to let him drive on the open road especially on Interstate sections that had been completed.

Rather than giving a full blown description of every day I will share some of the highlights.

We left early Saturday June 10. Each day we followed a daily schedule, which I had prepared in advance that showed the date, day of week, starting location, our destinations for the day, mileage point to point, estimated driving time, and place where we had overnight reservations, including directions and phone number. Reservations had been made for each day in advance and were confirmed. We had taken along a portable charcoal grill, charcoal, a two burner electric hotplate as well as a large cooler so we could help ourselves without stopping at restaurants as much as possible, except for our evening meal. There were no roadside parks as we know them today. Since we left the lodge, cabin or motel very early in the morning, breakfast was usually from the cooler in our room. We even used our hotplate despite there were always signs that cooking was prohibited. It was fast, convenient, and inexpensive. The children enjoyed the informality and adventure and so did Gert and I.

Whenever we were able to use stretches of the Interstate, Ronald relieved me in driving. It made driving so much easier for me. Near Oklahoma City we stopped briefly at a buffalo ranch to view these awesome animals. Next we took in Frontier City, a colorful replica of a frontier town of the last century, a welcome reprieve after sitting for hours in the car. We stayed at a Holiday Inn at Amarillo, Texas after driving through heavy rain followed by dust kicked up by strong winds. All of us longed to hit the pool, but in her eagerness to cool off, Karen dived in head first in the shallow end and chipped one of her front teeth. Luckily she did not hurt her head. It was a temporary disaster, but everybody got over it.

Staying in Gallup, New Mexico we had a chance to see real Indians to the delight of our three young ones. We visited Old Town Albuquerque, founded in 1707, and enjoyed the traces of Spanish influence and architecture. By now we had driven about 1575 miles all the while taking photographs, occasional movies, and enjoying a new world.

The next day turned into an unforgettable adventure that could have easily turned into a disaster. Many months ago I had written the Department of Indian Affairs in Washington D.C. asking them to give me the location of an Indian reservation in New Mexico that had not been commercialized and that would be interesting and educational to visit. Their answer was Acoma, the Sky City, an active Indian community since 1540 of about one thousand people, and the nearby Enchanted Mesa, both of which were well off the beaten path. After we turned off the main road we traveled on a dusty, unimproved sand and gravel road scattered with animal skeletons. The Acoma pueblo sat on an almost 400 foot high mesa reachable via a very steep stone and gravel incline that was until recently only passable with primitive wooden sleds. It was scary to drive up that steep incline, but we made it. As the only car there, we were greeted by a young Indian squaw who offered to take us around. Although she mentioned not to take pictures or movies, I could not resist the temptation. Later, as we were ready to leave our car was surrounded by many Indians who wanted to confiscate our movie camera. After a long hassle, I had to pay $25.00 in order to leave. It was their reservation, and we had to obey by their rules.

The temperature was high and the heat was suffocating; we were glad to have air conditioning in the car. After driving down the steep incline in the lowest gear and heavy on the brakes, we came to a handmade sign that showed two directions to get back to the highway. The children suggested to take the road we did not use on the way in, hoping that this other road would be more interesting. It certainly was! As we slowly drove the road became less discernable, rockier, and more treacherous, until the road completely disappeared. We were lost on a high plateau, in the hot desert, and no one around for help. Gert and the two girls in the back of the car were scared and started to cry. Ron and I were trying to stay calm, attempting to figure out what to do. We continued driving along the edge of the plateau until we could see the highway below in the distance. Would the radiator boil over? Would the air conditioner stop working? Would we run out of gas? Would we run out of drinking water? Those were thoughts that came to my mind.

We kept on driving, not faster than 2, perhaps 3, miles per hour, until we came to an abandoned stone quarry, at the near bottom of which we could see a road without any traffic. Ron and I got out of the car and noticed what looked like a hazardous, but passable stretch to descend to the bottom. There were many boulders that would have to be avoided. Therefore, Ron went ahead and signaled me to turn right or left to avoid them. We had to take a chance. With brakes on, only letting up now and then, we made to the bottom. The crying stopped, and my heart started to beat normally again. We took the road in the westerly direction until we saw a little hut with a small Red Cross flag. It was a First Aid station manned by an Indian aid who gave us directions back to the main highway, Route 66, famous for its history as put into song, "Get Your Kicks on Route 66."

We now were at an elevation of 7,200 ft. and had to turn the air conditioning off since all of a sudden it had become much cooler. We crossed the Continental Divide and arrived back in Gallup, New Mexico where we were staying at the Holiday Inn. Exhausted from our ordeal we all took a nap before going to a steak house for supper. Gallup was in the heart of Indian country with Navajo, Zuni, and Hopi Indian reservations nearby. We were told by people at the restaurant and at the motel that quite often tourists became lost in the desert and were found dead weeks or months later. We thanked the almighty that we were not one of them.

Five o'clock the next morning, after we packed the trunk and the luggage rack on top of the car, and had breakfast, we were on the road again. We took in the beauty of the Painted Desert and then the awesome Petrified Forest National Park in Arizona. The colorful petrified wood logs are a natural wonder and are estimated 200 million years old. Many of these wondrous logs bore hieroglyphics placed there by ancient people years before Columbus arrived. Before leaving I bought a small piece of petrified wood as a souvenir.

We drove on through Winslow, Flagstaff, and finally reached Grand Canyon National Park before checking in at the rustic Auto Cabin Lodge located at the South Rim of the Canyon. The sights were breathtaking. After a period of rain, I set up the charcoal grill and grilled several small chickens that we had bought earlier at a store. We had dinner and then took a leisurely drive along the Canyon, watching and photographing the sunset. Later that night, Ron slept in the sleeping bag, the girls in one bed, we in the other.

That morning Gert and I made breakfast, then we spent the rest of the day sightseeing and watching a Hopi Indian dance performance. Next morning like every other, up at five o'clock, breakfast in cabin, loading the car, and go. We drove around to the north side of the Canyon, crossed the Little Colorado River and headed and passed Glen Canyon Dam, Utah for Bryce Canyon National Park. We always made sure that we had enough fuel and supplies, since this was desolate country. We arrived mid afternoon after passing Indians alongside the road weaving beautiful blankets and rugs. Bryce Canyon Lodge at an altitude above 8000 feet, which at first gave all of us a headache since we were not used to the thin air. We got used to it just doing things, especially walking, albeit a little slower. We marveled at the weirdly sculptured and bright red colored rock formations as far as the eye could see. The spires were just awesome and at the same time beautiful.

Ron drove three additional hours and we arrived at Zion National Park, had a leisurely lunch, and took a long hike in what had become a sweltering heat. We went wading in a cool mountain stream in a most spectacular gorge. The park's 147,000 acres had the most colorful and deepest canyon walls and individual rock masses sprinkled with blooming cacti and other desert plants. We stayed at the Canyon Inn and relaxed with some good old fashioned ice cream. The next morning we were on our way to Las Vegas, first crossing back into Arizona and then into Nevada. Our reservations at the Lucerne Motor Hotel were just perfect on "the strip," located a little south of the Tropicana. Our room was very nice and two Olympic size swimming pools made the children and us feel very comfortable. It was unbearably hot and the air conditioning in our room, the car, and everywhere else was a gift from G'd. After an early supper we drove down the strip to visit the Dunes, Aladin, Caesar's Palace, the Tropicana, and looked into the casinos. Later in the evening, while Ron was baby sitting, Gert and I drove to the Sands Hotel to see the terrific Red Skelton Show. Afterwards we tried the slot machines, had some luck but went back to the hotel without any winnings. A long but wonderful day had come to an end.

After breakfast on Sunday morning June 19, we drove to see the miracle engineering feat of Hoover Dam, 726 ft. high, the highest ever constructed at the time. Coming back to Las Vegas, the streets were flooded from a heavy rain as there were no sewers so Gert did some laundry at the motel. After it had cleared up we drove to downtown Las Vegas to see all the bright flashing lights from hotels and casinos and drove back for a good night's rest. The next day was beautiful and all of us spent a good amount of time at the pool and sundeck and got sunburns as souvenirs. Later that evening Gert and I went to the "Stardust" for dinner and show.

Next morning, June 21, it was time to say good bye to the glittering lights. Ron did the driving on Interstate 15, which was also US Route 66. When we crossed the Nevada/California state line the children made a big yell of excitement. After all, everything that they had watched on television came from Hollywood, California, and therefore they had a dream image of the state on the far western side of our country. We passed the town of Baker from where the road leads to Death Valley, stopped to see Calico, a restored silver mining town, on to San Bernardino, and finally the town of Riverside through very scenic mountainous terrain interspersed with vast orange groves. There I took the family on a tour of the Mission Inn, a most unique and historic hotel built like a Spanish Mission. We all had a good laugh when we saw signs pointing toward a town named "Cucamonga," which sounded so funny that the young ones thought it was a hoax, and kept on repeating it.

Our destination was the Eden Rock Motel in Anaheim, which became our headquarters for the next few days. From there we made excursions to Knott's Berry Farm and Ghost Town, where we rode on a stage coach which was held up by desperados and Indians. We spent a whole day at Disneyland to try all the rides, some of which were scary, saw all the living exhibits, shows, the Magic Kingdom, Adventureland, Pirates of the Caribbean, and more. The following day we took in Marineland of the Pacific and see the seals, dolphins and whales perform after which we visited the all glass Wayfarer's Church. We passed many beautiful mansions on the way to Santa Monica where we all take a walk barefoot on the beach along the Pacific. Accidentally, we stepped into oil balls that would not come off our feet until we used kerosene from a nearby filling station. After this minor disaster we drove to the Farmer's Market, had a late lunch, and then drove through Beverly Hills to Grauman's Chinese Theater in Hollywood. There we watched movie stars drive up in their limousines to attend the premier of *The Happiest Millionaire*.

The next day, June 24 we drove back to Hollywood to visit the city of motion picture and television magic, known as Universal City. We took a tram tour of the 420 acre outdoor area where motion pictures and TV productions are made. We saw stunt men and women perform, saw how rain and snow was produced, and saw sound stages, dressing rooms, man-made lakes and waterfalls. The most exciting part, however, was when Karen was chosen from a large audience assembled in the make-up studio to be transformed by professional artists into a clown. It was fun to watch and she was in her glory when the make-up artists had completed her make-up. Later that evening, while Karen was very careful not to disturb her clown make-up including a hat, we went to see the fireworks at Disneyland above the Sleeping Beauty Castle. Of course everybody admired and chatted with Karen who looked like a performer from the amusement park, and she loved every minute of it.

EXHIBIT 19.4 Karen the clown.

The next morning was the beginning of the fifteenth day of this journey without having deviated from my original planned trip and schedule. The last three days had been especially enjoyable for the children with all the amusement parks and other entertaining sights. Still, we will never forget driving famous Route 66 that brought us across the country to Santa Monica and would hold our imagination and memories of the scenery of plains, mountains, desert and rivers.

In order to keep our intended schedule to San Simeon and stop at other sites, we had to get up at 4:30 a.m. when it is normally the best time to sleep. San Simeon, where we had reservations for touring the Hearst Estate at 3:00 p.m., was 250 miles away. However, we intended to stop at Solvang, or "Little Denmark," a Danish settlement established in 1911. There we saw Danish architecture, schools, churches, stores, and people wearing Danish dress. It was an unusual sight to see Denmark in California. From there, on fabled and beautiful Highway 1, we traveled up high along the cliffs of the blue Pacific Ocean. We arrived in San Simeon on time to tour the unbelievably beautiful estate of William Randolph Hearst, who named it La Cuesta Encantada, The Enchanted Hill. Located 1600 ft. above the Pacific Ocean, it truly is a sight for the gods. If you are ever in the vicinity of San Simeon, see it. Europe's castles can hardly compare.

We stayed at a motel in the vicinity overlooking the ocean, and later took a steep path down to the waterfront, which was thrilling. The next morning we started a bit later than usual because of a heavy fog. We drove very slowly along the coastal route because the fog greeted us now and again on this somewhat treacherous two lane curvy road. Once the fog lifted, the scenery from our vantage point was spectacular. We stopped many times at so called vista spots, left the car and ambled to the edge of the road to admire the colorful rocky coast below, with flowers everywhere and the white foamy waves disappearing into the sand or breaking up on the cliffs. The last stop before San Francisco wass Point Lobos Reserve, a small postcard-sized wonderland of nature. There a beautiful, lonely, and distinctive Monterey Cypress stands among others clinging to the sparse soil on the cliffs above the sea. There were sea lions with their hoarse barks and pelicans galore. From here it would be about 120 miles to San Francisco. It was a long day and we were really looking forward to a little rest at the Pacifica Motel on the water's edge, which overlooked the bay.

I telephoned my first cousin, Ilse Isaak Hertz (daughter of Ida, my mother's sister) who was expecting us for dinner. It was a wonderful reunion not having seen her, nor her husband Otto, since before I went overseas as a soldier in 1944. The meal, the first home cooked meal since we left Dayton, was delicious. After dinner the rest of the mischpocha showed up for dessert. It was overwhelming for Ronald, Susan, Karen, and Gert, none of whom had met Ilse and Otto, Ilse's brothers Norbert and Helmut Isaak plus their wives, as well as Judy, one of Ilse's twin daughters and her husband Dan. It was even overwhelming for me since I had never met Dan nor the wives of Norbert and Helmut who were being kindly referred to as "big" and "little" Ellen, since both shared that name.

The next morning Judy picked us up to show us the beautiful hilly city of San Francisco. The last time I saw Judy she and her twin sister were still in strollers. It was just amazing to see her now, a beautiful girl, married, driving us around in a car. It was as my mother and father always said, *Kinder werden Leute*, children become people.

We saw and admired the Golden Gate Bridge, the Japanese Gardens, the Arboretum, the Art Museum, followed by lunch at Fisherman's Wharf, sightseeing in China Town, the Haight Ashbury Streets area with all the hippies, and finally Lombard Street, billed as the most crooked street in the world. Again we had dinner at Cousin Ilse and Otto's home, and made it back for a well deserved night's rest at the Pacifica Motel. We got up a little later the next morning, which gave me a chance to read the newspaper and catch up with all the details of the war fought between Israel against the attacks initiated by Syria, Jordan and the Egyptian Armies. It appeared that sadly, Israel had lost 680 soldiers, but had recaptured Jerusalem, the entire Sinai Peninsula to the Suez Canal, as well as had destroyed more than 200 tanks and 400 planes of the Egyptian Air Force. Also, the strategic Golan Heights were captured from Syria. It was the biggest and best news I read. Everything else was of minor concern to me. It was then, and is still today, referred to as the Seven Day War. It showed the world that Israel's male and female soldiers and pilots are heroic fighters when it comes to protecting their little country. Now and then when we had the car radio on while driving, we heard the latest news and the tensions as they were staged by the Arab countries leading up to the fighting. The car radio was also important to obtain local news and weather reports, in addition to music which kept our kids from being restless at times.

After while we drove downtown San Francisco to visit Norbert in his jewelry store. He gave each of the girls a cable car charm for their bracelets and took us for lunch in a quaint restaurant named The Original Joe, on Taylor Street. From there we drove to Fisherman's Wharf where we bought tickets for an enjoyable bay cruise and went under the enormous Golden Gate Bridge, the Oakland Bay Bridge, passed close to the island of Alcatraz, and the infamous Federal Prison. Seeing the city from the bay was very special. Next we watched the cable cars, and then, like local folks, jumped on for the ride and then off again. It was a real thrill.

In the evening while Ron watched over the girls at the motel, Ilse and Otto picked us up and drove us to a friend's apartment where we had an excellent night view of the city and bay from high above. From there we all went to the swanky Fairmont Hotel where we had some drinks at the Tonga Room. It was a very unique place where an orchestra floated in a tropical lagoon and a simulated tropical storm surprised us. Next to the Bocce Ball on San Francisco's Broadway, where we had another drink and enjoyed listening to opera stars singing arias and more popular songs. If that wasn't enough for a night out, we went to see a topless show next door at the Peppermint Stick. After Gert and I were delivered back to our motel it only took a minute before we were asleep after a long day, and for a change a longer night.

The next morning we got ready to drive south to Sunnyvale to visit Joan, Judy's twin sister. We had a picnic in a park, drove back to the motel and packed so we could leave the next morning. That night we had our so-called last supper at the Hertz's, dessert at Norbert and Ellen's house, and said goodbye to everyone. Our stay in San Francisco was nice considering everything we did, saw, and of course meeting all the relatives after many years. While there, I tried not to think about the time that I was a patient at Letterman Army Hospital at the Presidio military reservation when I returned as an invalid from the war in the South West Pacific, and prior to my transfer to Danville in Kentucky. However, it was often on my mind as we drove around sightseeing. I had closed that chapter long ago and did not want to be reminded of the grim past.

From San Francisco, it was a drive of more than 200 miles to reach Yosemite National Park. The driving was slow and the views, left, right, and above were nature's wonders. Mountains, lakes, waterfalls, and snow high above were so extremely beautiful that I didn't mind driving slowly through the San Joaquin Valley and Mariposa. We finally arrived at Camp Curry, with our rustic log cabin set in a fragrant cedar grove. It cost $18.00 per night for four, but we had a sleeping bag for the fifth. As the children and I went out to look around, we saw our first bear and told Gert to come out to see this astounding sight. However, she had gotten a very bad migraine headache on the way to Camp Curry, so I carried her out of the cabin to witness the beast. Karen, Susan, Ronald and I then went for a bite to eat. Later we watched entertainment in the nearby amphitheater and the spectacle from high up Glacier Point where burning timbers were pushed over the edge and spectacularly floated to the valley below.

Thank G'd, Gert felt okay again in the morning and we registered at 8 a.m. to go on a two-hour horseback ride. Karen had to stand on her tip toes to be tall enough to qualify for the ride, and was assigned as big a horse as the rest of us. It was an enjoyable ride until the lead horse bolted because it spotted a bear, and all the other horses stampeded as well. Luckily, we all held on for life. Nevertheless, to see El Capitan, Yosemite Falls, the Half Dome, and Mirror Lake from above or below with snow everywhere, was simply breathtaking. In the afternoon we drove to Mariposa Groves to marvel in astonishment at the giant sequoias; one so huge that we could drive through its trunk. Known as the Tunnel Tree it was 27 feet diameter at its base. Unfortunately, Karen was stung by a mosquito, and her forehead swelled up like a melon. We took her to the Park Hospital where she received some helpful medication. I, too, received some medication since I had developed a sore throat.

It was a long day, and the next morning, July 2 we prepared to reach Lake Tahoe, Nevada via the Tioga Pass, which had been closed for the winter and had only opened days before. Originally a wagon trail, it was now a very hazardous road. Walls of snow and ice on either or both sides of the road were often obstructing any view as we drove up hill, where we finally reached an elevation of 9,943 ft. The road was winding, sometimes slippery, without guard rails or markings that would tell where the serpentine road was. Now and then we had to avoid snow on the road that was deposited by avalanches, and then there were occasional rock slides, but otherwise this white knuckle drive was as beautiful as it was scary. We stopped a few times to view the lakes and mountains around us. We even had a friendly snowball fight. There were no commercial services until we reached the small town of Lee Vining, which gave us a breather. Even so, they had only outhouses when we stopped for fuel and some hot chocolate. The trip to here was only about 65 miles, but to me it seemed like eternity.

From here it was a breeze driving to the Echo motel at Lake Tahoe where the weather was hot. Cousins Otto and Ilse were staying over the 4th of July at the nearby Marina Inn right on the lake. We all took advantage of that and went swimming in the lake and in the pool. After the seven of us had supper, Gert and I, as well as the cousins, went to some of the casinos on the Nevada side, while the kids watched TV back at our motel. According to a written log that Susan started for our trip, Gert noted both of us hit jackpots of $5.00. Big money! There was also excitement when the police chased a man, who had beaten someone up, and placed him in handcuffs. Then while police were busy with that fellow, someone supposedly ran off with a thousand dollars. We had a drink at the bar, said our goodbyes to Ilse and Otto, and went back to our motel. Continuing from the log, we noted that when we complained to the motel manager that we were kept awake because the people next door to us were partying, he gave us a $3.00 coupons to be cashed at a casino in Carson City, Nevada where we were headed on the way to Salt Lake City, Utah---a long 555 miles away. We cashed the coupons in the Carson City casino, then had a good breakfast in Reno, which was advertised as "the biggest little city in the world," also known for its quickie divorces. Yet Gert and I drove on, still married.

By 10:30 a.m. it was already 104 degrees in the shade as we approach the Great Salt Lake Desert. We were thankful that our air-conditioning, set at the highest speed, worked well. Coming down from elevations of about 7,000 ft. we stop in Wells, Nevada to tank up, buy some groceries, ice for the cooler, and fill up the jug with water. Ronald did a good job driving while I rested and watched the desolate expanse of the saltiest body of water in the world. The girls thought it looked spooky. We finally reach our Holiday Inn downtown Salt Lake City, Utah, having driven by the beautiful clad in white Mormon Temple. According to our plan we had not decided to do any specific sightseeing here.

The next morning the alarm clock woke us up to the traditional Fourth of July. After a while we were heading almost due north towards Yellowstone National Park. It was our 25th day on the road, and we were enjoying every bit of this great and grand country. We traveled fewer miles to our destination than yesterday because the two lane curvy road took us through mountainous country, so while we gained altitude, it was not designed for making good time. We crossed into Idaho to Montpelier, supposedly the oldest town in Idaho, at 6,000 ft. elevation, and the historic old Oregon Trail. Still gaining in altitude we crossed the Bear River and saw in the distance ahead of us Mt. Mead, towering at 10,000 ft. high. The girls and Ronald, when he was not driving, now and then studied the map to see where we were and noticed that we were coming to the town of Alpine that straddled the state line of Wyoming and Idaho.

As we crossed the Snake River numerous times the scenery became increasingly more breathtaking and like nature's fairyland. To our left were the Grand Teton Range and in the meadows of the Snake River we saw elks and bears crossing the road. After passing through a gatehouse, we entered Grand Teton National Park and next, the ranger station to Yellowstone National Park. With the National Parks permit bought before we left Dayton we were able to visit any National Park without paying the normal entry fee. We finally saw and were astonished by the huge log structure that turned out to be the Old Faithful Inn where we would stay for one night. I had developed a bad cold and struggled with it, but was able to carry on by taking some medications Gert had brought along with us, and continued to follow our pre-designed plan for all the sightseeing the rest of the afternoon and evening. Our room was similar to what we had seen on TV watching Wild West scenes. There was no TV or radio, and the bathroom facilities were dated. All the furniture, beds, chairs, closet, and chests of drawers were handmade over the years from native materials. The Lodge had been built back in 1903, had a total of 350 rooms, and employed about 250 student employees. There was an 85 ft. fireplace in the lobby and many other strange and interesting objects too numerous to describe.

Here we were located on a volcanic plateau at between 7,000 and 8,000 ft. above sea level, surrounded by about 3,000 geysers and hot springs. The largest and most predictable geyser, Old Faithful, was within walking distance from our Lodge. After we checked the probable eruption time, which was thought to be about 21 times per day, we went to watch with anticipation. We stood in awe as the spectacular eruption of scalding water took place, from a height of 105 to about170 ft. It happened like an explosion and scientists have not figured out yet the actual cause, except theoretically. The Park covers an area of 3,472 square miles mainly in Wyoming, and extending into Montana and Idaho. Because the

Grand Teton National Park was just 30 miles south, I made arrangements to stay overnight in three different areas so we could see the attractions of both parks.

The next morning, after we had checked out early, we followed the Grand Loop Road and had not driven far when we saw bison and moose having their fill of grass and other vegetation at the edge of Yellowstone Lake. On our drive we parked the car in several different places and walked to see boiling cauldrons of water, mud, and steam. We saw colored boiling terraces, all of them having a peculiar smell of sulphur. We saw many unusual small and big birds, as well as bighorn sheep, and people fishing in the Yellowstone River. In the distance we saw Mt. Washburn 10,350 ft. high with snow at the highest elevations. In the afternoon, we checked in at Canyon Village where a cabin was reserved for us. The Grand Canyon of Yellowstone, the so-called location where the Yellowstone River plunges over two high rocky cliffs. The walls surrounding those falls, approximately 1,200 ft. high, were of yellow color with tints of red, pink, purple and, if I remember correctly, also a bit of orange. The view was massive, beautiful, and indescribably colorful. That was certainly enough sightseeing for the day. After supper our three children spent the rest of the evening at the recreation center of the lodge. I can't describe how quickly and well we slept at night and every night, but after a very busy day, that is not hard to understand. For once, I did not have to tell any Hunkel Dunkel bedtime stories.

The next day was more sightseeing, this time to Mammoth Hot Springs with huge terraces of delicate shapes in different colors created by algae. We walk the Terrace Nature Trail and saw many more hot springs, and the odd, but amazing, terraces that were being shaped as we watched. You can tell me all about the beauty of Switzerland, but there is nothing like the wonders that we have seen so far of America!

When we spotted a herd of antelopes on a nearby hill we parked the car and approached them very slowly. Ron and I got fairly close to them and took movies and photos. As they ambled upwards, we followed, when suddenly Ron and I discovered a huge half of an antler from a wapiti elk. All of us were thrilled with the find and hoped to mount it on a wall when we got back home. In the meantime, we had to tie it to the top of the car and safeguard it every night wherever we stayed. As we drove through a wooded clearing we saw several grizzly bears rummaging in tied down garbage containers for leftovers from tourists. While there were signs reminding tourists not to feed the bears, I thought otherwise and encouraged one of the bears with a cookie to come closer so I could take some photos, and possibly movies. As the bear came closer I threw the cookie out the car window and closed it immediately while the beast enjoyed the treat. Not satisfied with one cookie, the bear climbed on the hood, tore the radio antenna off and pawed at us through the windshield. That was enough for me. I started the car and slowly drove away, shaking the bear off the car. It was scary because I had done something real stupid, and never heard the last off it from my wife and children. Nevertheless it was a lesson for us all to heed signs and above all use common sense.

The next morning, after the usual early breakfast in the cabin, we loaded the car, including the big elk rack on the top carrier, and were on our way to Grand Teton National Park where we would stay the night. On our way we saw a number of wapiti elks in a meadow and were able to view them up close and take some good photos. We also took a half mile walk on the Fountain Paint Pot Nature Trail from where we could see and watch many colorful so-called paint pots, fumaroles, geysers, and spouting pools, all natural elements with different characteristics and names. Driving farther south we saw some beautiful trumpeter swans and large birds we had never seen before, which we were told later were eagles. We said goodbye to Yellowstone National Park as we drove through the Ranger Station, and wondered whether we would have to leave the elk antler there.

Now we entered Jackson Hole country with its natural beauty. It had started to rain as we checked into our Colter Bay Cabin, which was situated on the shore of Jackson Lake. It was a one room cabin with bath, two double beds and one single, but no housekeeping facilities. There was a pot belly stove and kindling wood outside the front door. The rate for the night was $15.00 plus 3% tax. Since it was about noon, we had a sandwich from our cooler and afterwards took a nap, so we would be ready again later to explore the area. The size of the park is approximately 500 sq. miles, and the mountains of the Teton range, which are of solid granite, are more than 10,000 ft. tall, with the Grand Teton towering above at 13,700 ft. What makes this mountain range so unbelievably beautiful is its absence of foothills. Viewed from Jackson Hole, for which this area is called, it looks impenetrable, its peaks snow covered, and beautiful beyond imagination. As we ventured out of our cabin, the rain clouds had vanished. We drove up to Signal Mountain and from there to Jackson Lake Lodge, constantly observing the beautiful scenery over our right shoulders. On the way we saw some beavers in a small lake and some huge mean looking moose.

The Lodge overlooking Jackson Lake has as its centerpiece a 60 ft. panoramic window overlooking the sparkling lake and, as if a painting, the towering peaks of the Grand Tetons. All of us were fascinated by this breathtaking view. The Lodge, including guest cottages, was ultra-modern with about 400 rooms. That night we had dinner reservation in the dining room and enjoyed the food, the service, and the view at sunset. 500 or so other guests were having their meal in those special surroundings as well. It was a wonderful way to top the evening off.

Saturday July 8, is our last day at the Grand Tetons, and we had a lot yet to do and see. We paid for a motorboat trip across Jenny Lake for a guided tour in the lower areas of the Grand Teton. It was a beautiful trip on the lake, and flowers were everywhere on the ground when we landed. We decided to stay longer than the rest of the group, and the captain of the boat said he would pick us up in an hour or so. We relaxed and sat on some rocks and enjoyed the views around us until it became suddenly overcast with thunder rumbling in the distance. We became worried, but finally the boat arrived and were lucky to get back to our cabin for lunch before the storm hit.

By the time we had everything cleaned up and taken a little rest, it had cleared up and the sun was shining. We decided to take a leisurely boat ride around Jackson Lake, and were surprisingly the only passengers on the trip. Prior to our trip I had read that the town of Jackson Hole staged a Western shootout in the early evening hours. Only 25 miles away, I decided to surprise our three children. We drove there to see a typical western boom town, with cowboys and Indians on horseback, taverns, blacksmith shops, log houses, and cabins on the main street, just as in the movies. After walking around for a while we had supper in a place overlooking the area where I knew the event would take place. All of a sudden it happened. There was a lot of commotion in front of the bank, then some shooting, then some masked men on horseback shooting at men on the roof of the bank. It got pretty wild and noisy. Someone fell of the roof unto the street, and so on, until several bandits came out of the bank with bags, presumably filled with money. Some more shooting until one of the bandits got shot, while the others galloped down the street, being chased by others on horseback. The other hombre was bound, gagged, and then dragged away down the street behind a cowboy on a horse. It looked so natural that Ron, Susan, and Karen at first didn't believe me later when I told them that it was an act, performed here quite often for tourists like us. And so the last evening in Teton National Park came to an exciting conclusion.

We loaded up the car early in the morning, making sure not to leave the elk rack behind. We were going to cover some 460 miles to Colorado if all went according to plan, though none of that was on the Interstate. Before leaving the park we saw a huge eagle's nest on a sheltered rock and were surprised to spot the eagles flapping their enormous wings. Not far from the Southern exit to the park, we stopped to visit the tiny Chapel of Transfiguration and its small bell tower. It is unique because of its size, just 22 ft. by 50 ft., it is built entirely of native rustic logs. However, the most startling thing is the large window behind the altar which perfectly frames the magnificent Cathedral Group of the Grand Teton Mountain range. I took some movies to capture the beauty and serenity of the Chapel and its location. Leaving the park we drove a very scenic route, crossed the Shoshone Indian Reservation and cattle range country before stopping at the town of Rawlins for gas and groceries. The credit card system for gasoline was still in its infancy and often the pump operator went inside to take down the car's license plate number as a precaution. After a long day of driving and typical sibling spats, we decide to stay at a Holiday Inn motel in Fort Collins, Colorado. It was the first time that we deviated from our planned schedule, which had been to stay in Loveland, 29 miles farther. It was a good decision, since all of us were exhausted and had enough driving for a day. Four hundred and forty miles in all.

The next morning after a good night's sleep and a good breakfast in our room, we began our travels through the Rocky Mountain National Park. On the way to Estes Park, we reached Loveland from where thousands of Valentines are re-mailed on February 14th with a Loveland postmark. We took the Bear Lake Road to Bear Lake where we parked our car and start hiking to Nymph Lake. From there, we would be able to see Longs Peak, 14,256 ft. high and Glacier Gorge, both still covered with snow, although it was now the middle of July. This dramatic view was reflected in the water of the lake, a most spectacular sight. Then we all hiked up to Dream Lake, huffing and puffing because of the altitude. Ron and I decided to show off, and hiked up to Emerald Lake while Gert and the two girls rested. All the while we saw people climbing the mountain sides, while in other areas people were skiing. All in all, we saw the grandest of American mountain scenery and none of us have ever forgotten the beauty of flowered meadows, rugged gorges, plunging brooks, streams and animals.

Once we returned to our car and had some refreshments from our cooler, we drove along the Trail Ridge Road across the Continental Divide and continue to the resort town of Grand Lake. We stayed at a lodge by the same name, had dinner in town, walked along the beautiful lake, and played some miniature golf back at the Lodge where we had two adjacent rooms. Later, we watched the movie *Fail Safe* in the lodge lobby, before resting our tired heads on comfortable pillows for the night.

The next morning, Tuesday July 11, the alarm clock awoke us at 5:45 a.m. to continue our trip through the remainder of the Rocky Mountains, destination Colorado Springs. Before breakfast I lit the wood burning potbelly stoves in our rooms since it was very cold. We had a good breakfast using our portable electric range for toast and hot chocolate. Next we loaded the car up including our precious antler, and were ready to move out by 7:45 a.m. We were on a winding mountain road to Granby, and from there through small towns of Tabernash and Fraser to Winter Park, the scenery being spectacular on all sides. At Berthhould Pass, 11,307 ft. altitude, the road became so curvy that I decided to take over driving duties, but continued to drive slow to keep from going over the berm while at the same time enjoying the heavenly views. We didn't stop at Buffalo Bill's grave, which was near the town of Golden, and instead drove right to Sears in Denver where we took a well-deserved break while our well-worn two front tires were replaced.

With new front tires, we were now on our way to Colorado Springs which was to take us 4½ hours. It started to pour rain when we arrived at the Air Force Academy. Therefore we decided to drive on to our destination and checked in to the Yucca Lane Lodge from where we could see Pikes Peak through the haze and rain. I had imagined a peak as implied by the name, yet was disappointed to see a mountain that looked more like a bald head. It was then that I decided not to drive the next day up a strenuous road to the so-called Peak at an elevation of 14,110 ft., not knowing whether it was worth the effort and strain on the car, after all the beautiful sights we had experienced in the Rocky Mountain National Park. It was still raining when we went to bed, but we were delighted to get up in the morning with sunny skies.

We drove about seven miles north to the Air Force Academy where we visited the uniquely designed chapel for all denominations. Protestant services were conducted on the ground level, while Catholic and Jewish services were conducted on the second level. The structure has 17 spires thrusting high into the sky fashioned like airfoils or wings. It was certainly eye catching since this ultra-modern structure dominated the area as a symbol of man's devotion to G'd. We walked over the manicured grounds of the cadet area and looked at the Eagles Stadium, from where Pikes Peak was quite visible. We stayed to see the cadets march in formation to the dining hall while the band played. It was all quite interesting and quite a show. Next we went to see the ancient ruins of the Cliff Dwellings, which represented the remains of a vanished prehistoric civilization said to exist between 1000 C.E. and 1300 C.E. Overwhelmed by such history, we drove to our lodge for a refreshing swim, lunch, and a rest. In the afternoon we visited the Garden of the Gods where we marveled at the grotesque formations of red sandstone once sacred land to the Indians of the region. The oldest of the rock formations has been estimated to be about 3,750 years old.

For a change we slept a little longer the next morning, only to be awakened by another beautiful sunny day for sightseeing. We drove to Canyon City and approached the famous Royal Gorge of the Arkansas River. We were not disappointed in what we saw. Across the gorge, 1053 ft. above the river, was the world's highest suspension bridge. The setting was absolutely magnificent as we decide to walk over the bridge, at least part of the way, because the sensation of height, and the feeling of a sway made the walk kind of scary. Karen was really afraid and started the walk on her hands and knees. Yet it was amazingly beautiful as we took glimpses down below and were fortunate to see a Rio Grande train below winding its way through the narrow granite rock gorge, now and then blowing its whistle. It was an amazing sight and an unusual feeling experiencing the merger of awesome nature and latest technology. We walked back to the car, drove all the way across the 1,260 foot-long span and back because the road ended on the other end of the bridge. Indeed a bridge to nowhere, but no disappointment for us. To top it all off we bought tickets for the world's steepest incline railway, and took the lighter of our picnic carriers along. The descent to the bottom of the Royal Gorge was nothing short of amazing and so were the views as we came closer to the roaring sounding water of the Arkansas River. There we had an enjoyable picnic lunch, although visited by flying insects the likes we had not seen before.

Looking around and up, to see the bridge spanning the canyon walls from below, was an incredible sight. Around us were many flowers and a variety of cacti, some of which the children dug up to take home. Originally I had planned to drive to Cripple Creek, a picturesque mining camp famous for its gold mining in years gone by, using the scenic Ute Pass around Pike's Peak. Instead, I thought it was best to relax the rest of the afternoon surrounded by grandiose nature.

We returned to the lodge in Colorado Springs and enjoyed the swimming pool, before having supper at a nearby restaurant, and packing for our trip home via Kansas City, Missouri. All of us had seen so much, but now we were longing to come home and tell our friends how beautiful and exciting our country really is. It would be another two full days of driving, a total of 1,230 miles primarily on Interstate 70, before we arrived safe and sound back at Castano Drive, on Saturday July 15, 1967. The large antler trophy on top of the car carrier became the immediate curiosity of our friends in the neighboring homes. As we opened the trunk, like a miracle, some of the cacti were in full bloom. The experience of a lifetime had come to an end for five people, never to be forgotten!

We had explored a magnificent America with stunning views, events, history, people, traditions, lakes, parks, deserts, animals, forests, beaches, amusement parks, roads, technology, dams, flowers, gorges, waterfalls, vegetation, skies, canyons, mountains, trails, reservations, wilderness, farms, cities, monuments, wildlife, and more. Having driven a total of 7,901 miles, we had seen the personality of our country with every mile driven, we had witnessed the blessings of nature. We marveled at the remnants of past civilazations and the richness of their descendants, the Indians. All that time there was no work, study, or cleaning and no deadlines to meet, just a routine of restocking the two coolers with food, drink, and ice. We had turned the rite of just taking a trip into an exciting wonderful opportunity, especially for our three children, and thus awoke in them the element of curiosity so essential in later life.

I took out an insurance on my stamp collection, inclusive of Opa Wolff's collection which Oma had gifted me and kept all valuable stamps in a bank safe deposit. On July 31, we held a party at our house for my office personnel to premeire our 8mm films entitled "The Greatest Story Ever Told," or "How the West was Won." Nineteen people showed up. We had several intermissions and served refreshments. The small chunk of a petrified conifer tree bought from a vendor just outside the Petrified Forest is estimated to be 207 million old, according to a Smithsonian Museum Curator.

In August, my mother had a stroke and was confined to a wheel chair. She needed a full time caretaker while Dad still went to work. He had to, so he could pay for all the expenses. He cooked dinner in the evening and did all the shopping on weekends. Irene had to sell her house because of plans for an expressway being built there, and purchased a duplex on 6921 S. Merrill Avenue, across from

O'Keefe School, a block away from Mom and Dad. She had a job as a receptionist at University of Chicago Lying-In Hospital. From August to October, Ronald had a part-time job at Miller's Department Store, 101 Woodman Drive, as stock boy and sales clerk. He had another job for a while at The Treasure Chest in Salem Mall. Over Labor Day weekend, I drove to Chicago to visit my parents. Mother is very weak and Dad can no longer take care of her. A practical nurse is there to help.

In September, we bought a new Plymouth 4-door sedan, Belvedere model from Hilgeford Motors in Fairborn. It was titled to Gertrude. Also that fall, the musical "Hair" opened in New York and once a week, weather permitting, we would give Karen 50 cents so she could walk from Belle Haven School to McDonalds on Free Pike at lunchtime, buy a hamburger, french fries, and a drink, and with her friends go to the cemetery next to McDonald's, sit on a tombstone, and eat lunch. Susan is still a cheerleader at Meadowdale High School, and practicing diligently and enjoying it. December 4, a human heart was successfully transplanted into another person in Cape Town, South Africa by Dr. Barnard.

On December 26, I was notified by my Division Chief, Col. Gordon A. Spencer, that I had been again awarded an Outstanding Performance Rating which included a $250 bonus as ordered by Major General USAF, Kenneth O. Sanborn. The award did not take place until March 1968, and reads in part as follows: "The incumbents ability to consistently exceed the standard is exemplified by the high level products which have received higher echelon acceptance and culminated in published directives, plans, studies, and products. Most of these were developed under stress of too short deadlines established by Headquarters United States Air Force…Mr. Kahn's effectiveness in convincing his superiors, other staff agencies and Commands of the soundness of his approach to a problem and the reason, ability of implementing his proposals contribute to his outstanding capability in oral, written or graphic presentations. One of the first products which was developed to get mobilization of the ground and educated Air Force Logistics personnel on their subject, was producted by Mr. Kahn, i.e. the preliminary Plan for Mobilization Planning," etc. etc.

CHAPTER TWENTY

1968 and Beyond

It was 1989, believe I or not, 27 years ago that I started to think and agonize about this writing venture. Recently when the subject came up with several of my loved ones, the refrains was always, "I hope to see the finished biography before I die." Gleefully I gave assurances not knowing what the future had in in store that they would. This and the constant well-meaning reminders and lately nagging by my children, including my wife and others, prompted me to rethink my project. In a way it would have been a great relief to have it all done by the time I turned 92. However, that was not the case. The rest of my writing will therefore, at least for the most part, reduce or eliminate much of the less important events so I can bring my expanded autobiography to a satisfactory conclusion.

1968

January Received a letter from the Assistant Dean at the University of Oklahoma notifying me that my total score of the Social Science examination was above the score set by the faculty of the College. It was a long a difficult exam and I'm glad I passed it.

February 9 My dear Mother, Martha Kahn, age 75, passed away at 4 a.m. at South Shore Rest Home, Chicago, after many years of ailments. Many of those were due to torment and grief resulting from Nazi persecution; the hardships of life as immigrant in America the incarceration of my father at Dachau; the loss of her father, sister, brother-in-law and many other relatives murdered in Nazi death camps; the unknown fate of her daughter Irene for five years; and her worries about me being overseas fighting the Japanese. The list goes on. She died on 10 Shevat 5728. The death certificate listed the immediate cause of death as "terminal Broncho Pneumonia due to or as a consequence of a cerebral hemorrhage, non-traumatic." I loved her as none other could love his mother. Her funeral was plain, sad, and devastating. My eulogy was a combination of words and tears, shared by Gertrude who accompanied me. She was a great inspiration to me and will be to the end of my day.

February 22 We purchased a 4-unit furnished modern brick apartment building through Glen R. Smith Realty Co., in nearby Trotwood, 416-422 Burman Ave. The income was to help put Ronald through college, and it did.

March 19 Ron received results of a Civil Service Exam. He qualified for various positions.

April 4 Martin Luther King Jr. was assassinated in Memphis, Tennessee. A ghastly sign of racial hate.

After many years paying $251 for my $10,000 GI Life Insurance it was finally paid up. And Kodak put the "Instamatic Camera" on the market. A great improvement over cameras in use until now.

June 5 Ronald is awarded "Senior Recognition" at Meadowdale High School for his "Outstanding Service in National Honor Society, and Tennis on Varsity Team" and graduated from high school with ceremonies taking place at NCR (National Cash Register Co.) Auditorium. He had worked hard to make good grades, and we were proud of his accomplishments. Earlier he had applied for admission to the University of Cincinnati and was accepted. He was interested in Engineering. Through August 18, he worked second shift at Etched Products Corp., 1546 Stanley Avenue, as a production helper making $2.30/hour.

Also on June 5, Senator Robert Kennedy, the brother of the late President John F. Kennedy, was shot and killed by a Palestinian American in a Los Angeles Hotel. A senseless murder of a brilliant mind.

June 30 The world's largest troop and transport aircraft, the C-5 Galaxy was inaugurated by Lockheed Aircraft Co. Unfortunately, we can improve the tools for war, but are unable to develop or improve the tools for peace.

July All of us take a trip to Gettysburg, Pennsylvania, to see the battlefields of the Civil War and monuments. Although the war was fought to eliminate slavery in the South, we saw no black visitors.

August We drove to Massachusetts to visit Oma Wolff and took some excursions to Marblehead, Rockport, and Gloucester.

November 18-22 Received a letter of appreciation from Major General John L. McCoy for giving several presentations and participating in an Armed Services Procurements Planning Officers (ASPPO) conference and workshop.

General 1968 The war in Vietnam continues with heavy American casualties. As you know from other chapters, I deplore war and the heartache it often brings to innocent people.

We enjoy watching *I Love Lucy* show. The comedy skits made us forget the dark realistic world we live in.

Still busy being a Cubmaster for Cubscout Pack 65 exclusively for Jewish boys.

1969

January 20 Richard Nixon becomes President of the U.S.

March 12 Purchased a little used Klepper made kayak for two, with sailing equipment for $300. We were now able to go sailing at Kaiser Lake or Eastwood Park Lake, which we all enjoyed.

EXHIBIT 20.1
KlepperKayak with sails.

EXHIBIT 20.2 Loads of fun.

March 17 Golda Meir became Prime Minister of Israel.

March 28 General Dwight Eisenhower had died. He played a significant role in orchestrating the World War II invasion of Europe, and later became President from 1953-1957.

May 3 The 2000 year old Sequoia Redwood, also known as the Wawona Tunnel Tree, fell from its roots, leaving a big hole. We drove our car through it on our trip West, just about two years prior. It was 234 feet tall, just a sapling in Christ's time.

June 14 Miami Valley B'nai B'rith Lodge held a spectacular Dinner Dance at the Christopher Club, Kettering. Gert and I were in charge. It was much work for both of us, but it paid off. The cost per couple, including champagne, believe it or not, was only $9.50.

The wonderful Van Cleve Hotel located on the SW corner of First and Ludlow Street was demolished. It had 300 guest rooms and was famous for its Mayfair Dining Room with wonderful memories of special celebrations for us.

Susan received an Honors Certificate for sustained tenth grader Temple Israel Religious School scholarship, through several grading periods during the 1968-1969 school year. She was placed on the school's decade old Honors Megillah. She was in Mr. Green's Saturday class, and was confirmed later with 31 girls and 27 boys by Rabbi Selwyn D. Ruslander and Rabbi Joseph S. Weizenbaum.

July 20 American Neil Armstrong became the first man to walk on the moon after blasting off from Cape Kennedy, July 16 with Buzz Aldrin. An historic achievement of technological dimensions. "Aquarius" by the Fifth Dimension became the unforgettable song of the year.

August We all met the Salten family in the Smoky Mountains and did some fishing. The fish were turned over to the restaurant for the evening meal, but our Susan and Karen, as well as the Salten's Peggy, Roslyn and Rita didn't like eating the fish they caught. They felt sorry for them.

Next, Opa Kahn flew to Dayton for a visit. After a few days, we drove with Ron, Susan and Karen to General Butler State Park, Kentucky, overlooking the Ohio River. We all had a good time. Opa stayed at the Lodge while we stayed at a nice cabin and had a good time together.

August 20 Thousands of young people, mostly hippies, spend a rainy weekend at Woodstock, New York, making love, music, and smoking marijuana.

September 15 Ronald, now a freshman at the University of Cincinnati, became a Co-Op Student at National Cash Register Company. He was paid $128.90 per week and worked in the Manpower & Organization Development Department. He was able to live at home for room and board, 3639 Castano Drive. He and we were happy!

October 2 Made final payment on our loan for our house on Castano Drive to Gem City Savings Association. No more monthly payments! It's ours.

November Arthur Beerman, owner of Elder-Beerman stores in Dayton, began sponsoring a free Thanksgiving dinner for the poor, needy, and lonely, serving 4,000-5,000 people. It became a tradition for many years, and is still today. After his death, his foundation continued. Gert and I volunteered for several years to help at the event. Giving to others was the right thing to do.

B'nai B'rith performs invaluable service
Certificate of Recognition awarded

Colonel Robert M. Igleburger, Director of Police, presented a Certificate of Recognition to the Miami Valley Lodge of the B'nai B'rith. Accepting the Certificate in behalf of the Lodge was Mr. Norman Kimmel, Mr. Robert B. Kohn, and Mr. Gunther I. Jacobson.

The Certificate of Recognition was awarded by the Department of Police to express appreciation for services performed by the organization on December 24th and 25th, 1969. Thirteen members and one auxiliary member worked within the Department in order to permit personnel the pleasure of spending time with their families over that holiday period.

B'nai B'rith has performed an invaluable service to the Department for the past three years. During the ceremonies, Mr. Jacobson expressed a desire to expand their services to the Department of Police in the future.

EXHIBIT 20.3 Members of B'nai Brith accept a Certificate of Recognition in behalf of the Miami Valley Lodge of B'nai B'rith for service rendered to the Dayton Police Department on December 24 and 25, 1969. From left to right: Mr. Norman Kimmel (Electronics Engineer at DESC); Mr. Robert B. Kahn (Program Analyst at WPAFB); Mr. Gunter I. Jacobson (Editor of the Inland Division of General Motors); Colonel R.M. Ingleburger, Director of Police.

December 24-25 Thirteen members of Miami Valley B'nai B'rith Lodge, including myself, volunteered to work at the Dayton Police Department to permit some personnel to spend Christmas with their families. It was very well received and we felt good about it.

We watched the comedians Rowan and Martin's TV program, *The Laugh-In*.

1970

January/February My immediate supervisor and I were requested on short notice to travel to the Pentagon, to work with the Joint Logistics Review Board on a Top Secret project. It required working 11-12 hours each day, including Saturdays and Sundays. My boss left after several days and I had to stay on several weeks. Afterward, I received several letters of appreciation from Major General USAF, Thomas Jeffrey Jr., Director of Production, Pentagon, and Major General Fred J. Ascani, DCS, Plans and Operations Logistics Command. Of all the letters, the one which best captures the essence of my contribution reads in part: "your devotion to duty which required personal sacrifices on your part has not gone unnoticed," signed by Colonel USAF, Walter Gallagher, Director of War Plans.

January—July My studies at the University of Oklahoma have become much harder, requiring more time, research and writing, and burning the midnight oil. Also, the requirement to spend so much time on campus at Norman, Oklahoma, was hard on Gert and the children, on my bread and butter job at Wright Patterson and on our pocketbook. The Natural Science area of study, among others, required a review of Thales, the Catalyst of Scientific Thought, and writing extensive papers with my now considered-ancient portable typewriter. It required a review of the idea of scientific progress and other subjects demanding homework late into the night and forgoing weekends, often at the expense of spending much time with the family.

February 19 Purchased a Panasonic stereo/record player at Elder-Beerman with cabinet. Get much pleasure with it, especially since it plays 78", 45", and 33" records, of which we have many.

March Real Estate taxes for our home are $460 per year.

April 16 Apollo 13 had an explosion in space and had to abort mission. With extraordinary luck and handling the three astronauts are saved after making an emergency splash down in the South Pacific.

May 9 Gert and I did such a fantastic job organizing our first B'nai B'rith Lodge dinner dance last year that we were drafted to plan it again this year. We decided on a Hawaii motif and wrote to the Governor of Hawaii to have the ancient Gods bless our undertaking (see exhibit 20.4 in the appendix). The Governor, John Burns, mailed us his good wishes via a proclamation. Gert and I transformed the Christopher Club into a Hawaiian paradise with decorations, bought and borrowed. Pineapples, and orchids for each of the ladies, were flown in from the Island. We hired a Hawaiian guitarist. The evening was an outstanding success, and with food and a dance band, all for $12 per couple.

May 18 At Kent State University in Ohio, the National Guard's men wound eight and kill four students protesting the Vietnam War, causing general outrage by the American public.

Susan worked part time after school, twice a week and on weekends at The House of Fabrics. Her income savings at the end of the year was $1,498. I recorded her cheerleading at Meadowdale High School with my movie camera.

June Susan's 11th grade report card for the year was almost all *A*s. Her homeroom teacher was Mr. Martin. She also took driver's education lessons and had a boyfriend by the name of Steve Lipson. In her senior class, later that year, she served as Historian and designed the programs for the play *The Desk Set* by Willian Marchant, which was performed on November 21, 1970. Gert and I were one of the sponsors of the play.

August All of us take a nice vacation with Opa Kahn at Lake Cumberland State Park in Kentucky, near Jamestown. We all miss Oma. Opa gave Karen a gold ring with pearl setting, which my mother wore as a young woman. Engraved on the inside is the date: 10/31/1920. Later, Susan attends band camp since she was a cheerleader. Her clarinet had migrated to sister Karen.

August 20 We purchased our first full size freezer (Coldspot) at Sears. It was avocado color and had a miniscule dent, therefore the price was reduced to $270. It was placed in the garage.

September 14 Arab terrorists hijacked five passenger planes and blew up three in the Jordanian desert, holding passengers hostage.

October Gert and I take a week deserved, brief vacation with several other Jewish couples from Dayton to Nassau, Bahamas. We stayed at the Balmoral Beach Hotel where we played tennis, swam, and went sailing with Mel Kruger and wife.

November 3 Purchased a second 4-unit apartment building partially furnished at 4116 Merryfield Avenue for $43,000. I took out a loan for $2,500 from my VA Life Insurance to pay for the down payment with a 4% interest rate. Hade to take out a loan for the remainder at the bank at 8%.

November 19 150,000 people die in Pakistan as a result of a terrible typhoon.

December My salary: $20,068; Gert's salary working at Elder-Beerman, Trotwood: $1,324; Her income from selling jewelry: $358; income from both apartments: $6,199.

1971

January Sadly, America begins its 21st year of involvement in Vietnam.

Premiere of *All In the Family* on CBS. How can we forget Archie, Edith, Mike, and Gloria? The shows were wonderful and a delight to watch.

March 7 1,000 US war planes raid targets in Cambodia.

May We attend a *Musical Review* with Karen's participation at Belle Haven School.

We now owned a 1967 Plymouth and a 1970 Chrysler automobile.

May 11 Was appointed Group Leader of the Concepts and Guidance Group and Acting Division Chief of the Mobilization and Plans Division.

May 15 3rd annual B'nai B'rith Selwyn D. Ruslander Lodge Dinner Dance: "A night of the roaring twenties." Again, Gert and I were in charge and it was a blast.

May 29 For my studies at University of Oklahoma, wrote an extensive paper on "United States Foreign Policy," and other subjects.

1972

March 1 Ronald received a certificate of recognition and appreciation from the President of Grandview Hospital, Dayton, for seventy-six hours of volunteer service in the hospital.

March 15 War criminal Martin Borman, Hitler's secretary and a Nazi fanatic for the destruction of Jews, was caught in Columbia.

March 17 President Nixon requests Congress to terminate busing to achieve integration.

May 14 When you pour all of your strength into creating a new life for your parents, for yourself, and now for your own family, it is hard to think of new goals to accomplish. For some years I was so preoccupied with excelling at my job with the Air Force, even so I disliked (hated) the overall objective that I ignored my own goal which was to obtain a higher degree of learning from a university. After six years of struggling between studying and balancing my time and effort between job, family, and the University of Oklahoma, I finally finished my sixty-two page thesis study in depth titled "Projective Planning for Optimizing Defense Preparedness and Expenditures." What a relief when I received a letter from my professor: "I think you have done a superior job…I approved it, marked it superior." Next, I received the invitation to attend the graduation ceremonies to have the degree Bachelor of Liberal Studies officially conferred on Sunday, May 14. The 24 candidates for the BLS degree were to wear white gowns and black tassels. Because of travel cost, time, and other job commitments, I requested graduation in absentia. I was a happy and proud man having earned my Bachelor degree at age 48, a goal I promised to reach before my son Ronald would graduate, to set an example of determination, zeal, and self-esteem.

May 21 *The Pieta*, sculpture by Michelangelo in St. Peter's Basilica is damaged with a hammer by a deranged visitor.

June The play *Fiddler on the Roof* sets Broadway record with 3,225 performances. We saw it locally and loved it.

June 22 As President of Ruslander Lodge, B'nai B'rith recommended to the Executive Board and approved the donation of $500 to the Education Building Fund of Temple Israel.

August 13 Ron married Julie Zimmerman. The wedding ceremony took place at Beth Abraham Synagogue, Dayton. Rabbi Jack Riemer performed the most beautiful service. The rehearsal dinner took place at King's Table restaurant

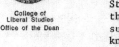

Mr. Robert B. Kahn
3639 Castano Drive
Dayton, OH 45416

Dear Mr. Kahn:

It is indeed a pleasure for me to inform you that you have fulfilled all requirements for the Bachelor of Liberal Studies degree. I am proud of your accomplishments and am pleased to include you in the ever increasing number of BLS graduates.

On behalf of the faculty of the College of Liberal Studies, I congratulate you on your achievement in the BLS program and extend our wishes for continued success in all future endeavors. Please let me know at any time when we can be of assistance to you.

Sincerely yours,

Roy Troutt
Dean

RT/pg

EXHIBIT 20.5 Letter from the Dean.

The Oklahoma State Regents for Higher Education acting through the

University of Oklahoma

have admitted

Robert Bernard Kahn

to the degree of

Bachelor of Liberal Studies

and all the honors, privileges and obligations belonging thereto, and in witness thereof have authorized the issuance of this Diploma duly signed and sealed.

Issued at the University of Oklahoma at Norman, Oklahoma on the fourteenth day of May, A.D. nineteen hundred and seventy-two.

For the State Regents:
Chairman
Secretary
Chancellor

For the University:
President, Board of Regents
President of The University
Academic Dean

EXHIBIT 20.6 Graduation diploma

attended among others by my dad from Chicago, and Gert's mom from Lawrence Massachusetts. We were happy to see that the young couple was happy.

August 30 We celebrate our 25th wedding anniversary with our first trip back to Europe. It was a hard decision to make. We rented a car in Frankfurt. It was difficult for me and Gert to speak German again after 31+ years not having spoken the language. With very mixed feelings, we drove to Mannheim, my former home town. This was the city that persecuted, tormented, and exiled me and my family. We checked into the well-known Park Hotel and walked to the places where we once lived. The first, now an IBM building, the other, a sex book store. The city which had been 80% destroyed showed no signs of earlier destruction. To the contrary, reconstructed buildings, churches, monuments, department stores, and new buildings had taken their place. One of the buildings not reconstructed was our beautiful and beloved synagogue. It had been bulldozed and was now a parking lot. Tears came to my eyes as I confronted the present with the past. We talked to no one, nor did I have the desire to. I was a stranger in the town I once loved and that hated me.

The next day we drove to Heidelberg where everything was the same and as beautiful as I remembered it. Then, by way of Meckenheim to Neustadt where Gert was born and lived. Had *Zwetschkenkuchen* at bakery Heizman. Gert's house where she once lived is the same with some updates. We were able to walk through it, which evoked an eerie feeling. On to Kreuznach, where Gert's cousin Peter Stern and his family were now living temporarily. In Sobenheim, everything looked the same, and Peter gave us a tour of the Mill which was now again in the hands of its former, and rightful, Jewish owners, the Marums.

From there we drive to Laufersweiler where nothing had changed. Stopped in front of my Dad's former home. People in the surrounding houses came out to see what was going on. I approached an elderly man and asked if he knew Joseph Kahn. His name was Stumm and his immediate reply was "Natürlich"—of course. "I used to play games of marbles with him." What remained of the synagogue which stood only a few houses away was being used as a community cold storage and laundry facility. A purposeful and sad desecration of a once holy site.

From there we crossed the border to Luxembourg and drove to the home of Aunt Marthe who was delighted to see us. While we stayed there several days, I saw the furniture, paintings, bookcases, two breakfronts, and figurines, all were our belongings which were hidden in Luxembourg before we left. Later they were gifted by my parents to Uncle Berny and Aunt Marthe when they returned after the war, and found their home plundered and ransacked by the Germans. She cried as she told us again how their son Georges was executed by the Nazis. Opa Raphael Joseph's house was no longer. It had been torn down by a lumber company. Gone was the house, but not my memories. We also visited Aunt Gaby and her son Marcel Kahn, and wife Lilliane, in nearby Roodt who as in former years

EXHIBIT 20.7 Marcel and Lilliane Kahn, Roodt s/Syr Luxembourg.

EXHIBIT 20.8 Aunt Gaby, mother of Marcel.

had cakes and tortes for us fresh from the bakery they operated. All of this brought back bitter sweet memories and tore at my heart with silent force. And yet I was glad that Gert and I were making this pilgrimage.

Next stop was Metz where we had lunch with cousin Eliane (nee Ehrlich) and her Rabbi husband, Jacques Ouaknin and children. On to Strasbourg where we visited cousin Claude and Pierrette Ehrlich and their eight children, with only one bathroom! Stayed there overnight.

From there we began our anniversary trip in earnest, leaving most memories behind.

Then something happened that no one had counted on and shook us all up. It happened during the Olympic Games in Munich, when on Tuesday morning, September 5, Arab guerillas invaded the village of the athletes. They penetrated the Israeli compound, shot several and took the rest hostage, all of whom were killed in a later unsuccessful raid by German police trying to save them. In all, 11 Israeli athletes, four guerillas, and one German police officer were killed. It saddened us and put us as Jews traveling through Germany doubly on the alert. It scared us to no end!

We drove back across the border to Germany, through the Black Forest, until we came to Lake Constance, where we spend our 25th Anniversary night at an ancient castle near the town of Lindau. It was unusual, but a romantic experience. Next we travelled to scenic Füssen, hence Neuschwanstein, Garmisch, and Innsbruck. Then across the Brenner pass into Italy and through breathtaking Dolomites to Cortina d'Ampezzo, then to Venice. All like fairy land, on to

Bergamo, and Milano where we went to see the famous Opera House La Scala. Scenery of beauty had no end at Lake Como, Lugano and Locarno, finally staying several days at Stresa on Lake Maggiore. Finally, through the Simplon Pass encountering a snowstorm to Tasch, parked the car and took the train to Zermatt where we marveled at the Matterhorn, 14,700 feet high covered in snow. Had to put our car on a train since the roads and passes were closed in order to get to Interlaken. From there we drove to Zurich, Schaffhausen, a long hike up the Feldberg, and our final destination Frankfurt for a smooth flight home to Dayton. We had been away 24 days, drove 1,860 miles, took 21 rolls of movie film and many photographs.

September 17 I was installed President of Selwyn D. Ruslander Lodge #2254 of B'nai B'rith by Max Kohnop District Past President. The installation took place at King's Table restaurant West First Street.

September 26 As President, I represented Ruslander and Kusworm Lodges of B'nai B'rith at a candle light ceremony at then known as Cox Municipal Airport, Dayton, in honor of the establishment and anniversary of the State of Israel.

October 16 Jacques Oaknin, husband of Eliane (nee Ehrlich) my first cousin, was installed as Grand Rabbi for the city of Metz, France and the entire French Mosel river area. The Grand Rabbi of France Jacob Kaplan conducted the installation.

November 5 Served as principal of the "Guardian of Menorah" at a dinner held at Temple Israel attended by more than 350 persons to bestow on Louis Goldman, president of the Jewish Community Council, this prestigious award by B'nai B'rith Sidney Kusworm and Selwyn D. Ruslander Lodges. Former astronaut and later (1974) senator John Glenn and his charming wife Annie were among the invited guests, also, James H. McGee, Mayor of the city of Dayton. Si Burick, sports editor and columnist for the Dayton Daily News was Master of Ceremonies, Victor Cassano, Sr., originator of "Cassano's Pizza King" restaurants, and philanthropist, was co-chairman. I gave the benediction. This event also served as a fundraiser and netted a total of $70,000. (See exhibit 20.9 in the appendix)

December 19 Apollo 17 astronauts had spent 75 hours on the moon.

December 21 My sister Irene took a solo trip to Israel with a stopover in Rome, and wrote a very detailed narrative of her trip.

1973

January 12 To my surprise, I received through the mail at my place of work at Wright Patterson Air Force Base a letter from the United States Secretary of Defense, the Honorable Melvin R. Laird, reading as follows: *Before I leave the position of Secretary of Defense, I want to thank you for the support you gave the*

President's Inter-Agency Economic Adjustment Committee in its efforts to alleviate the economic impacts of Defense decisions that adversely affected communities and individuals.

As Chairman of the Presidential Committee, I personally appreciate the help you have given us. Sincerely, [signed] Melvin R. Laird

No one in my office, nor in the entire Division ever received a letter from the Secretary of Defense. All of the chiefs and co-workers came to congratulate me, and I felt a certain pride having deserved such praise and recognition. (See exhibit 20.10 in the appendix)

January 22 Former US President Lyndon Johnson died.

January 27 President Nixon pulls American troops out of Vietnam.

February 25 My dad was admitted to Michael Reese Hospital, Chicago, suspected of having lung cancer. Biopsies of lymph nodes confirmed the malignancy and radiation treatments were started.

March-April Drove several times to Chicago to visit Dad at the hospital. On one occasion he asked me for a cigar. When I told the doctor, he said, "Give him anything he wants if he enjoys it." I realized then that there was no chance of recovery. A few days before he passed away, he held my hand and said: "Had I known that you would turn out to be as good a son, I would not have disciplined you as I did when you were young." I choked up and tears came to my eyes. Dad died at 4:20 p.m. April 15 (13 Nissan, 5733) at the age of 83. He was wise and good to everyone. A model father that everyone should have. He lived last with my sister Irene, who took care of him in an apartment at 7216 South Shore Drive, Chicago, 60649, overlooking the lake. (see exhibits 20.11 and 20.12 in the appendix)

April 8 Our B'nai B'rith Lodge sponsored an afternoon and evening program for Jewish students at the Hillel House of Miami University at Oxford, Ohio. Dinner, entertainment, and dance rounded out the program. It made me proud to be President of the Lodge.

June 9 My niece, Faye Diament, married Gregory High in Evanston, Illinois, whom she met when both were students at the University of Illinois. They were later divorced July 26, 1982.

June 30 Received an award in the form of a plaque from B'nai B'rith headquarters "for outstanding individual achievement and inspirational leadership he has rendered and devoted services on behalf of B'nai B'rith youth agencies.... etc. etc.

August 1 After Dad passed away, Irene moved to 1508 North Glenwood Avenue, Griffith, Indiana. She had remarried out of loneliness in summer of 1966 to Sidney Altman, an attorney. His son was on drugs, so she found out later, and for other reasons the marriage did not work out. The move by Irene to Indiana was to obtain a no fault divorce since he would not grant her a divorce in Illinois. However, she continued her job at the American College of Surgeons (1961-1981) although it required driving in a carpool a considerable distance.

Drove with Gert and Karen to visit Oma, staying at the Rolling Green Motel, Andover. Hans Marum, Gert's first cousin, invited me to go sailing with him at Marblehead.

October 4 We visit Gert's sister Ilse and brother-in-law Lester in Atlanta and on the holiday of Yom Kippur, October 6, we heard from the pulpit at synagogue the announcement that Arab forces, namely Syria, Egypt, Jordan with military assistance from the Soviet Union attacked Israel. As soon as I got back to Dayton, I was being dispatched to the Air Force Command Post, where supplies were immediately air lifted to Israel, including as I remember, flares to light up enemy positions at night. In the end Israel was victorious, in spite of the sneak attack from the Arab states.

November 13 Good neighbors deserve to be recognized when the opportunity presents itself. Thus, when I heard that Brad Kenney, the son of our neighbor across the street from us, aspired to become an Air Force officer, I wrote letters of recommendation to Ohio senators William Saxbe and Robert Taft to nominate Brad to become a cadet at the Air Force Academy. Although acceptance is on a highly competitive basis, his credentials resulted in Brad's nomination and acceptance to serve.

December Bought a $180 Israel Bond to mature in 1988 for each Karen and Susan as a way to add to their savings and a Chanukkah present.

1974

March 9 After 29 years, the last Japanese World War II soldier surrenders in the Philippines. They were sworn to fight to the death and as I found out, they did.

April 3 Xenia, 15 miles away from Dayton, experienced a tremendous tornado lasting 35 minutes and destroying much of the city, causing 34 deaths, injuring 1,500, and costing a huge amount of damage.

April 4 Next day, Gert, Karen and I fly to Tampa, rent a car and stay at St. Petersburg Beach for a vacation.

May Karen learns to drive.

May 7 Gave a lengthy and detailed briefing to high level Pentagon Air Force, Army, and Navy brass as well as high-level Pratt & Whitney executives at their engine production/assembly plant in West Palm Beach, Florida. It covered the war time surge requirement for the Air Force F100 engines powering the F-15 and F-16 fighter aircraft, the F117 Stealth fighter, the C-17 transport, as well as the TF33 engine powering the B-52 bomber and KC 135 cargo aircraft among others.

In recognition of my presentation, I received letters of appreciation from various Pentagon, Department of the U.S. Air Force Sources.

May 25 Reported to the police and insurance that one of Gert's rings was missing from the kitchen table. It was a white gold genuine Columbian emerald with two .05 point diamonds. Value, $450 paid by insurance. An open patio door was suspected.

May 27 6th of Sivan, 5734: Shavuot. Karen was confirmed at Temple Israel by Rabbis P. Irving Bloom and Samuel K. Joseph.

June 10-11 Some months ago, I was appointed to chair a study consisting of members from two commands to examine the requirements of spare parts under wartime flying hours for the TF-39 engine and the capability of General Electric Co. and its contractors to manufacture and deliver them on a stipulated time basis. This scenario would be crucial to reduce the downtime of aircraft such as the C-5 Galaxy cargo/transport, and the A-10 Thunderbolt attack aircraft. The completed study revealed numerous unacceptable situations and proposed remedial contractual actions. As chairman of the study, I was responsible for the final classified report. The significance of the findings and recommendations were acknowledged by Lt. General Edmund F. O'Connor, Vice Commander and Major General E.A. Rafalko, Hqs. Air Force Logistics Command and Major General Harold E. Collins, Hqs. Air Force Washington D.C. with high praises for me as chairman and letters of commendation.

Karen worked part-time at Friendly's Ice Cream Restaurant, earning $856 in wages and tips. She also was a teacher at Temple Israel, lower grade Sunday School for a while, and earned additional money.

August 9 President Nixon resigns to avoid impeachment.

Joined American Defense Preparedness Association and become active in its undertaking.

September 20 Bought a new Dodge Monaco custom automobile, color blue, for $4,127 including tax.

December 31 Karen wrecked the 1967 Plymouth 4-door bronze color, downtown near Sinclair College. Damage was $465, which insurance did not cover. As a result, she became a more careful driver.

1975

February 28 Karen has a lead role in her Junior Class high school play *You Can't Take it With You* as Rheba. We had lots of laughs.

April 30 A day after Gert's birthday, Saigon, Vietnam was captured by the Viet Cong, and the long war is over.

June 17 Sister Irene made her second trip to Israel, this time to Yad Vashem to attend the ceremony of the high award of a medal and certificate from the State of Israel to Canon Raymond Vancourt, and his niece Raymonde Lombard, in recognition of saving Irene's life by hiding her, and later also saving the lives of her aunt, uncle, and their two children from deportation. It saved them from ultimate death by the German occupiers during World War II. Also receiving this prestigious award in recognition were Jeanne and Alphonse Pattyn, Marie-Louise Siauve, and Miss Leroye for playing important roles in also saving Irene's life. Their awards were made later by an Israel Government representative in France. The title "Righteous Among Nations" one of the highest recognitions by the State of Israel is conferred on a person for saving the life of a Jew during the Shoah, upon meticulous examination of evidence submitted by the applicant. Irene had spent several years providing the required documentation and evidence.

EXHIBIT 20.13 Canon Raymond Vancourt.

EXHIBIT 20.14 Raymond Vancourt planted a Carob tree behind his monument. See exhibit 20.15 in the appendix.

June 21 Flew to Massachusetts to attend and celebrate Oma Wolff's 80th birthday. Ronald also attended, as well as Susan and Karen. Thereafter, we, i.e. including Susan and Karen, flew to Amsterdam, then via train to Rome where we rented a car and drove through Italy and Switzerland. This time we stopped at Mannheim with a purpose. I wanted to look up our grocer, Herr and Frau Klett who provided us with extra food without ration stamps and who clandestinely brought us milk, eggs, and bread after Kristallnacht at danger to their own life. I wanted to thank them and took Susan along. Knowing that they lived above the once small grocery store, I rang the bell, and the two of us climbed the stairs of the house, which was next to the police presidium. The elderly lady who opened the door didn't recognize me, nor did I recognize her. Frau Maria Krett, I said, I am Robert Kahn, your former Jewish customer. I continued, my father and mother were Joseph and Martha

Kahn, and I want to thank you for all your past good deeds. She choked as her eyes became moist and we embraced. Her husband, who had always rattled with his wooden leg, died some years prior. There was not much conversation as she and I were overwhelmed, so Susan and I left. What I set out do was done. Mannheim did not know I had been there. Departed again on July 13, back home from Amsterdam after seeing the Ann Frank house.

Summer The exciting movie *Jaws* hit the screens and was a huge success being directed by Steven Spielberg, and M*A*S*H hit the television screen.

Summer/Fall Our neighborhood is changing and hoodlums drive through our front yard at night leaving big ruts in the lawn. After I put large boards in the yard with spikes facing up, the incursions stopped. Then there were some local break-ins and several shootings, making us feel very uneasy. It was time to look for safer place to live.

August 26 A letter from my big boss, Brigadier General James P. Mullins to my immediate boss telling him that I was nominated as the "Planner of the Year" for the Command (of approximately 80,000 personnel) and that "such nomination is a signal honor and deserving of special recognition." He presented me with a certificate of Significant Achievement, in spite of the fact that someone else at our Oklahoma City Air Logistics Center received the actual honor.

1976

January 21 The supersonic passenger airline, Concorde, begins commercial flights.

March 9 We put our 4-unit Merryfield apartment complex up for sale, and sold it to Larry Kahn, of no relation, for a small profit.

April 20 Had to take a driver's test again since I had accidentally let my driver's license expire.

May 27 Karen graduates Meadowdale High School with commencement ceremonies at University of Dayton arena. We are proud of her just as much as we were when Ronald and Susan graduated.

June 10 It was on a Thursday afternoon when commencement exercises were held at Medical College of Ohio at Toledo. Ron was conferred the degree of Doctor of Medicine and could now officially show abbreviation of M.D. behind his name, Ronald S. Kahn. We are very proud of him as he enters his internship at Mercy Hospital, pursuing the specialty of family practice.

June 12-20 Vacation at Hilton Head Island, S.C. We drove; had Ronald with us in a rented apartment at South Beach Village. Gert, Ronald, and I played tennis every day.

July 4 Israel paratrooper commandos stormed the Entebbe, Uganda airport and rescued over 100 Israeli hostages held by Palestinian terrorists in an almost impossible operation. All hijackers were killed and four Israelis.

July 12 We signed a contract with Harold Haer Bldg Co 7130 South County Road, Tipp City, Ohio to build a three bedroom residence on Lot #78, 2702 Haverstraw Avenue. Later, we changed the building lot to #77. Initial cost: $54,204.50 with a loan of $36,000 at 7.5%. We made many modifications to the model home. The area is known as the "Iron Gate Plat" somewhat outside the city in Butler Township, away from the uncomfortable and unsafe area where we were living. Because of the energy crisis and unpredictable future, we asked the builder to design our new home with ceilings 6" lower than usual to conserve heat and cooling needs and the electricity. The home will be totally electric since the building of gas lines was restricted.

October 1 Moved into our new, beautiful home at 2694 Haverstraw Avenue, Dayton Ohio 45414. Street wasn't in yet, had to park on Hardwick Street, put on boots, and hike to our home since the street was not yet paved. Next morning, as we looked out the window, we saw sheep grazing in the field across from our house. Thank goodness our lot was not sodded yet. On a few lots from ours stood an old but beautiful barn with large hewn timbers, torn down later to make room for additional homes.

November 2 Appointed the Coordinator of our Division for the Combined Federal Campaign, which was much additional work. I received two letters of special recognition and an award from Major General USAF Gerald Post, Chief of Staff and James Mullins, Major General USAF Deputy Chief of Staff, Plans, Programs for having collected $104,757 or 106% of the monetary goal.

All year Used some of my free time hours now and in recent years to counsel Boy Scouts on achieving their "Personal Management" Merit Badge which required numerous sessions. Each scout was required to fulfill a number of written tasks, which I would certify upon completion.

1977

January 18 Temperature was -14 degrees, and most of our windows were frozen over solid.

January 21 It was somewhat eerie to be in a home without drapes. But who would look in, we were the only house on the street. We finally ordered drapes, including sheers for the living and dining rooms.

March Bought a 2" diameter, 7' tall Austrian Pine for $42, planted same in front yard in front of our guest bedroom. Also, bought an Ash tree, 1.5" in diameter for the front yard facing the street and two sculpted Yucca plants all for $81, planted by me on both sides of the garage.

May 18 Orin Cohen's wife, Adelle, both good friends, died after a long illness.

May 29 Rehearsal dinner and other festivities for Susan and Kenneth Rapoport's wedding at the Imperial House North. During the evening hours, we learned of the terrible fire at Beverly Hills Club, Southgate Kentucky, which consumed 164 people.

May 30 Susan and Ken's wedding and reception at Temple Israel. The bride looked ravishing. It was a great joy for Gert and me.

August 23 The King of Rock and Roll, Elvis Presley, was buried in Memphis, Tennessee.

September Gert and I drove to Chicago to celebrate Aunt Bella Danziger's 90th birthday. I danced with her.

Late September Irene had surgery for Stage 1 cancer of the uterus and ovaries.

December Julie, Ron's wife, suddenly left Ron and moved out of the house in Toledo. She had been seeing someone else behind Ronald's back. He was devastated.

December 28 Sold our four unit apartment building 416-422 Burman Avenue, Trotwood to Ted Miller. The income from all 8 apartment units helped considerably in funding all three of our children's college expenses.

1978

January 26 Severe blizzard with 12" piles of snow. Snow drifts were 8' around our house. Awful winter with a total of 75" of snowfall with freezing and below temperatures.

January 30 Raymond Vancourt, the priest who saved sister Irene from certain death by the Nazis, died. Irene had made a special trip in November 1977 to see him in Lille, knowing because of his cancer it would be the last time she would see him.

EXHIBIT 20.16 Ken Rapoport and his wife, our daughter Susan.

March Gert and I fly to San Francisco to visit cousins Ilse and Otto Hertz as well as Norbert and Helmut Isaak and their families.

April Planted a 6' Austrian Pine tree facing east in backyard

May 9 Taking Ronald along, we take a two week trip to Israel to celebrate the 30th year of Israel's independence. The land for which I had prayed each year, and before me, all my ancestors, was beautiful and inspiring. We stayed at the historic King David Hotel in Jerusalem, the Dan Hotel in Tel Aviv, the Dan Carmel in Haifa, and Laromme Hotel in Eilat. One of the high points was being able to pray and apply the ritual of teffilin at the Jewish section of the fortress like structure built by Herod the Great, now a mosque known by Jews as the Cave of Machpela. It is revered by all three faiths: Muslim, Christian, Jews, because Abraham, Isaak, Rebecca, Leah and Jacob are buried there. It is located at the town of Hebron a town in the West Bank inhabited primarily by Arabs, We attended the Independence Day concert at Mitchel Gardens at the foot of Mount Zion. Zubin Mehta, conductor, Itzhak Perlman, violinist; Leontyne Price, soprano; Jean Pierre Rampel, flutist; Mstislav Rostropovich, cellist and Isaak Stern, violinist. It was like music from heaven.

July Irene visits us in our new house.

September Gert and I visit Oma Wolff in Andover, Massachusetts. Marc Diament who at the time lived in Boston as well as Ernest and Marilyn Kahn from nearby Sharon came to visit with us and meet Oma. We drove to Marblehead with Oma, her favorite and most scenic place.

December 31 Big New Year's party at our house with our friends the Gilberts, Sanders, Rosses, Bogins, and Feists. Much fun, drinks, and food.

Became a member of the American Defense Preparedness Association

1979

January/February Industry executives and military planners became very interested in my idea of the contractual surge concept. As a consequence I was invited to make numerous presentations including to students of The National Defense University in Washington, D.C. Other presentations were made by myself and a coworker Robert Frey during January and February in St. Louis, MO, San Diego, CA, San Francisco, CA and Phoenix, AZ.

February 22 With General Mendell to Scottsdale, Arizona for presentation to Electronics Industry Association.

March 26 Peace Treaty signed between Egypt and Israel Prime Minister Menachem Begin and President Anwar Sadat.

March 28 Possibility of nuclear meltdown at Three Mile Island, PA, as a result of an accident at the nuclear reactor. Heard on the car radio on the way to attend John Sinsheinner and Erica Gold's wedding in Winnetka, IL. We were scared.

April 1 At the wedding I get to dance with 92 year old Aunt Leone again.

April 2 Bought a four globe modern floor lamp for our family room in Skokie, IL for $95 on return trip from Chicago.

Spring Irene, who now lived in an apartment in Skokie was still on oral chemo therapy, had several surgeries and was finally declared free of cancer. Her friend, Albert Poll, had become very supportive.

April 17 After Gert and I requested that a park be built in an acreage close to us which had been donated to the county by a Van Atta years prior, we had to submit a legal petition with neighborhood owners' signatures for park approval. Next, a preliminary design meeting was called. At that meeting, I suggested several important changes, namely to have only one drive in entrance from North Dixie and to move the baseball diamonds to the far side of the park with the tennis courts near a walk in the entrance. There will be a lake and walkways. It will be an enhancement for the entire neighborhood. We are excited. Additional design meetings will later finalize the park.

April 23 Meetings were held between County officials, park architects, township trustees, recreation personnel and residents to approve the park design and maintenance. I was in my glory and proud of what Gert and I had done.

April 24—25 While I was leaving to give a presentation on contractual surge clauses and the principle of methodology to the American Defense Preparedness Association, Washington D.C. Gert flew to visit Oma at Andover, MA, returning a week alter.

May 15 Was one of the main speakers at the American Industries Association National Conference, San Antonio, TX at the La Mansion Del Rio. All of the presentations were always accompanied by color slides projected on large screens, plus handouts.

May 29 Attended by invitation the Formal farewell dinner and retirement June 1 of my immediate boss Brig. Gen. Edward Mendel at the Wright Patterson AF Base Offices Club who was a Command Pilot with 4,200 flying hours. He died March, 2, 1992.

May 30-31 Briefed the Joint Secretariat, consisting of the highest Army, Air Force, and Navy generals and admirals at Andrews Airforce Base, MD. It was somewhat nerve-wracking for me to speak at that high a level.

June 11 David Kahn, son of Ernest and Marilyn Kahn, married Gayle Heffner. I went to attend the wedding which was held in a wooded area. It was the "in thing" not to do the traditional wedding.

June 18 Briefed General (4 star) Bryce Poe, Commander of the Air Force Logistics Command, on progress of Contract Surge concept. He is the highest ranking of my superiors. Dr. Morris Groban, our family physician, had prescribed a pill for me to settle down prior to making presentations etc. of this type. They worked a calming effect.

Spring/Summer Irene and her friend Albert Poll took various trips to France to meet with old friends, acquaintances, and family. The office of American

College of Surgeons gradually relieved her of certain department responsibilities. She was upset.

July Received a Significant Achievement Award with citation and best, a check with money.

June 29 We said farewell to Rabbi Joseph of Temple Israel.

July 2 Sold our apartment building 4116 Merrifield at a small profit at $49,500. The investment had served its purpose of providing some for our three children's college expenses.

August Ron and friend Kathy visit Oma Wolff in Andover and Susan did so later in the year. Gert and I attended Aunt Bella's 92nd birthday party in Chicago. Karen has a pet Cockatiel bird and makes the OSU honor roll for the spring quarter.

September 11 Even before that date I was working on a new presentation to be given at the upcoming Joint Logistics Commanders Conference. Received an invitation from Rear Admiral D.P. Hall, Commander, Naval Base Charleston to attend. Was advised locally to bring a tuxedo or a dark business suit since the conference would be preceded by formal "Dining-In" attended by the ranking Generals and Admirals, Army, Navy, Marine Corps, Air Force and DSA (Defense Supply Agency, no longer in existences), plus a few high ranking civilians and lowly me. The big surprise came when we were picked up at Wright Patterson by a Presidential fleet aircraft with "United States of America" in bold letters on its side. With all the other Air Force brass I walked, first time in my life, on a red carpet to the plane, greeted by Navy stewards in white dress uniforms, and later served lunch white gloved. It was overwhelming. The formal Dining-In was an unforgettable event. I followed prescribed etiquette by watching others. My presentation the next day went well and then with a few others I was piped onto and into the Ulyssess S. Grant SSBN 631, a Lafayette class Ballistic Missile nuclear submarine and personally greeted by Commander Donald E. Watkins. The tour of his ship was enlightening being informed how the nuclear reactor operates and how the Poseidon C-3 nuclear missiles are stored targeted and fired at a weight of 65,000 pounds, 34 feet length and a range of 2,500 nautical miles. Fantastic! A highly complimentary letter from my four star General Poe closed another chapter in my profession. (See exhbits 20.17-20.20 in the appendix)

October 21 Ordered a new 1980 Olds Cutlass Luxury Sedan and traded our 1970 Chrysler Newport Sedan.

November 4 49 American hostages taken in Iran.

December 9 Ronald married Kathy Austin at Toledo Country Club in a civil ceremony with about 21 people attending. Susan and Ken, and Karen, as well as Kathy's daughter, Heather, were present. A luncheon was served which all of us enjoyed.

December The beautiful NCR auditorium with many wonderful memories was being dismantled, and was finally demolished the following year.

1980

January 27 Ronald started his professional career with doctors Bahr and Nangle as associate practicing in the Kettering suburb of Dayton. We invited their entire office, and our friends at an open house to celebrate the occasion with Ron, his wife Kathy, and daughter Heather.

February As I was being complimented and praised for the innovative contributions to the Air Force and the Department of Defense it slowly dawned on me that my time was coming up to think about retirement. Not that was I was old enough being about 58, but being tired of dealing within an environment that contemplated the best way and means of conducting wars with men and equipment to inflict the greatest possible losses on others. Having been exposed to the tragedies of the Holocaust, then fighting myself during World War II, having to support the mayhem resulting during the Korean and then the Vietnam wars, being in the civilian capacity of the war machine, I knew that it was time for me to quit. Nevertheless there were so many other considerations. Because of all the fanfare of my work from the highest places there existed deep-seated jealousies by my coworkers and supervisors who tried and succeeded in preventing my promotion to a higher grade. Although, I never believed that there may have been an element of anti-Semitism it is not outside the realm of possibility. After all the accolades and honors received particularly in recent years, I came to the conclusion that it was best to cut the ties on high-notes. Without spreading the word at the office, except for discussing all of this with Gertrude, I prepared the required papers of which there were many including personal debriefings because of my Top Secret clearance. The die was cast and my retirement date was set for June 6, 1980. The day came and went and since I was told there would be an official and elaborate retirement ceremony I stayed on and briefed other coworkers so they would be able to continue my work and serve as an understudy.

1981

January 5 Finally, the day of my formal retirement was announced to take place on January 5. I really didn't think nor did I have any clue that this ceremony would be huge and unique, but it was. My entire family was to be invited as well as friends. Family sounded okay, but friends? Most of them would laugh and say you are making this a big deal. Our good and close friends, however, I did invite, namely Perry and Evelyn Ross. Ronald and Kathy, as well as Karen, honored me with their presence while Susan and Ken sent a congratulatory telegram. At best I was excited. First, Gert and I were ushered into the auditorium where we were told what was going to happen and in what order and where to stand. Next, the executive officer took us to the Commander's Office for greetings by General Poe and his staff of lower-ranking generals and their staffs. General Poe made some remarks about my outstanding service to the National Security Council, performance as Chair of specific advisory bodies, consisting of military and civilians from the Army, Navy, and Air Force. He then asked his aide de Camp to read a series of citations, i.e. accompanying the Certificate of Merit signed by all four star generals, Army General Guthrie, Navy Admiral Whittle, Air Force Generals Poe, and General Slay. All presented in a leather folder. Gert was presented with a beautiful bouquet of flowers. Back to the auditorium filled to the max of 350. There were the traditional ruffles and flourishes from the Air Force Band of Flight for the honored guests, the National Anthem, after which I with Gert in tow was ushered to the podium. A narrator gave a short introduction and read a long resume of my 36 years of illustrious and dedicated service. Again there were numerous commendations presented including one to Gert while receiving a beautiful rose. After a drum roll I was bestowed with a large bronze inscribed medal and two smaller ones from the Secretary of the Air Force for Exceptional Civilians Service to be worn on the

```
                    NARRATION
                  ACCOMPANYING
               CERTIFICATE OF SERVICE

ANNOUNCEMENT IS MADE OF THE RETIREMENT OF MR. ROBERT B. KAHN
EFFECTIVE 6 JUNE 1989 AFTER 36 YEARS OF FEDERAL SERVICE.
MR KAHN, A LOGISTICS MANAGEMENT SPECIALIST WITH THE DIRECTORATE
OF PROGRAMS, BEGAN HIS FEDERAL EMPLOYMENT WITH THE ARMY AIR
FORCES INTELLIGENCE, AIR DOCUMENTS DIVISION ON 1 JULY 1946.
HIS OUTSTANDING PERFORMANCE DURING HIS MANY YEARS OF SERVICE
HAVE RESULTED IN HIS RECEIVING NUMEROUS OUTSTANDING PERFORMANCE
AWARDS AND LETTERS OF APPRECIATION, INCLUDING ONE, IN 1973,
FROM THE SECRETARY OF DEFENSE MELVIN LAIRD, AND IN 1965,A PRESI-
DENTIAL CITATION FROM PRESIDENT LYNDON B. JOHNSON.
AS MR KAHN REVIEWS HIS RECORD OF SERVICE, HE CAN TAKE PRIDE IN
THE MANY ACCOMPLISHMENTS WHICH HAVE BEEN ACHIEVED THROUGH HIS
EFFORTS TO SUPPORT THE UNITED STATES AIR FORCE AND THE AIR FORCE
LOGISTICS COMMAND. HE TAKES WITH HIM THE BEST WISHES OF THE COM-
MANDER, HIS SUPERVISORS AND CO-WORKERS.
FOLLOWING HIS RETIREMENT, MR KAHN AND HIS FAMILY PLAN TO RESIDE
IN DAYTON OHIO
```

EXHIBIT 20.21 Aid de Camp to General Bryce Poe read this announcement and many to follow to the assembly.

EXHIBIT 20.22 General Bryce Poe presents the Department of the US Air Force Citation and decoration.

chest. In addition I also received a large oak plaque. The deafening applause was followed by the band playing the Air Force song and "Auld Lang Syne" while Gert and I endured handshakes, pats on my back plus hugs and kisses from a few ladies and then it was over! Relieved of a strenuous but exciting morning, we relaxed over brunch with the Ross's while the rest of the family went back to their place of work. It was indeed a memorable event. At a dinner party in my honor at the Officers Club several days later, Gert gave a speech and I was roasted by many, including Brigadier General Leo Marquez. (See additional exhibits 20.24, 20.25, 20.26 in the appendix). Since coming to work at Air Materiel Command Dayton, July 1946, I worked for the following 15 Commanding Generals:

Lt. Gen Donald Putt in 1946
Lt Gen Nathan F. Twining to October 1947
General Joseph T. McNarney to August 1949
Lt. General Benjamin W. Childlaw to August 1951
General Edwin W. Rawlings to February 1959
General Samuel E. Anderson to July 1961
General William F. McKee to June 1962
General Mark E. Bradley Jr. to July 1965

EXHIBIT 20.23 After I received the certificate from the four Armed Services Logistics Commanders, Gertrude was presented a bouquet of roses.

General Kenneth B. Hobson to July 1967
General Thomas P. Gerrity to February 1968
General Jack G. Merrell to September 1972
General Jack J. Catton to August 1974
General William V. McBride to August 1975
General F. Michael Rogers to January 1978
General Bryce Poe until my retirement

January 21 The remaining 52 U.S. Hostages held by Iran released after 444 days.

January—February Immediately after retirement I solicited employment as a technical consultant under the name of CTI Co., the abbreviation standing for Consultant to Industry, composing many letters primarily to defense contractors. Received an offer from the President of CFC Dayton Ohio, Larry Shpiner and signed a contract on February 12, 1981. The Company used to be known as Custom Film Communications but has now transformed itself into work for plant modernization, technology, and manufacturing method improvements, cost reduction and robotics. My reimbursement as an independent contractor was to be $150 per work day, inclusive of travel. Since Shpiner and another employee Lawrence Matthews were proficient commercial pilots travels to contractor sites were often via one or two leased single engine aircraft.

April 27-May 17 Took a wonderful vacation to Hawaii via San Francisco visiting Ilse and Otto, as well as Nobert's and Helmut's families. Rented a car on all of the islands and had a blast.

September 19 Attended a traditional Jewish wedding of our niece Peggy Salten to Albert (Bud) Schram in Atlanta, GA.

September 21 Aunt Marthe Joseph nee Michel died in Luxembourg. Sad that now that branch of the family has withered and was unable to be at her funeral.

EXHIBIT 20.27 Peggy and Bud Schram.

October Public Law 96-388 signed by President Reagan setting aside April 26-May 3 as Day of Remembrance for Victims of the Holocaust, Yom Hashoa.

December 31 A new leaf has been added to the family tree. Emily Beth Rapoport was born 6:37 p.m. at Hillcrest Hospital in Cleveland Ohio. Hopefully, there will be more leaves.

Peggy's sisters, Roslyn and Rita.

1982

January 5 Established our first IRA accounts at 15.25% interest.

January 16 On my new job with CFC, Gert and I travel to New Orleans, LA to attend an Industrial Modernization Conference, while Gert and other wives to go site-seeing.

March 20 Was given a mitzvah at Park Synagogue in Cleveland at the Hebrew naming of Emily. A great honor for Opa for his first grandchild.

April Freda Schlesinger, wife of Henry Schlesinger, and very good friends of ours since we moved to Dayton, passed away.

April 22-May 2 After receiving various letters from Mr. Jean Seckler lawyer of Aunt Marthe representing to administer her and her husband's last will in Luxembourg, Irene and I decided to meet him and the named heirs in Luxembourg to decide and agree on the liquidation and distribution of the estate. Named heirs: Monsieur Roger Michel of Nerac France (nephew), Renee Michel (niece) married name Wolarski of Strasbourg France, Irene Kahn (niece) married named Diament of Chicago, Claude Ehrlich (nephew) of Strasbourg France, and Eliane Ehrlich (niece) married name Ouaknin of Strasbourg France. Irene was accompanied by her friend Albert Poll and Gertrude accompanied me. After lengthy meetings and introductions, since we did not know any of the Michels, I decided and Irene agreed that we would opt to receive certain heirlooms which originally were the possessions of our parents, while the other heirs were primarily interested in the distribution of money pending the sale of other belongings and real estate. We hired an international shipper who packed specific furniture, carpets, paintings, sculptures and china for delivery to our home in Dayton and to Irene's apartment in Chicago. We did some visiting of friends and Aunt Gaby, Marcel and Roger Kahn in Roodt. Also did some visiting of old Jewish cemetery sites in Luxembourg and a brief visit of Paris, France.

April-May During our trip to Luxembourg and Paris we purchased a number of souvenir porcelain miniatures, several Hummel figurines and two Lladro figurines as presents for our children.

June Much travel as a consultant to Boeing Co. Wichita, Kansas; RMI, Niles, Ohio; General Electric Co., Evendale, Ohio and Madisonville, Indiana and companies out West.

July 19 Purchased a new Oldsmobile Cutlas.

August Ken's father, Sam Rapoport, passed away.

August 29 Swedish born Ingrid Bergman, actress, passed away.

August 30 Appointed Vice President of Operations at CFC with an increase of salary.

September 20 After Ronald had been practicing for about two years with Dr. Bahr and Dr. Nangle he opened up his own practice at 3080 Ackerman Blvd. Kettering, a suburb of Dayton.

September 30 Went to see and hear Kenny Rogers at UD arena

October 25 Took Gert to Deaconess Hospital Cincinnati for knee surgery, followed in Dayton with physical therapy, swimming, and other exercises.

November 2 Aunt Gaby, mother of Marcel and Roger Kahn, died of breast cancer in Luxembourg. Her husband, Uncle Sally, had died many years earlier.

Our son Ronald S. Kahn, M.D.

November 25 After trading in Karen's clunker, purchased a new '83 Buick Skyhawk for her in Cleveland.

December 2 Surgery performed for the first time to place an artificial heart successfully into a human body.

1983

February 28 – March 10 We vacationed at Cancun Mexico and stayed at the Sheraton.

June 8 Donated my 17' Klepper Kayak with sailing equipment to the Miami Valley Council of Boy Scouts.

Keep sending periodic contributions to USO since it was there that I met my wonderful wife Gertrude

June 22 Were visited by Louis and Lea Levy from Wales whom we met at Eilat Israel and enjoyed each other's company.

August 13 Visit Fairfield Glad Tennessee to inspect time shares.

August 21 Wedding of Mike Ross in Columbus, Ohio at a country club. His father, Perry was very sick. As his best friend, I attended to him so he could partake a few of the important parts of the ceremony He passed away September 5th, where I gave a short eulogy.

October 1 Wendy Yaross married Daniel Fischer at Stauffer's Hotel Dayton

October 24 Bought a Smith Corona word processer to serve as my first electronic typewriter.

November 6 Irene married Albert Poll in Skokie synagogue. Of course we attended and are happy for the couple.

Continue to counsel young Boy Scouts on earning their "Personal Management Merit Badge" from home.

1984

April 1-2 Gert and I assisted in setting up and serving as volunteer guides at large Israel exhibit at the downtown Arcade Rotunda. Eight thousand visitors viewed.

April 12 Oma Wolff admitted to hospital after she fell. We travel to see her.

April 25 Attended b'rith of Brett Altman in Centerville across from Ronald's house.

August 4 Gert and Ron flew to Massachusetts to attend to Oma and fly her back to Dayton where she will have her own room and care at our home. Oma walks with a walker. Loads of work! Her condominium apartment is put on the market.

August 18 Faye Diament married Charles Schulz at the University of Illinois at Champaign, Illinois. It was a somewhat unconventional affair with much enjoyable square dancing.

August 31 Oma has cataract surgery at St. Elisabeth's Hospital after many visits to Dr. Kunish

EXHIBIT 20.28 Faye and husband Charles Schulz married August 18, 1984.

September 13 After making all the necessary arrangements to sell Oma's condo in Andover, it was sold at a substantial profit.

November 6 Ronald Reagan re-elected to be our President

December Coldest day -20 F

All year My consulting work as Vice President of CFC include Magnovex Ft. Wayne, Indiana, Varian Inc. Palo Alto, CA, General Electric Co, Evendale Ohio and Madisonville Ky, as well as Menasco, Burbank CA and others. Cabbage Patch Dolls are the rage. They are ugly but cute. We gave one to Emily. Cost is $25 and up. They come with birth certificates and adoption papers. Crazy?

EXHIBIT 20.29 Marc Diament, Faye's brother.

1985

January 3 Oma Wolff, after months of constant care and love at our house her health has worsened that it has become difficult for Gert during the day and for me during the night to take care of her. She was admitted to Covenant House Nursing Home, Dayton, a Jewish Federation administered facility, and has a nice private room, TV and personal telephone.

January 5-6 temperature -22 degrees.

January 20 -24 degrees

February 6 Samuel Joseph Rapoport was born at Hillcrest Hospital Cleveland. Our first grandson! Tried to get to the airport to attend his b'rith on February 13, while working at Magnovox Fort Wayne, Indiana, but couldn't get to the airport only a couple of miles away because of an ongoing blizzard. Danny Sokol a co-worker, tried to get me there but failed in the high snow. Anyhow, all flights were cancelled and it took Danny and me three hours to get back to our motel. I was heartbroken to miss the b'rith of our first grandson, Sammy.

April 25- May 5 By air to Orlando, then by rental car to Sanibel Island Florida, staying at the Casa Ybel beach resort.

October 13 Our Karen and Dr. Ira Weiss were married at beautiful ceremony at Temple Israel with a reception, dinner and dancing at the Marriott Hotel. We are very proud of our children.

All year Gert and I, often both, visit Oma at Covenant House every day.

The music and chorus "We are the World" was composed and performed

EXHIBIT 20.30 Ira Weiss, and his wife, our daughter Karen.

1986

January 28 The space shuttle "Challenger" exploded after lift off and killed all of its 7 member crew.

January 30 Terminated my self-employment status as Consultant to Industry CTI and my stint as VP at CFC. I am finally really retired! Hurrah!

February Joined the Victoria Theater Association so Gert and I could enjoy Broadway plays, operas, ballet, and other types of performances.

March 12 Oma Wolff had a Pacemaker installed at Good Samaritan Hospital by Dr. Bozorgi.

March 18 Miamisburg rail disaster followed by large evacuations. CSX train involved. Sold our CSX stocks because of enormous lawsuits on the horizon.

May Gertrude finally retired from Elder-Beerman department store.

May 25 We joined hands with 6 million other Americans from LA to New York at the riverbank downtown Dayton. A project designed to show solidarity against hunger and homelessness in America. Gert and I had become a part of history.

May 26 Viewed the film *Shoah* by Claude Lanzman, a film of horror and sadness.

August 17 Frieda (Friedel) Salomon died at Isabella Home in New York. Her birthday was the same as mine. She was 86 years old, wife of Bruno Salomon and daughter Solange, now Sonya, married to Ernest Hartog. Bruno was a cousin of my mother living formerly in Luxembourg.

1987

January 2 Received my first Social Security check

January 5 Had a complete home security system installed by Brinks Inc. including motion and smoke detectors.

February – May Ever mindful of Oma's care at Covenant House, I became very sensitive to various complaints to Gert and me. Therefore I informed the Director and then the Board of observed deficiencies and improvement actions. The resultant nine page investigative report "A Review of Covenant House Improvement Areas" prepared by me May 27 for the Chairman of the Board brought new light on important areas for corrective action.

February 4-11 Vacation trip to Nassau, Bahamas Cable Beach. We had a great time.

March 17 Aunt Bella Danziger died. I gave a eulogy as well as her son-in-law Dick Sinsheimer. A sad day for her daughter, Alice, and for me.

April 20 Paid off mortgage on our home. It's ours, lock, stock, and barrel!

June Gert received her first Social Security check.

June 14 Jenna Rachel Weiss, our third grandchild, was born and we presented Karen and Ira a check for baby furniture.

June 16 Gert took Greyhound bus to Cleveland to take care of Susan, who was sick, the two grandchildren, husband, and household.

August 24- September 9 Trip to London England, Bath, and Cardiff Wales to visit Levys. Saw *Les Miserables* in London and bought an expensive Meissen Plate with gold border.

September 13 A new modern synagogue was dedicated at Mannheim Germany. Received an invitation to attend but was unable.

October 19-20 Stock Market crash, double the tumble in 1929. Biggest crash in all history took stocks down 508 points. From a high August 25 through October 19, Dow Jones dropped 1000 points. Shares, including ours, dropped almost 23%.

December 7 Renewed membership in the American Philatelic Society and insurances of my stamp collections. Purchasing stamps at auctions had to be discontinued since my retirement.

1988

January Signed up as Gallery Attendant of the Experiencenter at Dayton Art Institute each Wednesday afternoon. First exhibit: "Creative Camera."

March 10 Drove to Chicago/Skokie to visit Irene and Albert as we have done at least once and sometime twice over the past year. They had bought a nice home where we could comfortably stay overnight. Each visit includes our Chicago cousins and a visit to a Jewish delicatessen which unfortunately we don't have in Dayton. We visit again in May.

April 12-22 Vacation at Casa Ybel Resort, Sanibel Island, Florida.

May 29 Bought a beautiful metal and bronze dogwood leaf sculpture created by Thomas Yano for our bedroom.

June 2 Gert's photo was published in the *Dayton Daily Newspaper* showing her soaking up the sun at the JCC pool. It was an article about skin cancer.

July 15-17 Very high outside temperatures of above 100°F and 90°+ F for 46 days. During that period and beyond Dayton experienced the worst drought in 50 years.

July Joined, and now a member of the Leo Beck Institute. Their purpose is the study and collection of the history and culture of German speaking Central European Jewry. Their collection in New York, London, and Berlin are enormous.

October 15 Attended Walter and Barbara Kahn's daughter Hilde's wedding to Steve Bradbury Washington DC. Drove to Richmond VA where Gert visited Mr and Mrs Parish where she was a governess to their two children and where I fell for her as a hostess at the USO, 1943.

November 7 My life changed when watching TV *This Morning on CBS* I recognized my boyhood friend then of some 50 years ago Ernst Michel during the Holocaust years in Mannheim Germany. He was being interviewed because of Kristallnacht by CBS co-anchors Kathleen Sullivan and Harry Smith. We were both 15 on that day of November 9, 1938. After contacting CBS, Ernst returned my call and we had an exciting telephone conversation talking about our past, people and places. The most important thing, he was alive, and for him, I too had survived the Holocaust.

Next CBS producers called inviting me to be reunited with Ernest on the show and talk about the world then, events, and what brought us together. Flight to New York, accommodations, and more to be taken care of by CBS including Gert for several days.

November 14 Although the meeting of both of us was to take place the next day we couldn't wait and met at the Essex House where we stayed. A thrill of a life time was happening plus finding out from Ernie that other Mannheim friends including my dear Rabbi Max Grünewald (now Gruenewald) had survived and even lived in the greater NY area. Over lunch I broached the idea of arranging a "Mannheim Reunion." Ernie thought this to be a great idea. I was on a high looking forwarded to the possibility of meeting my Rabbi Grünewald. Later we met Harry Alkan and wife Suzanne. He and I had traveled together from Luxembourg to Barcelona and then the US in 1941 under very difficult circumstances. We had much to talk about, after all we had not seen each other since arriving in the US 47 years ago. Then came the day of the 15th when the saga of the two friends unfolded on CBS "This Morning" with all our friends and relatives watching on national TV. It was a morning to remember. Ernie and I have been and still are the best of friends. See additional exhibits 20.32 and 20.33 in the appendix.

After spending years tracking the Capells, the ones Irene and I often spent our summer vacation at Rommerskirchen Germany, finally was successful. Only the children are still living and was able to meet with Erich, Ilse and her husband Max Frey. Anne had passed on. Again it was a wonderful meeting with stories galore. Sadly Uncle Moritz and Aunt Johanna are only memories. After having a corned beef sandwich at the Carnegie Deli, we were picked up by my good Mannheim friend, Max'l Kaufmann and wife Lila who graciously offered their home in Livingston, N.J. for us to stay. Max'l and I who lived across the street

EXHIBIT 20.31 Harry Smith and next to him Kathleen Sullivan, across Ernest Michel, and me being interviewed on CBS This Morning.

from us in Mannheim talked about old times until past midnight. Both of us were in seventh heaven especially when Max'l offered to drive me and Gert to Milburn, N.J. the next day to meet with my long believed perished Rabbi Grünewald whom I had not seen since 1936. When the door to his apartment opened we fell into each other's arms as our tears were on each other's cheeks. He couldn't believe that of all things saved, I still had his Chumesh, the five books of Moses, with his handwritten dedication. Miracles have happened and I was told there were other Mannheimers in the area. Back to Dayton November 17 from an unforgettable journey where I was treated like a celebrity. Phone calls, letters, cards, speaking engagements, interviews etc. A neighborhood couple Reverend Elwood and Kim Rose asked to visit and meet me. They came and we became close friends until both passed away.

EXHIBIT 20.34 Reverend Elwood Rose and wife Kim.

December 7 Perhaps it was all the excitement, but during a trip to take care of Emily and Sammy while their parents were on vacation, I passed out in Higbee's department store and was taken to emergency room for treatment. Luckily no further complications.

1989

January Ernie Michel liked my suggestion to convene a "Mannheim Reunion" that after further consideration he informed me and we decided to establish a committee to bring it about. I had become the father of the Reunion. The committee consisted of Honorary Chairman, Rabbi Dr. Max Grünewald and Rabbi Dr. Karl Richter, who was our rabbi during Kristallnacht and beyond. Chairman Ernest Michel who has been Executive President Emeritus of UJA Federation of New York. Vice Chairs: Robert B. Kahn, who started this hornet's nest and Walter Salomon, whom I also knew from Mannheim since he was the lay cantor for the youth services on Shabbat and holidays. Treasurers: Max Kaufmann, boyhood friend and Max Liebmann, with whom I was not acquainted since he was two years older than I. Secretaries: Lotte Marshall: a distant relative who shares many memories with me and my beloved parents and Edith Ullmann in Mannheim. Public Relations: Joe Ullmann, husband of Edith.

January The Air Force finally revealed the existence and flight of the supersonic stealth bomber, the F-117 which was top secretly built at the so-called

"Skunk Works." While still employed prior to 1985 by the US Air Force I visited the Lockheed Skunk Works at Palmdale California AF Plant 42 on business and was aware of the TS technology and nightly testing for several years earlier.

January 22 I flew to New York attending the first Committee meeting at which it was decided on a date for the Reunion, namely June 14-17, 1990. Getting reacquainted with all the Committee members took a goodly while.

February-April Once back in Dayton, I saw a possibility of preparing a pamphlet with all the names and short biographies as a handout to all reunion attendees. Again the Committee agreed. In the meantime, they were feeding me names of Mannheim survivors and when I contacted them for their bio, they gave me additional names. Lo and behold the list got bigger until it mushroomed. As time went on I realized that my so-called pamphlet got so voluminous that I suggested to the New York Committee the possibility of a book. Their encouragement was enough for me to work on this project day and night. No exaggeration. Just ask my wife!

June 11 Attended Albert Poll's graduation. As "Master of Judaic Studies" from Spertus College, Chicago. Had dinner with Erich Dreifuss and wife. Erich was also a good friend of mine in Mannheim.

July Since I could not attend every committee meeting in N.Y., there were many phone calls and written communications both ways. The committee works flawlessly. Announcements of the reunion everywhere have brought 300 reservations so far and 170 rooms at Hotel Kutscher in Monticello, N.Y. in the Catskills Mountains. Reservations are from Australia, South America, Mexico, Israel, Europe and from all points in the US. We are thrilled. Laura Kessler a high school senior working at the Jewish Federation is typing the edited biographical sketches.

EXHIBIT 20.35 Irene's husband, Albert Poll, Master of Judaic Studies.

August 21 We greet the first Russian Jewish refugees at the Dayton airport and take them to their new apartments which were completely furnished and stocked with food through many volunteers including Gertrude.

October 14-15 A get together of the extended Kahn family dubbed "Kahnclave" was held at the Hyatt Hotel, Deerfield Ill. All except Helmut Isaak and wife Ellen were able to attend.

October 20 Five inches of snow, the earliest heavy snow on record. 25,000 residents are without power. Telephone out. Red Cross shelters open.

November 9 The Berlin Wall is destroyed and borders between West and East Berlin are once more open. Is November 9 1989 and November 9, 1938 a coincidence? After 40 years of the wall the two Germanies are one again. All in all Germany has lost 1/4th of its original area after World War II. East Prussia including Danzig is part of Russia. Pommern and Schlesien east of the river Oder and Neisse are part of Poland.

November 30 Signed contract for an addition to our front spare bedroom to make it big enough to serve as my study. It turned out beautiful.

December In order to take advantage of tax breaks by giving to charitable organizations I am donating considerable holding of my stamp collections to benefit those that need it more than us.

1990

January 10 We now have orders for 51 books, not published yet and cramming to get everything done. Mort New and wife Betty are helping with the final typing of "Reflections by Jewish Survivors from Mannheim." My recently purchased Smith Corona electronic word processor came in handy with my work. Made several important trips to attend Committee meetings and advised them of book publishing cost.

March Cut off date for submissions to me for book. Still they are coming and I try frantically to work them in.

March 15 Pledged $500 to the Project Exodus to support Russian Jewish immigrants.

April 1 The book is finished and turned out beautiful with a gold embossed cover showing a stylized version of the city. Four hundred copies are being sent to the Kutscher Resort Hotel to hold for the Reunion. We have 354 reservations inclusive of 225 originally from Mannheim. Additional countries represented are Germany and England. Nineteen US states are also represented.

June 2 Hurrah, Adam Weiss born at Cleveland to Karen and Ira Weiss. We attended his b'rith June 9 just in time to attend the reunion.

June 14-17 A lovefest as former Mannheimers find and meet friends, long thought lost, at the reunion. After much work and consternation, 500 copies of the beautiful book were created and given to attendees at the "Mannheim Reunion." The hardcover 198 page book, gold embossed "Reflections by Jewish Survivors from Mannheim" containing the biographical information and memoirs of 116 Mannheim survivors was an enormous hit for which I received unending compliments and standing ovations. Many of the attendees and others wished having contributed to the book, copyrighted with a Library of Congress 90-60674

EXHIBIT 20.36
The book.

EXHIBIT 20.37

EXHIBIT 20.38

Catalog Number. My dedication was a labor of love and silent oath to remember and tell of the Mannheimer Jews degradation and oppression under Nazi terror.

We wore badges with our current name under which we also wore a photo of what we looked like in Mannheim. I was mobbed for purchases of additional books and then there were constant hugs and tears of people that knew each other fifty years ago. There were bulletin boards of people seeking people. And there was a Shabbat Friday night prayer service conducted by Rabbi Karl Richter officiating in Mannheim in 1938, a service by Cantor Erwin Hirsch who served in

EXHIBIT 20.39 Rabbi Karl Richter **EXHIBIT 20.40** Postcard with reproduction of painting done by Luise Metzger

Mannheim 1937-1938, and then the tear jerking sermon by Rabbi Max Grünewald who served Mannheim Jews from 1925-1938.

There was an exciting program and there was time for activities. Golf and golf lessons, newspapers, swimming in a beautiful indoor pool; movies at a theater; tennis on a few courts; racquetball; health club; ice skating; aerobics and dance lessons; bocce tournament; line and folk dancing; ping pong; bingo; and more. Artist Luise Metzger nee Stiefel, now from Ramat Gan Israel presented each attendee with an Israeli postcard on which one of eight of her paintings was printed in color.

Another living souvenir was presented by Carl and Doris Landman (formerly Landmann), from Menlo Park CA consisting of packets, self-collected, of Giant Sequoia seeds, and packets of Eastern White Pine seeds, both with planting instructions.

Ernest (formerly Ernst Michel) entered into a lottery thirty souvenir Israel postcards with specially cancelled stamp from Jerusalem commemorating fifty years of Kristallnacht with a view of the Mannheim Synagogue 1855 – November 9, 1938. Through the generosity of the Jewish Community Mannheim every Reunion participant received a recording "Synagogue Gesänge" of songs by the choir. The food menu at the dining room was superb and kosher. All in all, the reunion of Mannheimers was a thriller for all of us having been reacquainted with at least three or four friends. I found seven. A final act of all that attended was to agree on a Resolution of concern regarding the resurrection of anti-semitism

```
GIANT SEQUOIA
    (Sequoiadendron giganteum)
The King of Plants..."It is, as a race, the
oldest & mightiest of living things. Not
even in past geological times, apparently,
were there any greater trees."
For its first hundred years this is a
beautiful yard tree (to 40-70 feet high),
densely pyramidal with lovely blue-green
foliage & wide-spreading trunk. Eventually,
after 1-2000 years it may grow to be 300'
tall and, if left to mature to its prime at
4000 years of age, who knows!
(hardy to -10 F)
```

```
A living souvenir of
the Reunion
with best wishes
from
Carl & Doris Landman
```

```
Giant Sequoia seeds
Planting directions inside
```

EXHIBIT 20.41 Envelope containing seeds and planting instructions inside.

to be presented to the Ambassador of West Germany, his Excellency, Juergen Ruhfuss in Washington DC. It was presented to the Ambassador with a copy of the book with an appropriate dedication. We also presented the Resolution to the Charge d'Affiar of East Germany, his Excellency, Norbert Reemer. I presented him also with the book of "Reflections…"

June 21 We celebrate Oma Wolff's 95th birthday.

July 16 Stayed with Walter Kahn and wife Barbara overnight. They took me for dinner at the very impressive and exclusive Cosmos Club 2121 Massachusetts Ave, NW.

December 6 On one of my trips to New York, I took Rabbi Grünewald for a belated birthday celebration in honor of his 90th birthday, which was December 4, 1990. It was the last time I saw him.

When my dear mother, Irene, I and my father would walk to shul for services at the synagogue in Mannheim, Dad often said to Irene and me "Follow your heart only when your mind tells you it's right." I have come to that point, the two namely my heart and my mind are one. Therefore I have decided on closing my memoirs although I could cover many more years since it is now 2016 and many things have happened since the end of my writings with year 1990. Important things like the birth of three more grandchildren, Aliza Weiss and Brennan and Cameron Kahn, my invitation and official visit to Mannheim and so many other important happenings to me, Gert, and to individual family members. Hopefully, they will be able to tell about themselves and perhaps they can tell some more details about me. I have some regrets, most of all that, with some exceptions, my Mannheim friends have passed on and I have never been able to find my good friend Günter Kaufmann in spite of many searches. Also that my dear sister and brother-in-law as well as several first cousins never saw my published autobiography. On the other hand, the life I have reestablished in American has been devoted to making the imperfect world a little less vulnerable to hate and create a life of fulfillment and happiness for my family.

Epilogue

The history of the extended Kahn family bears out that being born as Jews played a significant role in our destiny. In the nineteen thirties in Germany, and early forties having fled to Luxembourg, we couldn't just pack up again and run away after Luxembourg was invaded by Germany, and certainly we couldn't hide. Instead, in our dilemma of what to do we tried to adopt, at least for the time being, a coping mechanism which we hoped would help us deal with impending calamities. We did not yet realize that what the Nazis had in store would result in indescribable suffering and horrors with gruesome finality.

At first we resorted to disbelief, then denial that it could get worse. Then came resignation of realizing that we could not do anything about our lot. Last but most important came realism and with it defiance and the question: What can we do to survive? Without our mental strength and later my mental tenacity, I would not have.

Once having escaped to our new homeland America, the problem became one of rebuilding our lives while simultaneously struggling with the memories of the terror we had experienced ourselves, had heard about from others, or read about in the press. Also heavy on my shoulders was the survivor's guilt; that mysterious ever haunting thought that I, in leaving behind those who later perished or were murdered, was a coward, or even worse that I had betrayed them. These feelings created a long lasting and ever punishing aura of isolation that was not just imagined, but had become virtually real feelings that are still with me today. On top of this burden, my experiences as a soldier during the war years, coupled with the tragic facts that became known after the war primarily through the Nüremberg Trials, had resulted in a post-traumatic stress disorder (PTSD), which was always accompanied by nightmares and flashbacks that seemed and were real. One compartment of my brain, to no end, tried to reconstruct the awful events under which my loved ones were traumatized before being snuffed out, while the other compartment tried to suppress these thoughts instead concentrating on now and my future. Yet, the end result was a strengthening of my resolve to become whole again in all dimensions of my resurrected life.

This great desire to rebuild my life, and to assist that of my parents and sister Irene, became a relentless challenge and an exercise of conscious determination. As much as I was consumed by hate of those responsible for the persecution of my family, the murder of so many of our relatives and friends, and millions of other Jews, I tried to focus on our good fortune. I stubbornly created a new life with my wife Gertrude as proof that the Holocaust was not the end of Jewish life, and that even that terrible period of history was unable to destroy me. Although I had at times wavered in my belief in G'd, it has gradually been restored and with it my belief in the goodness of man, but not in all mankind.

Among all of us survivors there grew a deep sense of a silent camaraderie, an experience I never knew before and learned to cherish. Having been the so called father of the 1990 Mannheimer Reunion, I witnessed the miraculous discovery of persons long thought having gone up the chimney and the renewal of unraveled friendships. It became a wonderful time of bonding and a drying of tears.

Since the destruction of the first Temple, we Jews have always bounced back from every disaster brought upon us. As a matter of fact, we have become masters in rebuilding our lives, our culture, and with utter determination are continuing our contributions to world progress and mankind.

While working hard to avoid failure and to accomplish a peaceful, friendly coexistence with people around me, I have always tried to be respectful of others yet mindful of my checkered but proud past as a Jew. Throughout history we have always recorded the happy, exciting, but also often horrible events, as I have attempted to do herein. This custom has always given us the strength, hope and confidence for the future, and I hope it will do so here.

At first, writing my memoirs was just a wild idea, then it became a possibility with questions of how. Next came a preliminary outline that served me well as a statement of work. Now after many, too many, years of being a prisoner of my own decision, the "expanded autobiography" is finished but far from complete. The research required to describe the Kahn's early history took on a life of its own, but the value of its contribution is undeniable. The early chapters round out the story of my life since no individual is born in a vacuum. In those pages are revealed some most astounding and surprising information, not heretofore well-known. The life of Jews in the Hunsrück, particularly in the town of Laufersweiler, is described as researched and reported in various local records and sources. The life of my father and his eight siblings has been told forthright without distortion or unnecessary embellishment. However, my attempt to provide greater detail of the life of his brothers, sisters, as well as their offspring, my cousins and their families was not always successful. Some of that information, sadly, was not made available to me by everyone although I solicited same in writing and verbally on several occasions.

The years of my childhood, the many years of persecution, and my adult life received fairly detailed coverage while making certain that I did not mirror myself as a saint. In fact many instances and situations are described that show me as any other human being, not omitting delicate, painful, embarrassing, or foolish moments. In instances that I considered particularly important no words were spared to tell what took place, but also revealed my innermost feelings. Thus, I express contempt or affection wherever experienced without concern of the impressions conveyed. The biographical portions of my writings unlocked my memories and bared my soul to the bone, so that all that was left was my character. I leave it to the reader whether this character is of a quality to be scorned or admired.

Harder to write were the chapters of Nazi persecution encompassing the murder of eighteen relatives in addition to many friends during that part of history, the Holocaust. To recall the hurt and trauma of that era which my generation, including myself, has tried so desperately to suppress required a mental stamina which kept me up long hours at night and gave me nightmares when I finally fell asleep. It is a story that had to be told, and I did so from my peripheral vantage point. Over the years my writing became an obsession and at the same time I looked at it as a duty. "The Hard Road of Dreams" celebrates the extended Kahn family, their worldly tribulations and contributions, and yes, their hurt and mine.

There is something my memoirs were not designed to accomplish. They do not predict the future of the many related families spread out over the continent and beyond. What is worrisome ever since the last of the Laufersweiler generation departed is that the glue that held the "Kahn Clan" together has gotten old and brittle. There are even indications that the once strong values of family connections are starting to show hairline cracks. Further deterioration should not continue, and I urge the Kahn descendants, now with many different names, to search each other out, communicate, visit one another, so that this once mighty oak does not lose any more leaves or branches and eventually withers and disappears.

It is this special nourishing spirit that I have attempted to imitate throughout my later life and hope to have instilled in our three wonderful children, their families, including our seven loving grandchildren. Hopefully, the details of my expanded autobiography will convey this important message among many others, for generations to come.

Had I brought my writings up to the current year it would have included the wonderful and exhilarating years together with the bright, never flickering star, my wife Gertrude. Not only did we share our lives and love affair but we made it very special and inspiring for each other and our families. We enjoyed our travels to Hawaii and Alaska, as well as the old continent including England, Italy, Switzerland and countries in between. Nothing, however, can compare with the unforgettable African sights in Kenya and Tanzania, which I had always dreamt about. Yet the highlight of my life, as included in my prayers, was our pilgrimage to the land of my forefathers, Israel. A trip of unforgettable meaning and never-ending spiritual nourishment. Now my life is complete!

Hazak, hazak, v'nitchazeyk! Be strong, be strong, let us give strength to one another!

APPENDIX

Supporting Photos and Documents

The Appendix contains a multitude of photographs, documents, letters and maps. This affords the reader with uninterrupted enjoyment of the text. The Appendix enables the reader a more in depth understanding of certain details referenced in the text by furnishing photographic images supporting the author's research.

Each item has been provided with a sequence of numbers which refer to the Chapter and approximate location within the text. In reverse, the text may refer the reader to a specific item(s) in the Appendix using the same numbering system. This arrangement, plus a brief description (caption) of each item enables the reader to browse through the Appendix separate from the text.

CHAPTER TWO

EXHIBIT 2.3 An overview of Hunsrück that shows the small villages and towns, including Laufersweiler.

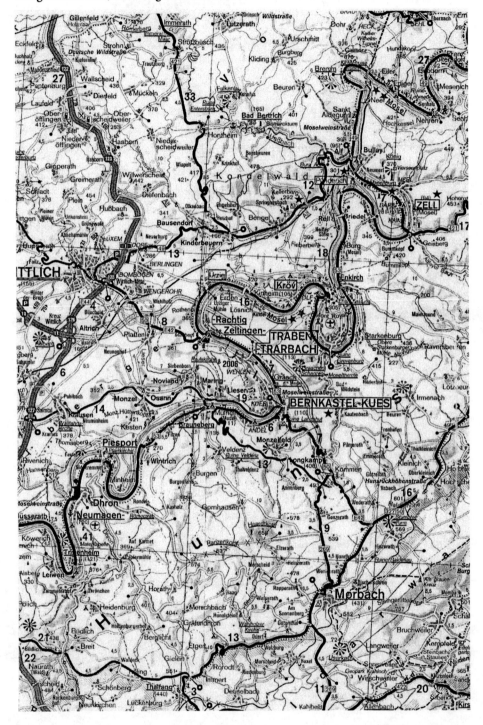

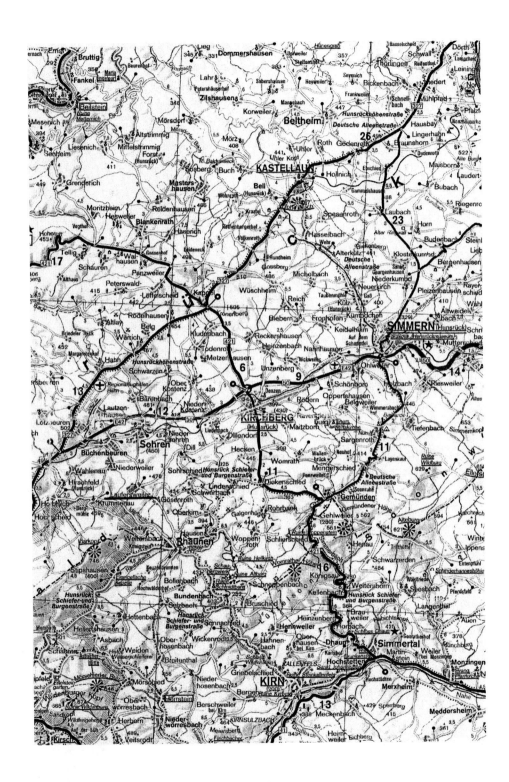

EXHIBIT 2.5 Translation of Exhibit 2.4. Translation of the document showing the changes in the family name. The original document shown in the text, exhibit 2.4.

Seal: Empire of France

Hinnele Low aka Rachel Kahn of Rhaunen

Appeared before us, Philippe Maull, assistant to the Mayor of Rhaunen, District of Rhaunen, county of Birkenfeld, Department of the Sarre, and presented herself to be Hinnele, widow Low of Rhaunen and declared to take for her family name, the name of Kahn, and for her first name of Rachel, and declared not to be able to sign; at Rhaunen.

11 November 1808

signature: P.Maull

Isaac Low aka Isaac Kahn of Rhaunen

Appeared before us, Philippe Maull, assistant to the Mayor of Rhaunen, District of Rhaunen, county of Birkenfeld, Department of the Sarre, and presented himself to be Isaac Low of Rhaunen and declared to take for his family name, the name of Kahn, and to keep his first name of Isaac, and signed in our presence at Rhaunen, 11 November 1808

signature: P.Maull

(signed Isaac Kahn in Hebrew)

Rebecca Low aka Rebecca Kahn of Rhaunen

Appeared before us, Philippe Maull, assistant to the Mayor of Rhaunen, District of Rhaunen, county of Birkenfeld, Department of the Sarre, and presented herself to be Rebecca Low, wife of Isaac Low of Rhaunen and declared to take for her family name, the name of Kahn, and for her first name of Rebecca, and declared not to be able to sign; at Rhaunen.

11 November 1808

signature: P.Maull

Low Issac aka Leopold Kahn of Rhaunen

Appeared before us, Philippe Maull, assistant to the Mayor of Rhaunen, District of Rhaunen, county of Birkenfeld, Department of the Sarre, and presented to be Isaac Kahn of Rhaunen and declared to give his minor son, eight years old, known as Low, the family name of Kahn, and for first name Leopold, and signed in our presence at Rhaunen.

11 November 1808

signature: P.Maull

(signed Isaac Kahn in Hebrew)

Getschlick Low aka Gottschalk Kahn of Rhaunen

Appeared before us, Philippe Maull, assistant to the Mayor of Rhaunen, District of Rhaunen, county of Birkenfeld, Department of the Sarre, and presented to be Isaac Kahn of Rhaunen and declared to give his minor son, eleven years old, known as Low, the family name of Kahn, and for first name Gottschalk, and signed in our presence at Rhaunen.

11 November 1808

signature: P.Maull

(signed Isaac Kahn in Hebrew)

Marx Low aka Jacob Marx

Appeared before us, Philippe Maull, assistant to the Mayor of Rhaunen, District of Rhaunen, county of Birkenfeld, Department of the Sarre, and presented himself as Marx Low, and declared that he will keep as family name of Marx and to take as first name Jacob and declared that he was unable to sign

11 November 1808

signature: P.Maull

Additional information on the history of the Laufersweiler *cheder*

According to Hans-Werner Johann, the history of the town's *cheder* began in 1802 when the hiring of the first Hebrew teacher, Elias Jacob, aged 22, was recorded. It was at that time that more Jews settled in Laufersweiler. Although most families were in favor of a publicly supported Jewish elementary school, a privately supported Jewish school for up to forty Jewish children operated for a short period of time. Financial shortcomings, discordance, disputes, and disharmony within the small Jewish community were the primary causes of the school's creation. Therefore, for a period of time around 1825, all elementary education took place in private homes of school-age children with a Jewish teacher in charge. Neither a Jewish school nor a schoolroom was available then. A year later the Jewish teacher made two rooms available in his own home for classes. However, the *cheder* was never recognized as a school by the government and the local courts. Later, a school room was established in the synagogue completed in 1844. In 1857, because of difficulties in obtaining qualified teachers, economic problems, and shenanigans from authorities and from the townspeople, about twenty-two Jewish children divided equally were sent to the two public parochial schools, one Catholic and the other Protestant.

The archival data gives more insight and specifics into the educational situation. Apparently, Elias Jacob was teacher for only two years, followed by Aron Anschel about 1804. Thereafter, until about 1859, eight different teachers were employed either to teach or supervise the teaching of Jewish children. Some of them had to resign because they failed the Royal Prussian government's proficiency tests which included German language, literature, arithmetic, and other subjects that were standard at that time in public elementary school education. Generally, certified teachers were hard to find, and in one instance, Michael Kilz, a Protestant, temporarily took over the administration of the Jewish school. Later, he also taught but was let go because of immoral behavior. As a result he taught Jewish children privately in the homes of their parents between eight a.m. and eight p.m. He was warned by the State that without government permission he could be punished. Finally, he received the necessary teaching permission. The Jewish congregation paid him per child per month, three Silbergroschen (a monetary unit of silver) and four Pfennige to teach each child two hours each day. School inspector Back faulted him for having a tendency of intoxication, which resulted in fits of anger. In 1826 when a certified Jewish teacher by the name of Scheuer was hired, two rooms in his own home were used as classrooms.

Many disputes ensued between Scheuer and the town council of Laufersweiler because the council would not furnish him firewood as was the customary for all townspeople. Many legal reasons were given along with others that had the ear-markings of blatant anti-Semitism, while referring to the firewood as Christian property: "And why should it (firewood) be shared with a people (Jews) who do not eat and drink with us, work little, and always scheme to bring doom to Christians as had been the case often in this town, and as can be proven."

After 1825, a schoolroom in the synagogue was furnished with three large tables, six benches and two slate boards. In 1831, two Jewish families from the nearby town of Sohren, who sent their children to the Jewish school of Laufersweiler, refused to pay the required fee even though there was no Jewish school at Sohren. While the Jewish school was being revamped, the government school official by the name of Eilers determined that the children were not being sufficiently instructed in all subjects, especially arithmetic, and that this was due to teacher Scheuer's lack of the necessary education. The school official requested that the Jewish Community Council of Laufersweiler dismiss Scheuer, which it did. Subsequent teachers fared similarly since any teacher with a combination of teaching skills for Judaic and other worldly subjects was very difficult to find. To retain such teachers was equally difficult especially since someone always found fault either with the person or his method of teaching. Finally from 1837 onward two teachers were hired, one to teach religion and Hebrew, the other, usually a Protestant, to teach the required elementary subjects. Still, complaints by parents were frequent, and constant squabbles were a heavy burden on teachers. The problems were elevated to the mayor of Kirchberg, and he sometimes passed the cases on to the higher county council at Simmern.

EXHIBIT 2.6 Open teaching position advertisement in the Allgemeinen Zeitung des Judentums general newspaper for Jewish people, August 3, 1857

> **Offene Lehrerstelle.**
> Bei der hiesigen israel. Gemeinde ist die Stelle eines Religions- und Elementarlehrers und Cantors mit einem jährlichen Gehalt von circa Thlr. 150., freier Wohnung, freiem Brennmaterial, nebst einigen Ländereien zum Bebauen und üblichen Nebeneinkünften, vacant.
> Bewerber, welche hierzu befähigt sind, wollen sich an den Oberrabbiner Herrn **Dr. Auerbach** in Bonn, oder an Herrn **David Rothschild**, Mitglied des israel. Consistoriums zu Simmern, wenden.
> Laufersweiler (Reg.-Bez. Coblenz), 20. Juli 1857.
> Der Vorsteher der israel. Gemeinde.
> **M. Frank.**

Translation:

> Our Jewish community has an opening for a teacher to teach religion as well as elementary subjects and serve as Cantor offering a yearly salary of approximately 150 Talers, including living quarters, free firewood, also some land for planting and additional income from the usual outside jobs.
>
> Applicants who meet the necessary requirements should apply to Chief Rabbi Mr. Dr. Auerbach at Bonn or to Mr. David Rothschild, member of the Jewish Council at Simmern.
>
> Signed and dated, Laufersweiler (District Koblenz) 20 July, 1857.
>
> The chair of the Jewish community,
>
> M. Frank.

The tenth teacher of Judaic and Hebrew studies was Herz Levy, who came from the nearby town of Hottenbach in 1859 (more about him in the text). In 1868, Mendel Mossbacher from the town of Gleicherweisen was hired with a yearly salary of 200 Talers. Shortly after, a big argument ensued between Mossbacher and Levy concerning their salaries. Levy gave lessons in Hebrew and other Judaic subjects to his own children. He then sent them to the Protestant school, for the other elementary subjects. The Royal Prussian government could not settle their salary disputes since there was no legal requirement to attend the private Jewish school.

In 1871, Moses Eisenkramer became the twelfth teacher. He went through difficult years, when during a governmental audit it was determined that sufficient funds were not available for salaries or teaching materials. He was finally dismissed in 1881 and was so angry that he warned potential applicants not to accept the position. Afterwards, he continued to teach seven local Jewish children while all others went to the Protestant school. The following is from the written memoirs (1944) of a former student, Bernhard Mayer: "We learned much from Mister Eisenkramer but were beaten much more from him. Although mister Eisenkramer was a small, wretched looking person, he worked us over with his cane as if he was the strongest man."

Four additional Jewish teachers were engaged between 1882 and 1895, but were dismissed or left on their own accord. In 1889, the Synagogue Council of Laufersweiler petitioned the government to grant the establishment of a Jewish public school in town, but their request was denied. Many reasons for this request underscored the problems of hiring and retaining qualified teachers to educate Jewish children in the prevailing private school environment. Since the number of Jewish children was still on the increase in 1895, a second petition was submitted to the government. Again the government refused, citing that adequate education was available through the existing Christian (public) schools in Laufersweiler.

Through governmental insistence, a new teacher, Aron Katz from the town of Waldgirmes, was hired in May 1896, to teach Judaism. His contract was cancelled in October of the same year when questions arose regarding his qualifications. He was followed by Hermann Ehrmann who resigned a year later and was replaced by Arnold Seliger from Gemünden near Wurzburg. Seliger was denied a portion of his fee as a *schochet* (Hebrew for kosher butcher) and was additionally insulted. As a result, he gave notice in June 1899 and left the community. The next teacher, Max Levite lasted from September 1899 until October 1901. At that time, the Laufersweiler Synagogue Council again made an attempt to set up a Jewish elementary school and requested that the town of Laufersweiler furnish appropriate financial support. After lengthy negotiations the Town Council agreed to support the establishment of the school with a yearly contribution of 200 Mark under the condition that no further requests would be made. The Synagogue Council welcomed the town's decision but turned down the offer and requested 300 Mark, as well as a free supply of lumber for the repair of the existing school. The Town Council considered this request too high a burden and shelved the entire matter. When one considers that the yearly salary paid to Aron Katz in 1896 was 800 Mark, the request by the Synagogue Council does not appear exorbitant.

Isidor Popper from Bohemia took over as teacher in October 1901, and a year later was succeeded by Julius Levy from the town of Illingen. Levy, in all probability, was the last Jewish teacher at the Laufersweiler *cheder* since the archives do not mention other teachers after 1911. When a renewed request for the establishment of a Jewish elementary school was made in 1903, area school inspector,

Mr. Liese, informed the *Landrat* (legal distric advisor) of the following. "The establishment of a Jewish (elementary) school at Laufersweiler cannot be recommended because of the unpleasant experiences of previous years of attempts at operating a Jewish school. Based on the quarreling character of the Jewish people there (Laufersweiler), who are primarily livestock dealers and butchers, there was never a lapse in annoying disputes with the hired teachers and therefore there was such a frequent turnover, that the teaching position became a pigeon roost (*Taubenschlag*). It cannot be expected that this situation improves in the future."

In 1904, the regional school inspector determined that the schoolroom on the ground floor of the synagogue below the sanctuary was far too small for forty-seven children. The room measured six meters by five meters (30 sq. m or 324 sq. feet) and allowed only .64 sq. meters (6.88 sq. ft) per child. The minimum government requirement was .74 sq. meters (796 sq. ft.) per child. The pupils were sitting practically on top of each other and very close to windows that were in disrepair. Also, the ceiling height of 2.4 meters (7.8 ft.) was unacceptably low. The building required major repair and structural modification, but the area architect considered these repairs impractical. Financial conditions in 1904 and later made it impossible to build a new Jewish elementary school, although, in 1907, the town offered to maintain the building and furnish living quarters for a married teacher. Additionally, the number of Jewish school-aged children had diminished, and by 1916, there were only six school-aged children, making the continuation of a *cheder* no longer viable.

EXHIBIT 2.7 The total population of Laufersweiler increased by only 232 over the period of 108 years. Protestants were always a considerable majority over Catholics, which was not always true in other towns in the area.

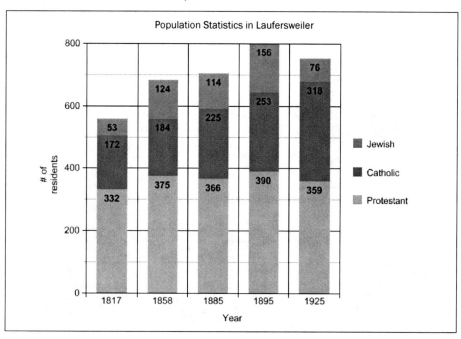

CHAPTER THREE

EXHIBIT 3.3 The Rathaus: Town hall in Laufersewiler dating back to the 18th century. Photo taken in 1980.

EXHIBIT 3.4 The Poststation: Post office is another of the oldest houses. Note the slate roof and the slate siding. Some remodeling had already taken place. Photo 1994.

EXHIBIT 3.5 Frederich Kehl's blacksmith shop, closed 1958.

EXHIBIT 3.15 Martha Joseph, standing, and her three siblings: Helene, sitting, Irma, standing, and her brother Bernard, later known as Berny or Benny.

EXHIBIT 3.18

Translation of a dedication by my father to my mother during their courtship while he was still in the military service at city Trier, better known as Treves, February 12, 1918. Unfortunately, the poetic rhyme in which the dedication is written is lost in the translation. Liberty has been taken to explain as much as possible the meaning of some of the sentences, which are noted in brackets.

"We saw each other many years ago, something you will certainly remember. However, then you didn't know me too well although you had a special nickname for me. Thereafter, in the year 1910, as if it was ordained, I found you again in our worthy land. Then I had the opportunity one evening to come to Hollerich [a specific area of the city in Luxembourg where Martha lived]. No evening was too far only the days became too long [he expresses his longing for her]. We spent nice days and hours together until you found a place [Martha was looking for a job, and found one in Paris, France). It was in Saabrüchen [a city in SW Germany on the Saar river where Josef had a job], where I received a letter from you that you had left home [presumably, she left for Paris]. From then on I have to tell you that I was very diligent in writing. So driven to write, I have to tell you, that I fell asleep doing so. That's how it happened. I took a weekday off because I had a longing for home. Suddenly I was able to get you out of Paris after we met at the train station and had a nice vacation. We had the wonderful time even so we sometimes had a quarrel. However, those squabbles never lasted too long because there was never a wall between us. Everything went along fine until August [1914] when I had to go into the war. We separated without being afraid, in the hope that we could be together again soon.

However, the war is still on today, otherwise we would be a married couple. When peace comes to Germany then our wedding will become the first thing. These lines shall be a reminder for all the times to come. Dedicated from your Josef, February 12, 1918"

EXHIBIT 3.19 Another sample of entries in Mother's Poesie Album.

EXHIBIT 3.20 Entries in Mother's Poesie Album were unique and colorful.

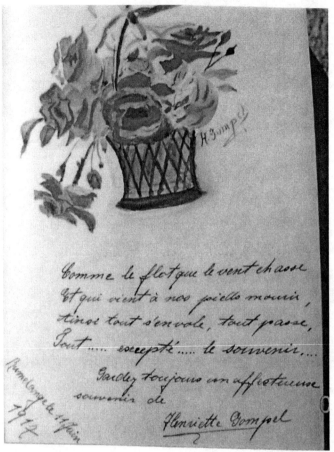

EXHIBIT 3.22

A poem written by hand in my mom's Poesie book by her Uncle Alphons to remember the day of her engagement to Joseph Kahn, my father, 12 December 1917. It is written in Letzebourgish, a dialect spoken in Luxembourg and translated by me to the best of my ability. (Luxembourgish: The national language of Luxembourg, and one of three administrative languages used today, in addition to French and German. It is a specific West Central German dialect with French loanwords, without any other derivations from the Romance dialects used in Belgium or France. German speakers might have difficulty understanding spoken, and definitely written, Luxembourgish if they are unfamiliar with West Central German dialects. It had no written standardization of spellings until 1956, and prior to that time, words were often spelled phonetically.)

    In Memory of Martha Joseph's Engagement to Joseph Kahn

    Why are we all here, you know it almost for sure. Believe it, not only to eat! We could get over that. We spoke of this engagement a long time ago. Now finally today the big day has come. You can see all the family here. They are all here to be witness to this engagement.

Joseph Kahn has permission from the German Army to show himself in civilian clothes to the mischpocha. From the war, from the front line, he came back, thank G'd, happy and in good health, he says.

My child, I thought of you all the time, involved in the war or at rest. It is not a joke, I prefer you staying here than being against the Russians in the East.

Now, all jokes aside, "Joseph Kahn is my name and I never disappointed any ones hopes. For a long time until now, I told you Martha, you are my dearest, my darling. We tell everyone the secret that we became engaged today as you all can see. In no time quickly, it has been done."

I certainly cannot complain. I had the honor to congratulate.

[Signed]

Dedicated to the engagement from Uncle Alphons, Hollerich (Luxembourg), December 12, 1917

EXHIBIT 3.23 On the back of the card translated from German: *A reminder of the New Year's celebration in enemy territory. War year 1916/1917 Your Josef* [note the spelling]. Dad is third from the left holding two mugs of beer.

EXHIBIT 3.24 Front of Postcard

EXHIBIT 3.25

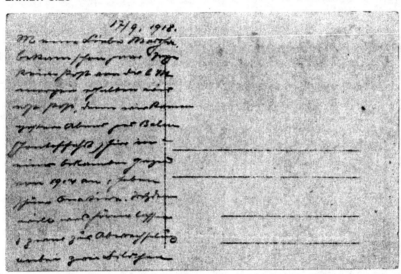

English translation of the back of the postcard:

September 17, 1918

My Dear Martha,

Did not receive mail from you for several days, dear Martha. We do not receive any mail tomorrow, because we arrived last evening for moving on to the front to a well known area since 1914 and have nice billets (accommodations). Nevertheless, I wanted you to hear from me and for a change enclose two photos.

CHAPTER FOUR

EXHIBIT 4.3 Castle, the Knight's Hall.

EXHIBIT 4.4 Haupt bahnhof. The main train station and postoffice.

EXHIBIT 4.5 The Marketplace.

EXHIBIT 4.6 Zeughaus and Moltke Monument.

EXHIBIT 4.7 The City Hall on Parade Square. Formerly shops, built between 1724 - 1746, a baroque building, since 1910 residence of the City Government.

EXHIBIT 4.8 A schematic of the city of Mannheim showing location of places described in text.

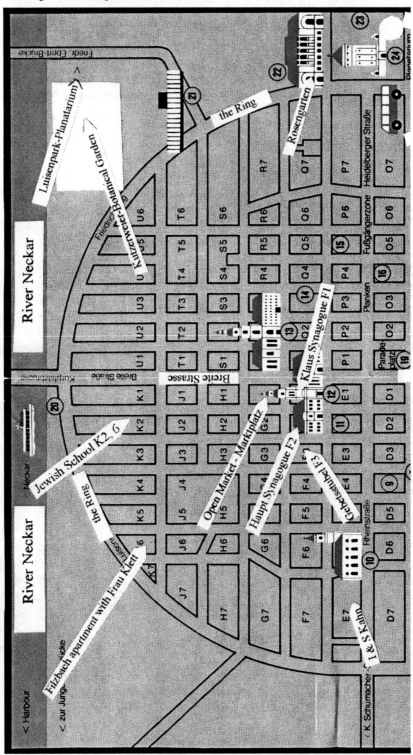

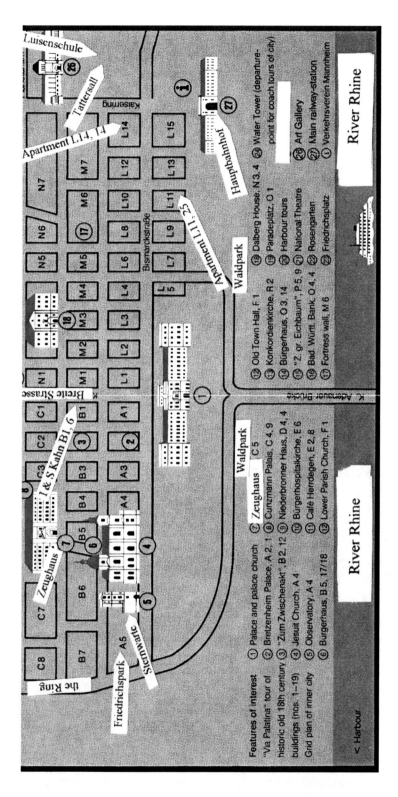

CHAPTER FIVE

EXHIBIT 5.10

Summer 1925 in the backyard of Opa Isaak Kahn's house, Laufersweiler, Germany. Opa is sitting in the chair; standing to the left in a white dress is Irene, 4 years old, and sitting on the blanket in front is Robert, 2 years old. Behind him is his mother Martha, and under the tree is Gerda Kahn Ackerman age 32. Far left is Kurt Strauss, next to him with glasses is Richard Kirchheimer, and the boy between Gerda and Martha may be Herbert Kirchheimer.

EXHIBIT 5.11

Family photo in front of Isaak and Lenchen Löser's house, Laufersweiler, Summer 1925. Lenchen's birth name was Magdalena, and she is standing on the far right. She and Malchen (Amalia), fourth from right, were sisters. Left to right: Martha Kahn holding Robert. Else Kirchheimer (with bangs) from America; Malchen Joseph née Levy from Luxembourg (Martha's mother); Isaak Löser with tie; Elsa Handel née Löser; Lenchen Löser née Levy. In front: Richard Kirchheimer, son of Else Kirchheimer; Irene Kahn, Robert's sister; Kurt Strauss, son of Leo Strauss and Jenny Strauss née Kahn.

Löser's house with Lenchen on the left and Isaak on the right. People in the doorway are not identifiable.

EXHIBIT 5.12 Opa Isaak Kahn with Robert and Irene. October 1925, Mannheim.

EXHIBIT 5.13 Opa Isaak and Robert (age 4), January 1927.

EXHIBIT 5.15 Robert (age 5), Irene (age 7), cousin Alice Danziger (age 3-1/2), Martin Joseph (age 5-1/2)

EXHIBIT 5.17 Irene and me dressed up in Purim costumes. Purim is a Jewish holiday commemorating the deliverance of the Jewish people in ancient Persia where a plot to destroy them was foiled. It's a holiday to rejoice and celebrate.

EXHIBIT 5.19 Manuel, as he was known, Isaak's younger brother, never married. He lived in a house in Laufersweiler by himself and as somewhat of a recluse. Not much else is known about him.

EXHIBIT 5.20 It was a sad day when Opa in Laufersweiler suddenly died on March 25, 1927. Both my dad and mom went to the funeral. Both monuments were erected a year later, but were desecrated during the Nazi period. These images show they were rededicated after World War II as were all the other graves in the Jewish Cemetery.

EXHIBIT 5.23 Theo and Erna Kiefer. Good friends of my parents. Photo taken at Arosa Switzerland, August 1935. Their daughter, Edith, and Irene were good friends. Edith later settled in Israel, but returned for the Mannheim reunion in 1990.

EXHIBIT 5.26 Certificate of the originality for "Mannemar Dreck" pastry.

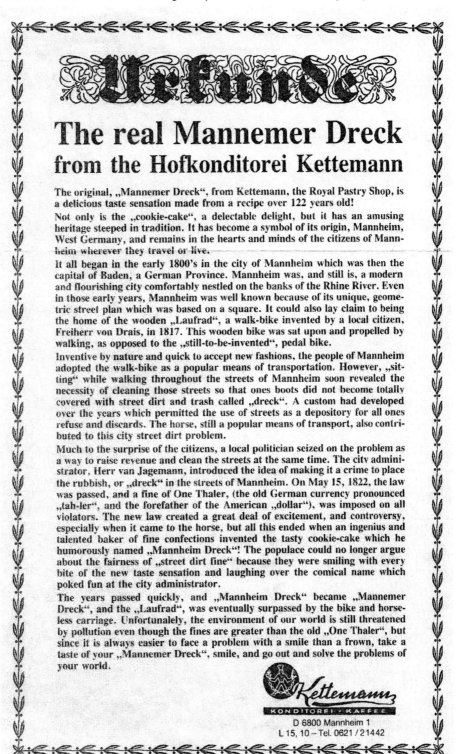

EXHIBIT 5.27 The carton in which the Mannemar Dreck is sold.

EXHIBIT 5.28 The individual pieces of confectionary are individually wrapped and are today produced by several bakeries in Mannheim.

EXHIBIT 5.29 Each piece of confectionary is approximately 3-1/2 inches in diameter.

EXHIBIT 5.30 Ingredients are listed on every wrapper.

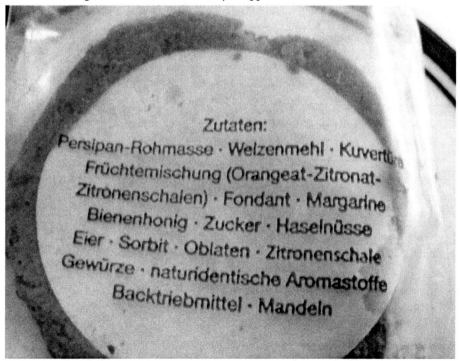

EXHIBIT 5.35 Map of Mannheim and environs

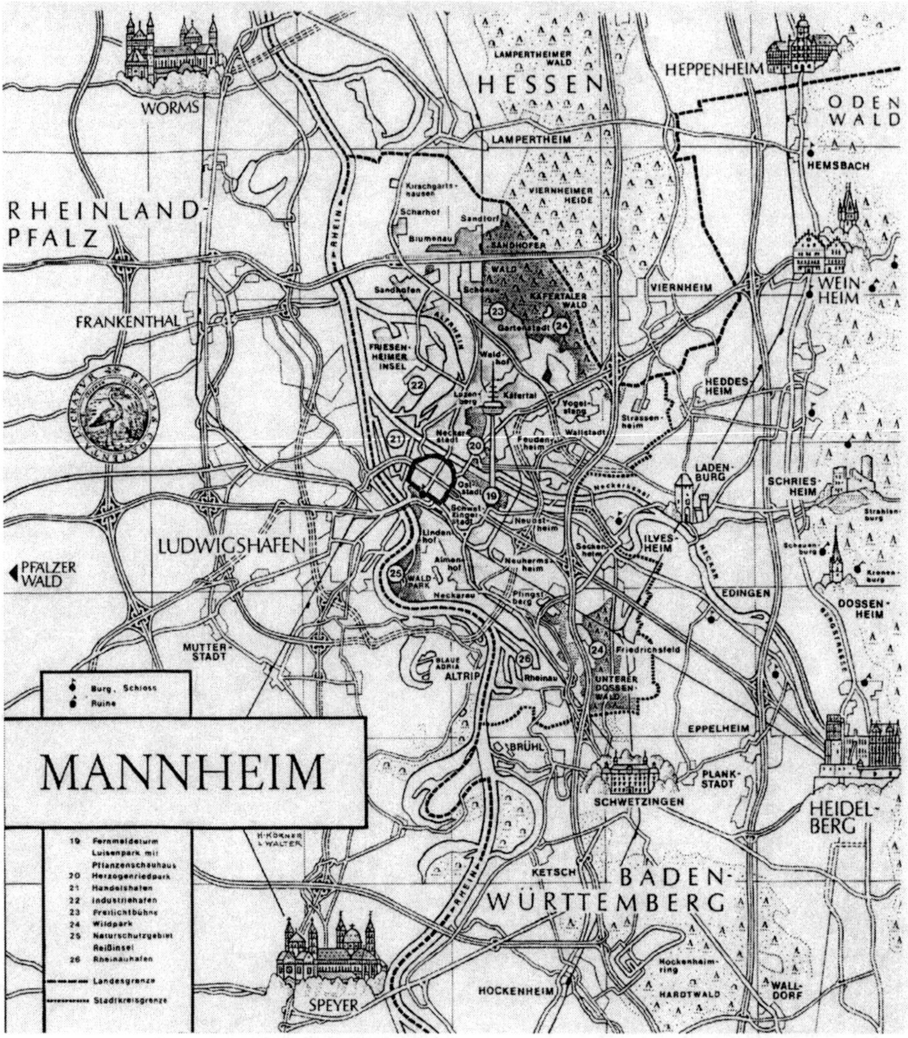

EXHIBIT 5.37
World's largest wine barrel with dance floor on top at Heidelberg Castle.

EXHIBIT 5.39
Heidelberg, the Neckar river and Castle at hillside.

EXHIBIT 5.40
Heidelberg Castle Courtyard.

EXHIBIT 5.49 A poem copied in her own handwriting and decorated by Irene for our mother. Title of the poem is "Mother's Eye" (1931/32).

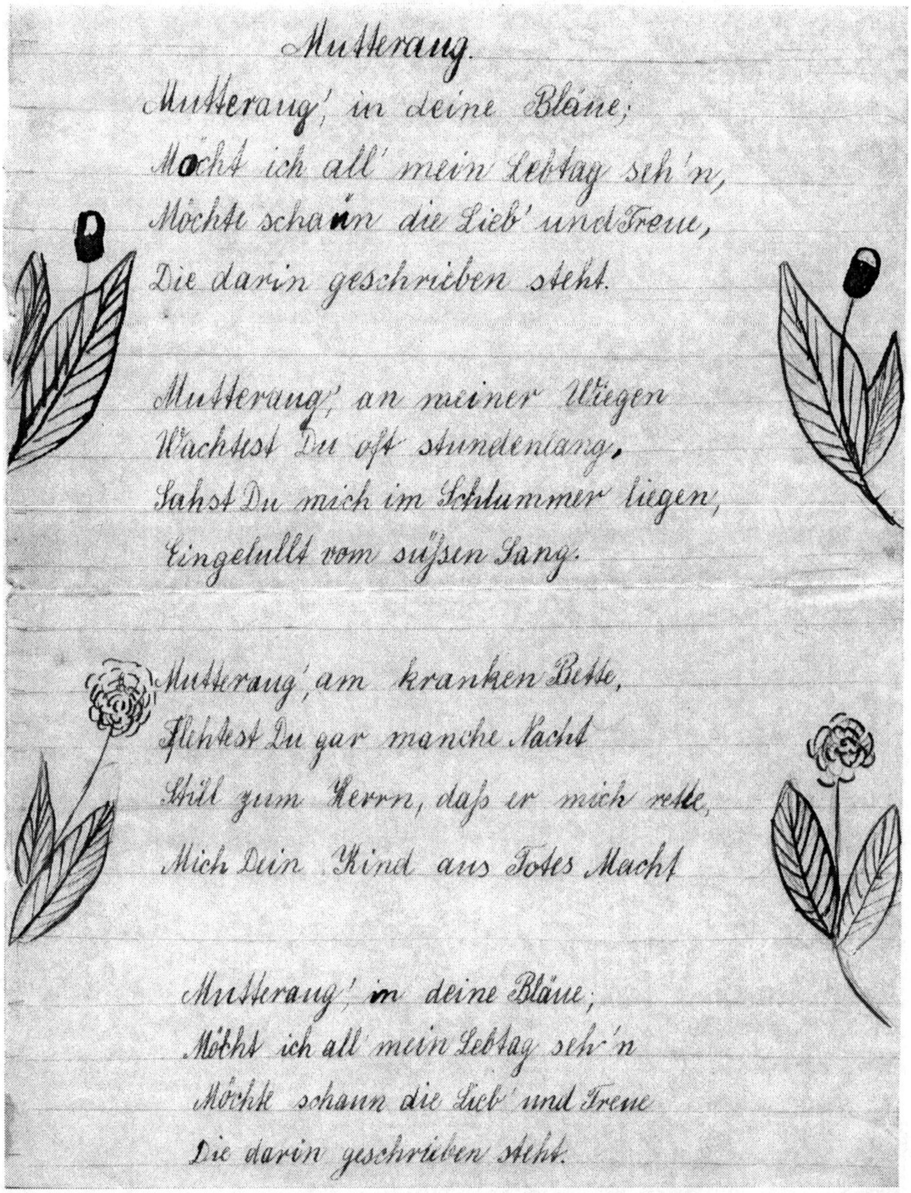

Mutteraug.

Mutteraug', in deine Bläue,
Möcht ich all' mein Lebtag seh'n,
Möchte schau'n die Lieb' und Treue,
Die darin geschrieben steht.

Mutteraug', an meiner Wiegen
Wachtest Du oft stundenlang,
Sahst Du mich im Schlummer liegen,
Eingelullt vom süßen Sang.

Mutteraug', am kranken Bette,
Flehtest Du gar manche Nacht
Still zum Herrn, daß er mich rette,
Mich Dein Kind aus Todes Macht

Mutteraug', in deine Bläue,
Möcht ich all' mein Lebtag seh'n
Möchte schau'n die Lieb' und Treue
Die darin geschrieben steht.

EXHIBIT 5.50 Photograph taken the week of March 31, 1930 on the occasion of Raphael Joseph's 70th birthday, in the courtyard in front of the livestock barn at Hollericherstrasse or Rue de Hollerich, Luxembourg.

Front row (L to R): Robert Bernhard (later changed to Bernard in 1943) Kahn, in sailor suit; Claude Ehrlich, son of Irma and Charles; Georges Joseph, also in a sailor suit, son of Bernard and Marthe Joseph. He would later be executed in Cuneo, Italy on April 26, 1945 by a German firing squad.

Middle row (L to R): Joseph Kahn, my father, who died April 15, 1973 in Chicago; Martha (Joseph), my mother, who died February 7, 1968 in Chicago; Oma Amalia (Levy) Joseph, known as Malchen, who died September 21, 1933 in Luxembourg; her husband, Opa Raphael Joseph, deported to Theresienstadt, Poland, reported dead February 6, 1943; Irma (Joseph) Ehrlich, Martha's sister and her husband, Charles Ehrlich, both of whom died after 1945.

Back row (L to R): Helen (Joseph) Cohen, my mother's sister, and her husband, Max Cohen, both deported April 23, 1942 to Izbica, Poland and subsequently murdered by the Nazis; Irene, my sister, also in a sailor suit, died September 7, 2009 in Chicago; Marthe (Michel) Joseph who survived the war and died September 21, 1981 in Luxembourg, and her husband/my mother's only brother, Bernard Joseph, who died January 20, 1961 in Nice, France.

EXHIBIT 5.51 A souvenir of the school year 1932/1933 and our teacher Mr. Weinreich before the Nazi era: harmonious relationships. I am the first boy in the last row, on left.

EXHIBIT 5.52 My dear sister Irene 1933. I often pulled on her braids and sometimes after she washed her hair I braided them.

EXHIBIT 5.64 Oma and Opa Joseph, 1930.

EXHIBIT 5.65 Oma Malchen Joseph, 1930.

EXHIBIT 5.66 A Neiderbronner sister attends to the very ill Malchen Joseph, my Oma, Luxembourg, 1932.

EULOGY (translation)

Held at the coffin of Frau Raphael Joseph, née Amelie Levy

September 24, 1933

So now it has been fulfilled what has been threatening this house for the last twenty months, what the inhabitants have feared for a long period: the honorable woman has gone to where there is no return. Her spirit has left this place. She was selfless in the fulfillment of her duties. The place where she was the source of highest joy for her husband, children, and grandchildren, and where she practiced genuine hospitality in welcoming her friends and acquaintances. She did this in a simple way that came from her heart. On Rosh Hashanah, the day of renewal and atonement, she passed away. She went home after a long a difficult illness. In spite of her suffering, she bore her pain stoically and with a faith in God. Futile were the attentions of her husband and children. They served her with love. Futile was the art of the doctors. The caring of the nurses was without example. Their concern, quiet patience, and loyalty made it possible for her to have joy and beauty at the end of her life. She has passed away. A valuable treasure of woman's virtue and motherly love has been lost with her passing. The pride and honor of her husband, and the joy and happiness of her children and grandchildren surround this coffin. And through our hearts rings the lamentation of the sufferer, Job: "*The zither turned into my sorrow, the sham (wind instrument) the tolling of the bell (the sound of mourning).*"

A Jewish woman in the best sense of the word, we bury her today, one who reflects the wonderful women of Bible stories. The stories from the happy days of Jewish history tell what women were like in the olden times of Israel. She put the sparkle into the eyes of the thankful people. The Hebrew psalms have again and again placed the ideal image of the Jewish woman into the eyes of the coming generations. As we sing about this on Friday nights in our Jewish homes: For six days the man is a slave of his job. On the Sabbath, he can lay his burden down. This holy day he is given time and rest and enjoys the blessings of being at home. And who does he extol at first when he comes home? His wife, who brings him joy in abundance. Rightly, the Jewish people are full of admiration for what she does and who she is. The Hebrew language is a witness of that. And in all of the areas in our history, the monuments speak of that. The holy language, in whose words the Jewish way of life has found its most concise expression, is full of boundlessly true recognition of the value of women. The Hebrew language has only one expression for both genders. In Hebrew it refers to man, as Man and the woman as, Woman. It has the same Hebrew word. It is a self-evident truth for the language that man and woman are one. Different expressions of the same divine thought by the creator.

We bury a Jewish woman here today, in the tradition of proud Jewish women. A wife and mother in whose life and deeds-the great and wonderful, the simple, and the uplifting, which you can also witness in the honorable women of the Bible.

"Three crowns," say our sages, "life can give to us: The crown of Torah, the crown of priestly service, the crown of the Kingdom, but the crown a good name on Earth radiates above all the others."

I knew the worth of this woman. And nevertheless I went out, following the advice our teachers had given: "Trying to find out what the people are talking about outside." I spoke to the people and everyone said to me, "You can't say enough good things about this woman." When we say these words in the morning while praying, "As long as the spirit and the soul are in me, I thank you, O God for your goodness," so was her whole life as long as her strength and spirit remained, a song of thanksgiving and praise of the Creator, by whose power and knowledge she was guided in her piety and fear of God. Her every word, and every deed, and every though was directed by her God.

Her whole life was nothing but a hymn of selflessness, and of devotion and service to her husband. In 44 years of a beautiful and harmonious marriage she developed the richness of her overflowing woman's heart out of the cornucopia of her personality and spirituality, she gave the best. She looked for and found her happiness in the happiness of her husband. With the same love and loyalty, she educated and raised her children. From the time that they were small she put into their hearts the seeds of their Jewish and religious thinking with her strong morals. And when her children were grown, and her son had established his own home, and the daughters had married brave and decent men far from Luxembourg, she knew no greater joy in life and no more beautiful a purpose than to continue to strengthen close family ties of unity. When she traveled to her daughters and sons-in-law, which was her greatest joy, she understood how to weave the fabric of the second and third generations with her warm and motherly heart and her Jewish soul. By doing this she was able to create even closer ties to the parental home in Luxembourg. In the circle of her children and grandchildren she created a comfortable atmosphere of unity that brought out the best in her.

But the fine character and personality of this woman were a well-known and positive influence, not only within the family circle, but with others as well. Her sense of charity and willingness to help at any time, as well as her deep compassion for any suffering have made her into a mistress of charity, in the true sense of the word. Within the women's charity organization, she was one of the most enthusiastic working and esteemed members. She was a member for many years. She developed activities which were an example and a blessing. With a tender hand and gentle mind, she tried to lessen and correct the discomfort of pain everywhere.

Like once for the prophet Ezekiel, who received the prophesy that his wife would die, and heard the call of the Eternal: "*O son of man, I will take the joy of your vision through illness but you may not complain nor cry and weep no tears*," this family today has to endure this difficult trial.

Therefore, I will say to you at this sorrowful time: Gather around your lonely father in child-like love and devotion, and comfort will blossom from the obedient fulfillment of your duties of children. By doing this, you will be upholding and carrying out the holy legacy of the prophets who have gone before and you'll strengthen the solidarity of the father, the children, and the grandchildren. By doing this, you will be following her example, dedicating the greatest fortitude of your lives with so much devotion.

The last words of this woman were for her grandchild. It was a wish that she mentioned on his/her birthday. It shall be a symbol for all of you. Her whole life was nothing but a wish, a blessing for her loved ones, selfless, putting others ahead of herself, her self-denying work for the family. In the quiet hours of reflection, you should tell your children about this woman, your grandmother. All of you will give the children with this the strongest morals and a Jewish foothold for life and you will put a memorial of her in the hearts of her descendants; a more beautiful memorial couldn't be built.

She leaves an indelible impression in the thoughts of her friends and neighbors and the wide circle of acquaintances. The image of this woman: this good and fine Jewish woman will live on in us. Our thankfulness and blessing lead her now into a world of pure joy and happiness, where she is accepted by the grace of the Eternal.

Amen.

Obituary (Translation from German)

Mr. Raphael Joseph, Mr. Josef Kahn and wife, née Martha Joseph, their children Irene and Robert; Mr. Max Cohen and wife, née Helene Joseph; Mr. Bernard Joseph and wife, née Marthe Michel and her son George, Mr. Charles Ehrlich and wife, née Irma Joseph and her children Claude and Eliane, the families Joseph, Kahn, Cohen, Löser, Salomon, Berney, Levy, and Ehrlich are fulfilling their sad duty by announcing the death of their deeply loved wife, mother, mother-in-law, grandmother, sister, sister-in-law, aunt, and cousin.

Mrs. Raphael Joseph

Née Amalia Levy

She died on the 22nd of September at 8:30 a.m. after a long, difficult illness. She was sixty-nine years old. The funeral will be in Luxembourg on Sunday, the 24th of September at 3:30 p.m. The funeral procession will start at the house where she died, Hollerich, Bahnhofstrasse No. 83, and continue to the Jewish cemetery at Belle-Vue.

Luxembourg, Hollerich, Mannheim, Köln, Lille, Chicago, Roodt/Syr, Junglinster, Laufersweiler, September 1933

Obituary (Translation from French)

Instead of Special Announcement

Mr. Raphael Joseph's children, grandchildren, and families are deeply touched at the numerous expressions of sympathy at the death of Madame Raphael Joseph and express their sincere appreciation to all her friends and acquaintances who showed their sorrow. Particular thanks for the beautiful flowers and wreath.

Luxembourg, November 20, 1933

EXHIBIT 5.69 Rheingrafenstein at Bad Münster am Stein (aka a Mountain).

EXHIBIT 5.70 My father's Cross of Honor and certificate awarded for his service during World War I.

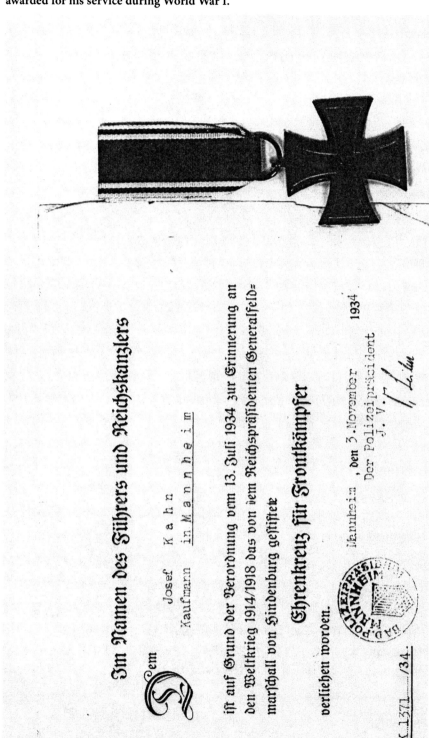

CHAPTER SIX

Nuremberg Laws description taken from Yad Vashem (yadvashem.org)

Racial laws implemented by the German Parliament in Nuremberg, on September 15, 1935. These laws became the legal basis for the racist anti-Jewish policy in Germany. Thirteen additional decrees were added to the Nuremberg Laws over the next 8 years. These included the first official definition of who was to be considered a Jew and who an Aryan. Jews with three or four Jewish grandparents were considered full-blooded Jews.

The first of the Nuremberg Laws was called the "Reich Citizenship Law," which declared that only Aryans could be citizens of the Reich. This stripped the Jews of their political rights and reduced them from *Reichsburger* (citizens of the Reich), to *Staatsangehorige* (state subjects). The second law, entitled the "Law for the Protection of German Blood and Honor," forbade marriages and extramarital sexual relations between Germans and Jews, the employment of German maids under the age of 45 in Jewish homes and the raising of the German flag by Jews.

In early anti-Jewish policy, exceptions were made for Jewish World War I veterans and state officials, who had worked for the government before the war's outbreak in 1914. The Nuremberg Laws nullified these exceptions, and Jewish war heroes were to be treated just as badly as any other German Jew.

By the summer of 1935, the need for laws like these had become urgent. The Nazi Party had a clear policy on the status of the Jews in Germany and party leaders and state officials were in conflict with each other about the "Jewish Question." Anti-Jewish rioting had broken out, the party and public were demanding clarification and Hitler felt pressed to provide a response. The Nuremberg Laws appeased those Nazi officials who had been calling for virulent anti-Jewish wording in the party's platform.

The Nuremberg Laws not only provided a "legitimate" legal mechanism for excluding the Jews from mainstream German culture, but also supplied the Nazi Party with a rationalization for the anti-Semitic riots and arrests they had carried out over the previous months.

EXHIBIT 6.6 The cover of a small advertisement notebook for our business, located at B1,6 tel.32935. Products: Ladies stockings, silk, wool, satin, velvet; Men's socks: of all types; Children's stockings: knee socks, ankle socks; Sport stockings; gloves: ladies, men's, children's; handkerchiefs, men's and women's undergarments (not shown)

J. & S. KAHN
Mannheim
B 1,6   Tel. 32935

Damen-Strümpfe
Seide, Wolle, Seidenflor, Maco

Herren-Socken
in allen Ausführungen

Kinder-Strümpfe
Kniestrumpfe, Söckchen

Sport-Strümpfe

Handschuhe
für Damen, Herren und Kinder

Taschentücher

EXHIBIT 6.8 Mannheim's members of the RJFS bowling league. Dad, second from left, back row. I, as honorary member, standing next to him. Circa 1935.

EXHIBIT 6.10 My grandfather Isaak's tombstone at the Laufersweiler cemetery.

CHAPTER SEVEN

EXHIBIT 7.3 Copy of Kurt Strauss's death certificate. He was committed to Concentration Camp Sachsenhausen on 16th March 1940, Prisoner's Number 17476.

```
Nr. 1797                                        533
                                                C 1
              Oranienburg, den 8. April 1940
      Der Schlosser Kurt, Israel Strauß - - - - - -
- - - - - - - - - - - - - - mosaisch - - - - - - -
wohnhaft in Grüsen bei Frankenberg - - - - - - -
ist am 5. April 1940 um 15 Uhr 15 Minuten - - - - -
in Oranienburg im Lager Sachsenhausen verstorben. -
      Der Verstorbene war geboren am 29. Januar 1918
in Frankfurt am Main - - - - - - - - - - - - - - -
(Standesamt - - - - - - - - - - - - - -Nr. - - -)
      Vater: Leo Strauß, wohnhaft in Frankfurt am
             Main Zeil 7 - - - - - - - - - - - -
                 nbekannt - - - - - - - - - - - -
                 orbene war nicht verheiratet. - - - -

             f schriftliche Anzeige des Lagerkom-
             Lagers Sachsenhausen in Oranienburg.

             ieser genehmigt und unterschrieben.
                    Der Standesbeamte
                    In Vertretung: Entreß
             - - - - - - - - - - - - - - - - - -
Todesursache: Körperschwäche
Die Übereinstimmung der obigen Abschrift mit den
Eintragungen im Sterbebuch wird hiermit beglaubigt.
          Oranienburg, den 2. Juli 1948
                    Der Standesbeamte
```

Translation:

> Oranienburg, April 8, 1940
>
> The mechanic Kurt Israel Strauss (---Mosaic (Jewish)) residing in Grüsen near Frankenberg died April 5, 1940 at 3:15 p.m. in Oranienburg in Sachsenhausen Camp.

The deceased was born January 29, 1918 in Frankfurt/Main

Bureau of Vital Statistics Father: Leo Strauss, residing at Zeil 7 Frankfurt/Main, Mother: unknown*.

The deceased was not married.

Entered by written entry of the Camp Commander of Camp Sachsenhausen in Oranienburg

Read, approved and signed by the official representative of the Bureau of Vital Statistics

Cause of death: body weakness

The above transcript is in agreement with the entry in the death record and is hereby certified. Oranienburg, July 2, 1948 Official Bureau of Vital Statistics

The above death certificate together with a box of ashes was sent to his father in 1940.

* his mother, Jenny, dad's sister, had died years earlier of natural causes

Kurt as a young adult

EXHIBIT 7.6 Hugo Adler, main cantor, Main Synagogue, 1924-1939. Born 1894 - Died 1955.

EXHIBIT 7.7 Erwin Hirsch. Cantor and teacher, Main Synagogue 1937-1939. Born 1914. Attended Mannheim Reunion, June 1990.

EXHIBIT 7.8 Rabbi Karl Richter, 1938-1939. Born 1910. Rabbi for all Jews. Remained in Mannheim. He attended the Mannheim Reunion, June 1990.

EXHIBIT 7.9 Manfred Kalbermann. Teacher of Jewish religion. Committed suicide March 22, 1939 being despaired. Born 1900.

EXHIBIT 7.15 Last row from left to right, my cousin Ernst Kahn, Günter Kaufmann, and Alfred Selig. In front row from right, Max Kaufmann, and my younger cousin, Walter Kahn. I don't remember the names of my other two friends.

EXHIBIT 7.19 Georges Joseph's bar mitzvah dinner with relatives and friends, August 28, 1937. Georges, left under chandelier between his mother and father, I am standing next to the door on the left. Mom, Dad, and Opa in back, right side of chandelier.

EXHIBIT 7.21 AND 7.22 Documents for Martha and Joseph in both French and English translations.

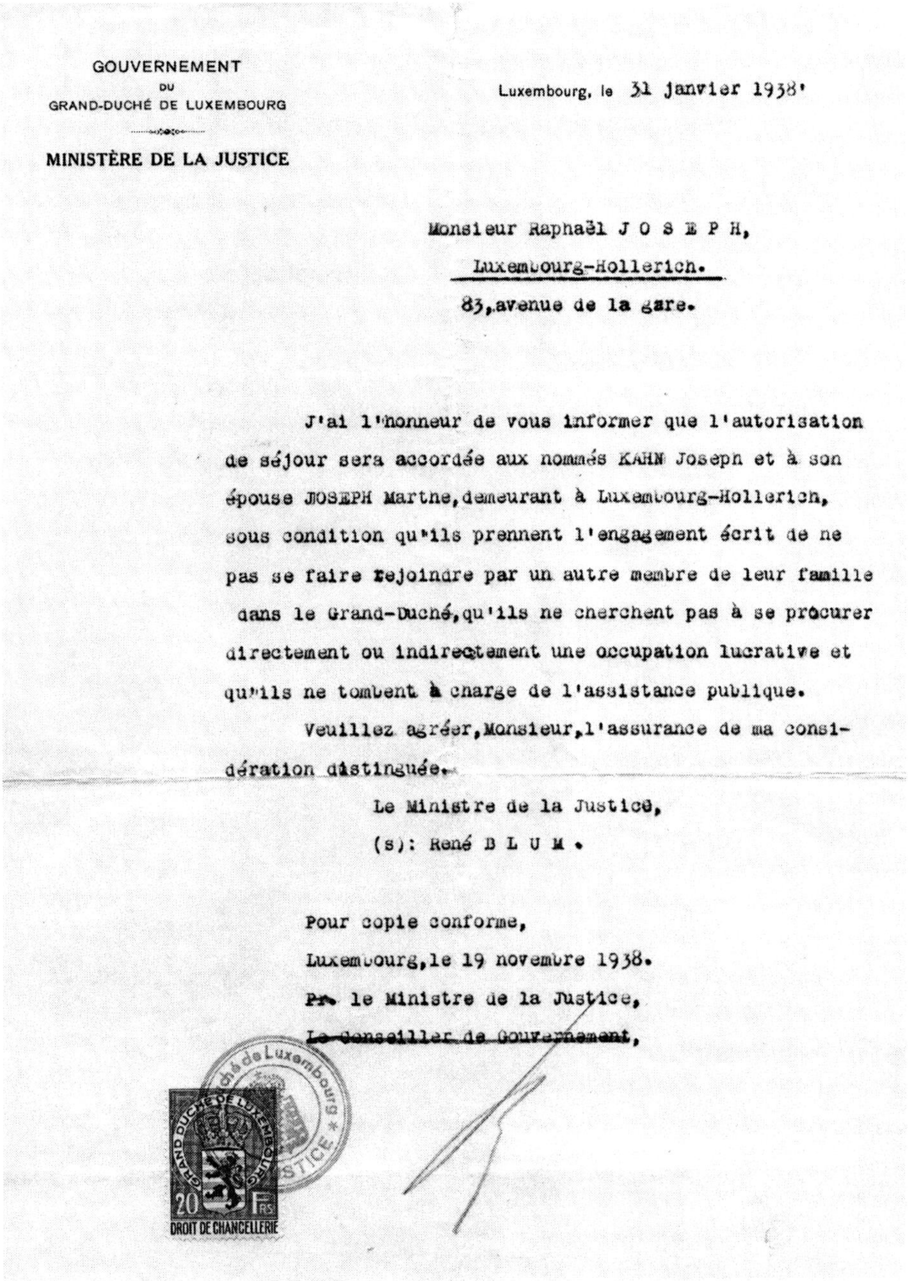

GOUVERNEMENT
DU
GRAND-DUCHÉ DE LUXEMBOURG

MINISTÈRE DE LA JUSTICE

Luxembourg, le 31 janvier 1938.

Monsieur Raphaël J O S E P H,
Luxembourg-Hollerich.
83, avenue de la gare.

J'ai l'honneur de vous informer que l'autorisation de séjour sera accordée aux nommés KAHN Joseph et à son épouse JOSEPH Marthe, demeurant à Luxembourg-Hollerich, sous condition qu'ils prennent l'engagement écrit de ne pas se faire rejoindre par un autre membre de leur famille dans le Grand-Duché, qu'ils ne cherchent pas à se procurer directement ou indirectement une occupation lucrative et qu'ils ne tombent à charge de l'assistance publique.

Veuillez agréer, Monsieur, l'assurance de ma considération distinguée.

Le Ministre de la Justice,
(s): René B L U M.

Pour copie conforme,
Luxembourg, le 19 novembre 1938.
P. le Ministre de la Justice,
Le Conseiller de Gouvernement,

Gouvernement du Grand-Duche de Luxembourg
Ministere de la Justice

Luxembourg, 31 January 1938

Mr Raphael Joseph
Luxembourg-Hollerich
83 Avenue de la Gare (Avenue of the Railroad Station)

I have the honor to inform you that the permission to stay will be granted to KAHN Joseph and to his wife JOSEPH Marthe, to reside at Luxembourg-Hollerich, providing that they agree in writing not to have any other member of their family join them in the Grand-Duche and that they will not attempt to secure a position which pays them either directly or indirectly and that they will not require public assistance.

Dear Sir, please receive my respectful regards,

The Minister of Justice,

(signed) Rene BLUM

Certified Copy,
Luxembourg, November 19, 1938
the Minister of Justice

GOUVERNEMENT
DU
GRAND-DUCHÉ DE LUXEMBOURG

MINISTÈRE DE LA JUSTICE

Luxembourg, le 13 octobre 1938.

Monsieur JOSEPH Raphaël,

Luxembourg-Hollerich.

83, avenue de la gare

    J'ai l'honneur de vous informer que l'autorisation de séjour accordée le 31 janvier 1938 aux époux Jos. KAHN - JOSEPH n'est pas périmée. Elle vaut toujours, à condition que les intéressés prennent les engagements exigés par cette autorisation, c'est-à-dire de ne pas se faire rejoindre par un autre membre de leur famille, de ne pas chercher à se procurer directement ou indirectement une occupation lucrative et de ne jamais avoir recours à l'assistance publique.

                        Le Ministre de la Justice,

Gouvernement du Grand-Duche de Luxembourg
Ministere de la Justice

Luxembourg, 13 October 1938

Mr Raphael Joseph
Luxembourg-Hollerich
83 Avenue de la Gare (Avenue of the Railroad Station)

I have the honor to inform you that the permission to stay which was granted January 31, 1938 to the spouses Jos. KAHN-JOSEPH has not lapsed. It is still valid providing that the people involved abide by the conditions set down in the authorization. That means that they will not be joined by another member of their family, that they do not attempt to secure a position which pays them either directly or indirectly and that they will not require public assistance.

The Minister of Justice.

EXHIBIT 7.27 Another view of the Mannheim cemetery, located at F,7 which dated back to 1661. Jews were buried here before the city fathers decided they needed the area to create a parking lot.

EXHIBIT 7.28 Some of the volunteers that dug up the remains of the dead and prepared them for reburial. Walter Oberländer, far right, had his bar mitzvah the same year I did. He was deported October 23, 1940 with all of the others.

EXHIBIT 7.33 The Jewish Home for the Aged of Neustadt, located at Karolinen Street 119. The Nazis set the building on fire with all 300 residents, plus staff, still inside, on the evening of November 9/10, 1938. Photo as shown taken of rebuilt facility after the war.

EXHIBIT 7.34

Gouvernment of Grand-Duche of Luxembourg

Justice Ministry

Herr District Attorney:

I have the honor to inform you that Mr. Robert Kahn born September 30 1923 at Mannheim living in Germany has received permission for a temporary stay in the Grand-Duche of Luxembourg.

The Justice Minister

(signed) Rene Blum

Certified Copy

Luxembourg, November 19 1938

EXHIBIT 7.37 Police certificate required for emigration purposes (that was only valid for a three month period), which indicated that Josef Israel Kahn had no criminal record whatsoever between March 11, 1920 and January 28, 1939. It was another method for the authorities to know your whereabouts and another shenanigan to make it tough on Jews to leave Germany.

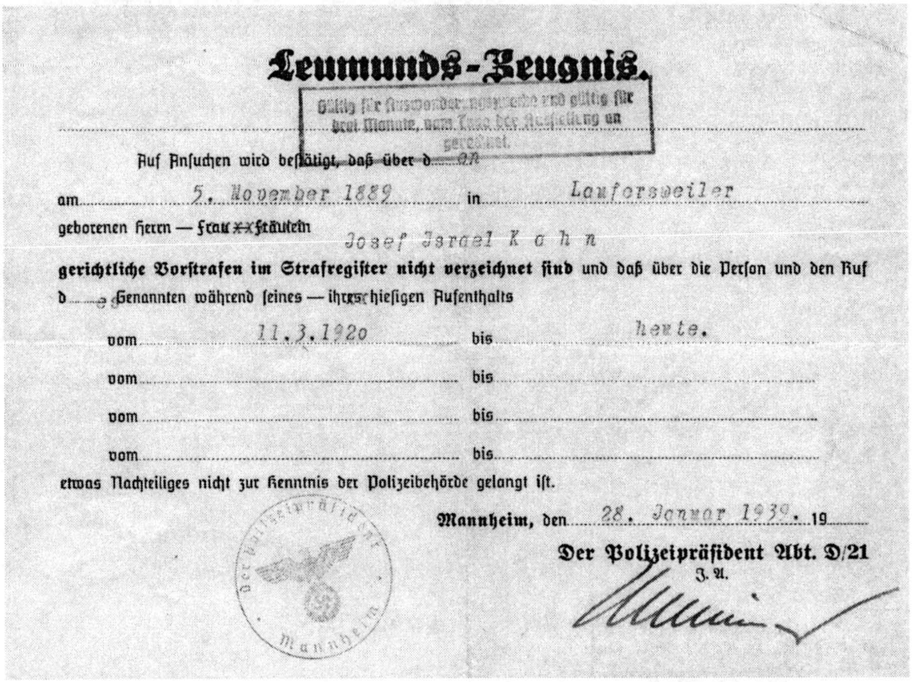

Leumunds-Zeugnis.

Gültig für Auswanderungszwecke und gültig für drei Monate, vom Tage der Ausstellung an gerechnet.

Auf Ansuchen wird bestätigt, daß über d en

am 5. November 1889 in Lauforsweiler

geborenen Herrn — ~~Frau — Fräulein~~ Josef Israel Kahn

gerichtliche Vorstrafen im Strafregister nicht verzeichnet sind und daß über die Person und den Ruf d es Genannten während seines — ~~ihres~~ hiesigen Aufenthalts

vom 11.3.1920 bis heute.

vom ... bis ...

vom ... bis ...

vom ... bis ...

etwas Nachteiliges nicht zur Kenntnis der Polizeibehörde gelangt ist.

Mannheim, den 28. Januar 1939. 19

Der Polizeipräsident Abt. D/21

I. A.

EXHIBIT 7.38 Reference letter for Robert (original document and translation).

JÜDISCHE WIRTSCHAFTSHILFE
MANNHEIM
E 7, 28

FERNSPRECHER Nr. 25388

Postscheck-Konto:
Karlsruhe I. B. Nr. 19313

Unser Zeichen: M/H.
Bei Beantwortung bitte anzugeben.

MANNHEIM, 18. April 1939

Z e u g n i s
=============

Robert K a h n , geb. 30.12.23 in Mannheim, war vom 20.4.38 bis 10.11.38 Schüler der Schlosserei der jüd. Anlernwerkstätte, Mannheim.

Während dieser Zeit hat er sich stets Mühe gegeben, sich die Handfertigkeiten und sonstigen Erfordernisse seines Handwerks anzueignen. Auch am Fachunterricht hat er regelmässig mit Interesse und gutem Verständnis teilgenommen.

Sein Betragen Vorgesetzten und Arbeitskameraden gegenüber war einwandfrei.

Infolge Schliessung der Anlernwerkstätte konnte Robert Kahn seine Lehrzeit nicht durchführen.

Wir wünschen ihm für sein ferneres Wohlergehen alles Gute.

Jüdische Wirtschaftshilfe
Abt. Berufsausbildung
Mannheim E 7, 28

Jewish Office for Economic Assistance

18 April 1939

Mannheim

E7,28

Telephone Nr. 25388

Banking: Karlsruhe I.B. Nr. 19313

Reference

Robert Kahn born 30.12.1923* in Mannheim, from 20 April 1938 to 11 November 1938 was an apprentice at the Jewish vocational school for metal fabrication, Mannheim.

During that time he always gave his best to follow instructions and other requirements of his trade. He attended classes regularly and showed interest and good understanding. His behavior toward his instructor and fellow apprentice students was perfect.

In view of the vocational school's closing, Robert Kahn was unable to complete his apprenticeship.

For his future we wish him further good tidings and good luck.

Jewish Office for Economic Assistane

Division of Occupational Guidance

Mannheim E7,28

signed: Engineer George Brauer

Adele Sara Horn

* author's note: the date is incorrect, should be 30.9.1923.

CHAPTER EIGHT

EXHIBIT 8.2 View of the Alzette river from above, also known as the "Grund." To the right are the ancient fortifications.

EXHIBIT 8.3 An old railroad bridge. In the background, the old fortifications and the city of Luxembourg.

EXHIBIT 8.4 Luxembourg from above, newer part.

EXHIBIT 8.5 View of parks and boulevards on top of old fortifications. Place de la Constitution and Pont Adolphe bridge.

EXHIBIT 8.15 Image of article in Der Stürmer newspaper, with the following translation:

Die Juden Kahn in Mannheim und ihr Nachfolger

Zwei sonderbare Empfehlungsschreiben

Lieber Stürmer!

Du hast Dich in Deiner Ausgabe 9 dieses Jahres mit jenen deutschen Geschäftsleuten befaßt, die jüdische Firmen übernommen haben. Zum besonderen hast Du darüber Klage geführt, daß sich diese deutschen Geschäftsleute in ihrem Empfehlungsschreiben auf das Vertrauen berufen, das man früher ihren jüdischen Vorgängern entgegenbrachte.

Vor mir liegt eine Werbeschrift der Firma Karl Grimm, vormals J. u. S. Kahn in Mannheim L 14. 14 Sie hat folgenden Wortlaut:

J. u. S. Kahn
Socken, Strümpfe, u. Handschuhe etc.
Trikotagen en gros
Mannheim L 14. 14
Telefon Nr. 23735

Mannheim, den 15. Jan. 1939.

P. P.

Wir beehren uns, Ihnen mitzuteilen, daß unsere Firma unter Ausschluß der Außenstände und Verbindlichkeiten mit dem heutigen Tage auf

Herrn Karl Grimm,
Mannheim L 14 14

übergegangen ist.

Wir danken Ihnen für das uns in so reichem Maße entgegengebrachte Vertrauen und bitten wir Sie, dasselbe auch auf unseren Nachfolger übertragen zu wollen.

Wir begrüßen Sie

mit aller Hochachtung

J. u. S. Kahn.

Karl Grimm
vorm. J. u. S. Kahn
Mannheim L 14. 14
Telefon Nr. 23735

Mannheim, den 15. Jan. 1939.

P. P.

Unter höflicher Bezugnahme auf die nebenstehende Mitteilung, habe ich mit heutigem Tage die Firma

J. u. S. Kahn

übernommen.

Ich werde wie bisher in gleicher Weise die verehrte Kundschaft bedienen und bestrebt sein, mit den günstigsten Angeboten aufzuwarten. Ich bitte, mir Ihr volles Vertrauen schenken zu wollen und werde ich dasselbe in jeder Beziehung zu rechtfertigen wissen.

Mit deutschem Gruß

Karl Grimm

vorm. J. u. S. Kahn.

Zu dieser sonderbaren Werbeschrift stellen wir folgendes fest:

1. Der Jude bittet, das Vertrauen, das man ihm bisher entgegenbrachte, auf seinen Nachfolger übertragen zu wollen. Er bittet also auch jene charakterlosen deutschen Kunden, die bis heute bei ihm gekauft haben, ihre Geschäftsbeziehungen zu seinem nichtjüdischen Nachfolger aufrecht zu erhalten.
2. Der Nachfolger **Karl Grimm** nimmt auf diese Mitteilung des Juden „höflichst" Bezug. Er bringt es sogar fertig, zu versichern, seine Kundschaft in der gleichen Weise zu bedienen, wie dies die beiden Kahns getan haben. Endlich besitzt er sogar die Frechheit, dieses Schreiben mit dem „deutschen Gruß" zu beschließen.

Lieber Stürmer! Du hast in Deiner Ausgabe 9 darüber geschrieben, welch große Erziehungsarbeit innerhalb unserer Geschäftswelt noch zu leisten ist. Wie recht Du damit hattest, das zeigt uns nun auch der „Fall **Kahn-Grimm**". D.

Two Strange Letters of Recommendation

Dear Stürmer: In issue #9 of this year (1939) you covered those instances in which German business people took over Jewish firms. You decried in particular that these business people when writing letters of recommendation (to their customers and those of the prior Jewish business owners) refer to the trust which the previous Jewish owners had earned.

In front of me is the announcement from Karl Grimm Company, formerly J. & S. Kahn at Mannheim L 14. 14. It contained the following text:

J&S Kahn, Wholesale of Socks, Hosiery, Gloves, Underwear, etc. Mannheim L 14. 14 Tel: 237 35 Mannheim, January 15, 1939.

We are honored to inform you that our Co. has ceased to exist and all assets as well as debts have been acquired as of this date by Karl Grimm, Mannheim L 14. 14. We thank you for the trust which you so richly extended to us, and we encourage you to extend the same to our successor We greet you with highest esteem J&S Kahn.

Karl Grimm, formerly J. & S. Kahn, Mannheim, L 14 14 Tel: 237 35 Mannheim, January 15, 1939

We refer respectfully to the information alongside, whereby I am the owner of J.&S. Kahn. I will, as heretofore, serve the esteemed customers, and will strive to present the most favorable offers. I plead with you to grant me your utmost confidence and will reciprocate as best I can.

With German Salute, Karl Grimm, formerly J. & S. Kahn

AUTHOR'S NOTE: Under normal circumstances, both translated letters above would have been most appropriate and not raised any eyebrows. However, that was not the intent of the published article, as can be gleaned from the discussion that followed in the hate monger tabloid, *Der Stürmer* as translated below:

> From this strange announcement, we can draw the following conclusion:
>
> The Jew asks that the confidence shown him in the past be granted his successor. He asks his unprincipled German customers, who until now made purchases from him, to switch their business connections to his non-Jewish successor.
>
> The successor Karl Grimm, refers politely to the letter of the Jew. He even has the shameless insolence to close the letter with the German Salute.
>
> Dear Stürmer! In your issue #9, you wrote about this, how much education is still necessary within our business world. How correct you were is now indicated by the Case Kahn-Grimm. Signed O.

Not only is this article full of antagonism, but it is completely silent on the coercive method by which Dad's business was acquired, or more accurately, confiscated.

EXHIBIT 8.16 *Der Stürmer* headlines

Author's Commentary: To give you a further idea of the hateful and detestable nature of this weekly paper, I have translated some of the headlines from the front page. On top indicates that the Stürmer's purpose was designed "For the Fight of the Truth." Headlines read: **The Oath of the Jew, a Remainder of the Past, The Laws of the Talmud Command Perjury.** Above the photo it reads: **Tearing down the Synagogues.** Under the photo it reads in rhyme: **The Jewish Mind Has No Right To Live In The Authentic German City.** On the bottom of the page: **The Jews Are Our Misfortune.**

EXHIBIT 8.18 Map of Luxembourg showing the different regions of the country.

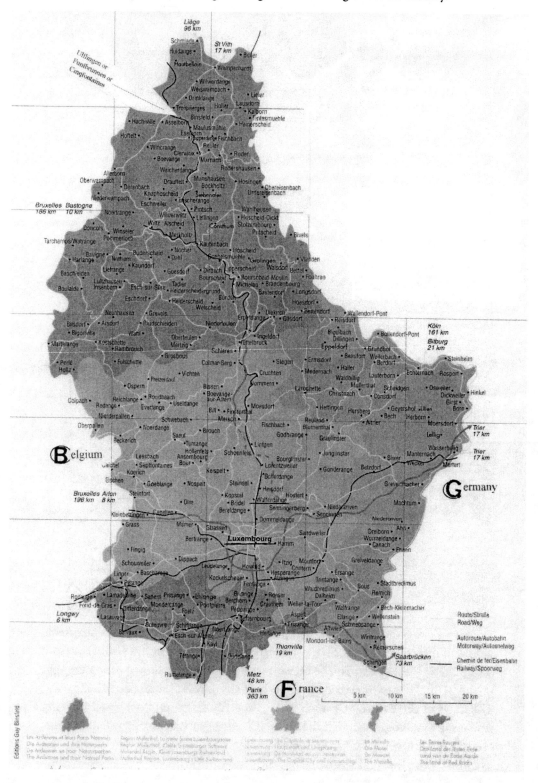

EXHIBIT 8.25 Villa Pauly, Gestapo Headquarters for interrogation and torture. Boulevard de la Petrusse #57

EXHIBIT 8.26 Letter from Feidert with the following translation:

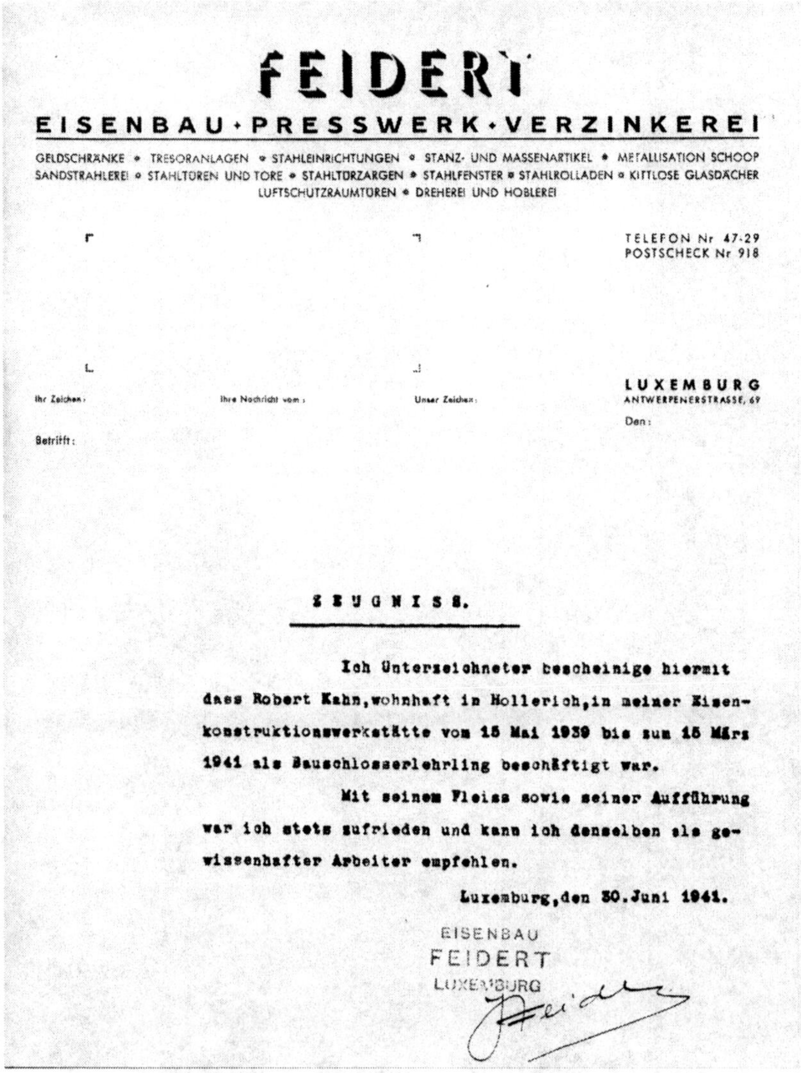

FEIDERT

EISENBAU • PRESSWERK • VERZINKEREI

GELDSCHRÄNKE • TRESORANLAGEN • STAHLEINRICHTUNGEN • STANZ- UND MASSENARTIKEL • METALLISATION SCHOOP
SANDSTRAHLEREI • STAHLTÜREN UND TORE • STAHLTÜRZARGEN • STAHLFENSTER • STAHLROLLADEN • KITTLOSE GLASDÄCHER
LUFTSCHUTZRAUMTÜREN • DREHEREI UND HOBLEREI

TELEFON Nr 47-29
POSTSCHECK Nr 918

Ihr Zeichen: Ihre Nachricht vom: Unser Zeichen:

LUXEMBURG
ANTWERPENERSTRASSE, 69
Den:

Betrifft:

ZEUGNISS.

Ich Unterzeichneter bescheinige hiermit dass Robert Kahn, wohnhaft in Hollerich, in meiner Eisenkonstruktionswerkstätte vom 15 Mai 1939 bis zum 15 März 1941 als Bauschlosserlehrling beschäftigt war.

Mit seinem Fleiss sowie seiner Aufführung war ich stets zufrieden und kann ich denselben als gewissenhafter Arbeiter empfehlen.

Luxemburg, den 30. Juni 1941.

EISENBAU
FEIDERT
LUXEMBURG

Letter of employment separation by Metal Manufacturer Feidert

The undersigned certifies that Robert Kahn residing in Hollerich was employed in my metal construction plant from May 15, 1939 to March 15, 1941 in the capacity of apprentice.

I was always pleased with his diligence and am able to recommend him as a conscientious worker.

Luxembourg June 30, 1941
Metal Construction
Feidert
Luxembourg
Signature

SUPPORTING PHOTOS AND DOCUMENTS

CHAPTER NINE

EXHIBIT 9.2 Translation of the forged safe conduct and travel pass.

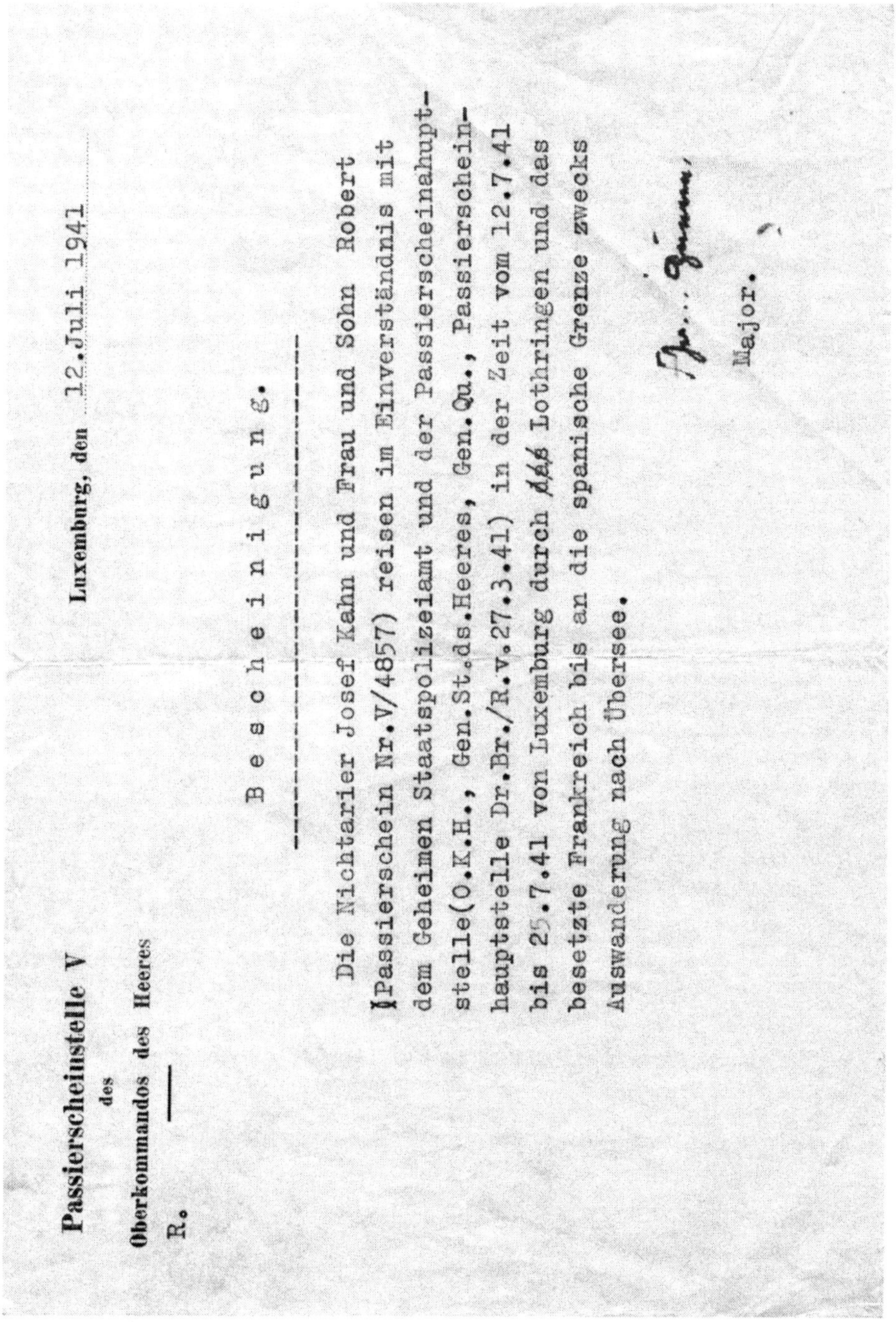

Passierscheinstelle V
des
Oberkommandos des Heeres
R.

Luxemburg, den 12. Juli 1941

B e s c h e i n i g u n g.

Die Nichtarier Josef Kahn und Frau und Sohn Robert (Passierschein Nr.V/4857) reisen im Einverständnis mit dem Geheimen Staatspolizeiamt und der Passierscheinhauptstelle(O.K.H., Gen.St.ds.Heeres, Gen.Qu., Passierscheinhauptstelle Dr.Br./R.v.27.3.41) in der Zeit vom 12.7.41 bis 25.7.41 von Luxemburg durch das Lothringen und das besetzte Frankreich bis an die spanische Grenze zwecks Auswanderung nach Übersee.

Major.

Travel pass Authority of the High Command of the Army

Luxembourg July 12, 1941

Certificate

The non-Arian Josef Kahn and wife and son Robert (travel-pass No. V/4857) travel with the permission of the Secret Police (GESTAPO) and the Main Travel Pass Authority (High Command of the Army, General Staff of the Army, General Quarters, Main Travel pass Authority Dr. Br./ R.v. 3.27.41) during the period of 12.July.41 until 25.July.41 from Luxembourg through Alsace Lorrain and occupied France to the Spanish border for the purpose of emigrating to overseas.

Signed,

Major (not legible)

CHAPTER TEN

EXHIBIT 10.8 The following examples (exhibits 10.8-10.14) depict the bureaucracy my father faced while trying to save our remaining relatives in Europe.

EXHIBIT 10.9

National Refugee Service, Inc.
139 Centre Street, New York

April 10, 1942

Mrs. Marion E. Schaar
Director, Chicago Section
National Council of Jewish Women
130 North Wells Street
Chicago, Illinois

Re: JOSEPH, Bernard-Martha-George
39 rue Verdi,
Dear Mrs. Schaar: Nice, France - case #A31,962

We received your letter correcting the information given us on the above named family's transportation problem. We have so informed the Joint Distribution Committee.

We feel that Mr. Kahn should know that the State Department is not likely to take any action in approving visas unless they can be assured that the family will be able to make use of visas. If Mr. Kahn deposits money with the Hias, his money is quite safe and would be returned to him in the event that the family could not complete their immigration. The decision, of course, must rest with him. We have had no word from the State Department as yet.

This case will probably have to go before the Interdepartmental Visa Review Committee. At such time Mr. Kahn would have an opportunity to either appear personally or to send a letter and in either event, he would have to meet the question of transportation. We feel that it would not be sufficiently assuring to the Interdepartmental Visa Review Committee if he merely stated that he might make the money available when the State Department has approved the documents. The action should be the other way around.

We will keep in touch with you.

Sincerely yours,

signed: Clara V. Friedman
Migration Department
Augusta Mayerson, Director.

EXHIBIT 10.10

NATIONAL COUNCIL of JEWISH WOMEN
CHICAGO SECTION
DEPARTMENT of SERVICE to the FOREIGN BORN

Franklin 9555
130 NORTH WELLS STREET

MRS. MARION E. SCHAAR
Executive Director

April 14, 1942

In reply refer to: JOSEPH, Bernhard-Martha-George
Nice, France

Mr. Ernst Kahn
20 East Kinzie Street
Chicago, Illinois

Dear Mr. Kahn:

In accordance with your request in our telephone conversation today, please find enclosed a copy of the letter we discussed.

Should you desire further information or advice, please do not hesitate to call upon us.

Sincerely yours,

Marion E. Schaar
Director, Chicago Section
Service to the Foreign Born

President
MRS. BENJAMIN I. MORRIS

First Vice-President
MISS EVLLYN SILVERSTINE

Second Vice-President
MRS. FRED BERNSTEIN

Third Vice-President
MRS. WILLIAM H. SAHUD

Treasurer
MRS. SAMUEL L. HERMAN

Recording Secretary
MRS. ISADORE PILOT

Corresponding Secretary
MRS. BENJAMIN BRAUDE
566 North Pine Avenue

Financial Secretary
MRS. MYRON I. INGRAM

Honorary President
MRS. HANNAH G. SOLOMON

Honorary Vice-Presidents
MRS. MARTIN BARBE
MRS. H. I. DAVIS
MRS. EMANUEL MANDEL

Council Camp
VERA TEPLITZ
Director

EXHIBIT 10.11

EXECUTIVE DIVISION **United States Post Office**
CHICAGO, ILLINOIS

Passport Section
OO:H

April 23, 1942

Re: #223

Mr. Joseph Kahn,
6728 Clyde Avenue,
Chicago, Illinois

Dear Sir:

You are requested to call at your earliest convenience at room 419, Main Post Office, Canal and Van Buren Streets, concerning a matter in which the Department of State, Washington, D. C., desires information. Please inquire for Mr. Orth.

Kindly be advised this office is closed on Saturdays.

Respectfully yours,

Ernest J. Kruetgen
Postmaster

EXHIBIT 10.12

Visa Form IVRC-3

DEPARTMENT OF STATE
WASHINGTON

In reply refer to
VD 811.111 Joseph, Bernhard (Nice)

May 8, 1942

Mr. Ernst Kahn,
   6819 Merrill Avenue,
      Chicago, Illinois.

Sir:

    With reference to your interest in the visa case of Bernhard Joseph and his family, there is enclosed for your information a copy of a letter which has been sent to the appropriate interested person explaining the procedure necessary to have the case considered by the Interdepartmental Visa Review Committee.

    Very truly yours,

A. M. Warren
Chief, Visa Division

EXHIBIT 10.13

ADDRESS OFFICIAL COMMUNICATIONS TO
THE SECRETARY OF STATE
WASHINGTON, D. C.

Visa Form IVRC 2

DEPARTMENT OF STATE
WASHINGTON

May 8, 1942

In reply refer to
VD 811.111 Joseph, Bernhard (Nice)

Mr. Joseph Kahn,
   6728 Clyde Avenue,
     Chicago, Illinois.

Sir:

    I refer to your interest in the visa case of Bernhard Joseph and his family.

    A preliminary examination of this case, with particular reference to sections 58.47 and 58.48 of the regulations covering the control of persons entering the United States (pages 26-27, Department of State Publication 1709, for sale by the Superintendent of Documents, Government Printing Office, Washington, D.C., price 10 cents), that were issued under the President's proclamation of November 14, 1941 has not resulted in a favorable recommendation to the American consular officer concerned.

    However, the case will be given further consideration by the Interdepartmental Visa Review Committee at Washington, as provided in section 58.57(c) of the aforementioned regulations. This provision gives an opportunity to interested individuals to appear in person, or through an attorney or other intermediary, before the Committee to make such additional statements as may be deemed appropriate.

    There are enclosed two copies of an Application for Appearance which should be completed and forwarded to the Department by the person particularly interested

    in

EXHIBIT 10.13

-2-

in appearing in the case at a hearing before the Committee. If it is desired that other interested persons or their intermediaries appear at the hearing, additional forms of Application for Appearance will be furnished upon receipt in the Department of a request stating the names of the persons who desire to appear, and the names of the alien visa applicants.

If, on the other hand, it is desired that the case be considered by the Committee without a hearing, it is requested that the Department be so advised.

Upon receipt of an Application for Appearance or a communication indicating that it is desired to have the case considered without a hearing, together with reasonable evidence that the persons seeking admission into the United States have made arrangements to travel to this country, the case will be entered for action by the Committee. Notice will be sent to the interested persons sufficiently in advance of the date set for hearing in order that they may make any arrangements necessary.

Very truly yours,

A. M. Warren
Chief, Visa Division

Enclosures:

Two Applications
for Appearance.

EXHIBIT 10.14

NATIONAL COUNCIL of JEWISH WOMEN
CHICAGO SECTION
DEPARTMENT of SERVICE to the FOREIGN BORN
Franklin 9555
130 NORTH WELLS STREET

MRS. MARION E. SCHAAR
Executive Director

November 10, 1942

Re: JOSEPH, Bernard and family
France

Mr. Ernst Kahn
6819 Merrill Avenue
Chicago, Illinois

Dear Mr. Kahn:

We are returning your money order for $3.00 made out to the Hebrew Immigrant Aid Society. This money order was returned to us by that agency as they cannot accept cable expenses unless a deposit for transportation is made. They write, "Our arrangements with the Cable and Radio Censor do not permit us to advise our office (abroad) of the issuance of the advisory approval unless funds for transportation are deposited with us."

In view of the recent developments in the war area we suggest that you wait a short time and then contact us for information on future possibilities to assist your relatives.

Sincerely yours,

Marion E. Schaar
Director, Chicago Section
Service to the Foreign Born

Reply attention:
I.N.Asheries
Enc.

EXHIBIT 10.17 Recommendation for letting me stay on defense work despite being an "Enemy Alien," written by Fred Gilson.

Consulat Général de Luxembourg

Chicago, Illinois
109 North Dearborn Street

January 21, 1943

Mr. Smily, Personell Mgr.
Ajax Engineering Co.
2451 S. La Salle St.
Chicago, Ill.

Dear Mr. Smily:—

    With reference to Mr. Robert Bernard Kahn, 2109 E. 65th St. wish to inform you that I have known him for approximately one year and I can vouch, that he is a fine young man, energetically and industrious. He has been in this country for one and one half year, arriving in New York in August 1941. Shortly thereafter he came to Chicago and has lived here ever since.

    His mother, who was born in the Grand Duchy of Luxembourg and whose family I have known over there, enjoyed the respect and the esteem of the Luxembourg people, who have known her. Robert B. Kahn lived for several years in Luxembourg with his parents previous to his entree in the United States of America.

    During the time Robert has lived in this country, I have had frequent contacts with him and his family and I can truthfully say, that he has the interest of his adopted country, the United States at heart and will do all he can to further the interest of this country.

    I am of the firm opinion, that if given an opportunity he will demonstrate his love for his adopted country and work hard to assist in producing the material needed during the present crisis and to further the cause it is fighting for at this time.

    I will be glad to give any further information desired in order to give service to him as well as your firm and our country, the United States of America.

Sincerely yours,

Fred A. Gilson
Chancellor

EXHIBIT 10.18 Letter of recommendation for citizenship from David Cohen, the father of a friend of mine.

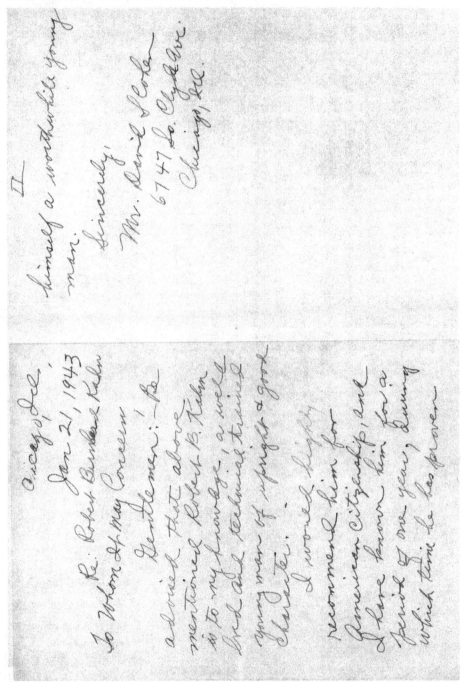

EXHIBIT 10.21 My notice of classification as 1a. Of course I did not appeal, as I was ready to go fight the Nazis.

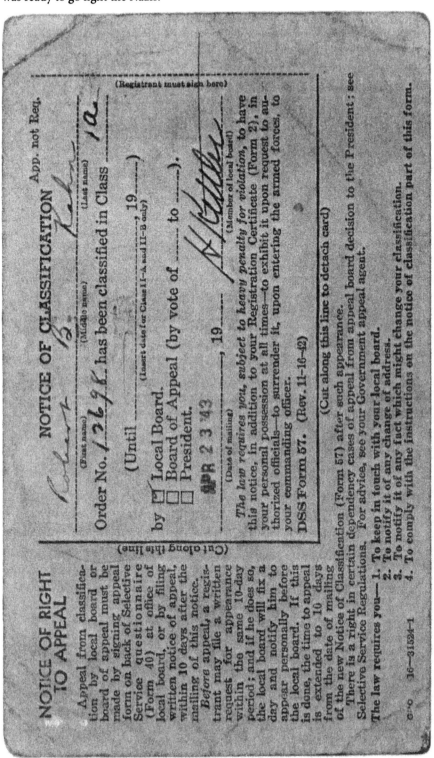

EXHIBIT 10.22 Letter from Ajax Engineering Company indicating the reason why I was let go.

AJAX ENGINEERING COMPANY
2451 S LA SALLE STREET
CALUMET 1740
CHICAGO

January 9, 1943

To Whom it May Concern:

This is to certify that Robert Kahn has been in our employ from March 20, 1942, to this date, as a Turret Lathe operator and Precision Bench Lathe hand. During this time he has shown himself to be a very competent operator of the above named machines.

He is being released only because the Government has denied approval for him to be employed on Classified Defense contracts.

Yours very truly,
AJAX ENGINEERING COMPANY

[signature]
Personnel Director

EXHIBIT 10.24 Documentation explaining the systems I would design.

IN THE AIR! ON LAND AND WATER!
ARENS CONTROLS GIVE DEPENDABLE SMOOTH TROUBLE-FREE SERVICE

It is a significant fact that ARENS CONTROLS are not only giving unusual satisfaction on the many installations but are establishing new records for trouble-free service and efficient operation.

In addition to these operating factors there is an initial cost saving due to the elimination of costly replacements.

ARENS CONTROLS combine advance principles of design with many mechanical advantages. These merits are reflected by an ever increasing number of repeat orders.

ARENS CONTROLS have been used on aeronautical installations since 1920. They have been used on many notable flights.

Dashboard of a Howard custom-built airplane. ARENS CONTROLS were used exclusively for operating the parking brake, fire extinguishers, cabin air and cabin heat, carburetor air and oil air; also for the throttle, mixture, propeller, ventilator, and wobble pump.

ARENS CONTROLS give unusual satisfactory service for operating the starter, choke, spark and throttle on every type of motor boat.

ARENS CONTROLS operate the choke and throttle on coaches of America's leading bus lines.

PAGE THREE

There can be no better testimonial to the dependability of ARENS CONTROLS than their repeated selection by well known builders for well known products

ARENS ROTATING PUSH-PULL CONTROLS in use on condensers in a broadcasting unit.

ARENS CONTROLS have been used on propellor pitch, throttle mixture, carburetor air and heat, oil radiator, ventilator and various other applications.

PAGE FOUR

CHAPTER ELEVEN

EXHIBIT 11.1 My dog tag with number 36691224 for identification. The little cut out on the left was to clean our fingernails. My blood type was O and my religion was J for Jewish. As I found out later, when a soldier died or was killed, one of the dog tags was sent to the next of kin, and the other remained on the soldier for burial.

EXHIBIT 11.20 Certificate of having crossed the Equator. Having been duly initiatied and transformed from a Pollywog into a Shellback by order of King Neptune.

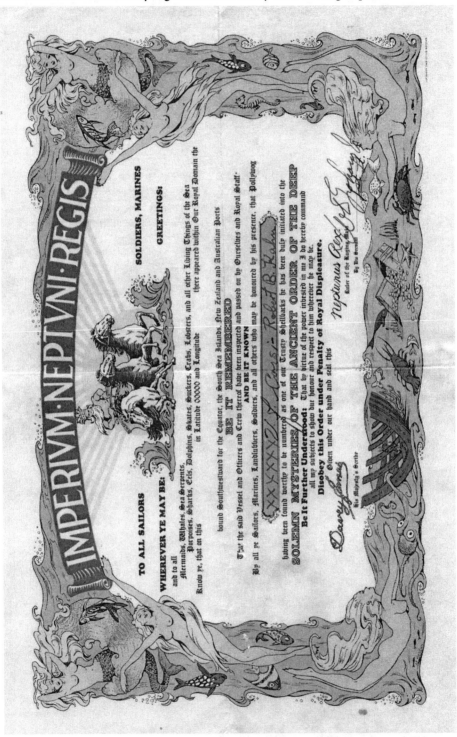

EXHIBIT 11.21 Jap Hunting License.

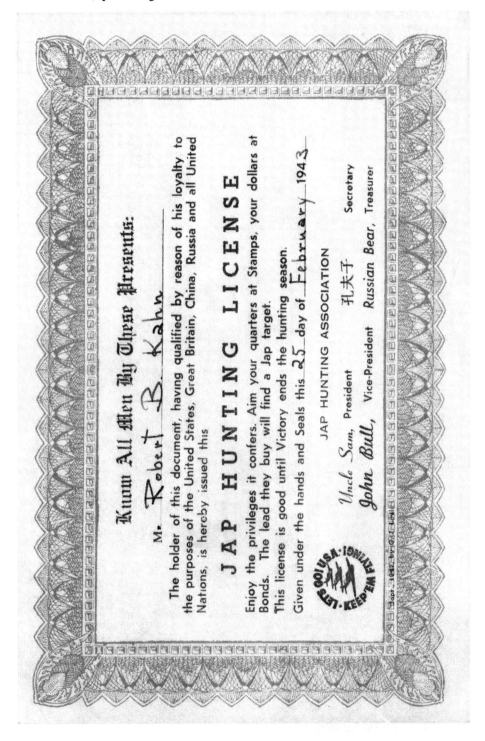

CHAPTER TWELVE

EXHIBIT 12.12 Most of them did not know what a camera was.

EXHIBIT 12.13 More New Guinea beauties.

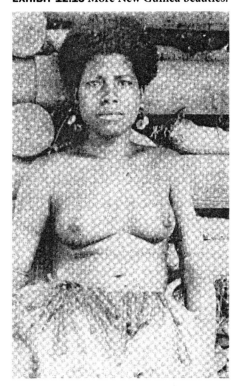

EXHIBIT 12.14 Doing laundry on top of a tree stump. Note a shower facility in the background.

EXHIBIT 12.15 We had the natives build us a primitive shower and pour the water over us.

EXHIBIT 12.16 We carried water to wash ourselves and to do laundry.

EXHIBIT 12.17 Sometimes I just looked into the distance.

EXHIBIT 12.18 Newspaper clipping regarding spoilage of film in *Yank Magazine*

SHUTTERBUG GIs in Guinea who get back a few designs on their pictures they didn't see in the view finder can blame New Guinea and the "wet." Some films sent for processing to the mainland bases of the Army's Photo Service are entirely ruined and as much as 30 percent of the stuff taken in the islands is "affected" by the excessive moisture.

That's a lot of ruined and damaged film. Army and commercial photogs alike say the thing to do is to get the film protected against moisture infiltration as soon as it arrives and keep it that way. Best suggestion, which some guys are now doing, is using those rubber devices from the pro kits. They'll handle a roll of film nicely and Army Exchange says it's OK by them. Besides, there's nothing much else can be done with them in Guinea. . . . —YANK's GHQ Bureau

EXHIBIT 12.19 After patiently explaining what we wanted them to do, they were a great help. We treated them well and gave them clothes to cover themselves up and paid them with a few cigarettes per day.

EXHIBIT 12.20 Japanese soliders carried specially printed money for use in the eastern part of New Guinea, which was the Australian Protectorate. Little could they buy with it here. Had they invaded Australia, it would have been a different story. Perhaps the bills were printed with this in mind.

EXHIBIT 12.21 Photos from dead Japanese soldiers. Although we were required to turn everything in for intelligence investigation, these were easy to hide.

EXHIBIT 12.22 Insignia ripped off a dead soldier's uniform.

EXHIBIT 12.23 AND 12.24 The stockade where the few Japanese prisoners were kept; The prisoners didn't trust our chow and cooked for themselves.

EXHIBIT 12.25 Occasionally enemy aircraft crashed nearby trying to make emergency landings on the beaches.

EXHIBIT 12.26 Standing in Kunai grass which can grow man high and was used by the natives to thatch their huts.

EXHIBIT 12.27 Deeper in the Jungle I came across this tatooed aborigine woman.

EXHIBIT 12.28 All native huts were built on stilts to cope with the heavy rains and floods.

EXHIBIT 12.32 Everything that could be salvaged was put to good use again.

EXHIBIT 12.33 The salvage or graveyard.

EXHIBIT 12.34 What was known as "the Mess" really was a mess!

CHAPTER THIRTEEN

EXHIBIT 13.2 The letter from America Soldier, Karl Loewenstein, with news to Chicago that my sister Irene is alive.

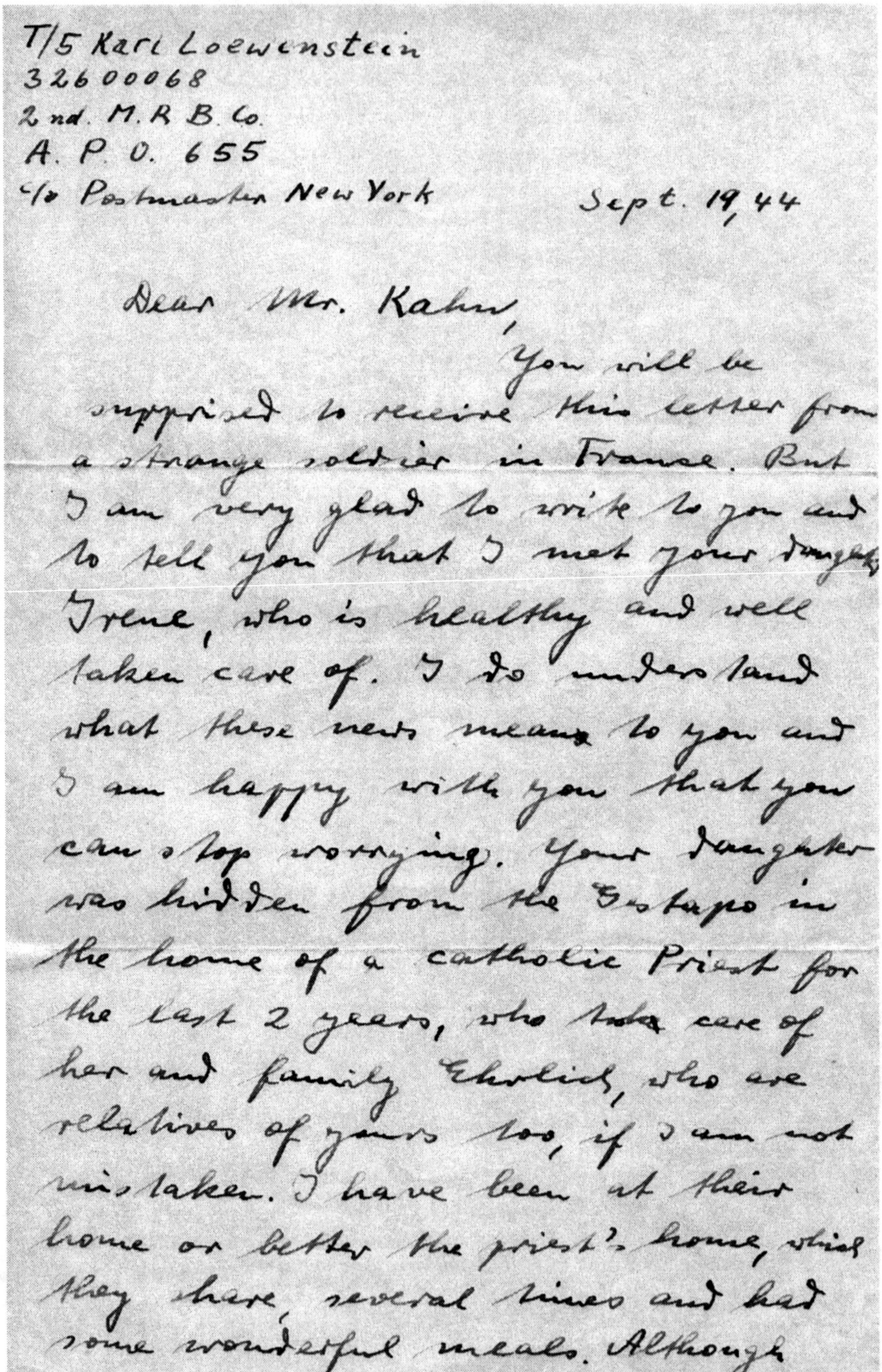

> T/5 Karl Loewenstein
> 32600068
> 2nd. M.R.B. Co.
> A.P.O. 655
> c/o Postmaster New York
>
> Sept. 19, 44
>
> Dear Mr. Kahn,
>
> You will be surprised to receive this letter from a strange soldier in France. But I am very glad to write to you and to tell you that I met your daughter Irene, who is healthy and well taken care of. I do understand what these news means to you and I am happy with you that you can stop worrying. Your daughter was hidden from the Gestapo in the home of a catholic Priest for the last 2 years, who takes care of her and family Ehrlich, who are relatives of yours too, if I am not mistaken. I have been at their home or better the priest's home, which they share, several times and had some wonderful meals. Although

everything is rationed in France, your daughter undertook to make some delicious meals, European dishes I had not eaten for years. I went on Rosh Hashonoh to the religious service and was amazed to find about 75 Jewish men, women and children, all of them had hidden somewhere. I heard a lot of terrible stories and I do not want to repeat them. You as well as I have had similar experiences in Germany. For the time being it is impossible for your daughter to write, as the postal service is operating for the army only. Your daughter's address is Miss Irene Kahn, 12 Rue de la Bassée, Lille (Nord France). I wish I could write a million similar letters, especially when we get to Germany. I shall see your daughter and family again to-night and maybe I can insert a foto.

Respectfully
Karl Loewenstein
4580 Broadway
New York.

EXHIBIT 13.3 Letter from Army Chaplain, Major Sandhaus.

13 Feb. 1945

Dear Mr. and Mrs. Kahn,

Your letter of the first arrived this morning and I immediatelt took it to Irene. She wasn't home, having gone to the university, so I left it with Mrs. Ehrlich. She read it as I wanted to know what to reply. The 100 dollars arrived and for the matter of sending packages, well you should have sent them directly to me. In fact I delieverd a package yesterday to one party. You write that you would like to have a Soldtat, I can be your soldat and anyhting you wish to send Irene or the Ehrlichs just buck it thorugh to me and you me assued that they will get it the same day if not the same hour that it arrives.

For me, besides doing the army work, it is a great source of satisfaction if I can help our people. Lord knows they suffered enouwh for four years and any littke thing I can do, and that goes for all our Chaplains on the continent, I consider a privilege. So don't hesitate to ask anyhting you want me to do and don't feel that you are imposing on me. I consider that as much of my army work as being in the field with the soldiers.

I don't know you at all and I don't know your circumstances. But I need help too. If you can give my address to men and women who can send me food, soap, childrens clothing I shall be grateful. I seek help all over and much has already come but the need is very great. I have undertaken to care ofr an orphan home in Brussels of fity children wgose parents are deported or dead. I do not expect you to do this but possibly throug buisnesx associations or contacts you may be able to do something. Every little bit counts. Best wishes and keep writng me. I shall keep delivering the letters as fast as they come.

Sincerely,
Morris. A. Sandhaus
Chaplain (Major) U.S. Army

JEWISH **W**ELFARE **B**OARD
Army and Navy Service Department

EXHIBIT 13.4 Letter from Irene to my parents, forwarded to me. Transcript follows.

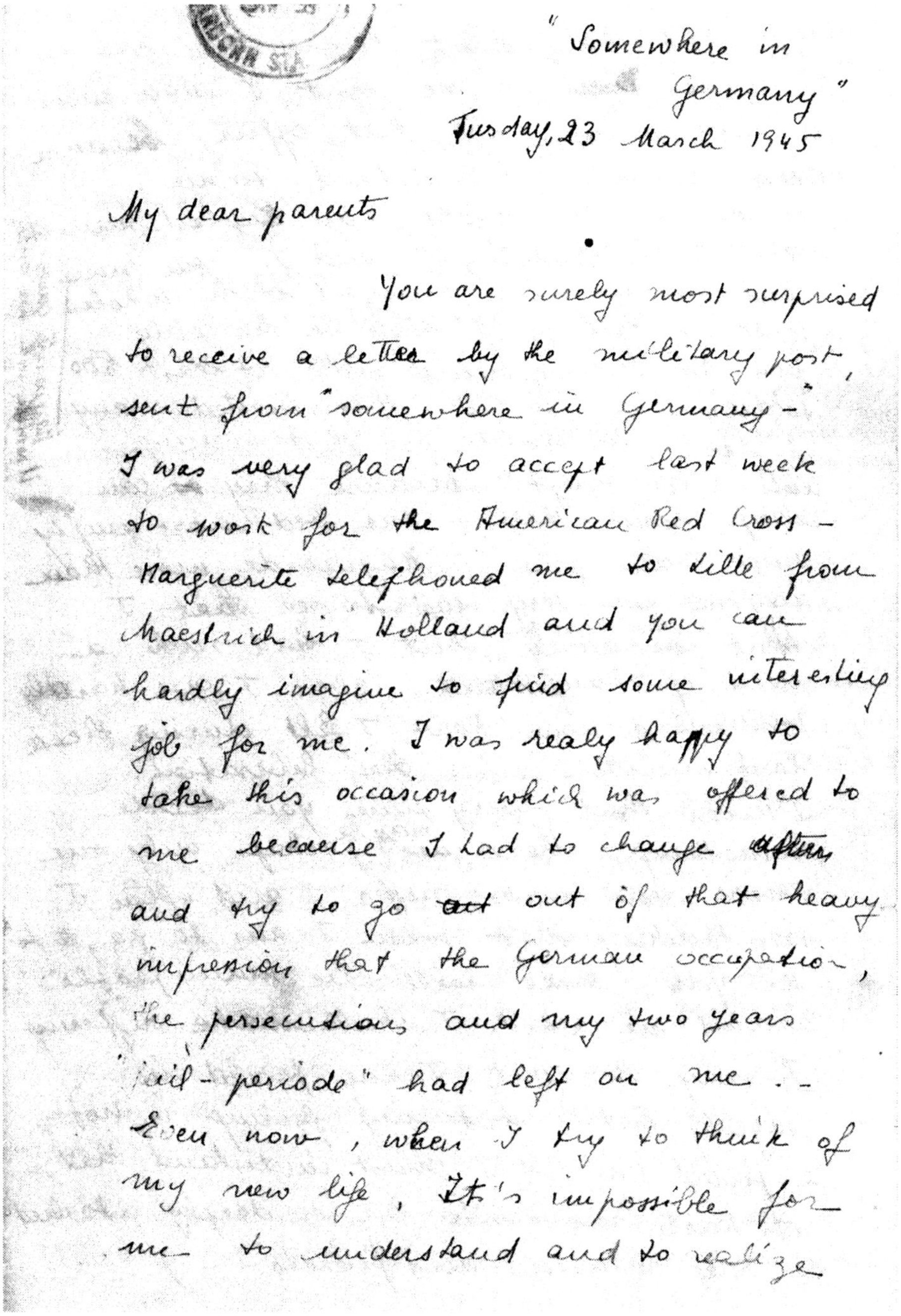

"Somewhere in Germany"
Tuesday, 23 March 1945

My dear parents

You are surely most surprised to receive a letter by the military post, sent from "somewhere in Germany". I was very glad to accept last week to work for the American Red Cross — Marguerite telephoned me to Lille from Maestrich in Holland and you can hardly imagine to find some interesting job for me. I was realy happy to take this occasion which was offered to me because I had to change after and try to go out of that heavy impression that the German occupation, the persecutions and my two years "jail-period" had left on me. — Even now, when I try to think of my new life, It's impossible for me to understand and to realize

how that change happened to me.
It seemes even to me that I stay since a long time with that office; because everbody is so kind to me.
We are 3 girls together: an English "married-girl", a Dutch girl and I. Am sure that I am the youngest in the whole sector. — Perhaps I shall be the only girl at Seder evening with at least 500 soldiers. — In Lille they invited many soldiers for that evening and even night because they can sleep now there — one bed more empty since I am gone... Raymonde more than anyone was very sad to see that I went far away, but I had such a need of change... even I can hardly understand now how I felt during these last month — since the liberation.
I know that every time you decide something, there may be perhaps only one person you make suffer, and often I was thinking that when I am to go to see you, there will be many people around me which I shall make suffering (It may be that I am proud in saying that — but my feeling is not a proud one, you must understand that, its hurts me too, to be so deeply attached to my relations and friends ---)

Tanta Irma said nothing when she saw me go away in Kaki uniforme - with two French soldiers who came to take me at home! She never tried to hinder me in my decision, but I felt during the whole time, that she struggled with herself; she said every time: I have a great daughter - and realy we understand so well. All that hard time during war brought us more nearer each other - And with Raymonde it is quite different; Her life and M. l'Abbé Vancourt's was exposed during the two years they had me in their house - and our understanding is more intellectual than the one existing between Marguerite and me. I met her for 2 days in Holland and she didn't change at all, and thinks the same of me. She has been decorated last month somewhere in Germany and all the military local newspapers spook about it. Now she is Lieutenant of the French Army and not far from us "some where in Germany". - Next I will try to meet her and if possible to go to see the country around where we are now.

Sunday evening. - Just I am back from a trip, and I saw Marguerite, and it's possible that she comes some evening to stay the night with me. We had only the time to see us, but not enough time to speak about all our common interests. —

— I should write you more often, but since we are here, "somewhere 30 miles behind de lines", we had much to do in the house and until now, we had every evening some military visitors, had parties and fun, as they call that evenings. — This is the first evening I am sitting quite and have a little very pleasant rest. My bed is very good, in a nice, clear room, with windows, what in our place is a luxe. In every room are flowers, and since yesterday we have electric light, before we moved with candle light through the house —

Write to Robert what I do now, I know that he is interested in my plays and doing. Answer me quickly — Here is my adres:

Miss Irene Kahn
Office of Field Director
American Red Cross
Headquarters Ninth U.S. Army, Fwd.
A.P.O. 339. U.S. Army % P.M.

With love and kisses
Give me Robert's I am your
adres. — In meantime I will write him to the last adres you sent to me. I would be very glad to get some parcel from you.

"Somewhere in Germany"

Tuesday, 23 March 1945

My dear parents,

You are surely most surprised to receive a letter by the military post sent from "somewhere in Germany"- I was very glad to accept last week to work for the American Red Cross—Marguerite telephoned me to Lille from (????) in Holland and you can hardly imagine to find some interesting job for me. I was really happy to take this occasion which was offered to me because I had to change and try to go out of that heavy impression that the German occupation—the persecutions and my two years "xxx-period" had left on me. Even know, when I try to think of my new life, it's impossible for me to understand and realize how that change happened to me. It seems even to me that I (slay juice) a long time with that office because everybody is so kind to me. We are 3 girls together: an English "married girl," a Dutch girl and I. * All xxx that I am the youngest in the whole sector—Perhaps I shall be the only girl at Seder evening with at least 500 soldiers. In Lille they invited many soldiers for that evening and even night because they can sleep now there—one bed more empty since I am gone....Raymonde more than anyone was very sad to see that I went far away but I had such a need for change...even I can hardly understand now how I felt during these last months since the liberation. I know that every time you decide something, there may be perhaps only one person you make suffer, and often I was thinking that when I to go to see you, there will be many people around me which I shall make suffering (It may be that I am proud in saying that—but my feeling is not a proud one, you must understand that, it hurts me too, to be so deeply attached to my relatives and friends--) Tante Irma said nothing when she saw me go away in kaki uniform- with two French soldiers who came to take me at home! She never tried to hinder me in my decision, but I felt during the whole time that she struggled with herself; she said everytime: I have a great daughter—and really we understand so well. All that hard time during war brought us more nearer each other—And with Raymonde it is quite different. Her life and Mr. l'Abbé Vancourt's was exposed to during the two years they had me in their house—and our understanding is more intellectual than the one existing between Marguerite and me. I met her for 2 days in Holland she didn't change at all, and thinks the same of me. She has be de?ted last month somewhere in

Germany and all the military local newspapers spook (sic) about it. Now she is Lieutenant of the French Army and not far from us "somewhere in Germany"—Next I will try to meet her and if possible to go see the country around where we are now.

Sunday evening—Just I am back from a trip and I saw Marguerite, and it's possible that she comes some evening to stay the night with me. We had only the time to see us, but not enough time to speak about all our common interest—I should write you more often, but since we are here "somewhere 30 miles behind the lines," we had much to do in the house and until now, we had every evening some military visitors, had parties, and fun, as they call that evenings—This is the first evening I am sitting quite [sic] and have a little very pleasant rest. My bed is very good, in a nice, clean room, with windows, what in our place is a luxe. Our every room are flowers, and since yesterday we have electric light, before we moved with candle light through the house—

Write to Robert what I do now, I know that he is interested in my plans and doings. Answer me quickly—here is my address [sic]:

Xxx Irene Kahn

Office of Field Director

American Red Cross

Headquarters Ninth U.S. Army Fwd.

A.P.P 339 U.S. Army

with love and kisses,

I am yours,

Irene

I thank you the most I can by letter, words for all those you have sent to Lille. Give me Roberts' adress: In the meantime I will write him to the last address you sent to me. I would be very glad to get some parcel from you.

* Marguerite comes if possible with her sisters*

EXHIBIT 13.5 Letter from my sister Irene.

THE AMERICAN RED CROSS

Somewhere in Germany,
21st April 1945

My dearest darling brother,

You cannot imagine how glad I was yesterday. I received the first letter from our parents here in Germany and it took only 10 days to go from Chcago to "where I am". They had not heard from you for a few days, but where not worried, because you advised them, that for a little time they shall not hear from you. I hope that everything is by the best and that you are in the best of health. Hope also that your life is not to hard, because I know that it musst be sometimes very difficult to live and especially to fight in so a unhealthy climat. Oh, how happy I would have been to see you come over to Europ, but now is nearly finished here, and I will go then to Chicago.o

    I am still working for the American Red Cross in the Office of the Field Director and am most interested in my job. We are three girls in that Office and occupied with correspondence, reports and other office busieness. As I told you perhaps in my first letter to you from Germyny one of the girls is Dutch and the other one is English. The French-Girl (that's myself) starts to get along much easier with the American language; it¢s quite different from the English, and everybody tells me that I have a real English accent when I speak English, but for myself I belief that it is more a French accent ; very often they laugh at me, not in a bad way, but make fun with the wrong sentences I built up when it is difficult for me to explain what I want to say (just as now). But on the other hand , I feel that I make progress and the only trouble is the unusual prononciation of some countries of the States, all the words seem to come out of their stomac or as if they have hot popatoes in their mouth. Often I must keep from laughing... I would like to hear you, dear Robert.
    I receive a few letters now from Lille; they seem very dad since I left them, but xxx anyway I cannot stay my whole life long next them, and if not now then later, I would go away from them. But also zhey are glad if I could find an occupation that interests me, because the last time in Lille I felt very disapointed of everything,and I felt that I had to change: change of country, occupation, people around me. I am trying and hope it will help. I understand myself quite well- when you stay so long in one house, with the same persons, even when they are your best freind, you need change of horizon. In the beginning I had many difficulties to get used to this life, we have now: Good food, strong

and

and plenty, different meal times and in Lille I was used to serve everybody, stand up, sat down again and never was siiting at table during a whole meal, and now you sit down and eat quitly everything you want as much you want and even have the possibility to waist food if you like. The first time, that made me very angry to see things spoiled and waisted here, and to think that not so far from here in Belgium, Holland and France they have nothing to eat!!!. But afterwards I said: when you start killing peopke, why should you you care about butter and bread!!!.

The children in Lille are very godd pupils. Claude is 16teen and is a very intelligent and industrious(I don't know if thj this is the right expression but I mean "eifrig"7 if you have not forgotten the language of the Deutschen Reichs).Eliane is also clever, but she likes still to play, she is now 13teen qbut asks question like a girl of 15teen sometimes. The German occupation mkes all the children older, because they heard of all the awfull things the German did during these years and how the treated the prisonners of any kind. Then they were themself near to be taken away and often afraid of alarms and bombardeemnts. We had the biggest one, last year in the night from Easter sonday to Monday. It was a marvelous moonlight night and the bombs fall during 50 minutes, about 2 miles from our house was the target, the nearest bombs fall 200 meters away from us. With the priest, my friend Raymonde and the rest of the family we went near the walls to the hospital neighbouring our house and laoded all the sick people on strechers and took them to the shelter. A part of this hospital ewas at that time occupaed by German dipensery and all the soldiers were sitting in the shelter, and we(the priest, the nurses and we two girls) did all this business alone accompanied by a terrible noise , without any light because it was the first of the bif RAF bombardements and we were not prepared to such a nught interruption. Since that day, I for myself feel very nervous, but much rest and change of everything would help to settle the situation.

We were in Munchen-Gladbach and now we are moved over the Rhin a on moving with the advancing armye . I hope to go quikly to . But even here in our country it is most interesting to look all through the destructed towns. But you must see every day the same pictures and you would surely l like to see a nice town, with straight walls, klean streets and roofs on the top of the houses. We came through a few towns here of which you only recognize the place where it was before but nothing left but rubbish and ruined dusty walls. Never they can built those towns and Germany will be the most modern country of the world with the most modern experiences of human living people, such as dissection, hanging, electrocuting and so on. Never the American Civilian couls belief how German treated the prisonners;...

I hope to hear soon from you, and that there will be no need to send a request for a health and welfare report on Pvt R.Kahn to the Commanding officer of your Bn!!!!..

I send you my best French kisses for both cheekes and wish you good luck and "baldiges Wiedersehn".

Your sister

Trem

EXHIBIT 13.9 Our ship and 200 GIs with full gear.

EXHIBIT 13.10 Other ships in our convoy.

EXHIBIT 13.11 Ships as far as the eye could see.

EXHIBIT 13.12 Our convoy is well protected.

EXHIBIT 13.13 After experiencing the destructive typhoon, we erected our tents on a not too distant hill to avoid flooding.

EXHIBIT 13.14 Farming with water buffalos.

EXHIBIT 13.15 Fishing boats in nearby harbor.

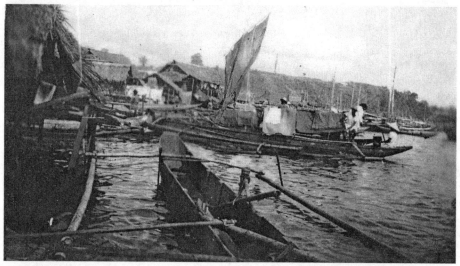

EXHIBIT 13.16 Japanese invasion money for Philippines.

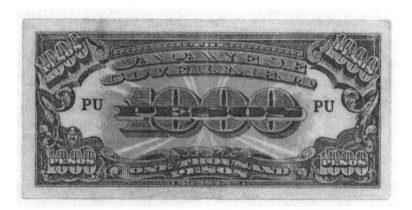

EXHIBIT 13.17 Photos from the metal box. Japanese soldiers with Samurai swords. Every soldier was issued a Samurai sword to commit suicide instead of being captured.

EXHIBIT 13.18 Also from the metal box, Japanese postcards depicting war sceneries.

EXHIBIT 13.19 More Japanese postcards in color from the found box. There were many more.

EXHIBIT 13.30 A red on white Japanese silk war flag in my possession, taken from a dead Japanese soldier. This flag was prohibited to be used after the peace treaty was signed following the end of the war.

CHAPTER FOURTEEN

EXHIBIT 14.4 Application for my father to travel.

```
                    UNITED STATES DEPARTMENT OF JUSTICE
             OFFICE OF THE UNITED STATES ATTORNEY, ROOM 450 U.S. COURT HOUSE
                            CHICAGO 4, ILLINOIS.

              APPLICATION FOR TRAVEL OF ALIEN OR ENEMY NATIONALITIES
                                       of
```

An alien/enemy nationality shall not travel or make trips or move from one locality to another except as herein provided. The alien shall file in writing with the United States Attorney of the district of his residence, a statement setting forth the particulars hereinafter enumerated. FIVE (5) COPIES SHALL BE FILED WITH THE UNITED STATES ATTORNEY AT LEAST SEVEN (7) DAYS PRIOR TO THE INTENDED DATE OF DEPARTURE. A SELF-ADDRESSED, STAMPED BUSINESS SIZE ENVELOPE MUST ACCOMPANY THIS APPLICATION. USE A TYPEWRITER IF POSSIBLE.

1. NAME: Joseph Kahn (Print) (first ~~a citizen of~~ (middle name) (last name)~~-Germany~~

2. NATIONALITY: None- Germany   PLACE & DATE OF BIRTH: Laupheim-Germany Nov. 5, 1889

3. HOME ADDRESS & TELEPHONE NUMBER: 2109 E 68th St - Tel. Hyde Park 8802

4. OCCUPATION: Shipping Clerk

5. ~~Chicago~~ ~~...~~ 20 ~~E.~~ Kinzie St. Superior 6825

6. HAVE YOU HAD PREVIOUS TRAVEL PERMISSION, IF SO, GIVE DATE & FROM WHOM: no

7. ALIEN REGISTRATION NO. 7630919 (As listed in pink book, inside).

8. DETAILED STATEMENT OF THE PURPOSE FOR WHICH THE TRIP IS TO BE MADE AND Visit my wounded son at Darnell Hospital-Danville, Kentucky

9. FINAL DESTINATION OF TRIP & ADDRESS: Darnell General Hospital-Danville, Ky

10. STOP-OVERS, IF ANY, ON WAY TO FINAL DESTINATION AND NAME & ADDRESSES OF PERSONS WHERE YOU CAN BE REACHED:

11. TRANSPORTATION USED (Via auto; give make & license No.): Train

12. INTENDED DATE OF DEPARTURE: Oct. 19th, 1945

13. INTENDED DATE OF RETURN: Sunday, Oct. 21st, 1945

14. HAVE YOU EVER BEEN CALLED BEFORE AN ALIEN ENEMY HEARING BOARD? IF ANSWER IS YES, STATE WHERE, WHEN & WHAT DISPOSITION WAS MADE OF YOUR CASE: NO

15. ARE YOU NOW ON PAROLE, OR SUBJECT TO DEPORTATION PROCEEDINGS: NO (yes or no)

16. (IF JAPANESE ENEMY ALIEN) HAVE YOU BEEN NOTIFIED OF BEING INDIVIDUALLY EXCLUDED FROM THE WEST COAST AREA? (yes or no)

                                        Joseph Kahn
                                   SIGNATURE OF APPLICANT

PERMISSION GRANTED TO TRAVEL AS INDICATED HEREIN:

OCT 12 1945
  (DATE)   J. ALBERT WOLL, UNITED STATES ATTORNEY FOR THE
                              NORTHERN DISTRICT OF ILLINOIS.

THIS PERMIT DOES NOT GRANT THE ALIEN THE RIGHT TO ENTER UPON ANY AREA PROHIBITED BY MILITARY, STATE OF LOCAL AUTHORITIES. WHEN AUTOMOBILE IS USED: THIS

EXHIBIT 14.5 Application for my mother to travel.

UNITED STATES DEPARTMENT OF JUSTICE
OFFICE OF THE UNITED STATES ATTORNEY, ROOM 450 U.S. COURT HOUSE
CHICAGO 4, ILLINOIS.

APPLICATION FOR TRAVEL OF ALIEN OF ENEMY NATIONALITIES
of

OCT 11 1945

An alien/enemy nationality shall not travel or make trips or move from one locality to another except as herein provided. The alien shall file in writing with the United States Attorney of the district of his residence, a statement setting forth the particulars hereinafter enumerated, FIVE (5) COPIES SHALL BE FILED WITH THE UNITED STATES ATTORNEY AT LEAST SEVEN (7) DAYS PRIOR TO THE INTENDED DATE OF DEPARTURE. A SELF-ADDRESSED, STAMPED BUSINESS SIZE ENVELOPE MUST ACCOMPANY THIS APPLICATION. USE A TYPEWRITER IF POSSIBLE.

1. NAME Martha   Kahn
   (Print)   (first name)   (middle name)   (last name)

2. NATIONALITY None- Last a citizen   PLACE & DATE OF BIRTH Shiaren-Luxembourg
               of Germany   Aug. 4, 1892

3. HOME ADDRESS & TELEPHONE NUMBER 2109 E 68th St- Tel. Hyde Park 8802

4. OCCUPATION   Housewife

5. EMPLOYERS NAME, ADDRESS & TELEPHONE NUMBER

6. HAVE YOU HAD PREVIOUS TRAVEL PERMISSION, IF SO, GIVE DATE & FROM WHOM NO

7. ALIEN REGISTRATION NO. 7630921   (As listed in pink book, inside).

8. DETAILED STATEMENT OF THE PURPOSE FOR WHICH THE TRIP IS TO BE MADE AND PERSONS TO BE VISITED WITH; THEIR ADDRESS:
   Visit wounded son at Darnell Hospital-Danville, Ky.

9. FINAL DESTINATION OF TRIP & ADDRESS Darnell General Hospital-Danville, KY

10. STOP-OVERS, IF ANY, ON WAY TO FINAL DESTINATION AND NAME & ADDRESSES OF PERSONS WHERE YOU CAN BE REACHED   NO

11. TRANSPORTATION USED (Via auto; give make & license No.)
    Train

12. INTENDED DATE OF DEPARTURE   Friday, Oct. 19, 1945

13. INTENDED DATE OF RETURN   Sunday, Oct. 21st, 1945

14. HAVE YOU EVER BEEN CALLED BEFORE AN ALIEN ENEMY HEARING BOARD? IF ANSWER IS YES, STATE WHERE, WHEN & WHAT DISPOSITION WAS MADE OF YOUR CASE   NO

15. ARE YOU NOW ON PAROLE, OR SUBJECT TO DEPORTATION PROCEEDINGS   NO
                                                              (yes or no)

16. (IF JAPANESE ENEMY ALIEN) HAVE YOU BEEN NOTIFIED OR BEING INDIVIDUALLY EXCLUDED FROM THE WEST COAST AREA?
                                                              (yes or no)

Martha Kahn
SIGNATURE OF APPLICANT

PERMISSION GRANTED TO TRAVEL AS INDICATED HEREIN:

OCT 12 1945   J. Albert Woll
  (DATE)   J. ALBERT WOLL, UNITED STATES ATTORNEY FOR THE
                NORTHERN DISTRICT OF ILLINOIS.

THIS PERMIT DOES NOT GRANT THE ALIEN THE RIGHT TO ENTER UPON ANY AREA PROHIBITED BY MILITARY, STATE OF LOCAL AUTHORITIES. WHEN AUTOMOBILE IS USED: THIS PERMIT DOES NOT GRANT THE APPLICANT TO EXTRA GAS RATION.

EXHIBIT 14.7 My honorable discharge certificate from the Army.

CHAPTER FIFTEEN

EXHIBIT 15.1 "Riegner Telegram" Sent to Rabbi Stephen S. Wise, August 26, 1942, informing the United States Jewish community of the beginning of the annihilation of all European Jews.

EXHIBIT 15.3 In between the tablets of Jews living in Laufersweiler that were murdered is a bronze relief sculpture. It portrays a mother holding her child tightly. Her demeanor symbolizes her anxiety of what is to come. The man with raised hands symbolizes his hopes of humane treatment which was taken away by the Nazi regime.

EXHIBIT 15.6 Email from the Mayor of Cuneo, Italy with specifics of Georges execution.

Cuneo, 14 marzo 2007

Dear Mr. KAHN,

I hope you appreciate this information I am sending you:

"Joseph George, son of Bernard and Michel Marthe, was a student born in Luxemburg and there resident, he was a Jewish French citizen, captured at Demonte in March 1945 by Italians and then taken to prison in Cuneo.

On April 26th 1945, at undetermined time, he was shot by Germans under the fifth arc of the "Ponte Nuovo" with Appelbaum Armand Moise born in Warsaw in 1901, civilian; Futterman Bernard born in Warsaw in 1903, civilian; Futterman Marcel (son of Bernard) born in Paris in 1927, civilian Giordano Biagio, born in Cuneo in 1924, civilian; Korbel Hugo, born in Vienna in 1894, civilian; Schwarz Siegfried, born in Vienna in 1902, civilian and Terrazzani Frencesco born in Pula (Istria) in 1892, partisan."

Yours faithfully,

Alberto Valmaggia

EXHIBIT 15.9 Memorial urn at the Jewish cemetery, Mannheim. "To those who found no grave."

EXHIBIT 15.10 The memorial cube of more than 20,000 perished (murdered) Jews of Mannheim with their names engraved.

EXHIBIT 15.20 March 15, 1946: *Chicago Times*. Irene wanted to see me in my uniform. I obliged happily.

Brother Robert Kahn, just out of the AAF, and father Joseph—neither of whom she had seen for seven years—greet 24-year-old Nazi fugitive Irene Kahn at long-awaited reunion in La Salle st. station. —*TIMES Photo*

EXHIBIT 15.20 Chicago newspaper article. Reunion of Irene Kahn with her family.

Swastika's shadow is gone

A German-born girl who didn't see the sun in two years she spent evading the Nazis was reunited today with her Chicago family.

When Irene Kahn, 24, stepped from the train in the La Salle st. station this morning she ran to the arms of the family from whom the Nazis had kept her separated for seven years.

Waiting to meet her were father, Joseph, and her brother, Robert, 22, wearing his AAF uniform because Irene wanted most of all to see him in "the uniform of a free country." Her mother was home at 2109 E. 68th, preparing a welcoming meal.

HID IN PARIS

The Kahn family saga, comprising an unbelievable story of a victory won against odds, dates back to the outbreak of the war. In that year—1939—Irene went to Lille, France, to attend the university and shortly afterward her father, Joseph, was sent to a concentration camp. He later was released. Robert was forbidden by the Germans to attend school.

Seeking to avoid the Nazi terror and a siege of forced labor in a concentration camp, the Kahns moved first to Luxembourg and then obtained passage to America. The parents and Robert were free of the German tide of conquest, but Irene was trapped in Lille.

She turned to a philosophy professor for help, he in turn appealed to a Catholic priest. She was smuggled into the priest's house one night and for the next two years never ventured out. Also hidden there were her aunt, uncle, and two children. The Germans who'd been searching for her never inquired at the clergyman's house.

After the liberation a cousin of hers in the American Army, later killed, accidentally found her and gave her the first news she'd had of her family.

Her first impression of America startled her. In the English she learned from GIs she explained: "Here everyone keeps talking about the next war. It's so different over there. Everyone hates war so much he can't realize it ever would happen again, or bear to think of it." She compared America's attitude with the little boy afraid he would drop a water pitcher he was carrying. He was so afraid he finally did.

While Irene was hiding from the Gestapo in Europe, Robert had troubles too with the air force in the Pacific.

First he suffered internal injuries when the plane in which he was flying crashed into a mountain near Manila during an electric storm. The only survivor of a crew of eight, he lay unattended for several days before being rescued. On his return to the United States in September after service in New Guinea, he was hospitalized for heart trouble incurred in the tropics.

Today, however, all was well with the Kahn family. They were well, together again, and dwelling in the land of sunshine and freedom.

Mrs. Joseph Kahn

CHAPTER SEVENTEEN

EXHIBIT 17.7 The new sanctuary of Temple Israel with the entrance on Salem Avenue. The curtain is drawn when the choir sings.

EXHIBIT 17.10 Ronald's Consecration by Rabbi Ruslander at Temple Israel. Ronald is third row, fourth from right, with bow tie.

CHAPTER EIGHTEEN

EXHIBIT 18.4 View of our new home on 3639 Castano Drive.

EXHIBIT 18.5 The house as originally designed with 3 bedrooms.

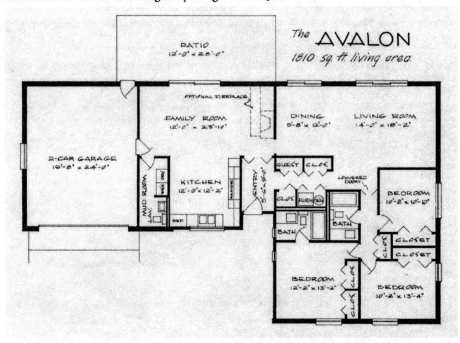

EXHIBIT 18.6 The home, as redesigned by me, with 4 bedrooms

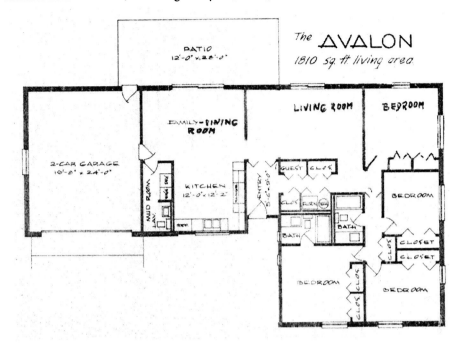

EXHIBIT 18.7 Irene had prepared readings for each of the children to recite on Opa Kahn's 70th birthday celebration. Faye and Marc on each end, with Susan and Ron in the middle, with Irene in the center.

EXHIBIT 18.8 Letter of commendation.

ASSISTANT SECRETARY OF DEFENSE
WASHINGTON 25, D. C.

SUPPLY AND LOGISTICS

DEC 1 1959

MEMORANDUM FOR THE ASSISTANT SECRETARY OF THE AIR FORCE (MATERIEL)

SUBJECT: Support of Net Evaluation Studies

This office has recently completed its work in support of the special studies conducted by the Net Evaluation Subcommittee of the National Security Council. This is written to express our appreciation for the support given by two Air Force employees, Mr. Thomas G. Baptist of Air Force Headquarters and Mr. Robert Kahn of the Air Materiel Command.

Mr. Kahn made a major contribution to our report by his excellent preparation of data prior to coming to Washington on temporary duty and by his intensive efforts while working with members of my staff in Washington. Mr. Baptist participated in successful efforts to expand our data on significant production facilities in preparation for this work and also gave us valuable assistance in the preparation of our report.

PHILIP L. MILLER, JR.
Deputy Assistant Secretary of Defense
(Supply and Logistics)

EXHIBIT 18.9 Letter of commendation.

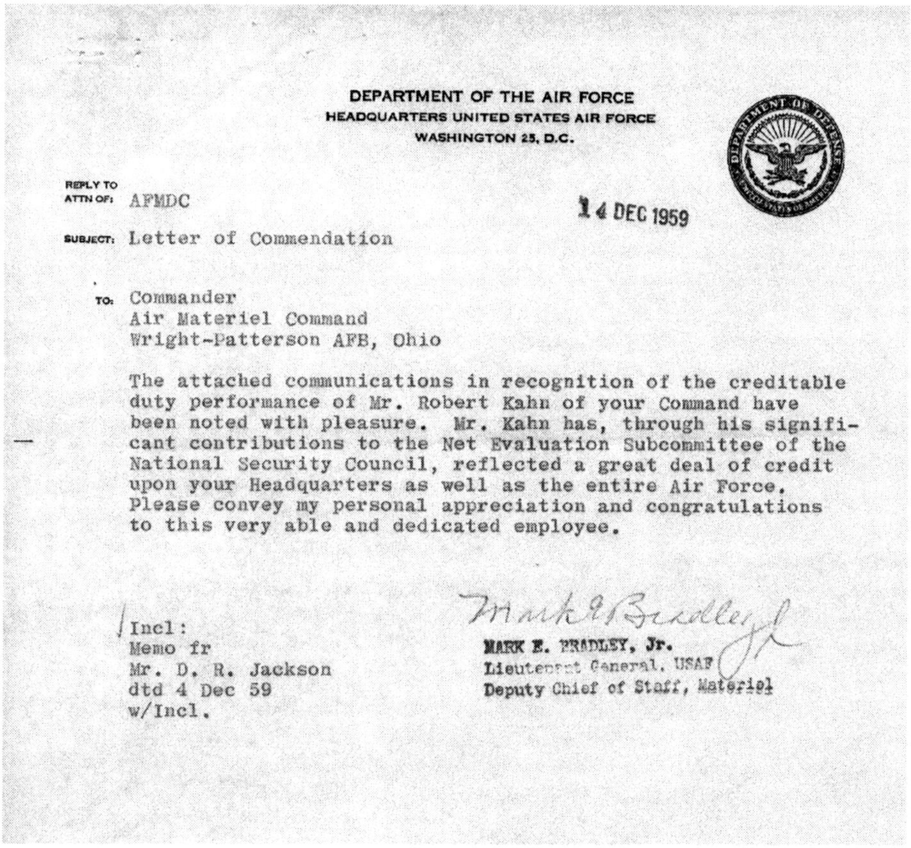

DEPARTMENT OF THE AIR FORCE
HEADQUARTERS UNITED STATES AIR FORCE
WASHINGTON 25, D.C.

REPLY TO
ATTN OF: AFMDC

14 DEC 1959

SUBJECT: Letter of Commendation

TO: Commander
Air Materiel Command
Wright-Patterson AFB, Ohio

The attached communications in recognition of the creditable duty performance of Mr. Robert Kahn of your Command have been noted with pleasure. Mr. Kahn has, through his significant contributions to the Net Evaluation Subcommittee of the National Security Council, reflected a great deal of credit upon your Headquarters as well as the entire Air Force. Please convey my personal appreciation and congratulations to this very able and dedicated employee.

MARK E. BRADLEY, Jr.
Lieutenant General, USAF
Deputy Chief of Staff, Materiel

Incl:
Memo fr
Mr. D. R. Jackson
dtd 4 Dec 59
w/Incl.

EXHIBIT 18.14: I had become a Boy Scout leader and was active for more than 50 years.

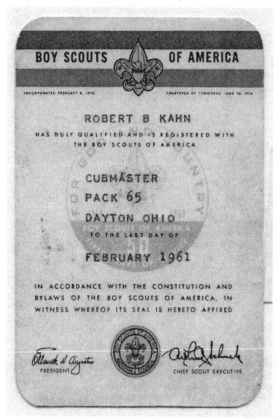

Kahn Cubmaster Of Pack No. 65

Robert Kahn has been appointed Cubmaster of Cub Pack 65, sponsored by the Jewish Community Activities Division of the Jewish Community Council. As one of his first duties, he presided at the Induction ceremony welcoming the following boys as Bob Cats to the Pack: Richard Block, Mike Cooper, Richard Cyge, Jim Finn, Richard Frank, Jon Graubarth, Tom Insel, Jim Mayer, Mark Miller and Charles Tiber.

In addition awards were made to: Jerry Baum, Marshall Beeber, Brad Donoff, David Fink, Jim Finn, Ben Goldberg, Norman Goldman, Jon Graubarth, Tom Insel, Sandy Jacobson, Eddie Kress, Mark Leeper, Philip Levy, Walter Maimon, Roy Marokus, Bruce Mendelson, Irvin Moscowitz, Leon Muler, Craig Ozer, Teddy Ozer, Steven Sax, Steve Schear, Michael Schlesinger, Larry Snyder, Bobby Tarsky, Sandy Wolfe and Howard Zusman.

Cub Pack 65 is seeking additional Den Mothers so that the boys waiting for admission to the pack may participate in this cubbing program. Special plans have been formulated for December, in keeping with the Chanukah theme.

Pack 65 Charter, Cub Master Robert B. Kahn

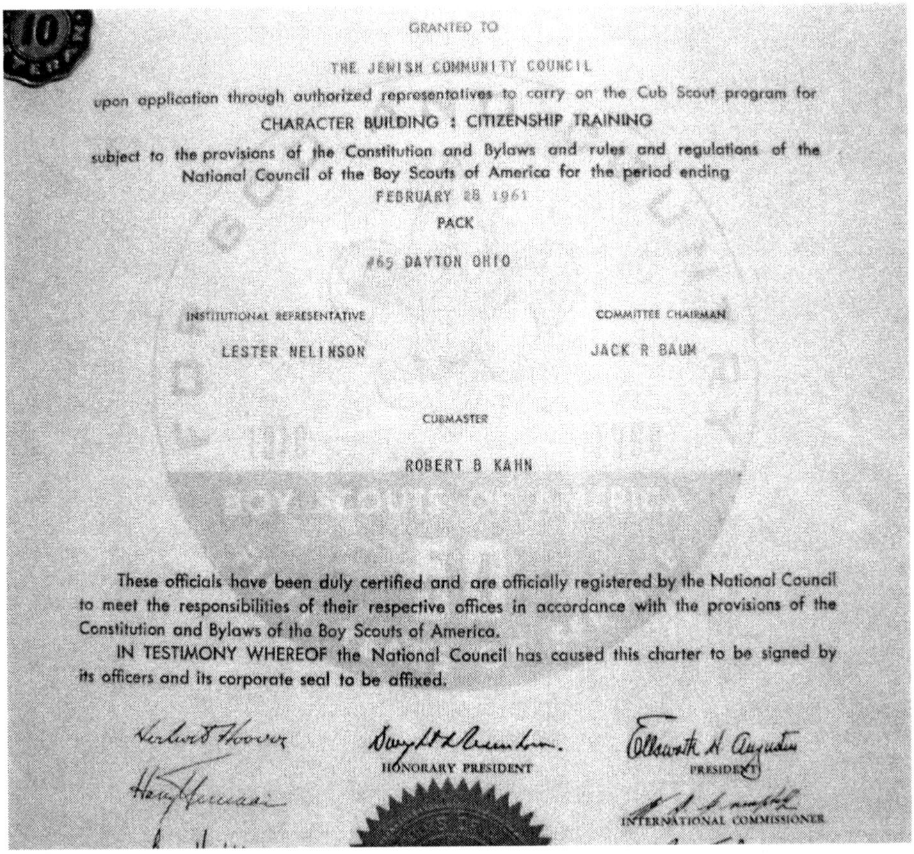

GRANTED TO

THE JEWISH COMMUNITY COUNCIL

upon application through authorized representatives to carry on the Cub Scout program for

CHARACTER BUILDING : CITIZENSHIP TRAINING

subject to the provisions of the Constitution and Bylaws and rules and regulations of the National Council of the Boy Scouts of America for the period ending

FEBRUARY 28 1961

PACK

#65 DAYTON OHIO

INSTITUTIONAL REPRESENTATIVE — LESTER NELINSON

COMMITTEE CHAIRMAN — JACK R BAUM

CUBMASTER — ROBERT B KAHN

These officials have been duly certified and are officially registered by the National Council to meet the responsibilities of their respective offices in accordance with the provisions of the Constitution and Bylaws of the Boy Scouts of America.

IN TESTIMONY WHEREOF the National Council has caused this charter to be signed by its officers and its corporate seal to be affixed.

HONORARY PRESIDENT — PRESIDENT — INTERNATIONAL COMMISSIONER

EXHIBIT 18.15 AND 18.16 Letters of recognition.

Office of the Commander

HEADQUARTERS
AIR FORCE LOGISTICS COMMAND
UNITED STATES AIR FORCE

Reply To Attn of: MCG

Wright-Patterson Air Force Base, Ohio

7 JUN 1961

Subject: Directory of Industrial Mutual Aid Associations

To: MCP (General Ruegg)

1. The Directory of Industrial Mutual Aid Associations, which was published in April by MCPM, has been called to my attention.

2. This publication obviously represents considerable effort on the part of the editor and other individuals in MCPM who assisted with the project. Please extend to all concerned my appreciation for a job well done.

S. E. ANDERSON
General, USAF
Commander

HEADQUARTERS
AIR FORCE LOGISTICS COMMAND
UNITED STATES AIR FORCE
WRIGHT-PATTERSON AIR FORCE BASE, OHIO

REPLY TO ATTN OF: MCPMC

14 June 1961

SUBJECT: Directory of Industrial Mutual Aid Associations

TO: Mr. R. B. Kahn

It is a pleasure to forward the attached correspondence commending your services in the preparation and publishing of subject directory. I wish to extend my personal thanks for a job well done.

ROBERT W. COCHRAN
Lt. Colonel, USAF
Chief, Industrial Capability Branch
Industrial Resources Division
Directorate of Procurement & Production

EXHIBIT 18.17 To attend the inauguration of John F Kennedy was a lifetime event.

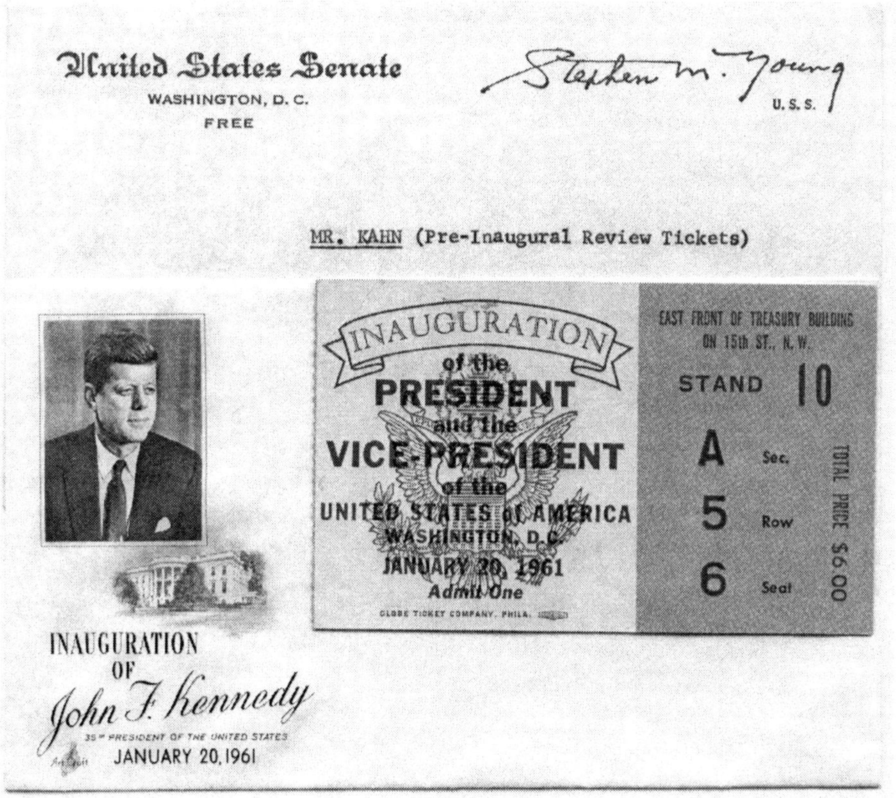

EXHIBIT 18.18 Letters of recognition, appreciation, and comment for nuclear attack assessment study

ASSISTANT SECRETARY OF DEFENSE
WASHINGTON 25, D. C.

March 22, 1961

INSTALLATIONS AND LOGISTICS

MEMORANDUM FOR ASSISTANT SECRETARY OF THE AIR FORCE (MATERIEL)

SUBJECT: Letter of Appreciation

We very much appreciate the assistance given to us by Mr. Robert B. Kahn and Mr. Harley C. Witham of the Air Materiel Command over the period January - February 1961.

Messrs. Kahn and Witham were made available at our request to participate in a special nuclear-attack assessment study. Their task was to evaluate the impact of the attack on Air Force production resources and schedules. This task they performed expeditiously, expertly and cheerfully despite transportation difficulties caused by inclement weather, our irregular work schedule and the serious interruption of their own work routines.

It would be appreciated if this note of thanks were forwarded to Messrs. Kahn and Witham. It is fair to say that without their competent assistance, completion of the special study within the specified time-limits would have been most difficult.

GLENN V. GIBSON
Deputy Assistant Secretary of Defense
(Requirements and Readiness Planning)

DEPARTMENT OF THE AIR FORCE
HEADQUARTERS UNITED STATES AIR FORCE
WASHINGTON 25, D.C.

REPLY TO
ATTN OF: AFMDC

11 APR 1961

SUBJECT: Letter of Appreciation

TO: AFLC

I have reviewed the attached complimentary communications and am most pleased to join Mr. Gibson and Mr. Jackson in an expression of appreciation to Mr. Robert B. Kahn and Mr. Harley C. Witham for their significant participation in the nuclear-attack assessment study.

1 Atch
Memo fr Donald R.
Jackson dtd 3 Apr 61,
w/Incl

MARK E. BRADLEY, JR.
Lieutenant General, USAF
Deputy Chief of Staff, Materiel

REMARKS Bob:

I want to reiterate what is said in the attached letter. To those of us who work with you it is just another illustration of the type of effort you consistently put out. This is why we have such a high opinion of you as a fellow worker.

FROM NAME OR TITLE: Charlie Rush
ORGANIZATION AND LOCATION: MCPMC-1
DATE: 5/2/61

DD FORM 95 Replaces DA AGO Form 895, 1 Apr 48, and AFHQ Form 12, 10 Nov 47, which may be used.

EXHIBIT 18.19 Cost Reduction and Improved Operating Effectiveness in Aircraft Flight Test and Acceptance Activities cover and acknowledgments.

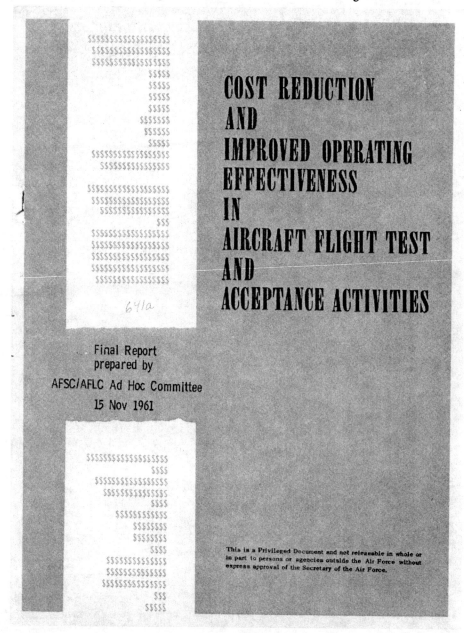

EXHIBIT 18.20

ACKNOWLEDGMENT

As editor of this report and Chairman of the AFSC/AFLC Ad Hoc Committee on Production Flight Test and Acceptance, I feel privileged in recognizing and commending the following individuals as having contributed significantly to the successful accomplishment of the Committee's mission.

Lt. Col. W. L. Alexander	Lt. Col. C. F. Monsell
Major I. H. Derrick	Lt. Col. J. E. Muldoon
Mr. R. J. Doyle	Col. H. W. Randall, Jr.
Mr. W. S. Klepper	Mr. H. Russell
Major R. W. Little	Major H. M. Watkins
Mr. R. L. Marderosian	Mr. H. Wolfe

Without exception and regardless of Command affiliation or rank, each member carried out his assignment in addition to his normal duties and in a spirit of cooperation motivated by a high sense of purpose. I am particularly indebted to Mr. Rex J. Doyle, who as the initial chairman, laid the cornerstone for the functioning of the committee and whose diligence and skill has won him the esteem of those associated with him. Recognized also is the able assistance of Mrs. Barbara Rankin, whose services as recording secretary throughout the life of the committee are greatly appreciated.

R. B. KAHN
Industrial Specialist
Chairman, Ad Hoc Committee

EXHIBIT 18.23 Letter of Commendation for participating in the Subcontract Management Task Group.

HEADQUARTERS
AIR FORCE SYSTEMS COMMAND
UNITED STATES AIR FORCE
ANDREWS AIR FORCE BASE
WASHINGTON 25, D. C.

DCS/Procurement & Production
~~XXXXXXXXXXXXXXXXXXXXXXXX~~
AIR FORCE SYSTEMS COMMAND
WRIGHT PATTERSON AF BASE, OHIO

REPLY TO
ATTN OF: ASXK (SCK)

SUBJECT: Letter of Commendation

27 August 1963

TO: Mr. Robert B. Kahn
Directorate of Production
DCS/Procurement & Production
Wright-Patterson AFB, Ohio

1. I wish to add my personal commendation for your significant contribution to the AFSC Subcontract Management Task Group as evidenced by the commendations attached from General Estes, General Keeling and Colonel Drobeck.

2. I recognize that much personal as well as official time and effort was necessary on your part to bring this team effort to a successful conclusion. This type of performance brings a great deal of credit to you as an individual and enhances the stature of our organization in the eyes of other AFSC offices.

JOHN E. TOLNITCH
Assistant for Contract Management
DCS/Procurement & Production

Atch
Gen Keeling's 1st Ind
20 Aug 63 w/atch

FORGING MILITARY SPACEPOWER

EXHIBIT 18.24 Wire from General Lemay of JFK's death.

Circulate thru all RCVA + RCVM

RCV Info

```
231158Z
FM AFSC
TO ALAFSC
BT
UNCLAS SCAM ALAFC 1418/63.
THE FOLLOWING ALMAJCOM MSG IS QUOTED FOR ACTION. QUOTE:
UNCLAS FROM SAF-OI ALMAJCOM 1838/63.
PERSONAL FROM ZUCKERT AND LEMAY. ONE
OF THE GREAT TRAGEDIES OF ALL TIME HAS TODAY TAKEN THE LIFE OF OUR
PRESIDENT AND COMMANDER-IN-CHIEF. SINCE 20 JANUARY 1961, HIS
LEADERSHIP HAS STRENGTHENED OUR FORCES AND BLENDED TOGETHER THE MIGHT
OF THE FREE WORLD. OUR NATION AND OUR ALLIES WILL EVER BE GREATFUL
FOR THE STRONG HAND WITH WHICH HE SO MAGNIFCENTLY STEERED THE COURSE
OF FREEDOM AND PEACE. AS MEMBERS OF THE ARMED SERVICES, YOU ARE


PAGE 2 RUEAGL 581 UNCLAS
TRAINED TO CARRY ON DURING TIMES OF STRESS AND GRIEF; WE ARE CONFI-
DENT YOU WILL DO SO NOW, IN THE TRADITION WHICH HAS MADE OUR NATION
GREAT. TO PRESIDENT KENNEDY'S FAMILY, TO THE NATION, AND TO THE
FREE WORLD, WE, ON BEHALF OF THE MEN AND WOMEN OF THE UNITED
STATES AIR FORCE, HAVE EXTENDED OUR DEEPEST SYMPATHY. IN THE KEEP
ING WITH OUR NATION'S GRIEF, THE NATIONAL FLAG WILL BE FLOWN AT HALF
STAFF UNTIL SUNDOWN, 22 DECEMBER 1963. UNQUOTE.
BT
```

EXHIBIT 18.25 Letter of appointment

ASX_K 5 February 1963

Top Secret Control Officer

ASAMCT

The following changes are to be made to Special Order
M-3, dated 3 January 1962:

Top Secret Control Officer	Alternate Top Secret Control Officer
Mr. Robert B. Kahn	Mr. Robert H. Dickman
vice Mr. William R. Frost	

JOHN C. TOLNITCH
Assistant for Contract Management
Directorate of Special Activities

EXHIBIT 18.26 Certificate of Merit

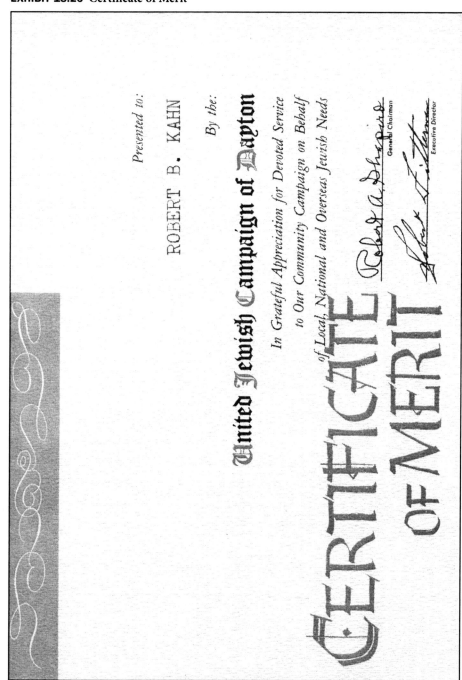

EXHIBIT 18.27 Wright Patt Credit Union letter.

March 23, 1964

Mr. Robert B. Kahn
3639 Castano Drive
Dayton 16, Ohio

Dear Mr. Kahn:

We, the Board of Directors of the Wright-Patt Credit Union, Inc., wish to express our sincere appreciation for your outstanding ability and cooperation in the performance of your duties as a member of the Board of Directors.

Sincerely,

EXHIBIT 18.28 Presidential Citation by President Lyndon B. Johnson for "Recognition of Significant Economy and Efficiency Achievements."

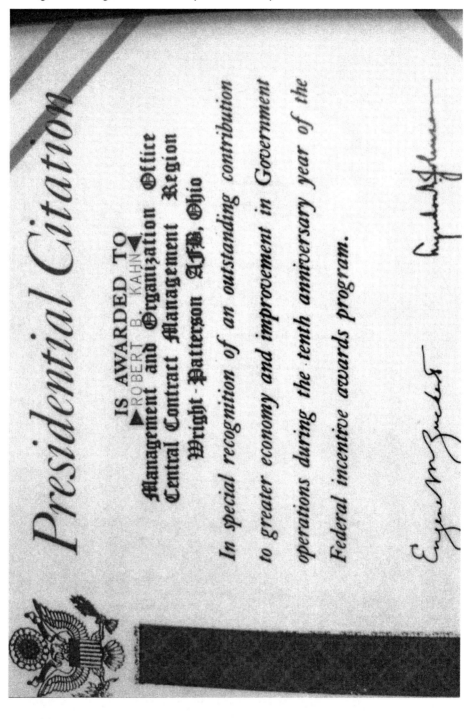

EXHIBIT 18.29 Directory of Industrial Mutual Aid Associations and Memo.

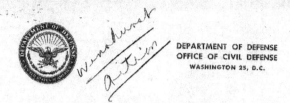

DEPARTMENT OF DEFENSE
OFFICE OF CIVIL DEFENSE
WASHINGTON 25, D.C.

AUG 6 1963

MEMORANDUM FOR DEPUTY CHIEF OF STAFF
        Systems and Logistics, USAF

ATTN: Directorate for Production, Room 4C-319

SUBJECT: Directory of Industrial Mutual Aid Associations

    In accordance with previous conversations, it will be appreciated if you would arrange to supply this office with 500 copies of the new Directory of Industrial Mutual Aid Associations.

    A review of the draft copy of the new Directory certainly indicates that it is an excellent document and fills a definite need for industry not only as a record of these organizations, but also as a fine reference and guide for those who are undertaking the development of such an association.

    Mr. Robert Kahn is to be congratulated on his effective efforts in preparation of the Directory.

                              V. L. Couch, Director
                              Industrial Participation

EXHIBIT 18.30 Major General William Veal.

CHAPTER NINETEEN

EXHIBIT 19.1

The News Tribune, Thursday, June 6, 1968 – Page 5

City League Tennis Scene

Pictured are members of the Meadowdale tennis team which won the City League championship this spring. They are, first row, left to right, Marvin Pierce, Dave Brown, Brad Hagen, Ron Kahn, John Scheu, Ken Kaplan, and Jim Jacobson. Second row, left to right, are Dave Gerkin, manager; Keith Donoff, Rick Fontaine, Jim Landis, David Spialter, Steve Cohen, and Bob Flacks. Not shown is Mike Casher. LOGAN STUDIO photo.

EXHIBIT 19.3 Trunk and luggage rack diagram

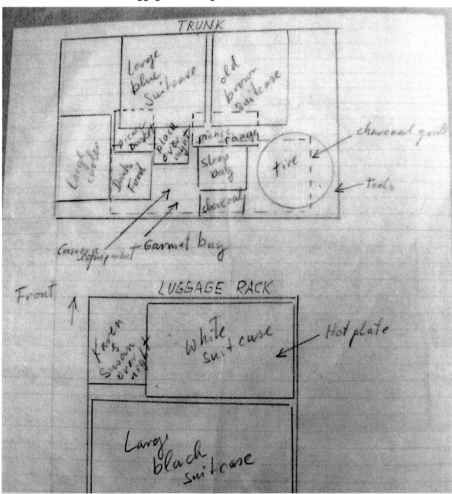

CHAPTER TWENTY

EXHIBIT 20.4 Governor of Hawaii sends his best wishes.

EXECUTIVE CHAMBERS
HONOLULU

JOHN A. BURNS
GOVERNOR

April 17, 1970

Dear Mr. Kahn:

We are happy to learn that the Miami Valley Lodge of B'nai B'rith is planning to stage a "Hawaiian Holiday" on the evening of May 9, in Dayton.

The State of Hawaii does indeed look with favor on your planned festivities.

The ancient gods of old Hawaii live on in legends, songs and dances of the Hawaiian people. If they were "alive" today they would surely be pleased with your undertaking.

In behalf of the people of Hawaii, I extend my best wishes for a highly successful "Hawaiian Holiday."

Aloha, to all the members of your Lodge and their families, and may the Almighty be with you and yours always.

Sincerely,

John A. Burns

Mr. Robert B. Kahn
Vice President
Miami Valley Lodge No. 2254
B'nai B'rith
3639 Castano Drive
Dayton, Ohio 45416

EXHIBIT 20.9 Guardian of the Menorah dinner with Louis Goldman and John Glenn and his wife. I am standing third from left. To my left are Vic Cassano and Si Burick.

EXHIBIT 20.10 Letter from Secretary of Defense.

THE SECRETARY OF DEFENSE
WASHINGTON, D.C. 20301

January 12, 1973

Mr. Robert Hahn
Headquarters, Air Force Logistics Command
XOXM
Wright-Patterson Air Force Base
Dayton, Ohio 45433

Dear Mr. Hahn:

Before I leave the position of Secretary of Defense, I want to thank you for the support you gave the President's Inter-Agency Economic Adjustment Committee in its efforts to alleviate the economic impacts of Defense decisions that adversely affected communities and individuals.

As Chairman of the Presidential Committee, I personally appreciate the help you have given us.

Sincerely,

Melvin R. Laird

EXHIBIT 20.11 Headstone for my mother, Martha Kahn.

EXHIBIT 20.12 Headstone for my father, Joseph Kahn.

EXHIBIT 20.15 Cover of French pamphlet recognizing Raymond Vancourt.

EXHIBIT 20.17 Invitation from Commander of Naval Base in Charleston, South Carolina.

COMMANDER, NAVAL BASE
CHARLESTON, SOUTH CAROLINA 29408

11 September 1979

Dear Mr. Kahn:

Welcome to Naval Base Charleston.

Charleston is the home of a naval complex which began as a tiny repair base established by the Federal fleet during the Civil War. It was enlarged in 1901, when most of the land occupied by the present base was acquired. Since then, the base has grown in size and importance until today, with 89 separate commands (including 58 ships), 35,000 people and an annual payroll of $518 million, Naval Base Charleston is the Navy's second largest east coast home port and greater Charleston's largest employer.

Although your schedule does not allow you time to take in all of the base or the historic Charleston area, we hope that while you are here you will be able to enjoy a little of the southern hospitality for which Charleston is so famous.

We are pleased to have you as our guests and we hope that you enjoy your visit.

Sincerely yours,

D. P. HALL
Rear Admiral, U. S. Navy
Commander, Naval Base Charleston

EXHIBIT 20.18 Brochure welcoming us aboard the United States nuclear ballistic missile submarine, the Ulysses S. Grant.

EXHIBIT 20.19 Autographed photo of Ulysses S. Grant submarine by the ship's Captain.

EXHIBIT 20.20 Letter of commendation from Air Force Commander General Bryce Poe.

Air Force Logistics Command
Wright-Patterson AFB, Ohio 45433
21 September 1979

Mr. Robert B. Kahn
Office of the Deputy Chief of Staff
 for Plans and Programs
Headquarters Air Force Logistics Command
Wright-Patterson Air Force Base, Ohio 45433

Dear Mr. Kahn

I want you to know how much I appreciate your representing AFLC in outstanding fashion at the 12 September 1979 Joint Logistics Commanders' (JLC) Meeting. Your briefing on our Contract Surge Concept was expertly tailored for a multi-service audience and delivered with clarity and enthusiasm.

Shared information leading to improved interservice efficiencies, savings, and readiness is a primary function of the JLC. Your superior briefing has certainly advanced this effort. I know I can count on your sustained outstanding contributions to AFLC and the Joint Logistics Commanders Organization.

Sincerely

BRYCE POE, II
General, USAF
Commander

Cy to: XR (Brig Gen Marquez)

EXHIBIT 20.24 General Poe presents me with a commemorative plaque of the Command.

EXHIBIT 20.25 Wearing the Secretary of the U.S. Air Force Exceptional Civilian Service Medal.

EXHIBIT 20.26 Kathy, Ronald, the proud retiree, his wife Gertrude, and Karen at the award ceremony.

EXHIBIT 20.32 AND 20.33 Newspaper articles about my reunion with dear friend, Ernest Michel.

THE RICHMOND NEWS LEADER, Tuesday, November 8, 1988

Boyhood friends who survived Holocaust are to be reunited

By The Associated Press

NEW YORK — As Robert Kahn listened to a Holocaust survivor tell his story on television, he had a flash of recognition. The man on the screen, he realized, was a boyhood chum he hadn't seen in 50 years.

Ernest Michel's face wasn't familiar, Kahn said, but the name rang a bell. When Michel told the "CBS Morning News" interviewer yesterday that he had grown up in Mannheim, Germany, "it all came back," Kahn said.

Michel, executive vice president of the United Jewish Appeal Federation of New York, was appearing on the program to discuss the 50th anniversary of Kristallnacht, the night when Nazis went on a rampage against Jews in Germany.

As Kahn watched from his home in Dayton, Ohio, he said he realized that Michel was a boyhood friend who had attended the same synagogue in Mannheim. The two hadn't seen each other at least since autumn 1938.

Kahn fled Germany with his parents in early 1939. Michel stayed and spent the war in labor and concentration camps, where almost all his family died.

"My young friends, most of them perished as far as I know," Kahn, a retired Air Force civilian employee, said in a telephone interview from Dayton. "So I was delighted to find out that here, in New York, was a former boyhood friend."

The two, who were 15 in 1938 and are 65 today, spoke by telephone yesterday evening, quickly catching up on the intervening years.

"It's real — we really know each other!" Michel exulted. "We traded stamps, we played soccer together. ... It's one of those incredible stories!"

"The excitement is not based on really having been close and longtime friends," Kahn said. "The excitement is that there is someone left whom I associated with. It has a tremendous meaning."

Michel said the two boys had dated two sisters, who now live in Florida. Those were the only surviving boyhood friends Michel was aware of, Kahn didn't realize the sisters were alive but knew of two other friends now living in the United States.

"We're going to get together as soon as we can work it out," said Michel.

"I'm sure he wouldn't recognize me," said Kahn. "I have white hair and I notice he has white hair, and we've put on a few pounds here and there."

TV TICKER

Holocaust survivors reunited

As Robert Kahn listened to a Holocaust survivor tell his story on the "CBS Morning News" yesterday, he suddenly had a flash of recognition. The man on the screen, he realized, was a boyhood chum he hadn't seen in 50 years.

Ernest Michel's face wasn't familiar, Kahn said, but the name rang a bell. And when Michel said he had grown up in Mannheim, Germany, said Kahn, "it all came back."

Michel, executive vice president of the United Jewish Appeal Federation of New York, was appearing on CBS to discuss the 50th anniversary of Kristallnacht, the night when German Nazis went on a nationwide rampage against Jews.

As Kahn watched from his home in Dayton, he said he realized that Michel was a boyhood friend who had attended the same synagogue in Mannheim. The two hadn't seen each other since the autumn of 1938.

Kahn fled Germany with his parents in early 1939; Michel stayed and spent the war in labor and concentration camps, where almost his entire family died.

"My young friends, most of them perished as far as I know," Kahn, a retired Air Force civil servant, said in a telephone interview from Dayton. "So I was delighted to find out that here, in New York, was a former boyhood friend." The two, who were 15 in 1938 and are 65 today, spoke by telephone yesterday evening, quickly catching up on the intervening years.

"It's real — we really know each other!" Michel exulted. "We traded stamps, we played soccer together. It's one of those incredible stories!" **AP**

EXHIBIT 20.42 Envelope containing seeds and planting instructions inside.

GIANT SEQUOIA

(Sequoiadendron giganteum)

The King of Plants..."It is, as a race, the oldest & mightiest of living things. Not even in past geological times, apparently, were there any greater trees."

For its first hundred years this is a beautiful yard tree (to 40-70 feet high), densely pyramidal with lovely blue-green foliage & wide-spreading trunk. Eventually, after 1-2000 years it may grow to be 300' tall and, if left to mature to its prime at 4000 years of age, who knows!

(hardy to -10 F)

A living souvenir of
the Reunion
with best wishes
from
Carl & Doris Landman

Giant Sequoia seeds
Planting directions inside

Additional Copyright Notes

Most photographs, Exhibits, and documents are primarily owned by the author. Permissions without monetary reimbursement have been granted limited to their use in this publication and media to publicize same. For specific photos and descriptions, the author appreciates having been given permission for their use in this publication and thanks the following institutions, entities, and individuals as follows:

Laufersweiler – Geschichte und Alltag eines Hunsrückdorfes von Fritz Schellack 1994. Permission by Christof Pies, Förderkreis Laufersweiler, Germany.

Die ehemalige Synagoge Laufersweiler – Ein Lern und Gedenkort by Hans-Werner Johann. Permission by Christof Pies, Förderkreis Laufersweiler, Germany.

Bilder vom jüdischen Leben in Mannheim by Volker Keller. Permission by Karen Strobel, M.A. Stadtarchiv Mannheim, Institut für Stadtgeschichte-Mannheim Germany.

Mannheim Einst und Jetzt 1933-1945 Nachdruck 1946 Edition Quadrat Mannheim 1989. First part (Einst) only. Permission by Karen Strobel, M.A. Stadtarchiv Mannheim, Institut für Stadtgeschichte-Mannheim Germany.

Mannheim ehemals, gestern und heute – Edition Quadrat by Ingeborg Riegl and Michael Caroli, 1987. Permission by Sylvia Rueckert, Fotoachiv der Reiss-Engelhorn-Museen, Mannheim Germany.

Maps and photographs and environs of Mannheim courtesy of Verkehrsverein Mannheim and Mannheimer Kongress und Touristik GmBH, Mannheim

Archival Sources and Literature

1. Sie Gehörten zu uns-Geschichte und Schicksal der Lauferseweiler Juden by Hans Werner Johann, 1988

2. Rhineland Pfalz-Synagogen und Denkmalpflege, Laufersweiler. Kreis Rhein-Hunsrück, ehemalige Synagoge, pamphlet

3. Statistische Materialien zur Geschichte der jüdischen Bevölkerung by Werner Knopp

4. Landeshauptarchiv, Koblenz, Auszug 655, 186 No. 777
Name changes in French and Hebrew dated November 11, 1808

5. Die Namenänderung der Juden im Jahre 1808 im Bereich der heutigen Verbandsgemeinde Kirchberg (Hunsrück) by Hans Werner Johann, Holzbach 1991

6. Amts-Blatt Nr. 53, September 4, 1839

7. Bernhard Mayer – Jugenderinnerrungen eines Laufersweiler Juden, und ergänzt by Hans Werner Johann

8. 22./23. October 1940, Deportation Mannheimer Juden mach Gürs Stadt Mannheim 1990

9. L'etoile Juive au Luxembourg by Paul Cerf, 1986

10. Hitler's Willing Executioners by Daniel Jonah Goldhagen, 1996

11. Pattern of Circles by John Dolibois, 1989

12. Die Jüdischen Opfer des Nationalsozialismus aus Köln, Gedenkbuch, 1995

13. Letters from Mrs. Alkan from Mini Ghetto Cinqfontaines, Luxembourg to her son Heinz, 1941-1942

14. Der Anfang nach dem Ende, 1945-49, by Christian Peters and Michael Caroli, 1985

15. Mannheim, ehemals, gestern und heute by Ingeborg Riegel and Michael Caroli, 1987

16. Memorial to the Jews deported from France from 1942-1944 by Serge Klarsfeld, 1983

17. Bilddokumente Mannheim 1933-1945: Mannheim Einst und Mannheim Jetzt Unveränderter Nachdruck der Ausgabe von 1946 mit einem Vorwort aus dem Jahne 1989

CPSIA information can be obtained
at www.ICGtesting.com
Printed in the USA
FFOW03n0708250417
34855FF